48347

Quantity
Food
Sanitation

Quantity
Food
Sanitation

FIFTH EDITION

Karla Longrée, Ph.D.

PROFESSOR EMERITUS
NUTRITIONAL SCIENCES
NEW YORK STATE COLLEGE OF HUMAN ECOLOGY
CORNELL UNIVERSITY, ITHACA, NEW YORK

Gertrude Armbruster, Ph.D.

ASSOCIATE PROFESSOR
NUTRITIONAL SCIENCES
NEW YORK STATE COLLEGE OF HUMAN ECOLOGY
CORNELL UNIVERSITY, ITHACA, NEW YORK

JOHN WILEY & SONS

New York • Chichester • Brisbane • Toronto • Singapore

4°347

N 0 3 7 7 1

This text is printed on acid-free paper.

Copyright © 1996 by John Wiley & Sons, Inc.

All rights reserved. Published simultaneously in Canada.

Reproduction or translation of any part of this work beyond
that permitted by Section 107 or 108 of the 1976 United
States Copyright Act without the permission of the copyright
owner is unlawful. Requests for permission or further
information should be addressed to the Permissions Department,
John Wiley & Sons, Inc., 605 Third Avenue, New York, NY
10158-0012.

This publication is designed to provide accurate and
authoritative information in regard to the subject
matter covered. It is sold with the understanding that
the publisher is not engaged in rendering legal, accounting,
or other professional services. If legal advice or other
expert assistance is required, the services of a competent
professional person should be sought.

Library of Congress Cataloging in Publication Data:

Longrée, Karla, 1905–
        Quantity food sanitation / Karla Longrée, Gertrude Armbruster.—
5th ed.
            p.   cm.
        "A Wiley-Interscience publication."
        Includes bibliographical references and index.
        ISBN 0-471-59660-4 (cloth : alk. paper)
        1. Food service—Sanitation.   2. Food handling.   I. Armbruster,
Gertrude.   II. Title.
TX911.3.S3L65   1996
647.95'0289—dc20   95-36504

Printed in the United States of America

10 9 8 7 6 5 4 3 2 1

Contents

v

Preface

Foodborne microbial pathogens have been recognized as causing illnesses in humans for more than 150 years. During this time, many studies have identified pathways by which the pathogens cause illnesses. From this knowledge, procedures and recommendations have become available to address this issue and minimize the illnesses resulting from exposure to these pathogens. During the same period of time, many changes have been made in the procurement, handling, and preparation of food. The use of prepreparation or advanced preparation practices has also increased. A larger variety of food is available, to include an increased use of imported foods and food components. This has modified the kinds and routes of contamination while expanding the opportunities for abuse.

While these changes have been developing, the foodservice industry has been growing in size. One of the biggest changes has been the robust growth of the fast-food sector of this industry. Fast food continues to grow both in volume as well as in acceptability by the consumer. Surveys show a continuing trend for consumers to eat more and more meals away from home. Supporting this trend is the growth of "to go" food that is prepared at a foodservice site but is consumed at home, work, or a recreation site. The food is transported by the consumer for a variable time and under variable conditions.

All of these changes have increased the chances for contamination and abuse of the food. Foods are prepared and processed in a variety of settings, transported to another site for consumption, and consequently exposed to increasing kinds and numbers of pathogens. Because a variety of individuals play a role in the food preparation chain, safe and appropriate procedures for handling foods may become lost or diminished in importance.

In the last two decades, pathogens that have caused some major outbreaks of foodborne illnesses included familiar organisms such as *Escherichia coli* and *Listeria monocytogenes*. Both have been recognized for years but were not associated with causing foodborne illnesses.

These changes and new directions affecting the foodservice industry underscore the need for a vigorous program to combat new and old microbial problems in the sanitary management of foodservice. It is necessary to emphasize microbial sanitation to the growing group of individuals who play a role in handling food. They must know about appropriate sanitation techniques and procedures that will assure the consumer of safe food.

This edition of *Quantity Food Sanitation* aims to bring to the attention of foodservice managers methods for controlling microbial problems of importance today.

KARLA LONGRÉE
GERTRUDE ARMBRUSTER

CHAPTER 1

Food Spoilage

S poilage of food may be due to chemical or biological causes; the latter include action of inherent enzymes, growth of microorganisms, invasion by insects, and contamination with trichinae and worms. About one-fourth of the world's food supply is lost through the action of microorganisms alone.

The "spoilage" concept includes concepts about edibility, or fitness to eat. Spoilage is decomposition. Many foods may not be decomposed, but harbor certain kinds of bacteria, or their toxins, in numbers or amounts which make the food poisonous and thus unfit for human consumption.

The criteria for assurance in foods suitable for consumption are:

1. The desired stage of development or maturity of the food.
2. Freedom from pollution at any stage in the production and subsequent handling of the food.
3. Freedom from objectionable chemical and physical changes resulting from action of food enzymes; activity of microbes, insects, rodents; invasion of parasites; and damage from pressure, freezing, heating, drying, and the like.
4. Freedom from microorganisms and parasites causing foodborne illnesses.

Enzymatic and microbial activities are undesirable when they are unwanted or uncontrolled. An example is the souring of milk; if unwanted, it is spoilage, yet the same process is purposely used in the production of certain cheeses and other fermented products made from milk.

STABILITY

Foods are frequently classified on the basis of their stability as nonperishable, semiperishable, and perishable. An example of the first group is sugar. Few foods are truly nonperishable. Hermetically sealed, heat-processed, and sterilized (canned) foods are usually listed among the nonperishable items. For all intents and purposes, they belong there. However, canned food may become perishable under certain circumstances, when, by accident, a chance for recontamination following processing is afforded: if the seams of the cans are faulty, or if through rusting or other damage the can is no longer hermetically sealed. Spoilage of canned goods may also take place when the canned items are stored at unusually high temperatures. Bacteria which are extremely resistant to heat must be expected to escape the killing effect of heat applied in routine canning. These thermophilic spore-forming bacteria may multiply at high temperatures, with an optimum near 113°F (45°C) and higher. Examples of these thermophiles are the *Bacillus* species which cause flat sour spoilage, the *Clostridium nigrificans* causing sulfide spoilage, and the *Clostridium thermosaccharolyticum.* It should be emphasized here that the organism causing botulism, *Clostridium botulinum,* is eliminated during the appropriate heat treatment given the foods in the canning operation. Certain heat-resistant molds have been found to escape thermal death in the routine canning of fruit, the most common one being *Byssochlamys fulva* (King et al., 1969; Splittstoesser et al., 1971; King et al., 1972).

Classified as semiperishables are usually the dry foods, such as flour, dry legumes, baked goods, hard cheeses, dried fruits and vegetables, and even waxed vegetables. Frozen foods, though basically perishable, may be classified as semiperishables provided they are freezer-stored properly.

The majority of our food materials must be classified as perishables. This group includes meat, poultry, fish, milk, eggs, many fruits and vegetables, and all cooked or "made" food items, except the dry and very acid ones.

MICROORGANISMS INVOLVED IN SPOILAGE

Microorganisms which may cause food to spoil include molds, yeasts, and bacteria. The contamination with molds, as a rule, is easily detected because of the presence of furry hyphae or threadlike structures which, in many instances, are colored. They often contribute a musty odor and flavor to the food they invade. Some molds, because of toxins they produce, are not altogether harmless. More will be said about aflatoxins later. Semimoist foods or foods with low water activity have been partially dehydrated, and the remaining water is sufficiently bound to hold the growth of bacteria, molds, and yeasts in check (Hollis et al., 1968).

Yeasts are unicellular bodies of small sizes which multiply by budding. In general, sugars are the best food for energy for yeast, carbon dioxide and alcohol being the end products of the fermentation they cause. Spoilage due to yeast may usually be recognized by the presence of bubbles and an alcoholic smell and taste.

Bacteria spoil food in many ways and it is not always possible to recognize the spoilage by sight, smell, or taste. Unfortunately, some of the bacteria that are important from a public health point of view may multiply to dangerously high numbers in food without changing the appearance, odor, or taste of the food. Disease-producing food has usually no decomposed appearance, but is certainly unfit for human consumption, and must be considered to be spoiled.

It is an important fact that almost any food will spoil if it is moist and not kept frozen. Spoilage must be expected within a wide temperature range. The various types of microorganisms as well as the genera, species, and strains vary in their temperature and food requirements. Thus the bacterial flora of a spoiled food item will vary greatly.

The origin of microorganisms varies also. The microorganisms may include the original flora of the particular food, as well as contaminants added in handling, processing, transporting, storing, preparing, and serving.

MULTIPLICATION

The multiplication of spoilage organisms on or in the food materials depends on many factors—the type of organism involved, its ability to gain nourishment from the food, competition from other microorganisms, initial load, and environmental conditions. Some important conditions are composition of the food, available moisture, pH level, oxygen tension, the presence of inhibitory substances, and temperature. For signs of spoilage consult Seeley, Vandermark, and Lee (1991) and Brock, Madigan, Martinko, and Parker (1994).

PROCESSING

Many food materials are processed to halt enzyme action and to destroy specific pathogens and spoilage organisms, thus prolonging the keeping quality for hours, days, months, or even years. Frazier and Westhoff (1978) have summarized the principles of food preservation as follows:

1. Prevention or delay of microbial decomposition:
   a. By keeping out microorganisms (asepsis)
   b. By removal of microorganisms, e.g., by filtration

   c. By hindering the growth and activity of microorganisms, e.g., by low temperatures, drying, anaerobic conditions, or chemicals
   d. By killing the microorganisms, e.g., by heat or radiation
2. Prevention or delay of self-decomposition of the food:
   a. By destruction of food enzymes, e.g., blanching
   b. By prevention or delay of purely chemical reactions, e.g., prevention of oxidation by means of an antioxidant
3. Prevention of damage because of insects, animals, mechanical causes, etc.

It is beyond the scope of this book to discuss the principles and methodology of commercial food preservation, such as pasteurization, canning, freezing, freeze-drying, dehydration, dehydrofreezing, curing, salting, pickling, use of chemical preservatives, and irradiation; the reader is referred to Frazier and Westhoff (1978), Potter (1986), Desrosier and Desrosier (1977), Decareau (1992), Gould, Brown and Fletcher (1983), and Mitchell (1988).

At this time federal regulations permit irradiation of potatoes for the prevention of sprouting, and irradiation of wheat grain and wheat flour for insect control. Also, irradiation of certain spices, herbs, and vegetable seasonings has been approved by the Food and Drug Administration (FDA) to control microbial load and insect infestation, provided that the total absorbed dose is not in excess of a certain limit set by the FDA.

In 1985 the FDA gave permission for irradiation of pork to control the presence of *Trichina spiralis,* the causative organism of trichinosis in humans. Foods treated by federally approved doses are completely wholesome. And in 1986 irradiation of fresh fruits and vegetables was approved. The use of radiation in food processing has not progressed as quickly as was hoped in the United States.

The microbial flora of public health significance that may be expected to occur in connection with processed foods are discussed in Chapter 6.

Persons entrusted with serving meals to the public must be familiar with the signs of incipient spoilage although, as was pointed out above, freedom from such signs is no guarantee of wholesomeness; unfortunately there are forms of illness-producing spoilage which do not give us the comfort of noticeable changes indicating that the food has become poisonous. When newly purchased food or stored food is being inspected, signs of incipient spoilage should be familiar to the one doing the job.

REFERENCES

Brock, T. D., M. T. Madigan, J. M. Martinko, and J. Parker (1991). *Biology of Microorganisms,* 7th ed. Prentice Hall, Englewood Cliffs, NJ.

Decareau, R. V. (1992). *Microwave Foods, New Product Development.* Food and Nutrition Press, Inc., Trumbull, CT.

Frazier, W. C. and D. C. Westhoff (1978). *Food Microbiology,* 3rd ed. McGraw-Hill Book Co., New York.

Gould, G. W., M. H. Brown, and B. C. Fletcher (1983). "Mechanisms of action of food preservation procedures." In *Food Microbiology: Advances and Prospects,* T. A. Roberts and F. A. Skinner, Eds., Academic Press, San Diego, CA, Chapter 3.

Hollis, F., M. Kaplow, R. Klose, and J. Halik (1968). "Parameters of moisture content for stabilization of food products." U.S. Army Natick Lab. Tech. Rpt. No. 69-26-FL.

King, A. D., Jr., H. D. Michener, and K. A. Ito (1969). "Control of *Byssochlamys* and related heat-resistant fungi in grape products." *Appl. Microbiol.,* 18:166–173.

King, A. D., Jr., A. N. Booth, A. E. Stafford, and A. C. Waiss, Jr. (1972). "*Byssochlamys fulva,* metabolite toxicity in laboratory animals." *J. Food Sci.,* 37:86–89.

Mitchell, E. L. (1988). "A review of aseptic processing of food." In *Advances in Food Research,* C. O. Chichester and B. S. Schweigert, Eds., Academic Press, San Diego, CA, Chapter 1.

Seeley, H. W., P. J. Vandemark, and J. J. Lee (1991). *Microbes in Action,* 4th ed. W. H. Freeman and Company, New York.

Splittstoesser, D. F., F. R. Kuss, W. Harrison, and D. B. Prest (1971). "Incidence of heat-resistant molds in Eastern orchards and vineyards." *Appl. Microbiol.,* 21:335–337.

ADDITIONAL READINGS

Ball, C. O. and F. C. W. Olson. *Sterilization in Food Technology: Theory, Practice and Calculations.* McGraw-Hill Book Co., New York. 1957.

Dack, G. M. *Food Poisoning,* 3rd ed. Univ. of Chicago Press, Chicago. 1956.

Heid, J. L., and M. A. Joslyn. *Fundamentals of Food Processing Operations: Ingredients, Methods, and Packaging.* Avi Publishing Co., Westport, CT. 1967.

The International Commission on Microbiological Specifications for Foods, *Microbial Ecology of Foods,* Vol. 1. Academic Press, New York. 1980.

Josephson, E. S. and M. S. Peterson, Eds. *Preservation of Food by Ionizing Radiation,* Vol. II and III. CRC Press, Boca Raton, FL. 1983.

Rose, A. H., Ed. *Food Microbiology.* Academic Press, London. 1983.

Russell, A. D. and R. Fuller, Eds. *Cold-Tolerant Microbes in Spoilage and the Environment.* Society for Applied Bacteriology, Techn. Services, No. 13. Academic Press, London, New York, San Francisco. 1979.

Sperber, W. H. "Influence of water activity on foodborne bacteria—a review." *Jour. Food Prot.,* 46:142–150. 1983.

Spiher, A. T. "Food Irradiation: an FDA report." *FDA Papers 2* (Oct.): 15–16. 1968.

CHAPTER 2

Some Basic Facts on Microorganisms Important in Food Sanitation

M icroorganisms and parasites may be transmitted through food and may cause illnesses in the persons who ingest the contaminated items. For some microorganisms the food may serve as a mere vehicle of transmission; for others, as a medium in which they multiply to tremendous numbers. Outbreaks of acute gastroenteritis caused by ingestion of food in which certain pathogens have multiplied profusely are popularly referred to as "food poisoning" outbreaks (see Chapter 4).

Microorganisms which may cause foodborne illnesses include bacteria, viruses, rickettsia, protozoa, and parasites such as trichinae. Although most of the microorganisms producing foodborne illnesses are bacteria, less than 1% of all bacteria are harmful to human beings and many are friendly.

This discussion is largely limited to bacteria. Among the bacteria are found some important pathogens transmitted by food—those that multiply profusely in food and are capable of causing outbreaks of food infections and food intoxications ("food poisoning").

Bacteria are plants. They are single-celled organisms and do not contain chlorophyll. The bacterial cell contains a wall through which the cell takes up simple nutrients in solution, which are combined by the cell for its utilization.

CLASSIFICATION, SIZE, SHAPE, MOTILITY, AND
ENDOSPORES OF BACTERIA

Classification

In contrast to the molds and yeasts, classification of bacteria on a morphological basis is difficult. In fact, bacteria are so small that morphological differences are inadequate as a basis for a workable classification. For larger grouping, some of the morphological characteristics used are shape, size, and
grouping of cells. Gram stain and formation of spores are used also. However, finer subdivisions into species and varieties are largely made on the
basis of physiological characteristics such as biochemical activities, pathogenicity, metabolic requirements, antigenic reactions, and reactions to the action of bacteriophages, which are viruses pathogenic to bacteria; these viruses attack the bacteria and kill them by lysis. Many phages are known, each
active against a specific species or even a strain of bacterium. This specificity
has an important practical application in the phage typing of bacteria. Thus
types may be distinguished which otherwise are known to look and react
alike.

The standard reference in the field of bacterial classification is Bergey's
Manual of Determinative Bacteriology, published by the American Society
for Microbiology.

Size

Bacterial cells are very small, with some variation among the different species. The majority of bacteria of importance in connection with food sanitation measure approximately $0.5–2.0 \times 2.0–10.0$ micrometers (μm), staphylococci having diameters 0.75 μm and larger; rods like salmonellae ranging in
width from 0.5 to 1 μm and in length from 2 to 3 μm. Filamentous bacteria
may be extremely long. The single cell is not visible to the naked eye, the
visual acuity of the naked eye being approximately 75 μm. One micrometer
equals 1/1000 mm or 1/25,400 inch.

When millions of bacterial cells are suspended in a clear substrate, the
suspension will assume a turbid appearance. Thus one may see the bacteria
as a population. Also, when bacteria cover a food surface in the form of a
slime they are visible to the human eye. Many times, however, the presence
of bacteria cannot be seen in food even if the contaminants are present in
sufficient numbers to make a person extremely ill.

Shape

In general, bacteria fall into three groups: cocci, rods, and spirilla. The rods are also referred to as bacilli. This is an unfortunate term since it may lead to confusion with the genus *Bacillus,* a spore former of the family Bacillaceae. The cocci are spherical; the rods are somewhat elongated; and the spirilla are comma-like or corkscrew-like in shape. The spirilla are not represented among the types causing foodborne diseases in man (Fig. 2.1).

Some bacteria form chains which may be short to quite long. Others cling together in various patterns, sometimes forming sizable aggregates or clumps. Examples among the cocci are: *Diplococcus,* a pair of cocci; *Sarcina,* eight spheres arranged in packet form; *Staphylococcus,* a grape-like aggregate of spheres; and *Streptococcus,* a chain of cocci. The rods may occur singly, in pairs, or in chains. The spirilla occur singly.

Motility

Some forms of bacteria carry whiplike appendages, termed flagella, by which some locomotion of the cells is made possible. Whereas all spirilla are motile, and practically none of the cocci are, the rods encompass motile as well

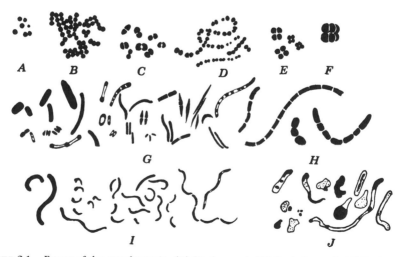

FIGURE 2.1.   Forms of the true bacteria. *(A)* Single cocci. *(B)* Staphylococci. *(C)* Diplococci. *(D)* Streptococci. *(E)* Tetrads. *(F)* Sarcinae. *(G)* Various forms of bacilli. *(H)* Streptobacilli. *(I)* Various forms of spirillae. *(J)* Involution forms. Reprinted with permission of Macmillan Publishing Co., Inc. from *Microbiology,* 6th ed., by K. L. Burdon and R. P. Williams. Copyright © 1968 by Macmillan Publishing Co., Inc.

as nonmotile forms. Examples of motile forms are *Proteus* and *Pseudomonas*. Although the flagella are relatively effective in helping bacteria to move about, they are not of practical importance in disseminating the cells. The distances traveled by bacteria with the aid of flagella are short indeed. Bacteria depend for distant dissemination on other means including dust particles, moisture droplets, direct contact, and the like.

Endospores

Some bacteria may form spores inside the cell wall, called endospores. One spore is formed in a cell. Of bacterial genera important in foods, *Clostridium* and *Bacillus* are spore formers. In general, bacterial forms other than rods do not produce spores. Spores are formed only in mature cells; they are thick walled and more resistant to high heat, low humidity, and other adverse conditions than vegetative cells.

The heat resistance of spores is very important in the food industry. The heat-resistant spores are used to develop heating temperatures and times for the production of safe canned goods. More will be said about the comparative heat resistance of vegetative cells and spores later on.

Spores may remain dormant for long times, even decades. When conditions become favorable, they will germinate into new, sensitive, vegetative cells which in turn start a new crop of vegetative cells.

Sublethal heating of spores has long been known to stimulate their germination. This fact is important in methods of food preservation involving the application of heat. It is also important in the cooking and holding of meats, since these are apt to be contaminated with the food-poisoning spore former *Clostridium perfringens*. The germination of spores can also be activated by other means, namely, by subjecting them to certain chemical agents under specified conditions and to ionizing radiation. The reader is referred to a review article by Berg and Sandine (1970).

REPRODUCTION AND DEATH OF VEGETATIVE CELLS

Reproduction of vegetative cells takes place by binary or transverse fission. In some cocci, division may take place along several planes. The rods divide along the short axis only. After a cell has divided into two daughter cells, each of these cells grows somewhat in size, quickly matures, and is ready for a new division. In fact, maturation may take as little as 15–30 minutes, this period being called the generation time. The length of generation time varies with the organisms as well as many other factors, among them medium and temperature.

When vegetative bacterial cells divide they multiply. Unfortunately, the term "growth" is also used to denote what in reality represents multiplication.

The Growth Curve

When bacterial cells multiply under favorable conditions they pass through various phases. When the number of cells is plotted against time, a curve results which illustrates these phases. To determine a growth curve, the investigator makes periodic counts of the number of cells and then plots the numbers per gram or milliliter of medium logarithmically on the ordinate, and units of time on the abscissa. A typical growth curve is illustrated in Figure 2.2.

Some bacteria produce toxins. The toxins may be excreted into the surrounding medium or food (exotoxins), or retained within the cell (endotoxins) and finally liberated when the cells disintegrate. Toxins capable of causing gastroenteritis or inflammation of the lining of the stomach and intestines are enterotoxins.

During the first phase no multiplication occurs. The phase is designated as stationary or as "lag" phase (A to B). It is possible for a decline to occur,

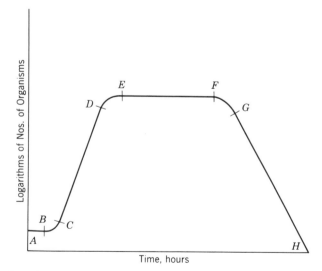

FIGURE 2.2.   Growth curve of microorganisms. *A—B:* Lag phase. *B—C:* Phase of positive acceleration. *C—D:* Logarithmic phase. *D—E:* Phase of negative acceleration. *E—F:* Maximum stationary phase. *F—G:* Accelerated death phase. *G—H:* Death phase. Reprinted with permission of McGraw-Hill Book Company from *Food Microbiology,* 3rd ed., by W. C. Frazier and D. C. Westhoff. Copyright © 1978 McGraw-Hill, Inc.

because some of the cells may fail to adjust to the new environment. The second phase *(B* to *C)* is that of "positive acceleration," during which the rate of multiplication is continuously increasing. The lag phase and the stage of continued increase are usually combined and referred to as "lag phase." Factors affecting this combination lag phase are: size of inoculum—if the inoculum is large, the lag phase is brief; age of cells—if the cells are young, the lag phase is brief; and general environmental conditions—if favorable, the lag phase is brief.

Perishable food items should be kept at temperatures conducive to holding the bacteria present in the "lag phase" as long as possible. This involves two major efforts: to keep the bacterial load low and to regulate the temperature of the food in such a fashion that it is far removed from the growth optimum. In a foodservice operation, suitable food is available to the bacteria at all times. Therefore, few alterations can be made in the environment, except changes in temperature.

During the third phase *(C* to *D)* the rate of cell increase is constant. This phase is referred to as the "logarithmic (or log) phase," since the number of bacteria increases in a geometric progression. If the logarithms of the numbers are plotted against time, a straight line results.

A generation time of 20–30 minutes is common for the bacteria that grow well at moderate and high temperatures, whereas the cold-loving bacteria have longer generation times.

The number of generations of bacteria during the logarithmic phase is calculated as follows:

$$n = \frac{\log c - \log b}{\log 2}$$

n = number of generations
$\log c$ = log of number of bacteria/ml at point *D*
$\log b$ = log of number of bacteria/ml at point *C*
$\log 2$ = log of 2

The duration of the logarithmic phase is affected by the factors controlling growth.

The fourth phase *(D* to *E)* is that of "negative acceleration," since the rate of multiplication is constantly decreasing. The fifth phase *(E* to *F)* is the maximum stationary phase; the increase and decrease cancel each other and thus the number of cells remains constant.

The length of the stationary phase is strongly affected by the kind of organism, depletion of nutrients, and accumulation of waste products of cells. The reasons for the stationary phase are not completely understood.

The sixth phase *(F* to *G)* is the "accelerated death phase," and the seventh

(G to *H)* is the "final death phase," during which the number of viable cells decreases at a steady rate. Eventually, all the cells of a culture die and become autolyzed or self-dissolving.

Some important factors besides kind of organism and its previous history affecting bacterial multiplication and death are: composition of substrate, moisture, osmotic pressure, oxygen tension, pH, temperature, and presence of inhibitors. Size of initial inoculum and competition from other microorganisms are other important factors.

Factors Affecting Growth

FOOD. Requirements for growth will vary with the kind of bacterium, sometimes down to the various strains of a species. Some bacteria have an extremely wide range and can multiply in many kinds of food; others are quite specific in their food requirements. Bacteria vary in their need for vitamins and other accessory growth factors in the medium. Although all bacteria need vitamins, some are able to synthesize the vitamins they need from other compounds present in the substrate.

Accessory growth factors are substances which do not furnish building materials or energy to the cells, but which are essential to growth. They are effective in minute or trace quantities. These substances are also called essential metabolites; they range from simple ionic forms such as Cu^{2+}, Mn^{2+}, and F^{3+} to complex organic materials.

The bacteria responsible for foodborne illnesses happen to thrive well in many of the foods we eat, especially in food items of proteinaceous nature. In general, if the quality of the growth medium is good, it widens the range of conditions, such as moisture, acidity, and temperature, within which an organism may grow.

MOISTURE AND OSMOTIC PRESSURE. Bacteria need food of high moisture content, in general. But the minimum moisture content necessary to support bacterial growth is not a definite value. By comparison, yeasts require high moisture for growth, and molds may develop on substrates of lower moisture content than is required by yeasts and bacteria. If the air surrounding the food is humid, molds may develop on substrates of rather low water content.

It has been emphasized that the amount of available moisture, not total moisture, affects bacterial multiplication. The available moisture may be expressed as "water activity" (a_w). Water activity is calculated by dividing the vapor pressure of the solution by the vapor pressure of the solvent; thus a value of 1.00 is assigned to pure water.

A medium of high osmotic pressure may adversely affect the bacterial cells by drawing water from the cells to an extent damaging to their metabolic processes. Sugar and salt are used in food preservation for this reason. Sensitivity to osmotic pressure varies with the kind of bacteria, whether the cells are vegetative or spores, and some other factors. Some microbial forms are very resistant to high osmotic pressure. Certain molds and yeasts grow in substrates of extremely high sugar content. Most bacteria are not highly sensitive to salt concentrations between approximately 0.5 and 3%. Some bacterial forms are quite tolerant to high salt, among them *Staphylococcus aureus,* a food-poisoning organism. Truly salt-loving, or halophilic, bacteria require high concentrations of salt in their growth media. Halophilics can be important in the spoilage of highly salted foods or curing brines of 20–30% salt content. Microorganisms that are merely tolerant to salt are salt resistant, or haloduric.

Water may become less available through the presence of solutes like salt and sugar as well as through the action of hydrophilic (water-loving) colloids. Water may also be tied up through freezing. In frozen foods the water is in the solid state and thus unavailable. Removal of water by dehydration is a common form of food preservation.

Once dried, some forms of microbes die more easily than others. Spores may survive longer periods of desiccation than vegetative cells. Even sensitive species can be kept viable in the dried condition if the cells are rapidly frozen, followed by rapid desiccation in a vacuum. This method of preserving bacteria, viruses, toxins, and enzymes is known as lyophilization.

OXYGEN REDUCTION POTENTIAL. Microorganisms vary in their response to oxygen. This characteristic has been used to classify them into three (or four) groups: the strict aerobes, which require free oxygen—to this group belong the molds, yeasts, and some bacteria; the strict anaerobes, which will multiply only where air is excluded except when strong substances are present or when associated with aerobic organisms; and the facultative forms, which multiply with or without free oxygen. Many bacteria belong here. Some bacteria require a definite, minute quantity of oxygen; these organisms are classified as being microaerophilic.

HYDROGEN ION CONCENTRATION (pH). The degree of acidity or alkalinity of a medium, or food, is expressed as the hydrogen ion concentration. The pH value represents the reciprocal of the negative logarithm of the hydrogen ion concentration. The pH scale extends from 0 to 14, a pH value of 7 expressing neutrality. Acid materials possess pH values below 7; basic or alkaline materials have pH values above 7. A difference of 1 pH unit corresponds to a tenfold difference in hydrogen ion concentration. The relationship between hydrogen ion concentration and pH is shown in Table 2.1.

The molds and yeasts are quite tolerant to acid, and some molds are able to grow in media of pH values near 2. Bacteria vary greatly in their reaction

TABLE 2.1. *Relationships Between Hydrogen Ion Concentration, pH, and Reaction*

Hydrogen Ion Concentration [H+] (moles per liter)	Logarithm of Hydrogen Ion Concentration	pH	Reaction
0.1	-1	1.0	Acid
0.01	-2	2.0	Acid
0.001	-3	3.0	Acid
0.0001	-4	4.0	Acid
0.00001	-5	5.0	Acid
0.000001	-6	6.0	Acid
0.0000001	-7	7.0	Neutral
0.00000001	-8	8.0	Alkaline
0.000000001	-9	9.0	Alkaline
0.0000000001	-10	10.0	Alkaline
0.00000000001	-11	11.0	Alkaline

Source: Adapted from Burdon and Williams (1968).

to pH. In general, they grow best at a pH near neutral. Some are quite sensitive to the pH of their substrate, others are not.

Some acid-forming bacteria are favored by a slightly acid medium. They are important in the food industry in that they are used in producing various acids in foods such as fermented milk, sauerkraut, butter, and cheeses. Certain proteolytic bacteria can grow in alkaline media such as egg white.

It is an important fact that slightly acid, neutral, and slightly alkaline food materials will support multiplication of the organisms causing food infections and food poisoning.

The food materials of pH near the neutral point are mostly the animal foods: meats and meat products, seafood, eggs, milk, and so on. Of the vegetables, some are rather low in acid; examples are corn, peas, and hominy. A very acid vegetable is the tomato, which is actually a fruit. The fruits are at the high-acid end of the scale, the citrus fruit being among the very acid fruits (Table 2.2).

Some food materials have a rather stable pH. The compounds which resist changes in pH are called buffers. Proteins have excellent buffering power.

Acid is used in food preservation to suppress bacterial multiplication. Within certain limits, acidification can also be used to suppress bacterial multiplication in menu items. This aspect is discussed in Chapter 11.

TABLE 2.2. *Hydrogen Ion Concentration and pH of Some Common Foods*

Hydrogen Ion Concentration	pH	Average pH Values for Common Foods
1.0×10^{-2}	2.0	Limes
8.0×10^{-3}	2.1	
6.3×10^{-3}	2.2	Lemons
5.0×10^{-3}	2.3	
4.0×10^{-3}	2.4	
3.2×10^{-3}	2.5	
2.5×10^{-3}	2.6	
2.0×10^{-3}	2.7	
1.6×10^{-3}	2.8	
1.3×10^{-3}	2.9	Vinegar, plums
1.0×10^{-3}	3.0	Gooseberries
	3.1	Prunes, apples, grapefruit (3.0–3.3)
	3.2	Rhubarb, dill pickles
	3.3	Apricots, blackberries
	3.4	Strawberries, lowest acidity for jelly
	3.5	Peaches
	3.6	Raspberries, sauerkraut
	3.7	Blueberries, oranges (3.1–4.1)
	3.8	Sweet cherries
	3.9	Pears
1.0×10^{-4}	4.0	Acid fondant, acidophilus milk
	4.1	
	4.2	Tomatoes (4.0–4.6)
	4.3	
	4.4	Lowest acidity for processing at 100°C
	4.5	Buttermilk
	4.6	Bananas, egg albumin, figs, isoelectric point for casein, pimientos
	4.7	
	4.8	
	4.9	
1.0×10^{-5}	5.0	Pumpkins, carrots
	5.1	Cucumbers
	5.2	Turnips, cabbage, squash
	5.3	Parsnips, beets
	5.4	Sweet potatoes, bread
	5.5	Spinach
	5.6	Asparagus, cauliflower
	5.7	
	5.8	Meat, ripened
	5.9	
1.0×10^{-6}	6.0	Tuna
	6.1	Potatoes
	6.2	Peas
1.0×10^{-6}	6.3	Corn, oysters, dates
	6.4	Egg yolk

TABLE 2.2. *Continued*

Hydrogen Ion Concentration	pH	Average pH Values for Common Foods
	6.5	
	6.6	Milk (6.5–6.7)
	6.7	
	6.8	
	6.9	Shrimp
1.0×10^{-7}	7.0	Meat, unripened
	7.1	
	7.2	
	7.3	
	7.4	
	7.5	
	7.6	
	7.7	
	7.8	
	7.9	
1.0×10^{-8}	8.0	Egg white (7.0–9.0)
	8.1	
	8.2	
	8.3	
	8.4	

Source: Handbook of Food Preparation, 9th ed., p. 21. Copyright © 1993, American Home Economics Association, Washington, D.C.

Acidity is not only important in relation to bacterial multiplication, it is also a factor in thermal death of bacteria. In canning, very acid foods may be given a relatively light heat treatment.

TEMPERATURE. Microorganisms have their specific temperature requirements for growth. At the *optimum temperature* a cell multiplies and grows most readily; at the *minimum temperature* it multiplies but ceases below that point; and at the *maximum temperature* it multiplies, but ceases above that point. It is well not to think of these temperatures as sharp points, since the medium in which the cells are suspended, as well as other factors, cause some degree of variation in optimum, minimum, and maximum temperatures of multiplication.

On the basis of their growth response to the various temperatures, bacteria have been classified into groups.

The thermophilic (heat-loving) bacteria have high optimum temperatures from 113 to 140°F (45–60°C) and a maximum of 167°F (75°C). The mesophilic (intermediate) bacteria have optimum growth temperatures between approximately 68 and 113°F (20 and 45°C), and a maximum of 114 to 131°F

(45 to 55°C). Psychrophilics are usually referred to as bacteria that are able to grow relatively rapidly at 32°F (0°C) or lower down to 19°F (−7°C), but usually have optima at 50–68°F (10–20°C), although a few have considerably lower optima, below 50°F (10°C). An effort has been made to more accurately define this group by dividing it into the true psychrophilics, which prefer low temperatures for growth, and psychrotrophics, which multiply fairly well at temperatures of 41°F (5°C) and below, whatever their optimum temperatures might be (Mossel and Zwart, 1960; Eddy, 1960). For a detailed discussion of temperature requirements of psychrophilics, see Morita (1975) and Herbert and Bhakoo (1979).

It should be reemphasized that much overlapping occurs within all the groups mentioned above. Organisms may vary greatly regarding the temperature range within which they are able to multiply. For example, some mesophilic bacteria may grow at very low temperatures and others at very high temperatures, although their optimum is in the medium-temperature range. Cold-loving bacteria play an important role in the spoilage of refrigerated food items.

When the maximum growth temperature of a bacterial cell is exceeded, the bacterium may survive for a while until eventually death takes place.

The heat resistance of microorganisms varies with genus, species, and strain. Therefore, only approximate data can be given. In general, spores of microorganisms are more heat-resistant than vegetative cells.

In the case of the yeast, the vegetative cells are usually killed by applying moist heat of 122–136°F (50–58°C) for 10–15 minutes; spores require exposure to 140°F (60°C) for the same length of time. In the case of the molds, vegetative cells and spores are usually killed by moist heating at 140°F (60°C) for 5–10 minutes. Some heat-resistant forms require a more vigorous heat treatment, and temperatures many degrees higher than those mentioned above must be applied to achieve kill.

In bacteria, resistance to heat varies widely. A few generalizations seem in order. Cocci are usually more heat resistant than rods, with exceptions. Bacteria that require high temperatures for optimum growth are likely to be resistant to heat, and so are bacteria that are shielded by capsules. Even strains of the same species may vary regarding response to heat. The heat resistance of bacterial spores varies with the species and the physiological condition of the spores. The concentration of cells has a definite effect on resistance to heat in that the higher the concentration or the larger the load, the greater is the heat treatment required for their destruction.

Age has an effect on heat resistance in that young cells in the lag or log stage are more easily killed than cells in the stationary growth phase. Old cells are again more easily killed. The previous history of cells, the temperature at which they were grown, seems to have an effect on their heat resistance also.

The type of medium in which the microbial cells are exposed has a profound effect on heat resistance. Microorganisms are killed more easily in moist than in dry media; in acid rather than neutral or somewhat akaline media, with exceptions; in the presence of antiseptic or germicidal substances; and in the absence of certain protective substances. The effect of certain protective substances has been established for specific organisms and generalizations cannot be made. Among protective substances are colloidal materials, especially proteins and fats, sodium chloride, and sugar.

Heating bacteria may damage the cells in such a way that they behave like dead cells in one medium, but again show viability when exposed to different conditions. It seems that a number of events contribute to the death of bacteria by heating.

Thermal death is a time–temperature effect. In general, as the temperature applied to the microorganisms is increased, the time needed to achieve death decreases. For example, milk can be effectively pasteurized at 145°F (63°C) by maintaining this temperature for 30 minutes, or at 161°F (72°C) by a 15-second exposure. Both temperature and time of heat application affect death of microorganisms.

Therefore, the heat resistance of microorganisms is usually expressed as thermal death time, which is the time required at a specified temperature to kill a specified number of vegetative cells, or spores, under highly specified conditions. In the older literature, the term "thermal death point" refers to the temperature necessary to kill all the organisms within a period of 10 minutes. This term is inexact because not all cells die at the very same instant.

Thermal death depends on the heat resistance of the organisms, the age and previous history of the organism, the temperature it is exposed to, the length of time for which heat is applied, the presence of moisture, the nature of the medium in which the cells are suspended, the number of vegetative cells or spores in the medium, and some other factors. There are differences in heat resistance within a given population.

The food-processing industry has developed time–temperature schedules for various products to satisfy the requirements of killing important contaminants of public health significance while preventing loss of culinary quality due to intense or prolonged heating.

Resistant forms are sometimes called "thermodurics." This is a practical term and serves to denote survivors resisting the heat treatments applied to foods in routine heat-processing operations.

At low temperatures the lag phase is prolonged, and when cell division has begun, generation times are very long and the bacterial population builds up at a very slow rate.

Below the freezing point, the degree of killing varies not only with type of organism, but with the nature of the surrounding medium. Injury to cells by freezing is also affected by the method and speed of freezing. In the freezing of foods, only part of the contaminating bacterial flora is eliminated. Vegetative cells are killed more readily than spores. Freezing is not a method of sterilization. In fact, bacterial cultures can be preserved by freezer-storing them at very low temperatures.

Low temperatures are used in refrigeration and in the storage of frozen foods. Low temperatures are, in general, inhibitors; their killing power is limited. Above the freezing point little multiplication takes place except for the psychrophiles.

To prevent perishable foods from remaining within the temperature range of bacterial multiplication is one of the most important duties of the food service manager in his endeavors to prepare and serve wholesome food to the public (Chapters 11 and 13).

INHIBITORS. Inhibitors may have a pronounced effect on bacterial multiplication and death. Inhibitors may be a part of the food; they may have developed as a product of the microorganism's metabolism; they may have developed during processing; or they may have been purposely added by the processor.

Some examples of inhibitors that are a natural part of the food are: benzoic acid in cranberries, lactenins and anticoliform factors in freshly drawn milk, and lysozyme in egg whites.

Inhibitory substances developed by microorganisms during their multiplication may accumulate and become toxic. An example is alcohol produced in the growth and fermentation of yeast, in fruit juices, or in the production of wine. Substances not inhibitory to the organism producing them may be inhibitory to other organisms. This fact is very important when different kinds of microorganisms are in competition while growing. Such inhibitory substances include acids, peroxides, alcohol, and antibiotics.

Seldom will a contaminant find itself without competition from other kinds of microorganisms with which it will interact in some way. These interactions fall into three general categories: metabiosis, synergism, and antagonism.

In a metabiotic relationship, one type of microorganism makes conditions favorable for the growth of the other. Many examples of these interactions are known such as fermentations and decompositions of raw food materials, and the reader is referred to books on food microbiology. One organism succeeds another, although some overlapping may occur.

In the natural souring of milk, a variety of different bacteria produce the acid at the early stage of souring. During the later stages, usually one *Streptococcus* survives.

In a synergistic relationship, organisms act cooperatively and achieve what neither can do alone. Colors may be produced in the medium which are different from what either organism can produce by itself. An item of interest in food sanitation concerns the food-poisoning organism *Clostridium botuli-*

num. The toxin *C. botulinum,* type E, when produced in a fish product was found to be greatly activated by the activity of another *Clostridium* which released an enzyme that enhanced the toxicity of the type E toxin (Sakaguchi and Tohyama, 1955a, b).

In an antagonistic relationship the microorganisms are in life-or-death competition, which may be for nutrients, change of pH to the disadvantage of the other, and even the production of antibiotics by one to the disadvantage of the other. An example of interest from a public health point of view is this: *Staphylococcus aureus* is adversely affected by a mixed population in milk, cream fillings, chicken pies, and other menu items (Peterson et al., 1962a, b). Graves and Frazier (1963) found that of 870 cultures of predominant microorganisms isolated from foods, over 25% were inhibitory to *S. aureus;* the remainder, however, had no stimulatory effects. According to Kraft and Ayres (1966), fluorescing spoilage organisms attained large populations on refrigerated chicken even when *S. aureus* initially outnumbered these spoilage organisms 100:1.

Clostridium botulinum may be adversely affected by other bacteria, which may limit the germination of spores and vegetative growth of this food-poisoning organism or may destroy its toxin as rapidly as it forms. An antibiotic active against *C. botulinum* is formed by *Brevibacterium lineus,* a bacterium important in the ripening of Limburger cheese (Grecz, 1961). Inhibition of *Clostridium botulinum* by strains of *Clostridium perfringens* was studied by Smith (1975), who found that several *C. perfringens* strains, isolated from soil, produced an inhibitor capable of affecting the majority of strains of *C. botulinum* type A, B, E, and F. In mixed culture, an inhibitory strain of *C. perfringens* interfered with growth and toxin production of *C. botulinum* type A in spite of the fact that the latter outnumbered it by about 40 times.

Inhibitory substances may develop during heat processing of foods. Examples are the substances resulting from the heating of lipids. An in-depth discussion of the interacting factors affecting mixed populations has been presented by the International Commission on Microbiological Specifications for Foods (1980).

Substances that are purposely added to foods by the processor to inhibit microbial growth are so manifold that a detailed discussion of these is beyond the scope of this book. Inhibiting agents may be physical or chemical in nature, or a combination. The chemicals may be inorganic or organic in nature.

Fungistatic or mycostatic agents inhibit, and fungicidal agents kill, fungi (molds). Bacteriostatic agents inhibit, and bactericidal agents kill, bacteria.

Sterilization denotes a process whereby a substance is freed of all living microorganisms, be it by chemical agents, heat, physical removal, radiation, or other means. Sanitizing reduces the microbial population to safe levels, as determined by public health requirements; usually 99.9% of the contaminants must be exterminated. Heat or chemical sanitizers are the agents.

The effect of the various agents employed in inhibiting or killing microorganisms is affected by such factors as their concentration and time of action, and by the kinds, numbers, age, and previous history of the microorganisms to which they are applied, as well as by the medium surrounding the microorganism. A protective action may be expected from the presence of colloidal matter or solids. More will be said about this later on.

OTHER MICROORGANISMS IMPORTANT IN FOOD SANITATION

Fungi

These are chlorophyll-free microorganisms which include, among other members, the molds and yeasts.

MOLDS.   Mold growth may appear as cottony, powdery, or fuzzy tufts and patches, often highly colored. Most molds smell "moldy." The tufts or patches are the mycelium which consists of threadlike structures called hyphae; on these hyphae spores are produced (Fig. 2.3). There is a great variation in the mode of spore formation. In contrast to spore-forming bacteria, in which only one spore is formed in one cell, the mold spores serve as reproductive bodies and disseminate the organisms. Practically all molds form spores of some kind.

In general, molds are not choosy regarding the substrate on which they grow, whether it is moist or dry, acid or nonacid, high or low in salt or sugar. Molds may grow over an extremely wide range of temperature. Optimal temperatures range from about 25 to 30°C (77–86°F) for most molds, but some will grow at higher temperatures, for example, *Aspergillus*. Others are capable of growing at refrigerator and freezer temperatures. Molds growing on foods are aerobic, requiring oxygen for growth.

Therefore, one finds molds on practically all foods at almost any temperature under which foods are held.

Among the molds important in food spoilage are species of *Aspergillus, Penicillium, Mucor,* and *Rhizopus.* Of these, *Aspergillus* has aroused concern because some species contain strains capable of releasing toxins into foods.

Metabolites of certain fungi are useful to us as antibiotics; others have proven to be toxic. Fungal metabolites that are capable of being toxic to humans and animals are referred to as mycotoxins. Of these, the aflatoxins are of great importance because of their carcinogenic capacity. They are produced by the common contaminants *Aspergillus flavus* and *Aspergillus parasiticus.*

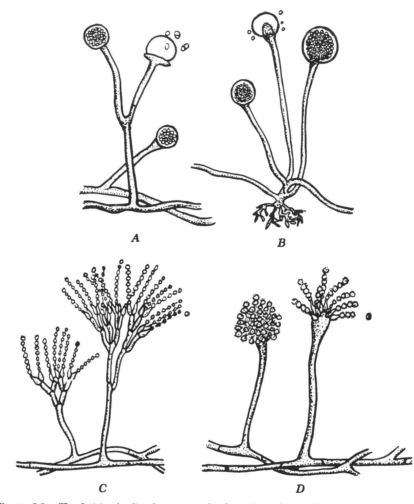

FIGURE 2.3. The fruiting bodies (structures for formation of asexual reproductive spores) in common molds. *(A) Mucor. (B) Rhizopus. (C) Penicillium. (D) Aspergillus.* Reprinted with permission of Macmillan Publishing Company, Inc., from *Microbiology,* 6th ed., by K. L. Burdon and R. P. Williams. Copyright © 1968 by Macmillan Publishing Co., Inc.

YEASTS.   Yeasts are not known to cause foodborne illnesses. The yeasts are one-celled bodies propagating by budding (Fig. 2.4), and are very ubiquitous. Because they need moisture and sugar for their metabolism, they cause spoilage of sugar-containing foodstuffs. The yeasts are very useful in the food industry for processing food requiring fermentation and leavening, as in the manufacture of beer, wine, and bread. In general, the temperature require-

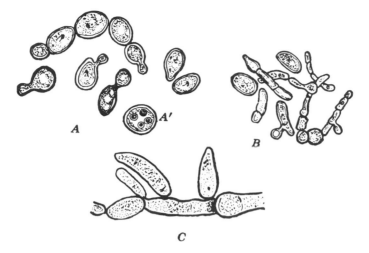

FIGURE 2.4.   Yeasts. *(A)* Common harmless yeast *(Saccharomyces),* showing budding. *(A')* An ascospore, a special reproductive body sometimes formed by true yeasts. *(B) Blastomyces,* a pathogenic yeast. *(C) Candida albicans,* a yeastlike fungus causing thrush. Reprinted with permission of Macmillan Publishing Co., Inc., from *Microbiology,* 6th ed., by K. L. Burdon and R. P. Williams. Copyright © 1968 by Macmillan Publishing Co., Inc.

ments of yeasts are similar to those of the molds. Yeasts may grow under aerobic or anaerobic conditions.

Viruses

Since it has been shown that viruses can be foodborne, a brief discussion is in order. Viruses are capable of causing diseases in plants, animals, and humans. They do not multiply outside the living cells of their hosts. They are of extremely small (ultramicroscopic) size, and most forms will pass through filters, which retain bacteria. They are very specific in their host relationship and consist essentially of genetic material, that is, nucleic acids. A virus genome contains two or three chemical compounds: a single molecule either of DNA (deoxyribonucleic acid) or RNA (ribonucleic acid) and a protein coat around the nucleic acid. Some viruses possess, in addition, an envelope (around the protein coat) which contains a structural lipid essential to the infectivity of the virus particle. Viruses are acellular and have no cytoplasm, nucleus, cell wall, or cell membrane. They do not undergo fission. The more complex viruses contain nucleoproteins and other compounds such as carbohydrates, lipids or lipoproteins, trace metals, and substances of vitamin-like nature.

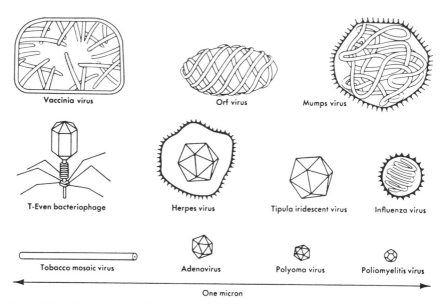

Vaccinia virus   Orf virus   Mumps virus

T-Even bacteriophage   Herpes virus   Tipula iridescent virus   Influenza virus

Tobacco mosaic virus   Adenovirus   Polyoma virus   Poliomyelitis virus

One micron

Figure 2.5. Relative sizes and structure of viruses. Drawings represent the objects magnified 175,000 times. The herpes virus, adenovirus, polyoma and poliomyelitis viruses, and tipula iridescent virus (an insect virus) have a polyhedral structure and possess cubic symmetry. The tobacco mosaic virus and the internal components of the mumps and influenza viruses have helical symmetry. The others have a more complex structural symmetry. From R. W. Horne: *The Structure of Viruses.* Copyright © 1963 by Scientific American, Inc. All rights reserved.

An electron microscope* is required to study their structure. It has been found that they are of various shapes and sizes (10–450 mμm) (Fig. 2.5); some are shaped like cocci or rods, some have peculiar "tails." Some viruses are shown to be of crystalline structure. Examples of human diseases caused by viruses are influenza, measles, mumps, poliomyelitis, chicken pox, yellow fever, the common cold (in part), hepatitis, and AIDS, a disease with no known cure at this time. Some of these viruses have been associated with foodborne outbreaks.

Many viruses seem to be inactivated by heating at 65°C (149°F) for one-half to one hour, or by very brief heating at 72°C (161.6°F). Some viruses require boiling for destruction (Mosley and Galambos, 1969). The type of food and its constituents also seem to have an important bearing on the efficacy of heat to destroy viruses in food. Therefore, generalizations are risky.

---

*In an electron microscope, structures of 10 mμm are visible, whereas with the ordinary light microscope, the limit of visibility is approximately 200 mμm.

Rickettsiae

The rickettsiae are rod-like, ovoid, or spherical in shape, and are much smaller than bacteria. Like the viruses, they multiply in living tissues only. They are, in size, intermediate between the large viruses and the bacteria. They range in size up to 0.5×2 μm, at the most, and can be seen with the

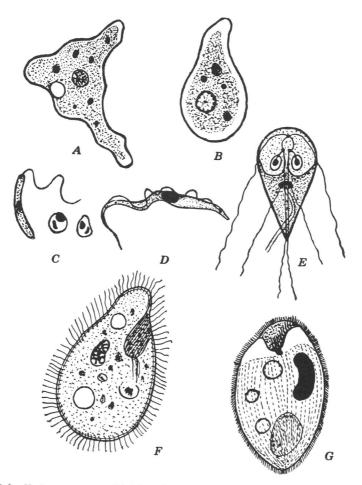

FIGURE 2.6.   Various protozoa. *(A)* A harmless amoeba. *(B) Entamoeba histolytica,* the cause of amoebic dysentery. *(C)* Forms of *Leishmania,* a kind of protozoan causing sores on the skin. *(D)* A trypanosome, a flagellated protozoan of the type causing African sleeping sickness. *(E) Giardia (lamblia) intestinalis,* a common intestinal parasite of man. *(F) Colpuda,* a harmless ciliated protozoan common in nature. *(G) Balantidium coli,* a ciliate sometimes found in the intestine of man. Reprinted with permission of Macmillan Publishing Co., Inc., from *Microbiology,* 6th ed., by K. L. Burdon and R. P. Williams. Copyright © 1968 by Macmillan Publishing Co., Inc.

ordinary microscope. They are believed to multiply by fission, and their mode of nutrition and multiplication is not fully understood. Examples of human diseases caused by rickettsiae are: typhus fever, Q fever, and Rocky Mountain spotted fever.

Cows infected with the organism causing Q fever many transmit the disease to humans through the milk, unless the milk has been properly heat treated.

Some members of the rickettsiae have been shown to have a definite metabolic activity. They are susceptible to antibiotics; in this respect they resemble the larger viruses, the small viruses being resistant to antibiotics. Rickettsiae are primarily parasites of insects, and some are pathogenic to their insect hosts. Many of them are pathogenic to humans, to whom they are transmitted by the bite of the insects carrying the rickettsiae—the so-called vectors.

Protozoa

The protozoa need mentioning since certain forms may be carried by food and may cause illness when ingested. Protozoa are one-celled animal-like forms, usually of microscopic size (Fig. 2.6).

Protozoa are widely distributed in nature, especially in sea water, but also in lakes, ponds, and streams. Soil, especially soil rich in organic matter, contains large numbers of these animals. Nearly all animals carry protozoa in their intestinal tract, most of them harmless. *Entamoeba histolytica* is a pathogenic form which has been shown to cause amoebiasis or amoebic dysentery and is spread by water and food. Amoebae multiply by fission.

Giardia lamblia is an inhabitant of the human intestinal tract; it is capable of causing an enteritis known as giardiasis. The organism may get into the food and water with human feces. Another disease-producing protozoan capable of causing intestinal disorders is *Dientamoeba fragilis*.

REFERENCES

American Home Economics Association (1993). *Handbook of Food Preparation,* 9th ed. American Home Economics Association, Washington, D.C.

American Society for Microbiology (1974). *Bergey's Manual of Determinative Bacteriology,* 8th ed. Williams and Wilkins Co., Baltimore, MD.

Berg, R. W. and W. E. Sandine (1970). "Activation of bacterial spores. A review." *J. Milk Food Technol.,* 33:435–441.

Burdon, K. L. and R. P. Williams (1968). *Microbiology,* 6th ed. Macmillan Co., New York.

Eddy, B. P. (1960). "The use and meaning of the term 'Psychrophilic.'" *J. Appl. Bacteriol.,* 23:189–190.

Frazier, W. C. and D. C. Westhoff (1978). *Food Microbiology,* 3rd ed. McGraw-Hill Book Co., New York.

Graves, R. P. and W. C. Frazier (1963). "Food microorganisms influencing the growth of *Staphylococcus aureus.*" *Appl. Microbiol.,* 11:513–516.

Grecz, N. (1961). "Natural Antibiotics in Limburger Type Cheese and Its Possible Use in Food Preservation." Activities Report, *Quartermaster Food Container Inst. Armed Forces,* 13:152–159.

Herbert, R. A. and M. Bhakoo (1979). "Microbial growth at low temperatures." In *Cold Tolerant Microbes in Spoilage and the Environment,* A. D. Russel and R. Fuller, Eds. The Soc. Appl. Bact. Tech. Ser. No. 13.

Horne, R. W. (1963). "The structure of viruses." *Sci. Am.,* 208:48.

International Commission on Microbiological Specifications for Food (1980). *Factors Affecting Life and Death of Microorganisms. Microbial Ecology of Foods,* Vol. I, Chapter 13.

Kraft, Allen A. and J. C. Ayres (1966). "Competitive growth of microorganisms and fluorescence development on inoculated chicken." *J. Food Sci.,* 31:111–117.

Morita, R. Y. (1975). "Psychrophilic bacteria." *Bacteriol. Rev.,* 39:146–167.

Mosley, J. W. and J. T. Galambos (1969). "Viral hepatitis." In *Diseases of the Liver,* J. B. Schiff, Ed., 3rd ed. Lippincott, Philadelphia, PA. p. 417.

Mossel, D. A. A. and H. Zwart (1960). "The rapid tentative recognition of psychrophilic types among *Enterobacteriaceae* isolated from foods." *J. Appl. Bacteriol.,* 23:185–188.

Peterson, A. C., J. J. Black, and M. F. Gunderson (1962a). "Staphylococci in competition. I. Growth of naturally occurring mixed populations in precooked frozen foods during defrost." *Appl. Microbiol.,* 10:16–22.

Peterson, A. C., J. J. Black, and M. F. Gunderson (1962b). "Staphylococcus in competition. II. Effects of total numbers and proportion of staphylococci in mixed cultures on growth in artificial culture media." *Appl. Microbiol.,* 10:23–32.

Sakaguchi, G. and Y. Tohyama (1955a). "Studies on the toxin production of *Clostridium botulinum* Type E. I. A strain of genus Clostridium having the action to promote Type E botulinal toxin production in a mixed culture." *Jap. J. Med. Sci. Biol.,* 8:247–253.

Sakaguchi, G. and Y. Tohyama (1955b). "Studies on the toxin production of *Clostridium botulinum* Type E. II. The mode of action of the contaminant organisms to promote toxin production of Type E organisms." *Jap. J. Med. Sci. Biol.,* 8:255–262.

Smith, L. D. S. (1975). "Inhibition of *Clostridium botulinum* by strains of *Clostridium perfringens* isolated from soil." *Appl. Microbiol.,* 30:319–323.

ADDITIONAL READINGS

Ayres, J. C., J. O. Mundt, and W. E. Sandine. *Microbiology of Foods.* W. H. Freeman and Co., San Francisco. 1980.

Horne, R. W. *Structure and Function of Viruses.* E. Arnold, London. 1978.

Ingraham, John L. "New concepts of psychrophilic bacteria." *Low Temperature Microbiology Symposium, Proceedings, 1961.* Campbell Soup Co., Camden, NJ. 1962.

Riemann, H., Ed. *Food-Borne Infections and Intoxications.* Academic Press, New York. 1969.

Rose, A. H., Ed. *Food Microbiology.* Academic Press, London. 1983.

CHAPTER 3

Foodborne Illnesses

F oodborne illnesses are usually caused by bacteria or their toxins. "Ptomaine poisoning" is an outdated term sometimes used to denote foodborne illnesses.

Foodborne illnesses may result from consumption of water, milk, other beverages, and solid food items in uncooked or cooked form, provided they contain the disease-producing agent in sufficient quantity. The quantity required to produce illness varies with the susceptibility of the individual and a number of other factors. The causative agents may be: (1) a native part of the offending food, such as poisonous plants and animals; (2) chemicals, which may be added purposely during processing to assure quality or to enhance certain quality characteristics, or which may be added accidentally to the food materials at any stage of production, harvesting, transport, processing, storage, preparation, and service; (3) radionuclides, resulting from atomic fission; (4) parasites; (5) pathogenic microorganisms such as protozoa, viruses, rickettsiae, and bacteria; the latter may or may not profusely multiply in the food and may or may not release exotoxins into the food.

For the sake of simplification of discussion, the causes of gastrointestinal disturbances following the ingestion of food are divided into three groups:

Group I   Poisonous plants and animals.
Group II   Agents for which the food is simply a vehicle of transmission.

Group III   Microbial pathogens which multiply profusely in the food caus-
             ing explosive gastrointestinal upsets. (To be discussed in
             Chapter 4.)

GROUP I: POISONOUS PLANTS AND ANIMALS

Poisoning from plants and animals is in this country largely restricted to food
prepared in the home. Even then it occurs relatively seldom. A few examples
of poisonous plants and animals are given below.

PLANTS

Many plants contain toxic compounds, but the potential toxicity of these compounds under normal conditions of human consumption is very small (Singleton, 1981). Yet there are exceptions. Phytates in legumes and cereals interfere with absorption of minerals such as calcium, magnesium, zinc, and iron
(Reddy et al., 1982).

Such common foods as rutabagas, turnips, cabbage, kale, broccoli, mustard, and some other related vegetables contain goitrogens. These are substances capable of blocking the human body's ability to absorb iodine in
adequate amounts. When eaten in normal amounts, these foods are perfectly
wholesome. However, excessive and prolonged consumption may create an
abnormal condition (Van Etten and Wolff, 1973; Coon, 1975). The goitrogenic
activity in foods is largely destroyed by cooking. In spite of the great number
of toxic substances naturally present in plant foods, few hazards seem to exist
for the healthy individual consuming a normal diet.

Some forms of mushrooms are extremely poisonous. Mushroom poisoning is relatively uncommon in this country, but, for example, *Amanita* species
have been mistaken for edible mushrooms. The active principles in poisonous mushrooms are phalloidine and other alkaloids.

Potato poisoning from green potatoes has been reported in the literature.
There are several glycoalkaloids present in potato tubers. The glycoalkaloid
causing greening is solanine, and much research has been devoted to it. Exposure to light, be it in the field or in storage, makes tubers turn green.
Solanine is insoluble in water and not destroyed in the cooking process
(Whitaker and Feeney, 1973). Solanine is also present in the sprouts of stored
potatoes. Foodservice managers should reject greened and sprouted potatoes
upon delivery. The effect of baking and drying on the total glycoalkaloid content of potatoes was studied by Ponnampalam and Mondy (1983). It was
found that the content of this chemical was highest in the outermost (cortex)
tissues of tubers of the varieties studied and exceeded the level considered

safe. The amounts were particularly high in the outermost tissues of fried items. The authors warn that because of the high total of glycoalkaloid content of fried potato peels and the resulting possible toxicity, caution in eating fried potato peels is advised.

Food toxicants of natural origin are listed in Rodricks and Polhand (1981), the *Handbook of Naturally Occurring Food Toxicants* (1983), and the National Academy of Sciences' publication *Toxicants Occurring Naturally in Foods* (1973).

Rhubarb poisoning has occurred from eating rhubarb leaves, the active principle being oxalic acid, and, possibly, some toxic agents other than oxalates. Snakeroot poisoning has resulted from drinking milk drawn from cows which feed on snakeroot; the active principle is trematol. Favism is caused by fava beans *(Vicia fava);* it is uncommon. Ergot poisoning is produced by the fungus *Claviceps purpurea,* which forms its fruit bodies on rye. If these bodies are not removed before the grain is ground, the ergot will poison the flour. Ergot poisoning is now very rare in this country.

Poisoning caused by molds (which are plants) is discussed in Chapter 4.

Combinations of certain natural chemicals occurring in foods when combined in the human body with certain medications can create a problem. For example, bananas contain substances known as pressor amines which are held in check and rendered harmless by an enzyme, monoamine oxydase. Certain antidepressant drugs inhibit this enzyme and enable the toxic nature of the pressor amines to go into effect. Naturally occurring toxicologic substances in plant products were discussed by Weisburger (1984).

ANIMALS

Some animals' tissues are naturally toxic to man, even when they are entirely fresh. Their poisonousness cannot be determined by such simple signs as appearance, odor, discoloration of metal, or other hard-and-fast criteria. Most animal toxins are heat stable and cannot be rendered harmless by cooking.

Most probably, more poisonings are caused by toxic animals than by toxic plants. Marine toxins are of special interest. It is known that many species of shellfish and fish may contain chemicals toxic to humans. Even seafood that is normally harmless may become toxic under certain conditions (Hashimoto, 1979).

Poisonous Shellfish

Paralytic shellfish poisoning may result from eating mussels *(Mytilus)* and clams *(Saxidomus),* which have become poisonous by feeding on poisonous plankton, namely, various species of *Gonyaulax,* a dinoflagellate. The active principle is a neurotoxin which is not inactivated by cooking. Certain areas of the Pacific Coast of the United States and Canada, part of the Gulf Coast and the Atlantic Coast, the Bay of Fundy, and the Gulf of the St. Lawrence, are all valuable shellfish areas where this trouble has occurred. Paralytic shellfish poisoning has been reported from as far north as Alaska (Cladouhos, 1977). The toxin is not inactivated by cooking. Paralytic shellfish poisoning is controlled by government agencies through direct and systematic checking of the harvesting grounds.

The reddish-brown discoloration of waters invaded by a "population explosion" of certain dinoflagellates is popularly called "red tide." Examples of shellfish poisonings connected with red tide were reported in *Morbidity and Mortality Weekly Report,* 1973 and 1974. For more detailed information the reader is referred to Schantz (1973) and Harsanyi (1973).

Poisonous Fish

A number of tropical fish are known to be poisonous to man and must be considered inedible. Among these are puffers, parrot fish, trigger fish, surgeon fish, porcupine fish, and goat fish. These fish feed on poisonous marine organisms. Even wholesome fish may occasionally prove poisonous when they are harvested in certain localities. Barracuda, perch, mackerel, sea bass, snapper, and pompano are examples of fish that have been found to be at times unfit to eat because of the toxicity of their flesh. Fish poisoning may be classified into seven types: tetraodon, ciguatera, scombroid, clupeoid, chimaeroid, gemphylid, and hallucinary mullet.

Ciguatera poisoning is one of the largest public health problems in connection with poisoning from fish. It is common in much of the Pacific area and throughout the Caribbean. The species implicated in ciguatera poisoning have been enumerated by Halstead (1965). The cause of the poisoning is heat stable ciguatoxin. From 1966 to 1973 three outbreaks of ciguatera poisoning were reported to the Center for Disease Control (CDC), whereas 26 outbreaks were reported in *Morbidity and Mortality Weekly Report* in 1974. Large (over 15 pounds) fish are more likely to contain great amounts of toxin than small ones. The poisonous fish look and smell perfectly normal. Four to eight hours may elapse between ingestion of the poison and the onset of symptoms, which include weakness and abnormal sensory phenomena (*Morbidity and Mortality Weekly Report,* Feb. 3, 1978).

Fish may also become poisonous through their ingestion of metals (see Chapter 6).

GROUP II: AGENTS FOR WHICH FOOD SERVES AS A SIMPLE VEHICLE OF TRANSMISSION

A variety of agents belong here: chemicals, radionuclides, parasites, and those pathogenic microorganisms for which the food serves as a vehicle of transmission to man. For the agents included in Group II, food is a mere vehicle for the pathogens, as are hands, money, doorknobs, and the like. The bacteria included in this group do not necessarily have to multiply to large numbers in the food in order to cause disease in man; they are so highly infectious that a small number will suffice for illness to ensue, and these pathogens are usually not associated with the food supply, although exceptions occur, and borderline cases exist.

CHEMICALS

Many chemicals may become poisons when ingested in large amounts. Chemicals that are quite harmless when present in traces have caused severe illness or death when ingested in quantity, an example being monosodium glutamate (MSG).

When used in large amounts (it is a popular ingredient in Chinese menu items), monosodium glutamate can cause poisoning. The incubation time is short, usually less than 1 hour. The symptoms often include burning sensations in the chest, neck, and abdomen. The extremities and face may feel abnormal. The reader is referred to an article by Schaumburg et al. (1969).

Toxic chemicals in food that are not of natural origin are considered synthetic. In this category belong certain additives (including antimicrobial preservatives and antibiotics), agricultural chemicals (such as pesticides and drugs) fed to meat animals, accidental contaminants, and metals originating from equipment used in the preparation and service of foods and beverages.

Additives

Chemical additives have been used in foods for many years and contribute to the high quality and shelf life of our food supply. The definition of the term "additive" varies, unfortunately, and the difference needs to be understood. As defined by the World Health Organization (WHO) and the Food and Agriculture Organization (FAO) the term is restricted to substances added to food with the intention that they perform specific functions, like improving the nutritive value, color, flavor, texture, and shelf life of the food; it does not include chemicals which enter the food unintentionally, like residues of pesticides.

In the United States, legal control of food additives is made possible through the Federal Food, Drug and Cosmetic Act through laws enacted about 20 years ago and amended in 1976. The legal definition is as follows:

> Any substance, the intended use of which results or may reasonably be expected to result, directly or indirectly, in its becoming a component of or otherwise affecting the characteristics of any food (including any substance intended for use in producing, manufacturing, packing, processing, preparing, treating, transporting or holding a food; and including any source of radiation intended for any such use), if such substance is not generally recognized, among experts qualified by scientific training and experience to evaluate its safety, as having been adequately shown through scientific procedures (or, in the case of substances used in food prior to January 1, 1958, through either scientific procedures or experience based on common use in food) to be safe under the conditions of its intended use except that such term does not include (1) a pesticide chemical in or on a raw agricultural commodity; or (2) a pesticide chemical to the extent that it is intended for use or is used in the production, storage, or transportation of any raw agricultural commodity; (3) a color additive; or (4) any substance used in accordance with a sanction or approval granted prior to the enactment of this paragraph pursuant to this Act, the Poultry Products Inspection Act . . . or the Meat Inspection Act . . . or (5) a new animal drug.

Exempted from the requirement of proving safety are substances which by previous scientific evaluation or from long years of common usage as additives in food are generally recognized by experts as being safe. These substances make up the so-called GRAS ("generally recognized as safe") list.

The safety evaluation of an additive is a most difficult task. It is almost impossible to provide absolute proof that an additive is nontoxic to all persons under all conditions. Animal tests have been designed for testing the safety of specific additives at specified levels of consumption. To be passed as safe, the level of intake must—in the best judgment of highly qualified scientists—lie considerably below the level which could prove harmful to the consumer. In spite of this margin of safety, some degree of uncertainty remains; namely, the applicability to humans of data gained from research with animals.

The Food and Drug Administration (FDA) enforces the tolerances of additives pertaining to the safety of all foods except meats, including poultry and their products. These are under the administration of the U.S. Department of Agriculture.

The much-debated Delaney Clause of 1958 was incorporated into the Food Additives Amendment. This clause requires that no additive may be permitted in food if, at any level, it can produce cancer in humans or animals; or, if it can be demonstrated to be cancer forming by any other appropriate testing method (Federal Food, Drug and Cosmetic Act, 1976b). After over a decade of debating this controversial clause, there is still no general agreement in regard to safety criteria and methodology for testing, and it seems that there is a general demand for greater flexibility than the Delaney Clause allows.

The Delaney Clause is applicable to food additives and color additives; it does not apply to substances generally recognized as safe (GRAS) or to substances sanctioned previously. However, a periodic examination of GRAS listings for their safety and updating of the list on the strength of current, pertinent findings is necessary.

Safety standards for the reevaluation of additives are becoming increasingly rigorous, partly because of improved methodology for determining very low levels of toxicants. There also is concern regarding hazards resulting from a build-up of toxicants caused by long-term ingestion (Federation of American Societies, 1977).

The Food and Drug Administration (1979) is active in evaluating a "sensitivity-of-method" approach to determine cancer-producing capability of a compound prior to its approval. The aim of this approach is to determine the level of residue which would not present a significant risk of cancer.

Antimicrobial Preservatives

From a food sanitation point of view, additives that enhance the keeping quality, or stability, of food are of special interest and concern. Many chemicals are able to inhibit or kill microorganisms, causing spoilage, but the use of most in food is prohibited.

Antimicrobial preservatives were grouped by Frazier and Westhoff (1978). They are:

> Preservatives not defined as such by law, such as the natural organic acids and their salts; vinegars; sodium chloride; sugars; spices and their oils; wood smoke; carbon dioxide, and nitrogen. Substances generally recognized as safe (those on the GRAS list) for use in food. Examples are: Propionic acid and sodium and calcium propionates; caprylic acid; sorbic acid; potassium, sodium and calcium sorbates; benzoic acid, benzoates, and certain derivatives of benzoic acid; sulfur dioxide and sulfites; potassium and sodium bisulfite; and others, such as methylparaben and propylparaben. Chemicals that are being considered as food additives and have not been listed under the above categories. These can only be used if and when they have been proven to be safe for man or animals. If proven safe, they move on to this category: Chemicals proven safe and approved by the Food and Drug Administration.

Preservatives are used to inhibit or kill contaminating microorganisms present in the food. The effectiveness of antimicrobial preservatives depends on several factors, among these: the kind, age, and previous history of the organism; the number of cells present; type and concentration of the chemical used; the nature of the material which is to be preserved; and time and temperature of exposure.

Chemical compounds and elements that can be used as preservatives may be grouped as inorganic and organic substances. Among the organic preservatives are certain inorganic acids and their salts; certain alkalies and alkaline salts; certain metals, halogens, peroxides, and gases. Among the organic preservatives are certain organic acids and their salts; sugars; alcohols; formaldehyde; spices; and wood smoke.

Antimicrobial additives are used in a great variety of solid food items and beverages, examples being cheese and cheese products, margarine, pie crust and pastries, pie fillings, sausage, salads and salad dressings, fresh and dried fruits and vegetables, pickles, sauerkraut, olives, carbonated beverages, fruit drinks and fruit juices. Information on what kinds of antimicrobial additives are used in what foods and beverages is available in the *Handbook of Food Additives,* compiled by Furia (1972).

There is need for more research data on possible interaction of food additives, on their influence under different dietary patterns, and on the interaction of food additives and drugs which a person may take.

Sulfites

Sulfur dioxide, in the form of sodium and potassium sulfites, metabisulfites, and bisulfites, has been in long-time use as an antimicrobial agent and/or as a substance preventing food discoloration caused by oxidation. Sulfiting food was considered a safe procedure, when the chemicals were applied by appropriate methods, until the 1980s. Sulfiting has been used for holding fresh fruits and vegetables, including prepeeled potatoes; for fresh and processed shellfish; for dried fruit; and for a long list of other products.

However, beginning in the early 1980s, an increasing number of food-related illnesses were traced to the consumption of sulfited foods, the symptoms of the illnesses being allergic in type (Simon, 1982). Items such as raw fruits and vegetables and cooked shrimp are popular items served in restaurants, frequently displayed on salad bars. They are also offered on special counters in supermarket-type stores. To keep their appearance fresh and appealing, sulfiting is frequently used—or was. However, as the number of illnesses traced to sulfited food items increased, steps were taken to warn the public. For packaged foods, the answer is proper labeling, now required for sulfited foods. The solution for nonpackaged sulfite items is as follows.

In 1985, the Food and Drug Administration made it known that the use of sulfites when applied to fresh fruits and vegetables intended to be served or sold raw to consumers should cease; use of sulfites for these particular purposes no longer deserves GRAS status. Thus, the use of sulfites on fresh fruits and vegetables has been banned. As an alternative, restaurants and supermarkets have resorted to using lemon juice or citric acid. Regulations for other items now routinely sulfited may follow.

The sulfiting of shrimp has not been banned, but the FDA has taken steps toward standardizing procedures for sulfiting so as to ensure safer sulfited products of lesser variability than formerly found. The FDA, after having surveyed the shrimp industry, is advising the industry on procedures and labeling.

Nitrites

The use of nitrites and nitrates in curing meat, especially pork, is of long standing. Nitrites, when decomposing, form nitric acid which in turn reacts with the heme pigments in meat, forming a stable red color, so desirable in ham and bacon. The nitrites are added as sodium or potassium salts. Nitrates serve as a reservoir for nitrites and their use is largely discontinued. Nitrates are naturally present in many foods, especially vegetables. Bacteria present in the human digestive system produce nitrite from nitrate and other nitrogen-containing compounds.

Besides its effect on the color of curing meat, nitrites are known to have an inhibitory effect on *Clostridium botulinum*. They have also been shown to inhibit growth of *Clostridium perfringens* (Riha and Solberg, 1975; Ingram, 1976). In spite of these favorable effects of nitrites, there is a strong effort made to discontinue the use of nitrites for the following reason.

Nitrites, upon reacting with secondary and tertiary amines, may form nitrosamines, known to be carcinogenic to laboratory animals. Besides, sodium nitrite itself may be a carcinogen. Thus the future for their use is a questionable one. Nitrites in bacon have received special attention because the high temperatures used in cooking bacon favor the formation of nitrosamines (Sen et al., 1974; Gray and Collins, 1978; Gray and Randall, 1979; Scanlan, 1983).

In 1975 the Food and Drug Administration sponsored a large study (as a contract with the Massachusetts Institute of Technology, MIT) which led to data indicating that, in laboratory animals, nitrite induced a statistically significant increase in cancer of the lymphatic system. The controversy over the use of nitrites in curing meat is not over. A cooperative effort is being made by the Food and Drug Administration and the U.S. Department of Agriculture to solve this multifaceted problem (Hopkins, 1978b). As an important step, the USDA has required that bacon be cured with no more than a specified, much-reduced amount of nitrite salts plus a specified amount of potassium sorbate plus ascorbate or erythorbate, and that tests be made on samples from bacon processors by the Food Safety and Quality Service of the USDA. Nitrite is regulated under the Federal Meat Inspection Act.

However, the use of nitrites in curing meats has not been banned; to date the USDA and FDA are permitting continued use of these chemicals with the proviso that the level of use in some products not exceed certain prescribed limits. Research on alternative ways of preserving is encouraged.

Nitrites are also used in further-processed poultry and fish products. Since 1977 the Food and Drug Administration has required processors of poultry products to request permission for the use of these chemicals. The same agency, FDA, is working out regulations in connection with the use of nitrates and nitrites in the processing of smoked fish. Regulations are aimed at reducing the amounts of nitrites to low levels which still give the desired protection against the danger from botulism. It is reasonable to expect that the use of nitrites will gradually be phased out in these products also, when safe and feasible alternative preservatives have been found.

A committee charged with evaluating alternatives to the current use of nitrite in foods was established in 1980 by the National Academy of Sciences–National Research Council at the request of the Food and Drug Administration and the U.S. Department of Agriculture. Various recommendations were made (Widdus and Busta, 1982).

The Food and Drug Administration has actively cooperated with industry in an effort to reduce nitrosamine levels in products such as bacon, nonfat dry milk, soy protein, beer, malt and malt-containing products. The FDA's activities were reviewed by Havery and Fazio (1985). See also Chapter 7.

Drugs

Drugs such as *hormones* and *antibiotics* are useful to farmers as a means of improving the health and/or growth rate of their meat animals. A large proportion of the meat and poultry eaten in the United States originates in animals that had received drugs with their feed. It is essential that no harmful residues of these chemicals are passed on to the consumer. Information on antibiotics in food has been summarized in a report by the International Commission on Microbiological Specifications for Foods (1980).

The use of antibiotics in food is now prohibited in the United States. Several antibiotics have been used experimentally, and two were actually approved and commercially used for a while, but their safe use was reconsidered in 1967. These antibiotics were chlortetracycline and oxytetracycline. They had been approved first for use as a dip for chilled raw poultry and, later on, for use with chilled raw fish. Although residues of these antibiotics were shown to be inactivated by cooking the food, there were other considerations sufficiently convincing to scientists which led to the decision to prohibit the use of these substances in food. Among others, the considerations were that the extended use of antibiotics might give rise to large numbers of bacteria resistant to the antibiotics through selection and that these resistant forms might prove harmful to the consumer. Also, that antibiotics might be misused, in that they might serve to cover up the poor quality of a food produced under unsanitary conditions.

While antibiotics may not be added as a preservative to food, they are still permitted as an additive to animal feeds. The use of certain antibiotics in the feeding of certain meat animals is common because of their effect of promoting the animal's weight gain during its growth. The risks of feeding antibiotics to meat animals have been discussed by Crawford (1985), Director of the FDA's Center for Veterinary Medicine. Besides the risk of residues left in the meat, there is the awesome risk connected with the possibility that certain pathogens, common to animals and humans, may become resistant to antibiotics used in treating human diseases—antibiotics such as penicillin and tetracycline. Therefore, the FDA discourages the use of these substances, especially because other growth promoters for meat animals are available that are not used in human medicine.

Included in the growth-promoting, metabolic drugs used in food animals are the estrogens and progesterones. A widely used drug is DES (diethylstilbestrol), which is either mixed into the feed or implanted into the flesh of the animal in the form of a pellet. Diethystilbestrol has been demonstrated to cause cancer in laboratory test animals and in humans. The question of how much residue of the drugs should be allowed in the meat has been raised, and it is a sticky problem indeed. It is tied up with the question of methodology for detecting residue, which is being constantly improved and which makes very slight residues detectable. It is a problem of great economic importance to farmers raising meat animals.

Diethylstilbestrol was introduced in 1947 as a pellet to be implanted in the necks of poultry. Then in 1954, DES was added to the feed of beef cattle, and approved by the FDA on the basis of data indicating that residues of the drug would not be found in the edible flesh of the treated animal, if the drug was withdrawn 48 hours prior to slaughter. Several years later, however, data were made available which proved that although DES residues could not be found in the edible flesh of treated cattle (provided DES was withdrawn at a specified time before slaughter), this did not apply to poultry: DES was found in the liver and skin fat of poultry.

In 1958 the Delaney Clause, which prohibits the use of cancer-causing substances in food for man and animals, was enacted. Under this clause, the FDA could not approve new applications for feed containing DES. Poultry growers voluntarily discontinued sale of birds treated with DES. However, the meat-processing industry has put up a long and desperate fight, lasting for years, against the rulings dealing with the use of DES. In January of 1976, the FDA again proposed to withdraw approval of all outstanding DES applications, at this time giving meat manufacturers a chance to request a hearing, which did take place in May 1977. On the basis of these hearings, it was decided that DES, when used to promote growth in meat animals, was not shown to be safe. It was also decided that DES causes cancer, and that there is no known amount below which it can be shown not to cause cancer in animals or man. Residues of DES are being found in flesh from animals which have been treated with the drug; and public health, environmental, and economic benefits from continued use of DES as a promotent of animal growth do not outweigh the risk to human health (Hecht, 1979). The use of DES in meat animals was banned in 1979.

Pesticides

The term pesticide is being used to include insecticides, fungicides, herbicides, and—in part—germicides. These chemicals, when ingested in large amounts, may cause poisoning. In the United States spray schedules have been carefully worked out to avoid adherence of deleterious deposits to the crops at the time of harvest. Regulations pertaining to interstate commerce are aimed at protecting the consumer from dangerous levels of residues of pesticides.

Legal control of these chemicals is administered under the regulations of the Federal Food, Drug and Cosmetic Act. The Miller Pesticide Amendment of 1954 deals specifically with insecticides and provides procedures for establishing tolerances for residues of those used with agricultural products. Regulations of the Environmental Protection Agency (EPA) require that the manufacturer of the pesticide produce evidence of safety at certain levels of intended use. Tolerances of permitted residues are established by the Environmental Protection Agency, but the Food and Drug Administration is entrusted with the enforcement of these tolerances.

In recent years, new attention has been focused on certain pesticides that had been used by fruit and vegetable growers for many years; their safety is being reevaluated to ensure that no cumulative toxic effects can be expected.

The fumigant ethylene dibromide (EDB), which over many years had been employed in the control of insects damaging grains and certain fruits, was banned by the Environmental Protection Agency in 1984. This pesticide is a carcinogen.

According to Thompson (1984) many shipments of food—both domestic and imported—are sampled during a year's time by the FDA for unsafe residues. Examples of items sampled are dairy products, fish, fresh and processed fruits and vegetables, and animal foods. As stated by Thompson

(1984), almost all samples commonly comply with the limits prescribed.

Substances vary regarding legal classification. As an international effort, the World Health Organization (WHO) Expert Committee on Pesticide Residues, working in cooperation with the Food and Agriculture Organization (FAO) Working Party of Experts on Pesticide Residues, makes evaluations and develops recommendations concerning acceptable daily intakes and allowable residue limits (WHO-FAO, 1975).

Germicides are used as chemical sanitizers in the food processing and food service industry. Their main function is to eliminate, as a follow-up to cleaning, residual contaminants adhering to food-contact equipment and working surfaces. Germicides must be used in the prescribed concentrations by the prescribed methods of application.

Metals

Metals may get into food by using utensils, pots, and pans of unsuitable material. For example, cookingware containing cadmium (plated utensils), antimony (grey enamelware), and zinc may render food poisonous. Shelves in refrigerators may contain cadmium. Food such as meats placed directly on such shelves may be rendered poisonous. Tin has been indicated where tinned milk cans were used to store highly acid fruit punches or juices. Zinc used in galvanized food containers may render acid foods poisonous, examples being fruit juices and acid salads. The cadmium, tin, and zinc are dissolved through the action of the acid, and containers containing cadmium, tin, and zinc which make contact with food are unsuitable for food preparation. Unfortunately, potentially hazardous containers are sometimes used "in a pinch" when community meals are served.

Copper has caused gastric upsets when it was in contact with acid food and carbonated liquids. The vending industry recently has voluntarily discontinued all post-mix carbonation systems which did not completely guard against the possibility of backflow and copper poisoning.

The use of certain earthenware has caused food poisoning. Although earthenware is not likely to be used by the commercial food service industry, it might be used in community meal service. A surveillance of the FDA has shown that earthenware imported from a number of foreign countries proved to be unsafe because of the acid-extractable lead, or cadmium, it contained. A surveillance of the domestic market has revealed some unsafe pottery also (Krinitz and Hering, 1971). Pottery found to be unsafe cannot be imported or sold. Actually, the hazard is slight unless acid foods are stored in pieces whose glaze or decal (decoration applied over the basic glaze and bonded by firing) is not properly formulated, applied, and fired (Food and Drug Administration, 1971). The importance of mercury as a contaminant of seafood is discussed in Chapter 6. The literature on the toxic potential of trace metals in foods was reviewed by Somers (1974).

Miscellaneous Poisonous Chemicals

Miscellaneous poisonous chemicals may get into food "by accident," and some of the descriptions of such poisonings make gruesome reading. Such incidences may be due to actual accidents, but in most instances they are the result of negligence. When rat poison is mixed into breadcrumbs, when sodium fluoride is confused with baking powder and dishwashing compound with paprika, when liquid detergent is taken for cooking oil, something is radically wrong with the housekeeping.

If animal feed becomes accidentally contaminated with PCBs, large-scale contamination of human food may be the result. PCBs (polychlorinated biphenyls) are synthetic compounds insoluble in water, but soluble in oil and many organic compounds, that are useful to industry in capacitors and transformers. PCBs are able to enter the body by way of ingestion, inhalation, and percutaneous absorption. They may accumulate in body lipids of humans and animals. PCB-contaminated meat and eggs, for example, are important sources of PCBs ingested by humans. Excessive exposure to PCBs may cause chloracne (a skin lesion), hyperpigmentation, abnormal liver function, and elevated triglycerides in man, and cancer in test animals. Therefore, the manufacture and distribution of PCBs was banned in 1976. Unfortunately, much equipment containing PCBs is still in use. As recently as 1979, accidental contamination with PCBs of animal feed, and subsequent contamination of meat and eggs, has been reported (*Morbidity and Mortality Weekly Report,* 1979).

Although PCBs are no longer manufactured in the United States, large quantities are still present in the environment. The sediments of some lakes and streams continue to be a reservoir for these poisons and find entry into the food chain by way of fish harvested from these waters (Sawhney and Hankin, 1985).

RADIONUCLIDES

Fallout in connection with testing of atomic weapons has caused concern in recent years. Radionuclides are products of atomic fission; some of the important sources of radionuclides in connection with fallout are strontium-89, strontium-90, iodine-131, and cesium-137. Among foods, milk and plant foods are the most important vehicles of transmission of radionuclides to man.

Eisenbud (1963), in his discussion of the distribution of radioactivity in foods, states that doubtlessly every living cell everywhere in the world today contains some of the radioactive substances produced by the tests of nuclear and thermonuclear weapons, but that the radioactivity of nature is probably no less ubiquitous than the radioactivity produced by man. Some radionuclides occur naturally. The element delivering the largest share, 20%, is potassium.

Radionuclides originating from fallout may contaminate grass, vegetable crops, and fruits. The mode of contamination from fallout varies. Radionuclides may form deposits on foliage or other plant parts; man or animal becomes contaminated eating these deposits along with the plant parts. Radionuclides may be translocated from foliage to other parts of the plant. Another mode of plant contamination is by way of soil. Radionuclides may contaminate the soil first, then the root system, and eventually the whole plant. Milk becomes contaminated when contaminated vegetation is consumed by cows, and the radionuclides from milk can be transferred to products such as cheese, made from milk. Factors affecting the biological availability of radionuclides for plants were discussed by Menzel (1963). The effects of radioactive contamination of the environment on public health are presented by Chadwick (1962).

The symptoms in the person ingesting radionuclides depend on the nature of the source and the tendency of certain radionuclides to concentrate in the tissues of important organs. Symptoms therefore vary. Also, the age of the person and his or her resistance to the toxic effect of the radionuclides are said to play a role in the severity of illness resulting from ingesting radionuclides.

Through the past years much progress has been made by the federal government in developing effective radiation surveillance. In this effort, many agencies have participated, including the U.S. Public Health Service and the U.S. Atomic Energy Commission. Protective measures have been discussed by Read (1963). Research is seeking answers to questions on how to minimize the effects of fallout in connection with contamination: means of reducing the uptake of radionuclides from soil, preventing entry of radionuclides to animals, and removal of radionuclides from milk and food.

PARASITES

Trichinae

Trichinella spiralis is the cause of trichinosis, which is a not uncommon but preventable disease of public health significance. The trichinae belong to the round worms, *Nematoda*. Trichinosis occurs usually as a sporadic disease, but outbreaks have been reported when many persons were served a disease-producing menu item. The early stages of trichinosis have been confused with food poisoning (Dack, 1956). *Trichinella* is classified among the Helminths, which are parasitic worms of medical significance.

The trichina larvae in the tissues give rise to the pathologic picture. The main source of the parasite is infested pork, other reported sources being bear and rabbit meat. Possibly an early clue to the existence of trichinosis in man and pork is the Mosaic rule against eating pork. Trichinosis has a worldwide distribution, being especially prevalent in countries where pork is eaten in the raw state, and least frequently found where eating pork is prohibited, as in Jewish and Mohammedan countries.

Trichinosis has been found to have seasonal incidences. In the seasons during which much pork is consumed more frequent incidences occur. In the United States, the incidence of trichinosis has been shown to be somewhat variable. In 1930, approximately one out of six persons (17%) carried the disease. Since then trichinosis has been declining. In 1990, Bean and Griffin reported that outbreaks due to Trichinella spiralis infections decreased between 1973 and 1987. Hogs should be fed heat-treated garbage only, but this rule is difficult to enforce in this country. It has been reported that many other countries have succeeded in almost eliminating trichinosis in humans (Schantz, 1983).

The parasite takes the following path. The pork harboring the larvae is eaten by a person. When eaten, the encysted larvae are released and penetrate the duodenum of the human host. They mature within a few days. The females are fertilized and the males die. The female trichinae then invade the mucosa, where they produce hundreds of embryos and subsequently die. This period of discharging embryos may take 5–6 weeks. The young larvae gain entrance to the bloodstream of the human victim and finally encyst in the victim's muscles. After 4–5 months the capsule which encases the embryo will calcify and the embryo will die.

The onset of symptoms is usually about 2 days after the victim has eaten pork contaminated with the larvae. The symptoms of trichinosis vary with the life history of the parasite and with the number of larvae ingested. Intestinal invasion is usually accompanied by abdominal pain, nausea, vomiting, and diarrhea. At this stage the symptoms may resemble those caused by bacterial "food poisoning." When large numbers of larvae invade the bloodstream, fever may result. There may be other symptoms, such as edema of the eyelids, spastic paralysis of the muscles, and edema of face and hands. Death may occur in very severe infections.

In the past it was a practice to inspect meat for trichinae at the processing plants, but this practice led to false security, since the presence of the parasite is difficult to ascertain.

A widely used method is to prevent the meat from becoming infected in the first place. The most successful methods to achieve this goal are to cook all garbage fed to hogs, and to control rats and mice since these may be host to the parasites.

Irradiation of pork to eliminate trichinae is now permitted by the FDA.

Heating pork to at least 137°F (58°C) will kill the larvae. However, the margin of safety is very narrow. Viable larvae have been demonstrated by Carlin et al. (1969) in roasts cooked to an end point of 135°F (57°C)—a temperature dangerously close to 137°F (58°C). In the FDA Food Service Sanitation Manual (1976), a terminal temperature of at least 150°F (66°C) is recommended for cooking pork; at this low internal temperature the meat is still pink. Unless a thermometer is used and used properly, the endpoint of safety cannot be determined accurately. It is, therefore, a good rule to cook pork to 170°F (77°C), or a grey color, to provide a margin of safety.

The larvae are also destroyed by freezing. Times and temperatures required by the U.S. Department of Agriculture (1960) are, for pieces and layers not exceeding 6 inches: 5°F (−15°C) for 20 days; −1°F (−18.3°C) for 10 days; −20°F (−28.9°C) for 6 days. For pieces or layers exceeding a thickness of 6 inches, longer holding times are required by these regulations at each temperature.

The former Bureau of Animal Industry (USDA) has worked out a processing method for pork products which, when followed, assures a safe product. This procedure involves treating of the meat with a certain percentage of salt, and holding the salted meat in the drying room under refrigeration for 3 weeks. The length of smoking time and the temperatures applied are specified also. The smoking is to be followed by a certain storage period at specified temperatures.

Government regulations cover the manufacture of frankfurters and other processed pork products to assure their freedom from trichinae.

Recontamination of cooked meat from equipment may occur. Pocock et al. (1963) described an outbreak of trichinosis involving a hospital population in Ohio. The most probable source was a ham salad prepared from ground smoked ham. On the basis of an investigation into the preparation and heating procedures it was concluded that the ham was probably sufficiently heated to kill the trichinae, but that recontamination from raw pork took place when the cooked meat was ground using equipment previously used for raw pork.

The odds of acquiring trichinosis are small. Only about 1:3000 U.S. swine are significantly infected. Heating, freezing, or curing markedly reduces the number of trichinae in pork products. Recommendations made were:

1. Use slow-cooking procedures.
2. Use roasts 5 pounds or less in weight.
3. Allow stand or hold time.
4. Take temperature of roast at several places.
5. Make visual observations.

Strict adherence to these procedures could virtually eliminate the possibility of acquiring trichinosis (Zimmerman, 1982).

The control measures to be applied in the institutional kitchen include the procurement of meat from approved sources, rendering pork safe by adequate cooking, and taking precautions against contamination of cooked meat with trichinae originating from raw pork.

Tapeworms

The beef and the hog tapeworm, *Taenia,* may cause disease in humans when larva-infested meat is ingested. Humans are a host of both the beef and the hog tapeworms. The adult worm is a parasite of humans while the larva infests the animal tissues (Brandly et al., 1966); infested meat is referred to as being "measly." The cycle is this: humans pass the eggs or proglottids ("tapes") of the worm with their stool. Whether people defecate in a pasture or hayfield or whether they spread raw sewage on an area used to raise feed, the end effect is that eggs and proglottids are passed on to livestock. The eggs hatch within the animal host and develop into larvae which settle in the muscle. This stage is called cysticercosis, "measles." If a person consumes raw or undercooked larva-infested meat the larvae develop in his or her intestinal tract into adulthood and breed. This stage is called human taeniasis. With the passing of the ova in the feces, the cycle is completed. Infestation of humans with pork tapeworm, although rare, can be a serious affliction, because it may develop in the human brain (Healy and Juranek, 1979; Hird and Pullen, 1979).

The exact incidence of *Taenia* in humans has been difficult to ascertain. Identification of the bovine form made in 43 states from 1963 through 1967 showed an incidence of 23 per 100,000 stool samples examined. The true incidence is believed to be higher than that. The number of incidences in slaughtered cattle inspected by federal agents ranged from 12,000 to 16,000 during the period of 1959 to 1967 (Schultz et al., 1970). To prevent taeniasis/cysticercosis, the host cycle must be broken by applying sanitary measures. Contamination of pastures and hayfields with human feces and sewage effluent must be prevented. Federal regulations (adopted in 1970) prohibit carcasses of cattle infected with *Taenia* cysts from being marketed as human food if the lesions prove to be extensive. Carcasses with a very few lesions may be marketed after the lesions have been removed, and provided that these carcasses be continuously exposed to freezing temperatures of 15°F (-9.4°C) or lower for at least 10 days. For boned meat, freezer storage for at least 20 days is required. As an alternative to low-temperature treatment, carcasses and boned meat must be heated throughout to an endpoint of 140°F (60°C) to render the meat safe.

The World Health Organization has published guidelines for the surveillance, prevention, and control of taeniasis/cysticercosis (WHO, 1984). An update on the problem was published by Flisser (1985).

Anasakis

Anasakis spp., a nematode, is a contaminant of fish. Raw or insufficiently processed fish may cause anasakiasis in humans. Japan and the Netherlands have reported a fairly large number of cases of anasakiasis, but some incidences have occurred in North America also (Jackson, 1975). The incubation period, the time required for signs and symptoms to appear after consuming contaminated fish, is several days. Signs and symptoms are an irritation of the throat and the digestive tract. The anasakine larvae, either remaining free or becoming attached to the human digestive tract, are the cause of irritation, inflammation, or ulceration. The larvae do not mature in the patient and are eventually expelled—sometimes by vomiting and coughing. Jackson et al. (1978) analyzed over 1000 fresh whole fish of 14 families, 20 genera, and 23 species, bought in retail markets, in the Washington, D.C. area (Chesapeake Bay). In all, 6547 nematodes were produced from dissecting these fish. Only two nematodes came from the flesh of fish, the others were of intestinal origin. The nematodes recovered from flesh were both *Anasakis* larvae. Myers (1979) recovered anasakine nematodes from fresh commercial fish (but not from shellfish) harvested from the waters along the Washington, Oregon, and California coasts. The larvae are killed by prolonged freezing and holding at $-20°C$ ($-4°F$), depending on the type (Bier, 1976).

Protozoa

Entamoeba histolytica is a member of the protozoa. This species causes a disease in humans which is called amoebiasis or amoebic dysentery.

Contamination of food with this pathogen, although worldwide, is more prevalent in high-temperature regions. Amoebic dysentery usually occurs sporadically, but has been found to occur in epidemics also. It is, in general, spread by human-to-human contact but may be food- and waterborne.

The symptoms vary from mild to violent diarrhea, alternating with constipation, and abdominal pain is usually present. Occasional fatalities do occur.

The amoebae may infect rats and flies. The organisms get into the soil from human and animal feces. Food becomes contaminated from soil, rats, flies, or unclean hands of infested persons, especially if they do not wash their hands after visiting the toilet. Therefore, food handlers may play an important role in the spread of amoebae.

Raw foods grown on contaminated soil are an important vehicle of the contaminant. Vegetables should be cooked before they are eaten, and fruits should be thoroughly washed and peeled. Infested persons should not handle food.

Other potentially dangerous protozoa are *Dientamoeba fragilis, Giardia lamblia,* and *Cryptosporidium.* They may cause enteritis with symptoms of diarrhea and in the case of giardiasis, cause presence of mucus in the stool. For giardiasis, infection is most common in children. The source of the pathogens is human feces. Food and water may become contaminated from sewage or from feces adhering to the bodies of insects (flies, cockroaches) and rodents (rats, mice), and to the hands of the food handler.

PATHOGENIC MICROORGANISMS (VIRUSES, RICKETTSIAE, BACTERIA)

Viruses

Viruses can multiply only in the living cell. Outbreaks of certain virus-produced diseases that have been reported point to food and water as important vehicles in virus transmission (Berg, 1964; Cliver, 1967). Outbreaks of serious diseases, such as infectious hepatitis and poliomyelitis, have been linked to these vehicles of transmission. Another important vehicle is an infected food handler, either acutely ill or a carrier, who excretes the organism in the feces. Other vehicles implicated were food or water contaminated with raw sewage. Such contamination can happen in the foodservice establishment when plumbing is faulty and sewage is leaking out from pipes or backing up into sinks or onto floors (see Chapter 8).

Enteroviruses invade the gut of humans, while certain other viruses *(Echo, Coxsackie)* are capable of causing respiratory illnesses. Enteroviruses reproduce in the intestinal tract and are expelled with feces and urine. Hepatitis virus A is a pathogen of great importance in connection with the sanitary handling of food, since through faulty hygienic measures of an infected food handler (lack of washing hands after a visit to the restroom) the organism may be spread to many persons consuming the contaminated food. A virus that lodges in an infected person's respiratory tract is likely to be passed on to food, and thus the consumer, by way of droplet contamination.

Infectious hepatitis has the highest incidence of food-associated viral illnesses. An early record of food-associated hepatitis dates back to 1946, when Read et al. linked infectious hepatitis to food eaten at a certain fraternity house. A description of 36 outbreaks was given by Cliver (1966, 1967). It was shown that uncooked food as well as a variety of cooked foods were involved. Uncooked shellfish was a frequent offender. Contamination of seafood with the virus usually stems from sewage-polluted harvesting areas (see also Chapter 6).

The persistence of enterovirus in meat products was investigated by Herrmann and Cliver (1973). They found that in the meat products studied, sausage and ground beef, the virus was quite stable. The probable vehicle of transmission in such products is the food handler. Raw vegetables may be sources of pathogenic viruses also, and have been implicated in foodborne illnesses. Survival of enteric viruses on vegetables was studied by Konowal-chuk and Speirs (1975).

Animals may carry viruses also. Cattle, swine, and sheep may be infected with a number of viruses, some of these seemingly specific, others not. Viruses that infect animals may be present in the apparently healthy tissues of meat. We have at present little knowledge about the specificity of the viruses and the ability of viruses of other than human origin to cause infection in man. However, it is a known fact that Newcastle disease, a poultry disease caused by a virus, may be contracted by workers handling poultry through splash, causing infection of the workers' eyes.

Also, outbreaks of ornithosis, or psittacosis, are on record, involving patients employed in poultry plants and handling turkey. Berg (1964) has suggested that food, animals, or plants might be investigated as reservoirs of viruses possibly dangerous to man. Important research is now being conducted on the relationships among human and animal viruses. There is at present a lack of knowledge about the ability of viruses to cross from animal to man.

The stability of viruses in food is affected by many factors. Among these are food composition, the concentration of the virus, and temperature. Viruses, although incapable of multiplying in food, may remain viable in food for a while. The period of viability is longer at refrigeration temperatures than at room temperature. In general, enteroviruses are quite stable when in frozen condition, as shown by Lynt, Jr. (1966).

From a public health point of view, the susceptibility of viruses to heating is important. Many viruses seem to be inactivated by heating to 65°C (149°F) for ½ to 1 hour, or by brief heating to 72°C (161.6°F), but others require boiling. On the basis of a survey of available data, Cliver (1966) concluded that the hepatitis virus is evidently not inactivated by "limited heating." More research data are needed on the thermal inactivation of foodborne viruses, in different foods, and under various conditions of time and temperature.

Inactivation of viruses in food by heating has been discussed by Cliver and Konowalchuck (1983), who emphasize that transmission of virus is more likely to occur by way of unheated food items and by items that are intimately handled during their final preparation and that receive no further heating after handling, such as salads or sandwiches. Chemical inactivation of viruses has been discussed by Cliver (1979).

Rickettsiae

The rickettsiae may be looked upon as being somewhat akin to the bacteria, but they radically differ from bacteria and resemble viruses in that they need the living cell to reproduce and are truly parasitic in nature. Food is not a vehicle of transmission for the rickettsiae, with the exception of the organism causing Q fever. Cows infected with the organism causing Q fever, *Coxiella burnettii,* may transmit it to the milk; therefore, the heating times and temperatures for pasteurization of milk were adjusted to eliminate this contaminant.

Bacteria: Pathogens for Which Food Serves Merely as a Vehicle of Transmission

Pathogens causing communicable diseases may be transmitted through food just as they are through other vehicles on or in which bacteria may land. The pathogens are passed on from person to person via food, money, hands, and so on. These agents may stem from humans, either acute cases or carriers, or from animals.

It is difficult to arrive at a hard-and-fast rule as to which pathogens transmitted by food should be included in this category or in the category of organisms causing acute gastroenteric outbreaks. The latter category includes the organisms which multiply profusely in the food and cause illnesses of an explosive nature. Infectious diseases and epidemics, however, are characterized as illnesses developing over a period of several days, and contact with relatively small numbers of bacteria brings on the illness.

Examples of pathogens that may be foodborne and belong in the category of pathogens for which food serves merely as a vehicle of transmission are those causing tuberculosis, undulant fever, scarlet fever, septic sore throat, diphtheria, and cholera. Of the pathogens causing these diseases, some are capable of developing powerful exotoxins, the most important being *Streptococcus pyogenes, Corynebacterium diphtheriae,* and several species of *Shigella.* These organisms may be sustained in the food that serves as their vehicle in the spread of communicable diseases. They are specific pathogens one would not find in a healthy person, except for the chronic carriers. A carrier is a person who, without apparent symptoms of a communicable disease, harbors and disseminates the specific organisms.

Since some of these pathogens may multiply profusely in milk, the basis for grouping them here may be questioned. However, for all practical purposes, milk nowadays is a food somewhat set apart from other foods because in the United States it is presently marketed under highly controlled regulations of sanitation. Pasteurization temperatures and times are regulated to free milk of the important human pathogens that in the distant past were frequently transmitted through milk.

Examples of borderline cases with respect to grouping into the two categories are the pathogens causing bacillary dysentery and typhoid fever.

Dack (1956), an early authority on "food poisoning," has set the gastrointestinal disturbances caused by these organisms apart from other "food poisoning" forms, since "food poisoning" organisms were classified as those causing illnesses of an explosive nature. However, typhoid fever is an illness that develops over a period of several days; the pathogen is highly infective since a small number of cells may cause the disease in the person who ingests them, and the exclusive host is man.

Since the pathogens causing typhoid fever and bacillary dysentery would not be found in a healthy person or commonly in the food supply delivered to the kitchen, these organisms are included in Group II.

The foods involved in the transmission of pathogens may be many. For animals as well as man, foodstuffs of animal origin are the usual vehicle. In the case of human pathogens, the organisms get into the food when it is handled by a person suffering from the disease producing the pathogen. The pathogens may also be transmitted through sewage and sewage-polluted water. Streams, lakes, and ocean waters that have become polluted with raw sewage in turn contaminate fish and seafood living therein. Sewage may directly contaminate food through faulty plumbing.

PATHOGENS OF ANIMAL AND HUMAN ORIGIN. *Mycobacterium tuberculosis,* especially the bovine type, has caused tuberculosis primarily in children. It is no longer a major problem because of vigilance in detecting and eliminating infected cows, and because of heat treatment during pasteurization of milk and cream. However, the human pathogen may be transmitted by a food handler suffering from tuberculosis.

Brucella abortus, B. melitensis, and *B. suis* cause brucellosis, or undulant fever, in man. These organisms stem from cattle, goats, and hogs, respectively. They are killed by proper pasteurization of milk and cream and have been shown to remain viable in cream stored at 50°F (10°C) for several days. Control over the disposal of infected milk animals seems the most fundamental measure for eradication of brucellosis from animals and humans.

PATHOGENS OF HUMAN ORIGIN. For the sake of simplification, the pathogens of human communicable disease are discussed as three groups based on the site of infection: pathogens of the skin; pathogens of the mouth, nasal passages, throat, ear, and chest; and intestinal pathogens.

Skin. A discussion of the many diseases of the skin is beyond the scope of this book. Any of the pathogens causing skin diseases may be transmitted through food, which serves as a simple vehicle of transmission.

Hemolytic streptococci of group A, which cause erysipelas, are worth mentioning because the disease is not uncommon and is very contagious. The organism causes an inflammation of the superficial lymphatic vessels of skin or mucous membranes. Discharges from these lesions carry large loads of the streptococci. Other diseases of the skin include leprosy, lupus, and syphilis.

Staphylococcus aureus causes furuncles and carbuncles of the skin and is also associated with acne and common pimples. This organism is not only transmitted through food, it also has the ability to multiply freely in the food. Unfortunately, certain strains release a toxin into the food that is capable of causing gastroenteric outbreaks or true food poisoning. Therefore, the organism is discussed further later on.

Mouth, Nose, Throat. From the mouth, nose, and throat a great number of pathogens may be transmitted through food. The food handler's saliva and discharges are the source of the pathogens.

Hemolytic streptococci of group A cause sore throat, or pharyngitis, tonsillitis, scarlet fever, and other ailments of the throat. They also cause ear infections. Another important bacterial infection of the mouth and throat is Vincent's angina, caused by two kinds of organisms, *Fusobacterium fusiforme* and *spirochetes,* which may be transmitted through food.

Pathogens associated with colds, sinusitis, and influenza, although usually transferred directly from one person to another, may be transmitted through food also. Among these pathogens may be viruses and *Staphylococcus aureus.*

Corynebacterium diphtheriae is the pathogen causing diphtheria, and it may be transmitted through food. Diphtheria was once among the most feared of all communicable diseases. Its pathogen causes severe inflammation of the throat and other portions of the upper respiratory tract. Other vital organs, the heart and the kidneys in particular, are poisoned by a very powerful toxin secreted by the bacterial cells.

Pathogens associated with bronchial and lung diseases may also be transferred through food. The principal specific diseases of the lungs are tuberculosis, mentioned earlier, and pneumonia, caused by *Diplococcus pneumoniae.* Some other organisms involved in pneumonia are *S. aureus, Klebsiella pneumoniae, Streptococcus pyogenes,* and viruses.

Intestinal Tract. Pathogens of intestinal origin have a good chance to contaminate food when it is touched by contaminated hands. Food handlers may transmit these pathogens to ingredients and menu items when they do not wash their hands properly after visiting the toilet. Important bacterial pathogens of the intestinal tract are those causing cholera, bacillary dysentery, typhoid fever, and infectious hepatitis.

Vibrio cholerae, the causative organism of cholera, which may be transmitted by food and water, infects the human intestinal tract. Cholera is a disease characterized by vomiting, diarrhea, and severe prostration. Patients often die from severe dehydration. Since about 1875, cholera epidemics have no longer been a menace in the United States, but continue to occur in the warmer countries of the world (Finkelstein, 1973; Gangarosa and Mosley, 1974).

The shigellae are frequently transmitted by food. Bacillary dysentery, or shigellosis, may be caused by several species: *Shigella dysenteriae, boydii, sonnei,* and *flexneri.* The disease is an acute infection of the intestines, causing diarrhea and bloody stool containing mucus. The period of incubation is commonly less than 4 days, but may be as long as 7 days. Fever and cramps are often present. The organisms are transmitted in the same manner as *Salmonella.* Of the three shigellae species *S. dysenteriae* is the only one capable of producing exotoxins, but it is less prevalent than the two other species. In a report made by Eichner et al. (1968) on the status of shigellosis in the United States from fall 1963 to mid-1966, it is stated that the majority of isolations of *Shigella* from humans came from children under 10 years of age.

Transmission is commonly through food and water that have become contaminated with feces, and the food handler may play an important role in the transmission. Any item that has been contaminated and brought in contact with food may serve to transmit the pathogen.

Among the salmonellae is the powerful intestinal pathogen of man, *Salmonella typhi,* the cause of typhoid fever. This disease presents an interesting chapter in the history of public health in the United States. Before 1900, typhoid fever was one of the principal causes of severe illness and death. At present, it has an insignificant place in the mortality statistics in the United States. In cities where the water supply is under strict sanitary control, few cases of this disease occur; however, in rural regions, it does occur in isolated cases, mostly as epidemics limited to a family.

The source of infection is the infected human. The pathogen causes an infection of the intestinal tract, especially in the lower ileum. Continued fever is an important symptom, also headache, abdominal pain, and anorexia. The bacteria invade the lymph nodes, then the bloodstream, and eventually various organs and tissues such as the kidneys, liver, bone marrow, and spleen.

The incubation period is from 1 to 3 weeks. The recovered patient may become a carrier and remain a carrier for many months.

To prevent transmission of pathogens, the sanitation of food and drink and sanitary sewage disposal are important. Patients who are suffering from communicable diseases, or who are carriers, should not handle food to be served to others. It is necessary to ascertain that a person who is employed in food service is not a carrier. It is important to remember that convalescent patients of certain diseases may remain carriers for long periods of time.

REFERENCES

Bean, N. H. and P. M. Griffin (1990). "Foodborne disease outbreaks in the United States, 1973–1987: Pathogens, vehicles and trends." *J. Food Prot.,* 53:804–817.

Berg, G. (1964). "The food vehicle in virus transmission." *Health Lab. Sci.,* 1:51–59.

Bier, J. W. (1976). "Experimental anasakiasis: cultivation and temperature tolerance determinations." *J. Milk Food Technol.,* 39:132–137.

Brandly, P. J., G. Migaki, and K. E. Taylor (1966). *Meat Hygiene,* 3rd ed. Lea & Febiger, Philadelphia, PA.

Carlin, A. F., C. Mott, D. Cash, and W. Zimmermann (1969). "Destruction of *Trichina* larvae in cooked pork roasts." *J. Food Sci.,* 34:210–212.

Chadwick, D. R. (1962). "Effects of radioactive contamination of the environment on public health." *J. Dairy Sci.,* 45:1552–1557.

Cladouhos, J. W. (1977). "Paralytic shellfish poisoning reported in Alaska." *J. Environ. Health,* 39:256–257.

Cliver, D. O. (1966). "Implications of foodborne infectious hepatitis." U.S. Public Health Rep., 81:159–165.

Cliver, D. O. (1967). "Food-associated viruses." *Health Lab. Sci.,* 4:213–221.

Cliver, D. O. (1979). "Viral infections." In *Foodborne Infections and Intoxications,* H. Riemann and F. L. Bryan, Eds., 2nd ed. Academic Press, New York.

Cliver, D. O. and J. Konowalchuck (1983). "Viruses as agents of foodborne diseases." In *Food Microbiology,* A. H. Rose, Ed., Chapter 9. Academic Press, New York, London.

Coon, J. M. (1975). "Natural toxicants in foods." *J. Am. Diet. Assoc.,* 67:213–218.

Crawford, L. (1985). (untitled). *FDA Consumer,* 19(Feb):15–17.

Dack, G. M. (1956). *Food Poisoning.* 3rd ed. Univ. Chicago Press, Chicago, IL.

Eichner, E. R., E. J. Gangarosa, and J. B. Goldsby (1968). "The current status of shigellosis in the United States." *Am. J. Public Health,* 58:753–763.

Eisenbud, M. (1963). "Distribution of radioactivity in foods." *Fed. Proc.* 22:1410–1414.

Federal Food, Drug and Cosmetic Act (1976a) as amended October 1976. Sec. 409 (c)(3)(A). U.S. Government Printing Office, Washington, D.C.

Ibid. (1976b), Sec. 201(s).

Federation of American Societies for Experimental Biology (1977). "Evaluation of the health aspects of GRAS food ingredients: Lessons learned and questions unanswered." *Fed. Proc.,* 36:2519.

Finkelstein, R. A. (1973). "Cholera." *CRC Critical Rev. Microbiol.,* 2:553–623.

Flisser, A. (1985). "Cysticercosis: A major threat to human health and livestock production." *Food Tech.,* 39(3):61–64.

Food and Drug Administration (1971). "Toxic metals in dinnerware." *FDA Fact Sheet,* OCAG14 (FDA) 72–1001.

Food and Drug Administration (1979). "Carcinogenic residues in food producing animals." *Fed. Reg.,* 44(March 20):17070.

Frazier, W. C. and D. C. Westhoff (1978). *Food Microbiology,* 3rd ed. McGraw-Hill Book Co., New York.

Furia, T. E. (1972). *Handbook of Food Additives.* The CRC Press, Cleveland, OH.

Gangarosa, E. J. and W. H. Mosley (1974). "Epidemiology and surveillance of cholera." In *Cholera,* D. Barua and W. Burrows, Eds. W. B. Saunders Co., Philadelphia, PA.

Gray, J. I. and M. E. Collins (1978). "Formation of N-nitrosopyrrolidine in fried bacon." *J. Food Prot.,* 41:36–39.

Gray, J. I. and C. J. Randall (1979). "The nitrite/N-nitrosamine problem in meats: An update." *J. Food Prot.,* 42:168–179.

Halstead, B. W. (1965). *Poisonous and Venomous Marine Animals,* Vol. 1. U.S. Government Printing Office, Washington, D.C.

Handbook of Naturally Occurring Food Toxicants (1983). M. Recheigl, Ed. CRC Press, Boca Raton, FL.

Harsanyi, Y. L. (1973). "Paralytic shellfish poisoning." *FDA Consum.,* 7(July–Aug.):22–23.

Hashimoto, Y. (1979). *Marine Toxins and Other Bioactive Marine Metabolites.* Japan Scientific Societies Press, Tokyo.

Havery, D. C. and T. Fazio (1985). "Human exposure to nitrosamines." *Food Technol.,* 39(1):80–83.

Healy, G. R. and D. Juranek (1979). "Parasitic infections." In *Foodborne Infections and Intoxications,* H. Riemann and F. L. Bryan, Eds., 2nd ed. Academic Press, New York.

Hecht, A. (1979). "DES: The drug with unexpected legacies." *FDA Consum.,* 13(May):14–19.

Herrmann, J. E. and C. O. Cliver (1973). "Enterovirus persistence in sausage and ground beef." *J. Milk Food Technol.,* 36:426–428.

Hird, D. W. and M. M. Pullen (1979). "Tapeworms, meat and man: A brief review and update on cysticercosis caused by *Taenia saginata* and *Taenia solium.*" *J. Food Prot.,* 42:58–64.

Hopkins, H. (1978a). "The GRAS list revisited." *FDA Consum.,* 12(4):13–15.

Hopkins, H. (1978b). "Nitrites: focusing on safety." *FDA Consum.,* 12(1):9–11.

Ingram, M. (1976). "The microbiological role of nitrite in meat products." In *Microbiology in Agriculture, Fisheries, and Food,* F. A. Skinner and J. G. Carr, Eds. Academic Press, London, New York, San Francisco.

International Commission on Microbiological Specifications for Food (1980). *Factors Affecting Life and Death of Microorganisms. Microbial Ecology of Foods,* Vol. 1, Chapter 9.

Jackson, G. J. (1975). "The 'new disease' status of human anasakiasis and North American cases: A review." *J. Milk Food Technol.,* 38:769–773.

Jackson, G. J., J. W. Bier, W. L. Payne, T. A. Gerding, and W. G. Knallenberg (1978). "Nematodes in fresh market fish of the Washington, D.C. area." *J. Food Prot.,* 41:613–620.

Konowalchuk, J. and J. I. Speirs (1975). "Survival of enteric viruses on fresh vegetables." *J. Milk Food Technol.,* 38:469–472.

Krinitz, B. and R. K. Hering (1971). "Toxic metal in earthenware." *FDA Pap.,* 5(3):21–24.

Lynt, R. K., Jr. (1966). "Survival and recovery of enterovirus from foods." *Appl. Microbiol.,* 14:218–222.

Menzel, R. C. (1963). "Factors influencing the biological availability of radionuclides for plants." *Fed. Proc.,* 22:1398–1401.

Morbidity and Mortality Weekly Report (1973). U.S. Department of Health, Education and Welfare, Public Health Serv., Center for Disease Control, 22, Dec. 1.

Morbidity and Mortality Weekly Report (1974). U.S. Department of Health, Education and Welfare, Public Health Serv., Center for Disease Control, 23, Sept. 14.

Morbidity and Mortality Weekly Report (1978). U.S. Department of Health, Education and Welfare, Public Health Serv., Center for Disease Control, 27, Feb. 3.

Morbidity and Mortality Weekly Report (1979). U.S. Department of Health, Education and Welfare, Public Health Serv., Center for Disease Control, 28, Sept. 28.

Myers, B. J. (1979). "Anasakine nematodes in fresh commercial fish from waters along the Washington, Oregon, and California coasts." *J. Food Prot.,* 42:380–384.

National Academy of Sciences (1973). *Toxicants Occurring Naturally in Foods,* 2nd ed. Washington, D.C.

Pocock, D. G., P. R. Schnurrenberger, A. D. Ziegler, F. H. Wentworth, and J. Basche, Jr. (1963). "Trichinosis. A point source outbreak." *Ann. Int. Med.,* 59:323–331.

Ponnampalam, R. and N. I. Mondy (1983). "Effect of cooking on the total glycoalkaloid content of potatoes." *J. Agr. Food Chem.,* 31:493–495.

Read, M. S. (1963). "Countermeasures against radionuclides in foods." *Fed. Proc.,* 22:1418–1423.

Read, M. R., H. Bancroft, J. A. Doul, and R. F. Parker (1946). "Infectious hepatitis—presumedly foodborne outbreak." *Am. J. Public Health,* 36:367–370.

Reddy, N. R., S. K. Sathe, and D. K. Salunkhe (1982). "Phytates in legumes and cereals." *Advances in Food Res.,* 28:1–92.

Riha, W. E. and M. Solberg (1975). "*Clostridium perfringens* inhibition by sodium nitrite as a function of pH, inoculum size, and heat." *J. Food Sci.,* 40:439–442.

Rodricks, J. V. and A. E. Pohland (1981). "Food hazards of natural origin." In *Food Safety,* H. R. Roberts, Ed., Chapter 5. Wiley-Interscience, New York.

Sawhney, B. L. and L. Hankin (1985). "Polychlorinated biphenyls in food: A review." *J. Food Prot.,* 48:442–448.

Scanlan, R. A. (1983). "Formation and occurrence of nitrosamines in food." *Cancer Res.,* 43:2435.

Schantz, E. J. (1973). "Seafood toxicants." In *Toxicants Occurring Naturally in Foods,* 2nd ed. National Academy of Sciences, Washington, D.C.

Schantz, P. M. (1983). "Trichinosis in the United States." *Food Technol.,* 37(3):83–86.

Schaumburg, H. H., R. Byck, R. Gerstl, and J. H. Mashman (1969). "Monosodium L-glutamate: Its pharmacology and role in the Chinese restaurant syndrome." *Science,* 163:826–828.

Schultz, M. G., J. A. Hermos, and J. H. Steele (1970). "Epidemiology of beef tapeworm infection in the United States." *U.S. Public Health Rep.,* 85:169–176.

Sen, N. P., J. R. Iyengar, B. A. Donaldson, and T. Panalaks (1974). "Effect of sodium nitrite concentration on the formation of nitrosopyrrolidine and dimethylnitrosamine in fried bacon." *J. Agr. Food Chem.,* 22:540–541.

Simon, R. A. (1982). "The incidence of ingested metabisulfite sensitivity in an asthmatic population." *J. Allergy Clinic. Immunol.,* 69(Jan.):118.

Singleton, V. L. (1981). "Naturally occurring food toxicants: Phenolic substances of plant origin common in foods." *Adv. Food Res.,* 27:149–242.

Somers, E. (1974). "The toxic potential of trace metals in foods. A review." *J. Food Sci.,* 39:215–217.

Thompson, R. C. (1984). "The search for pesticide residues." *FDA Consum.,* 18(July/Aug.):6–11.

U.S. Department of Agriculture, Agricultural Research Service, Meat Inspection Division (1960). *Regulations Governing the Meat Inspection of the United States Depart-*

ment of Agriculture, edition of June 1, 1959. U.S. Government Printing Office, Washington, D.C.

Van Etten, C. H. and I. A. Wolff (1973). "Natural sulfur compounds." In *Toxicants Occurring Naturally in Foods,* 2nd ed. National Academy of Sciences, Washington, D.C.

Weisburger, J. H. (1984). "Naturally occurring toxicologic substances: Nutragens and carcinogens in food." In *Proceedings of the Second National Conference for Food Protection,* U.S. Department of Health and Human Services, FDA contract no. 223–84–2087. Pages 73–93.

Whitaker, J. R. and R. E. Feeney (1973). "Enzyme inhibitors." In *Toxicants Occurring Naturally in Foods,* 2nd ed. National Academy of Sciences, Washington, D.C.

Widdus, R. and F. F. Busta (1982). "Antibotulinal alternatives to nitrite in foods." *Food Technol.,* 36(12):105–106.

World Health Organization (1984). FAO/UNDP/WHO, 1984. *Guidelines on Surveillance, Prevention and Control of Taeniasis/Cysticercosis.* Document VPH/84, 49.

World Health Organization (WHO); Food and Agriculture Organization of the United Nations (FAO)(1975). *Pesticide Residues in Food,* Report of the 1974 Joint Meeting of the FAO Working Party of Experts on Pesticide Residues and the World Health Organization Expert Committee on Pesticide Residue. WHO Technical Report Series No. 574; FAO Agricultural Studies No. 97.

Zimmerman, W. J. (1982). "Effect of microwave roasting on *Trichinella spiralis* in pork." *J. Microwave Power,* 17:250–251.

ADDITIONAL READINGS

Celeste, A. C. and C. G. Shane. "Mercury in fish." *FDA Pap.,* 4(9):27–30. 1970.

Greenland, S. "The interaction of nitrites with food, drugs and contaminants." *J. Environ. Health,* 41:141–143. 1978.

Greger, J. L., W. Goetz, and D. Sullivan. "Aluminum levels in foods cooked and stored in aluminum pans, trays and foil." *J. Food Prot.,* 48:772–777. 1985.

Hopkins, H. "Countdown on color additives." *FDA Consum.,* 10(Nov.):5–7. 1976.

Institute of Food Technologists' Expert Panel on Food Safety and Nutrition. "Naturally occurring toxicants in foods." *J. Food Sci.,* 40:215–222. 1975.

Institute of Food Technologists' Expert Panel on Food Safety and Nutrition. "Sulfites as food additives." *Food Technol.,* 29(10):117–120. 1975.

Liener, I. E., Ed. *Toxic Constituents of Animal Foodstuffs.* Academic Press, New York. 1974.

McFarren, E. F. "Assay and control of marine biotoxins." *Food Technol.,* 25:234–244. 1971.

Middlekauff, R. D. "Food safety review in Congress." *Food Technol.,* 35(12):84–87. 1981.

Potter, N. N. *Food Science.* Avi Publishing Co., Westport, CT. 1986.

U.S. Department of Agriculture. "An Analysis of a Ban on Nitrite Use in Curing Bacon." U.S. Department of Agriculture, Economics, Statistics, and Cooperative Service. ESCS-48. Washington, D.C. 1979.

Van Houweling, C. D. "Use of antibiotics in food animals." *FDA Pap.,* 3(4):21–25. 1969.

Foodborne Illnesses

GROUP III. PATHOGENS MULTIPLYING PROFUSELY IN FOODS AND CAPABLE OF CAUSING OUTBREAKS OF ACUTE GASTROENTERITIS

Acute gastroenteritis caused by microbial pathogens which multiply profusely in food are popularly called "food poisoning" outbreaks. These outbreaks are either foodborne intoxications or foodborne infections. The symptoms are violent reactions and include nausea, vomiting, diarrhea, and intestinal cramps.

The label "food poisoning" should be restricted to incidences in which a poison or toxin causes the illness. Foodborne poisonings or intoxications are, in general, of a more explosive nature than foodborne infections. The time elapsing between partaking of the toxin-containing food and the appearance of the first symptoms may be as short as a couple of hours. In the infectious type of foodborne illness, the symptoms are caused by the activity, within the gastrointestinal system of the victim, of large numbers of bacterial cells, and the incubation time of the infection is longer than that of the intoxication.

Both types of the illnesses under discussion are more explosive in nature than illnesses in which food plays merely the role of a transmitting vector. An exception is botulism, a foodborne intoxication with a long incubation period.

From an economic point of view, the cost of foodborne disease must not be underestimated. The discussion of economic loss resulting from microbial contamination of food by Todd (1984) brings out the fact that losses can be very high. The author stresses the need for a systematic approach elucidating this multifaceted problem, and the need, in particular, for data now missing for the costs of small outbreaks and single cases. The author, in evaluating the problem, suggests possible solutions. Weiss in 1993 stated that his estimate of medical costs and productivity losses as a result of foodborne pathogens in 1992 was 5–6 billion dollars.

Paramount to effectual sanitary control of menu items prepared in quantity is an understanding of the reservoirs of these potentially dangerous organisms, the conditioning favoring contamination of food in the areas where menu items are prepared and served, and the factors allowing for profuse multiplication of the contaminants during preparation and storage of menu items under conditions of quantity food service.

The Centers for Disease Control (CDC) have defined a foodborne outbreak as an incident in which, first, two or more persons experience similar illness, usually gastrointestinal, after ingestion of a common food; and, second, epidemiologic analysis implicates the food as the source of the illness. There are these exceptions: one case of botulism or of chemical poisoning is considered to be an outbreak also. A discussion of the epidemiology of foodborne disease was presented by Bryan (1979).

INCIDENCE OF OUTBREAKS

Relative Importance of Causative Agents

Important pathogens responsible for foodborne intoxications are *Clostridium botulinum* and *Staphylococcus aureus.* Pathogens responsible for foodborne infections include, before all, the salmonellae. *Vibrio parahaemolyticus,* which is responsible for a great number of foodborne infections in Japan, is gaining in importance in the United States also. Fecal streptococci are occasionally associated with outbreaks of foodborne infections. An impressive number of foodborne illnesses is ascribed to *Clostridium perfringens.* The organism releases an enterotoxin into the victim's intestinal tract when sporulating. Other pathogens known to be associated with gastroenteric outbreaks are *Bacillus cereus, Yersinia enterocolitica,* and enteropathogenic forms of *Escherichia coli.* Many outbreaks are, unfortunately, of unknown etiology. And many others are never even reported.

Among the fungi, *Aspergillus flavus* is capable of releasing powerful toxins into foods on which certain strains grow.

The microorganisms most frequently indicted as the causes of foodborne illnesses are bacteria. *Staphylococcus, Salmonella,* and *Clostridium perfringens* are at the top of the list of offenders (Table 4.1). The cause of many outbreaks is unknown. Fortunately, the number of "unknowns" is constantly

TABLE 4.1.   *Confirmed Foodborne Disease Outbreaks, by Etiologic Agent, United States, 1978–1982*

Etiologic Agent	1978 No.	1978 (%)	1979 No.	1979 (%)	1980 No.	1980 (%)	1981 No.	1981 (%)	1982 No.	1982 (%)
Bacterial										
B. cereus	6	(3.9)	—	—	9	(4.1)	8	(3.2)	8	(3.6)
Brucella	—	—	2	(1.3)	—	—	—	—	1	(0.5)
C. jejuni	—	—	—	—	5	(2.3)	10	(4.0)	2	(0.9)
C. botulinum	12	(7.8)	7	(4.0)	14	(6.3)	11	(4.4)	21	(9.5)
C. perfringens	9	(5.9)	20	(11.6)	25	(11.3)	28	(11.2)	22	(10.0)
E. cloacae	—	—	1	(0.6)	—	—	—	—	—	—
E. coli	1	(0.7)	—	—	1	(0.5)	—	—	2	(0.9)
Salmonella	45	(29.3)	44	(25.5)	39	(17.7)	66	(26.4)	55	(25.0)
Shigella	4	(2.6)	7	(4.0)	11	(5.0)	9	(3.6)	4	(1.8)
S. aureus	23	(14.9)	34	(19.7)	27	(12.2)	44	(17.6)	28	(12.7)
Streptococcus Group A	—	—	—	—	—	—	2	(0.8)	1	(0.5)
Streptococcus Group D	1	(0.7)	—	—	—	—	1	(0.4)	—	—
Streptococcus Group G	—	—	1	(0.6)	—	—	—	—	—	—
V. cholerae 01	1	(0.7)	—	—	—	—	—	—	1	(0.5)
V. cholerae non-01	—	—	1	(0.6)	—	—	1	(0.4)	1	(0.5)
V. parahaemolyticus	2	(1.3)	2	(1.3)	4	(1.8)	2	(0.8)	3	(1.4)
Y. enterocolitica	—	—	—	—	—	—	2	(0.8)	2	(0.9)
Other	1	(0.7)	—	—	1	(0.5)	1	(0.4)	—	—
Total	105	(68.5)	119	(69.2)	136	(61.7)	185	(74.0)	151	(68.7)
Chemical										
Ciguatoxin	19	(12.3)	18	(10.4)	15	(6.8)	15	(6.0)	8	(3.6)
Heavy metals	1	(0.7)	1	(0.6)	1	(0.5)	2	(0.8)	5	(2.3)
Monosodium glutamate	—	—	—	—	—	—	2	(0.8)	3	(1.4)
Mushroom poisoning	1	(0.6)	1	(0.6)	—	—	11	(4.4)	4	(1.8)
Paralytic shellfish	4	(2.6)	—	—	5	(2.2)	—	—	1	(0.5)
Scombrotoxin	7	(4.5)	12	(7.0)	29	(13.0)	7	(2.8)	18	(8.2)
Other	5	(3.2)	4	(2.3)	16	(7.2)	14	(5.6)	8	(3.6)
Total	37	(23.9)	36	(20.9)	66	(29.7)	51	(20.4)	47	(21.4)
Parasitic										
Trichinella spiralis	7	(4.5)	11	(6.4)	5	(2.3)	7	(2.8)	1	(0.5)
Other	—	—	—	—	2	(0.9)	1	(0.4)	—	—
Total	7	(4.5)	11	(6.4)	7	(3.2)	8	(3.2)	1	(0.5)
Viral										
Hepatitis A	5	(3.2)	5	(2.9)	10	(4.5)	6	(2.4)	19	(8.6)
Norwalk virus	—	—	1	(0.6)	2	(0.9)	—	—	2	(0.9)
Total	5	(3.2)	6	(3.5)	12	(5.4)	6	(2.4)	21	(9.4)
Confirmed total	154	(100.0)	172	(100.0)	221	(100.0)	250	(100.0)	220	(100.0)

Source: Centers for Disease Control, U.S. Department of Health and Human Services, Public Health Service (1985). *Foodborne Disease Surveillance, Annual Summary, 1982.*

decreasing because of improvements in methodology of identification and expansion of laboratory facilities devoted to this effort.

Outbreaks caused by chemicals, parasites, viruses, rickettsiae, and bacterial pathogens for which food serves as a mere vehicle of transmission, rather than as a medium for multiplication to great numbers, are discussed in Chapter 3.

Reports from States

The number of outbreaks and cases listed in Table 4.1 presents by no means an accurate picture. The actual number of stricken victims may amount to several millions per annum. Reporting is poor in many states. Fortunately, the trend is toward better participation of states in reporting.

Outbreaks of foodborne illness as reported by states are shown in Figure 4.1. In New York State, the reported number of outbreaks is high, but this is

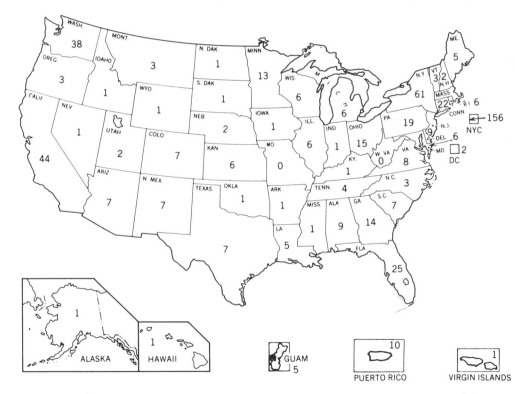

FIGURE 4.1. Outbreaks of foodborne disease reported to the Centers for Disease Control, by state, 1981. *Morbidity and Mortality Weekly Report* (1984). U.S. Department of Health and Human Services, Centers for Disease Control, 32(54):16.

known to be a result of good reporting, indicating an interest in matters of food sanitation. Many family incidents go by without being reported to the health authorities, probably because the individual outbreak is restricted to one family at a time and lacks the dramatic impact of an outbreak at a public gathering, where hundreds of people might be involved. Even outbreaks which take place in foodservice establishments remain largely unreported because of "poor publicity" for the organization, loss of customers and profit, and fear of possible legal involvements.

Difficulties in identification of the causative agent are manifold. They include delayed reporting, inability to secure samples of the suspected menu items, inadequate history of the incident, inadequate facilities for laboratory studies, and poor cooperation of foodservice personnel.

The U.S. Public Health Service is well aware of the inadequacies of assessing the incidence of the hazards caused by incomplete reporting, incomplete diagnosis, and lack of uniformity in state regulations, and is working to improve this situation.

Reliable data on gastroenteric eposides are important because they form a basis for developing successful measures to protect the consumer. It is the duty of the food manager to report foodborne gastroenteric episodes to the appropriate health authorities.

Foods Involved

Table 4.2 lists foodborne outbreaks in 1982 by vehicles of transmission and specific etiology. Meat, poultry, fish, and shellfish are items frequently implicated. However, the category "unknown" has the highest number of reported outbreaks.

It has been shown that circumstances often associated with outbreaks of foodborne illnesses are: employees suffering from intestinal upsets, colds, sinusitis, acne, sores, infectious burns, and boils; employees having unsanitary personal habits; obtaining food from unsafe sources; prolonged holding of cooked food in warm places; inadequate refrigeration; insufficient heating; unclean food preparation equipment; and presence of flies, cockroaches, and rodents.

Foodservices Involved

Incidents have been reported from homes and from many types of foodservice establishments, such as restaurants, cafeterias, delicatessens, schools, colleges, hospitals, and private clubs; also from camps; social gatherings such as picnics and church suppers; and from vehicles of public transportation. The

TABLE 4.2. Foodborne Outbreaks by Specific Etiologic Agent and Vehicle of Transmission, United States, 1982

Etiologic Agent	Beef	Ham	Pork	Sausage	Chicken	Turkey	Other Meat	Shellfish	Tuna	Mahi-Mahi	Other Fish	Milk	Eggs	Ice Cream	Baked Foods
Bacterial															
B. cereus	1	—	—	—	—	—	—	—	—	—	—	—	—	—	1
Brucella	—	—	—	—	—	—	—	—	—	—	—	—	—	—	—
C. jejuni	—	—	—	—	—	—	—	—	—	—	—	2	—	—	—
C. botulinum	1	—	—	—	—	—	—	—	—	—	1	—	—	—	—
C. perfringens	6	—	—	—	—	4	2	—	—	—	—	—	—	—	—
E. coli	2	—	—	—	—	—	—	—	—	—	—	—	—	—	—
Salmonella	1	—	2	1	2	4	1	—	—	—	1	1	2	—	—
Shigella	—	—	—	—	—	—	—	—	1	—	—	—	—	—	—
S. aureus	5	3	2	1	4	3	1	—	—	—	—	1	—	—	2
Streptococcus Group A	—	—	—	—	—	—	—	—	—	—	—	—	—	—	—
V. cholerae 01	—	—	—	—	—	—	—	—	—	—	—	—	—	—	—
V. cholerae non-01	—	—	—	—	—	—	—	1	—	—	—	—	—	—	—
V. parahaemolyticus	—	—	—	—	—	—	—	3	—	—	—	—	—	—	—
Y. enterocolitica	—	—	—	—	—	—	—	—	—	—	—	1	—	—	—
Other	—	—	—	—	—	—	—	—	—	—	—	—	—	—	—
Total	16	3	4	2	6	11	4	4	1	—	2	4	2	—	3

Chemical														
Ciguatoxin	—	—	—	—	—	—	—	—	—	8	—	—	—	—
Heavy metals	—	—	—	—	—	—	—	—	—	—	—	—	—	—
Monosodium glutamate	—	—	—	—	—	—	—	—	—	—	—	—	—	—
Mushroom poisoning	—	—	—	—	—	—	—	—	—	—	—	—	—	—
Paralytic shellfish	—	—	—	—	—	—	1	—	—	—	—	—	—	—
Scombroxtoxin	—	—	—	—	—	—	—	3	5	10	—	—	—	—
Other	1	—	—	1	—	—	—	—	—	—	—	—	—	—
Total	1	—	—	1	—	—	1	3	5	18	—	—	—	—
Parasitic														
Trichinella spiralis	—	1	—	—	—	—	—	—	—	—	—	—	—	—
Total	—	1	—	—	—	—	—	—	—	—	—	—	—	—
Viral														
Hepatitis A	—	—	—	—	—	—	5	1	—	—	—	—	—	1
Norwalk virus	—	—	—	—	—	—	—	—	—	—	—	—	—	1
Total	—	—	—	—	—	—	5	1	—	—	—	—	—	2
Confirmed total	17	3	5	3	6	11	4	10	5	5	20	4	2	1	5
Unknown	5	2	1	1	7	—	—	56	2	—	1	—	1	—	5
Total 1982	22	5	6	4	13	11	4	66	7	5	21	4	3	1	10

TABLE 4.2 *(continued)*

Etiologic Agent	Fruits and Vegetables	Potato Salad	Poultry, Fish, Egg Salad	Other Salad	Fried Rice	Chinese Food	Mexican Food	Carbonated Beverage	Nondairy Beverage	Multiple Foods	Mushrooms	Other Foods	Unknown	Total
Bacterial														
B. cereus	—	—	—	1	3	—	—	—	—	—	—	1	—	8
Brucella	—	—	—	—	—	—	—	—	—	—	—	—	1	1
C. jejuni	—	—	—	—	—	—	—	—	—	—	1	1	—	2
C. botulinum	16	—	—	—	—	—	—	—	—	—	1	—	1	21
C. perfringens	—	—	—	—	—	—	2	—	—	1	—	—	7	22
E. coli	—	—	—	—	—	—	—	—	—	1	—	—	—	2
Salmonella	—	—	1	2	—	—	1	—	—	—	—	3	29	55
Shigella	—	—	1	1	—	—	—	—	—	—	—	—	2	4
S. aureus	—	2	1	1	—	—	1	—	—	1	—	—	2	28
Streptococcus Group A	—	—	—	1	—	—	—	—	—	1	—	—	—	1
V. cholerae 01	—	—	—	—	—	—	—	—	—	1	—	—	—	1
V. cholerae non-01	—	—	—	—	—	—	—	—	—	—	—	—	—	1
V. parahaemolyticus	—	—	—	—	—	—	—	—	—	—	—	—	—	3
Y. enterocolitica	1	—	—	—	—	—	—	—	—	—	—	—	—	2
Other	—	—	—	—	—	—	—	—	—	—	—	—	—	—
Total	17	2	2	5	3	—	4	—	—	3	1	5	42	151

													Total
Chemicals													
Ciguatoxin	—	—	—	—	—	—	—	—	—	—	—	—	8
Heavy metals	—	—	—	—	—	—	4	—	1	—	—	—	5
Monosodium glutamate	—	—	—	—	2	—	—	—	1	—	—	—	3
Mushroom poisoning	—	—	—	—	—	—	—	4	—	—	—	—	4
Paralytic shellfish	—	—	—	—	—	—	—	—	—	—	—	—	1
Scombrotoxin	—	—	—	—	—	—	—	—	—	—	—	—	18
Other	1	—	—	—	—	—	1	—	1	—	—	3	8
Total	1	—	—	—	2	—	5	4	2	1	4	3	47
Parasitic													
Trichinella spiralis	—	—	—	—	—	—	—	—	—	—	—	—	1
Total	—	—	—	—	—	—	—	—	—	—	—	—	1
Viral													
Hepatitis A	—	—	1	—	—	—	—	—	1	—	—	10	19
Norwalk virus	1	—	—	—	—	—	—	—	—	—	—	—	2
Total	1	—	1	—	—	—	—	—	1	—	—	10	21
Confirmed total	18	2	6	3	2	4	5	5	5	2	8	52	220
Unknown	1	3	6	1	1	2	—	5	5	—	9	325	436
Total	19	5	12	4	3	6	5	10	10	2	17	377	656

Source: Centers for Disease Control, U.S. Department of Health and Human Services, Public Health Service (1985). *Foodborne Disease Surveillance, Annual Summary,* 1982.

relative frequency of outbreaks in some selected places where food was eaten is shown in Table 4.3, which indicates that the place where outbreaks occurred most frequently were "restaurant, delicatessen or cafeteria," followed by "home" and "other."

According to the CDC, outbreaks frequently involve food that was prepared well in advance of service and held without the benefit of adequate facilities for keeping the items either hot enough or cold enough to discourage bacterial multiplication.

REPORTING AND INVESTIGATION OF OUTBREAKS

Gastroenteric outbreaks caused by food have been reported to the authorities for over 50 years. Beginning in the early 1920s, reports, limited to milk, were summarized by the Public Health Service. In 1938, waterborne and foodborne outbreaks were added. The decision to expand the reports grew out of concern over outbreaks of typhoid fever and infant diarrhea. In 1951 the Centers for Disease Control, then called the Communicable Disease Center, began to publish reports on foodborne illness in the *Morbidity and Mortality Weekly Report*. In 1966, annual summaries were published by this agency. The cooperation with state agencies greatly advanced the success of the effort of the CDC in the investigation of food- and waterborne outbreaks.

According to a statement by the CDC (1985), the surveillance of such outbreaks has traditionally served three objectives:

1. *Disease control,* through identification of contaminated products from the market, through correction of faulty food preparation practices in food service establishments and in the home, and through the appropriate treatment of human carriers of foodborne pathogens. Rapid reporting and subsequent investigation are essential at every step.
2. *Knowledge of disease causation,* through constant improvements in laboratory techniques for the identification, isolation, culturing, and tests for pathogenicity of the suspected pathogens. The responsible pathogen has not been identified in 30–60% of foodborne disease outbreaks reported to the CDC in recent years, in spite of the fact that great advances have been made in the area of identification. Sometimes tentative identification of unknowns can be made on the basis of incubation periods.
3. *Administrative guidance,* which is given on the basis of data collected from outbreak investigations. Common errors in the handling of food and water can be analyzed and corrective measures developed and passed on to state and local health agencies for guidance in their work in food protection and preparation of educational materials to be used in training programs.

TABLE 4.3. *Foodborne Disease Outbreaks, by Specific Etiologic Agent and Place Where Food Was Eaten, United States, 1982*

Etiologic Agent	Home	Delicatessen, Cafeteria, or Restaurant	School	Picnic	Church	Camp	Other	Un-known	Total
Bacterial									
B. cereus	—	3	2	—	—	1	2	—	8
Brucella	1	—	—	—	—	—	—	—	1
C. jejuni	1	—	—	—	—	—	1	—	2
C. botulinum	21	—	—	—	—	—	—	—	21
C. perfringens	—	9	1	—	—	—	12	—	22
E. coli	—	—	—	—	—	—	2	—	2
Salmonella	12	17	6	3	4	1	12	—	55
Shigella	1	2	—	—	1	—	—	—	4
S. aureus	4	7	2	2	2	1	10	—	28
Streptococcus									
Group A	—	—	—	—	—	—	1	—	1
V. cholerae 01	1	—	—	—	—	—	—	—	1
V. cholerae non-01	1	—	—	—	—	—	—	—	1
V. parahaemolyticus	1	—	—	1	—	—	1	—	3
Y. enterocolitica	1	—	—	—	—	—	1	—	2
Total	44	38	11	6	7	3	42	—	151
Chemical									
Ciguatoxin	3	5	—	—	—	—	—	—	8
Heavy metals	1	3	—	—	—	—	1	—	5
Monosodium glutamate	1	2	—	—	—	—	—	—	3
Mushroom poisoning	3	—	—	—	—	—	1	—	4
Paralytic shellfish	1	—	—	—	—	—	—	—	1
Scombrotoxin	7	9	—	—	—	—	2	—	18
Other chemical	4	4	—	—	—	—	—	—	8
Total	20	23	—	—	—	—	4	—	47
Parasitic									
Trichinella spiralis	1	—	—	—	—	—	—	—	1
Total	1	—	—	—	—	—	—	—	1
Viral									
Hepatitis A	5	6	—	1	—	1	6	—	19
Norwalk virus	—	1	—	—	—	—	1	—	2
Total	5	7	—	1	—	1	7	—	21
Confirmed total	70	68	11	7	7	4	53	—	220
Unknown	127	221	17	16	2	1	49	3	436
Total 1982	197	289	28	23	9	5	102	3	656

Source: Centers for Disease Control, U.S. Department of Health and Human Services, Public Health Service (1985). *Foodborne Disease Surveillance, Annual Summary, 1982.*

Reports

Family-limited gastrointestinal episodes are frequently unreported, an exception being suspected or confirmed cases of botulism. For many upsets, a physician is not called in. However, when meals that are served to the public cause illness, the impact may be dramatic.

When an outbreak of foodborne disease is suspected by the management of a foodservice establishment or when management has a suspicion that one of the food handlers has, or is coming down with, a communicable disease, the local health authorities must be informed at once. The regulatory authority may require that any, or all, of several measures be taken. These measures include: the immediate removal of the employee from the foodservice establishment; restriction of the employee's services to some area where no danger of transmitting his disease exists; the immediate closure of the foodservice establishment until no more danger of disease outbreak exists; and follow-up with medical examination of the employee, of other employees, and, possibly, of patrons of the establishment.

The initial report may be made through various channels of communication. Some of the basic data asked for are: date, time, and place of the suspected meal; names, addresses, and telephone numbers of at least some of the victims; symptoms of the victims; and the name of the person making the report. If the onset of the symptoms is slow, as is true for infection-type outbreaks, it may be difficult to even pinpoint the food service establishment where the illness-producing food was consumed, let alone the meal or particular item.

Some patients are very slow to report. When the onset of symptoms is brief, however, as in *Staphylococcus* food poisoning, the victims may be still present in the building or compound, such as in a school or industrial park. The principal or manager would be the person reporting to the local authorities.

For success in follow-up and eventual control, reporting to the health authority should be as prompt as possible. The unsatisfactory outcome of many investigations is caused by a delay in reporting, which makes it impossible for the epidemiologist or sanitarian to get all the facts he or she needs to pinpoint the case. A full knowledge of all pertinent facts is immediately helpful in limiting the spread of the outbreak and in treating the victims. In addition, it serves to deepen the understanding of the causes and effects at play in foodborne outbreaks. At the time of an outbreak, foodservice personnel and the public are probably most receptive to information on the subject of sanitary handling of foods. The reasons for poor reporting may some day be overcome by leadership education.

Investigations

Local health departments carry out most epidemiological investigations and pass their findings on to the appropriate state health departments who may assist in the investigations; or they may seek the cooperation of the Centers for Disease Control, which are well equipped with laboratory facilities and personnel. The CDC are always involved in implicated food products which move in interstate commerce.

Many outbreaks require the knowledgeable services of an entire team: the physician, the epidemiologist, the engineer, the sanitarian, the veterinarian, and the laboratory personnel (McCutchen, 1963). After the initial report has been received, immediate action is paramount to success. The objects of the investigation of foodborne illness are to: (1) determine the responsible meal; (2) determine the responsible item within the meal; (3) determine the nature and source of the contaminants; (4) determine the circumstances leading to contamination of and growth in the food; and (5) establish, in case of infections, proof that the pathogen has infected the patient.

The actual steps to take are: interview the victims, locate and visit the foodservice establishment suspected of having served the illness-producing food, impound the suspect food, take samples, and determine the causative agent.

Persons who ate the suspected meal, both ill and healthy, are interviewed as to what they ate. Also interviewed are physicians and nurses in charge of the ill victims and the food managers and/or employees of the suspected establishment. Samples of suspect food items are collected and transmitted to the laboratory team for analysis.

The food establishment is scrutinized for detailed information on the source of the suspect food, storage condition, length of storage, preparation, holding, and other pertinent information in connection with the history of the suspect meal and its components. The health of the employees and the sanitary conditions of the premises, including washroom facilities, are also surveyed. The cooperation of the foodservice staff, dietitian, manager, and other employees is extremely important if the survey is to be successful. All this information is entered on the appropriate forms.

The detailed food report usually includes: a copy of the suspected menu and a list of the ingredients used; preparation and holding conditions; brand and manufacturer and/or packer of ingredients; method of and circumstances pertaining to transportation, especially time; time of arrival and history after arrival; place, conditions, and length of storage; holding time and method of holding between preparation and service; and other information of importance in specific cases.

In the laboratory the food samples are subjected to chemical and microbiological analyses and a report is made on those findings. Specimens may also be obtained from patients and food handlers. The leader of the investigation team, an epidemiologist or sanitarian, interprets the information gained from interviews and laboratory tests as to the cause and source of the agent causing the outbreak.

Thus, the investigation calls for close cooperation of such agencies and persons as health officers, epidemiologists, physicians, nurses, sanitarians, laboratory technicians, and at times, even veterinarians. The combined data of the field and laboratory investigations are carefully evaluated for their use in pinpointing the incriminating food and identifying the locale of the episode and circumstances leading up to the actual outbreak. Often circumstantial evidence has to be substituted for hard-and-fast proof.

Once the source of the agent has been established, the agent identified, and the circumstances leading to the outbreak elucidated, control measures can and must be taken to prevent future outbreaks. Although great advances are being made all the time, too many outbreaks remain in the "etiology unknown" class.

An update on foodborne disease surveillance in the United States was presented by MacDonald (1984). The author points to improvements in the quality and quantity of reporting. For example, one improvement in the quality of epidemiologic investigation was the revision of "Procedures to Investigate Foodborne Illness of the International Association of Milk, Food and Environmental Sanitarians"; another was in the area of laboratory methodology used in identifying pathogenic organisms.

Only one of the purposes of this book is to make foodservice managers, present and future, aware of the inherent dangers of foodborne illnesses, and the various agents causing them. In addition, the book is designed to give information on possible sources of contamination with the various pathogenic agents, whether these may originate from the food itself, the food handler, environment, or food preparation equipment, and to suggest appropriate sanitary methods to keep them under control. This is what quantity food sanitation is all about.

BACTERIA CAUSING FOODBORNE INTOXICATIONS

Two important pathogens known to cause foodborne intoxications are *Clostridium botulinum* and *Staphylococcus aureus*.

Clostridium botulinum

ORGANISM. The food poisoning referred to as botulism is caused by *Clostridium botulinum*. Botulism is a disease of humans and animals. An excellent treatise on botulism has been published by Sakaguchi (1979). The organism is an anaerobic, Gram-positive, gas-producing spore former that is able to grow over a wide range of pH and temperatures and tolerates high salt concentrations.

C. botulinum is capable of producing a powerful toxin, a protein. Seven types are distinguishable on the basis of the serological specificity of the toxins. Six of the types are now known in more or less purified form: types A, B, C, D, E, and F. Type G has been recovered from soil in Argentina and from dead persons in Switzerland. The similarity of the strains isolated was discussed by Solomon et al. (1985).

The toxins are exotoxins in the sense that they are released into the medium or food after the death, or lysis, of the cell. The physical and chemical properties of type A are known best, because extensive studies have been made of this particular toxin. It is more toxic to humans than type B. The main features of the different types are shown in Table 4.4. *Clostridium botulinum* is antigenic, causing the production of antitoxins specific for the type of toxin. The toxins are the active agents causing the food poisoning. They are the most potent toxins known, and may persist in food for long periods of time, especially under low-temperature storage. Spores or vegetative cells will not cause ill effects in the human being when ingested.

DISTRIBUTION AND SOURCE. *Clostridium botulinum* exists as a saprophyte in soil, the sediment of lakes and oceans, and the intestinal tract of man and animals. The distribution of the pathogen is worldwide. In the United States, type A is very common in soils of the West, while type B, also a soil inhabitant, has a wider distribution. Type E, an inhabitant of the sediments of lakes, stream estuaries, and oceans, is widely distributed also.

Human botulism is most often caused by types A, B, and E, type F being a rare cause. Type A is also toxic to chickens, and type B to horses and hogs. Types C and D cause botulism in various animals. Type C causes botulism in fowl and other birds, but also in cattle, horses, sheep, and mink. Type D is the cause of forage poisoning of cattle in South Africa; it has been known to affect humans occasionally.

Type E is pathogenic to man, wild birds, and mink. It is found all over the world, but mostly in northern countries. It can be of terrestrial as well as of marine origin.

Type F is rare. The first episode caused by this type happened in Denmark. In the United States, this type has been recovered from marine sediment, fish, and crab (Eklund and Paysky, 1965; Craig and Pilcher, 1966; William-Walls, 1968). For more detailed information on botulism, the reader is referred to Sakaguchi (1979). Purification and properties of type F were described by Yang and Sugiyama (1975).

Types A and B have been known for decades to cause food poisoning, and

TABLE 4.4. *Main Features of the Different Types of C. Botulinum*[a]

Type	Differentiated By	Year	Species Mainly Affected	Most Common Vehicles	Highest Geographic Incidence
A	Leuchs Burke	1910 1919	Humans, chickens ("limberneck")	Home-canned vegetables and fruits, meat, and fish	Western United States, Soviet Ukraine
B	Leuchs Burke	1910 1919	Humans, horses, cattle	Prepared meats, especially pork products	France, Norway, Eastern United States
Cα	Bengston	1922	Aquatic wild birds ("western duck sickness")	Fly larvae (*Lucilia caesar*); rotting vegetation of alkaline ponds	Western United States and Canada, South America, South Africa, Australia
Cβ	Seddon	1922	Cattle ("Midland cattle disease"), horses ("forage poisoning"), mink	Toxic forage, carrion, pork liver	Australia, South Africa, Europe, North America
D	Theiler and Robinson Meyer and Gunnison	1927 1929	Cattle ("lamziekte")	Carrion	South Africa, Australia
E	Gunnison, Cummings, and Meyer Kushnir	1936 1937	Humans	Uncooked products of fish and marine mammals	Northern Japan, British Columbia, Labrador, Alaska, Great Lakes region, Sweden, Denmark, USSR
F	Moeller and Scheibel Dolman and Murakami	1960 1961	Humans	Home-made liver paste	Denmark

Source: Adapted from Dolman (1964).
[a]A seventh type, G, was isolated from soil in Argentina in 1969 (Gimenez and Ciccarelli, 1970).

these toxins have been found to be associated with meats and vegetables. Type E has become the major cause of botulism from commercially prepared foods, especially processed fish.

SYMPTOMS. *Clostridium botulinum* affects the nervous system; the symptoms appear from 2 hours up to 8 days, usually in 3–6 days, following the ingestion of the contaminated food. Among them are dry mouth, difficulties in swallowing and speech, double vision, and difficulty in breathing. The cause of death is a paralysis of the muscles of respiration. Botulism has a high death rate in the United States, in that approximately 65% of afflicted persons die. Humans are very susceptible to the botulinum toxins, and a "small taste" of toxin-containing food may suffice to make a person ill or cause him to die. This high death rate is probably the reason botulism is much feared, in spite of the fact that it occurs rarely in this day and age. Complete recovery of the nonfatal cases is very slow and may extend over several months.

The illness is treated by administering an antitoxin specific for the particular type of toxin involved. Despite the availability of antitoxins, botulism therapy is still not satisfactory due to the lag times between the ingestion of the food, the appearance of symptoms, the diagnosis, and the procurement of the specific antitoxin. The general availability of the specific antitoxins is limited. Most hospitals do not stock the antitoxins because of the rarity of botulism incidences.

Wound infection caused by *C. botulinum* is possible and has been reported in the United States. Treatment with antitoxins is indicated here also.

INCIDENCE. Before 1925, commercially canned foods in the United States were implicated in 32 cases. Since 1925, the implicated foods have been shown to be home-canned items; commercially canned foods have had an excellent record of safety, thanks to research efforts that resulted in the adoption of safe processing practices by the canning industry. Therefore, it was a shock when in the early 1960s some outbreaks occurred in the United States and were traced to commercially processed foods. These were canned tuna and vacuum-packed smoked freshwater fish (whitefish, chubs, ciscoes), the latter originating from the Great Lakes.

The incidence of botulism in the United States was low from 1938 to 1953 inclusive, an average of less than seven outbreaks per year being reported. A graph illustrating the number of reported cases (not outbreaks) by year in the United States is given in Figure 4.2.

Beginning in 1971, an increase in botulism outbreaks caused by commercially canned items was noticed with alarm. *Clostridium botulinum* and/or its toxins were found in vichyssoise, chicken vegetable soup, beef stew, tuna fish, peppers, chicken pie, marinated mushrooms, and in 41 cans of mush-

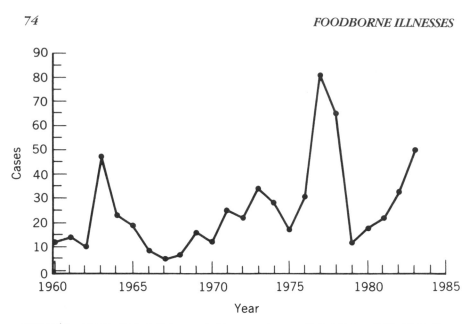

FIGURE 4.2.   Foodborne botulism reported by cases, by year, United States, 1960–1983. *Morbidity and Mortality Weekly Report* (1984). Annual Suppl., Summary for 1983.

rooms from 20 lots packed by domestic and foreign packing companies. In general, the presence of *C. botulinum* and/or its toxins in canned foods indicates faulty processing (Lynt et al., 1975).

FOODS IMPLICATED.   Inadequately processed, usually home-canned, foods such as meats and many kinds of vegetables, especially green beans, sweet corn, beets, asparagus, and spinach, have frequently been associated with botulism; tomatoes and fruits have been indicted also.

Smoked products, among them smoked fish, sausage, and other products made from meat, have caused botulism when inadequately processed.

Frozen foods have not been indicted in botulism. However, it is known that the spores of *C. botulinum* may survive long storage periods in raw and precooked frozen foods, and that during warm holding, after thawing, the spores are able to germinate and form toxins.

The appearance of foods carrying the toxins of *C. botulinum* is not necessarily indicative of the presence and activity of the organism. Frequently the food has been described by the victims as looking normal, even when the proteolytic strains of A and B were involved. Usually, the proteolytic strains of type A and some of type B noticeably change the appearance and odor of the invaded foods. The appearance may become more or less slimy and cheesy, and the odor foul and obnoxious. However, when the protein content of the medium is low, as is true for many vegetables, changes in appearance and odor may not be detectable. Also, gas production is not always in evidence. Type E will not visibly change the appearance of the food in which it multiplies.

FACTORS AFFECTING GROWTH AND PRODUCTION OF TOXINS. Toxin production goes hand in hand with growth. Both have been shown to be affected by the strain of organism, the composition, moisture, pH, oxygen, and salt content of the food; by the temperature and time of food storage; and by combinations of these. The botulinum toxin is stable in acid but unstable in alkali.

Food. Many foods may serve as substrates. Meats, shellfish, fish, low-acid vegetables, and some medium-acid vegetables support growth and toxin formation of *C. botulinum.* Most of the outbreaks were attributed to vegetables. Inadequately heat-processed home-canned foods are most frequently the cause of outbreaks of botulism, whereas commercially processed foods were indicted in a small percentage of outbreaks. Botulism in commercially canned foods has also been discussed by Lynt et al. (1975).

For type A, the potency of the toxin has been found to differ with the food, the more potent toxin being formed by media containing glucose, casein, and milk. The toxin formed in certain vegetables was found to be more potent than in others; corn and peas are among the vegetables supporting the formation of a very potent toxin.

Moisture. A certain amount of moisture has been demonstrated to be required for toxin production of types A and B. The critical water activity seems to be 0.935.

Salt and Sugar. Type E spores are much less salt-tolerant than type A and B spores (Segner et al., 1964). It is generally agreed that approximately 50% sugar or 10% salt (NaCl) completely inhibits types A and B. However, the exact inhibitory concentration is dependent on the strain of the organism, the nature of the medium in which the cells are suspended, and temperature.

Oxygen. *Clostridium botulinum* is an anaerobe, but may grow under certain conditions of reduced oxidation–reduction potential. The organism is able to grow and produce toxin in sealed cans and other hermetically sealed containers. For example, on fresh mushrooms, which are likely to be naturally contaminated with *C. botulinum* spores, outgrowth of spores followed by formation of a crop of vegetative cells is possible when the mushrooms are wrapped in air-proof plastic overwraps, unless the wraps are equipped with holes allowing access of oxygen into the package (Sugiyama, 1982). Smoked fish and other mildly heated food must undergo prescribed heat treatments. Exclusion of oxygen inhibits aerobic microorganisms, such as the lactic acid bacteria, which—when air is available—tend to suppress growth of *C. botulinum.*

A case of botulism reported from Puerto Rico in 1978 is an interesting one. Type A toxin was identified, and marinated fish was the implicated food; usually type E is associated with botulism in fish. Another interesting fact was that the fish was marinated in closed, narrow-mouthed jars, not in shallow trays, as it is customarily done. Perhaps the thick oil layer on top precluded access of oxygen, and it may also have protected the fish from the acid marinade (*Morbidity and Mortality Weekly Report,* 1978).

It has been shown (Kautter, 1964) in laboratory experiments that smoked ciscoes inoculated with type E spores and held at 30°C (86°F) in packages open to access of air were rendered toxic in about the same time as those held under anaerobic conditions. In vacuum-packaged inoculated fish, toxin production was demonstrated after 5 days' storage at 10°C (50°F) with no visible signs of quality reduction; at higher storage temperatures a greater percentage of fish contained toxin. The studies proved that type E is able to produce toxin in open packages as well as under vacuum. However, vacuum packaging is perhaps more hazardous because molds and contaminating aerobes are suppressed, giving *C. botulinum* more time and a more favorable environment for toxin formation.

A food poisoning outbreak (Seals et al., 1981) caused by *C. botulinum,* type A toxin, that had developed in foil-wrapped potatoes, which were held at room temperature for several days before they were used in potato salad, is an excellent example of a situation where botulinum spores were first stimulated by heating to germinate, and thereafter were provided warm conditions for a sufficiently long period so that cell multiplication and toxin formulation could occur.

There is also a potential risk of toxin production in vacuum-packed and subsequently cooked potatoes unless these are kept under refrigeration following the cooking process (Notermans et al., 1981).

pH.   *Clostridium botulinum* favors a pH near neutrality, but spores may germinate, vegetative cells divide, and toxin be produced over a considerably wide pH range. The lowest pH at which toxin is produced varies with the type of food, and also with the organism and temperature. Thus, no definite limits can be given. In general, at a pH of 4.6, growth and toxin production of types A, B, and E ceases, so that food of a pH 4.5 should be safe. Within the range of pH 5 to pH 8, growth and toxin production are excellent. It is important to remember that molds growing in an originally acid food, such as tomatoes, may render the food less acid and thus enable *C. botulinum* to start growing (Huhtanen et al., 1976).

Temperature. The temperature requirements of the various strains vary somewhat. Spores require a somewhat higher temperature for germination than the vegetative cells for fission. For spore germination, the minimum temperature for type A and B is approximately 15.5°C (60°F). The optimum for growth and toxin formation is near 35°C (95°F), the maximum approximately 48°C (118°F). As demonstrated by Schmidt et al. (1961), type E is quite different in that its minimum temperature requirement for growth is low: 38°F (3.3°C) for spore germination and subsequent outgrowth and toxin formation. Optimum growth temperature is 86°F (30°C), and the maximum is 113°F (45°C). Type F also can multiply at low temperatures, 39°F (3.9°C) being the minimum (William-Walls, 1968).

Freezing prevents growth and toxin formation of *C. botulinum,* but does not kill the organism or inactivate its toxins.

In quantity food service, to avoid botulism these precautions should be taken: (1) the procurement of a safe food supply; (2) rejection of canned goods exhibiting defects such as swell, rust, or leakage; (3) storage of canned goods under conditions recommended for these items, practicing reasonably frequent turnover of canned goods; (4) storage at 37°F (3°C), or below, of all perishable fish items that have received light heat treatment and are labeled "keep refrigerated"; and (5) the use of appropriate procedures for the storage and thawing of frozen food items.

The spores of *C. botulinum* vary in their resistance to heating. Thermal death is affected by many factors, a discussion of which is beyond the scope of this book; the reader is therefore referred to textbooks on food preservation. Some of the factors are: type and strain of organism, conditions under which the spores were formed, the age of the spores, the kind of food in which the organism is suspended during heating, and the number of spores present. To kill spores of types A and B, several hours of boiling are required, but much shorter heating will suffice at higher temperatures, for example, 10 minutes at 250°F (121°C). But these are theoretical considerations. Under actual canning conditions, a multitude of factors have to be taken into consideration to assure killing of *C. botulinum* spores. The National Canners Association and other agencies which set up specifications for the canning industry allow a wide margin of safety in the time–temperature requirements for the killing of *C. botulinum* spores.

The spores of type E are less resistant to heating than those of type A and B. Crisley et al. (1968), working with five strains of type E, found that under the conditions of the experiment, spores of the strain most resistant to heating were killed when exposed to 180°F (82°C) for 17 minutes; the spores were tested in a medium of ground whitefish chubs.

Subjecting spores to temperatures somewhat below the lethal level may actually stimulate them to germinate. Spores of type A and B are stimulated by exposure to 185°F (85°C) for 10–20 minutes; and type E spores when subjected to 140°F (60°C) for 13 minutes (Schmidt, 1964).

Spores of *C. botulinum* are very resistant to adverse conditions other than heat and may remain viable for extremely long periods of time.

The toxins are not very resistant to heat, and are readily denatured at temperatures above 176°F (80°C). Types A and B are more heat-resistant than type E. Type A toxin is inactivated by 5–6 minutes of heating at 176°F (80°C), and type B by 15 minutes of heating at 194°F (90°C). Therefore, for foods suspected of containing toxins A and B, 15 minutes of boiling is recommended. This treatment provides a margin of safety, since in laboratory experiments shorter times were sufficient to inactivate the toxins. Heat resistance has been shown to vary with the pH of the substrate, resistance decreasing with decreasing pH. To destroy type E in fish, FDA regulations require that the fish be heated to specified temperatures and held for a specified length of time (see Chapter 6). The heat sensitivity of toxin type A in several freezer-stored menu items was investigated by Woolford et al. (1978). The pH of the samples ranged from 4.1 (tomato soup) to 6.2 (cream of mushroom soup). During 180 days of storage at −20°C (−4°F), the toxin did not change its behavior in regard to heat; also, its toxicity remained stationary. A summary of information concerning requirements of *C. botulinum* for growth and on its toxin production was published by Sperber (1982).

Staphylococcus aureus

Staphylococcus food poisoning (enterotoxemia) is caused by the toxins of *Staphylococcus aureus,* a facultative aerobic organism. The toxins set off an inflammation of the lining in the stomach and the intestinal tract of the victim, causing gastroenteritis. Thus they are enterotoxins.

ORGANISM.   As the name *Staphylococcus* indicates, the organism is characterized by a group of cocci combined in grape-like clusters. The cells may also occur in pairs and short chains. The cocci are tiny, less than 1 μm in diameter.

Many strains of *S. aureus* are known, some being extremely pathogenic. The cultures are golden yellow in color, nearly always liquify gelatin, and ferment lactose and mannitol. Many virulent strains coagulate oxalated blood plasma. Strains associated with food poisoning are usually coagulase-positive. The various *S. aureus* strains elaborate a number of toxins that are proteins. Several enterotoxins are distinguishable. Of these, only two seem to be most frequently associated with food poisoning. The toxins are exotoxins since they are diffusible and are eliminated into the substrate, whether it is a culture medium or food. Staphylococcal enterotoxins are weakly antigenic. A characterization of the various types was given by Bergdoll and Robbins (1973) and Bergdoll (1979).

The staphylococci are susceptible to specific bacteriophages. Phage typing has been given much study, and has been used for the determination of the relationship between strains and their sources. However, phage typing as a tool for linking strains of staphylococci to food poisoning has been found to have its limitations.

Proof of the pathogenicity of the toxins has been a stumbling block in the past. Although most, if not all, of the enterotoxic staphylococci were known to produce coagulase, this was not a foolproof test for pathogenicity, since there was the possibility that some strains of coagulase-negative staphylococci might produce enterotoxin, and this indeed is the case (Bergdoll et al., 1967).

Many investigators therefore relied on testing the pathogenicity on human volunteers or on laboratory animals—especially on monkeys but also on cats and kittens. The tests consist of feeding filtrates of the media on which the isolates were grown to the volunteers or animals and observing the reaction regarding vomiting and diarrhea. Intravenous and intraperitoneal injection tests were also made on test animals.

Assays performed on rhesus monkeys are considered quite reliable. The suspected food or other test medium is fed to the animal by stomach tube. Vomiting is the accepted symptom for a positive reaction. However, the acquisition and maintenance of these animals is costly.

Serological tests have largely replaced animal assays (Hall et al., 1963, 1965; Casman and Bennett, 1965; Read et al., 1965a, b). Trends in methodology for the detection of toxins in food were discussed by Minor and Marth (1971), Crowther and Holbrook (1976), and Saunders and Bartlett (1977).

DISTRIBUTION AND SOURCE.   The distribution of *S. aureus* is worldwide. Although the organism does not form spores, it is relatively resistant to injurious environmental conditions. In dust, soil, or frozen foods or on cloth, floors, or walls, the cells may survive for a considerable length of time, even months.

The most important source of *S. aureus* is probably the human body. Healthy people harbor the organism on their skin, in their mouths and throats, and in their nasal passages. Skin abrasions, wounds, and cuts are commonly a rich source of the organism. Infected sinuses, pimples, furuncles, and carbuncles abound with *S. aureus*. The human reservoir of the staphylococci is discussed more fully in Chapter 5.

Another important source of *S. aureus* may be the food supply. Other sources of the organism are man's pets, especially cats and dogs.

SYMPTOMS.   The ingestion of toxin-containing food causes the symptoms. The toxins build up in a food when *S. aureus* cells are allowed to multiply profusely in it. When the toxin-containing food is ingested, it usually causes acute gastroenteritis in the victim, the severity of the symptoms varying with the susceptibility of the individual, the concentration of the toxin in the food, and the amount consumed.

The symptoms appear on an average of 2–3 hours after ingestion of the toxic food, but the times vary from ½ to 6 hours. The symptoms include salivation, nausea, vomiting, abdominal cramps, diarrhea, headache, muscular cramps, sweating, chills, prostration, weak pulse, and shallow respiration.

The duration of the illness is 24 hours to 2 days; the mortality is extremely low. Medical treatment is usually not indicated, for the illness runs its course. In severe poisoning, saline solutions are administered. The minimum amount of enterotoxin necessary to evoke symptoms in man is not known. Considerable variation in susceptibility has been noted in tests performed with human volunteers and animals.

INCIDENCE.   Staphylococcal intoxication outbreaks occur frequently. Sometimes hundreds of persons are involved in one outbreak. The cause of this form of foodborne illness was not recognized until 1880, when Pasteur detected the organism in pie.

Since 1930, great strides have been made in understanding the cause of and the circumstances favoring foodborne staphylococcal intoxications. Unfortunately, this knowledge has not been put into good practice, as the high incidence of outbreaks proves.

FOODS IMPLICATED.   The foods involved in staphylococcal episodes are of great variety; food items high in protein are most frequently involved (Minor and Marth, 1972). Examples of indicted items are: custards, cream-filled bakery goods, meat sauces, gravies, meats and meat products, meat-filled sandwiches, roast turkey and dressing, chicken salad, fish and fish products, milk, cheese, butter, ice cream, and other dairy products and cream items. Regarding preparation procedures, the items frequently indicted are menu items that have been handled a great deal and, therefore, have had a good chance of becoming contaminated with the bacteria clinging to human hands and unsanitary equipment. Endangered are items cut, sliced, and cubed, then placed in a sauce and not sufficiently reheated; items which are allowed to cool slowly and therefore remain in the danger zone of bacterial growth for long periods of time; and items which are "warmed over" several times without ever getting hot enough for the contaminants to be killed. More will be said about that in later chapters.

The appearance, flavor, or odor of the food items in which *Staphylococcus aureus* multiples are often not noticeably altered, and the invaded food does not seem spoiled, although some fermentative or proteolytic activity might be noticeable.

FACTORS AFFECTING GROWTH AND PRODUCTION OF TOXINS

Food. *Staphylococcus aureus* multiplies extremely well in proteinaceous foods, but there are differences. For example, meats and custards support growth better than salmon.

Being a facultative aerobe, it is able to grow in liquid foods as well as on solid foods of suitable moisture content. The staphylococci are tolerant of sugar.

Many strains are salt tolerant and grow well in media of moderately high (10%) salt concentrations; others multiply in brine of very high (up to 20%) concentration of NaCl. Staphylococci are also tolerant of nitrites, and so they have the faculty to contaminate curing and cured meats. In addition, the staphylococci are quite tolerant of dissolved sugar. The literature dealing with the effect of water activity on the growth and enterotoxin production of *S. aureus* has been reviewed by Tatini (1973).

pH. *Staphylococcus aureus* is capable of growing in substrates of a wide range of pH, from acid (4.5) to alkaline (above 7). Growth media of near neutral reaction are most favorable, in general. The minimal pH for growth is lower under aerobic than under anaerobic conditions.

Competition from Other Microorganisms. *Staphylococcus aureus* has been demonstrated to be sensitive to competitors. For example, repressive effects have been shown to be exerted by psychrophilic saprophytes. These interactions were found to be very complex. They were affected not only by temperature, but also by the composition and pH of the media (Peterson et al., 1964). Some lactic acid bacteria inhibit, others stimulate, the growth of *Staphylococcus,* depending on conditions (Kao and Frazier, 1966). In heated foods, competitors have been largely eliminated.

Temperature. The temperature range within which *S. aureus* may grow and produce toxins is affected by, among other factors, strain, number of cells, and the medium in which the organism is suspended. The minimum temperature for growth and toxin production was given as approximately 4°C (39°F) by Frazier and Westhoff (1978). According to research by Angelotti et al. (1961a), temperatures between 44 and 114°F (6.7 and 45.6°C) may be expected to support growth of *S. aureus.* For growth and toxin formation the optimum temperature range is 70–98.7°F (21–37°C); the organism grows profusely with elaboration of toxins within a wide range of temperatures.

Under favorable growth conditions, the toxin becomes evident after 4–6 hours of active multiplication. At lower temperatures, longer time is required. As is true for growth, the production of the toxin is affected by a number of factors. In general, it is accepted that a prerequisite for appreciable amounts of toxin to be formed is active multiplication of cells to high numbers, which means, several millions per gram or milliliter of food. However, Tatini (1973) has reported that a population of *S. aureus* cells, in spite of attaining high numbers, might be subjected to inhibition in toxin formation by the independent and interactive effects of pH, oxygen tension, temperature, water activity, and competitive growth of other microorganisms.

Staphylococcus aureus is fairly resistant to heat and is not always killed in the pasteurization of milk. Heat resistance varies with, among other things, the strain and the nature of the medium in which the cells are suspended.

Angelotti et al. (1961b) reported on survival of cells of a heat-resistant strain when these were suspended in custard and ham salad and exposed to temperatures up to 150°F (66°C). The authors concluded from their data that heating these perishable foods to 150°F (66°C) and holding every particle of the food at this temperature for at least 12 minutes rendered the food practically sterile. The same degree of destruction was achieved when the foods were held at 140°F (60°C) for 78–83 minutes.

The heat stability of the toxins can be considerable. Type B is the most resistant type. Thermal inactivation is affected by many factors; therefore, hard-and-fast rules about destroying possible toxins present in food are not reliable. The thermostability of the various toxins under varying conditions was discussed by Tatini (1976) and Lee (1977).

Staphylococci are potentially very dangerous as food contaminants, and should be prevented from multiplying in food. Temperatures must be carefully controlled.

Multiplication of the organism is possible under refrigeration, when the cooling process does not proceed fast enough and if the bacteria find the temperatures conducive to multiplication. Storage in a refrigerator for a long period has been found to keep the toxin intact.

Viable cells of food-poisoning *Staphylococcus* withstand freezing well; freezing will not even reduce the potency of the toxins.

The control of foodborne illnesses caused by *S. aureus* should include: first, sanitary precautions in connection with the food handler, because the human body is the main reservoir of *S. aureus;* second, efficient measures to preclude the multiplication of the organism in the food during its preparation, service, and storage; and third, using heat for the destruction of the contaminants before they have formed toxins.

Clostridium perfringens (welchii)

This organism is steadily gaining in importance as a pathogen capable of causing foodborne illness, in this country as well as abroad. The gastrointestinal illness caused by foods containing this organism in large numbers was first described in the late 1890s, and then 50 years later, by McClung (1945). However, the organism did not attract much attention as a foodborne pathogen until Hobbs et al. (1953) described several outbreaks associated with *C. perfringens* in England.

ORGANISM. The bacterium *Clostridium perfringens* is an anaerobic, Gram-positive, spore-forming rod.

Forms of *C. perfringens* have been known to cause gas gangrene in man and various intestinal diseases in animals, especially young lambs, pigs, and calves. Sporulation and heat resistance of the spores vary with strains and many other factors. The strains may be differentiated on the basis of pattern of toxin formation typical for the various strains. Of five toxigenic strains known at present, type A is most commonly associated with foodborne illness in the United States. Angelotti et al. (1962) studied 83 strains of *C. perfringens,* 30 from England, the European continent, and Asia, and 28 from the United States; all of these had been associated with gastrointestinal illness. Another group of 25 came from other sources. On the basis of the results, these workers concluded that the American food-poisoning strains vary widely in their characteristics. They also stated that it does not seem likely that *C. perfringens* strains causing gastroenteritic outbreaks in the United States are restricted to the criteria for food-poisoning strains set up for England. Relatively few of the enteritis-causing strains isolated in the United States are very resistant to heat.

Which agent is ultimately responsible for causing enteritis symptoms has been shrouded in uncertainty for a long time. Although toxins are produced, experimental evidence from studies with human volunteers seemed to show that toxins were not responsible and that bacterial cells must be ingested in large numbers to cause typical enteritis in human volunteers. However, it was later documented that cell-free enterotoxin given to human subjects and monkeys can cause symptoms of enteric food poisoning (Duncan and Strong, 1971; Strong, Duncan, and Perna, 1971; Uemura et al., 1975; Duncan, 1976).

DISTRIBUTION AND SOURCE. The organism is extremely widespread in nature here and abroad. It is a common inhabitant of the intestinal tract of healthy animals and human beings. It occurs in large numbers in soil, sewage, manure, water, and dust; therefore, many foods, especially meats, reaching the kitchen are likely to be contaminated with *C. perfringens.*

Hobbs et al. (1953) isolated *C. perfringens* from every batch of blowflies which was examined. The sources of these flies included a hospital, a fried-fish shop, a refuse sorting depot, a butcher shop, and a slaughter house.

Canada et al. (1964) recovered *C. perfringens* from 26% of 100 bovine liver samples purchased in retail markets and in 12% of the livers from freshly slaughtered animals. The strains were typed as producing toxins, but it was not known whether they were able to cause gastrointestinal disturbances in man.

Hall and Angelotti (1965) studied the incidence of *Clostridium perfringens* in meat and meat products in the Cincinnati area. Some of the items studied were raw, some partially cooked, and some fully processed, requiring no cooking. The organism was isolated from 43.1% of 262 specimens, the highest percentage of contamination being found in veal cuts, and the lowest in sandwich cuts and spreads. Only 2 of the 113 isolates produced heat-resistant spores.

Dehydrated soups and sauces were analyzed for *C. perfringens* by Nakamura and Kelly (1968), who found that 18.2% of the samples were so contaminated. This points toward the importance of treating the reconstituted products as "vulnerable," keeping them either hot or cold until they are served.

SYMPTOMS.   The symptoms begin between 8 and 22 hours, usually 8–15, after the ingestion of the contaminated food and may continue for 6–12 hours. They are somewhat similar to those of staphylococcal intoxication, but are milder. Symptoms include nausea (rarely accompanied by vomiting), intestinal cramps, and diarrhea. Fever, chills, and headache are rarely experienced. The illness is seldom fatal.

INCIDENCE.   In the United States, the reported incidence of this foodborne illness is relatively high (see Table 4.1). The actual figures are believed to be much higher. A high rate of incidents has been reported from England for years. Other reports have come from continental Europe, Canada, and Asia.

FOODS IMPLICATED.   Listed in connection with gastrointestinal episodes believed to be caused by *C. perfringens* were meats, items in which meat served as an ingredient, and gravy. The organism may be carried into the kitchen on the hands of the food handlers as well as on many foodstuffs. It has also been isolated from other uncooked and cooked food products, such as vegetables, dairy products, eggs, and condiments such as pepper. Here are examples of some outbreaks: An outbreak was reported in 1960, which originated from a turkey dinner served on a train. Approximately one-half of 450 passengers became ill (Hart et al., 1960). In 1962, a large outbreak in which creamed turkey was implicated occurred in a mental institution in California. The circumstances have been described by Kemp et al. (1962). In a later outbreak in a high school cafeteria, roast beef was the incriminated menu item (*Morbidity and Mortality Weekly Report*, 1965).

Another example of an outbreak is one that was associated with a "Meals on Wheels" program in California (*Morbidity and Mortality Weekly Report*, 1981). Chicken was implicated as the cause; it had been cooked six days earlier, frozen, thawed, held refrigerated, then reheated on a steam table.

The danger of reheating cold food on hot-holding equipment is discussed in Chapter 11. A general discussion of *C. perfringens* food poisoning in the United States was presented by Shanders et al. (1983).

Contamination of food with the pathogen is common, but the counts have, in general, been low and the spores largely of the nonheat-resistant type; therefore it follows that opportunity is afforded in the kitchen for the organism to build up to dangerously high numbers and that recontamination of cooked foods occurs frequently. Obviously, this has been the case when outbreaks due to *C. perfringens* have occurred. To cause illness, the critical dose seems to be several hundred million organisms, or 5–10 million organisms per gram of food.

FACTORS AFFECTING GROWTH AND DEATH

Food.   Meats and menu items made with meat support the multiplication of this organism extremely well. The organism is inhibited by approximately 5% NaCl in the substrate. The effect on growth of the water activity (a_w) of the medium was studied by Strong et al. (1970). Various solutes were used in the substrate. These workers found that, as the water activity was lowered, and pH was decreased within each a_w level, the rate and amount of bacterial growth were decreased also.

pH.   Multiplication can take place within a wide range of pH, 5–9, and is most rapid within a pH range of 6–7.5. But there is no clear-cut optimum.

Temperature.   The temperature range for growth and sporulation depends greatly on strain and substrate (Ray et al., 1975). Smith (1962) reported the effect of temperature on generation time of *C. perfringens* using five strains, and a temperature range of 5–50°C (41–122°F). None of the strains grew appreciably at 15°C (59°F) and none grew at 5°C (41°F), but they grew well over a wide range of 20–50°C (68–122°F). Under most favorable conditions, the shortest generation time may be as brief as 10 minutes (Smith, 1971). Solberg and Elkind (1970) established the minimum temperature for growth as 12°C (54°F).

The ability of the organism to multiply profusely at high temperatures was also reported by Hall and Angelotti (1965), who obtained excellent growth at 35–46°C (95–114.8°F). At the lower temperature, rapid growth was found to be preceded by a 2–4 hour lag period, whereas no lag phase was observed at 46°C (114.8°F). The authors point out the dangers of holding meat items at these higher temperatures for even brief periods of time. Complete inhibition was observed at 49 and 52°C (120.2 and 125.6°F). No multiplication was observed by these workers at a temperature range of 5–15°C (41–59°F).

Canada et al. (1964) determined the response of *C. perfringens* spores and vegetative cells to low temperature, using four strains. Exposure to freezing at −17.7°C (0°F), and a refrigeration temperature of 7.1°C (45°F), killed a large percentage of the vegetative cells. The spores of *C. perfringens* are resistant to freezing and freezer storage.

Death by Heat.   Both heat-sensitive and heat-resistant spore-producing strains may cause food poisoning. Subjecting the spores of *C. perfringens* to sublethal temperatures stimulates them to germinate. The thermal resistance of spores varies considerably. Some strains are very resistant to heating, others not so. Heat-resistant strains are common in England, but in the United States the percentage of such strains seems much lower. Hall and Angelotti (1965) found heat-resistant strains to constitute less than 1% for the Cincinnati area.

The spores of heat-resistant strains may require several hours of boiling for kill, whereas exposure to temperatures below boiling will suffice for the less resistant strains.

Canada et al. (1964), using four strains of *C. perfringens,* exposed the vegetative cells to temperatures lower than boiling. Essentially, no vegetative cells and few spores survived a heat treatment of 10 minutes at 80°C (176°F). Boiling for 5–10 minutes eliminated most spores of nonheat-resistant strains. However, the spores of heat-resistant strains have been reported to be extremely resistant to heat and to resist boiling for several hours (Hobbs and Wilson, 1959).

In this connection, the 1965 outbreak involving roast beef should be mentioned again. According to the report (*Morbidity and Mortality Weekly Report,* 1965), a bacteriological examination of the roast beef yielded a viable count of 80,000 cells per gram, and numbers seen on a direct microscopic smear proved that the count had previously been much higher. These findings may indicate that the contaminant was present before roasting and survived the heating applied during the roasting process. In 1966 an outbreak ascribed to heat-resistant *C. perfringens* was reported from Wisconsin (*Morbidity and Mortality Weekly Report,* 1966). In this case, gravy was implicated. The organism had multiplied in the gravy at some time during preparation or inadequate refrigeration. Bringing the gravy to a "rolling boil" did not kill the contaminant.

Thermal resistance also varies with the presence or absence of protective substances, such as meat (Collee et al., 1961).

Furthermore, resistance to heat is dependent on previous heat treatment. Nishida et al. (1969) submitted strains of the organism, isolated from samples that had been held at different temperatures, to heating; the authors found that almost all strains from unheated or lightly heated samples gave rise to spores that were sensitive to heat; however, samples that had been submitted to 100°C (212°F) for 1 hour produced heat-resistant spores.

Circumstances frequently associated with outbreaks of *C. perfringens*-associated enteritis are poor time–temperature control in the handling of cooked meat and gravy and recontamination of cooked meat with the contaminant lodging on food preparation equipment and utensils. Since the spores of some strains are very heat-resistant, and since the spores are ubiquitous in soil, in dust, and in the air, we simply must face the likelihood that cooked food was either not sterilized by the cooking process, or was recontaminated after cooking. Therefore, the control of this organism in quantity foodservice lies mostly in preventing its multiplication by strict time–temperature control and meticulous sanitary care of equipment, utensils, and workers' hands.

Bacillus cereus

As a cause of foodborne illness, *Bacillus cereus* was first reported from Norway (Hauge, 1950). Since then, it has been indicted in other countries also, especially in Scandinavia. Few outbreaks are reported in the United States (see Table 4.1), and very few are well documented.

Bacillus cereus is distributed all over the world. It is a large, aerobic spore former that is capable of growing under anaerobic conditions also. It is frequently associated with grains, flour, starch, and other cereal products. The spores are ubiquitous and are easily recovered from soil and dust.

The organism has been isolated from a variety of foodstuffs. In Sweden Nygren (1962) found a 47.8% incidence of *B. cereus* in several thousand samples of various foods. In the United States, Kim and Goepfert (1971) reported that 25% of 175 samples of dry food, distributed nationally, yielded the organism. *Bacillus cereus* seems to be a common contaminant of spices also. Powers et al. (1976) tested 110 processed spices and found that over half of the samples were contaminated with this organism, and that 89% of the isolates were toxigenic to rabbits. Each kind of spice was contaminated with *B. cereus*.

The symptoms of *B. cereus*-induced illness include abdominal pain, diarrhea, nausea, and vomiting; they appear approximately 8–16 hours following the ingestion of the offending item. The symptoms are apt to be milder than those typical of *Staphylococcus* intoxication or *Salmonella* infection. Food containing cells must be ingested before illness ensues. Gilbert and Taylor (1976) doubt that *B. cereus* food poisoning is an infection and postulate that the relatively sudden onset of symptoms and the short duration of the illness indicate an intoxication. Goepfert (1973) and Goepfert et al. (1973) have demonstrated that the organism is capable of producing an enterotoxic substance causing overt diarrhea in rhesus monkeys. Two toxins, one described by Terranova and Blake (1978) as a heat-stable emetic toxin, and another described by Turnbull et al. (1979) to be a heat-labile diarrheal toxin, may be the causative agents involved in food-poisoning outbreaks.

Foods implicated in the outbreaks are of great variety; this is not surprising in view of the ubiquitous presence of this spore former. Examples are meat and items made with meat, soups, mashed potatoes, minced meat, liver sausage, rice dishes, including fried rice, puddings, vanilla sauce, and cream sauce (Gilbert and Taylor, 1976; Mortimer and McCann, 1974).

In many foodservice operations it is a common practice to leave cooked rice out at room temperature, in preference to storing it under refrigeration, because when cooked rice is chilled, the kernels tend to cling together and the rice becomes "sticky." This regrettable practice of holding cooked rice at room temperature has caused outbreaks of foodborne illness due to excessive multiplication of *B. cereus.* The solution to the problem is one of management.

Bacillus cereus may grow over a wide range of pH, 4.35–9.3. Temperatures for growth range from 10 to 50°C (50–122°F), with an optimal range of 35–40°C (95–104°F). As is true for *Clostridium* spores, the spores of *B. cereus* can be stimulated to germinate when they are first exposed to sublethal temperatures, and the temperature is thereafter decreased to appropriate lower levels. Therefore, strict temperature control must be exercised in the cooling and holding of cooked food. This subject is discussed further in later chapters.

For more detailed information on *B. cereus* the reader is referred to Goepfert et al. (1972), Gilbert and Taylor (1976), Gilbert (1979), and Johnson (1984).

BACTERIA CAUSING FOODBORNE INFECTIONS

Among the bacteria causing foodborne infections are the salmonellae, *Vibrio parahaemolyticus,* and the fecal streptococci.

Salmonella

Salmonellae have been associated with foodborne illnesses for a long time. In the past, salmonellae probably have, at times, been indicted in outbreaks when the cause may have been *S. aureus* or *C. perfringens.* Salmonellosis is an infection. Except for *Salmonella typhi,* a highly infectious pathogen, most victims must ingest large numbers of *Salmonella* cells before they are stricken. Salmonellae do not release toxins into the food in which they multiply; rather, the ingested cells multiply in the small intestine of the victim, causing illness that way. In most years salmonellae have been very high on the list as causes of foodborne gastroenteritis.

ORGANISM.   In the United States, the first salmonellae typing center was established in 1934 by the Public Health Service. The serotyping of salmonellae from the animals was later taken over by the Animal Disease Eradication Division of the Agricultural Research Service.

The Public Health Service, through the activities of its Centers for Disease Control (formerly the National Communicable Disease Center) in Atlanta, Georgia, conducts a very active *Salmonella* surveillance program. Cooperating in this effort are state and local health authorities and other federal authorities.

Through the work of typing centers, great strides have been made in the identification of the many forms of this organism and its many sources. An international *Salmonella* Center has been established at the State Serum Institute in Copenhagen, Denmark.

Approximately 1600 serotypes of *Salmonella* are known at this time. The native habitat of the salmonellae is the intestinal tract of humans and animals. The salmonellae may be grouped on the basis of their hosts:

1. Salmonellae pathogenic to humans only. Here belongs *S. typhi,* cause of typhoid fever.
2. Salmonellae primarily pathogenic to animals. Examples are *S. pullorum,* a pathogen of poultry, and *S. abortusequi,* a pathogen of horses.
3. Salmonellae adaptable to both humans and animals. These are mostly serotypes of *S. enteritidis.*

The salmonellae are Gram-negative facultative aerobic rods which ferment glucose, usually with gas, and do not form spores. Serotypes are characterized on the basis of their antigen content.

Of the approximately 1600 serotypes of *S. enteritidis* known, only about 50 occur commonly. Of these, serotype *typhimurium* heads the list of those implicated in gastroenteric outbreaks. Others include *heidelberg, derby, java, infantis, saint paul, newport, agona,* and *hadar;* the latter two appeared in the 1970s (Silliker, 1981).

The illness caused by the unadapted serotypes may be characterized as follows:

1. The serotypes produce, at least usually, gasteroenteritis rather than enteric fever, and the infection is largely localized in the intestine.
2. The incubation time is relatively short.
3. Relatively large numbers of bacteria are necessary in order to make healthy adults ill.

DISTRIBUTION AND SOURCE. The salmonellae are distributed over the world. The fact that unusual serotypes have appeared in countries far apart has indicted foods and feeds as vehicles.

The primary source of *Salmonella* is, before all, the intestinal tract of animals, whether these are acute cases or carriers. A carrier is an individual harboring causative organisms of a particular illness, who appears to be well and shows no symptoms or signs of being ill. A person once infected may also act as a reservoir. A carrier eliminates these organisms from his body and thus serves as a source of infection for weeks, months, or years. Man's enemies, such as rodents, flies, and cockroaches, as well as his pets, such as cats, dogs, turtles, chicks, and ducklings, seem to be frequent reservoirs of salmonellae. Food animals are very important reservoirs; hogs, chickens, turkeys, and ducks are all sources of salmonellae, and cattle and sheep have also been shown to harbor salmonellae. Poultry feed and dog food have been reported to be heavily contaminated with *Salmonella.*

Salmonellae are discharged into sewage and manure. They have been found in soil contaminated with raw sewage and are known to survive in soil for months. They also survive in dry foods such as dry milk and cocoa powder, and in feed, such as poultry feed, and meat and bone meal (Juven et al., 1984). Survival of the organism in frozen foods has also been demonstrated (see Chapter 6).

The reader of the literature dealing with *Salmonella* and the salmonelloses cannot help being appalled by the seemingly endless host cycles which encompass humans, feces, sewage, food animals, manure, pets, rodents, insects, processed meats and poultry, prepared food items, animal feed, and pet food. The interrelated facets of the problems connected with salmonellosis are elucidated in the report of the committee on *Salmonella,* National Research Council (1969); and Bryan et al. (1979). A discussion of animal-to-man transmission of antimicrobial-resistant *Salmonella* was presented by Holmberg et al. (1984).

SYMPTOMS.   The symptoms of salmonellosis resemble those of *Staphylococcus* food poisoning. The onset is not as rapid, because there is no toxin present in the food. The illness results from an ingestion of large numbers of bacteria. The incubation time varies from 3 to 72 hours, with an average of 12–24 hours. The incubation time of typical "food-poisoning" salmonellae is shorter than that of the salmonellae species capable of causing typhoid fever and that of the pathogens causing bacillary dysentery.

The severity of the disease depends on the strains of *Salmonella* involved, the individual's susceptibility to the organisms, and the total number of cells ingested with the food. The minimal infective dose of salmonellae is not known.

The symptoms include: nausea, vomiting, abdominal pain, diarrhea, headache, chills, marked prostration, watery and foul-smelling stools, muscular weakness, faintness, drowsiness, and thirst; there may be fever and septicemia. Mortality is less than 1%.

The illness usually lasts 2 or 3 days, but it may linger. A small percentage of persons may become carriers; numerous *Salmonella* species have been isolated from the stools of seemingly healthy persons.

INCIDENCE. Salmonellosis is largely spread by contaminated food. While typhoid fever is easily transmitted by person-to-person contact, this is not typical for the other salmonelloses.

The number of *Salmonella* food infections, as shown in Table 4.1, may not seem impressively large. These data indicate, however, that in comparison with other outbreaks of foodborne illnesses, salmonellosis ranks relatively high. It is agreed that the actual number of outbreaks and cases is considerably higher. In a report on the *Salmonella* problem prepared by the committee referred to above, it is stated that salmonellosis is one of the most important communicable diseases in the country, and that there are an estimated two million human cases annually. There is reason to suspect that relatively more outbreaks occur in the summer and autumn than in the other months of the year. The incidence of salmonellosis has risen more than 20-fold since 1946. One reason may lie in the expansion of centralized processing and bulk distribution of processed food items. An example is an outbreak of salmonellosis from eating contaminated shrimp, involving 9000 persons attending 190 parties, all served by a single catering service. The raw shrimp had been purchased at one not very sanitary outlet, then transported to another place for boiling. The boiled shrimp was—while still warm—returned to the containers in which the raw shrimp had arrived. They were then transported in an unrefrigerated truck to the places of service and, finally, served. By then, 7–8 hours had elapsed. Obviously, the cooked shrimp were recontaminated when they were placed in the containers in which the raw shrimp had been packed (*Morbidity and Mortality Weekly Report,* 1973). The detection and reporting of salmonellosis is being constantly improved. The number of outbreaks reported to the CDC between 1963 and 1975 can be ascertained in an article by Cohen and Blake (1977). During the 1980s, it became clear that shell eggs were involved in *Salmonella* outbreaks (*Morbidity and Mortality Weekly Report,* 1990). Gast and Beard (1992) showed the presence of *S. enteritidis* in fresh and stored eggs laid by experimentally infected hens.

FOODS IMPLICATED. A variety of raw and processed foods have been found to carry *Salmonella,* some important ones being raw meat and poultry; shellfish; cracked shell eggs and egg removed from the shell; processed meat, poultry, and egg products; pasteurized and unpasteurized milk; dried milk; and cheese made from unpasteurized milk. Some other miscellaneous foods that have been incriminated occasionally are dried coconut, dried cereal, smoked fish, spices, nuts, vegetable gum, and others (Committee on *Salmonella,* 1969; Foster, 1969).

The list of prepared menu items frequently implicated in salmonellosis is a long one. It is headed by proteinaceous menu items such as meat and poultry; mixtures containing meat, poultry, eggs and seafood; dressings and gravy; salads made with meat, poultry, egg, and seafood; puddings;

cream-filled pastries; custards; cream-filled cakes; meringued pies; and many others.

The appearance, odor, and flavor of *Salmonella*-contaminated food items are usually not noticeably altered.

Examples of circumstances frequently associated with *Salmonella* outbreaks are: food handlers who are carriers; poor personal hygiene of food handlers; poor supervision; poor general sanitation practices in the preparation, storage, and service of food; poor maintenance of equipment; presence of rodents, flies, and cockroaches; long holding of food at warm temperatures; slow cooling due to refrigeration of large batches; cutting boards used for raw as well as cooked meats and poultry; and poor cleaning of cutting boards, to name just a few.

FACTORS AFFECTING GROWTH

Food. The great variety of foods involved in outbreaks of salmonellosis indicates that the causative organisms are able to multiply to large numbers in many commonly served menu items.

pH. The organism grows best in nonacid substrates, up to a pH of 9. However, under certain conditions growth is possible at quite low pH levels. The growth-limiting effect of low pH is dependent on many factors, such as temperature, relative oxygen supply, level of inoculum, and nature of the acid molecule. Chung and Goepfert (1970), who studied the effect of 13 different acidulants on the growth of *Salmonella,* found the more "permissive" acids to be citric, hydrochloric, and tartaric. The authors also reported that, under specific conditions, the test organisms multiplied at pH levels as low as 4.05. Acid foods, such as tomatoes, have been reported to allow growth of *Salmonella.* Segalove and Dack (1944) inoculated cans of asparagus, spinach, string beans, tomato juice, peaches, shrimp, salmon, corn, and peas with a strain of *S. enteritidis* and incubated the samples at two temperatures, 71.6°F (22°C) and 98.6°F (37°C). Multiplication took place at the lower temperature in all the foods except the peaches, and at the higher temperature in all the foods except the peaches and asparagus.

Temperature. The salmonellae multiply over a rather wide range of temperature, but there is some variation due to strains. Angelotti et al. (1959, 1961a) studied the time–temperature effects on salmonellae using *S. manhattan, enteritidis, typhimurium, senftenberg, cubana,* and *montevideo (typhimurium* and *senftenberg,* heat-resistant strains) suspended in broth. They found that these organisms did not multiply at 41°F (5°C) but that good growth occurred at 50, 59, and 68°F (10, 15, and 20°C). Some of the strains were also inoculated into custard, ham salad, and chicken à la king. The lowest temperature at which multiplication was observed was 44°F (6.7°C).

The same authors (1961b) conducted a study on the behavior of salmonellae at warm holding temperatures. The test strains were *S. senftenberg, enteritidis,* and *manhattan.* The foods in which the bacteria were suspended were custard, ham salad, and chicken à la king. It was shown that the salmonellae were able to multiply in certain foods at temperatures as high as 112–114°F (44.5–45.6°C). Maximum growth temperatures of 110–115°F (43.3–46°C) were also demonstrated by Elliott and Heiniger (1965) for 34 selected strains of *Salmonella;* among the species represented were *S. typhimurium, senftenberg, derby,* and *anatum.*

The results of these studies have an important bearing on refrigeration and holding of prepared menu items. The implications are discussed in more detail in Chapter 13.

The optimum temperature for growth of the salmonellae is about 98.6°F (37°C); at this temperature the generation time may be expected to be 15 minutes.

Thermal death of the salmonellae depends on many factors, as is true for other microorganisms. Among these are: the heat resistance of the strain; the number of cells in the medium exposed to heating; the type of medium, in particular, the presence of substances protecting the cells from the heat; the water activity of the environment; and the temperatures and times applied in the heat treatment.

The various serotypes are similar in their thermal resistance, except *S. senftenberg* 775 W, which is extremely resistant.

Regarding the relation of the heat resistance of salmonellae to the water activity of the environment, Goepfert et al. (1970) studied the behavior of eight strains of *Salmonella,* among others, *S. senftenberg* 775 W, *S. anatum, S. infantis,* and *S. typhimurium.* They found that heat resistance increased as the water activity of the substrate in which the cells were exposed to heating was reduced, but a direct correlation could not be established. As the environment became drier, all strains showed a greater increase in heat resistance than *S. senftenberg* 775 W.

Angelotti et al. (1961b), using a heat-resistant strain of *S. senftenberg* and a nonheat-resistant strain of *S. manhattan,* in the same three foods mentioned above, exposed these salmonellae to temperatures up to 150°F (65.5°C). They found that no instantaneous kill resulted from this exposure. Holding the inoculated foods at 150°F (65.5°C) for several minutes resulted in the death of the inoculum. The authors suggest that to effect a 90% reduction in numbers of salmonellae, heating at 150°F (65.5°C) for 12 minutes is necessary. The same degree of destruction was achieved by heating at 140°F (60°C) for 78–83 minutes.

Salmonellae have been shown to survive freezing and freezer storage. The relationship of the frequency of salmonellae and their resistance to freezing was studied by Enkiri and Alford (1971). The authors found that the strains which had a tendency to be more susceptible to the cold and dry environment to which they were exposed in the tests were also low-incidence strains. In conclusion it was suggested that the ability of certain serotypes to survive might be a factor in their higher incidence of causing salmonellosis.

Salmonellae are serious food contaminants and their control is extremely important. Principles of control involve, first, the production of a wholesome food supply that carries the smallest load of *Salmonella* attainable and, second, the production of safe menu items in the kitchen. The production of a wholesome food supply must be the effort of the processing industry which is effectively supported by governmental agencies such as the U.S. Department of Health and Human Services and the U.S. Department of Agriculture. However, the production of safe meals is, with some exceptions such as "factory-prepared" convenience items, largely in the hands of all those who purchase, store, prepare, and serve food to people at home, in institutions, and in public eating places.

To assess the potential hazards from salmonellae of a product, the product's ultimate usage as a food should be considered: namely, whether the product will most probably be served and eaten without having been subjected to heating in its preparation, whether it is likely to be subjected to holding at temperatures at which bacterial growth is possible, or whether it is intended as a food for persons particularly susceptible to salmonelloses—the very young, the aged, the frail, the sick, and convalescents.

In the preparation of safe food, sanitary measures must be applied at every step, from the purchase of wholesome food and its sanitary storage, to safe handling of ingredients and menu items during actual preparation and service, and the handling of leftovers.

Methodology for rapid detection of *Salmonella* in foods has been researched for years and is now available. Rapid detection makes possible quick response to contamination problems, eases the testing of food items for the presence of *Salmonella,* and enables the food buyer to procure raw meats, poultry, and other perishable food items that have been tested and found to be free of this pathogen. Methods of rapid detection have been described by Swaminathan et al. (1985).

Vibrio parahaemolyticus

Halophylic *Vibrio* infections are estimated to represent a large percentage of all cases of bacterial gastroenteritis in Japan (Sakazaki, 1979). The vibrios are said to have been first isolated following an outbreak of food poisoning in 1951, but to have been wrongly identified at the time. Since then, foodborne illnesses due to halophylic vibrios have occurred repeatedly in Japan, where they are confined to the warm season of the year.

The first two reported outbreaks caused by *V. parahaemolyticus* that occurred in the United States took place in August of 1971. However, it is possible that earlier incidents escaped identification; *V. parahaemolyticus* cannot be cultured on media routinely employed for the isolation of enteric pathogens from food. Steamed crabs were implicated in both reported outbreaks (*Morbidity and Mortality Weekly Report,* 1971b).

ORGANISM. *Vibrio parahaemolyticus* is a Gram-negative facultative anaerobe, which needs 2–4% NaCl in its substrate to grow and will tolerate up to 7% NaCl. The organism multiplies most actively at a pH level of 7.5–8.5, but growth is possible at a pH range from 5 to 11. The temperature range for growth is 59–104°F (15–40°C), with the optimal growth temperature somewhat below the maximum.

When normal coóking procedures are used, the organism succumbs. Its response to environmental conditions is dependent upon complex interactions and physical forces. It is sensitive to both heat and cold (Beuchat, 1975; Johnson and Liston, 1973). However, it is able to withstand freezing to a certain extent. According to Liston (1974), deep-freezing is not as injurious to the organism as chilling at 0–5°C (32–41°F).

Vibrio parahaemolyticus, and the foodborne illness it causes, have been studied chiefly by Japanese investigators. The organism is pathogenic to humans only, and the illness it causes is an infection. The organism is not found in the feces of healthy individuals but can be recovered in large numbers from the stools of victims. A discussion of the organism as a food-spoilage organism was given by Sakazaki (1983).

DISTRIBUTION. The organism is associated with sea water. Marine studies have revealed the presence of *V. parahaemolyticus* in Japan, Germany, Hong Kong, the Philippines, Taiwan, and the United States. In the United States, the organism has been found mostly in the waters of temperate regions. However, it was also recovered from Alaskan waters (Vasconecelos et al., 1975).

FOODS IMPLICATED. Seafoods such as oysters, shrimp, and blue crabs, and products made from them, are the main offending food items. Commercially produced crabmeat is frequently removed from the shell by hand and therefore is more exposed to contamination than seafoods not so handled. In countries where much seafood is eaten raw, for example, Japan, contamination with *V. parahaemolyticus* poses an especially serious problem (Sakazaki, 1979). In the United States, most outbreaks have been traced to cooked seafood that had been contaminated through contact with raw seafood or contaminated hands, working surface, and equipment. Outbreaks of gastroenteric illness caused by *V. parahaemolyticus* have been discussed by Barker (1974).

The sensitivity of this organism to spices was investigated by Beuchat (1976). Certain spices and organic acid were added to the growth media, all at reasonable levels compatible with normal use in cookery. An inhibitory effect was noted in a number of cases. Certain spices, especially oregano, thyme, and sassafras, had bactericidal effects.

SYMPTOMS. The symptoms of a *V. parahaemolyticus* infection appear approximately 12 hours after the ingestion of the offending food; the time may vary from 2 to 48 hours. The symptoms include abdominal pain and diarrhea, usually accompanied by nausea and vomiting. Mild fever occurs occasionally. Recovery occurs usually within 2–5 days. Fatality is low and is restricted to frail and old persons. For details of the history, bacteriology, and epidemiology of *V. parahaemolyticus,* the reader is referred to Barrow and Miller, 1976; Beuchat, 1975; and Sakazaki, 1979, 1983.

Yersinia enterocolytica

ORGANISM. *Yersinia enterocolytica* is a pathogen capable of causing a foodborne infection, yersiniosis, in the victim. It is a Gram-negative, facultative anaerobic rod.

DISTRIBUTION AND SOURCE. The illness has been prevalent in Japan, Europe, the United States, and Canada (Asakawa et al., 1973; Toma and Lafleur, 1974; Toma and Deidrick, 1975). The first outbreak reported to the CDC in which foodborne transmission was documented occurred in 1976 among school children in Oneida County, New York (*Morbidity and Mortality Weekly Report,* 1977). Chocolate milk was the indicted food. Previous similar outbreaks had been suspected to be due to *Yersinia,* although their foodborne nature could not be clearly documented (Asakawa et al., 1973; Laboratory Centre for Disease Control, 1976).

Later, major outbreaks in the United States included one that occurred in 1981 in a summer camp in New York State (Shayegani et al., 1983) (milk reconstituted from powder as well as a turkey chow mein were implicated) and a multistate outbreak that took place in 1982 (Morse et al., 1984) in which the infections were associated with pasteurized milk, an unusual occurrence indeed. Unfortunately, the organism is capable of multiplying at chilling temperatures and is ubiquitous throughout the animal world. It has been suggested that cattle and swine may be important reservoirs of *Yersinia* (Toma and Deidrick, 1975), and humans have been shown to harbor it also (Shayegani et al., 1981; Shayegani et al., 1983; Morse et al., 1984). In 1994, Reed reported that human infections developed as a result of contact with household pets, particularly puppies and kittens (Reed, 1994a).

Naturally, a careless food handler would be able to contaminate many kinds of raw foods and prepared menu items. An assessment of *Y. enterocolitica* and its presence in foods was presented by Lee (1977).

SYMPTOMS. The symptoms of yersiniosis appear approximately 2–5 days after ingesting the contaminated food. They include fever, headache, nausea, general malaise, abdominal pain, and diarrhea.

FACTORS AFFECTING GROWTH OF ORGANISM. The organism is able to multiply at low temperatures, even under refrigeration. Hanna et al. (1977) studied the growth of this organism on raw and cooked beef and showed it capable of multiplying on raw beef at 0°C (32°F), 1°C (34°F), and 5°C (41°F), and on raw and cooked beef and pork at 7°C (45°F) and 25°C (77°F).

Thorough cooking of food and pasteurization of milk will destroy the contaminants and so will adequate chlorination of water. Since *Y. enterocolitica* may be present on raw meats, shellfish, and raw vegetables, meticulous sanitizing of food preparation surfaces, equipment, and utensils must be practiced to forestall transfer of contaminants to foods eaten raw or prepared menu items. The organism is tolerant to salt (NaCl) and is able to multiply at a concentration of 5% when tested under conditions of refrigeration (Stern et al., 1980). The same authors state that the pH and salt levels that commonly inhibit enterobacteriaceae under refrigeration do not appear adequate to inhibit *Y. enterocolitica*. The pH range for growth is wide, from 4.6 to 9.

Campylobacter jejuni

This pathogen had been well known in veterinary medicine before it appeared as a human pathogen (Levy, 1946). It was formerly referred to as *C. fetus* subsp. *jejuni,* known to cause abortion in cattle and sheep, hepatitis in poultry, and dysentery in cattle. It was first cultured from a human being in 1947, but it was not until 1978 that the organism became a human pathogen of concern. It is now recognized as one of the most common causes of gastroenteritis in humans (Mandal et al., 1984), its importance being similar to that of *Salmonella*. A treatise of *Campylobacter* in animals and humans is available in book form, edited by Butzler (1984). In 1994, DeMol stated that *C. jejuni* has become one of the most common causes of bacterial diarrheal illness, and in the United States it is estimated that over 2 million infections occur per year (DeMol, 1994). The pathogen is a Gram-negative, slender, curved to spiral rod carrying flagellae; it is motile.

DISTRIBUTION AND SOURCE. The distribution of the organism is worldwide. Being a pathogen of cattle, sheep, pigs, and poultry, it follows that it is present on the flesh of these food animals and thus introduced to the kitchen with the food supply. Other animal reservoirs are dogs, cats, and rodents. In animals, sources may be soil and water. In general, the modes of transmission to humans much resemble those of the salmonellae.

SYMPTOMS. Incubation time varies from 2 to 10 days; usually it is 4–7 days. Gastrointestinal symptoms are abdominal pain, from slight to severe. Bloody diarrhea is common. The symptoms may last from 2 to 7 days.

FOODS IMPLICATED. The occurrence of *C. jejuni* in foods has been discussed by Doyle (1981, 1984), Blaser (1982), and Istre et al. (1984). Because of the pathogen's ubiquity, its presence in the areas where raw meats and poultry are handled must be expected, and techniques of sanitary handling of these items and the food preparation surfaces with which they come in contact must be practiced. Besides flesh foods, raw milk has been implicated (Doyle, 1984) in outbreaks of gastroenteritis caused by *C. jejuni*. Even certified raw milk has been implicated, albeit rarely. *Campylobacter jejuni* in foods was reviewed by Doyle (1984).

FACTORS AFFECTING GROWTH AND SURVIVAL

Food. The variety of menu items that have been involved in foodborne outbreaks attests to the fact that multiplication of the organism is possible in many different foods and food mixtures.

pH. The response of *C. jejuni* to pH varies with the strain and the temperature of the substrate. Good growth has been found to take place at a pH range from 6.0 to 8.0, but depending on the strain, growth was found to take place in more acid substrates also (Doyle, 1984).

Sodium Chloride. The response of the organism to salt is dependent on temperature, highest concentrations being tolerated as temperatures are reduced from optimal growth temperature to refrigerator temperatures.

Oxygen. *Campylobacter jejuni* requires for growth oxygen levels well below the atmospheric level, which is actually inhibitory to its growth. It is therefore classified as a microaerophile.

Temperature. In laboratory culture media, growth of *C. jejuni* was restricted to a temperature range of 30°C (86°F) to below 47°C (114.8°F), growth at 42°C (107.6°F) being excellent for growth on some substrates, but not on others. Refrigerator temperatures did not support growth, but survival was better under refrigeration than at room temperature. Studies on meats stored under refrigeration have shown that, depending on strain, degree of contamination, and storage conditions, campylobacters may survive on raw foods for a long time. These studies were summarized by Doyle (1984). Under refrigeration, it may survive at least 1 week, while freezing temperatures are not very well tolerated by this organism. Yet survival has been detected after several months of frozen storage (Svedhem et al., 1981).

Heating.   Properly pasteurized milk should be free from *C. jejuni* cells, and roasts heated to internal temperatures of 50–55°C (122.0–131.0°F) should also be free from living cells, according to studies reported by Christopher et al. (1982). According to their study, heating at 53°C (127.4°F) was insufficient to kill all contaminants. Poultry meat heated to, and held at, 60°C (140°F) for 10 minutes should be rendered practically free from this organism, according to Blankenship and Craven (1982). More research is needed to elucidate time–temperature relationships required for thermal death using a variety of food items and preparation procedures. According to Svedhem et al. (1981), the organism tolerated heating to 60°C (140°F) for a maximum of 15 minutes.

Fecal Streptococci

Several fecal streptococci have been indicted in foodborne gastrointestinal illness on circumstantial evidence, in that these streptococci represented the predominant flora of the foods ingested in connection with the outbreaks. No toxins have been associated with the illness-producing capacities of these bacteria which are linked, by association, with outbreaks of foodborne infections. The reader is referred to a review by Bryan (1979a).

Several species and varieties of *Streptococcus* are of interest as possible causes of foodborne illnesses. They are: *S. faecalis, faecalis* var. *zymogenes, faecalis* var. *liquefaciens, durans,* and *faecium.* These species are generally referred to as the enterococci. Enterococci were first associated with foodborne gastroenteritis outbreaks by Linden et al. (1926).

Dack (1956) reported on several food-poisoning outbreaks with human volunteers. Using live cultures and also filtrates of the organisms isolated in connection with these outbreaks, it was proven that the cultures caused gastroenteritis in the subjects, whereas the filtrates did not.

A number of other bacteriologists have attempted to establish experimentally the enterococci as the cause of gastroenteritic symptoms in man. Using volunteers, food poisoning has been achieved at times. A literature review on the subject is presented by Deibel and Silliker (1963). These authors call attention to the fact that a clear distinction must be drawn between food poisoning attributable to this group and *Streptococcus* disease transmission in which food may play a role as a simple vehicle of transmission. More research is needed to elucidate the conditions necessary for the fecal streptococci to cause enteritis in man. The current thought is that the fecal streptococci are most probably innocuous.

DISTRIBUTION AND SOURCE.   As the name indicates, the enterococci are inhabitants of the intestinal tract. They are harbored by man and animals. When discharged with the feces they may contaminate whatever has contact with the feces, sewage, and manure, such as meat animals, hide, the abdominal cavity of the freshly slaughtered animal, soil, water, air, and the hands of the food handler. In processing, the meat may become heavily contaminated when sanitary standards in the packing plants are low. Distribution of the enterococci is wide.

Insalata et al. (1969) analyzed 5719 industrially processed food samples for fecal streptococci and recovered these organisms from 10.6% of the samples; frozen foods had a higher incidence than other foods.

SYMPTOMS.   The symptoms in persons who ingest food items containing large numbers of the enterococci include nausea, occasionally also vomiting, colic, and diarrhea. Incubation time may vary from 3 to 18 hours. Symptoms are milder than those caused by *Salmonella* and *Staphylococcus*.

INCIDENCE.   Few incidences are reported. Because of their relative mildness the illness may easily escape recognition.

FOODS IMPLICATED.   A variety of items have been mentioned, among them pasteurized canned ham, vienna sausage, beef croquettes, pork sausage, barbecued beef, bologna, turkey dressing, turkey à la king, dried eggs, evaporated milk from rusty and leaky cans, charlotte russe, cheese, chocolate pudding, and whipped cream.

FACTORS AFFECTING GROWTH.   Conditions favoring growth vary somewhat with species and strains.

Food.   A variety of foods are able to serve as substrates. Enterococci, in general, need complex substrates and grow poorly on many culture media. Their salt tolerance is high, approximately 6.5% or more being tolerated. *Streptococcus faecium* grows well on salt-cured hams.

pH.   The organisms may grow over an extremely wide range of pH. Especially unusual is their capability to grow in alkaline media of pH 9 and higher.

Temperature.   The organisms are capable of growing over a very wide range of temperature. The widest range is 42–126°F (5.5–52°C). Angelotti et al. (1963) have studied the time–temperature effects on fecal streptococci in foods at refrigeration temperatures as well as at warm-holding temperatures. Mixtures of enterococcal species were incubated in custard, chicken à la king, and ham salad, at temperatures ranging from 40°F (4.4°C) through 128°F (53.3°C). In custard, growth was slight at 42°F (5.5°C), but good growth was observed at 48°F (9°C) through 115°F (46°C). In chicken à la king no growth was noted at 42°F (5.5°C) or below, but good growth occurred at the temperature range between 50°F (10°C) and 115°F (46°C). In ham salad, no growth occurred at 48°F (9°C) and below; at 50°F (10°C) growth was slight; and excellent growth was observed at 60°F (15.5°C) through 115°F (46°C).

The enterococci are thermoduric and are able to survive pasteurization of milk. Shannon et al. (1970) exposed *S. durans* suspended in milk to high temperatures for 16 minutes and reported the following survival: at 161°F (71.7°C) a 55.2% survival; at 170°F (76.7°C), a 46.4% survival; and at 180°F (82.2°C), a 32.5% survival. *Streptococcus faecalis* and *S. faecium* have been shown to survive the pasteurization treatment given certain canned hams. In general, processors aim at a terminal internal food temperature of 158°F (70°C) to preclude the hazard from bacterial spoilage.

Surgalla et al. (1944) demonstrated that *S. faecalis* remained viable for at least 30 days at 98.6°F (37°C) in foods of varying acidity. At below-freezing temperatures, the cells remained viable for long periods of time. This property has been claimed to be of some value as a microbiological index of food quality for foods such as water, milk, and frozen foods stored at low temperatures. The role of the enterococci as indicators of food quality is questionable.

OTHER BACTERIA ASSOCIATED WITH FOODBORNE GASTROENTERIC OUTBREAKS

Escherichia coli

Escherichia coli, a common inhabitant of the intestinal tract of man and warm-blooded animals, was long regarded as a harmless saprophyte. However, in November of 1971, Camembert and Brie cheeses imported from France caused outbreaks of foodborne illness; *E. coli* was found to be the culprit. This is the first well-documented occurrence of foodborne illness in the United States of which this organism was the cause (*Morbidity and Mortality Weekly Report,* 1971c). Since then, *E. coli* has been associated with outbreaks involving apple cider (Besser et al., 1993), hamburger (Tarr, 1993), unpasteurized milk (Hedberg and Pokarney, 1993), and contaminated water (Rice, 1993).

Serotypes of *E. coli* that are capable of causing foodborne gastroenteritis are designated as enteropathogenic. Four major categories of enteropathogenic *E. coli* have been defined: (1) classical serogroups that have been historically associated with diarrhea in infants and young children; (2) facultatively enteropathogenic *E. coli* that are serogroups associated with sporadic diarrhea and the normal flora of the intestinal tract; (3) enterotoxigenic *E. coli* associated with travelers' diarrhea; and (4) strains that are enteroinvasive, since they cause an invasive infection of the gastrointestinal tract (Kornacki and Marth, 1982).

A large dose of *E. coli* must be ingested regardless of the group they belong to, before signs or symptoms of illness occur. The mean incubation period for the enterotoxigenic type is 26 hours, for the invasive type, 11 hours. Symptoms for the enterotoxigenic type are diarrhea, vomiting, dehydration, and shock—similar to those of cholera. Symptoms for the invasive type are abdominal cramps, watery stool, fever, chills, and headache.

The optimal conditions for growth are a temperature of 37°C (98.6°F), with a range of 10–40°C (50–104°F), and a pH of near neutral, with a possible range of pH 4–8.

The ubiquitous nature of this organism causes the contamination to originate from many sources: air, dust, water, food handler, kitchen utensils, flies, rodents, and many more. The organism is easily killed by pasteurization and cooking temperatures of at least 71°C (160°F).

The potential public health significance of non-*E. coli* coliforms in food was discussed by Twedt and Boutin (1979), Kornacki and Marth (1982), and Reed (1994b).

Listeria monocytogenes

Listeria monocytogenes was responsible for one of the most deadly outbreaks in the United States, accounting for more than 40 deaths in 1985. The organism is widely distributed in nature and has been isolated from fruits, vegetables, milk, cheese, meats, and seafood. When consumed in contaminated food by humans, the bacterium will multiply in the gastrointestinal tract, causing listeriosis. The organism will grow in a wide range of pH levels, from 5 to 9, and can grow at refrigerator temperatures as low as 1.7°C (35°F). It is killed at 45°C (113°F) or higher. Thus, thorough cooking will kill contamination by this bacterium. However, frozen or refrigerated foods should be heated thoroughly before tasting. Cross contamination should also be avoided. Raw milk or unripened cheese made from unpasteurized milk should not be consumed, especially by compromised individuals or those who are at high risk for opportunistic pathogens causing illnesses.

FUNGI

The fungi include molds, yeasts, and mushrooms. Many fungi are useful. We are concerned with those that may become dangerous because they are capable of releasing toxic products into food. Mushroom poisons were discussed in Chapter 3.

Increasing attention is being paid to the real and potential dangers arising from the contamination of our feed and food supplies with toxins elaborated by molds.

Fungal toxins, also called mycotoxins, may cause disease in animals and man. Mycotoxicoses are poisonings caused by the ingestion of fungus-contaminated feed or food, such as moldy grain and other seeds, moldy nuts, and other fungus-infested materials (Busby and Wogan, 1979). Important contaminants of stored feed and food products are members of the genera *Aspergillus* and *Penicillium,* which are capable of producing mycotoxins. The syndrome resulting from consuming food containing sufficient amounts of mycotoxin is called mycotoxicosis.

The production of mycotoxin is favored by high humidity and water activity. The acute form of mycotoxicosis is characterized by hemorrhages in many tissues. The chronic form also includes changes in the blood and bone marrow; damage to liver and kidneys is frequent. The molds capable of forming toxins and causing mycotoxicosis in man and animals are distributed all over the world. They grow, produce toxins, and multiply on a wide variety of foods over wide ranges of temperature and humidity.

The potential danger to man arising from eating moldy food has stimulated much research in recent years, but many facets need to be explored before the question of which mycotoxins represent a health hazard to humans is answered. Some of the toxins are carcinogenic, and the possible association of incidence in liver disease with the consumption of food materials contaminated with mold toxins is ominous. Until more is known about the dangers to man of consuming moldy food, certain precautions seem in order. Acute illness following the ingestion of moldy food was mentioned by van Walbeek et al. (1968) in a review on mycotoxins from foodborne fungi. One of the cases was a child who had become ill after having consumed spaghetti which contained aflatoxins. Although aflatoxins are the most widely known of the fungal toxins, others have been reported and are under investigation. Other mycotoxins that may be significant in food are patulin, penicillic acid, ochratoxin A, alimentary toxic aleukia (ATA), and roquefortine.

Aflatoxicosis

Aflatoxicosis was first discovered in England (Blount, 1961), when turkeys became poisoned by aflatoxins present in peanut meal. A subsequent study of feed materials revealed that an active principle could be extracted from many of them. In the course of the investigations it was found that samples from at least 14 peanut-producing countries were contaminated with the toxic agent. After the turkey incident, similar poisonings were found in ducklings, chickens, hogs, and calves (Gray, 1970). Feedstuffs other than peanuts found to contain aflatoxins were oilseeds, such as cottonseed and soybeans, and grains, such as corn, rice, wheat, millet, and barley. The reader is referred to a review by Busby and Wogan (1979).

Selected physical and chemical data are now available for several aflatoxins. Toxicity studies on animals (in vivo) and on animal tissues (in vitro) have resulted in important information on the damaging effect of the toxins. Studies on human liver tissue, in vitro, have shown damage to human cells. Of major interest and concern are the carcinogenic properties of certain metabolites (Enomoto and Saito, 1972).

Many of the aflatoxins have a potential for being toxic, or carcinogenic, to a variety of mammals, poultry, and fish. Cooking food containing aflatoxins will not destroy the poison—it is extremely heat stable. It seems that the optimum temperature for toxin production ranges from 25 to 40°C (77–104°F). Below 8–10°C (46–50°F), aflatoxin production is possible, but slow. Therefore, storage temperatures of 5°C (41°F) or lower are recommended for commodities on which toxin-forming aspergilli may grow.

Many common foods have been found to be able to serve as substrates for toxin-producing *Aspergillus flavus*. Peanuts were mentioned earlier as a feedstuff, but peanuts are also an important food for humans. To protect the consumer from the danger of aflatoxins which might be present in diseased kernels, peanut growers of the United States are taking great care in the handling of their crop by preventing them from being attacked by mold. In addition, precautions are applied to prevent diseased nuts from being included in shipments to consumers; one is mechanical sorting by size and another is elimination of discolored nuts by electronic screening. In countries of humid and warm climates a potential hazard exists when the harvesting and subsequent handling of peanuts is not carried out so as to preclude conditions favoring the growth of molds.

A listing of other foods which may serve as substrates to *A. flavus* has been assembled by van Walbeek et al. (1968). Crops as well as processed and prepared foods were included. Among the processed foods were egg noodles, cheese, powdered milk, various kinds of nuts, poppy seed, apple juice, paprika, smoked bacon, cured ham, dried peas, lentils, plums, apple slices, peaches, figs, spaghetti, kippers, orange juice, and ham. Among the prepared foods were meat pie, apple squares, bread and other baked goods, cooked (comminuted) meat, and rice (TV dinners).

Also, nuts have come under scrutiny. Moldy pecans were found to be contaminated with aflatoxins by Koehler et al. (1975). Brazil nut and pistachio imports are carefully checked by the FDA for freedom from molds because these nuts, too, have been found contaminated with aspergilli.

In this country, the Federal Food, Drug and Cosmetic Act has made moldy foods illegal in interstate commerce since 1906. At present, they fall in the category of adulterated foods, since they contain a filthy, putrid, or decomposed substance, or are otherwise unfit for food.

The FDA began surveillance for the presence of aflatoxins in human food and animal feed in 1963. As was mentioned earlier, the peanut industry and the USDA initiated a certification program for aflatoxin-free peanuts in cooperation with the FDA. During 1973, a surveillance program for various dairy products was also set up. To eliminate aflatoxins in milk, it must be kept out of the feed given cows. Also, moldy materials fed to animals may leave residues of toxin in meat. Since the FDA can prove unfitness by demonstrating the presence of mycotoxins in significant concentrations, research on mycotoxins is being pushed ahead. Other research involves tests dealing with fungus–host relationships, breeding for varieties resistant to molds, and developing effective fungicides. Also, attention is being given to the improvement of harvesting methods, storage, processing, and plant sanitation. The food industry is cooperating with government agencies to safeguard the country's food supply against toxins from molds; similar efforts are being made abroad.

Although the significance of aflatoxins on human health has not yet been fully established, the FDA removes products containing aflatoxins from food channels. In its control program, the FDA is joined by the USDA and industry. For a detailed discussion of the subject, the reader is referred to Busby and Wogan (1979), van Walbeek (1973), Rodricks (1976), Goldblatt (1969, 1977), Campbell and Stoloff (1974), and Bullerman et al. (1984). The last reference includes a useful listing of earlier publications.

Roquefortine

A word should be said about the safety of food items like Gorgonzola and Roquefort cheeses, in the processing of which molds have been used for centuries with no evidence of harm to consumers. No cause for worry seemed to exist for the wholesomeness of such products. However, a toxic substance has now been detected in commercial blue cheeses from several countries, and this toxin was extracted primarily from the heavily molded portions. The fungus that is used to produce Roquefort (or blue) cheese is *Penicillium roqueforti*. The toxin is a neurotoxin. It has been tested in the laboratory on mice, and when injected into the animals it caused convulsions. Any ill effects on humans, however, are not known at this time.

Implications for Foodservice

In foodservice, the prolonged and improper storage of perishable food supply items and of cooked food invites the danger from mold growth and elaboration of toxic metabolites. Van Walbeek et al. (1969) studied the effect of refrigeration on the formation of toxins from *Aspergillus flavus*. Inoculated media were stored at temperatures of 45.5–50°F (7.5–10°C) for one day to a week. Aflatoxins were produced in the media within a day, in small amounts. After a week, the amounts were significant. When the inoculated media were allowed to remain for 24 hours at room temperature before they were refrigerated, the amount of aflatoxin produced was increased in each instance. The authors warn that at refrigeration temperatures sporulation may be absent, and so would be the tell-tale green color of the mold. Therefore, the presence of the mold might not even be noticed, although the mycelium is there.

Even when mold spots are visible, they are not a sure sign of how far the toxin has penetrated into the food. Cutting off moldy spots from solid foods, and skimming off the mold colonies from fluid foods such as fruit juices, is most probably not an effectual method of ridding the food of these toxins (Frank, 1968). At this time, we really do not *know* what harm might be done to man by consuming toxins present in moldy food. Until more is known on this subject we should—without being alarmists—do our utmost to manage food in such a way that it does not have a chance to get moldy. The information we have points toward the importance of storing vulnerable foods at low temperatures and for as brief a period as is feasible. The presence of moldy food is a sure sign of poor management in any foodservice.

On the international scene, the problem of mycotoxins is of great importance in connection with development of high-protein plant foods for the populace of developing countries suffering from a lack of animal protein in their diets (Milner, 1965). Such food plants include peanuts, soya beans, cottonseed, rice, and other crops known to be substrates for *Aspergillus flavus*. Some of these countries have warm and humid climates conducive to mold growth. Improvement in methods of harvest, storage, and transit of crops is essential to safeguard the wholesomeness of food and feed plants susceptible to fungal attack. To monitor the level of aflatoxins in food, guidelines have been established through cooperative efforts of FAO, WHO, and UNICEF, Protein Advisory Board (Rodricks, 1976).

REFERENCES

Angelotti, R., E. Wilson, M. J. Foter, and K. H. Lewis (1959). "Time–temperature effects on salmonellae and staphylococci in foods. I. Behavior in broth cultures and refrigerated foods." The Robert A. Taft Sanitary Engineering Center Technical Report No. F 59-2. Cincinnati, OH.

Angelotti, R., M. J. Foter, and K. H. Lewis (1961a). "Time–temperature effects on salmonellae and staphylococci in foods. I. Behavior in refrigerated foods. II. Behavior at warm holding temperatures." *Am. J. Public Health,* 51:76–83; 83–88.

Angelotti, R., M. J. Foter, and K. H. Lewis (1961b). "Time–temperature effects on salmonellae and staphylococci in foods. III. Thermal death time studies." *Appl. Microbiol.,* 9:308–315.

Angelotti, R., H. E. Hall, M. J. Foter, and K. H. Lewis (1962). "Quantitation of *Clostridium perfringens* in foods." *Appl. Microbiol.,* 10:193–199.

Angelotti, R., K. H. Lewis, and M. J. Foter (1963). "Time–temperature effects on fecal streptococci in foods. I. Behavior in refrigerated foods and at warm-holding temperatures." *J. Milk Food Technol.,* 26:296–301.

Asakawa, Y., S. Akahane, N. Kagota, M. Noguchi, R. Sakazaki, and K. Tamura (1973). "Two community outbreaks of human infection with *Yersinia enterocolitica.*" *J. Hyg. (Camb.),* 71:715–723.

Barker, W. H. (1974). "*Vibrio parahaemolyticus* outbreaks in the United States." *Lancet,* 1:551–554.

Barrow, G. I., and D. C. Miller (1976). "*Vibrio parahaemolyticus* and seafoods." In *Microbiology in Agriculture, Fisheries, and Food,* F. A. Skinner and J. G. Carr, Eds., Academic Press, London, New York, San Francisco.

Bergdoll, M. S. (1979). "Staphylococcal Intoxications." In *Food-Borne Infections and Intoxications,* H. Riemann and F. L. Bryan, Eds., 2nd ed. Academic Press, New York.

Bergdoll, M. S. and R. N. Robbins (1973). "Characterization of types of staphylococcal enterotoxins." *J. Milk Food Technol.,* 36:610–612.

Bergdoll, M. S., K. F. Weiss, and M. J. Nuster (1967). "Production of Staphylococcal Enterotoxin by a Coagulase Negative Microorganism." A–68 (Abstract) *Proc. Am. Soc. Microbiol.,* 67th Annual Meeting.

Besser, R. E., S. M. Lett, J. T. Weber, M. P. Doyle, T. J. Barrett, J. G. Wells, and P. M. Griffin (1993). "An outbreak of diarrhea and hemorrhagic uremic syndrome from *Escherichia coli* 0157:H7 in fresh-pressed apple cider." *J. Am. Med. Assoc.,* 269:2217–2220.

Beuchat, L. R. (1975). "Environmental factors affecting survival and growth of *Vibrio parahaemolyticus.* A review." *J. Milk Food Technol.,* 38:476–480.

Beuchat, L. R. (1976). "Sensitivity to *Vibrio parahaemolyticus* to spices and organic acids." *J. Food Sci.,* 41:899–902.

Blankenship, L. C. and S. E. Craven (1982). "*Campylobacter jejuni* survival in chicken meat as a function of temperature." *Appl. Environ. Microbiol.,* 44:88–92.

Blaser, M. J. (1982). "*Campylobacter* and food." *Food Technol.,* 36(3):89–92.

Blount, W. P. (1961). "Turkey 'X' disease." *Turkeys (J. Brit. Turk. Fed.),* 9(2):52; 55–58; 61; 77.

Bryan, F. L. (1979a). "Infections and Intoxications Caused by Other Bacteria." In *Food-Borne Infections and Intoxications,* H. Reimann and F. L. Bryan, Eds., 2nd ed. Academic Press, New York.

Bryan, F. L. (1979b). "Epidemiology of Food-Borne Disease." In *Food-Borne Infections and Intoxications,* H. Riemann and F. L. Bryan, Eds., 2nd ed. Academic Press, New York.

Bryan, F. L., M. J. Fanelli, and H. Riemann (1979). *"Salmonella* Infections." In *Food-Borne Infections and Intoxications,* H. Riemann and F. L. Bryan, Eds., 2nd ed. Academic Press, New York.

Bullerman, L. B. L., L. L. Schroeder, and K. J. Park (1984). "Formation and control of mycotoxins in food." *J. Food Prot.,* 47:637–646.

Busby, W. F., Jr. and G. N. Wogan (1979). "Food-Borne Mycotoxins and Alimentary Mycotoxicoses." In *Food-Borne Infections and Intoxications,* H. Riemann and F. L. Bryan, Eds., 2nd ed. Academic Press, New York.

Butzler, J. P., Ed. (1984). *Campylobacter Infection in Man and Animals.* CRC Press, Boca Raton, FL.

Campbell, T. C. and L. Stoloff (1974). "Implication of mycotoxins for human health." *J. Agric. Food Chem.,* 22:1006–1015.

Canada, J. C., D. H. Strong, and L. G. Scott (1964). "Response of *Clostridium perfringens* spores and vegetative cells to temperature variation." *Appl. Microbiol.,* 12:273–276.

Casman, E. P. and R. Bennett (1965). "Detection of staphylococcal enterotoxin in food." *Appl. Microbiol.,* 13:181–189.

Centers for Disease Control (1985). *Foodborne Disease Surveillance,* Annual Summary, 1982. U.S. Department of Health and Human Services, Washington, D.C.

Christopher, F. M., G. C. Smith, and C. Vanderzant (1982). "Effect of temperature and pH on the survival on *Campylobacter fetus." J. Food Prot.,* 45:253–259.

Chung, K. C. and J. M. Goepfert (1970). "Growth of *Salmonella* at low pH." *J. Food Sci.,* 35:326–328.

Cohen, M. L. and P. A. Blake (1977). "Trends in foodborne salmonellosis outbreaks: 1963–1975." *J. Food Protect.,* 40:798–800.

Collee, J. G., J. A. Knowlden, and B. C. Hobbs (1961). "Studies on the growth, sporulation and carriage of *Clostridium welchii* with special reference to food poisoning strains." *J. Appl. Bacteriol.,* 24:326–339.

Committee on *Salmonella,* National Research Council (1969). "An evaluation of the *Salmonella* problem." A Report of the USDA and the FDA National Academy of Sciences Publication No. 1683, Washington, D.C.

Craig, J. M. and K. S. Pilcher (1966). *"Clostridium botulinum* type F: Isolation from salmon from the Columbia River." *Science,* 153(3733):311–312.

Crisley, F. D., J. T. Peeler, R. Angelotti, and H. E. Hall (1968). "Thermal resistance of spores of five strains of *Clostridium botulinum* type E in ground whitefish chubs." *J. Food Sci.,* 33:411–416.

Crowther, J. S. and R. Holbrook (1976). "Trends in methods for detecting food poisoning toxins produced by *Clostridium botulinum* and *Staphylococcus aureus."* In *Microbiology in Agriculture, Fisheries, and Food,* F. A. Skinner and J. G. Carr, Eds. Academic Press, London, New York, San Francisco.

Dack, G. M. (1956). *Food Poisoning,* 3rd ed. Univ. Chicago Press, Chicago, IL.

Deibel, R. H. and J. H. Silliker (1963). "Food poisoning potential of the enterococci." *J. Bacteriol.,* 85:827–832.

DeMol, P. (1994). "Human campylobacteriosis: Clinical and epidemiological aspects." *Dairy, Food and Environ. Sanit.,* 14:314–316.

Dolman, C. E. (1964). "Botulism as a world problem." In *Botulism*. U.S. Department of Health, Education and Welfare, Public Health Serv., Publication No. 999–FE–1, Cincinnati, OH.

Doyle, M. P. (1981). "*Campylobacter fetus* subsp. *jejuni:* An old pathogen of new concern." *J. Food Prot.,* 44:480–488; 454.

Doyle, M. P. (1984). "*Campylobacter* in foods." In *Campylobacter Infection in Man and Animals,* J. P. Butzler, Ed. CRC Press, Boca Raton, FL.

Duncan, C. L. (1976). "*Clostridium perfringens.*" In *Food Microbiology: Public Health and Spoilage Aspects,* M. P. Defigueiredo and D. F. Splittstocsscr, Eds. Avi Publishing Co., Westport, CT.

Duncan, C. L. and D. H. Strong (1971). "*Clostridium perfringens* type A food poisoning. I. Response of the rabbit ileum as an indication of enteropathogenicity of strains of *Clostridium perfringens* in monkeys." *Infect. Immunol.,* 3:167–170.

Elliott, R. P. and P. K. Heiniger (1965). "Improved temperature-gradient incubation and the maximal growth temperature and heat resistance of *Salmonella.*" *Appl. Microbiol.* 13:73–76.

Eklund, M. W. and F. Paysky (1965). "*Clostridium botulinum* type F from marine sediments." *Science,* 149(3681):306.

Enkiri, N. K. and J. A. Alford (1971). "Relationship of the frequency of isolation of salmonellae to their resistance to drying and freezing." *Appl. Microbiol.,* 21:381–382.

Enomoto, M. and M. Saito (1972). "Carcinogens produced by fungi." *Ann. Rev. Microbiol.,* 26:279–312.

Foster, E. M. (1969). "The problem of salmonellae in foods." *Food Technol.,* 23:1178–1182.

Frank, H. K. (1968). "Diffusion of aflatoxins in foodstuffs." *J. Food Sci.,* 33:98–100.

Frazier, W. C. and D. C. Westhoff (1978). *Food Microbiology,* 3rd ed. McGraw-Hill Book Co., New York.

Gast, R. and C. W. Beard (1992). "Detection and enumeration of *Salmonella enteritidis* in fresh and stored eggs laid by experimentally infected hens." *J. Food Prot.,* 55:152–156.

Gilbert, R. J. (1979). "*Bacillus cereus* Gastroenteritis." In *Food-Borne Infections and Intoxications,* H. Riemann and F. L. Bryan, Eds., 2nd ed. Academic Press, New York.

Gilbert, R. J. and A. J. Taylor (1976). "*Bacillus cereus* food poisoning." In *Microbiology in Agriculture, Fisheries, and Food,* F. A. Skinner and J. G. Carr, Eds. Academic Press, London, New York, San Francisco.

Gimenez, D. F. and A. S. Ciccarelli (1970). "Another type of *Clostridium botulinim.*" *Zentralbl. Bakteriol. Parasitenkd. Infektionskr. Hyg. Abt. 10 rig.,* 215:221–224.

Goepfert, J. M. (1973). "Pathogenicity patterns in *Bacillus cereus* food-borne disease." *Abst. 1st Int. Congr. Bacteriol., Int. Assoc. Microbiol. Soc., Jerusalem,* 1:140.

Goepfert, J. M., I. K. Iskander, and C. H. Amundson (1970). "Relation of the heat resistance of salmonellae to the water activity of the environment." *Appl. Microbiol.,* 19:429–433.

Goepfert, J. M., W. M. Spira, B. A. Glatz, and H. U. Kim (1973). "Pathogenicity of *Bacillus cereus.*" In *The Microbiological Safety of Food,* B. C. Hobbs and J. H. B. Christian, Eds. Academic Press, London.

Goepfert, J. M., W. M. Spira, and H. U. Kim (1972). *"Bacillus cereus:* food poisoning organism. A review." *J. Milk Food Technol.,* 35:213–227.

Goldblatt, L. A., Ed. (1969). *Aflatoxin: Scientific Background, Control, and Implications.* Academic Press, New York.

Goldblatt, L. A. (1977). "Mycotoxin—past, present, and future." *J. Am. Oil Chem. Soc.,* 54:302A–309A.

Gray, W. D. (1970). *The Use of Fungi as Food and in Food Processing.* CRC Press, Cleveland, OH.

Hall, H. and R. Angelotti (1965). *"Clostridium perfringens* in meat and meat products." *Appl. Microbiol.,* 13:352–357.

Hall, H., R. Angelotti, and K. H. Lewis (1963). "Quantitative detection of staphylococcal enterotoxin B in food by Gel-Diffusion methods." *U.S. Public Health Rep.,* 78:1089–1098.

Hall, H. E., R. Angelotti, and K. H. Lewis (1965). "Detection of the staphylococcal enterotoxin in food." *Health Lab. Sci.,* 2:179–191.

Hanna, M. O., J. C. Stewart, D. L. Zink, Z. L. Carpenter, and C. Vanderzant (1977). "Development of *Yersinia enterocolitica* on raw and cooked beef and pork at different temperatures." *J. Food Sci.,* 42:1180–1184.

Hart, C. H., W. W. Sherwood, and E. Wilson (1960). "A food poisoning outbreak aboard a common carrier." *Public Health Rep.,* 75:527–531.

Hauge, S. (1950). *"Bacillus cereus* as a cause of food poisoning." *Nordisk Hyg. Tidskr.,* 31:189–206.

Hedberg, K. and B. Pokarney (1993). *"Escherichia coli* 0157:H7 cluster in Portland linked to raw milk." *Oregon Hum. Res. News/Health Division,* April 21.

Hobbs, B. C. and J. G. Wilson (1959). "Contamination of wholesale meat supplies with *Salmonella* and heat resistant *Clostridium welchii." Mon. Bull. Min. Health, Public Health Lab. Serv.,* 18:198–206.

Hobbs, B. C., M. E. Smith, C. L. Oakley, H. G. Warrack, and J. C. Cruikshank (1953). *"Clostridium welchii* food poisoning." *J. Hyg.,* 51:75–101.

Holmberg, S. D., J. G. Wells, and M. L. Cohen (1984). "Animal-to-man transmission of antimicrobial-resistant *Salmonella:* Investigations of U.S. outbreaks, 1971–1983." *Science,* 225 (Aug. 24):833–835.

Huhtanen, C. N., J. Naghski, C. S. Custer, and R. W. Russell (1976). "Growth and toxin production by *Clostridium botulinum* in moldy tomato juice." *Appl. Environ. Microbiol.,* 32:711–715.

Insalata, N. F., J. S. Witzeman, and F. C. A. Sunga (1969). "Streptococci in industrially processed foods—an incidence study." *Food Technol.,* 23:1316–1318.

Istre, G. R., M. J. Blaser, P. Shillam, and R. S. Hopkins (1984). *"Campylobacter* enteritis associated with undercooked barbecued chicken." *Am. J. Publ. Hlth.,* 74:1265–1267.

Johnson, H. C. and J. Liston (1973). "Sensitivity of *Vibrio parahaemolyticus* to cold in oysters, fish fillet, and crabmeat." *J. Food Sci.,* 38:437–441.

Johnson, K. M. (1984). *"Bacillus cereus* foodborne illness—an update." *J. Food Prot.,* 47:145–153.

Juven, B. J., N. A. Cox, J. S. Bailey, J. E. Thomson, O. W. Charles, and T. V. Shutze (1984). "Survival of *Salmonella* in dry food and feed." *J. Food Prot.,* 47:445–448.

Kao, C. T. and W. C. Frazier (1966). "Effect of lactic acid bacteria on growth of *Staphylococcus aureus." Appl. Microbiol.,* 14:251–255.

Kautter, D. A. (1964). "*Clostridium botulinum* type E in smoked fish." *J. Food Sci.,* 29:843–849.

Kemp, G. E., R. Proctor, and A. Browne (1962). "Foodborne disease in California with special reference to *Clostridium perfringens (welchii).*" *Public Health Rep.,* 77:910–914.

Kim, H. U. and J. M. Goepfert (1971). "Occurrence of *Bacillus cereus* in selected dry food products." *J. Milk Food Technol.,* 34:12–15.

Koehler, P. E., R. T. Hanlin, and L. Beraha (1975). "Production of aflatoxin B_1 and G_1, by *Aspergillus flavus* and *Aspergillus parasiticus* isolated from market pecans." *Appl. Microbiol.,* 30:581–583.

Kornacki, J. L. and E. H. Marth (1982). "Foodborne illness, caused by *Escherichia coli:* A review." *J. Food Prot.,* 45:1051–1067.

Laboratory Centre for Disease Control (1976). *Can. Dis. Wkly. Rep.,* 2:41–44; 73–74.

Lee, W. H. (1977). "An assessment of *Yersinia enterocolytica* and its presence in foods." *J. Food Prot.,* 40:486–489.

Levy, A. J. (1946). "A gastro-enteritic outbreak probably due to a bovine strain of *Vibrio.*" *Yale J. Biol. Med.,* 18:243–258.

Linden, B. A., W. R. Turner, and C. Thom (1926). "Food poisoning from a *Streptococcus* in cheese." *U.S. Public Health Rep.,* 41:1647–1652.

Liston, J. (1974). "Influence of U.S. seafood handling procedures on *Vibrio parahaemolyticus.*" In *Proceedings of the International Symposium on Vibrio parahaemolyticus.* T. Fujino, G. Sagaguchi, R. Sakazaki, and Y. Takeda, Eds. Saikon Publishing Co., Tokyo.

Lynt, R. K., D. A. Kautter, and R. B. Read (1975). "Botulism in commercially canned foods." *J. Milk Food Technol.,* 38:546–550.

MacDonald, K. (1984). "Foodborne disease surveillance in the United States." In *Proceedings of the Second National Conference for Food Protection,* published by the U.S. Department of Health and Human Services, FDA Contract No. 223–84–2087. Pages 167–171.

Mandal, B. K., P. DeMal, and J. P. Butzler (1984). "Clinical aspects of *Campylobacter* infections in humans." In *Campylobacater Infection,* J. P. Butzler, Ed. CRC Press, Boca Raton, FL.

McClung, L. S. (1945). "Human food poisoning due to growth of *Clostridium perfringens (welchii)* in freshly cooked chicken: Preliminary note." *J. Bacteriol.,* 50:229–231.

McCutchen, J. H. (1963). "Investigation of foodborne diseases." *J. Environ. Health,* 25:339–346.

Milner, M. (1965). "Significance of Mycotoxins in International Protein Food Efforts." In *Mycotoxins in Foodstuffs.* G. N. Wogan, Ed. The MIT Press, Cambridge, MA.

Minor, T. E. and E. H. Marth (1971). "*Staphylococcus aureus* and staphylococcal food intoxications. A review. II. Enterotoxins and epidemiology." *J. Milk Food Technol.,* 35:21–29.

Minor, T. E. and E. H. Marth (1972). "*Staphylococcus aureus* and staphylococcal food intoxications. A review. IV. Staphylococci in meat, bakery products, and other foods." *J. Milk Food Technol.,* 35:228–241.

Morbidity and Mortality Weekly Report (1965). U.S. Department of Health, Education and Welfare, Public Health Serv., 14, June 5.

Morbidity and Mortality Weekly Report (1966). U.S. Department of Health, Education and Welfare, Public Health Serv., 15, March 26.

Morbidity and Mortality Weekly Report (1971b). U.S. Department of Health, Education and Welfare, Public Health Serv., 20, Oct. 2.

Morbidity and Mortality Weekly Report (1971c). U.S. Department of Health, Education and Welfare, Public Health Serv., 20, Dec. 11.

Morbidity and Mortality Weekly Report (1973). U.S. Department of Health, Education and Welfare, Public Health Service, Center for Disease Control, 22, Dec. 8.

Morbidity and Mortality Weekly Report (1977). U.S. Department of Health, Education and Welfare, Public Health Service, Center for Disease Control, 26, Feb. 18.

Morbidity and Mortality Weekly Report (1978). U.S. Department of Health, Education and Welfare, Public Health Serv., Centers for Disease Control, 27, Sept. 22.

Morbidity and Mortality Weekly Report (1981). U.S. Department of Health and Human Services, Centers for Disease Control, 30(14):171–172.

Morbidity and Mortality Weekly Report (1984). U.S. Department of Health and Human Services, Centers for Disease Control, 32(54):16.

Morbidity and Mortality Weekly Report (1990). U.S. Department of Health and Human Services, Centers for Disease Control, 39:909–912.

Morse, D. L., M. Shayegani, and R. J. Gallo (1984). "Epidemiologic investigation of a *Yersinia* camp outbreak linked to a food handler." *Am. J. Publ. Hlth.,* 74:589–592.

Mortimer, P. R. and G. McCann (1974). "Food poisoning episodes associated with *Bacillus cereus* in fried rice." *Lancet,* 1:1043–1045.

Nakamura, M. and K. D. Kelly (1968). "*Clostridium perfringens* in dehydrated soups and sauces." *J. Food Sci.,* 33:424–426.

Nishida, S., N. Seo, and M. Nakagawa (1969). "Sporulation, heat resistance, and biological properties of *Clostridium perfringens.*" *Appl. Microbiol.,* 17:303–309.

Notermans, S., J. Dufrenne, and M. J. H. Keijbets (1981). "Vacuum-packed cooked potatoes toxin production by *Clostridium botulinum* and shelf life." *J. Food Prot.,* 44:572–575.

Nygren, B. (1962). "Phospholipase C-producing bacteria and food poisoning." *Acta Patl. Microbiol. Scand. Supp.,* 160:11–88.

Peterson, A. C., J. J. Black, and M. F. Gunderson (1964a). "Staphylococci in competition. III. Influence of pH and salt of staphylococcal growth in mixed populations (1964b). IV. Effect of starch and kind and concentration of sugar on staphylococcal growth in mixed populations (1964c). V. Effect of eggs, eggs plus carbohydrates and lipids on staphylococcal growth." *Appl. Microbiol.,* 12:70–76; 77–82; 83–86.

Powers, E. M., T. G. Latt, and T. Brown (1976). "*Bacillus cereus* in spices." *J. Milk Food Technol.,* 39:668–670.

Ray, C. R., H. W. Walker, and P. L. Rohrbaugh (1975). "The influence of temperature on growth, sporulation, and heat resistance of spores of six strains of *Clostridium perfringens.*" *J. Milk Food Technol.,* 38:461–465.

Read, R. B., Jr., W. L. Pritchard, J. Bradshaw, and L. A. Black (1965a). "In vitro assay of staphylococcal enterotoxins A and B from milk." *J. Dairy Sci.,* 48:411–419.

Read, R. B., Jr., J. Bradshaw, W. L. Pritchard, and L. A. Black (1965b). "Assay of staphylococcal enterotoxin from cheese." *J. Dairy Sci.,* 48:420–424.

Reed, G. H. (1994a). "Foodborne illness: *Yersiniosis.*" *Dairy, Food Environ. Sanit.,* 14:536.

Reed, G. H. (1994b). "Foodborn illness: *Escherichia coli.*" *Dairy, Food Environ. Sanit.,* 14:327.

Rice, E. (1993). "Drinking water associated with waterborne disease: Hemorrhagic colitis." *Dairy, Food Environ. Sanit.,* 13:603.

Rodricks, J. V. (1976). "The occurrence and control of mycotoxins and mycotoxicoses." *Food Nutr. (FAO),* 2:9–14.

Sakaguchi, G. (1979). "Botulism." In *Food-Borne Infections and Intoxications,* H. Riemann and F. L. Bryan, Eds., 2nd ed. Academic Press, New York.

Sakazaki, R. (1979). "*Vibrio* Infections." In *Food-Borne Infections and Intoxications,* H. Riemann and F. L. Bryan, Eds., 2nd ed. Academic Press, New York.

Sakazaki, R. (1983). "*Vibrio parahaemolyticus* as a food-spoilage organism." In *Food Microbiology,* A. H. Rose, Ed. Academic Press, New York, London.

Saunders, G. C. and M. L. Barlett (1977). "Double antibody solid-phase enzyme immunoassay for the detection of staphylococcal enterotoxin A." *Appl. Environ. Microbiol.,* 34:518–522.

Schmidt, C. F. (1964). "Spores of *C. botulinum.*" In *Botulism,* U.S. Department of Health, Education and Welfare, Public Health Service Publication No. 999–FP–1, Cincinnati, OH.

Schmidt, C. F., R. V. Lechowich, and J. F. Folinazzo (1961). "Growth and toxin production by type E *Clostridium botulinum* below 40°F." *J. Food Sci.,* 26:626–630.

Seals, J. E., J. D. Snyder, T. A. Edell, E. L. Hatheway, C. J. Johnson, R. C. Swanson, and J. M. Hughes (1981). "Restaurant-associated type S botulism: Transmission by potato salad." *Am. J. Epidemiology,* 113:436–444.

Segalove, M. and G. M. Dack (1944). "Growth of a strain of *Salmonella enteritidis* experimentally inoculated into canned foods." *Food Res.,* 9:1–5.

Segner, W. P., C. F. Schmidt, and J. K. Baltz. (1964). "The effect of sodium chloride and pH on the outgrowth of spores of type E *Clostridium botulinum* at optimal and suboptimal temperatures." *Bacteriol. Proc., Am. Soc. Microbiol.,* 1964:3.

Shanders, W. X., C. O. Tacket, and P. A. Blake (1983). "Food poisoning due to *Clostridium perfringens* in the United States." *J. Inf. Dis.,* 143:167–170.

Shannon, E. L., G. W. Reinbold, and W. S. Clark, Jr. (1970). "Heat resistance of enterococci." *J. Milk Food Technol.,* 33:192–196.

Shayegani, M., D. L. Morse, I. DeForge, T. Root, L. M. Parsons, and P. S. Maupin (1983). "Microbiology of a major foodborne outbreak caused by *Yersinia enterocolitica* sero group 0:8." *J. Clin. Microbiol.,* 17:35–40.

Shayegani, M., I. DeForge, D. M. McGlynn, and T. Root (1981). "Characteristics of *Yersinia enterocolitica* and related species isolated from human, animal and environmental sources." *J. Clin. Microbiol.,* 14:304–312.

Silliker, J. H. (1981). "The *Salmonella* problem: Current status and future direction." *J. Food Prot.,* 45:661–666.

Smith, L., DS. (1962). "*Clostridium perfringens* Food Poisoning." In *Microbiological Quality of Foods,* L. W. Slanetz, G. D. Chichester, A. R. Gaufin, and Z. J. Ordal, Eds., Proceedings of a Conference held at Franconia, New Hampshire, Aug. 1962. Academic Press, New York.

Smith, L., DS. (1971). "Factors affecting the growth of *Clostridium perfringens.*" In *SOS/70 Proc. 3d Int. Congr. Food Sci. Technol., Inst. Food Technol.,* Chicago, IL.

Solberg, M. and B. Elkind (1970). "Effect of processing and storage conditions on the microflora of *Clostridium perfringens*—inoculated frankfurters." *J. Food Sci.,* 35:126–129.

Solomon, H. M., D. A. Kautter, and R. K. Lynt (1985). "Common characteristics of the Swiss and Argentine strain of *Clostridium botulinum* Type G." *J. Food Prot.,* 48(1):7–10.

Sperber, W. H. (1982). "Requirements of *Clostridium botulinum* for growth and toxin production." *Food Tech.,* 36(12):89–94.

Stern, N. J., M. D. Pierson, and A. W. Kotula (1980). "Effect of pH and sodium chloride on *Yersinia enterocolitica* growth at room and refrigeration temperatures." *J. Food Sci.,* 45:64–67.

Strong, D. H., C. L. Duncan, and G. Perna (1971). "*Clostridium perfringens* type A food poisoning. II. Response of the rabbit ileum as an indication of enteropathogenicity of strains of *Clostridium perfringens* in human beings." *Infect. Immunol.,* 3:171–178.

Strong, D. H., E. F. Foster, and C. L. Duncan (1970). "Influence of water activity on the growth of *Clostridium perfringens*." *Appl. Microbiol.,* 19:980–987.

Sugiyama, H. (1982). "Botulism hazards from nonprocesssed foods." *Food Technol.,* 36(12):113–115.

Surgalla, M., M. Segalove, and G. Dack (1944). "Growth of food-poisoning strain of alpha-type *Streptococcus* experimentally inoculated into canned foods." *Food Res.,* 9:112–114.

Svedham, Å., B. Kaijser, and E. Sjögren (1981). "The occurrence of *Campylobacter fetus jejuni* in fresh food and survival under different conditions." *J. Hyg.,* 87:421–425.

Swaminathan, B., J. A. G. Aleixo, and S. A. Minnich (1985). "Enzyme immunoassays for *Salmonella:* one day testing is now a reality." *Food Technol.,* (3):83–89.

Tarr, P. I. (1993). "*E. coli* 0157:H7 outbreak in the Western United States." *Dairy, Food Environ. Sanit.,* 13:592.

Tatini, S. R. (1973). "Influence of food environment on growth of *Staphylococcus* and production of various enterotoxins." *J. Milk Food Technol.,* 36:559–563.

Tatini, S. R. (1976). "Thermal stability of enterotoxins in food." *J. Milk Food Technol.,* 39:432–438.

Terranova, W. and P. A. Blake (1978). "*Bacillus cereus* food poisoning." *New Eng. J. Med.,* 298:143–144.

Todd, E. C. D. (1984). "Economic loss resulting from microbial contamination of food." In *Proceedings of the Second National Conference for Food Protection,* published by the U.S. Department of Health and Human Services, FDA Contract No. 223–84–2087. Pages 151–165.

Toma, S. and L. Lafleur (1974). "Survey on the incidence of *Yersinia enterocolitica* infection in Canada." *Appl. Microbiol.,* 28:469–473.

Toma, S. and V. R. Deidrick (1975). "Isolation of *Yersinia enterocolitica* from swine." *J. Clin. Microbiol.,* 2:478–481.

Turnbull, P. C. B., J. M. Kramer, K. Jorgensen, R. J. Gilbert, and J. Melling (1979). "Properties and production characteristics of vomiting, diarrheal, and necrotizing toxins of *Bacillus cereus*." *Am. J. Clin. Nutr.,* 32:219–228.

Twedt, R. M. and B. K. Boutin (1979). "Potential public health significance of non-*Escherichia coli* coliforms in food." *J. Food Prot.,* 42:161–163.

Uemura, T., G. Sakaguchi, T. Itoh, K. Okazawa, and S. Sakai (1975). "Experimental diarrhea in cynomolgus monkey by oral administration with *Clostridium perfringens* type A viable cells or enterotoxin." *Japan J. Med. Sci. Biol.*, 28:165–177.

van Walbeek, W. (1973). "Fungal toxins in foods." *Can. Inst. Food Sci. Technol. J.*, 6:96–104.

van Walbeek, W., P. M. Scott, and F. S. Thatcher (1968). "Mycotoxins from foodborne fungi." *Can. J. Microbiol.*, 14:131–137.

van Walbeek, W., T. Clademenos, and F. S. Thatcher (1969). "Influence of refrigeration on aflatoxin production by strains of *Aspergillus flavus.*" *Can. J. Microbiol.*, 15:629–632.

Vasconecelos, G. J., W. J. Strong, and R. H. Laidlow (1975). "Isolation of *Vibrio parahaemolyticus* and *Vibrio alginolyticus* from estuarine areas of Southeastern Alaska." *Appl. Microbiol.*, 29:557–559.

Weiss, M., T. Roberts, and H. Linstrom (1993). "Food safety issues: Modernizing meat inspection." *Agricultural Outlook.* A0–197. Economic Research Service, U.S. Department of Agriculture, Washington, D.C.

William-Walls, N.J. (1968). "*Clostridium botulinum* type F: Isolation from crabs." *Science,* 162(3851):375–376.

Woolford, A. L., E. J. Schantz, and M. J. Woodburn (1978). "Heat inactivation of botulinum toxin type A in some convenience foods after frozen storage." *J. Food Sci.,* 43:622–624.

Yang, K. H. and H. Sugiyama (1975). "Purification and properties of *Clostridium botulinum* type F toxin." *Appl. Microbiol.*, 29:598–603.

ADDITIONAL READINGS

Ahmed, A. A. H., M. K. Moustafa, and E. H. Marth. "Incidence of *Bacillus cereus* in milk and some milk products." *J. Food Prot.*, 46:126–128. 1983.

Ahmed, M. and H. W. Walker. "Germination of spores of *Clostridium perfringens.*" *J. Milk Food Technol.*, 34:378–384. 1971.

Baird-Parker, A. C. "Factors affecting the production of bacterial food poisoning toxins." *J. Appl. Bacteriol.*, 34:181–197. 1971.

Blaser, M. J., I. D. Berkowitz, F. M. Laforce, J. Cravens, L. B. Reller, and W. L. L. Wang. "*Campylobacter* enteritis: Chemical and epidemiologic features." *Am. Intern. Med.,* 91:179–185. 1979.

Blaser, M. J., P. Checko, C. Bopp, A. Bruce, and J. M. Hughes. "*Campylobacter* enteritis associated with foodborne transmission." *Am. J. Epidemiol.*, 116:886–894. 1982.

Bullerman, L. B. "Significance of mycotoxins to food safety and human health." *J. Food Prot.,* 42:65–86. 1979.

Christiansen, L. N., R. W. Johnston, D. A. Kautter, J. W. Howard, and W. J. Aunan. "Effect of nitrite and nitrate on toxin production by *Clostridium botulinum* and on nitrosamine formation in perishable canned comminuted cured meat." *Appl. Microbiol.,* 25:357–362. 1973.

Christiansen, L. N., B. B. Tompkins, A. B. Shaparis, T. V. Kueper, R. W. Johnston, D. A. Kautter, and O. J. Kolari. "Effect of sodium nitrite on toxin production by *Clostridium botulinum* in bacon." *Appl. Microbiol.*, 27:733–737. 1974.

Delmore, R. P., Jr., and F. D. Crisley. "Thermal resistance of *Vibrio parahaemolyticus* in clam homogenate." *J. Food Prot.,* 42:131–134. 1979.

Doupnik, B., Jr. and D. K. Bell. "Toxicity to chicks of *Aspergillus* and *Penicillium* species isolated from moldy pecans." *Appl. Microbiol.,* 21:1104–1106. 1971.

Doyle, M. P. and D. J. Roman. "Growth and survival of *Campylobacter fetus* subsp. *jejuni* as a function of temperature and pH." *J. Food Prot.,* 44:596–601. 1981.

Duggan, R. E. "Controlling aflatoxins." *FDA Papers,* 4(3):13–18. 1970.

Fischer, L. H., D. H. Strong, and C. L. Duncan. "Resistance of *Clostridium perfringens* to varying degrees of acidity during growth and sporulation." *J. Food Sci.,* 35:91–94. 1970.

Graham, H. D., Ed. *The Safety of Foods,* 2nd ed. Avi Publishing Co., Westport, CT.

Hackling, A. and J. Harrison, "Mycotoxins in Animal Feeds." In *Microbiology in Agriculture, Fisheries and Foods,* F. A. Skinner and J. G. Carr, Eds. Academic Press, London, New York, San Francisco. 1976.

Hobbs, B. and J. H. B. Christian, Eds. *The Microbiology of Foods.* Academic Press. New York, 1973.

Holmberg, S. D. and P. A. Blake. "Staphylococcal food poisoning in the United States: New facts and old misconceptions." *J. Am. Med. Assoc.,* 251(4):487–489. 1984.

Jarvis, B. "Factors affecting the production of mycotoxins." *J. Appl. Bacteriol.,* 34:199–213. 1971.

Jarvis, B. "Mycotoxins in Food." In *Microbiology in Agriculture, Fisheries and Foods,* F. A. Skinner and J. G. Carr, Eds. Academic Press, London, New York, San Francisco. 1976.

Karmali, M. A. "*Campylobacter* enteritis in children." *J. Pediatr.,* 94:527–533. 1979.

Markus, Z. H. and G. J. Silvermann. "Factors affecting the secretion of staphylococcal enterotoxin A." *Appl. Microbiol.,* 20:492–496. 1970.

Minor, T. E. and E. H. Marth. *Staphylococci and Their Significance in Foods.* Elsevier Scientific Publishing Co., Amsterdam, New York. 1976.

Moreau, C. *Moulds, Toxins and Foods.* Transl. with add. material by M. Moss. John Wiley & Sons, Chichester. 1979.

Nelson, K. J. and N. N. Potter. "Growth of *Vibrio parahaemolyticus* at low salt levels and in nonmarine foods." *J. Food Sci.,* 41:1413–1417. 1976.

Racvuori, M. and C. Genigeorgis. "Effect of pH and sodium chloride on growth of *Bacillus cereus* in laboratory media and certain foods." *Appl. Microbiol.,* 29:68–73. 1975.

Roberts, H. R., Ed. *Food Safety.* John Wiley and Sons, New York. 1981.

Saunders, G. C. and M. L. Bartlett. "Double-antibody solid-phase enzyme immuno assay for the detection of staphylococcal enterotoxin A." *Appl. Environ. Microbiol.,* 34:518–522. 1977.

Schlech, W. F. III, P. M. Lavigne, R. A. Bortolussi, A. C. Allen, E. V. Haldane, A. J. Wort, A. W. Hightower, S. E. Johnson, S. H. King, E. S. Nicholls, and C. V. Broome. "Epidemic listeriosis—Evidence for transmission of food." *N. Engl. J. Med.,* 308:203–206. 1983.

Thomas, C. T., J. C. White, and K. Longrée. "Thermal resistance of salmonellae and staphylococci in foods." *Appl. Microbiol.,* 14:815–820. 1966.

Wilson, B. J. "Hazards of mycotoxins to public health." *J. Food Prot.,* 41:375–384. 1978.

CHAPTER 5

Reservoirs of Microorganisms Causing Foodborne Gastroenteric Outbreaks: People, Animals, Environment

R eservoirs of the bacteria that cause foodborne gastroenteric illnesses are human beings and the animals they keep, sewage, manure, soil, water, air, rodents, insects, and the food supply. Water and soil frequently acquire pathogens from sewage (human source) and manure (animal source); in turn, the food supply may acquire pathogens from all the above-named sources. Thus, humans and animals emerge as the fundamental sources of the organisms that are responsible for foodborne gastrointestinal illnesses.

PEOPLE

Of special interest to the foodservice manager is the inherent danger from the bacterial flora of the healthy person and carrier. Persons suffering from obvious communicable diseases are not as likely to prepare food for the public as is the carrier. A carrier is a person who harbors and disseminates the disease-producing microbes without having the symptoms of the disease. He or she may have recovered from the disease or may never have been ill at all. Carriers are immune to the organisms that they harbor in their system.

Skin

The human skin is never free of bacteria; even clean skin carries some organisms. But, when skin is not clean, an impressive number and variety of microorganisms are present, including bacteria, molds, yeasts, and protozoa. Since people use their hands for many different purposes, they touch a great many things, acquiring the microbial population from almost everything they contact. This population of microorganisms is apt to include pathogens capable of causing various foodborne gastroenterites.

The bacteria clinging to the skin may multiply there, especially near the sebaceous glands. Although thorough washing removes many bacteria from the skin, some microorganisms are apt to remain.

The common flora of the human skin includes representatives of the genus *Staphylococcus,* one being the nonpathogenic *S. epidermidis; S. aureus,* however, includes strains that are able to multiply in food and form toxins, which, when such food is ingested, cause the dreaded intoxications or food poisonings. Other common bacteria associated with the human skin are micrococci and other aerobics. The reader is referred to an extensive study by Kloos and Musselwhite (1975).

It has been estimated that at least one-half of the normal, healthy population harbors virulent, or potentially virulent, staphylococci. Staphylococci are generally found in connection with pimples, acne, skin wounds, and other inflamed skin conditions. Some pyogenic strains of *S. aureus* may cause skin infections of various kinds. The resistance of the body to staphylococci varies with the virulence of the organisms and the resistance of the invaded tissues.

Furunculosis is a type of infection that follows a cut or simple abrasion. Carbuncles are a more severe skin disorder that follow the invasion of the staphylococci into the deeper tissues. While the furuncle is characterized by a single superficial abscess, the carbuncle involves a large area of deeper tissues characterized by the formation of several "heads" containing pus and staphylococci. Impetigo contagiosa is a contagious skin infection characterized by small pustules which occur on the face but may also spread to other parts of the body. Paronychia is an infection of the nail bed of either fingers or toes. Scratching of infected skin transfers the staphylococci to the hands, especially the nails.

From the foregoing discussion it is obvious that, in foodservice, the person afflicted with pyogenic infections of the skin is a menace; unfortunately, the person who is so afflicted is usually not ill enough to stay away from work. Furthermore, since the infections are largely localized on the exposed body parts, the fingers, hands, arms, and face, an infected food handler is in a particularly excellent position to spread these organisms around, contaminating the food and equipment he or she touches and sowing the seeds of food poisoning in the food preparation area.

Seligman and Rosenbluth (1975) studied the complex etiological relationships in food production as a permanent interaction among three factors: Food, environment, and food handler. Interestingly, coagulase-positive staphylococci changed their status of transient bacteria and became permanent residents on the food handlers' skin.

Mouth, Nose, Throat, Eyes, and Ears

The areas of the mouth, nose, and throat of a healthy human abound with microorganisms of various kinds. The environment is moist and warm, and acceptable nutrients are available to the bacteria in the form of remnants from food consumed by the human.

Among the numerous kinds of microorganisms represented, one is of outstanding significance here, namely *Staphylococcus aureus,* which lodges in the respiratory passages of many healthy individuals. According to a review by Williams (1963), the rates of healthy carriers ranged from 30 to 50%. If persons associated with a hospital were included in the tabulation, the incidence of nasal carriage was higher yet—60 to 80%. Virulent strains of the organism are associated with ailments such as sinusitis and the common cold. Persons recovering from these ailments may remain carriers for extended periods. *S. aureus* is also frequently associated with infections of the eyes and ears.

Persons suffering from infections of the respiratory tract, eyes, and ears, or who are carriers while or after recovering from these diseases, must be suspected of being a rich source of virulent staphylococci and should be prevented from handling food.

Obviously, individuals who suffer from, or are recovering from, serious illnesses, such as tuberculosis, scarlet fever, septic sore throat, and diphtheria, are very liable to contaminate food if allowed to handle it. The causative organisms may be discharged from the patients for varying periods of time after the acute stage has passed. The reader is referred to Chapter 3.

Intestinal Tract

The composition of the intestinal flora of the healthy human body may vary with certain external factors. The first part of the small intestine has, like the stomach, no natural microbial flora. In the jejunum and ileum, microorganisms begin to appear. It is in the lower end of the small intestine that a variety of bacteria are found in large numbers. The major representatives are the coliforms, *Escherichia coli* and *Aerobacter aerogenes.* Bacteria important in connection with foodborne illnesses are *Clostridium perfringens,* fecal streptococci (enterococci), salmonellae, and occasionally staphylococci. The salmonellae are particularly plentiful in the intestinal tracts of persons recovering from salmonelloses.

It is important for foodservice management to realize that some of the pathogens for which food is a vehicle of transmission may remain in the human carrier for prolonged periods of time, as in the case of typhoid fever, the dysenteries, the salmonelloses, and hepatitis. In typhoid fever, convalescent carriers usually discharge the bacteria for 8–10 weeks following recovery, but some patients become chronic or permanent carriers for the rest of their lives. Following salmonellosis victims may remain carriers for several weeks; *S. derby* has been found to persist for months in the victims' intestinal system (Sanders and Friedman, 1965).

Patients who have recovered from bacillary dysentery or shigellosis are carriers for a while, but no chronic carriers result from this infection. Patients who have recovered from amoebic dysentery may become chronic carriers for the rest of their lives. The hepatitis virus has been found to remain with patients from one to five years.

Since a food handler would be, in general, without symptoms when most infectious, he or she would be a menace when handling food, be it in the area of preparation, service, or storage (*Morbidity and Mortality Weekly Report,* 1977). Peak excretion of the hepatitis virus by way of elimination of feces occurs prior to the onset of symptoms.

It is readily understandable that the principles of control include these important items: (1) exclusion of carriers from the area of food preparation and service; (2) education of foodservice workers in the importance of sanitary habits; and (3) unrelenting supervision.

ANIMALS

Livestock

Staphylococcus aureus is an inhabitant of the nose, mouth, throat, and skin of farm animals. However, Morrison et al. (1961), who reviewed the literature on the subject and studied the incidence of staphylococci in cattle and horses, concluded that the majority of the forms are coagulase-negative and therefore not likely to be potentially virulent.

Fecal streptococci, *Clostridium perfringens,* and coliforms are natural inhabitants of the intestinal tract of livestock.

Salmonellae have been shown to be frequent inhabitants of farm animals, including horses, cattle, and hogs (Moran, 1961; Galton, 1963). These animals may become carriers.

According to a report by Galton (1963) of a survey made in Florida, hogs frequently harbor salmonellae. The organisms spread when the animals are crowded together in barns during the months when pasturing is not possible. Crowding during shipment to the abattoirs and in the corrals near abattoirs increases salmonellae incidence up to tenfold the normal amount found in farm animals.

In a study made in Florida, Galton and Hardy (1953) found that the relative prevalence of most common *Salmonella* types isolated from man, swine, and dogs was similar. This seems to indicate that infections were either spread from one host to the other, or that these salmonellae came originally from the same source.

Poultry

Poultry may become an important reservoir of *Staphylococcus aureus* when the skin of the live bird has been injured and the bruises have become infected with staphylococci. Hamdy and Barton (1965) demonstrated that multiplication of *S. aureus* is related to the severity of the bruise.

Poultry is the greatest single animal reservoir of *Salmonella,* including strains pathogenic to man. A high proportion, approximately one-half, of the *Salmonella*-caused gastroenteric outbreaks in man are traced to poultry products.

It seems that poultry has an unusual susceptibility to salmonellae. One of the species, *S. pullorum,* seriously affects baby chicks and poults, causing many fatalities. The organism invades practically all of the internal organs. In the United States the poultry-raising industry has made a supreme effort to eradicate *S. pullorum* from flocks and has been quite successful by testing birds for carriers, eliminating carriers, hatching eggs from sources known to be free of the disease, and maintaining high sanitary standards in the plants. *Salmonella pullorum* does not seem to be pathogenic to man. However, it has been demonstrated in some instances that the ingestion of massive doses of the organism caused gastrointestinal disorders in the volunteers participating in the experiments.

Other species and strains of *Salmonella* harbored by poultry, among these *S. typhimurium,* are also pathogenic to man. Poultry, especially turkeys, are known to become carriers of these organisms. The adult carriers usually look healthy and escape culling for disease. Therefore, they represent a constant source of infection to other birds and a source of contamination to eggs (Quist, 1963). When the birds are processed into meat, the flesh is likely to become contaminated with salmonellae originating from the intestinal tract.

The shells of eggs become a source of *Salmonella* and may contaminate the contents when the shell and membranes are injured, or when the shell is deliberately opened in the egg-processing plant and kitchen.

Control measures include, for all livestock and poultry, the elimination of carriers of *Salmonella,* high sanitary standards in the care of farm animals and poultry flocks, and the use of feedstuffs known to be free from *Salmonella* (Morehouse and Wedman, 1961).

Pets

Morrison et al. (1961) studied *Staphylococcus aureus* in dogs and cats. They found that carrier rates of coagulase-positive, antibiotic-resistant staphlococci on the skin and nose were high in the canine and feline species. The authors concluded that domestic animals may serve as sources of pathogenic staphylococci.

These companions of humans are known to harbor many serotypes of *Salmonella* (Mackel et al., 1952). In a study involving greyhounds in Florida, Stucker et al. (1952) were able to relate the extent of incidences to the sanitation in the kennels. Even family dogs have been shown to be extensively infected with salmonellae. *Salmonella* incidences in dogs have been related to intake of *Salmonella*-contaminated, underprocessed dog food (Galton et al., 1955).

Salmonella from turtles has also been reported to cause foodborne gastroenteric outbreaks. Case histories showed that the contaminated agent was the turtles' water, which was discarded into the kitchen sink. Although the chances are remote that food prepared in public eating places becomes contaminated from such a source, opportunities might be afforded when food is prepared in the family kitchen for community meal service, or when children handling pets are taking part in meal preparation, as may happen in a camp situation.

The potential health hazards arising from transmission of *Salmonella* from household pets to humans should not be taken lightly. In 1975, the FDA imposed a ban on interstate shipment of pet turtles of certain sizes, excepting shipments to zoos and scientific or educational institutions (*Morbidity and Mortality Weekly Report,* 1975).

Pets do not belong in an area where food is prepared, served, and stored. Persons who have handled pets should change clothing and wash up thoroughly before handling food. Although these hygienic practices are obligatory for personnel employed by foodservice establishments, they are not always enforced and they are not always likely to be followed when food is prepared in the home for community food service.

The control of salmonellae in pet food is another means of reducing the incidence of salmonelloses in pets and indirectly in man.

Rodents

Rats and mice may contaminate food during harvest, in transport, in storage, and in the food preparation area. These animals carry disease-producing organisms on their feet and/or in their intestinal tracts. Rats, in particular, have a habit of feeding in places of filth, like garbage dumps and sewers.

These rodents are known to harbor salmonellae of serotypes frequently associated with foodborne infections in man, such as *Salmonella typhimurium, enteritidis,* and *newport.*

Poultry producers in this country are plagued by rats and suffer great losses from their activity caused not only by loss of feed eaten by the rats, but also by the disease which rats pass on to poultry. Rats infect, by their droppings, poultry feed and eggs with *Salmonella.* Rats are largely nocturnal animals and are among the most prolific of mammals. Their appetite for food is tremendous. The control of rats is most essential but, unfortunately, is more difficult than the control of mice. Rats are very suspicious animals and evade trapping.

Rats and mice must be kept out of places where food animals, feed, and food are housed. They should be exterminated from appropriate access places where they like to feed, like garbage cans; these places should be protected. Rodents must be kept out of the areas where food is stored, prepared, and served.

Insects

FLIES. The fly most frequently associated with people is the housefly, *Musa domestica.* This species is the predominant one found in food establishments. During warm weather, two or more housefly generations per month may be produced. The female lays large numbers of eggs each time and populations increase at a tremendous rate. In the winter, the housefly seeks protected areas. In temperate climatic zones, the fly passes the winter months by a combination of adult hibernation and semicontinuous breeding.

Animal manure, human feces, sewage, and garbage are favored breeding places of flies. Open garbage cans and dumps are, therefore, a menace to sanitation.

Flies frequently carry disease-causing organisms in their mouth parts, intestinal tracts, and on their leg hairs and feet. Since flies feed on feces, animal manure, and human filth, all of which may contain intestinal pathogens of human and animal origin, they are an important reservoir of microorganisms causing many foodborne illnesses; among these are the salmonelloses, typhoid fever, and dysenteries. Flies are attracted to many foods. Carbohydrates are needed as well as proteins, the latter being required for production of eggs. Flies are constantly moving about, taking nourishment here and there. Since they are attracted to feces as well as to food, they are a menace to food sanitation; as the fly feeds on the materials on which it alights, it periodically regurgitates liquid from the crop. This liquid may contain pathogens picked up from fecal material on which the animal fed previously. Therefore, it is extremely important that the food supply be protected from flies at all times.

COCKROACHES.   Cockroaches are one of the most common and trouble-some pests in food establishments. There are several kinds—the American, German, Brown-Banded, and Oriental are most frequently seen.

Cockroaches are nocturnal in habit and scurry away to hide when disturbed. They may leave a musty odor on objects on which they rest for a while; another sign of their presence is a stain which they leave with their rather liquid feces. When dry, droppings resemble mouse pellets, but they are distinguished by lengthwise ridges.

Cockroaches are able to contaminate more food than they are able to eat. They are particularly fond of starchy foods, cheese, and beer; but they will also feed on dead animals, leather, wallpaper, and the like. They contaminate food, equipment, and utensils by carrying filthy material that may contain pathogens on their legs and bodies. Also, while feeding on food, cockroaches may regurgitate filthy material previously eaten which may be laden with bacteria capable of causing foodborne illnesses.

ANTS AND SILVERFISH.   Ants are frequently pests in some food establishments, including camps. Ants may carry disease organisms around and thus may contaminate the food. Their life cycle consists of eggs, larvae, pupae, and adults.

Silverfish are related to the centipedes. They like warmth and are often found to infest warm places, such as the neighborhood of bakery ovens where they feed on crumbs. Silverfish like starchy foods.

In summary, foods must be protected from insects at all times. To achieve this, basic sanitation must be constantly applied because it deprives the insects of food and shelter. For chemical control, the services of professional exterminators should be sought. However, only permanent methods such as pestproofing and sanitation can achieve long-time control (Johnson, 1960).

ENVIRONMENT

Sewage

COMPOSITION.   Sewage consists of fecal matter of human origin, much diluted with water, and other wastes such as laundry water, bath water, and residues resulting from comminuted household garbage, mostly vegetable matter and similar wastes. Sewage is approximately 99% water and has a pH near neutral.

FLORA.   The flora of sewage includes aerobes, strict anaerobes, and facultative anaerobes. The bacteria include forms that stem from soil and the intestinal tract of humans. Examples of bacteria are fecal streptococci, *Clostridium perfringens, Salmonella, Shigella,* micrococci, Pseudomonadacae, and Lactobacillaceae. Also present may be viruses, yeasts, molds, algalike forms, and slime-forming organisms often called "sewage fungi." These organisms aid in one way or another to decompose the organic matter in sewage.

Sewage is thus a potential source of human pathogens, especially those of intestinal origin. Sewage plays a most important role in the contamination of water and food.

CONTAMINATION OF WATER AND FOOD.   The chances for contamination are manifold. Excellent opportunity is afforded when sewage is used to fertilize fields in which vegetable crops are raised. In this country, the use of raw sewage for the purpose of fertilization of truck crops is not practiced.

When sewage is allowed to flow into rivers, lakes, and seas, it contributes its flora, including pathogens, to the fish, shellfish, and other potential foods native to these waters. Sewage also creates a nuisance; when raw domestic sewage is not properly treated by oxidation and is allowed to flow directly into natural waters such as ponds, lakes, and streams, the microorganisms furnished by the raw sewage soon deplete these waters of oxygen and other hydrogen acceptors. In consequence, anaerobic processes develop, creating foul-smelling products and making conditions for natural biologic life of these waters very unfavorable. A most undesirable situation is thus created. Besides these waters not being usable for drinking or recreational purposes, they have spoiled much of the surrounding areas because of their distasteful odor.

Drinking water may become contaminated with sewage in various ways. In some rural and suburban areas the water supply is not as strictly and permanently controlled as in most cities. Also, in dwellings that have their own water source as well as sewage disposal tanks, cross-connection sometimes occurs.

TREATMENT.   In most communities, raw sewage is rendered safer by these steps: (1) collection in septic tanks or central sewage disposal plants; (2) separation of the organic materials by gravity as the sewage is held for several hours; (3) digestion of the sludge through mostly anaerobic microorganisms; (4) processing of the sludge to a powder which serves as a fertilizer; (5) treating the supernatant fluid part by aeration and oxidation with the aid of aerobic bacteria; (6) filtering the residual oxidized fluid; and (7) as a possible final step, chlorination of the fluid. The major steps in sewage treatment have been illustrated by Pelczar and Reid (1965).

Control measures should be directed at preventing the contact of sewage with food and water.

Perfectly pure and wholesome food and water may be recontaminated on the premises of a food service establishment through faulty plumbing and leaky sewer connections.

Soil

The soil abounds with microorganisms, abundant in kind as well as in number. The microorganisms from soil affect the microbial flora of air, water, plants, and animals. In turn, soil may become contaminated by sewage and manure.

All microorganisms of importance in connection with foodborne illness may come from soil. Of bacteria causing foodborne illnesses, *Clostridium botulinum* and *perfringens* are natural inhabitants of soil and may survive there for very long periods of time.

Soil may enter the areas of food preparation and storage in many ways: with the food and its wrappings, on the employees' shoes, and in the air. Most "dust" is actually soil.

Water

In the United States sanitation of drinking water is well controlled, in general, by agencies concerned with public health. In fact, the present generation must find it rather difficult to visualize the seriousness of a situation when a public water supply becomes contaminated with pathogens. Waterborne outbreaks of typhoid and paratyphoid fevers have almost disappeared from the records.

Unfortunately, industrial waste has gradually become a real problem and a threat to the quality of drinking water in certain areas (see Chapter 3).

FLORA.   Water found in nature is seldom sterile. Water coming down as rain or snow picks up contaminants from the air, and as it contacts the ground it picks up contaminants from the soil and other surfaces. Thus, surface waters of streams, lakes, and seas contain these microorganisms also. As water penetrates the ground the soil has a filtering effect, and many of the contaminants that move downward with the water are removed. The deeper the water goes, the cleaner it becomes, although seldom is water rendered sterile by this kind of filtration.

Surface waters usually contain more organic matter than deep waters and thus support microbial life better. Near cities, surface waters are frequently contaminated with sewage, and in the country with sewage as well as manure. Other miscellaneous contaminants are contributed as industrial wastes.

After making a worldwide review of the literature dealing with microbial pollution of water, Bryan (1977), concluded that typhoid fevers, infectious hepatitis, and cholera are among the diseases most frequently transmitted by water and food that had been contaminated through contact with sewage or by irrigation water, in agricultural or aquacultural practices.

Most microorganisms, including the pathogens, do not multiply profusely in pure water. They may sustain life for a while and then die. Spores, however, may survive for months or years in water.

Although natural waters have a capacity to assimilate as well as transport waste, increase in wastes from the population and industrial plants is making it increasingly important that ways other than simple dilution be found to dispose of these wastes. The water of some streams and rivers is already being used over several times, especially at periods of low flow.

People should not rely upon self-purification of streams for pure supply of water. The popular belief that streams clarify themselves within a distance of 20 miles from the source of pollution has numerous loopholes. Purification is strongly affected by rate of flow; in fast-flowing streams the dilution of organic matter and of microorganisms is much more efficient than in slow-flowing ones. In ponds and reservoirs, water becomes purified by sedimentation. It has been stated that up to 90% of the bacteria can be removed in this manner.

Although industrial wastes seriously reduce the quality of our water supply, an extremely important source of pollution of public health significance is sewage. Fecal coliforms, fecal staphylococci, enterococci, salmonellae, and clostridia are even discharged from healthy persons, and, of course, from carriers, and are transferred with sewage into the water. Persons who suffer from acute cases of intestinal diseases contribute tremendous numbers of virulent pathogens into sewage. Serious and widespread epidemics of communicable diseases have resulted from fouled water supplies. Today, waterborne epidemics of typhoid and dysentery are rare in the United States but are still found in other parts of the world.

Pathogenic bacteria and viruses do not multiply in water. To be a hazard, a water supply must either be freshly contaminated or possess a continuous source of contaminants.

The numbers of waterborne disease outbreaks reported to the Centers for Disease Control (CDC) for the years 1971–1983 are shown in Table 5.1. Table 5.2 gives a breakdown of waterborne disease reported in 1983, by etiology and type of water system.

According to the CDC (1984), a waterborne disease outbreak is an incident

TABLE 5.1.   *Waterborne Disease Outbreaks, by Year and Type of System, United States, 1971–1983*

	Community	Noncommunity	Private	Total	Total Cases
1971	5	10	4	19	5,182
1972	10	18	2	30	1,650
1973	5	16	3	24	1,784
1974	11	10	5	26	8,363
1975	6	16	2	24	10,879
1976	9	23	3	35	5,068
1977	12	19	3	34	3,860
1978	10	18	4	32	11,435
1979	23	14	4	41	9,720
1980	23	22	5	50	20,008
1981	14	16	2	32	4,430
1982	22	12	6	40	3,456
1983	29	6	5	40	20,905
Total (%)	179 (41.9)	200 (46.8)	48 (11.2)	427	106,740

Source: Centers for Disease Control, U.S. Department of Health and Human Services, Public Health Service (1984). *Water-Related Disease Outbreaks. Surveillance—Annual Summary 1983.*

in which (1) two or more persons experience similar illness after consumption or use of water intended for drinking, and (2) epidemiologic evidence implicates the water as the source of illness. In addition, a single case of chemical poisoning constitutes an outbreak if laboratory studies indicate that the water was contaminated by the chemical. Only outbreaks associated with water intended for drinking are included.

In 1983, 40 waterborne disease outbreaks involving an estimated 20,905 persons were reported to the CDC and the Environmental Protection Agency (EPA). This represents the largest number of cases reported since surveillance began in 1971.

The bacteriology of water supplies, drinking water as well as plant water, has also been discussed in brief form by Frazier and Westhoff (1978) and Lehr (1975).

Waterborne outbreaks of acute gastrointestinal disease on oceangoing vessels, reported for 1975–1978, were significantly less frequent on vessels with sanitation scores that met the Public Health Standards than on vessels that did not (Dannenberg et al., 1982).

TABLE 5.2. *Waterborne Disease Outbreaks by Etiology and Type of Water System, 1983*

	Public Water Systems				Private Water Systems		Total	
	Community		Noncommunity					
	Outbreaks	Cases	Outbreaks	Cases	Outbreaks	Cases	Outbreaks	Cases
AGI[a]	8	4,612	6	11,875	1	11	15	16,498
Giardia	16	2,203	0	0	1	4	17	2,207
Hepatitis A	1	6	0	0	2	158	3	164
Salmonella	2	1,150	0	0	0	0	2	1,150
Shigella	0	0	0	0	1	12	1	12
Campylobacter	1	871	0	0	0	0	1	871
Chemical	1	3	0	0	0	0	1	3
Total	29	8,845	6	11,875	5	185	40	20,905

[a]Acute gastrointestinal illness of unknown etiology.
Source: Centers for Disease Control, U.S. Department of Health and Human Services, Public Health Service (1984). *Water-Related Disease Outbreaks. Surveillance—Annual Summary 1983.*

OTHER CONTAMINANTS.   A variety of nonmicrobial contaminants are furnished by household wastes (i.e., detergents), industrial wastes of many kinds, and products used in farming (i.e., pesticides, mineral fertilizers). Some of these have been recognized as harmful agents for years, and action was initiated to have these wastes pretreated at the source before they are discharged into streams, lakes, and other places where they would be likely to contaminate the drinking water supply. Unfortunately, these attempts to stave off increasing pollution at the source have so far met with only partial success.

Pesticides may find their way into wells, streams, and lakes through runoff of rain, or through gradual soil percolation. Some of these compounds are very stable and do not break down and "disappear." And they may not become completely removed from the water during its purification for drinking purposes. An example of water contamination by inorganic fertilizers is the undesirably high nitrate content of some water which is apt to be caused by high applications to field crops of nitrogen fertilizers; however, high nitrate content of spring water has also been detected in largely forested areas (Smith, 1967). It seems that the danger of high nitrate concentration in the drinking water lies in the conversion of nitrate to nitrite in the intestinal tract, by the action of certain intestinal bacteria. Infants seem to be particularly prone to suffer from the toxic effects of the nitrites, which may cause methemoglobinemia (Marienfeld, 1965; Winton, 1970). Research to elucidate these and other problems pertaining to the purity of our water supply is very active at present.

The impact of pesticides on the quality of drinking water is hotly debated. It is well documented that numerous fish kills have resulted from pesticides present in their habitat. It is another question if, or at what level of contamination, pesticides will endanger human beings. There is the possibility of a long-term toxic effect (Huang, 1972).

The drinking water supply is endangered by many factors in addition to pesticides. These include the dumping of landfills, sewage, garbage, wastepiles, stockpiles, and highway salt, and oil and gas leakage. The reader is referred to Lehr (1975) and his discussion of the Safe Drinking Water Act. It was estimated in 1978 that governments and industry had already spent many billions of dollars on water pollution control. Although the EPA pushes the effort, much more cooperative effort, money, and goodwill must be invested in the future.

TREATMENT.   To safeguard the water supply it is essential that the disposal of sewage be strictly controlled. Improper disposal of sewage is, in particular, a menace to private water supply systems, which may escape the constant scrutiny to which the public water supply is subjected. The treatment of sewage was discussed above. In the United States the water supply is generally of excellent quality, thanks to strict sanitary supervision and treatment.

Requirements for a public water supply are listed by Weiser (1971) as the following:

1. That it shall contain no organisms which cause disease
2. That it be sparkling clear and colorless
3. That it be good tasting, free from odors and preferably cool
4. That it be neither scale-forming nor corrosive
5. That it be reasonably soft
6. That it be free from objectionable gas, such as hydrogen sulfide, and objectionable minerals, such as iron and manganese
7. That it be plentiful and low in cost

The test for freedom from pathogens is the presumptive test for coliform bacteria, which comprise two species, *Escherichia coli* and *Aerobacter aerogenes*. The former is an intestinal organism, the latter is found more frequently in soils and on plant surfaces.

In the test for presence of these indicators, dilutions of the water are cultured in fermentation tubes of lactose broth at a temperature of 98.6°F (37°C). If acid and gas are produced, it is assumed that coliforms are present, and more detailed tests are performed.

Almost all our drinking water undergoes treatment before it is released to the public. Although water may purify itself under certain conditions, this purification is rather inefficient and cannot be relied on for a supply of safe water. In the United States, aeration, coagulation, filtration, and chemical treatment are used. Aeration helps to purify the water from dissolved gases and to oxidize iron as well as organic matter.

The chemical treatments serve to adjust the hardness of the water and to control the bacterial population. Chlorine has characteristics that make it desirable as a chemical agent in the treatment of water; it is highly bactericidal and not expensive. Viruses and the protozoa *Entamoeba histolytica* resist chlorination.

Failure to chlorinate water resulted in a serious and extensive outbreak of gastroenteritis caused by *Salmonella typhimurium* in Riverside, California (*Morbidity and Mortality Weekly Report,* 1965). The community water supply consisted of deep wells inside and outside the city. The water had always been pure and had never been chlorinated. Regular testing for the presence of *Escherichia coli* did not reveal high counts, even during the time of the *Salmonella* outbreak.

Water used in the processing and preparation of food should be of drinking quality. Water is used in food as an ingredient and as a cleaning agent for ingredients and equipment. Water must, therefore, be free from pathogens.

Drinking water must meet public health standards when tested by the methods recommended in the latest edition of *Standard Methods for the Examination of Water and Wastewater* (American Public Health Association, 1977).

When a food establishment does not receive a piped-in supply of pure water, it may have to transport water from an approved outside supply in approved containers. In an emergency, boiling may be used to destroy pathogens present in water. Certain chemicals of bactericidal effect may be used for small quantities of water, if the directions are followed meticulously. Treatment of large amounts is to be entrusted to a trained person.

Ice manufactured from contaminated water, and ice manufactured, stored, or shipped under unsanitary conditions may contaminate food and drink in which it is used.

A comprehensive treatise on the subject of water pollution is beyond the scope of this book, and the reader is referred to texts on this complex subject, such as that by Mitchell (1972).

Air

Air does not contain a natural flora of microorganisms, but dust particles or moisture droplets present in air may pick up microorganisms. Therefore, air may serve as a reservoir of contaminants. If forced air is used on foods, contamination of food from air is greater than in still air.

The kinds and numbers of microorganisms present in air are so varied that enumeration is beyond the scope of this book. The numbers and kinds of microorganisms depend on many factors, among them location and season. Rain and snow remove organisms from the air. On mountaintops the air is generally low in microbial counts.

AIR IN FOOD PREPARATION AREA.   The kinds of microorganisms found in the air in a given area depend on many factors. Droplets of moisture from persons talking, coughing, and sneezing may contribute microorganisms to the air. Soil clinging to shoes and other clothing and soil adhering to materials brought into a room are examples of the sources of microorganisms that may be transmitted through air. Diseases that are typically transmitted through air are the common cold and some other respiratory illnesses spread by droplets discharged by the affected person. It is known that bacteria may be spread through coughs and sneezes to considerable distances, up to 15 feet.

The number of microorganisms present in a given air space depends on many factors, among them presence of dust and droplets of moisture and air movement brought about by ventilation breezes or persons moving about.

The bacterial content of air can be diluted by simply opening a window and letting in fresh air. However, admitting dusty air would not achieve much or may make matters worse. Air conditioning can be used to control the bacteriological quality of air in a food service establishment. Removal of microorganisms from air can be achieved by methods such as filtration, heat, electrostatic precipitation, and treatment by chemicals. Filtration involves the passing of air through filters. Chemicals used for reducing the microbial load of air include di- or triethylene glycol, propylene glycol, formaldehyde, *o-p-*benzyl phenols, and hypochlorites.

Ultraviolet rays are also used to reduce the bacterial load of air. Rays of wavelengths 136–3,900 Ås are germicidal, those between 2500 and 2800 Å are particularly effective. Each kind of microorganism has a specific resistance to these rays. It may take several times as much exposure to kill vegetative cells of one kind of bacteria as of another. Spores are more resistant to the killing effect than vegetative cells.

Ultraviolet rays are used very little in food service, but are to some extent employed in processing rooms. Some of the examples of successful uses are, among others, treatment of water for beverages, aging of meat, treatment of knives for slicing bread and cakes, sanitizing of eating utensils, and treatment of air for, or in, storage and processing rooms.

REFERENCES

American Public Health Association (1977). *Standard Methods for the Examination of Water and Wastewater,* 14th ed. American Public Health Association, New York.

Bryan, F. L. (1977). "Disease transmitted by waste water." *J. Food Prot.,* 40:45–56.

Centers for Disease Control, U.S. Department of Health and Human Services, Public Health Serv. (1984). *Water-Related Disease Outbreaks, Surveillance—Annual Summary 1983.*

Dannenberg, A. L., J. C. Yashuk, and R. A. Feldman (1982). "Gastrointestinal illness on passenger cruise ships, 1975–1978." *Am. J. Publ. Health,* 72:484–488.

Frazier, W. C. and D. C. Westhoff (1978). *Food Microbiology,* 3rd ed. McGraw-Hill Book Co., New York.

Galton, M. M. (1963). "Salmonellosis in livestock." In *Epidemiology of Salmonellosis, U.S. Public Health Rep.,* 78:1066–1070.

Galton, M. M. and A. V. Hardy (1953). "The distribution of *Salmonella* infections in Florida during the past decade." *Public Health Lab.,* 11:88–93.

Galton, M. M., M. Harless, and A. V. Hardy (1955). "*Salmonella* isolations from dehydrated dog meals." *J. Am. Vet. Med. Assoc.,* 126:57–58.

Hamdy, M. K. and N. D. Barton (1965). "Fate of *Staphylococcus aureus* in bruised tissue." *Appl. Microbiol.,* 13:13–21.

Huang, J. C. (1972). "Pesticides in water—Effects on human health." *J. Environ. Health,* 34:501–508.

Johnson, W. H. (1960). "Sanitation in the control of insects and rodents of public health importance." Public Health Service Publication No. 772, Part IV, Government Printing Office, Washington, D.C.

Kloos, W. E. and M. S. Musselwhite (1975). "Distribution and persistence of *Staphylococcus* and *Micrococcus* species and other aerobic bacteria on human skin." *Appl. Microbiol.,* 30:381–395.

Lehr, J. H. (1975). "The Safe Drinking Water Act—First 180 days." *J. Environ. Health,* 38(Sept.–Oct.):88–91.

Mackel, D. C., M. M. Galton, H. Gray, and A. V. Hardy (1952). "Salmonellosis in dogs. IV. Prevalence in normal dogs and their contacts." *J. Infect. Dis.,* 91:15–18.

Marienfeld, C. J. (1965). "Water forum—Nitrates in human health." *Missouri Agric. Exper. Sta. Spec. Rep.,* 55:37–38.

Mitchell, Ralph, Ed. (1972). *Water Pollution Microbiology.* Wiley-Interscience, New York.

Moran, A. B. (1961). "Occurrence and distribution of *Salmonella* in animals in the United States." In *Proceedings, 65th Annual Meeting, U.S. Livestock Sanitary Association,* Minneapolis, MN, Oct. Pages 441–448.

Morbidity and Mortality Weekly Report (1965). U.S. Department of Health, Education and Welfare, Public Health Serv., Center Dis. Contr.,14, June 5; 14, June 12.

Morbidity and Mortality Weekly Report (1975). U.S. Department of Health, Education and Welfare, Public Health Serv., Center Dis. Contr., 24, May 31.

Morbidity and Mortality Weekly Report (1977). U.S. Department of Health, Education and Welfare, Public Health Serv., Center Dis. Contr., 26, July 29.

Morehouse, L. G. and E. E. Wedman (1961). "*Salmonella* and other disease-producing organisms in animal by-products. A survey." *J. Am. Vet. Med. Assoc.,* 139:989–995.

Morrison, S. M., J. F. Fair, and K. K. Kennedy (1961). *"Staphylococcus aureus* in domestic animals." *U.S. Public Health Rep.,* 76:673–677.

Pelczar, M. J., Jr. and R. D. Reid (1965). *Microbiology,* 2nd ed. McGraw-Hill Book Co., New York.

Quist, K. D. (1963). "Salmonellosis in Poultry." In *Epidemiology of Salmonellosis, U.S. Public Health Rep.,* 78:1071–1073.

Sanders, E. and E. A. Friedman (1965). "Epidemiological Investigation of the Outbreak." In *Proceedings of National Conference on Salmonellosis.* March 11–13. U.S. Public Health Service Publication No. 1262. Pages 111–116.

Seligman, R. and S. Rosenbluth (1975). "Comparison of bacteria flora on hands of personnel engaged in non-food and in food industries: A study of transient and resident bacteria." *J. Milk Food Technol.,* 38:673–677.

Smith, G. E. (1967). "Fertilizer Nutrients as Contaminants in Water Supplies." In *Agriculture and the Quality of Our Environment,* N. C. Brady, Ed. American Association for the Advancement of Science, Publication No. 85. Pages 173–186.

Stucker, C., M. M. Galton, J. Cowdery, and A. V. Hardy (1952). *"Salmonella* in dogs. II. Prevalence and distribution in greyhounds in Florida." *J. Infect. Dis.,* 91:6–11.

Weiser, H. H., G. J. Mountney, and W. A. Gould (1971). *Practical Food Microbiology and Technology,* 2nd ed. Avi Publishing Co., Westport, CT.

Williams, R. E. O. (1963). "Health carriage of *Staphylococcus aureus:* Its prevalence and importance." *Bacteriol. Rev.,* 27:56–71.

Winton, E. F. (1970). "The variables in infant methemoglobinemia from nitrate in drinking water." Paper presented at the 12th Annual Sanitary Engineering Conference, Univ. Illinois, Feb. 11.

ADDITIONAL READINGS

Aly, R. and H. I. Maibach. "Aerobic microbial flora of intertrigenous skin." *Appl. Environ. Microbiol.,* 33(1):97–100. 1977.

Giefer, G. J. *Sources of Information in Water Resources: An Annotated Guide to Printed Materials.* Water Information Center, Inc., Port Washington, NY. 1976.

Gloyna, E. F. and W. W. Eckenfelder, Jr., Ed. *Water Quality Improvement by Physical and Chemical Processes.* Univ. Texas Press, Austin, TX. 1970.

Hamilton, W. J. "Rats and Their Control." *Cornell Ext. Bull.,* 353, May 1950.

Pike, E. B. "The classification of staphylococci and micrococci from the human mouth." *J. Appl. Bacteriol.,* 25(3):448–455. 1962.

Ruddock, J. C. "Cockroach control." *J. Environ. Health,* 25(6):17–420. 1963.

Scott, H. G. "Household and Stored-Food Insects of Public Health Importance." U.S. Public Health Service Publication No. 772. 1962.

Scott, H. G. and K. S. Littig. "Flies of Public Health Importance and Their Control." U.S. Public Health Service Publication No. 772. 1962.

Skinner, F. A. and J. G. Carr, Eds. *The Normal Microbial Flora of Man.* Society for Applied Bacteriology, Symposium Series No. 3. Academic Press, London, New York, San Francisco. 1974.

Tartakow, I. J. and J. H. Vorperian. *Foodborne and Waterborne Diseases, Their Epidemiologic Characteristics.* Avi Publishing Co., Westport, CT. 1981.

Taylor, D. N., M. Brown, and K. T. McDermott. "Waterborne transmission of *Campylobacter* enteritis." *Microb. Ecol.,* 8:347–354. 1982.

U.S. National Technical Advisory Council on Water Quality Criteria. "Water Quality Criteria." Report to the Secretary of the Interior, Federal Water Pollution Control Administration, Washington, D.C. 1968.

CHAPTER 6

Reservoirs of Microorganisms Causing Foodborne Gastroenteric Outbreaks: Food Supply

FOOD SUPPLY OF ANIMAL ORIGIN

MILK AND OTHER DAIRY PRODUCTS

Fluid Milk and Cream

These foods are highly perishable, yet in the United States milk and cream are seldom associated with foodborne illnesses under the present conditions of milk production. The market milk produced in this country is, generally, of excellent quality, due to elimination of disease from dairy herds, sanitary milk production, pasteurization, and care in transportation and delivery to the consumer. The situation is not as favorable in many other countries.

CONTAMINANTS.   At the time milk leaves the udder of the healthy cow, it contains few bacteria; these stem from milk ducts and cisterns. During the milking process, bacteria are usually added from various sources. In hand milking, the sources are air, the hair of the animal, manure, the milker, equipment such as pails, flies, feed, and many others.

Fewer microorganisms contaminate milk when it is drawn by milking machines rather than by hand, provided, of course, that the equipment is properly cleaned and sanitized. In fact, one of the most important sources of contamination in milk can be milk-contact surfaces, such as milking machines, milk cans, pipelines, and bulk-milk coolers. Dairy utensils that are not properly cleaned and sanitized represent a breeding ground for all kinds of contaminants, including the "thermodurics," which are heat-resistant bacteria that are resistant to pasteurization.

Among the contaminants originating from the intestinal tract of the cow are the salmonellae and the fecal streptococci (enterococci). *Campylobacter jejuni,* a causative agent of abortion in cattle, can be another contaminant (Blaser and Reller, 1981; Robinson et al., 1979). Staphylococci may be contributed by the skin, respiratory tract, and the udder. Contaminants known to originate from the handler, in the barn as well as the dairy, are manifold; among them are *Staphylococcus aureus* and salmonellae (Sunga et al., 1970). A variety of undesirable contaminants are contributed by dust, flies, and rodents.

When milk cows suffer from certain diseases, microorganisms injurious to public health may be released into the milk. Mastitis is a common disorder of the udder. Microorganisms associated with this disease include *S. aureus,* micrococci, and streptococci.

After the milk has been drawn it is rapidly cooled to 45°F (7.2°C) to prevent contaminants from multiplying. Further processing is given the milk at the creamery. Certified raw milk is not pasteurized, but is produced under very strict conditions of sanitation following standards adopted by the American Association of Medical Milk Commissions (1976). But even certified milk has been demonstrated to be, at times, contaminated with pathogens (U.S. Department of Health, Education and Welfare, 1974; Potter et al., 1983).

After the milk leaves the farm, other sources of contamination come into play, such as transfer pipes, transfer trucks, and equipment at the place of further processing with its multitude of processing equipment.

PASTEURIZATION AND ULTRAPASTEURIZATION. To eliminate pathogens from milk and cream, the process of pasteurization is applied. This involves application of heat below the boiling point, since the physical and culinary quality of these important foods must be kept intact.

Pasteurization procedures have been devised to eliminate, before all, important pathogens and at the same time to kill the majority of other microorganisms in the raw milk. Milk may be treated either at a relatively low temperature for an extended period of time or at a higher temperature for a brief period. The slow, or holding, treatment is a process of heating every particle of milk, or milk products, to at least 145°F (62.8°C) and holding at such temperature continuously for at least 30 minutes. The high temperature, short time or flash method (HTST) requires that the product be heated to at least 161°F (71.7°C) and held at that temperature for at least 15 seconds. Actually, the trend now is to use even higher temperatures and longer holding times, such as 174°F (79°C) for 20–25 seconds. Approved and properly operated equipment is required for any method. After heating, the milk is promptly and efficiently cooled to 45°F (7.2°C) or lower.

In ultrapasteurization or ultra-high-temperature processing (UHT), the product is exposed to at least 137.8°C (280°F) for 2 seconds or more. Heating is usually done by injection of steam. The product is packaged aseptically. The products so treated have a very long shelf life—as long as several weeks, if kept under refrigeration (Aggarwal, 1974). For shorter storage, no refrigeration is required.

Milk may be sterilized instead of pasteurized. Such milk is sometimes referred to as ultra-high-temperature (UHT) processed milk. It can be stored at room temperature.

Some important pathogens that should be destroyed by pasteurization include *Mycobacterium tuberculosis* causing tuberculosis; *Brucella* species causing brucellosis; and *Streptococcus* species and *Micrococcus pyogenes,* which are involved in causing chronic mastitis, as well as other organisms associated with acute mastitis including *Staphylococcus aureus, Clostridium perfringens,* and *Streptococcus pyogenes.* Pasteurization also kills yeasts, molds, and bacteria, which grow readily at low temperatures. Thus, pasteurized milk should keep well under refrigeration and usually does unless mishandled.

The percentage of survivors varies with many factors, such as the method used for pasteurization, the holding time, the total bacterial load, and the percentage within the bacterial load of those microorganisms that resist heating, namely, the spore formers and the thermodurics. Conventional pasteurization should first kill all molds, yeasts, and the majority of the vegetative cells of the thermoduric bacteria. (Thermoduric is a term used for a mixed group of bacteria, namely, the high-temperature lactics, and certain species of *Micrococcus.*) Then it should kill spore formers, including *Bacillus cereus,* among many others. Spores are very heat-resistant, and as pasteurization temperatures are raised, spores tend to represent an important percentage of the surviving thermodurics (Martin, 1974).

Ice cream mix usually receives a heating treatment at 160°F (71.1°C) for 30 minutes, or at 180°F (82.2°C) for 16–20 seconds. Cream for whipping, half and half, and coffee cream are processed by the UHT method.

It should be remembered that the pasteurized product devoid of its natural flora is a more agreeable medium to *S. aureus* than the raw product because of the antagonistic effects which the natural flora exerts. An interesting example of antagonistic contaminants interfering with growth of *S. aureus* was given by Post et al. (1961), who studied growth of this organism in cream and cream products. The authors sought an explanation for the fact that although these potentially perishable products were carried for hours in warm trucks in Southern California, they were not known to have caused illnesses.

For years the dairy industry has endeavored to prevent the dissemination of pathogens through milk, cream, and other products made from milk. The health of dairy herds is generally good and elimination of pathogens by pasteurization compulsory. Efforts are made to prevent contamination of pasteurized milk from the human reservoir by eliminating as far as possible direct contact between the employee of the dairy plant and the pasteurized product, to control flies and rodents, to maintain the equipment in sanitary condition, and to keep sanitary standards high at all times.

In spite of precautions and generally high standards of milk sanitation found in the United States, outbreaks of milk-associated gastroenteritis do occur occasionally. Milkborne diseases of contemporary importance are salmonellosis, campylobacteriosis, staphylococcal intoxication, brucellosis, and yersiniosis. The causative contaminants have usually been associated with ingestion of raw milk, certified raw milk, homemade ice cream containing fresh eggs, dried milk, and pasteurized milk that was either under-processed or recontaminated after processing (Bryan, 1983). An example of an outbreak associated with pasteurized milk caused by *Yersinia enterocolitica* was discussed by Tacket et al. (1984). One rare occurrence was an outbreak of listeriosis in Massachusetts that occurred in 1983; it was associated with the consumption of pasteurized milk that came from a farm where listeriosis in dairy cows was detected. Proper pasteurization methods should have eliminated the contaminant, *Listeria monocytogenes* (Bradshaw et al., 1985).

In spite of precautions and generally high standards of sanitation found in the United States, some outbreaks of foodborne gastroenteritis are occasionally caused by milk and other dairy products. The incidence is very low. Causative organisms have included *Staphylococcus aureus,* salmonellae, enterococci, and *Clostridium perfringens.*

The FDA administers a very active Milk Sanitation Program, which covers Grade A fluid milk and fluid products, frozen desserts, evaporated and dried milks, and dry milk products used in the reconstitution of fluid milk and milk products. The purpose of the program is to assist state and local agencies, and the milk industry as well, with those problems that have a bearing on public health. Although the laws pertaining to milk and their enforcement are formulated by state and local agencies, the program provides encouragement, advice, and actual technical assistance.

In general, the dairy industry of the United States has developed standards for dairy products to a high degree of efficacy, and quality standards have been furthered on local, state, and federal levels.

At the local level, the county or municipality entrusts the health department with this responsibility. On the state level, the departments of health or agriculture are entrusted. On interstate carriers, the supervision of the milk supply is under the U.S. Public Health Service Ordinance and Code, published in 1924, amplified in 1927, and constantly revised to keep up with current developments. The code has been adopted widely by cities and counties and serves as a guide for the milk laws of many states. The code is concerned with all the aspects of safe production, processing, transporting, and handling of milk.

Milk is easily contaminated with radionuclides from atomic fallout.

STORAGE. Properly pasteurized milk that has not been recontaminated and is held at appropriate temperatures will not readily spoil and will keep for up to 2 or 3 weeks, or even more, if the UHT method, described above, is used (see Table 6.1). For details concerning microbiological spoilage of milk, consult Frazier and Westhoff (1978).

Evaporated Milk

This canned product is prepared from milk that conforms to established high standards. Before condensing, the milk is pasteurized, usually at temperatures near boiling, for a short time. The milk is then subjected to evaporation, homogenization, and cooling processes, and is eventually canned at temperatures designed to obtain the required viscosity and to destroy enzymes and bacteria.

In another process, the concentrated product is sterilized outside the can by the HTST technique and then canned aseptically.

Bacteriological defects of evaporated milk occur occasionally, the main reason being leaky cans. A variety of contaminants may enter a leaky can and

TABLE 6.1. *Storage Temperatures and Shelf Life of Milk*

Product	Temperature		Approximate Storage Period
	°C	°F	
Canned			
Evaporated	0	32	+1 year
and	4.4	40	6–12 months
Condensed	10	50	Few months
	21.1	70	Few weeks
Pasteurized			
HTST	1.6–4.4	34–40	2–3 weeks
	4.4–7.2	40–45	1–2 weeks
UHT	1.6–4.4	36–40	+1 month
Dehydrated			
Nonfat dry	4.4	40	10 months
	21.1	70	5 months
	37.7	100	2 months

Source: Adapted from Refrigeration Research Foundation (1974).

quickly spoil the contents; if the entering contaminants are pathogens, the consequences may be serious. Another reason for spoilage is insufficient heat treatment during the canning process, thermophilic and thermoduric organisms being associated with these defects. Sometimes underprocessed milk has a coagulated appearance, several spore formers being associated such as *Bacillus subtilis, B. coagulans, B. cereus,* and *Clostridium.* These organisms may also cause bitterness.

If leaky and bulging cans are discarded, the storage time is brief, and opened cans are kept under sanitary conditions and refrigerated, few troubles should result from evaporated milk (see Table 6.1 for storage).

Condensed Milk

If sugar is added to evaporated milk, which is usually done at the end of the condensing process, and the mixture is cooled, condensed milk results. The average amount of sugar in the finished product is 55–60% lactose plus added sugar. Packaging is done in hermetically sealed cans using a separate sanitary room, and no further heat treatment is applied. Bacteriological defects depend a great deal on plant sanitation. In spite of extensive precautions, microorganisms such as yeasts, molds, micrococci, coliforms, and spore-forming aerobes can become contaminants of condensed milk. The yeasts, which are quite tolerant of sugar, may cause gas, which leads to bursting of the cans' seams. Thickening may be caused by micrococci, and so-called "buttons" by molds, such as *Aspergillus* and *Penicillium.*

Dried Milk

MANUFACTURE.   Whole milk, skim milk, cream, whey, buttermilk, malted milk, and ice cream mix are dried. Either the spray or the roller process can be used. In connection with the bacteriological quality of the powders, the temperatures used in the drying process are of interest. The clarified homogenized liquid is preheated, the terminal temperatures ranging from 65 to 85°C (149–185°F) for the roller process, and 68.8–93.3°C (156–199°F) for the spray process. The length of exposure depends on the temperature employed. The temperatures during the drying process vary with the method. In the spray process, the milk is briefly subjected to dry air at high temperatures. Thermoduric bacteria may survive this treatment.

During the concentration of the milk to a high solid content, surviving thermodurics, especially the streptococci, may multiply if the temperature remains at a level favorable to their growth for a sufficiently long time. This has been found to occur in exceptional cases.

CONTAMINANTS.   Among the factors affecting the bacterial flora of the finished powder are kind and number of bacteria originally present in the raw milk; plant sanitation; preheating temperatures; and the drying process used. It is difficult for a plant practicing poor sanitation to obtain a low-count powder, because of heat-resistant bacteria that build up in the plant. The flora of dried milk would, for the greatest part, consist of thermodurics, such as heat-resistant micrococci, streptococci, microbacteria, and both anaerobic and aerobic spore formers. Thus, drying cannot be relied upon to destroy all bacteria under all conditions. Recontamination of the finished product is also possible. These facts are important to remember when dried milk is reconstituted because it is at that time that moisture will be restored and the powder again becomes a highly perishable item.

McDivitt et al. (1964) made a field study on the manufacture of nonfat dry milk in two plants. Similar equipment was used in these plants, but modifications in processing procedures were possible in that the operation varied regarding temperatures used and regarding the coordination of the steps used in processing. The raw milk supply varied in quality and volume.

The main difference in the plants was the handling of the concentrated product previous to the actual drying. The results from analyses made at different stages of processing led the authors to the conclusion that efficient equipment and well-controlled practices are prerequisites to a safe quality product, and that low bacteria counts of a milk powder could be misleading as a sole indicator of safety.

In the mid-1960s the detection of salmonellae in milk powders caused the recall of several nationally distributed brands. Through a joint effort of the FDA and industry the sources of the contamination were searched. Several possibilities for contamination presented themselves: *Salmonella*-contaminated milk, insufficient heat treatment, and recontamination of the finished powder with bacteria lodging on poorly sanitized processing equipment. Since then a very watchful eye has been kept on these vulnerable areas of dried-milk production. The USDA and the FDA have been cooperating with industry in a continuous sampling program (Schroeder, 1967).

Dangers from toxins exist when staphylococci are allowed to build up to high numbers before the milk is subjected to the drying process. Since heat-stable toxins will resist inactivation by heat, the dried product may contain these toxins. This has been dramatically demonstrated by a series of food-poisoning outbreaks in Puerto Rico in 1956 (Armijo et al., 1957), the first such cases reported in the United States. Sixteen schools were involved; 775 of 4094 children became violently ill but recovered within 24 hours. Through the cooperation of human volunteers the toxic batches were identified and were traced to certain manufacturing plants (in the continental United States) where sanitary standards were found to be low.

The bacterial population of milk powder declines gradually during storage, but spores will survive for long periods of time.

The American Dry Milk Institute and the United States Army have set up bacterial standards for dry milk. Also, the Agricultural Marketing Service of the USDA has set up standards for standard plate counts, and also for direct microscopic clump counts (per gram of milk powder). For storage of dried milk products see Table 6.1.

RECONSTITUTED MILK. When powder has been reconstituted with water and becomes a fluid, it has all the prerequisites of a highly perishable food item and must be handled accordingly. Milk reconstituted from powder will contain the bacterial population of the powder plus the contaminants added by handling. In general, good-quality powder reconstituted with potable water, using clean equipment, by a food handler employing high standards of hygiene, should be a satisfactory product. Reconstituted milk should be kept under refrigeration unless used immediately following reconstitution. It is important for the kitchen supervisor to educate employees regarding the perishability of this item.

Ice Cream and Other Frozen Desserts

Ice cream, frozen custards, sherbets, ice milks, and ices are examples of this category.

Ice cream mixes are given more rigorous heat treatments than those used for milk (Frazier and Westhoff, 1978). With a well-controlled sanitation program, organism counts should be low.

The types of organisms found in ice cream are of a wide variety, and include streptococci, micrococci, spore formers, coliforms, and *Pseudomonas*.

One important reservoir of contaminants is the employee in the ice cream plant, since he may contribute bacteria of public health significance. The list of pathogens isolated from ice cream includes salmonellae and staphylococci. *Mycobacterium* and *Brucella* have been recovered occasionally. These pathogenic contaminants survive for considerable periods of time. Control measures include the use of high-quality supplies, excellent sanitation during preparation of the product, protection from recontamination, and storage at appropriate, low temperatures. Any of the ingredients may contribute microorganisms to the product. Examples of commonly used ingredients (their use varies with the product to be made) are milk, evaporated milk, condensed milk, dried milk, eggs and egg products, stabilizers and coloring agents, and an array of flavoring materials such as vanilla, fruits, nuts, chocolate, and coconut. Actually, the only spoilage of importance might occur before these are added to the mix, or in the mix before it is frozen. The mix is pasteurized before it is frozen, and as long as this process is properly performed and immediately followed by freezing and proper freezer storage, no problems should result.

High sanitary standards of the industry and strict control of the agencies entrusted with food protection are powerful tools for making ice cream produced in the United States the safe and delightful dessert it is.

Butter

In general, the conditions prevailing in butter are not conducive to bacterial growth, although molds may grow on butter. The moisture content of butter is low and is restricted to droplets.

Survival of bacteria has been observed occasionally in butter, however. The organisms studied varied regarding length of survival time from a few weeks to several months. The source of contaminants was usually the cream. Sims et al. (1969) inoculated salted and unsalted butter with *Salmonella typhimurium* var. *copenhagen* and held the samples at 77, 40, 0, and −10°F (25, 4.4, −17.8, and −23.3°C). Actual multiplication was found to occur in all samples kept at room temperature, but no increase was noted in the 40°F (4.4°C) samples. A significant decline occurred in the frozen butter.

A rare case of staphylococcal food poisoning caused by butter was reported in 1970. The offending item was prepared by whipping milk into softened butter. The product, a regionally distributed item, was implicated as the food-poisoning agent in incidences occurring in two cities in the South. The manufacturer voluntarily recalled a large consignment of this product (*Morbidity and Mortality Weekly Report,* 1970). Commonly, butter is kept under refrigeration. For commercially stored butter, freezer storage at 0°F (−17.8°C) is usually employed.

Cheese

There are many different kinds of cheeses and the reader is referred to books on dairy microbiology for information on the bacterial flora of cheeses.

Bacteria of importance to public health have been found in cheese, and cheeses have occasionally been indicted in outbreaks of foodborne illnesses, several outbreaks having been caused by Camembert and Brie imported from France; the causative organism was *Escherichia coli* (*Morbidity and Mortality Weekly Report,* 1971). An outbreak of listeriosis was associated with Mexican-style cheese in California (*Morbidity and Mortality Weekly Report,* 1985).

The presence of fecal coliforms and serotypes of enteropathogenic *Escherichia coli* in soft and semisoft cheeses was emphasized as a potential danger by Fantasia et al. (1975), Frank and Marth (1978), and Bryan (1983).

Use of unpasteurized milk and recontamination of pasteurized milk have been two of the reasons for the presence of pathogens in cheese. Another cause has been direct contamination of the finished product. Because of the long holding periods that many cheeses undergo and because of wide shipping distances, the original source of the pathogens is usually difficult to determine.

Among the contaminants of public health significance reported are coagulase-positive staphylococci. Donnelly et al. (1962) investigated the occurrence of these organisms in Cheddar cheese. Samples from several lots of cheese incriminated in foodborne gastroenteritis, and 343 samples of cheese procured over a period of 3 years in retail markets, were analyzed for the presence of these bacteria. Of the 13 food-poisoning samples, 11 contained coagulase-positive staphylococci; the contamination ranged from low to very high. The market cheeses labeled "pasteurized" were contaminated 20% of the time, some with bacteria being capable of causing food poisoning. Of the cheeses that were not labeled "pasteurized," a similar percentage was contaminated with *Staphylococcus aureus*. The incidence of potentially pathogenic staphylococci in cheese has been discussed by Mickelsen et al. (1961).

The presence of these contaminants in the cheeses made from unpasteurized milk is not surprising in view of the fact that *Staphylococcus aureus* is among the causative organisms of mastitis in milk cows. But their presence in the cheeses made from pasteurized milk is baffling, since the organisms should be eliminated in common pasteurization treatment. Insufficient pasteurization may be one explanation, and recontamination from various sources may be another.

Survival of pathogens in cheese may last for a long time (Nevot et al., 1963; Hargrove et al., 1969; Park et al., 1970a, b; White and Custer, 1976). Either pasteurization or curing may be prescribed by law. Curing times may be at least 2 months or longer.

Mycotoxin-producing molds have been isolated from Cheddar cheese (Bullerman and Olivigni, 1974) and Swiss cheese (Bullerman, 1976).

A toxic condition has been demonstrated for Roquefort (or blue) cheese in those portions that showed very heavy growth of the fungus *Penicillium roqueforti*. Although the toxin is a neurotoxin and has been demonstrated to be injurious to small laboratory animals, adverse effects on humans are not known at this time (see Chapter 4).

MEAT AND MEAT PRODUCTS

Animals on farms are, as a rule, healthier than when crowded in abattoirs, since healthy animals become infected during transit to markets and in the pens. Cross-infection may take place from diseased animals or carriers to the healthy specimens during this period. By direct contact or through manure, the bacteria become disseminated. For example, fecal specimens taken from animals at the farm showed that a small percentage of the animals harbored salmonellae. Specimens taken from animals penned at the packing plant indicated that the incidence had increased tenfold. Infection of meat animals prior to slaughter may even cause certain bacteria to penetrate into the muscle fiber although the tissues of normal and healthy meat animals do not harbor them. This may be true for salmonellae, streptococci, *Brucella,* and *Mycobacterium tuberculosis.*

Processing of Fresh Meat

Thanks to a very effective inspection service in the United States, diseased animals are excluded from processing for human consumption. The 1967 Amendments to the Federal Meat Inspection Act require that all states adopt and enforce inspection of meat. Before that time, only meats shipped in interstate commerce were to be federally inspected as required by the Federal Meat Inspection Act. The 1967 Amendments rule that all states adopt and enforce inspection using standards comparable to, and not lower than, federal ones. Inspection is continuous and thorough. Certain parts of all animals are examined before and after slaughter. In addition, all ingredients used in processing of meats and meat products are subject to inspection for wholesomeness.

Prepared meats, such as sausages, franks, and meat dinners, are inspected also. During the 10 years following the 1967 Amendments, the number of meat processing plants submitting to inspection increased markedly. In several more years, it is hoped, according to Angelotti (1978), that all states may turn over their inspection programs to the federal government. In the same publication, the author describes quality assurance programs for the meat-processing industry that should contribute to further improvement in the sanitary quality of meat and further processed meat products.

The flesh of healthy living meat animals is practically sterile. Microorganisms have been isolated occasionally from flesh and more readily from lymph nodes and bone marrow (Lepovetsky et al., 1953).

When the animal is killed, the walls of the intestines and other mucous tissues lose resistance to bacterial penetration; intestinal bacteria are known to have contaminated sterile tissues by this method of penetration. Injection of the live animal with papain for the purpose of tenderization makes the meat more vulnerable to bacterial penetration (Gill and Penny, 1977).

The excited or fatigued condition of the animal prevents the pH of the tissues to go down as it should, the glycogen being used up in fatigue. With a smaller glycogen reserve, less lactic acid is produced in the tissues. Normally the pH would fall from near neutral to approximately pH 5.7. Failure of drop in pH will also result when incomplete bleeding is practiced.

Injury during dehairing may carry microorganisms into the flesh of the animal. The hide of the animal is apt to be contaminated with many species of bacteria, among them *Staphylococcus aureus, Salmonella* species, *Clostridium perfringens,* and fecal streptococci.

The main and massive contamination of meats occurs, however, after the animal carcass has been opened. The sources of the contaminants of public health significance are the animal itself, the handler, the abattoir, and the surroundings.

The rate of cooling the carcass has an effect also. When the animal is cooled rapidly, the rate at which the microorganisms invade the tissue is reduced.

The following factors are known to affect the chance for, and degree of, contamination of the carcass:

1. Bacterial flora of the animal, including the bacterial load in the gut
2. State of fatigue and excitement
3. Method of slaughter and degree of bleeding
4. Injury during dehairing
5. Rate of cooling the carcass
6. Degree of sanitation in operations during killing and opening of carcass; contact of meat with fecal matter, hide, hoofs, hair; sanitation of knives; sanitation of scalding and skinning operations
7. Sanitation in operations during cutting of meat, possible contacts with diseased meats and other contaminated surfaces
8. General sanitary state of plant as a whole; freedom from rodents and insects; effectiveness of cleaning operations
9. Health, working habits, and personal hygiene of workers
10. Competency of supervision

The effect of sanitary operations during the entire process is so obvious that a detailed discussion would seem unnecessary, if it were not for the fact that surveys of bacterial contamination of market meat have shown a great need for improvement of sanitation in the packing plants, involving every step of the operation.

CONTAMINANTS. Although the organisms causing foodborne disease are of greatest interest here, many kinds of microorganisms are found on meat. These include molds, yeasts, and bacteria of the genera *Achromobacter, Clostridium, Escherichia, Flavobacterium, Pseudomonas, Micrococcus, Salmonella, Sarcina, Staphylococcus, Streptococcus, Lactobacillus, Streptomyces, Leuconostoc, Proteus, Yersinia,* and *Campylobacter.* Many of the contaminants can multiply at temperatures used for chilling (refrigeration). For a detailed discussion of the spoilage of different kinds of meat consult Frazier and Westhoff (1978), Hurvell et al. (1981), and Svedhem et al. (1982).

The contaminants that are potential hazards in connection with foodborne gastroenteric episodes are of greatest concern to those entrusted with quantity food production and service.

Many studies have been made of total counts of bacteria found on market meats, usually from retail stores, including large supermarkets and small neighborhood stores. In general, the smaller the stores, the higher the counts. Meat that has been federally inspected and passed tends to have lower counts than noninspected meats. Very high counts are frequently associated with ground meat. Even if "scraps," a rich source of contaminants, are excluded and pure meat is ground, the large surface and available air in ground meats favor bacterial growth.

Total bacterial counts reported in the literature vary so much that no attempt is made here to present the voluminous literature on the subject. Bacterial counts of meats other than ground meats may vary from 100 per gram to 1 million per gram and of ground meat up to 100 million per gram. High total counts do not prove the presence of pathogens, but they indicate that the meat was either of poor sanitary quality to begin with or has been exposed to conditions favoring bacterial proliferation.

Before federal law required, in 1967, that all states adopt and enforce inspection of meat using standards at least as high as federal standards, the picture representing surveys of conditions as they existed was pretty grim. It showed a great necessity for rigorous sanitary improvement in the processing of our meat supply. Quality assurance programs for meat inspection and processing are a joint effort of the meat processing industry and the federal government to produce safe, wholesome, quality food. These programs involve the adoption and use, universally within the meat-processing industry, of quality assurance programs that result in the continuous production of meats and further-processed products that are in compliance with regulatory requirements as well as with industry's specifications (Angelotti, 1978).

An appreciation of bacterial counts in beef patties processed under federal inspection will be gained by reading the article by Surkiewicz et al. (1975) of the microbiology staff of the U.S. Department of Agriculture. The data show that the bacteriological quality of ground meat can indeed be improved when scrupulously sanitary practices are used from the time of slaughter to the consumer. For other data see references listed under "Additional Readings." A study of frozen ground patties was made by Goepfert (1977), who determined the aerobic plate counts and *Escherichia coli* counts of over 600 samples. He concludes that the same principle holds for frozen ground beef as for fresh, namely, that without concurrent inspections and enforcement of sanitary practices, bacterial counts per se are not very meaningful. The same author (Goepfert, 1976) had studied aerobic plate counts, coliform counts, and *Escherichia coli* content of raw ground beef at the retail level.

Goepfert and Kim (1975) investigated the behavior of pathogens such as salmonellae, enterococci, staphylococci, *Clostridium perfringens, Bacillus ce-*

reus, and *Escherichia coli* in raw ground beef when in competition with the natural flora of the meat. Among the inoculated pathogens, only *E. coli,* the salmonellae, and the enterococci multiplied, and then only at the highest of the four temperatures employed: 1, 4.5, 7, and 12°C (33.8, 39.6, 44.6, and 53.6°F). The authors concluded that the natural flora largely suppressed the pathogens, the feasibility of protecting the public by establishing microbiological standards for raw ground beef at the retail level being an exercise in futility. As said above, for a number of years, a controversy has been alive over the value, meaning, and practicability of setting up and legally enforcing bacterial counts in ground raw meat. In 1973, the state of Oregon set up, and subsequently enforced, maxima for aerobic plate counts per gram of meat, and for allowable numbers of *Escherichia coli.* The legally enforceable standards were revised to become only guidelines in 1977. Microbiological criteria are discussed further in Chapter 7.

Ground raw meat, mixed with proteinaceous "extenders" such as soy and cottonseed products, has been analyzed by Kokoczka and Stevenson (1976). They found that, under the conditions of their experiments, the addition of cottonseed retarded multiplication of *Clostridium perfringens,* whereas soy products had no effect. Concerning spoilage bacteria, Keeton and Melton (1978) determined that the growth of spoilage bacteria was favored by soy products. Foster et al. (1978) studied the bacterial population of ground beef, textured soy protein, and mixtures of these under refrigeration. They concluded that under proper handling and cooking conditions, these products are not likely to present a public health hazard.

The ability of *Listeria monocytogenes* to survive various times and temperatures of postpasteurization in precooked beef roasts was investigated by Hardin in 1993. Pasteurization temperatures used were 91°C (196°F) and 96°C (205°F) for 3- and 5-minute dwell times. Storage times used were 1–56 days at 4°C (104°F) and 10°C (50°F). Survivors were encountered for every treatment used.

Staphylococcus aureus. The incidence of this organism in market meats has been studied by Jay (1961a, b; 1962), who was particularly interested in those meats that are commonly cooked to uncertain and varying degrees of doneness such as hamburger, beef steaks, and liver. The investigations were concerned with the number of coagulase-positive *S. aureus* in various meat cuts. The meat markets were located in the Baton Rouge, Louisiana, area. Twenty-eight stores and markets, representing 10% of all such stores in that area, were sampled. Of these 28 outlets, 16 yielded coagulase-positive strains of *S. aureus* in hamburger, 11 on round steak, 15 on beef liver, and 14 on pork chops. Prepackaged meat obtained from large chain stores contained relatively fewer coagulase-positive organisms. The author suggests that these results may be due to several factors, including the prepackaging per se as well as the fact that the chain stores kept available fresher meats.

The same author, surveying retail grocery stores and markets, found that 38.7% of 174 samples obtained from 27 stores yielded coagulase-positive *S. aureus.* The meats from which this contaminant was recovered most frequently were, in order of frequency, chicken, pork, liver, fish, spiced ham, round beef steak, hamburger, beef liver, pork chops, veal steak, and lamb chops.

In 1971, staphylococcal food poisoning outbreaks were traced to salami manufactured by two meat-packing companies which distribute nationally (*Morbidity and Mortality Weekly Report,* 1971).

Contamination of the meat from human sources is a great problem in meat-packing plants and retail stores, and so is the reverse situation: contamination of humans with staphylococci originating from the animal source. A very interesting study by Ravenholt et al. (1961), involving meat workers in the Seattle, Washington, area pointed to the importance of this type of cross-contamination.

Salmonellae. Several studies have shed light on the incidence of *Salmonella* in market meats. In general, pork cuts and products made from pork have shown the highest incidence.

According to Felsenfeld et al. (1950), the incidence of *Salmonella* in uninspected pork was higher (27%) than in inspected pork (14%). These figures are somewhat higher than recoveries reported elsewhere. Cherry et al. (1943) found an incidence of 6% and Wilson et al. (1961) reported 4%. However, some very high recovery rates were found by Galton et al. (1954) for fresh pork sausage; these rates averaged from 8% in samples from national distributors to as high as 58% from local sources. The same authors reported that up to 37% of fresh pork sausage sampled from retail markets in Florida was contaminated with *Salmonella.*

Wilson et al. (1961) found that the types of pork products from which salmonellae were most frequently isolated were, besides sausage, the assorted cheap parts such as feet, tails, neckbones, chitterlings, and stomach.

The incidence of *Salmonella* was also studied by Weisman and Carpenter (1969), who analyzed 100 carcasses from five abattoirs in the state of Georgia. They also studied the incidence of *Salmonella* in sausages purchased from local and national processors. The incidence was 74% in beef, and 56% in pork carcasses; and was 38% in fresh, and 9% in smoked pork sausages.

In a survey made in 1974, Ladiges and Foster found no salmonellae in 129 quarters of carcass beef surveyed in retail stores in the Denver area. They attributed these findings to high sanitary standards maintained in processing.

Salmonellae have been reported as contaminants in beef liver powder, marketed as a "health food" (Thomason et al., 1977).

Although salmonellae are frequently associated with raw meat and meat parts from which sausages are made, and also are a fairly common contaminant of fresh (unprocessed) sausage meat, they are much less frequently found in other processed meat items.

Fresh sausage is apt to have higher *Salmonella* counts than processed smoked or cooked products. Weisman and Carpenter (1969) found the incidence in samples of fresh pork sausage to be 38%, but only 9% in smoked samples.

The Centers for Disease Control has published (*Morbidity and Mortality Weekly Report*, 1975) surveillance data gathered (1972–1975) by the USDA on the presence of salmonellae in (among other food products) raw beef patties (Table 6.2). They have also published data gathered (1967–1973) on the food-handling errors in foodservice establishments and homes leading to 15 outbreaks of food poisoning attributed to ground beef (Table 6.3). In this connection it is worth mentioning that ground beef, because it is usually thoroughly heated, has a fairly good record as a cause of gastroenteric foodborne outbreaks. From 1966 through 1973, 2464 foodborne outbreaks were reported to CDC; of these 1827 (74%) were identifiable as to food vehicle and only 3.6% of these were attributable to ground beef. The relatively few outbreaks due to ground beef are particularly interesting in view of the large volume consumed by the public. Mishandling of the product occurred more frequently in public eating establishments than in the home. Fortunately, ground beef is, in general, cooked to the well-done stage. In the report cited above (*Morbidity and Mortality Weekly Report*, 1975), it is concluded that in the prevention of disease due to this meat product, an effective means of control should be health education directed to the foodservice industry and the consumer, and that this approach, combined with foodborne disease sur-

TABLE 6.2. *Surveys for Salmonellae in Raw Beef Patties, Frankfurters, and Sliced Luncheon Meat, 1972–1975 (Conducted by USDA)*

Product	Samples Examined	Samples Positive
Raw beef patties		
Raw trimmings used	690	1
Raw finished patties	735	3
Frankfurters		
Raw trimmings used	842	56
Cooked finished frankfurters	690	0
Sliced luncheon meat		
Raw trimmings used	936	69
Cooked sliced luncheon meat	456	0

Source: Morbidity and Mortality Weekly Report (1975).

TABLE 6.3.   *Food-handling Errors in Foodservice Establishments and Homes in 15 Outbreaks Attributed to Ground Beef, 1967–1973*

Error	Occurrence
Improper storage or improper handling temperature	9
Inadequate cooking	2
Contaminated equipment or working surfaces	2
Poor personal hygiene of food handler	2
Other	4

Source: *Morbidity and Mortality Weekly Report* (1975).

veillance and with unrelenting investigation of outbreaks, would most probably be a more effective method of control than requiring microbiological standards for raw ground beef as well as for frankfurters and cold cuts.

Clostridium perfringens (welchii).   Strong et al. (1963) analyzed American foods for the presence of this organism in Wisconsin and included various meats in their study. Samples positive for this organism were found on most meats. Of 26 beef cuts, 2 were contaminated; of 23 pork cuts, 1; of 5 lamb cuts, 2; of 3 veal cuts, 0; of 28 spiced meats, 5; of 14 organ meats, 6; and of 9 ground meats, 4.

Canada and Strong (1964) reported that 26% of 100 bovine liver samples purchased from retail markets within the Madison, Wisconsin, area were positive for *C. perfringens* type A. An examination of liver and bile samples from newly slaughtered cattle revealed the presence of the organism in 12% of the livers, but in none of the bile samples.

It appears that nearly 50% of minced beef is contaminated with this organism.

Fecal Streptococci.   The fecal streptococci, or enterococci, are also common contaminants of meats. They are a special problem in pasteurized hams, and are therefore discussed under "Heat-Processed Meats."

Yersinia enterocolitica.   This organism, capable of causing a type of food poisoning called yersiniosis, has been occasionally identified as a contaminant of raw meat (see Chapter 3). An assessment of this organism as a contaminant of food was published by Lee (1977).

Campylobacter jejuni.   This pathogen, known as a cause of abortion in cattle and sheep for many years (formerly referred to as *Vibrio fetus*) and for the first time cultured from a person in 1947, must now be counted as a fairly common contaminant of meat (Blaser and Reller, 1981). Freezing reduces the degree of contamination (Stern et al., 1984).

Heat-Processed Meats

CANNED MEATS. Included in this category are the canned products that have had rigorous heat treatment and are considered sterile for all intents and purposes, since pathogens are eliminated. This category contains the smaller hams. Today, large hams are usually pasteurized to avoid over-cooking.

Canning of meat is difficult because of poor heat penetration. Temperatures and times sufficient to kill *Clostridium botulinum* spores are used in commercial canning operations. However, some thermophilic organisms may escape death. Canned meats, like other canned goods, must be stored at cool temperatures. At temperatures over 113°F (45°C), danger of deterioration from thermophilic bacteria arises. Frequent turnover and cool storage of canned meats is indicated in a foodservice operation.

Canned meat shipped interstate must be inspected and passed by the federal government. The packing and processing of canned meat has to be inspected for required sanitary standards.

CURED AND SMOKED MEATS. The curing process is applied to much pork and some beef. Although years ago the curing process was designed to preserve meats with salt, or salt and sugar, without refrigeration, this is no longer the process. At present, most cured meats are also smoked. The curing agents permitted include salt (NaCl), sugar, vinegar, sodium nitrite, and sodium nitrate. The reader is referred to books on food preservation for detailed information on curing. The curing brines are not devoid of halophylic contaminants, the micrococci being frequently among these. *Staphylococcus aureus,* being salt-tolerant, and *Clostridium botulinum* have also been known to survive curing of meat.

An assessment of botulism hazards from cured meat products was given by Hauschild (1982) who in his conclusions calls attention to the questionable safety of turkey rolls, which are traditionally manufactured without nitrite in the United States and Canada. For a discussion of nitrates, nitrites, and nitrosamines in meats the reader is referred to Chapter 3.

In 1963 the U.S. Food and Drug Administration approved sterilization of bacon by irradiation, but the approval was revoked in 1968. A discussion of irradiation procedures and its implications in connection with the wholesomeness of food is found in Potter (1978).

Eddy and Ingram (1962) studied the occurrence and growth of staphylococci on bacon. These workers reported that *Staphylococcus aureus* could survive in curing brine, although only small numbers were found in "normal" or in vacuum-packed bacon. The organisms grew well on bacon stored anaerobically at 77°C (170.6°F). There was little growth below 50°F (122°C).

Another organism of public health significance that is quite salt tolerant is *Streptococcus faecalis*. Resistance to both salt and heat enables this organism to be among the flora of cured and smoked meat products.

At present, many cured meats are smoked and thus dried to some extent. In present-day methods of smoking, the heat treatment is light. The combined effects of curing, heating, and drying, as well as the action of chemicals from the smoke, aid in preservation. Research results have shown that these treatments do not guarantee complete sterilization and that microorganisms capable of spoilage as well as pathogens may remain viable. This is also true for products that are smoked without previous curing. Sources of contaminants of public health significance have been shown to be the meat itself; spices; personnel; and contaminated, poorly maintained processing equipment. The problem arising from the use of nitrates and nitrites in cured meat is discussed in Chapter 3.

The effects of time and temperature of smoking on microorganisms present in sausages were studied by Heiszler et al. (1972), Tatini et al. (1976), and Palumbo et al. (1977).

A survey by the Centers for Disease Control of salmonellae in frankfurters and sliced luncheon meats, before and after processing, is presented in Table 6.2 (*Morbidity and Mortality Weekly Report,* 1975). The data show that the processing (heating) of these products reduced the *Salmonella* content to zero. In the same report, it is stated that, of 1827 gastroenteric outbreaks (1972–1975) identified as to vehicle, only 0.3% were caused by cold cuts, and 1.1% by frankfurters. Mishandling of meat products after they left the processing plants may have been a contributing factor in causing whatever outbreaks did occur. Now, with commonly practiced inspection within the meat-processing industry, great strides have been made toward providing wholesome products to the consumer.

Packages made of films of poor gas penetration that contain sliced bacon and other sliced, cured meats occasionally show swelling, especially when vacuum treated. The usual cause is the action of fermentative lactobacilli. Opened packages or packages with faulty seams are vulnerable to spoilage by molds.

Wrapping films that allow good penetration of gases (oxygen, carbon dioxide) favor the growth of aerobes, which is accompanied by the development of slime, off-flavors, and other signs of spoilage typical of unwrapped meat.

PASTEURIZED HAMS.   Pasteurized hams are given a mild cure and light heat treatments. In contrast to the processing of "country-style" hams, which involves dry curing, slow smoking, and gradual drying, modern methods of processing ham are short and result in milder, more tender hams. The curing solution is pumped into the hams, and the hams are then rolled in brine for additional curing. Heat processing follows; it varies according to the type of product desired. Hams labeled "Tenderized" or "Smoked" have been heated to an internal temperature of 140°F (60°C). At that temperature the majority of bacteria and all trichinae have been killed. But these hams are not sterile, not completely free from bacteria. Hams labeled "Fully-Cooked" or "Ready-to-Eat" have been heated to a temperature of 150°F (65.6°C). Most bacterial contaminants have been killed, and of course trichinae; but the possibility exists that thermoduric microorganisms survive. Therefore, these hams, too, must be treated as perishables and not as hams which have undergone sterilization by pressure cooking. All tenderized hams require refrigeration at all times, regardless of whether they are packaged in cans or in other wrappings.

The fate of *Staphylococcus aureus* during the processing of hams was studied by Silliker et al. (1962). Twenty-two of 53 strains of the organism were killed, in excess of 99% kill of cells, after a 10-minute exposure to 137°F (58.5°C). Thirty-one strains were more resistant and were destroyed after 1 hour exposure to 137°F (58.5°C). *Staphylococcus aureus* originating from the hands of packers handling the finished, pasteurized, cured meats may be an important contaminant also.

The bacterial flora of packaged perishable hams before and after heating to 150°F (65.6°C) was studied by Brown et al. (1960). They found that the average total count of 210,000 per gram of meat was reduced to 451 per gram by the heat treatment given the hams. Survivors were cocci, bacilli, and clostridia. The heat-resistant cocci were able to multiply slowly at refrigerator temperatures. The authors also studied the heat resistance of some of the surviving cocci, comparing them with fecal streptococci, among them *Streptococcus faecium* and *durans*. One of the surviving cocci was comparable in resistance to the heat-resistant streptococci.

Thermal death studies (unpublished data) were made by Angelotti et al. (1962), who found that *Streptococcus faecalis* became inactivated when exposed to 150°F (65.6°C) for 40 minutes, 155°F (68.3°C) for 14 minutes, or 160°F (71.1°C) for 5 minutes. It may therefore be concluded that, although Angelotti's studies were not made on canned hams, the possibility of streptococcal survival is not precluded when hams are heated up to 150°F (65.6°C) without additional holding at that temperature. There is no doubt that fecal streptococci are extremely important contaminants of pasteurized meat products. They are heat resistant, may multiply under anaerobic conditions and grow at a pH under 5, are salt-tolerant, and are able to multiply at very low and very high temperatures.

Another pathogen known to be a contaminant of pasteurized hams is *Clostridium perfringens* (Fruin, 1977). This spore former may, if canned pasteurized hams are allowed to be held at warm temperatures, cause swelling of the cans and breaking of seams.

Molds occurring on hams cured by the country-cured method were studied by Sutic et al. (1972); they found that only a small percentage of the molds were aspergilli and that there was no definite evidence of harmful amounts of toxin present in these hams. To check multiplication of survivors, canned hams that are labeled "keep under refrigeration" must be kept cold at all times.

Frozen Meats

Freezing is frequently used to safeguard the keeping quality of meat during transit. The freezing process may kill approximately one-half of the contaminants. Further decrease in bacterial numbers may be expected during subsequent freezer storage. Bacteria subjected to freezing in or on meat seem to be more resistant to salt and heat than cells not so treated. Frozen meat is not sterile.

The conditions of thawing are important because bacterial numbers may increase considerably during this process. There is little difference between thawing in air or water, provided that temperatures below 50°F (10°C) are used in defrosting.

General Precautions

Boned meat and other products that have undergone extra handling, such as meat mixtures, ground meats, and meat trimmings, are known to have picked up pathogens from various sources. They must be handled with caution so that multiplication of these contaminants is kept in check, and strict temperature control must be exercised at all times. Curing and smoking procedures must conform to government meat inspection regulations and thus meet the requirements for the quality and safety of these products.

The problem of pathogens in large roasts is discussed in Chapters 11 and 13.

An overview of the microbiological safety of processed meat was presented as a symposium by the Institute of Food Technologists' 45th Annual Meeting in 1985 and published in *Food Technology* (1986).

POULTRY AND POULTRY PRODUCTS

Poultry is very high on the list as an offender in food-poisoning outbreaks. There is general agreement among the authorities that poultry is an important reservoir of organisms causing foodborne disease, especially salmonellae.

Poultry meat is ideally suited as a culture medium for bacteria, including those causing foodborne illnesses. It is rich in nitrogenous substances, carbohydrates, and other growth factors. It is high in moisture and the pH is favorable to bacterial multiplication. The pH of the white meat is somewhat lower than that of the dark.

The skin of poultry abounds with bacteria. To the natural flora are added contaminants from feathers, which in turn are apt to be contaminated with bacteria from manure, especially when the poultry are kept in dusty and unsanitary quarters.

Bruises in poultry are condemned by federal meat and poultry inspectors. A microbiological examination of poultry bruises conducted by McCarthy et al. (1963) revealed that 61–74% of the tissues harbored aerobic as well as anaerobic bacteria. Age of bruise, sanitation of batteries, temperature, moisture, and severity of the bruise were all factors affecting the microbial content and the growth of the microbes in the bruises. Among the organisms recovered from experimentally inflicted bruises, staphylococci were prominent. Approximately one-half of these were *Staphylococcus aureus* and *epidermidis*. It was shown that fecal matter and poultry feed were important sources of the predominant contaminants of the bruises.

Hamdy et al. (1964) reported that the source of the staphylococci was often normal tissue, air sac, and skin; also feed, gut, and droppings. They found that the extent of staphylococcal multiplication was related to the severity of the bruise.

The intestinal tract of healthy poultry is likely to contain, before all, numerous species of *Salmonella;* also staphylococci and fecal streptococci, with *Clostridium perfringens* being found in smaller numbers. Some members of the *Salmonella* group that are at home in the intestinal tract of poultry are capable of causing infections in human beings too, provided the number of cells ingested is sufficiently large.

Processing of Fresh Poultry

For a sizable poultry-processing plant to operate efficiently, a great number of live animals must be housed prior to killing and processing. This increases the likelihood of spreading pathogens such as salmonellae among them, unless great care is taken to exercise meticulous sanitation of the batteries. Government inspection is carried out by the Poultry Products Inspection Division, Agricultural Marketing Service, USDA, to eliminate obviously sick birds, but carriers remain a problem. Through the Wholesome Poultry Products Act of 1968, federal assistance is provided to the states for strict sanitary inspection of the plants that process poultry for sale within the states' boundaries. Quality assurance programs ("Food Safety and Quality Safety") for poultry inspection are a joint effort of the poultry processing industry and the federal government to produce wholesome and safe poultry and further-processed poultry products (Angelotti, 1978).

In the 10-year period from 1968 to 1977, the number of poultry plants requiring federal inspection increased tremendously, especially in the area of further-processed poultry. According to Angelotti (1978), in several more years all states will probably turn their inspection programs over to the federal government. A proposed quality assurance program for the processing of poultry is described in the publication above by Angelotti.

The steps in processing are briefly discussed since they are important for an understanding of contamination of poultry meat.

STEP 1. *Killing and bleeding.* The methods used affect quality and flavor of the meat.

STEP 2. *Plucking.* Dry plucking is more apt to leave the skin intact than wet plucking, and this method is less likely to cause decomposition. However, in this method pin feathers are apt to remain. At present a semiscald method, which consists of immersion or spraying of the carcasses at 128–132°F (53.3–55.6°C) for 30 seconds, is used most often. If the water is replenished frequently, it is not an important source of spreading contaminants. If precautions are taken to maintain the required temperatures, a mild pasteurization effect is achieved without adding microorganisms. Bacterial counts have been shown to average 250,000 cells per gram of skin and to be very low under the skin. Steam scalding is more effectual than hot-water scalding in reducing the number of contaminants, including salmonellae.

STEP 3. *Removal of pin feathers,* if necessary. Final finishing requires human hands to pick out pin feathers. Rough picking will break the skin.

STEP 4. *Singeing* is performed to remove fine feathers. Some bacteria may possibly be killed then and there.

STEP 5. *Washing* is a very important step. This process serves to remove dirt, debris, and surface bacteria. Actual scrubbing is done with some machines. Scrubbing removes bacteria more efficiently than spraying alone. After Step 5, the chickens have arrived at the "New York dressed" state. They may now be treated in one of several ways: (1) sold as is; (2) frozen, then sold; (3) eviscerated at once; or (4) frozen, then eviscerated at special plants.

STEP 6. *Evisceration.* Birds may be eviscerated warm, an easy procedure; or cooled before evisceration, either chilled on racks to get rid of animal heat (this is a slow-cooling process); or chilled on slush ice (this is a poor sanitary procedure whereby contacts can be made from contaminated to clean birds).

STEP 7. *Washing following evisceration.* These washing operations, usually by spray, are very important since by now the intestinal tract has been handled and bacteria have been released.

Washing should be done by running water, in order to prevent water from becoming a source of contamination. A study of Salzer et al. (1967) showed that by using running water for washing giblets, their bacterial count could be cut to a fraction.

STEP 8. *Inspection* for blemishes.

CONTAMINANTS. Salmonellae and *Clostridium perfringens* are potentially hazardous pathogens frequently associated with poultry. Gunderson et al. (1954) have made a careful study of poultry flora during the processing operations from freshly killed, warm-eviscerated birds and found the average counts to be 4812 per square centimeter of skin. From freshly killed, chilled, iced, cold-eviscerated birds the average counts were 60,625 per square centimeter of skin, and from frozen, defrosted, or cold-eviscerated birds, the average counts were 37,233. The reason for the high counts was that the bacteria spread from heavily contaminated birds to clean ones. Total viable bacterial counts of birds arriving at the evisceration line averaged over 26,000 per square centimeter of skin. The authors reported that the washing, and to a slight extent the singeing, resulted in a marked reduction in bacterial numbers of all types on the skin and the cavity surfaces of the carcasses passing through evisceration. All other procedures, particularly those involving handling or damage to intestines, resulted in additions. A total of over 2000 cultures was studied. Numerous strains of *Salmonella* were isolated from the evisceration line and associated procedures; other contaminants were *Klebsiella, Vibrio, Alcaligenes, Proteus,* and coliforms. *Staphylococcus aureus* was evidently contributed by the human source, since strains of this organism were isolated, at the end of the line, from the packaged product.

A special study was made on the role of the plant worker and the equipment. It was demonstrated that the workers' hands passed the contaminants from bird to bird. This was true even though they frequently rinsed hands in fresh running water; there simply was no time available for a thorough washing with soap.

Equipment was found to be contaminated with representatives of the intestinal flora of the chickens.

Human pathogens most frequently associated with poultry meat were discussed by Hobbs (1971) and Todd (1978, 1980). They include *Staphylococcus aureus,* salmonellae, *Clostridium perfringens, Yersinia,* and *Campylobacter.*

Chilled Poultry

Rapid chilling is essential to maintain a high bacteriological quality of the bird. Chilling periods should be kept brief, preferably less than a week. If longer storage is desired, freezing is the proper method for maintaining high meat quality during storage.

When poultry is refrigerated, psychrophilic bacteria will gradually crowd out other bacteria. Nagel and Simpson (1960) determined the types of bacteria associated with the spoilage of chilled poultry. Cultures were isolated from chilled, cut-up fryers that had been allowed to remain chilled at 40°F (4.4°C) for 7 days. One hundred and three cultures were isolated. Of these, 81 were of the genus *Pseudomonas;* next in line of frequency were *Achromobacter* and *Alcaligenes.* These psychrophilic bacteria are apt to outnumber others in prolonged cold storage.

Walker and Ayres (1956) reported that storage of poultry at 4.4°C (40°F) in polyethylene bags generally resulted in spoilage in 4–6 days. The spoilage was associated with organisms with characteristics of the *Pseudomonas–Achromobacter* group.

When the carbon dioxide concentration in the atmosphere is increased to 10 or 20%, growth of cold-loving bacterial contaminants is inhibited.

The shelf life of chilled poultry is brief, 12 days at the most, depending on degree and kind of contamination, and storage temperatures.

Canned Poultry

Dressed poultry may be preserved by canning—either whole or in pieces. The processing follows the general principles that are applied for the canning of meat.

Frozen Poultry

Much poultry is merchandised in the frozen state because of the good keeping quality of the frozen item. Yet frozen poultry is not sterile and may contain microorganisms capable of causing foodborne illnesses. The staphylococci and fecal streptococci especially are quite resistant to freezing and freezer storage, but even the salmonellae have been shown to survive freezing preservation for over a year. Hagberg et al. (1973) studied the effect of 31 days of frozen storage at $-20°F$ ($-29°C$) on the survival of four pathogens with which the turkey meat was contaminated: *Clostridium perfringens, Staphylococcus aureus,* salmonellae, and coliforms. Survival rates were high in all instances. According to Ostovar et al. (1971), the effect of prolonged freezer storage at $-15°F$ ($-26°C$), for three, six, and nine months, of mechanically deboned poultry, was a significant reduction in the numbers of contaminants, some of them pathogens.

In one study, the presence on frozen chickens of enteropathogenic bacteria such as *Campylobacter fetus* spp. *jejuni* and *Yersinia enterocolitica* were detected in approximately one-fourth of samples taken from frozen chickens for sale in retail stores (Norberg, 1981). In another study, it was shown that frozen items were lower in counts of *Campylobacter jejuni* (Stern et al., 1984). The microflora of fresh and thawed frozen fryers has been shown to be similar (Sauter et al., 1978).

Frozen poultry, after it has warmed up to the extent that bacterial multiplication is possible, is as perishable as the fresh product. The thawed product and the thaw water can be sources of adhering microorganisms and therefore must be kept from contact with other foods.

Further-Processed Poultry

Many poultry convenience items are now produced in processing plants. Some are marketed raw; some are fully cooked. Examples are deboned breasts, rolls, logs, and steaks. The additional handling to which further-processed items are subjected offers opportunities for increasing the number of contaminants which may come from soiled food-contact surfaces and equipment, utensils, and workers' hands. In rolling pieces of meat, the contaminants may be made a part of the center of a finished product, whereas an unboned item would be contaminated on the outside only. In cooking, the outside will be more thoroughly heated than the inside. Unless precautions are taken to cook rolled poultry items to specific safe endpoints, pathogens might survive the cooking process.

Smoked ready-to-eat turkey was the cause of a typical outbreak of a *Salmonella* infection. The turkey was traced to a smoke house that dealt largely in mail-order business. The items had most probably been contaminated at the processing plant, since raw and smoked products were held in the same room and handled by the same personnel (*Morbidity and Mortality Weekly Report,* 1969).

Under the heat treatment required by federal regulations for smoked poultry, heat-resistant spores of *Clostridium perfringens* might escape destruction. According to research data by Strong and Ripp (1967), some of the spores used as inoculum in turkey rolls were able to survive heating to endpoints of 165 and 183°F (74 and 84°C).

The processes of deboning and comminution require strict observance of high sanitary standards at all times (Gutherz et al., 1976; Zottola et al., 1971). In studying *Clostridium perfringens* in broiler processing and in further-processing operations, Lillard (1971) found that this pathogen was isolated most frequently from samples of flour and batter used for covering raw parts before cooking. However, only a small percentage of the cooked samples (2.6% of 118 samples) were positive for the contaminant.

Whether poultry items are raw, smoked, or fully cooked by any other method, they must be kept under strict refrigeration at all times.

EGGS

Shell Eggs

The majority of the hens' eggs are sterile inside. If the ovary is infected with bacterial pathogens, the egg may become infected before it is laid. An example of such a pathogen is *Salmonella pullorum,* which used to be a common inhabitant of chicken flocks but has largely been eradicated. The organism is not pathogenic to man unless massive doses are ingested. Another *Salmonella* that has been associated with hens' eggs is *S. gallinarum,* which has not been proven to be pathogenic to man either.

The egg is formed as follows: the yolk is developed in the ovary; it passes through the oviduct, and albumen or egg white is added; when the egg arrives in the uterus the final shell is added. Following this, the egg is moved toward the cloaca. Before it is passed out, the shell is coated with a waxlike substance, the cuticle or so-called "bloom." The shell represents the container, so to speak, for the liquid portion of the egg. On the inside of the shell is a membrane consisting of two layers, the outer and inner membranes. The egg white is composed of several layers, thin, thick, and again thin. The yolk is separated from the whites by the vitelline membrane.

CONTAMINANTS.   Outside, eggs are not sterile. When the egg passes through the cloaca of the hen, it becomes contaminated immediately. It has been estimated that the shell of an egg carries from 100 to 10,000,000 bacteria. Since poultry frequently carry *Salmonella* in their intestines, these contaminants may, and usually do, become part of the bacterial flora of the egg shell. Other sources of contamination include the nest, the hens' feathers and feet, the hands of the person handling the eggs, and previously used, soiled containers. The fecal matter of the hen is a very important source of *Salmonella enteritidis* and other enteric organisms including fecal streptococci. Poultry are very resistant to the salmonellae and may carry them in their intestinal tracts without showing signs of illness. Research has shown that chicken feed, especially fish meal, may be heavily contaminated with salmonellae. As long as this is true, it is almost impossible to eliminate *Salmonella* from poultry and the eggs they produce.

Rats and mice, which are common pests in poultry plants, are also important sources of salmonellae, and if present, contribute to the contamination of the hens' living quarters, the feed, nests, and eggs.

Contaminants are constantly added as the eggs are handled for marketing. Washing water has been indicted as an important source of contamination. Bacteria that have been associated with eggs are, besides salmonellae and fecal streptococci: *Achromobacter, Alcaligenes, Flavobacterium, Serratia, Bacillus, Proteus, Pseudomonas, Micrococcus,* and *Escherichia.*

Lifshitz et al. (1965) made a study to determine whether or not the exterior structures, namely, cuticle, shell, and membranes, are able to support the growth of two common egg-spoiling bacteria species and of a pathogen, *Salmonella paratyphi*. They reported that these structures supported extensive growth of the three species tested.

PENETRATION. The shell and the outer and inner membranes aid in resisting bacterial penetration. Lifshitz et al. (1964) studied penetration of *Pseudomonas fluorescens* into the egg. Three sets of egg shell models were used to measure the resistance time of penetration. Of three exterior structures resisting penetration—shell, outer membrane, and inner membrane—the inner membrane ranked first, the shell second, and the outer membrane third.

In a subsequent study (1965), these authors investigated penetration through the shell by three organisms: *Pseudomonas fluorescens, Alcaligenes bookeri,* and *Salmonella paratyphi*. *Ps. fluorescens* was the first organism recovered from inside the model, after 5 days of incubation. It was found that *A. bookeri* required 17 days to penetrate 4 of 6 models, and *S. paratyphi* required 23 days. Bacterial spores were not able to penetrate. Stokes et al. (1956) also demonstrated that salmonellae are able to penetrate the shell.

According to a study made by Vadehra et al. (1970), the blunt end of the egg was most vulnerable to penetration of the test organism, *Pseudomonas aeruginosa*. Thickness of shell membranes was not a critical factor affecting penetration; but the authors suggest that the air cell might cause a vacuum or suction effect on the bacteria.

Certain environmental conditions may affect ease of penetration. When moisture is present and when the temperature is favorably high, penetration is favored. Under commercial egg production an effort is made to strictly control these conditions as much as feasible, using principles of scientific management.

When the shell has been penetrated, the two membranes that separate the shell from the egg white form barriers, the inner membrane being very effective. This membrane is rich in lysozyme, which is inhibitory to Gram-negative bacteria. However, penetration of the membranes may eventually take place. At refrigeration temperatures, penetration is retarded.

Duck eggs are usually produced under "natural" conditions. Being water birds, ducks are prone to lay eggs in wet places that may be heavily contaminated. When the eggs are gathered and handled the moisture aids in the bacterial penetration. Duck eggs contaminated with *Salmonella* have been frequently indicted as a cause of salmonellosis in man.

TREATMENT. Various methods are constantly explored, and some are commercially used, to remove the contamination from the shell of the egg or to discourage bacterial penetration. Among these are sandblasting, washing with water, washing with solutions of various sanitizers, use of heat, and use of cold. A combination of some methods of cleaning and disinfecting the shell, followed by storage at low temperatures, is the most common method of preserving the quality of freshly laid eggs.

To make the washing process effective, a sanitizer should be present. In the research, Lifshitz et al. (1965) imply that eradication of the bacteria, not of dirt alone, is essential, since bacteria may, in the absence of dirt, use the components of the shell as nourishment and multiply.

When washing the eggs, the wash water must be kept within a prescribed temperature range. If the wash water is cooler than the egg, the bacteria will be drawn into the egg; water temperatures above 130°F (54.4°C) may partially coagulate the egg white. The eggs are dried immediately after washing. Properly washed eggs have most of their former bacterial flora removed.

An additional precaution sometimes used to keep the shell surface dry is coating the eggs to be stored with a mineral oil that is colorless and odorless. This treatment is also an aid in retaining other quality characteristics of the egg such as preserving the natural moisture content and slowing down physical and chemical changes within the egg. This treatment can have little, if any, effect on the activity of microorganisms already present in the egg before it is treated. In a method called "thermostabilization," the eggs are dipped in hot water, which is just hot enough to slightly coagulate the outermost portion of the egg white, thus creating a barrier by which evaporation of moisture through the shell is reduced. The heat should be applied within the 24-hour period following collection of the eggs to forestall penetration. Microorganisms that have already penetrated will not be destroyed by the relatively mild heating applied in the process of thermostabilization.

MULTIPLICATION OF CONTAMINANTS.   Egg white is not a favorable medium for bacterial multiplication. This is partly due to its alkaline pH; partly to inhibiting substances such as lysozyme, conalbumin, and avidin; partly to its lack of free water and nutrients; and partly—according to Yadav and Vadehra (1977)—because it possesses a physical structure not conducive to bacterial growth. The microorganisms that succeed in penetrating into the yolk, however, find a medium extremely favorable for their multiplication.

In summary, freshly laid intact eggs coming from healthy flocks free from *Salmonella* infections and produced under sanitary conditions may well be considered as sterile inside. However, the possibility exists that bacteria, among those salmonellae pathogenic to man, may be present if bacterial penetration through the shell has taken place. Ample opportunity is afforded when the shell is cracked and the membranes injured. For example, shell eggs have been indicted by circumstantial evidence to have caused gastroenteritis in hospital patients as was described in a report on a series of incidences traced to *S. derby* by Sanders et al. (1963). Raw or undercooked eggs originating from cracked specimens were implicated as the common source vehicle of infection which involved many hospitals in 13 states; extensive secondary spread followed. A discussion of the various aspects of this somewhat controversial topic is presented in the Proceedings (1965) of the National Conference on Salmonellosis held in 1964 at what is now the Centers for Disease Control, Atlanta, Georgia.

Cholesterol-free and low-cholesterol egg substitutes now on the market are of interest to persons on low-cholesterol diets. Research data on bacterial growth in two commercially produced egg substitutes as compared with whole egg were presented by Paul and Potter (1978), who found that the bacterial growth patterns of the liquid egg and the two substitutes were similar.

CHILLED STORAGE.   Only specimens free from visible internal defects are stored. Selection is made by the method of "candling," a process by which the egg is subjected to light and examined. For best results, storage conditions are carefully controlled regarding temperature and relative humidity. For commercial storage, 6 months or more, temperatures of 29–31°F (-1.7 to -0.58°C) and relative humidities of 80–90% are commonly used. The air is constantly moved to avoid possible condensation of moisture on the shells, which would favor the penetration of microorganisms.

Gas storage involves the use of carbon dioxide. Recommendations for concentrations vary widely. Concentrations sufficiently high to delay microbial activity are apt to unfavorably affect some other quality characteristics of the egg. Ozone has also been used for gas storage of eggs.

Frozen and Dried Eggs

A considerable portion of the total egg production in the United States goes into frozen and dried eggs.

Frozen and dried eggs are available as whole eggs, whites, and yolks. High-quality processed eggs of low bacterial count are available on specification for preparing lightly heated items such as scrambled eggs and French toast.

The main bacteriological problem in the freezing and drying of eggs is securing raw material worthy of processing. The contaminating bacteria are most usually the kinds that cause spoilage of eggs at low temperatures such as representatives of the genera *Alcaligenes, Pseudomonas, Proteus,* and *Flavobacterium.* However, *Salmonella* may be present also, and occasionally hemolytic bacteria.

Constant vigilance is necessary to insure that specimens containing bacteria will not be incorporated, thereby contaminating an entire batch. Parts of contaminated shell must be kept out. An extremely important precaution is to exercise excellent general plant sanitation. Unless the highest standards prevail as to selection of sound material, healthy and clean personnel, and frequent cleaning of equipment, the finished product may not be acceptable bacteriologically. Another reason for high counts may be excessive multiplication of contaminants occurring prior to processing, caused by delays along the processing line.

PASTEURIZATION.   As a safeguard against *Salmonella* it is required by federal law that all liquid egg that is to be frozen or dehydrated, must be pasteurized to render it *Salmonella*-free. Before this law went into effect, many outbreaks of *Salmonella*-caused food poisonings resulted from the use of unpasteurized egg magma and products made from it. The Egg Products Inspection Act, an ordinance and code for the processing of eggs and egg products, was enacted by the U.S. Department of Health, Education and Welfare, Public Health Service, as the United States Public Law 91-597, 1970.

Pasteurizing eggs is a delicate process, since the temperatures required for the killing of bacterial contaminants are close to those at which the egg proteins coagulate. Egg white is particularly sensitive to coagulation.

The pasteurization process employs the following temperatures: for whole, liquid egg, 60°C (140°F) for at least 3.5 minutes; for yolk liquid, 61.1°C (142°F) for at least 3.5 minutes, or 60°C (140°F) for at least 6.2 minutes; for yolk with carbohydrate, 63.3°C (146°F) for at least 3.5 minutes, or 62.2°C (144°F) for at least 6.2 minutes; for yolk with salt, 63.3°C (146°F) for at least 3.5 minutes, or 62.2°C (144°F) for at least 6.2 minutes (Frazier and Westhoff, 1978).

Although the pasteurized eggs are rendered free from salmonellae, recontamination may well happen afterward. Therefore, sanitary precautions are always indicated. Low levels of *Listeria* species were found in blended raw egg before pasteurization by Moore in 1993. After pasteurization, 500 samples were negative for *Listeria.* The pasteurization process used was 60°C (140°F) for 3.5 minutes.

A process for ultrapasteurized liquid whole eggs was reported by Hamid-Samimi in 1984. The patent for the process was issued in 1986. The product *Salmonella, Listeria,* and *E. coli* negative may be easily poured from the container and is more convenient than frozen eggs, which have to be thawed for use. In addition, the product has all the functional properties of fresh eggs. It is rapidly replacing fresh eggs in foodservice.

FROZEN EGGS.   Frozen eggs should be kept solidly frozen until the time for defrosting has come.

The method of thawing is important. If the frozen egg is thawed at a high temperature, or if the thawed product is held at temperatures favorable for bacterial growth, possible contaminants may multiply. When defrosting takes place under refrigeration, the process may take days in eggs packaged in large bulk but is a bacteriologically safe method.

DRIED EGGS.   As is true for eggs to be frozen, eggs to be dried must be pasteurized beforehand.

Most of the dried egg in this country is processed in the spray dryer. The magma is sprayed into a dry, heated air current. The aim is to withdraw almost all moisture and to leave approximately 1% in the product. Another method is the roller or drum process.

Before pasteurization of all processed eggs became law, powdered eggs and mixes made from unpasteurized egg powder caused rather frequent outbreaks of salmonellosis. Cake and frosting mixes, pancake and waffle mixes, meringue powders, whip-powder mixes, batter mixes, pie crusts and cookie mixes, and biscuit and gingerbread mixes are examples of mixes that were implicated.

The U.S. Department of Agriculture has recommended (USDA, 1971) that dried eggs be used in thoroughly cooked menu items only. Examples are baked goods, baked custards, and long-cooking casseroles. Cooked salad dressing may also be made with dried eggs, in spite of the short cooking time used, since the product is of high acidity.

Dried eggs are not to be used in scrambled eggs made on top of the stove, omelets, soft custards, cream puddings, uncooked salad dressings, and egg–milk drinks.

RECONSTITUTED EGG.   When reconstituted with water, powdered egg assumes the properties of fluid egg, including its vulnerability to bacterial activity. Reconstituted egg should therefore be carefully protected from recontamination and held at temperatures preventing microbial multiplication. It is amazing to observe how carefully shell eggs are routinely treated with regard to refrigeration, while reconstituted egg is found standing for hours in kitchens and bakeshops where the chances for contamination and multiplication are dangerously great.

The production of the highly perishable commodity, eggs, must be guided by stringent principles of sanitation, beginning at the hen house and ending at delivery to the consumer. The consumer, in this case the manager of a foodservice establishment, must again apply highest standards of sanitation at every step of storage, preparation, and service. Cracked eggs should not used.

Government-inspected egg products carry the official inspection mark, which indicates that the items have been produced according to strict sanitary standards under continuous inspection.

FISH AND SHELLFISH

Fish and shellfish are extremely susceptible to microbial spoilage. They carry a varied bacterial flora, most of it harmless; however, organisms of public health significance may be present.

Much fresh fish and shellfish is immediately absorbed by the local markets but transportation from one locality to another requires icing. Fish eviscerated under hygienic conditions and well iced will tolerate icing for a couple of days without apparent loss in quality. Much fish is frozen and marketed in that state.

Contaminants

The slime covering fish and shellfish may contain bacteria of the genera *Pseudomonas, Achromobacter, Micrococcus, Flavobacterium, Corynebacterium, Sarcina, Serratia,* and *Vibrio,* all of which are found in water. If the water from which the fish and shellfish originate contains raw sewage, human pathogens are likely to be among the microbial flora associated with the fish and shellfish. An inhabitant of some waters, fresh and salt water, is *Clostridium botulinum* type E.

In the intestinal tract of fish are found representatives of *Alcaligenes, Bacillus, Clostridium, Escherichia,* and *Pseudomonas.* These intestinal bacteria may become quite prevalent as contaminants of opened fish. This is the reason why fish "in the round" have been claimed to keep fresh somewhat better than opened fish, at least for a while.

Fish may be contaminated with nematodes; some invade the intestinal tract, others the flesh. They can cause a foodborne illness, provided the fish is eaten raw or underprocessed. The reader is referred to Chapter 3.

Shellfish such as oysters, clams, and mussels pass large amounts of water through their bodies. In general, the majority of the bacteria found in and on unprocessed shellfish consists of the water bacteria mentioned above.

Oysters and clams, which prefer to live in sheltered bays, are liable to grow in waters that become easily contaminated from freshwater runoffs and even sewage. Places where shellfish grow have plankton, microscopic animals, and plant life, which serve as food to shellfish.

Pathogens that may be contained in the water of their origin and that are important from the viewpoint of public health include bacteria and viruses.

Clostridium botulinum spores, type E, are inhabitants of many waters where fish are caught. They have been found to be associated with tuna prior to canning, but proper canning methods will kill them. The slow heat penetration into fish, especially oily fish, presents a problem. However, the information on heat transfer into these products is available to the food technologist and care is taken to obtain a safe canned product. Kautter et al. (1974) surveyed fresh crabmeat for the presence of *Clostridium botulinum*. Of 986 samples, 6 were found to harbor the organism; 4 of these were type E, and 2 were proteolytic type B.

Salmonellae may cause a serious problem in shellfish when these are harvested from polluted waters. The dangers are particularly serious in oysters and other marine foods that are often eaten raw, or only slightly heated, as in stews and soups. Typhoid bacteria have been found to survive in shell oysters and shucked oysters for months.

Vibrio parahaemolyticus occurs in sea water and has been associated with seafood of the Chesapeake Bay area and the states of Hawaii, Washington, Texas, Louisiana, and New Hampshire. It is very prevalent in Japanese waters.

In 1993, Abeyta reported that consumption of raw Pacific oysters harvested from a Washington State recreational bed was associated with a *Campylobacter jejuni* outbreak (Abeyta et al., 1993).

A review of *Listeria* in seafoods was reported by Dillon and Thakor in 1992.

Hepatitis virus may be present in sewage-polluted waters and is known to have contaminated seafood many times. As has been warned by Metcalf (1982), the fact that the bivalve shellfish is a virus carrier has evolved as the most important consequence of the virus pollution of waters from which shellfish are harvested. Metcalf emphasizes the fact that the nonculturable human enteric viruses are responsible for most if not all of foodborne illnesses transmitted by virus-carrying shellfish. Over 100 outbreaks have been reported in the United States during the past 50 years, and it is now a fact that reported cases of shellfish-associated enteric virus illnesses are on the increase, while bacterial illnesses associated with ingestion of shellfish are declining (Richards, 1985).

Contamination of fish and fish products with *Clostridium perfringens* was studied by Nakamura and Kelly (1968) in Missoula, Montana, markets. The incidence was very low or absent on fresh and frozen fish. Further-processed items were more frequently contaminated with the organism.

The presence, growth, and survival of *Yersinia enterocolitica* in oysters, shrimp, and crab was studied by Peixotto et al. (1979). This pathogen is not only able to survive at refrigeration temperature, it may even multiply. Contaminated seafood eaten raw or lightly heated is capable of causing yersiniosis illness when consumed.

Because cholera had not been epidemic in the United States since 1911, it was a shock to learn in 1978 that in Louisiana a person became infected with gastroenteritis and diarrhea after having eaten crabmeat that was either insufficiently heated in cooking or recontaminated after cooking, or both. Thereafter, a survey was made by the Food and Drug Administration of oysters harvested along the East and Gulf coasts of the United States. Of 791 oyster samples analyzed for *Vibrio cholerae,* the causative organism of cholera, 14% yielded this pathogen (Twedt et al., 1981; Madden et al., 1982).

Staphylococci are not members of the typical flora of fresh seafood, but coagulase-positive forms have been isolated from fillets and other fish cuts. Evidently, these contaminants were added in the cutting operation, their source being the food handler.

In the past, some serious outbreaks of typhoid fever were traced to shellfish from sewage-infested waters. Following this, health departments and the shellfish industry asked the Public Health Service for aid in the sanitary control of the shellfish industry. Effective sanitary supervision was initiated in all shellfish-producing states in 1925.

Sanitary measures in seafood production and distribution were discussed by Liston (1965). For many years now, the National Shellfish Sanitation Program has been active as a cooperative effort of the U.S. Public Health Service, state agencies, and industry.

In July of 1968, the federal responsibility was transferred to the Food and Drug Administration. Basic to the activities of the program is a mutual agreement between the various shellfish-harvesting states that individually bear the chief responsibility for the sanitary control of the shellfish industry. The FDA coordinates program activities. An effort is being made to eliminate some of the difficulties arising from the fact that inspection is monitored by each state on a somewhat different level of strictness, some states being less effectual in their inspection than others. Therefore, an effort is being made to establish uniform national administrative procedures for the control of shellfish harvesting and marketing (Corvin, 1975).

In recent years, the presence of relatively large amounts of toxic metals such as copper, lead, zinc, and mercury in seafood has become a matter of concern. There are many sources of direct and indirect pollution of water from toxic metals. Seafood harvested from waters polluted with such substances may show an accumulation of the metals in their organs and flesh. In the 1950s, in the Minamata area of Japan, some people were stricken with a new neurological ailment in which the victims lost control of their limbs and that some went insane. A second outbreak occurred 10 years later in another location of that country. The cause was identified to be the ingestion of mercury-poisoned seafood. In the United States, through the efforts of the FDA and cooperating agencies, fishing waters have been surveyed for their potential of being contaminated with mercury; the levels of mercury residues in fish from these waters have been determined, and state fishing restrictions have been imposed where necessary. Swordfish that proved to have high levels of mercury in its flesh has been practically removed from our markets.

Since fresh fish and shellfish are highly perishable, they are consumed or processed as fast as possible. The catch is often processed on the boat, or it is packed in ice, or frozen, prior to transit to the processing plant or market.

For an excellent discussion of fish and shellfish and their relation to human health, the reader is referred to an article by Brown and Dorn (1977).

Processed Fish and Shellfish

CANNED. Many kinds of canned fish and other seafood are available. As is true for other canned products, canned seafood is devoid of disease-producing organisms but may harbor some thermophilic types, which will not cause problems unless the cans are stored at high temperatures.

Incidences of food poisoning from commercially canned fish and other seafood have not been on record for many years until a recent episode occurred involving botulism from canned tuna, which was probably caused by recontamination in the can owing to faulty seals.

Oysters do not lend themselves to the high heat treatment of canning, except when smoked. Canning practices are subject to the FAO Code of 1973 which ensures the safety of canned seafood.

SALTED, DRIED, SMOKED, PASTEURIZED. Salting, marinating, and smoking fish will dry the tissues to some extent. A combination of salting and smoking is frequently used. The heat treatment applied in smoking is nowadays only light. The effect of drying may be intensified by using flowing air. Smoking may be done at fairly low temperatures or at temperatures as high as 200°F (93.3°C). Wood smoke contains certain chemicals, which seem to act to some extent as a preservative. However, most of the preserving effect of the smoking process is due to heating, and also to drying, especially on the surface. The germicidal effect of smoking is not completely understood. Smoked fish was the cause of several episodes of type E botulism (*Morbidity and Mortality Weekly Report,* 1963), and the possibility was voiced that light smoking followed by anaerobic packaging might prove a dangerous combination. The

FDA then ruled that fish smoked by hot process must be heated to an internal temperature of 180°F (82.2°C) for 30 minutes, the minimum acceptable level of sodium chloride being 3.5%. Relative humidity is strictly controlled. As an additional precaution, smoked fish is to be kept under constant refrigeration, below 36°F (2°C). Pace and Krumbiegel (1973) have shown occasional contamination with *Clostridium botulinum* of "sterile" products. This is a dangerous situation, regardless of whether the smoked product was not sterile at the end of the processing or whether it was recontaminated later on.

The significance of *Clostridium botulinum* in fishery products preserved short of sterilization was reemphasized by Ecklund (1982), who stresses the importance of low-temperature storage (3.3°C, 38°F) of such items.

"Liquid smoke," a solution of chemicals similar to those occurring in smoke of burning wood, has little if any bactericidal value, but it enhances flavor.

Pasteurization of crab and shrimp is a popular method of preparing them for the market. Chilling and freezing follows pasteurization. The pasteurization process used for blue crab has been described by Dickerson and Berry (1974); heating temperatures may range from 186 to 189°F (85.6–87.2°C); heating times, from 92 to 150 minutes. It is important that the pasteurized items be immediately chilled or frozen, as specified. A study by Ward et al. (1977) showed that a pasteurization process at a lower temperature, 185°F (85°C), did not completely sterilize the crabmeat; however, the survivors were not pathogens. Kautter et al. (1974) surveyed 1000 samples of pasteurized crabmeat for *Clostridium botulinum* and found only one sample contaminated with type F, which was heat-resistant.

Maintenance of high sanitary standards in the processing plants is extremely important. Unsanitary handling of shellfish after it has been cooked may recontaminate the items with pathogens from workers' hands, contact with the raw product, and soiled equipment, especially when the items are eaten without reheating, as are seafood cocktails, salads, sandwiches, and the like. A survey of 47 crabmeat plants in the United States located along the Atlantic Coast and the Gulf Coast was made by Wentz et al. (1985).

Keeping pasteurized seafood chilled at all times is very important because much of it is eaten as a cocktail, or in salads, without further heat treatment.

FROZEN.   Raw fish is seldom frozen whole but, rather, is frozen as fillets and steaks. Raw shrimp, scallops, clams, oysters, and lobster tails are frequently marketed frozen. Shrimp, crabmeat, and lobster meat are also marketed cooked in the frozen state.

The freezing kills part, but certainly not all, of the contaminants. Upon thawing, if time–temperature conditions permit, the survivors will resume multiplication.

Fish sticks and similar products are marketed either as an uncooked or precooked product. Through the addition of bread crumbs, spices, batter, and other coverings, more contaminants are apt to be added. Their source could be human hands, machinery, packaging materials, and work surfaces. Spices in themselves might add numerous contaminants (see Chapter 7). A study of the microbiological quality of frozen breaded fish and shellfish was made by Baer et al. (1976).

COOKED FISH AND SHELLFISH.   Items that are frequently marketed in the cooked stage include crab, shrimp, and lobster. The process of cooking renders them almost sterile. Unfortunately, however, recontamination with staphylococci and salmonellae is not uncommon (Silverman et al., 1961; Nickerson et al., 1962). In fact, the percentage of samples contaminated with *Staphylococcus aureus* was reported to be extremely high, up to 75%, in some instances.

An extensive study was made by Raj and Liston (1963) on the effect of processing on bacteria of public health significance in frozen seafoods. These authors found that frozen raw seafood, including fish and oysters, when entering the processing plant, carried rather low levels of bacteria of public health significance. The initial cutting operation of the frozen fish caused a tenfold increase in counts. The staphylococci count in the samples increased from 7 to 64%; among these staphylococci were coagulase-positive strains.

Battering and breading operations added more significant contaminants, among them hemolytic streptococci, coagulase-positive staphylococci, enterococci, coliforms, and miscellaneous anaerobes; batter was shown to be an excellent medium for multiplication of contaminants. In 73% of the battered samples, staphylococci were found. The precook operation, done in oil, reduced the counts of some forms, namely hemolytic streptococci and the coliforms. However, this heat treatment hardly affected the staphylococci, enterococci, and anaerobes.

Research results of other workers have also pointed to the dangers of introducing great numbers of bacteria, including pathogenic contaminants, with the breading operation, especially when it is performed by hand. Contaminants of significance include coagulase-positive staphylococci, salmonellae, shigellae, and enterococci. In a study by Appleman et al. (1964), coagulase-positive staphylococci were isolated in a high percentage of unfrozen crab cakes. Frozen crab cakes were not as high in viable staphylococci.

The importance of sanitary standards is evident from data by Slocum (1960) presented in Table 6.4.

The same author stressed that efficient terminal heat treatment killed a large proportion of the contaminants. The danger of recontamination of

TABLE 6.4.   *Effect of Sanitary Handling on Total Bacterial Counts of Fish Sticks Before Final Cooking and on Bacterial Counts per Gram of Substrate (Fish, Batter, or Both)*

Material	Plant A—Poor Sanitation	Plant B—Above Average Sanitation
Raw fish	560,000	65,000
Batter	12,000,000[a]	210,000[b]
Fish and batter	2,000,000	260,000

[a] Batter used for 10 hours.
[b] Batter used for 30 minutes.
Source: Adapted from Slocum (1960).

cooked items is present wherever food is prepared, including quantity food-service. The application of the principle of efficient terminal heat treatment deserves more attention than it now gets in many establishments where food is prepared and served to the public.

A study made by Duran et al. (1983) investigating the microbiological quality of breaded shrimp during processing in plants of 33 shrimp-breading firms revealed, after 63 inspections were made, that all firms were using good manufacturing practices. The Good Manufacturing Practice regulation of the Food and Drug Administration is basic to using excellent sanitary control in processing plants, and compliance is determined by FDA investigators who spot-check conditions during processing and quality control of the final product.

In 1956, the Agricultural Marketing Act was extended, and under this act the standards for quality were developed, including fish. The administration is the responsibility of the Bureau of Commercial Fisheries, U.S. Fish and Wildlife Service, Department of the Interior.

Shellfish are under the jurisdiction of the Food and Drug Administration (U.S. Public Health Service), and this jurisdiction extends to catching, processing, and marketing. The product must come from beds that are certified to be pure.

Only fish and shellfish from uncontaminated waters should be purchased. Local health authorities are helpful when it comes to choosing vendors for fish and shellfish.

To safeguard high-quality fresh fish and shellfish, they should be stored on ice or at 30–32°F (−1.1 to 0°C) and for the shortest periods possible. Smoked and otherwise heat-pasteurized items must be kept refrigerated below 38°F (3.3°C) at all times. Frozen products should be kept frozen, and precautions taken during thawing to prevent the items from warming up to temperatures supporting bacterial multiplication.

FOODS OF PLANT ORIGIN

FRUITS AND VEGETABLES

Fruits and vegetables are marketed as fresh, frozen, pasteurized, canned, dried, and fermented products.

Contaminants

Fruits and vegetables carry a natural flora, which ordinarily does not include types pathogenic to man. The organisms causing spoilage in fresh and stored foods are not pathogenic to man either; for information on microbial spoilage of fresh and refrigerated plant foods, the reader is referred to Vaughn (1963).

The natural bacterial flora varies with the type of plant. The genera frequently encountered are *Achromobacter, Alcaligenes, Flavobacterium, Micrococcus,* the coliforms, and the lactics.

Plants may acquire human pathogens from contact with contaminated soil, water, human hands, animals, air, harvesting equipment, and so forth. The nature of the contamination depends on many factors. An important source of contamination is soil containing raw sewage.

Sewage-contaminated irrigation water has been found to contaminate vegetable crops with enteric bacteria, viruses, protozoa, and eggs of parasitic worms (Bryan, 1974a). Fortunately, in the United States, raw sewage is rarely used for fertilizing soil; and if it is used, it is by persons raising vegetable garden crops for their own use. However, in some other parts of the world, fertilization with raw sewage is still practiced; vegetable foods grown on such soil must be expected to be contaminated with human pathogens. Soil may also become contaminated from surface waters into which sewage has been directed.

Fresh Fruits and Vegetables

The term "fresh" here implies that the plant materials were not processed, but they may have been cold stored.

Fresh fruit may become contaminated from soil dust in the orchard. Fruit collected from the ground, and low-growing fruit, often becomes heavily contaminated with soil organisms. Dust from the road may be an important source when fruit is displayed on roadstands. One of the important sources from a public health point of view is human hands. During harvesting, subsequent sorting, and storing, fruit may acquire the flora adhering to the handlers' hands. Certain species of molds can penetrate the skin of certain fruit and produce mycotoxins in the fruit (Wilson and Nuovo, 1973; Alderman and Marth, 1974).

In the case of vegetables, contact with the ground makes contamination with organisms from the soil likely. Spore formers such as *C. botulinum* and *C. perfringens* are inhabitants of soil. When the ground has been fertilized with night soil or similar products, the soil flora may include salmonellae originating from the human intestinal tract. For example, the outer leaves of lettuce and cabbage have been found to contain, on occasion, typhoid organisms and other species of *Salmonella*.

Solid waste–disease relationships have been reviewed by Hanks (1967). Information on fecal contamination of fruits and vegetables during cultivation and processing for market was assembled in a review by Geldreich and Bordner (1971). The contaminants of raw vegetables used in salads and sandwiches, such as lettuce, cabbage, spinach, and parsley, deserve attention. Maxcy (1978) studied lettuce as a possible carrier of microorganisms of public health significance. He found a broad spectrum of microbial contaminants, the load being greatest on the outer leaves of a head. To test lettuce for its potential as a substrate for the multiplication of pathogenic organisms, he experimentally added suspensions of *Escherichia coli, Salmonella typhimurium,* and *Staphylococcus aureus* to torn lettuce leaves. The inoculated lettuce was then held for several hours in serving bowls of wood, plastic, and glass, placed on a bed of ice. It was found that this commonly used method of holding lettuce for service did not keep the product really chilled. After a lag of 2 hours, the inoculum multiplied. The author concluded that the environmental conditions prevailing in the salads (no dressing) could be conducive to the multiplication of microorganisms of public health significance, when lettuce should be contaminated with these.

The load of *Escherichia coli* on fresh parsley was investigated by Käferstein (1976) who found it to be heavy in many instances.

Epidemic listeriosis, probably brought about by eating cole slaw, was reported by Schlech et al. (1983). The contaminant, *Listeria monocytogenes,* is only infrequently indicated as a pathogen of humans, although it is frequently isolated from soil, water, and vegetation. In the case reported above, the cabbage used to prepare the incriminated cole slaw had been obtained from a farm known to have had cases of listeriosis in sheep; sheep manure was used to fertilize the soil on which the cabbage was grown.

Because cases are on record in which raw vegetable materials were implicated as the source of gastrointestinal illness, Konowalchuk and Speirs (1975) studied the survival of enteric viruses on raw vegetable surfaces. The authors compared the rapidity of decay of viruses when placed on glass with that of viruses placed on vegetable surfaces. They found that virus decay was considerably slower when the viruses were in contact with the vegetable surface rather than with glass. In light of this study, vegetables have a potential for harboring viral pathogens for a while, and their possible presence must be taken into account in connection with their use in salads and sandwiches.

WASHING.   In the case of fruit, mechanical washing is quite an efficient method for removal of soil, chemical residues, and microorganisms adhering to the outside, but washing does not render plant tissue sterile. Sometimes chlorinated water or borax solution, with or without the addition of detergents, are used to remove soil and lower the load of contaminating microorganisms. Since washed fruit is by no means sterile when it reaches the consumer, additional thorough washing is necessary to assure a clean product earmarked for consumption as a raw item.

In the case of vegetables, washing may remove much of the gross soil, but additional thorough washing remains to be done by the consumer. It is difficult to clean certain vegetables from all traces of gross soil; green vegetables are particularly stubborn in releasing dirt.

Along with the gross soil, microorganisms and animal parasites are only partially removed, complete removal being impossible. Therefore, vegetables to be consumed raw must never originate from sewage-polluted soil. Utmost care must be given to the handling of all vegetables to be served raw. This will require careful management regarding washing and temperature control. And finally, it should be remembered that raw vegetables added to cooked items which already have received a terminal heat treatment may recontaminate these items.

For celery to be used in salads, Shahidy et al. (1970) found this treatment effective in reducing bacterial counts: dipping the washed vegetable for 30 seconds in boiling water, immediately followed by chilling under running cold tap water. For parsley, Käferstein (1976) also recommended blanching, since ordinary rinsing in water had little effect on the bacterial load of this vegetable.

CHILLED STORAGE.   Fresh fruits and vegetables that are not processed further are cooled promptly by appropriate means, including use of cold air, cold water, ice, or vacuum cooling. The vacuum cooling process is frequently used for lettuce. It involves moistening and evacuation. Relatively stable vegetables such as potatoes and other root crops are less liable to succumb during chilled storage than produce of soft and fragile tissues, therefore, their storage poses fewer problems.

In storing fresh mushrooms, plastic overwraps covering them should be provided with holes to permit access of air to the mushrooms and prevent the formation of toxin of *Clostridium botulinum,* a pathogen that frequently contaminates fresh mushrooms (Suiyana and Rutledge, 1978).

Many fruits and vegetables may be kept fresh for long periods of time if stored under appropriate conditions, which include atmosphere controlled with respect to composition, temperature, and relative humidity. The reader is referred to the literature dealing with the science of pomology and vegetable crops.

Processed Fruits and Vegetables

CANNED FRUIT.   Canned fruit is safe from a public health point of view. Spore formers which may survive include some gas-producing butyric anaerobes, such as *C. pasteurianum,* and the aciduric flat sours (e.g., *Bacillus coagulans*), which are not pathogenic to man. Fruits are placed in two groups: the acid, such as pineapples, pears, and tomatoes; and the very acid, such as berries. Very acid fruits require less rigid heat treatment in canning than the acid.

CANNED VEGETABLES.   Vegetables, except tomatoes, which are really fruits, are low in acid, and this is taken into account when they are heat processed.

In properly canned vegetables the spores of *C. botulinum* have been destroyed. Commercially canned vegetables have had an excellent record for decades. Heat-stable survivors may prove a nuisance and spoil canned vegetables under "tropical" conditions of storage. The thermophilic anaerobes are most frequently encountered in the medium-acid group of vegetables; the thermophilic flat sours and putrefactive anaerobes represent the more common survivors in the low-acid group of vegetables such as corn and peas.

However, as was pointed out in Chapter 4, the last two decades have shown an upswing in botulism caused by commercially canned vegetables. Faulty processing was to blame for these incidents (Bryan, 1974b). To forestall future occurrences, the Food and Drug Administration (FDA) has taken a forceful step by setting up recommendations to promote quality assurance at the plant level, where the primary responsibility rests. The processing industry, in an effort to preserve the culinary quality of the canned products, has shown a tendency to use minimum processing times and temperatures, and this may have dire consequences. The FDA, in its role as a monitoring agency, must motivate compliance with its regulations, assuring a safe product.

The FDA has in recent years promulgated several regulations in which current good manufacturing practices (GMPs) in the manufacture and packing of human foods are specified. Part of these regulations, referred to as the "umbrella GMPs," cover many common aspects of food processing. Other parts deal with specific items, among them processing of low-acid foods. The FDA (1976a) has also published proposed GMPs for pickled, fermented, and acidified foods.

The trend is toward application of the principles of hazard analysis critical control points (HACCP), a principle applicable not only to the canning process but also to other food-processing activities. Briefly, hazard analysis serves to identify sensitive ingredients and products. Once these have been established, various critical control points are identified (Bauman, 1974; Kauffman, 1974). Critical control points are concerned with the processing techniques themselves. Microbiological critical control points for canned foods were discussed by Ito (1974). Some food manufacturers have set up their own strict controls. The Pillsbury Company was among the first concerned with the development of the HACCP concept. Others were the U.S. Army Natick Laboratories and the National Aeronautics and Space Administration.

The FDA motivates compliance with its regulations by various means: through inspection of the canners' establishments; by collecting samples at critical stages of processing and by analyzing them. The FDA also offers a system of surveillance intended to pinpoint new problems and to appraise the significance of problems due to a variety of causes (Angelotti, 1975).

DRIED FRUIT. Excellent dried fruit is available on the market, and much of it is pasteurized. Fruit that has been sulfured has some of its microbial content reduced by that process. Molds constitute the greater percentage of the flora of dried fruit. Moldy fruit should not be consumed because of the potential danger from aflatoxins.

DRIED VEGETABLES. Vegetables may be dehydrated from the raw stage, or they may be blanched before processing.

Raw dehydrated vegetables may be used to make fresh-like salads. Examples of vegetables processed in this way are peppers, carrots, and cabbage. These are first washed to reduce soil contaminants. Obviously, the kinds and numbers of microorganisms remaining on the product will depend on many factors including kind of soil, kind of vegetable, number of microorganisms, thoroughness of cleaning, and general sanitation during the operation. Germicidal rinses are sometimes used as an aid in reducing the number of bacteria remaining on the vegetable after washing. If the flora includes *Escherichia coli,* human or animal contamination must be suspected, and use of these vegetables as a raw item must be questioned.

Blanched dehydrated vegetables are more common. Blanching inactivates the enzymes and reduces the microbial content considerably. Sulfuring of vegetables also reduces total counts. The flora of the finished product is therefore largely acquired during processing following blanching. Contaminants often originate with the raw vegetables brought into the processing plant. These contaminants include *Aerobacter, Achromobacter, Bacillus, Clostridium, Escherichia, Micrococcus, Streptococcus, Pseudomonas, Lactobacillus, Leuconostoc,* and many others. Spores, micrococci, and microbacteria are quite resistant to drying and will linger, while other forms of bacteria gradually decrease in number. No multiplication of bacteria takes place in the dehydrated product if it is stored properly. The microbiology of various dehydrated foods has been discussed by Goresline (1963).

FROZEN FRUIT AND JUICE.   These items have not proven to be a problem from a public health point of view. Vaughn et al. (1957) reviewed the significance of microorganisms in frozen citrus products and found no known health hazard of bacterial origin.

Microorganisms of public health significance have been seen to survive for a while in fruit products. Larkin et al. (1955) found fecal streptococci after 147 days storage at $-10°F$ ($-23.3°C$) in orange concentrate. On the other hand, Hahn and Appleman (1952) found that these organisms disappear rather quickly. The initial bacterial load may have something to do with this discrepancy of results; possibly, with a larger initial bacterial load, the chance that survivors will be detected is greater.

Fecal streptococci were also isolated from commercially frozen grape juice, peaches, melon balls, and various citrus juices. As reported by Tressler et al. (1968), survival after several months of freezer storage was noted by Wallace and Tanner for several pathogenic strains of *Salmonella, Escherichia coli,* and *Proteus vulgaris* when these were introduced into cherries and frozen at 0 and $-40°F$ (-17.8 and $-40°C$). Survival in the juice was less than 4 weeks. The survival periods for several salmonellae in strawberries have been known to be as long as 6 months.

FROZEN VEGETABLES.   Vegetables are washed and blanched before freezing. Germicides may be used in the washing process. Washing and blanching remove much of the natural flora as well as the contaminants from soil and water.

Larkin et al. (1955) found that blanching with 190°F (87.8°C) water destroyed *Streptococcus faecalis* in 1 minute. Recontamination of the blanched product may occur during cooling and further handling. Fecal streptococci in sufficient numbers to possibly be of public health significance were isolated from commercially frozen vegetables including green beans, corn, lima beans, and spinach.

Splittstoesser et al. (1965) determined the incidences of coagulase-positive staphylococci in 112 samples of peas, green beans, and corn collected at various stages of processing for freezing. The greatest percentage of contaminated samples (65%) was obtained with corn; the highest counts (7.3 per gram) were found in peas. Major sources of the staphylococci were the hands of employees. The gravity separator used in the processing procedure was found to be a potential area for staphylococcal buildup.

DEFROSTING.   Fruits and vegetables to be used without further heating are defrosted. The possibility that pathogenic contaminants may survive freezing and freezer storage points to danger when thawing is allowed to proceed at room temperature for a prolonged period. The fact that fruits and vegetables lose their textural quality quickly when allowed to remain warm for hours after thawing is fortunately a safeguard. With fruit, acidity is a safeguard also.

Vegetables to be cooked are, as a rule, cooked from the frozen state; this is a good practice.

GRAINS AND FLOURS

Several types of undesirable microorganisms may be associated with starch and flour, but none are of public health significance except *Bacillus cereus,* which is capable of releasing enterotoxins and causing foodborne illness. Foods prepared with starches must not be allowed to remain at temperatures favorable to bacterial growth for any length of time. The spores of this organism are resistant to heating given to foods in routine cooking operations (see also Chapter 13).

Given the proper environmental conditions, grains may be afflicted with certain molds capable of producing toxins. Aflatoxin, zearalanone, and deoxynivalenol are three mycotoxins that can contaminate a wide variety of grains used for human as well as animal consumption. Methods of detoxification are currently being researched (Huff and Hagler, 1985).

SPICES

Spices have a reputation for possessing germicidal qualities. It is a fact, however, that few spices seem to have this property. Some have some bacteriostatic action, however.

Oils from ground mustard, cinnamon, and cloves possess some bactericidal power toward certain bacteria. Garlic and onion have been shown to exert bactericidal power also. The bactericidal action of horseradish was investigated by Foter and Gorlick (1938), who reported that the active principle is allyl isothiocyanate. The activity of the vapors was dependent on temperature, the most favorable temperature being 99.5°F (37.5°C). These vapors were found to have a greater bactericidal power than garlic and onion. The oil (volatile) of mustard is most inhibitory to yeasts.

The resistance of different bacteria to a particular spice varies; differences also exist in the reaction of a specific organism to different spices (Fabian, et al., 1939).

Commercial spices not only are apt to be heavily contaminated with insect fragments and other gross particles but also harbor great numbers of microorganisms that may contaminate the menu items in which they are incorporated, unless the spices have been heat-treated sufficiently to reduce their bacterial load. The microbial content of untreated spices was studied by Yesair and Williams (1942), who found staggering numbers in some. The microbial contents of common spices were reviewed by Weiser (1971). Strong et al. (1963) examined 20 spices for the presence of *Clostridium perfringens;* they isolated the organism from paprika, savory, and poultry seasoning. In studying the microflora of black and red pepper, Christensen et al. (1967) found, among many other contaminants, aspergillae capable of producing aflatoxins.

Julseth and Deibel (1974) undertook a study to determine a partial microbial profile for 113 documented samples of imported and domestic spices; these were black pepper, cassia, celery seed, ginger, mace, mustard seed, nutmeg, oregano, paprika, and rosemary, chosen on the basis of their popularity and common use in food preparation. An attempt was made to determine the origin, port of entry, and some other significant data. Standard plate counts and bacterial spore counts were made; analyses were made for thermophilic anaerobes, proteolytic and amylolytic organisms, yeasts, and molds. Interestingly, no microorganisms of public health significance were detected. Also, there was no apparent correlation between the country of origin and microbiological quality. However, the authors warn that the absence of pathogens in their particular samples does not mean a guarantee that this is always so. Some pathogenic species may well be expected as contaminants of spices and herbs because of the diversity of the sanitary conditions under which they are cultivated, harvested, dried, and subsequently handled in different countries, some of which do not adhere to high standards of sanitation. Powers et al. (1975) studied the microbiology of processed spices procured for the United States Armed Forces. Included were bay leaves, red pepper, chili powder, mustard powder, cinnamon, garlic powder, and oregano. The authors found that *Clostridium perfringens* was present in 15% of 114 samples of seven types of spices. Oregano was high on the list of contaminated samples in that 53% of the oregano samples carried the *perfringens* organism. No other bacteria of public health significance were found in these spices.

Powers et al. (1976) also studied the incidence and levels of contamination in spices with *Bacillus cereus*. Counts varied from 50 to 8500 per gram of spice. Interestingly, 89% of the isolates tested for toxicity were toxigenic in animal (rabbit) tests. Toxigenic *B. cereus* was detected in each kind of spice.

NUTS

Nuts harbor a variety of microorganisms on their shells when harvested. In processing nuts, these organisms should be eliminated to prevent contamination of the nut meats. The source of the outside contaminants varies, but contact with the ground seems to be important. Marcus and Amling (1973) studied the incidence of *Escherichia coli* harvested from grazed and ungrazed orchards and found that nuts from grazed orchards were more heavily contaminated. They also showed that contact with moisture allowed the nuts to crack their seams, thus offering contaminants access to the nut meats. When nuts are processed, the outside is usually heat treated to reduce or eliminate the microbial load. Beuchat and Heaton (1975) investigated the survival of *Salmonella (senftenberg, anatum, typhimurium)* as influenced by processing and storage conditions as practiced commercially. They reported that thermal treatments normally applied were inadequate to completely and in all instances destroy the salmonellae. Heavily contaminated nuts were a special problem. Packing material treated with an antimicrobial chemical afforded some protection, as did prolonged storage at certain temperatures.

Nut meats removed from the shell may harbor a variety of bacteria in large numbers. The presence of enterococci and staphylococci on broken nut meats has been demonstrated by Smith and Iba (1947) and Hyndman (1963). Salmonellae have been demonstrated in shredded coconut. Since nuts are not natural hosts of salmonellae, the contaminants must have been added in the processing or in transport, storage, or other handling. Moldy nuts should not be consumed because of the danger from aflatoxins.

The FDA (1976b) has developed and published good manufacturing practice regulations for tree nuts and peanuts.

Since nuts are frequently added to highly perishable items such as puddings and other desserts at the end of the cooking process, they may well be expected to recontaminate the items after these have received their terminal heat treatment. Precautions have been suggested, which aim at the removal and/or killing of contaminants through immersion of the nuts in hot (180–190°F) (82–88°C) water immediately followed by cooling. Aflatoxins are heat stable and cannot be eliminated by this procedure.

Perishable items into which nuts have been incorporated should be kept safely chilled at all times. The problem in connection with aflatoxins in peanuts was discussed in Chapter 4.

REFERENCES

Milk and Other Dairy Products

Aggarwal, M. L. (1974). "Commercial sterilization and aseptic packaging of milk products." *J. Milk Food Technol.,* 37(5):250–254.

American Association of Medical Milk Commissions (1976). *Methods and Standards for the Production of Certified Milk.* Alphareta, GA.

Applebaum, R. S., R. E. Brackett, D. W. Wiseman, and E. H. Marth (1982). "Aflatoxin: Toxicity to dairy cattle and occurrence in milk and milk products—A review." *J. Food Prot.,* 45:752–777.

Armijo, R., D. A. Henderson, R. Timothee, and H. B. Robinson (1957). "Food poisoning outbreaks with spray-dried milk—An epidemiologic study." *Am. J. Public Health,* 47:1093–1100.

Blaser, M. J. and L. B. Reller (1981). "*Campylobacter* enteritis." *N. Engl. J. Med.,* 305:1444–1452.

Bradshaw, J. G., J. T. Peeler, J. J. Corwin, J. M. Hunt, J. T. Tierney, E. P. Larkin, and R. M. Twedt (1985). "Thermal resistance of *Listeria monocytogenes* in milk." *J. Food Prot.,* 48:743–745.

Bryan, F. L. (1983). "Epidemiology of milkborne disease." *J. Food Prot.,* 46:637–649.

Bullerman, L. B. (1976). "Examination of Swiss cheese for incidence of mycotoxin-producing molds." *J. Food Sci.,* 41:26–28.

Bullerman, L. B. and F. J. Olivigni (1974). "Mycotoxin-producing potential of molds isolated from Cheddar cheese." *J. Food Sci.,* 39:1166–1168.

Donnelly, C. B., L. A. Black, and K. H. Lewis (1962). "The occurrence of coagulase-positive staphylococci in Cheddar cheese." A Preliminary Report, Society of the American Bacteriologists, *Bacteriol. Proc.,* 62nd Annual Meeting, p. 23.

Fantasia, L. D., L. Mestrandea, J. P. Schrade, and J. Yager (1975). "Detection and growth of enteropathogenic *E. coli* in soft ripened cheeses." *Appl. Microbiol.,* 29(2):179–185.

Frank, J. F. and E. H. Marth (1978). "Survey of soft and semi-soft cheese for presence of fecal coliforms and serotypes of enteropathogenic *Escherichia coli.*" *J. Food Prot.,* 41(March):198–200.

Frazier, W. C. and D. C. Westhoff (1978). *Food Microbiology,* 3rd ed. McGraw-Hill Book Co., New York.

Hargrove, R. E., F. E. McDonough, and W. A. Mattingly (1969). "Factors affecting survival of *Salmonella* in Cheddar cheese." *J. Milk Food Technol.,* 32:480–484.

Martin, J. H. (1974). "Significance of bacterial spores in milk." *J. Milk Food Technol.,* 37:94–98.

McDivitt, M. E., P. P. Huppler, and A. M. Swanson (1964). "Bacteriological changes during the manufacture of non-fat dry milk." *J. Dairy Sci.,* 47:936–941.

Mickelsen, R., V. D. Foltz, W. H. Martin, and C. A. Hunter (1961). "The incidence of potentially pathogenic staphylococci in dairy products at the consumer level. II. Cheese." *J. Milk Food Technol.,* 24:342–345.

Morbidity and Mortality Weekly Report (1970). U.S. Department of Health, Education and Welfare, Public Health Serv., 19, July 18.

Morbidity and Mortality Weekly Report (1971). U.S. Department of Health, Education and Welfare, Public Health Serv., 20, Dec. 11.

Morbidity and Mortality Weekly Report (1985). U.S. Department of Health, Education and Welfare, Public Health Serv., 34, June 21.

Nevot, A., G. Mocquot, P. Lafont, and M. Plommet (1963). "Studies on the survival of pathogenic bacteria in ripened soft cheese." *Dairy Sci. Abst.,* 25:1170.

Park, H. S., E. H. Marth, J. M. Goepfert, and N. F. Olson (1970a). "The fate of *Salmonella typhimurium* in the manufacture and ripening of low-acid Cheddar cheese." *J. Milk Food Technol.,* 33:280–284.

Park, H. S., E. H. Marth, and N. F. Olson (1970b). "Survival of *Salmonella typhimurium* in cold-pack cheese food during refrigerated storage." *J. Milk Food Technol.,* 33:383–388.

Post, F. J., A. H. Bliss, and W. B. O'Keefe (1961). "Studies on the ecology of selected food poisoning organisms in food. I. Growth of *Staphylococcus aureus* in cream and cream products." *J. Food Sci.,* 26:436–441.

Potter, M. E., M. J. Blaser, R. K. Sikes, A. F. Kaufman, and J. G. Wells (1983). "Human *Campylobacter* infection associated with certified raw milk." *Am. J. Epidem.,* 117(4):475–483.

Refrigeration Research Foundation (1974). *Commodity Storage Manual.* Refrigeration Research Foundation, Washington, D.C.

Robinson, D. A., W. J. Edgar, G. L. Gibson, A. A. Matchett, and L. Robertson (1979). "*Campylobacter* enteritis associated with consumption of unpasteurized milk." *Brit. Med. J.,* 1:1171–1173.

Schroeder, S. A. (1967). "What the sanitarian should know about salmonellae and staphylococci in milk and milk products." *J. Milk Food Technol.,* 30:376–380.

Sims, J. E., D. C. Kelley, and V. D. Foltz (1969). "Effects of time and temperature on salmonellae in inoculated butter." *J. Milk Food Technol.,* 32:485–488.

Sunga, Fe. C. A., D. R. Heldman, and T. I. Hedrick (1970). "Microorganisms from arms and hands of dairy plant workers." *J. Milk Food Technol.,* 33(5):178–181.

Tacket, C. O., J. P. Narain, R. Sattin, J. P. Lofgen, C. Konigsberg, Jr., R. C. Rendtorff, A. Rausa, B. R. Davis, and M. L. Cohen (1984). "Multistate outbreak of infections caused by *Yersinia enterocolitica* transmitted by pasteurized milk." *J. Am. Med. Assoc.,* 251(Jan. 6):483–486.

U.S. Department of Health, Education and Welfare (1974). "Human *Salmonella dublin* infections associated with consumption of certified milk." *Morbidity and Mortality Weekly Report,* 25:175–176.

White, C. H. and E. W. Custer (1976). "Survival of *Salmonella* in Cheddar cheese." *J. Milk Food Technol.,* 39:328–331.

Meat and Meat Products

Angelotti, R. (1978). "Quality assurance programs for meat and poultry inspection and processing." *Food Technol.,* 32(Oct.):48–50.

Angelotti, R., K. H. Lewis, and M. J. Foter (1962). "Time–temperature effects on fecal streptococci in foods." Unpublished paper presented before the Laboratory Section, 90th Annual Meeting, American Public Health Association, Miami, FL., Oct.

Blaser, M. J. and L. B. Reller (1981). "*Campylobacter* enteritis." *N. Engl. J. Med.,* 305:1444–1452.

Brown, W. L., C. A. Vinton, and C. E. Gross (1960). "Heat resistance and growth characteristics of microorganisms isolated from semi-perishable canned hams." *Food Res.,* 25:345–350.

Canada, J. C. and D. H. Strong (1964). "*Clostridium perfringens* in bovine livers." *J. Food Sci.,* 29:862–864.

Cherry, W. B., M. Scherago, and R. H. Weaver (1943). "The occurrence of *Salmonella* in retail meat products." *Am. J. Hyg.,* 37:211–215.

Eddy, B. P. and M. Ingram (1962). "The occurrence and growth of staphylococci on packed bacon, with special reference to *Staphylococcus aureus.*" *J. Appl. Bacteriol.,* 25:237–247.

Felsenfeld, O., V. M. Young, and T. Yoshimura (1950). "A survey of *Salmonella* organism in market meat, eggs, and milk." *J. Am. Vet. Assoc.*, 116(874):17–21.

Foster, J. F., R. C. Hunderfund, J. L. Fowler, J. T. Fruin, and L. S. Gutherz (1978). "Bacterial populations of ground beef, textured soy protein, and ground beef extended with soy protein after 3 and 10 days of refrigerated storage." *J. Food Prot.*, 41:647–653.

Frazier, W. C. and D. C. Westhoff (1978). *Food Microbiology*, 3rd ed. McGraw-Hill Book Co., New York.

Fruin, J. T. (1977). "Significance of *Clostridium perfringens* in processed foods." *J. Food Prot.*, 40:330–332.

Galton, M. M., W. D. Lowrey, and A. V. Hardy (1954). "*Salmonella* in fresh and smoked pork sausage." *J. Infect. Dis.*, 95:232–235.

Gill, C. O. and N. Penny (1977). "Penetration of bacteria into meat." *Appl. Environ. Microbiol.*, 33:1284–1286.

Goepfert, J. M. (1976). "The aerobic plate count, and *Escherichia coli* content of raw ground beef at the retail level." *J. Milk Food Technol.*, 36:375–377.

Goepfert, J. M. (1977). "Aerobic plate count and *Escherichia coli* determination on frozen ground-beef patties." *Appl. and Environ. Microbiol.*, 34:458–460.

Goepfert, J. M. and J. U. Kim (1975). "Behavior of selected foodborne pathogens in raw ground beef." *J. Milk Food Technol.*, 38:449–452.

Hardin, M., S. Williams, and M. Harrison (1993). "Survival of *Listeria monocytogenes* in post-pasteurized precooked beef roasts." *J. Food Prot.*, 56:655–660.

Hauschild, A. H. W. (1982). "Assessment of botulism hazards from cured meat products." *Food Technol.*, 36(12):95–104.

Heiszler, M. G., A. A. Kraft, C. R. Rey, and R. E. Rust (1972). "Effect of time and temperature of smoking on microorganisms on frankfurters." *J. Food Sci.*, 37(Nov.–Dec.):845–849.

Hurvell, B., M.-L. Danielsson-Tham, and E. Olsson (1981). "Zoonotic aspects of *Yersinia enterocolitica* with special reference to its ability to grow at low temperatures." In *Psychrotrophic Microorganisms in Spoilage and Pathogenicity*, T. A. Roberts, G. Hobbs, J. H. B. Christian, and N. Skovgaard, Eds. Academic Press, London, New York.

Institute of Food Technologists (1986). "Microbiological safety of processed meats. An overview." *Food Technol.*, 40:133–176.

Jay, J. M. (1961a). "Incidence and properties of coagulase-positive staphylococci in certain market meats as determined on three selective media." *Appl. Microbiol.*, 9(3):228–232.

Jay, J. M. (1961b). "Some characteristics of coagulase-positive staphylococci from market meats relative to their origins into the meats." *J. Food Sci.*, 26:631–634.

Jay, J. M. (1962). "Further studies on staphylococci in meats. III. Occurrence and characteristics of coagulase-positive strains from a variety of non-frozen market cuts." *Appl. Microbiol.*, 10:247–251.

Keeton, J. T. and C. C. Melton (1978). "Factors associated with microbial growth in ground beef extended with varying levels of textured soy protein." *J. Food Sci.*, 43:1125–1129.

Kokoczka, P. J. and K. E. Stevenson (1976). "Effect of cottonseed and soy products on the growth of *Clostridium perfringens*." *J. Food Sci.*, 41:1360–1362.

Ladiges, W. C. and J. F. Foster (1974). "A research note: Incidence of *Salmonella* in beef and chicken." *J. Milk Food Technol.,* 37:213–214.

Lee, W. H. (1977). "An assessment of *Yersinia enterocolitica* and its presence in foods." *J. Food Prot.,* 40:486–489.

Lepovetsky, B. C., H. H. Weiser, and F. E. Deatherage (1953). "A microbiological study of lymph nodes, bone marrow and muscle tissue obtained from slaughtered cattle." *Appl. Microbiol.,* 1:57–59.

Morbidity and Mortality Weekly Report (1971). U.S. Department of Health, Education and Welfare, Public Health Serv., Center Dis. Contr., 20, July 17; July 24; Oct. 9.

Morbidity and Mortality Weekly Report (1975). U.S. Department of Health, Education and Welfare, Public Health Serv., Center Dis. Contr., 24, July 5.

Palumbo, S. A., J. L. Smith, and J. C. Kissinger (1977). "Destruction of *Staphylococcus aureus* during frankfurter processing." *Appl. Environ. Microbiol.,* 34:740–744.

Potter, N. N. (1986). *Food Science,* 4th ed. Avi Publishing Co., Westport, CT.

Ravenholt, R. T., R. C. Eelkema, M. Mulhern, and R. B. Watkins (1961). "Staphylococcal infection in meat animals and meat workers." *U.S. Public Health Rep.,* 76:879–888.

Silliker, J. H., C. E. Jensen, M. M. Voegeli, and N. W. Chmura (1962). "Studies on the fate of staphylococci during the processing of hams." *J. Food Sci.,* 27:50–56.

Stern, N.J., S. S. Green, N. Thaker, D. I. Krout, and J. Chiu (1984). "Recovery of *Campylobacter jejuni* from fresh and frozen meat and poultry collected at slaughter." *J. Food Prot.,* 47:372–374.

Strong, D. H., J. C. Canada, and B. B. Griffith (1963). "Incidence of *Clostridium perfringens* in American foods." *Appl. Microbiol.,* 11(1):42–44.

Surkiewicz, B. F., M. E. Harris, R. P. Elliott, J. F. Macaluso, and M. M. Strand (1975). "Bacteriological survey of raw beef patties produced at establishments under federal inspection." *Appl. Microbiol.,* 29(3):331–334.

Sutic, M., J. C. Ayres, and P. E. Koehler (1972). "Identification and aflatoxin production of molds isolated from country cured hams." *Appl. Microbiol.,* 23(3):656–658.

Svedhem, Å., B. Kaijser, and E. Sjögren (1982). "The occurrence of *Campylobacter fetus jejuni* in fresh food and survival under different conditions." *J. Hyg.,* 87(3):421–426.

Tatini, S. R., R. Y. Lee, W. A. McCall, and W. M. Hill (1976). "Growth of *Staphylococcus aureus* and production of enterotoxins in pepperoni." *J. Food Sci.,* 41(March–April):223–225.

Thomason, B. M., W. B. Cherry, and D. J. Dodd (1977). "Salmonellae in health foods." *Appl. Environ. Microbiol.,* 34(5):602–603.

Weisman, M. A. and J. A. Carpenter (1969). "Incidence of salmonellae in meat and meat products." *Appl. Microbiol.,* 17:889–902.

Wilson, E., R. S. Paffenbarger, Jr., M. J. Foter, and K. H. Lewis (1961). "Prevalence of salmonellae in meat and poultry products." *J. Infect. Dis.,* 109:166–171.

Poultry and Poultry Products

Angelotti, R. (1978). "Quality assurance programs for meat and poultry inspection and processing." *Food Technol.,* 32(10):48–50.

Gunderson, M. F., H. W. McFadden, and T. S. Kyle (1954). *The Bacteriology of Commercial Poultry Processing*. Burgess Publishing Co., Minneapolis, MN.

Gutherz, L. S., J. T. Fruin, D. Spicer, and J. L. Fowler (1976). "Microbiology of fresh comminuted turkey meat." *J. Milk Food Technol.,* 39:823–829.

Hagberg, M. M., F. F. Busta, E. A. Zottola, and E. A. Arnold (1973). "Incidence of potentially pathogenic microorganisms in further-processed turkey products." *J. Milk Food Technol.,* 36:625–634.

Hall, H. and R. Angelotti (1965). "*Clostridium perfringens* in meat and meat products." *Appl. Microbiol.,* 13:352–357.

Hamdy, M. K., N. D. Burton, and W. E. Brown (1964). "Source and portal entry of bacteria found in bruised poultry tissue." *Appl. Microbiol.,* 12:464–469.

Hobbs, B. C. (1971). "Food poisoning from poultry." In *Poultry Diseases and World Economy,* R. F. Gordon and B. M. Freeman, Eds. Br. Poult. Sci., Edinburgh.

Lillard, H. S. (1971). "Occurrence of *Clostridium perfringens* in broiler processing and further processing operations." *J. Food Sci.,* 36:1008–1010.

McCarthy, P. A., W. Brown, and M. K. Hamdy (1963). "Microbiological studies of bruised tissues." *J. Food Sci.,* 28:245–253.

Morbidity and Mortality Weekly Report (1969). U.S. Department of Health, Education and Welfare, Public Health Serv., 18, Feb. 22.

Nagel, C. and K. Simpson (1960). "Microorganisms associated with spoilage of refrigerated poultry." *Food Technol.,* 14:21–23.

Norberg, P. (1981). "Enteropathogenic bacteria in frozen chicken." *Appl. Environ. Microbiol.,* 42(1):32–34.

Ostovar, K., J. H. MacNeil, and K. O'Donnell (1971). "Poultry product quality. 5. Microbiological evaluation of mechanically deboned poultry meat." *J. Food Sci.,* 36:1005–1007.

Salzer, R. H., A. A. Kraft, and J. C. Ayres (1967). "Microorganisms isolated from turkey giblets." *Poultry Sci.,* 46:611–615.

Sauter, E. A., C. F. Petersen, and J. F. Parkinson (1978). "Microfloral comparison of fresh and thawed frozen fryers." *Poultry Sci.,* 57(2):422–424.

Stern, N. J., S. S. Green, N. Thaker, D. J. Krout, and J. Chiu (1984). "Recovery of *Campylobacter jejuni* from fresh and frozen meat and poultry collected at slaughter." *J. Food Prot.,* 47:372–374.

Strong, D. H. and N. M. Ripp (1967). "Effect of cookery and holding on hams and turkey rolls contaminated with *Clostridium perfringens.*" *Appl. Microbiol.,* 15:1172–1177.

Todd, E. D. C. (1978). "Foodborne disease in six countries—A comparison." *J. Food Prot.,* 41:559–565.

Todd, E. D. C. (1980). "Poultry associated foodborne disease—Its occurrence, cost, source, and prevention." *J. Food Prot.,* 43:129–139.

Walker, H. W. and J. C. Ayres (1956). "Incidence and kinds of microorganisms associated with commercially dressed poultry." *Appl. Microbiol.,* 4:345–349.

Zottola, E. A. and F. F. Busta (1971). "Microbiological quality of further-processed turkey products." *J. Food Sci.,* 36:1001–1004.

Eggs

Frazier, W. C. and D. C. Westhoff (1978). *Food Microbiology,* 3rd ed. McGraw-Hill Book Co., New York.

Hammid-Samimi, M., K. Swartzel, and H. Ball (1984). "Flow behavior of liquid whole egg during thermal treatments." *J. Food Sci.,* 49:132–136.

Lifshitz, A., R. C. Baker, and H. B. Naylor (1964). "The relative importance of chicken egg exterior structures in resisting bacterial penetration." *J. Food Sci.* 29:94–99.

Lifshitz, A., R. C. Baker, and H. B. Naylor (1965). "The exterior structures of the egg as nutrients for bacteria." *J. Food Sci.,* 30:516–519.

Moore, J. and R. Madden (1993). "Detection and incidence of *Listeria* in blended raw egg." *J. Food Prot.,* 56:652–654.

Paul, M. E. and N. N. Potter (1978). "Bacterial growth in whole egg and egg substitutes including inoculation with *Staphylococcus aureus* and *Clostridium perfringens.*" *J. Food Sci.,* 43:803–806.

Proceedings (1965). National Conference on Salmonellosis, March 11–13, 1964. Communicable Disease Center, Atlanta, GA. pp. 111–151.

Sanders, E., F. J. Sweeney, E. A. Friedman, J. R. Boring, E. L. Randall, and L. D. Polk (1963). "An outbreak of hospital-associated infections due to *Salmonella derby.*" *J. Am. Med. Assoc.,* 186:984–986.

Stokes, J. L., W. W. Osborne, and H. G. Bayne (1956). "Penetration and growth of *Salmonella* in shell eggs." *Food Res.,* 21:510–518.

U.S. Department of Agriculture (1971). *Quantity Recipes for Type A School Lunches.* USDA Food and Nutrition Services, PA 631, revised.

Vadehra, D. V., R. C. Baker, and H. B. Naylor (1970). "Infection routes of bacteria into chicken eggs." *J. Food Sci.,* 35:61–62.

Yadav, N. K. and D. V. Vadehra (1977). "Mechanism of egg white resistance to bacterial growth." *J. Food Sci.,* 42:97–99.

Fish and Shellfish

Abeyta, C., F. G. Dieter, C. A. Kaysner, R. R. Stott, and M. M. Wekell (1993). "*Campylobacter jejuni* in a Washington state shellfish growing bed associated with illness." *J. Food Prot.,* 56:323–325.

Appleman, M. D., N. Bain, and J. M. Shewan (1964). "A study of some organisms of public health significance from fish and fishery products." *J. Appl. Bacteriol.,* 27:69–77.

Baer, E. F., A. P. Duran, H. V. Leininger, R. B. Reid, Jr., A. H. Schwab, and A. Swartzentruber (1976). "Microbiological quality of frozen breaded fish and shellfish products." *Appl. Environ. Microbiol.,* 31:337–341.

Brown, L. D. and C. R. Dorn (1977). "Fish, shellfish, and human health." *J. Food Prot.,* 40:712–717.

Corvin, E. (1975). "For safer shellfish." *FDA Consum.,* 9(8):8–11.

Dickerson, R. W. and M. R. Berry (1974). "Temperature profiles during commercial pasteurization of meat from the blue crab." *J. Milk Food Technol.,* 37:618–621.

Dillon, R. and R. Thakor (1992). "*Listeria* in seafoods: A review (1992)." *J. Food Prot.,* 55:1009–1015.

Duran, A. P., B. A. Wents, J. M. Lanier, F. D. McClure, A. H. Schwab, A. Swartzentruber, R. J. Barnard, and R. B. Read, Jr. (1983). "Microbiological quality of breaded shrimp during processing." *J. Food Prot.,* 46:974–977.

Ecklund, M. W. (1982). "Significance of *Clostridium botulinum* in fishery products preserved short of sterilization." *Food Technol.,* 36(12):107–112.

Kautter, D. A., T. Lilly, Jr., A. J. LeBlanc, and R. K. Lynt (1974). "Incidence of *Clostridium botulinum* in crabmeat from the blue crab." *Appl. Microbiol.,* 28:722.

Liston, J. (1965). "Sanitation in seafood production and distribution." *J. Milk Food Technol.,* 28:152–158.

Madden, J. M., B. A. McCardell, and R. B. Read, Jr. (1982). "*Vibrio cholerae* in shellfish from U.S. coastal waters." *Food Technol.,* 36(3):93–96.

Metcalf, T. G. (1982). "Viruses in shellfish growing waters." *Environ. Int.,* 7:21–28.

Morbidity and Mortality Weekly Report (1963). U.S. Department of Health, Education and Welfare, Public Health Serv., 12, 378.

Nakamura, M. and K. D. Kelly (1968). "Incidence of *Clostridium perfringens* in fish and fish products." *Health Lab. Sci.,* 5(2):84–88.

Nickerson, J. T. R., G. J. Silverman, M. Solberg, D. W. Duncan, and M. M. Joselow (1962). "Microbial analysis of commercial frozen fish sticks." *J. Milk Food Technol.,* 25:45–47.

Pace, P. J. and E. R. Krumbiegel (1973). "*Clostridium botulinum* and smoked fish production: 1963–1972." *J. Milk Food Technol.,* 36:42–49.

Peixotto, S. S., G. Finne, M. O. Hanna, and C. Vanderzant (1979). "Presence, growth and survival of *Yersinia enterocolitica* in oysters, shrimp and crab." *J. Food Prot.,* 42:974–981.

Raj, H. and J. Liston (1963). "Effect of processing on public health bacteria in frozen seafoods." *Food Technol.,* 17:1295–1301.

Richards, G. (1985). "Outbreaks of shellfish-associated enteric virus illness in the United States: Requisite for development of viral guidelines." *J. Food Prot.,* 48:815–823.

Silverman, G. J., J. T. R. Nickerson, D. W. Duncan, N. S. Davis, J. S. Schachter, and M. M. Joselow (1961). "Microbial analysis of frozen raw and cooked shrimp. I. General results." *Food Technol.,* 15:455–458.

Slocum, G. G. (1960). "Microbiological limits for frozen precooked foods." In *Conference on Frozen Food Quality.* U.S. Department of Agriculture, Western Utilization Research and Development Division, Albany, CA. ARS-74-21. pp. 70–73.

Twedt, R. M., J. M. Madden, J. M. Hunt, D. W. Francis, J. T. Peeler, A. P. Duran, W. O. Hebert, S. G. McCoy, C. N. Roderick, G. T. T. Spite, and T. J. Wasenski (1981). "Characterization of *Vibrio cholerae* isolated from oysters." *J. Appl. Environ. Microbiol.,* 41:1475–1478.

Ward, D. R., M. D. Pierson, and K. R. Van Tassell (1977). "The microflora of unpasteurized crabmeat." *J. Food Sci.,* 42:597–600; 614.

Wentz, B. A., A. P. Duran, A. Swartzentruber, A. H. Schwab, F. D. McClure, D. Archer, and R. B. Read, Jr. (1985). "Microbiological quality of crab meat during processing." *J. Food Prot.,* 48:44–49.

Fruits, Vegetables, Cereals, Spices, Nuts

Alderman, G. G. and E. H. Marth (1974). "Experimental production of aflatoxin on intact citrus fruit." *J. Milk Food Technol.,* 37:451–456.

Angelotti, R. (1975). "FDA regulations promote quality assurance." *Food Technol.,* 29(11):60–62.

Bauman, H. E. (1974). "The HACCP concept and microbiological hazard categories." *Food Technol.,* 28(9):30, 32, 34, 74.

Beuchat, L. R. and E. K. Heaton (1975). "Salmonella survival on pecans as influenced by processing and storage conditions." *Appl. Microbiol.,* 29(6):795–801.

Bryan, F. L. (1974a). "Diseases transmitted by food contaminated by waste-water." *Proceedings of the Conference on the Use of Waste Water in the Production of Food and Fiber.* Oklahoma State Department of Health, Oklahoma City, OK.

Bryan, F. L. (1974b). "Microbiological food hazards today—based on epidemiological information." *Food Technol.,* 23(9):52–66, 84.

Christensen, C. M., H. A. Fanse, G. H. Nelson, F. Bates, and C. J. Mirocha (1967). "Microflora of black and red pepper." *Appl. Microbiol.,* 15:622–626.

Fabian, F. W., C. F. Krehl, and N. W. Little (1939). "The role of spices in pickled food spoilage." *Food Res.,* 4:269–286.

Food and Drug Administration (1976a). "Proposed good manufacturing practices for pickled, fermented, acidified, and low-acid foods." *Federal Register,* July 23.

Food and Drug Administration (1976b). "Good manufacturing practices for tree nuts and peanuts." *Federal Register,* June 30.

Foter, M. J. and A. M. Gorlick (1938). "Inhibitory properties of horseradish vapors." *Food Res.,* 3:609–613.

Geldreich, E. E. and R. H. Bordner (1971). "Fecal contamination of fruits and vegetables during cultivation and processing for market: A review." *J. Milk Food Technol.,* 34:184–195.

Goresline, H. E. (1963). "A Discussion of the Microbiology of Various Dehydrated Foods." In L. W. Slanetz et al., *Microbiological Quality of Foods,* proceedings of a conference held at Franconia, New Hampshire, Aug. 27–29, 1962. Academic Press, New York, pp. 179–192.

Hahn, S. S. and M. C. Appleman (1952). "Microbiology of frozen orange concentrate." *Food Technol.,* 6:156–158.

Hanks, T. G. (1967). *Solid Waste Disease Relationships.* U.S. Department of Health, Education and Welfare, Public Health Service Publication No. 999-UIH-6. Washington, D.C.

Huff, W. E. and W. M. Hagler, Jr. (1985). "Density segregation of corn and wheat naturally contaminated with aflatoxin, deoxynivalenol and zearalenone." *J. Food Prot.,* 48:416–420.

Hyndman, J. B. (1963). "Comparison of enterococci and coliform microorganisms in commercially produced pecan nut meats." *Appl. Microbiol.,* 11:268–272.

Ito, K. (1974). "Microbiological critical control points in canned foods." *Food Technol.,* 28(9):46, 48.

Julseth, R. M. and R. H. Deibel (1974). "Microbial profile of selected spices and herbs at import." *J. Milk Food Technol.,* 37:414–419.

Käferstein, F. K. (1976). "The microflora of parsley." *J. Milk Food Technol.*, 39:837–840.

Kauffman, F. L. (1974). "How FDA uses HACCP." *Food Technol.*, 28(Sept.):51, 84.

Konowalchuk, J. and J. I. Speirs (1975). "Survival of enteric viruses on fresh vegetables." *J. Milk Food Technol.*, 38:469–472.

Larkin, E. P., W. Litsky, and J. E. Fuller (1955). "Fecal streptococci in frozen foods. I. A bacteriological survey of some commercially frozen foods. II. Effects of freezing storage of *Escherichia coli*, and some fecal streptococci inoculated onto green beans. III. Effects of freezing storage of *Escherichia coli, Streptococcus faecalis* and *Streptococcus liquifaciens* inoculated into orange concentrate. IV. Effect of sanitizing agent and blanching temperatures on *Streptococcus faecalis*." *Appl. Microbiol.*, 3:98–101; 102–104; 104–106; 107–110.

Marcus, K. A. and H. J. Amling (1973). "*Escherichia coli* field contamination of pecan meats." *Appl. Microbiol.*, 26:279–281.

Maxcy, R. B. (1978). "Lettuce salad as a carrier of microorganisms of public health significance." *J. Food Prot.*, 41:435–438.

Powers, E. M., R. Lawyer, and Y. Masuoka (1975). "Microbiology of processed spices." *J. Milk Food Technol.*, 38:683–687.

Powers, E. M., T. G. Latt, and T. Brown (1976). "Incidence and levels of *Bacillus cereus* in processed spices." *J. Milk Food Technol.*, 39:668–670.

Schlech, W. F. III, P. M. Lavigne, R. A. Bortolussi, A. C. Allen, E. V. Haldane, A. J. Wort, A. W. Hightower, S. E. Johnson, S. H. King, E. S. Nicholis, and C. V. Broome (1983). "Epidemic listeriosis evidence for transmission by food." *N. Engl. J. Med.*, 308:203–206.

Shahidy, S. A., H. A. Hershey, C. Reisberg, and H. R. Berkowitz (1970). "Celery implicated in high bacteria count salads." *J. Environ. Health*, 32:669–673.

Smith, W. W. and S. Iba (1947). "Survival of food poisoning staphylococci on nut meats." *Food Res.*, 12:400–404.

Splittstoesser, D. F., G. E. R. Hervey II, and W. P. Wettergreen (1965). "Contamination of frozen vegetables by coagulase-positive staphylococci." *J. Milk Food Technol.*, 28:149–151.

Strong, D. H., J. C. Canada, and B. B. Griffith (1963). "Incidence of *Clostridium perfringens* in American foods." *Appl. Microbiol.*, 11:42–44.

Suiyana, H. and K. S. Rutledge (1978). "Failure of *Clostridium botulinum* to grow in fresh mushrooms packaged in plastic film overwraps with holes." *J. Food Prot.*, 41:348–350.

Tressler, D. K., W. B. van Arsdel, and M. J. Copley, Eds. (1968). *The Freezing Preservation of Foods,* Vol. 4. Avi Publishing Co., Westport, CT.

Vaughn, R. H. (1963). "Microbial spoilage problems of fresh and refrigerated foods." In L. W. Slanetz, et al., *Microbiological Quality of Foods,* proceedings of a conference held at Franconia, New Hampshire, Aug. 27–29, 1962. Academic Press, New York, pp. 193–197.

Vaughn, R. H., D. I. Murdock, and C. H. Brokaw (1957). "Microorganisms of significance in frozen citrus products." *Food Technol.*, 11:92–95.

Weiser, H. H. (1971). *Practical Food Microbiology and Technology,* 2nd ed. Avi Publishing Co., Westport, CT.

Wilson, D. M. and G. J. Nuovo (1973). "Patulin production in apples decayed by *Penicillium expansum*." *Appl. Microbiol.*, 26:124–125.

Yesair, J. and M. H. Williams (1942). "Spice contamination and its control." *Food Res.,* 7:118–126.

ADDITIONAL READINGS

Al-delaimy, K. S. and M. E. Stiles. "Microbiological quality and shelf-life of raw ground beef." *Can. J. Public Health,* 66:317–321. 1975.

Applebaum, R. S., R. E. Brackett, D. W. Wiseman, and E. H. Marth. "Aflatoxin: Toxicity to dairy cattle and occurrence in milk and milk products—A review." *J. Food Prot.,* 45:752–777. 1982.

Barnard, A. "The reorganization of the shellfish sanitation program under FDA." *Assoc. Food Drug Of. U.S., Q. Bull.,* 34(2):90–96. 1970.

Baumann, D. P. and G. W. Reinhold, "Enumeration of psychrophilic microorganisms. A review." *J. Milk Food Technol.,* 26:81–86. 1963.

Beuchat, L. R. "*Vibrio parahaemolyticus:* Public health significance." *Food Technol.,* 36:(3)80–83, 92. 1983.

Cavett, J. J. "The microbiology of vacuum packed sliced bacon." *J. Appl. Bacteriol.,* 25:282–289. 1962.

Chambers, J. V., D. O. Brechbill, and D. A. Hill. "A microbiological survey of raw ground beef in Ohio." *J. Milk Food Technol.,* 39:530–535. 1976.

Clem, J. D. "Certified shellfish." *FDA Pap.,* 3(4):8–12. 1969.

DiGirolamo, R., J. Liston, and J. R. Matches. "Survival of virus in chilled, frozen, processed oysters." *Appl. Microbiol.,* 20:58–63. 1970.

Duitschaever, C. L., D. R. Arnott, and D. H. Bullock. "Bacteriological quality of raw refrigerated ground beef." *J. Milk Food Technol.,* 36:375–377. 1973.

Duitschaever, C. L., D. H. Bullock, and D. R. Arnott. "Bacteriological evaluation of retail ground beef, frozen beef patties, and cooked hamburger." *J. Food Prot.,* 40:378–381. 1977.

Duran, A. P., B. A. Wentz, J. M. Lanier, F. D. McClure, A. H. Schwab, A. Swartzentruber, R. J. Barnard, and R. B. Read, Jr. "Microbiological quality of breaded shrimp during processing." *J. Food Prot.,* 46(11):974–977. 1983.

Goepfert, J. M. and K. C. Chung. "Behavior of salmonellae in sliced luncheon meats." *Appl. Microbiol.,* 19:190–192. 1970.

Hill, W. M., J. Reaume, and J. C. Wilcox. "Total plate count and sensory evaluation as measure of luncheon meat shelf life." *J. Milk Food Technol.,* 39:759–762. 1976.

Hobbs, B. and J. H. B. Christian, Eds. *The Microbiology of Food.* Academic Press, New York. 1973.

Hobbs, G. "Food poisoning and fish." *J. Roy. Soc. Health,* 103:144. 1983.

Kemp, J. D., B. E. Langlois, J. D. Fox, and W. Y. Varney. "Effects of curing ingredients and holding times and temperatures on organoleptic and microbiological properties of dry-cured sliced ham." *J. Food Sci.,* 40:634–636. 1975.

Kraft, A. A., J. L. Ablinger, H. W. Walker, M. C. Kawal, N. J. Moon, and G. W. Reinbold. "Microbial interactions in foods: Meats, poultry and dairy products." In *Microbiology in Agriculture, Fisheries and Food.* F. A. Skinner and J. G. Carr, Eds. Academic Press, London, New York, San Francisco. 1976.

Lahiry, N. J., M. M. Moojani, and B. R. Baliga. "Factors influencing the keeping quality of fresh water fish in ice." *Food Technol.*, 17:1203–1205. 1963.

Maxcy, R. B. "Fate of microbial contaminants in lettuce juice." *J. Food Prot.*, 45:335–339. 1982.

Mayer, F. J. and M. A. Takeballi, "Microbial contamination of the hen's egg: A review." *J. Food Prot.*, 46:1092–1098. 1983.

Miller, L. and J. A. Koburger. "*Plesiumonas shigelloides:* An opportunistic food and waterborne pathogen." *J. Food Prot.*, 48:449–457. 1985.

Payne, W. L., A. P. Duran, J. M. Lanier, A. H. Schwab, R. B. Read, Jr., B. A. Wentz, and R. J. Barnard. "Microbiological quality of cocoa powder, dry instant chocolate drink mix, dry nondairy creamer, and frozen nondairy topping obtained at retail markets." *J. Food Prot.*, 46:733–736. 1983.

Oblinger, J. L. and A. A. Kraft. "Inhibitory effects of *Pseudomonas* on selected *Salmonella* and other bacteria isolated from poultry." *J. Food Sci.*, 35:30–32. 1970.

Ostovar, K., J. H. MacNeil, and K. O'Donnell. "Poultry product quality. 5. Microbiological evaluation of mechanically deboned poultry meat." *J. Food Sci.*, 36:1005–1007. 1971.

Palumbo, S. A., C. N. Huhtanen, and J. L. Smith. "Microbiology of the frankfurter process: *Salmonella* and natural aerobic flora." *Appl. Microbiol.*, 27:724–732. 1974.

Peel, J. L. and J. M. Gee. "The role of microorganisms in poultry taints." In *Microbiology in Agriculture, Fisheries and Food*, F. A. Skinner and J. G. Carr, Eds. Academic Press, London, New York, San Francisco. 1976.

Powers, E. M., T. G. Latt, D. R. Johnson, and D. B. Rowley. "Occurrence of *Staphylococcus aureus* in and the moisture content of precooked canned bacon." *J. Food Prot.*, 41:708–710. 1978.

Raj, H. and J. Liston. "Survival of bacteria of public health significance in frozen seafoods." *Food Technol.*, 15(10):429–434. 1961.

Solberg, M. and B. Elkind. "The effect of processing and storage conditions on the microflora of *Clostridium perfringens*-inoculated frankfurters." *J. Food Sci.*, 35:126–129. 1970.

Stern, N. J., M. P. Hernandez, L. Blankenship, K. E. Deibel, S. Doores, M. P. Doyle, H. Ng, M. D. Pierson, J. N. Sofos, W. H. Sveum, and D. C. Westhoff. "Prevalence and distribution of *Campylobacter jejuni* and *Campylobacter coli* in retail meats." *J. Food Prot.*, 48:595–599. 1985.

Stewart, A. W., A. F. Langford, C. Hall, and M. G. Johnson. "Bacteriological survey of raw 'soul foods' available in South Carolina." *J. Food Prot.*, 41:364–366. 1978.

Taclindo, C., T. Midura, G. S. Nygard, and H. J. Bodily. "Examination of prepared foods in plastic packages for *Clostridium botulinum*." *Appl. Microbiol.*, 15:426–430. 1967.

Vadehra, D. V., R. C. Baker, and H. B. Naylor. "Role of cuticle in spoilage of chicken eggs." *J. Food Sci.*, 35:5–6. 1970.

Westhoff, D. and F. Feldstein. "Bacteriological analysis of ground beef." *J. Milk Food Technol.*, 39:401–404. 1976.

Wilkinson, R. J., W. L. Mallman, L. E. Dawson, T. F. Irmiter, and J. A. Davidson. "Effective heat processing for the destruction of pathogenic bacteria in turkey rolls." *Poultry Sci.*, 44:131–136. 1965.

CHAPTER 7

Control: Procurement of Sound Food Supply and Appropriate Storage of Purchased Items

The procurement of food must involve assessment of food choices in terms of cost, all aspects of quality (including sanitary quality), convenience, and nutritional value. The food field is undergoing change on a continuing basis. Thus, there is always a need to keep abreast of a rapidly fluctuating situation.

A number of state and federal agencies are concerned with protecting the food supply and are responsible for controlling the sanitary quality of food. Products that may be injurious to health could be embargoed, seized, or recalled.

AGENCIES AND ORGANIZATIONS CONCERNED WITH PROTECTION OF FOOD SUPPLY

The government agencies concerned with the protection of the food supply available to the consumer officiate as representatives at three levels—federal, state, and local—many times in close cooperation with industry. Other agencies that concern themselves with the sanitary aspects of foods are trade associations and institutes, professional societies, private associations, and foundations. The fundamental concern of all these agencies is the wholesomeness of the food supply as it reaches the consumer. The food-processing industries, and their associations, are increasingly active and effective in the promotion of the high sanitary quality of their products.

INTERNATIONAL AGENCIES

Under the umbrella of the United Nations, several branches are concerned with food protection on an international scale. They are the Food and Agriculture Organization of the United Nations (FAO); the World Health Organization (WHO); and the United Nations International Children's Emergency Fund (UNICEF). However, these are not control agencies. Their common interest in healthful and safe foods led to the creation of a forum, the joint FAO/WHO Food Standards Commission, which serves to stimulate and further cooperation among nations regarding international standards for the food-processing industry.

The FAO/WHO Expert Committee on Food Additives establishes acceptable daily intakes for various products commonly added to food.

FEDERAL AGENCIES

Although a number of U.S. Government departments are involved in regulating the food supply, these stand out as being much concerned with the sanitary aspects of food protection: the U.S. Department of Health and Human Services through its agencies, which include the U.S. Public Health Service (PHS) and the Food and Drug Administration (FDA); the Environmental Protection Agency (EPA), which dovetails with the FDA in the responsibility for certain areas (e.g., pesticides in foods); and the U.S. Department of Agriculture, which in turn cooperates closely with the FDA and the EPA.

U.S. Department of Health and Human Services

Under the umbrella of this large department, the U.S. Public Health Service and its subdivisions, the U.S. Food and Drug Administration and the Centers for Disease Control (CDC), are specifically charged with promoting the highest quality of health for every American and the safety of the country's food supply.

PUBLIC HEALTH SERVICE (PHS). The major functions of the PHS are to identify health hazards and to aid in the control of these; to render health services in the field of physical and mental health; and to conduct and support research in medical and related health services, promote the dissemination of research data, and further education and training in matters of health.

The Public Health Service Act of July 1, 1944, substantially revised all legislation concerning the Public Health Service, which has been constantly broadened since, through inclusion of vital statistics, health services for

American Indians and natives of Alaska, the National Library of Medicine, and (in 1968) the Food and Drug Administration.

The PHS is charged by law to promote and assure the highest health attainable for every individual and family in this country, and to cooperate with other nations in projects dealing with health. These are some of the major functions of the PHS:

1. Stimulate and assist in the development of health resources on state and local levels
2. Assist in the development of education for the health professions
3. Further the delivery of health services to all Americans
4. Support and conduct research in the medical sciences
5. Protect the health of all citizens against unsafe and impure foods, drugs, cosmetics, and other potential hazards
6. Provide leadership for the prevention of communicable diseases

The PHS consists of six agencies: Agency for Toxic Substances and Disease Registry; Alcohol, Drug Abuse, and Mental Health Administration; Centers for Disease Control; Food and Drug Administration; Health Resources and Services Administration; and National Institutes of Health.

FOOD AND DRUG ADMINISTRATION (FDA). The name was first provided by the Agriculture Appropriation Act of 1931, although some of its functions had been carried on (under different titles) since 1906. The FDA directs its efforts toward protecting the nation's health against unsafe and impure foods, unsafe drugs and cosmetics, and other potential hazards.

The FDA administers the Federal Drug and Cosmetic Act, the Fair Packaging and Labeling Act, the Tea Act, and the Import Milk Act. The Federal Drug and Cosmetic Act was originally enacted in 1906 and amended in 1938.

The Fair Packaging and Labeling Act was enacted in 1966 as an amendment to the 1938 act. Three major amendments to the 1938 law are the Miller Pesticide Amendment of 1954, the Food Additives Amendment of 1958 (which includes the Delaney clause), and the Color Additives Amendment of 1960.

The Federal Food, Drug, and Cosmetic Act of 1938 as amended applies to interstate shipment of food (except meat and poultry) and also to food items than are produced in—or shipped into—territories and the District of Columbia. In connection with matters of food sanitation, it is important to know that the act includes authorization for standards of quality for foods except butter, vegetables, and fruits (with some exceptions), and classification of violations into *adulteration* and *misbranding.*

Meat, poultry, and egg products are exempt in all points covered by the Meat Inspection Act, the Poultry Inspection Act, and the Egg Products Inspection Act; these acts are regulated through the U.S. Department of Agriculture.

The activities of the FDA that have to do with food protection are carried out by the Center of Food Safety and Applied Nutrition. Food-related activities of the Center are divided into food sanitation and quality control; chemical contamination and pesticides; food additives; interstate travel; nutrition and nutrition labeling; and foodservice, shellfish, and milk safety (Read, 1982).

As part of its charge of policing the purity, quality, and labeling of foods, the agency makes periodic inspections of food-processing and storage facilities and examines samples; enforces regulations that specify the kinds and quantities of microbial contaminants, additives, and pesticides allowable in foods; checks imports of foods into the United States; cooperates with state and local agencies in the inspection of and—if indicated—the removal from the market of foods contaminated in the course of disasters; requests recalls of foods known or suspected to contain ingredients known or suspected to be injurious to human health; and assists industry in voluntary compliance with the Federal Food, Drug, and Cosmetic Act.

In connection with the microbiological aspects of food quality, the requirement that the food not be "adulterated" is of interest, since the presence of certain microorganisms and/or their toxins falls into the category of "adulterated foods."

Certainly, microorganisms capable of causing foodborne illnesses, and their toxins, are "injurious to health." Thus, it takes little imagination to see that the FDA can exert considerable power in forcing many foods so contaminated out of the market, at least those shipped in interstate commerce. The microorganisms, the toxins they produce, and other evidence of unsanitary processing need not be proved; the mere fact that their presence can be shown to be possible may lead to condemnation.

The FDA has set a vigorous and effective control project in operation. An effectual approach taken in the inspection of food-processing plants employs the system of hazard analysis and the pinpointing of critical control points (HACCP). Hazard analysis is a system of food product classification on the basis of potential health hazard. The critical control point concept can be defined to describe the points (or locations) in a food-processing operation at which failure to prevent contamination or bacterial growth results in a product that represents a potential food safety risk. By this method, the inspectors determine the points in processing that are critical ones for the safety of the product they produce and where processors fail to control these critical points (see also Chapters 6 and 14).

The FDA keeps a sharp eye on food shipments made across state lines to assure food safety. Acidified or low-acid canned foods are a case in point, since these items could provide excellent environments for the growth of *Clostridium botulinum.* The FDA requires manufacturers of low-acid or acidified foods to register their processing plants and file their processes with the FDA. If a firm fails to comply, it may be required to obtain an emergency permit before releasing its product into interstate commerce. There are special regulations for imported foods also.

When contamination of processed food with microorganisms such as *Clostridium botulinum, Clostridium perfringens, Salmonella, Campylobacter jejuni, Vibrio parahaemolyticus, Yersinia enterocolitica,* and *Listeria monocytogenes,* or other important foodborne pathogens is discovered, the FDA locates the source and removes the contaminated items from the market unless the processors of the contaminated items have already withdrawn them voluntarily. There is close cooperation between the FDA and industry in their concern for the wholesomeness and safety of the nation's food supply.

A good example of the cooperative actions of the food industry and the FDA is the voluntary recall in 1985 of all 44 dairy products manufactured by Jalisco Mexican Products, Inc., Artesia, California. The recall resulted from an investigation by the California Department of Health, the County of Los Angeles, and the Centers for Disease Control, which linked infant deaths to the fact that the babies' mothers had eaten Mexican-style soft white cheeses contaminated with the pathogen *Listeria monocytogenes,* an organism routinely killed during pasteurization. The cheeses had been distributed nationwide. A thorough inspection of the plant for faults in the method of milk pasteurization made by the FDA and the state and county health organizations followed, and then the plant was closed.

The FDA also ensured that following the recall of the product by the manufacturers, wholesale and retail distributors did their share in removing the products from warehouses and shelves. Listeriosis is not a common illness in adults, and symptoms of the illness are similar to those of a mild flu. However, in fetuses and newborns, the disease is life threatening (Special Communication, FDA, June 17, 1985). Within the organizational structure of the FDA, it is the Center for Food Safety and Applied Nutrition* that is largely concerned with matters of foodservice sanitation and safety. The Office of Compliance is concerned with regulatory guidance, food and color additives, and cooperative programs.

The FDA offers, in its own facility,** training courses for persons concerned with food safety, for example, sanitarians, inspectors, regulatory officials, sanitary engineers, investigators, and administrative personnel responsible for food-protection programs in government and industry.

Since the FDA is legally responsible for interstate travel sanitation, federal inspectors will check on the sanitary conditions of foodservice on public conveyances such as trains, planes, buses, and ships operated under the U.S. flag, and on the safety of the food and drink served.

Problems connected with sanitary handling of food served in flight are

*Address: 200 C Street, SW, Washington, D.C.
**Address: 5600 Fishers Lane, Rockville, MD 20857.

not too surprising, considering the multitudes of persons served meals on airplanes each day combined with the fact that the kitchens where the meals are prepared are often a great distance away from airports, not to mention unforeseeable delays in holding and serving the meals to the public. Food-poisoning outbreaks have occurred owing to such causes as improper preparation or subsequent handling (McLearn and Miller, 1985). Investigation of foodborne disease outbreaks and/or spot inspections by the FDA personnel have prompted the FDA to offer guidance to the industry. Information on interstate travel sanitation conveyances and support facilities is available through FDA offices.

The FDA works closely with state and local health agencies in matters of food protection. Such cooperation was initiated by the Public Health Service many years ago. One example is the cooperative Program for the Certification of Interstate Milk Shippers; the Milk Sanitation Program is under the FDA.

Another cooperative example between federal and state agencies and industry is the National Shellfish Program. Initiated almost 50 years ago by the PHS, this program, too, is part of the FDA, in cooperation with state agencies and industry.

Model codes and ordinances have been, and are being, developed; they serve nonfederal agencies as models for the production of safe, potentially hazardous foods such as milk, frozen desserts, smoked fish, processed egg products, drinking water, and ice. Model ordinances and codes have also been developed for sanitary foodservice and the sanitary vending of food (Food and Drug Administration, 1978a, b); and, in cooperation with the Association of Food and Drug Officials,* a retail food store sanitation code (Association of Food and Drug Officials, 1982).

In 1993, the Public Health Service published the *Food Code 1993*. This publication combines the information incorporated in the Food Service Sanitation, Vending of Food and Beverages, and Retail Food Store Sanitation publications. An introduction states that the publication was aimed at safeguarding public health by assuring that food is unadulterated and safe wherever it is offered to the consumer. The strategy used is to emphasize prevention of problems as well as the detection of them in the finished product. The *Food Code 1993* includes the following subjects: purpose and definitions; management and personnel; food; equipment, utensils, and linens; water, plumbing, and waste; physical facilities; poisonous and toxic materials; and compliance and enforcement. The *Food Code 1993* is available in printed form or on diskette from the U.S. Department of Commerce (NTIS).**

The Division of Cooperative Programs, Retail Food Protection Branch, has the important function of aiding the foodservice industry in producing and

---

*Address: P.O. Box 3425, York, PA 17402.
**Telephone number: 703-487-4650 or 800-553 NTIS.

serving wholesome, safe food to the public. This division also includes the Shellfish Sanitation Branch and the Milk Safety Branch. Its activities are:

1. To develop national sanitary standards (model ordinances) for the operation of retail food establishments
2. To promote the legal adoption of the model ordinances by state regulatory agencies that have responsibility for the sanitation level of retail food operations
3. To standardize and certify state persons who satisfactorily demonstrate competence through field and written examinations
4. To evaluate foodservice sanitation programs
5. To provide technical assistance to those persons, associations, or organizations who request such service in matters pertaining to the retailing of foods
6. To inspect foodservice facilities in government-owned buildings, as well as those in the Interstate Travel Sanitation (ITS) program
7. To participate in national committee work where food equipment construction criteria are determined
8. To work with the retail food industries in the development, promotion, and implementation of management-level sanitation training programs

These FDA regulations promote quality assurance (Angelotti, 1975; Majorack, 1982).

Another regulatory area of the FDA is establishment of microbiological quality standards. Acceptable microbial levels for food products are developed at the retail or consumer level, bringing into account abuses that are to be expected under normal conditions. To arrive at these levels, several steps are taken:

1. Nationwide (statistical) survey of the food being evaluated
2. Critical review of the data assembled
3. Development of realistic, workable standards
4. Publication of the proposed standard in the *Federal Register*
5. Finalizing of the proposed standard, which then becomes a mandatory standard

Regarding toxins in food, the FDA has set action levels for aflatoxins in peanuts, certain dairy products, and other commodities. The action level is that level of adulteration below which the agency will generally not prosecute (Labuza, 1983).

The FDA works in close cooperation with the Centers for Disease Control. The two federal regulatory agencies that have major responsibilities for food protection—the FDA and the USDA—report incidences of foodborne illnesses to the Centers for Disease Control in Atlanta, Georgia. The CDC and local health authorities, in turn, report to the FDA and the USDA any disease outbreaks that might have arisen in connection with commercial products.

It is evident that the FDA is concerned with the sanitary quality of foods on the processors' as well as the retailers' level, which includes the foodservice industry.

Although the overall safety of the food products used in foodservice is controlled by the FDA, the actual food-handling operations are controlled through local and state agencies.

U.S. Department of Agriculture (USDA)

The USDA engages in food protection in that it establishes, administers, and enforces a number of food standards through the branch agency known as the Food Service and Inspection Service (FSIS).

This office aids in making the tremendous national food marketing operation more orderly, efficient, and economical. A considerable part of the research effort and regulatory activity of this agency is devoted to the goal of reducing the incidence of pathogenic and otherwise harmful bacteria in livestock, poultry, and food products. For example, through the efforts of the cooperative poultry improvement programs, *Salmonella pullorum* was practically eradicated from poultry flocks. USDA specialists were successful in developing a workable method for pasteurizing egg white, and the USDA scientists have developed a recommended procedure for isolating salmonellae from meat products and animal feed.

THE MEAT INSPECTION ACT.   The Meat Inspection Branch of the FSIS enforces the Meat Inspection Act of 1906 and regulations in connection with inspection of meat, that all meat and meat products shipped in interstate commerce, produced in the District of Columbia or in the U.S. territories, or imported from foreign countries must be inspected as regulated by the act and must be packed under a license. Among important activities are ante- and postmortem inspections of the animal for disease, and inspection for sanitation pertaining to processing procedures, plant maintenance, and personnel. Since 1967, federal law requires that all states adopt and enforce inspection of meat using standards at least as high as federal standards.

THE POULTRY PRODUCTS INSPECTION ACT.   Regulations similar to those applied to meat are used for poultry through enforcement of the Poultry Products Inspection Act of 1957. They involve ante- and postmortem inspection of the animals and inspection for sanitation regarding processing, personnel, and plant maintenance. The Poultry Division of the FSIS gives this service. The act, which first went into effect on a voluntary basis, became mandatory in 1959.

THE EGG PRODUCTS INSPECTION ACT.   This act, passed in 1970 (U.S. Public Law), provides for the inspection of certain egg products by the USDA, restriction of the disposition of certain qualities of eggs, uniformity of standards for eggs in interstate or foreign commerce, and cooperation with state agencies in administration of the act. No egg-processing plant is permitted to sell eggs or egg products—in local or out-of-state markets—that are not pasteurized. Inspection regulations are stringent.

ACCEPTANCE-TYPE INSPECTION SERVICE.   This service provides, on request, an inspection service that allows an institutional food buyer to write specifications to suit needs.

COMMODITIES OTHER THAN MEAT, POULTRY, AND EGG PRODUCTS.   Continuous inspection services are available for fruit and vegetable products, dairy products, egg products, and rabbit meat. Processing plants must at all times measure up to strict requirements for quality and sanitation, or service will be withdrawn.

GRADING.   A large percentage of all the grading in foods is done on the basis of U.S. grades set up by the FSIS. The grading service will provide certification of quality based on these grades.

Environmental Protection Agency (EPA)

In the realm of food safety as affected by pesticides and additives, this agency dovetails some of the responsibilities that were formerly carried out by the U.S. Department of Health and Human Services (Food and Drug Administration) and the U.S. Department of Agriculture. One very important responsibility of the EPA is registering pesticides and establishing pesticide tolerances on both raw agricultural commodities and processed foods.

U.S. Department of Commerce (USDC)

The National Marine Fisheries Service of the U.S. Department of Commerce administers the Agricultural Marketing Act as it extends to fish. Products that meet the official standards carry the U.S. shield, indicating the grade of the product and that it was packed under continuous supervision of a government agent. The Division of Seafood Research, Inspection and Consumer Services houses the USDC quality inspection services. The inspection service of the National Marine Fisheries Service is also concerned with microbiological criteria; it does not establish criteria but examines fishery products for conformance with criteria of other agencies, such as the FDA, the Department of Defense, industry, and/or institutional purchasers.

FEDERAL REGISTER SYSTEM

Pronouncements of agencies of the federal government that pertain to standards and inspection are published in the Federal Register System. The system consists of two parts: the *Federal Register,* which is published on a frequently scheduled basis, and the annually revised *Code of Federal Regulations.* These two publications together provide an up-to-date version of agency regulations.

The creation in 1935 of the *Federal Register* by congressional legislation has resulted in a much-needed central system for the publication of government regulations. A new dimension was created in 1946 through the Administrative Procedure Act, by which the element of public participation was added. In the *Federal Register* as we know it today, interested persons are given an opportunity to react to, and make comments on, agency proposals before final regulations are issued. Notices of proposed regulations should be closely watched by food industry and trade associations.

Documents published in the *Federal Register* may be grouped as follows:

1. Presidential documents
2. Rules and regulations, codified, as they will appear in the *Code of Federal Regulations*
3. Proposed rules, giving the public an opportunity to react to them and make comments
4. Notices, which are miscellaneous announcements (not codified). Since 1977, a further breakdown of notices is grouped under "Sunshine Act Meetings"

STATE AND LOCAL AGENCIES

The food laws laid down by states and municipalities are, in general, fashioned after the regulations or recommendations set up by federal agencies.

State and local agencies are active to assure that foodservice establishments:

1. Are operated under the supervision of a person knowledgeable in sanitary food-handling practices
2. Are equipped, maintained, and operated to offer minimal chance for food hazards to develop
3. Use, at all times, ingredients and food products that are wholesome as well as safe

State food laws are usually enforced through the state's Department of Public Health. On the municipal level, the Department of Health and/or Board of Health may be involved. Some states publish a state-level equivalent of the *Federal Register.*

The FDA, although cognizant of the fact that state and local governments have jurisdiction over the sanitary aspects of a foodservice establishment's operation, is very active in assisting states in their efforts.

OTHER AGENCIES AND PROFESSIONAL SOCIETIES

Some trade associations and institutes are active in upgrading and maintaining the sanitary quality of their products. The National Canners Association, the American Meat Institute, and the American Dry Milk Institute are examples of such organizations. Many processing plants set up their own sanitary standards, which are frequently fashioned after federal recommendations.

The Armed Services set up their own criteria and recommend special laboratory procedures to assure the high sanitary quality of the ingredients and products they use. In this connection, a radiometric method for rapid screening of cooked foods for microbial acceptability was developed by Rowley et al. (1978).

The Institute of Food Technologists also offers short courses on food safety.

One of the influential semiprivate agencies concerned with sanitation is the National Sanitation Foundation, which was organized by a group of industrial leaders and Public Health officials. It is a nonprofit, noncommercial organization that seeks solutions to problems involving cleanliness, and it sponsors and conducts research to find answers to sanitation problems. On the basis of results from research, minimum sanitation standards are developed for equipment, products, and devices that are generally acceptable to the health authorities. A manufacturer or producer may apply for the use of the National Sanitation Foundation Testing Laboratory Seal of Approval.

The American Public Health Association, the International Association of Milk, Food and Environmental Sanitarians, and the Association of Food and Drug Officials are examples of professional societies that have published recommendations pertaining to methodology for investigation of food-poisoning outbreaks and the microbiological examination of foods. The Association of Food and Drug Officials also publishes recommendations for uniform codes pertaining to the sanitary quality of foods.

MICROBIOLOGICAL CRITERIA

Rapid developments in the processing and distribution of foods that need little or no additional preparation in the kitchen are constantly creating new opportunities for potential hazards to public health. In connection with the concern over potential hazards (Slanetz et al., 1963), microbiological criteria have been, and still are, ardently discussed.

In 1985, a report titled *Evaluation of the Role of Microbiological Criteria for Foods and Food Ingredients* was published. It contains the findings of the Subcommittee on Microbiological Criteria, Committee on Food Protection, Food and Nutrition Board, National Research Council (National Research Council, 1985). Under discussion were definitions, purposes, and needs for microbiological criteria; selection of foods for criteria related to safety; selection of pathogens as components of microbiological criteria; selection of indicator organisms and agents as components of microbiological criteria; consideration of sampling associated with a criterion; consideration of the decision (action) to be taken when a criterion (limit) is exceeded; current status of microbiological criteria and legislative bases; application of microbiological criteria to foods and food ingredients; expansion of the HACCP system in food-protection programs; and plans of action for implementation of the HACCP system and of microbiological criteria for foods and food ingredients.

DEFINITIONS

These are the definitions given by the above-named committee studying the role of microbiological criteria:

> A *standard* is part of a law or ordinance and is a mandatory criterion.
>
> A *guideline* is a criterion used to assess microbiological conditions during the processing, distribution, and marketing of foods. Guidelines are mandatory in that they signal when there are microbiological problems that require attention.
>
> A *specification* is used in purchase agreements between buyers and vendors of a food ingredient.

They may be mandatory or advisory.

The discussion that follows is based on some of the highlights of the committee's evaluation. The committee's report states with emphasis that a microbiological criterion should be established (and implemented) only in cases where there is a need for it and when it can be shown to be effective as well as practical.

Concerning standards, it is stated that they be considered only when, based on evidence, the standard would alleviate a problem existing between a food and foodborne disease outbreaks; when it is evident that the food contains decomposed ingredients; when the food was evidently grossly mishandled during preparation, packaging, or storage; and/or when, in the case of certain imported foods, the standard would eliminate dangers to health; or when the standard would constitute a basis for rejecting items produced under possibly poor conditions.

Concerning guidelines, it is stated that these function as alerting mechanisms whenever microbiological conditions prevail while an item is processed and distributed.

Concerning specifications set up in connection with purchasing food, a need for certain specifications should exist and these should be based on sound data.

FOODS

Foods for which microbiological criteria are meaningful and useful need to be selected on the basis of certain prerequisites: there should be epidemiological evidence that they are significant vehicles for transmission of foodborne disease; that opportunities for survival of contaminants in the food exist; that it is to be expected that growth of contaminants occurs sometime during the manufacture, storage, and distribution of the food and its final handling during meal preparation and prior to service.

PATHOGENS

Concerning pathogens to be selected as a meaningful part of a microbiological criterion, it is stated that the pathogen must be one likely to be found in a particular food or ingredient and be of a hazardous nature. Some important pathogens and toxins are listed next.

For *Salmonella,* microbiological criteria have been set and applied by official agencies and industry, being used for sensitive food as well as animal feed.

For *Staphylococcus aureus,* microbiological criteria that are feasible for assessing the extent of contamination with cocci and/or toxins formed by these should be established and applied.

Regarding *mycotoxins,* standards have already been set by the FDA for aflatoxins B_1 and M_1 for sensitive foods fed to animals.

Concerning *Clostridium perfringens,* the report stated that microbiological criteria would not contribute significantly to preventing foodborne disease caused by this organism, since the presence of low numbers is, in many foods, unrelated to unsanitary handling. However, suspect food incriminated in outbreaks should be checked for presence of *C. perfringens.*

In regard to *Clostridium botulinum,* the committee suggested that the organism should not be used as a test organism in the routine surveillance of potentially hazardous foods, but that, following outbreaks of botulism, a thorough investigation should be made.

Other pathogens that, at this time, were not considered to be eligible for serving as microbiological criteria in routine surveillance of foods were the following: *Bacillus cereus, Vibrio parahaemolyticus, Yersinia enterocolitica, Campylobacter jejuni, Shigella,* and *Vibrio cholerae.*

Regarding *V. cholerae,* strict adherence to the requirement set by the National Shellfish Sanitation Program would prevent contamination with the pathogen of raw oysters, mussels, and clams.

Regarding *viruses,* present methods of analysis were considered to be impractical for routine surveillance of foods.

Concerning pathogenic *Escherichia coli,* it was stated that procedures that would be practical for the detection and enumeration of *E. coli* are not available at the present time for routine programs of surveillance.

In regard to *Trichinella spiralis,* the committee suggested that, in view of the procedures specified by the USDA and the accepted procedure of cooking pork to temperatures ensuring freedom from live trichinae, no routine examination of meat for larvae is recommended.

INDICATOR ORGANISMS AND AGENTS

Certain microorganisms and metabolic products produced during microbiological growth have been much used to assess food safety, either as a sole test or in conjunction with others.

Aerobic plate counts (APCs), providing an estimated number of microorganisms present in a food, can be a valuable tool if used for certain purposes, for example, to indicate microbial survival following certain processing methods, or growth at critical control points, or the shelf life of a food.

However, APCs also have limitations because they do not accurately determine the total number of bacteria in a sample. Actually, they determine only that portion of the bacterial population that will form colonies in the test medium on which they are tested, and under other environmental conditions provided during the test. To obtain meaningful data, methodology has to be strictly standardized. A discussion of the value of aerobic plate counts for assessing safety, sanitary quality, and organoleptic quality was given by Silliker (1963).

Use of thermoduric, psychrotrophic, thermophilic, proteolytic, and lipolytic counts was discussed also. Thermoduric pasteurization counts are used in the milk industry to assess the efficacy of pasteurization and also effective cleaning and sanitizing of equipment. Psychrotrophic microorganisms are able to multiply under conditions of refrigeration and are useful indicators of proper refrigeration. High numbers of proteolytic and lipolytic bacteria can cause objectionable odors and flavors in seafood, poultry, dairy products, and meat, and indicate poor quality.

Direct microscopic counts (DMCs) are a valuable component of microbiological criteria for eggs (liquid, frozen, and dried) and raw milk. By direct count, however, viable and dead cells cannot be distinguished.

Other methods worth mentioning are *microscopic mold counts,* used for raw horticultural products; *yeast and mold counts,* which are part of microbiological standards for certain dairy products; counts of *heat-resistant molds,* used for heat-processed fruits; and *thermophilic spore counts,* employed in the canning industry.

Metabolic products, which are produced during the growth of microorganisms, can also be a useful tool in assessing the effect of microbial activity in food. It is beyond the scope of this book to elaborate on these. The reader is referred to the committee's report mentioned earlier (National Research Council, 1985).

ASSESSMENT OF INDICATORS OF HUMAN OR FECAL CONTAMINATION

Some foodborne pathogens deserve special consideration because they are indicators of human or fecal contamination.

Staphylococci are useful indicators of contamination by a human source and applicable to foods that are handled after heat processing such as pasteurization or cooking, and to foods that are handled much in preparation. Large numbers of the organism may indicate the presence of toxins.

Escherichia coli is a commonly used indicator of fecal contamination. Small-number contamination of raw foods of animal origin is to be expected, but large numbers indicate mishandling and unsanitary procedures in slaughtering. Heat-processed foods should be free from *E. coli;* therefore, their presence in heat-processed foods usually indicates recontamination. The presence of *E. coli* raises suspicion that other intestinal organisms, including enteric pathogens, might be present.

Fecal coliforms are used as indicator organisms for evaluating shellfish and water in which they grow, for wholesomeness. But they are used for evaluating other foods also.

Enterococci are useful as indicator organisms in certain foods because they are fairly salt-tolerant and are relatively resistant to freezing. However, enterococci counts are not regarded as providing a reliable index of fecal contamination.

Coliforms may originate from an environment of plants, soil, water, and feces. They frequently find their way into the processing plant. Therefore, they are useful indicators for assessment of postprocessing contamination or the efficacy of heat treatment.

LEGISLATIVE ASPECTS

Microbiological criteria are developed and applied at international and national levels. In the United States, federal and state health and agriculture departments, local (city, county) agencies, and the food industry are involved.

International Level

On this level, microbiological criteria are handled through the Joint FAO/ WHO Food Standards Program (Olson, 1978; Clark, 1978), implemented as the Codex Alimentarius Standards Commission.

National Level (U.S.A.)

FEDERAL AGENCIES. *The Food and Drug Administration* has the power of specifying certain microbiological criteria for certain food items (FDA, 1982). The criteria pertain to foodborne pathogens, aflatoxins, bacterial toxins, and indicator bacteria. Some imported items such as shrimp and frog legs are tested for the presence of salmonellae. The FDA endeavors to establish close cooperation with industry to assure food quality through its quality assurance assistance program (Majorack, 1982).

The U.S. Department of Agriculture (USDA) has set up microbiological standards for raw milk, for processed milk products, and for frozen and dried egg products. The USDA egg program requires that *Salmonella* be absent from eggs.

At present, the *Food Safety and Inspection Service (FSIS)* of the USDA is responsible for the wholesomeness of meat and poultry. The agency has not set up microbiological criteria, but used informal, advisory criteria (National Research Council, 1985).

The U.S. Department of Commerce, National Marine Fisheries Service (NMFS), established in 1970, has an inspection program for fishery products that is a voluntary program of inspection and grading. The quality inspection activities of NMFS have been described by Sackett (1982). The development and use of microbiological criteria are the responsibility of the Division of Seafood Research.

The Defense Standardization and Specification Program, administered by the *U.S. Army Natick Research and Development Center,* includes several hundred food specifications of which approximately one-tenth involve microbiological criteria (Department of Defense, 1978).

State Agencies

On the state level, great variation exists regarding microbiological criteria for a great number of foods (Wehr, 1982). However, regarding milk, the cooperation between the FDA and the states has led to good uniformity; and most state and local regulatory agencies use the Grade A Pasteurized Milk Ordinance (USPHA/FDA, 1978).

Close cooperation also exists between federal and state agencies regarding sanitation of shellfish and seafood. The microbiological criteria applying to seafood can be found in the National Fisheries Institute *Handbook* (Martin and Pitts, 1982).

Numerous agencies (state level) are listed by Wehr (1982). The microbiological criteria reported lack uniformity from state to state.

Food buyers who wish to use microbiological criteria should seek guidance from their own states. Examples of agencies concerned with matters of food sanitation might be a Department of Public Health, a Department of Consumer Protection, a Department of Agriculture, a Department of Human Resources, a County Board of Health, or a City Department of Health. The local health agency should be able to direct the food buyer to the appropriate office.

Local (County, City) Level

Local agencies concentrate mainly on the safety of locally produced and/or consumed food products, frequently those from specialty food-processing operations.

Industry

The food-processing industry sets up microbiological guidelines and specifications of raw materials and other ingredients used in further processing in order to assess their wholesomeness. Microbiological criteria are also used by processors throughout the operation, especially for the monitoring of critical control points. The finished product should satisfy the goal of microbiological limits that will indicate its safety.

However, processors vary regarding use of microbiological limits. The importance of good manufacturing practices to achieve finished products that are bacteriologically safe is of very great importance. In fact, according to the Subcommittee on Microbiological Criteria (National Research Council, 1985), the HACCP concept is considered a rational and effective approach to assuring safety and preventing spoilage of foods. The committee report also emphasizes that—in the application of HACCP—the use of microbiological criteria is a very effective tool, at least in the manufacture of some products; in others, critical control points would be monitored by other tests. The HACCP concept application of foodservice is discussed in Chapter 14.

THE ROLE OF THE DIETITIAN, FOODSERVICE MANAGER, OR OTHER BUYER

The person entrusted with the purchasing of food carries the responsibility for obtaining the best for a given amount of money, one important quality factor being the wholesomeness or sanitary quality of the items purchased.

In the FDA *Food Service Sanitation Manual* (1978a), it is stated that "food shall be in sound condition, free from spoilage, filth, or other contamination and shall be safe for human consumption. Food shall be obtained from sources that comply with all laws relating to food and food labeling. The use of food in hermetically sealed containers that was not prepared in a food processing establishment is prohibited." It is the responsibility of the institutional food buyer to find out which sources are safe.

Wholesome food from safe sources can be subjected to contamination and spoilage. It is the responsibility of the food buyer to write into his or her specifications sanitary packaging and protection during transit against physical damage resulting from lack of time–temperature control. It is also the responsibility of the buyer to check and inspect the incoming purchases.

The steps to effective institutional food buying, as listed by Frooman (1953), are these: (1) find out what the food industry is offering the institutional market; (2) determine what best fits your needs; (3) compile written specifications covering your selections; (4) work out a buying procedure and decide on a course of action; and (5) check and inspect all deliveries.

In many institutions, the dietitian or foodservice manager is the person who carries out all of these activities in addition to other responsibilities which involve supervision of the storage of the purchased goods, the preparation and service of menu items, and the storage of leftovers. In some large organizations, a purchasing agent may do the actual ordering and checking. Yet the dietitian or foodservice manager may even then exert an influence by requesting that the purchasing agent specify certain quality characteristics of the various items he orders or by requesting the purchase of "new" items placed on the market. Therefore, the first step, "find out what the food industry offers," is indeed an important one.

This is a relatively easy task for the more conventional line of foods, but not so for some of the "new" foods, the products of recent and current developments in the food-processing field. Criteria of wholesomeness have not been developed for many of these new items.

DEVELOPMENTS IN THE FOOD-PROCESSING INDUSTRY

One of the most remarkable developments in the food industry has been the transfer of menu item preparation from the institution kitchen to the factory. The factory-prepared items include partially prepared as well as ready-to-eat products. Improvement in speed of transportation and extensive use of refrigeration and freezing are making this development possible.

By keeping abreast of new developments in the food field and research on the sanitary quality of new products, dietitians and foodservice managers can not only further their knowledge—if they put this knowledge to work by using it in specifications when contracting for food, if they request products produced under conditions of high sanitary standards—but also contribute toward a high goal of sanitation in the food field as a whole.

The dietitian or foodservice manager can use various resources to gain information on what industry has to offer. Some important sources of information are professional organizations such as the American Dietetic Association, the American Hospital Association, the American School Food Service Association, the National Restaurant Association, and the various professional state associations. These associations sponsor meetings at which eminent speakers present, among other material, pertinent information on newly developed foods, including the microbiological aspects of their processing and packaging. Also, these national associations have professional journals that publish articles with pertinent information regarding problems related to the sanitary aspects of the food supply.

Information on new developments in the food field is also made available by Cooperative Extension Services of the various states which transmit foodmarketing information. Hospital management magazines, foodservice magazines, and trade association publications all bring food news to the customer. Very little information on the sanitary aspects of newly developed food products is actually conveyed to the potential buyer to use as a basis for writing specifications insuring sanitary quality.

PURCHASING BY SPECIFICATIONS

Specifying exactly what is wanted is of greatest importance in purchasing food of high sanitary quality. Precise specifications can and should be made for the food itself as well as the packaging whenever possible. The federal or trade grade, or the brand, of the food should be stated. The size, nature, and sanitary conditions of the container may be specified. There may be specific factors required for specific commodities that are important from the viewpoint of sanitation; these may concern sanitary standards of the food itself, sanitary condition of containers, conditions of shipping, and other factors.

The writing of specifications is made easier by the establishing of grades and familiarity with the product. Governmental agencies and local health authorities may help set up specifications for food items that lack established standards or criteria. Specifications set up by the institutional food buyer should cover the wholesomeness of the product at the source, nature of packaging, handling, and time–temperature control during transit.

The use of microbiologic criteria in writing specifications for potentially hazardous items is on the increase. Meaningful and achievable criteria should be employed.

The Committee on Microbiological Criteria (National Research Council, 1985) expresses with regret that "unfortunately, purchase specifications are frequently written by a purchasing agent whose knowledge of the relevance of such specifications to the microbiological acceptability of the finished product concerned, is insufficient for selection of appropriate specifications."

It is advisable that help be sought by contacting the public health agency of the respective state for information on criteria established by that agency regarding a specific food item and the type and allowable number of microorganisms (usually per gram) present, and/or the regional FDA office. Negative counts for *Salmonella* are established for a great number of items. However, in the case of raw meat, microorganisms of public health significance such as *Salmonella, S. aureus, C. perfringens, Y. enterocolitica,* and *C. jejuni,* are part of the natural microbial flora of live animals and cannot be completely eliminated.

Microbiological specifications are useful and meaningful for cooked ready-to-eat shellfish such as shrimp and crabmeat. The guidelines should include aerobic plate count (APC), *E. coli,* and *S. aureus* (National Research Council, 1985). There are also other different criteria and even standards for fresh seafood, *E. coli* being a useful indicator of polluted waters.

The sound condition and safe source of a food are basic to the protection of the consumer from a public health point of view, particularly food considered "potentially hazardous." According to the definition of the U.S. Public Health Service (FDA, 1978a):

> Potentially hazardous food means any food that consists in whole or in part of milk or milk products, eggs, meat, poultry, fish, shellfish, edible crustacea or other ingredients, including synthetic ingredients, in a form capable of supporting rapid and progressive growth of infections or toxigenic microorganisms. The term does not include clean, whole, uncracked, odor-free shell eggs or foods which have a pH level of 4.6 or below or a water activity (a_w) value of 0.85 or less.

The reader is referred to Chapter 6 for a discussion of the microflora of different kinds of foods, and to Chapter 10 for a discussion on effects of pH and moisture (a_w) on multiplication of bacteria in food.

In the FDA *Food Service Sanitation Manual* (1978a) mentioned earlier, specific requirements were set up for milk, eggs, and shellfish, because these items are particularly favorable media for growth of pathogenic contaminants. Nondairy creaming and whitening agents are given attention also.

The reason for prohibiting the use of hermetically sealed, noncommercially processed and packaged food is based on the fact that these items have frequently been the cause of outbreaks of foodborne diseases.

Dairy Products

According to the U.S. Public Health Service (FDA, 1978a):

> Fluid milk and fluid milk products used or served shall be pasteurized and shall meet the Grade A quality standards as established by law. Dry milk and dry milk products shall be made from pasteurized milk and milk products.

> Milk and milk products for drinking purposes shall be provided to the consumer in an unopened, commercially filled package not exceeding 1 pint in capacity, or drawn from a commercially filled container stored in a mechanically refrigerated bulk milk dispenser. Where a bulk dispenser for milk and milk products is not available and portions of less than ½ pint are required for mixed drinks, cereal, or dessert service, milk and milk products may be poured from a commercially filled container of not more than ½ gallon capacity.

> Cream or half and half shall be provided in an individual service container, protected pour-type pitcher, or drawn from a refrigerated dispenser designed for such service.

> Reconstituted dry milk and dry milk products may be used in instant desserts and whipped products, or for cooking and baking purposes.

The Grade A Pasteurized Milk Ordinance 1978 Recommendations is the most recent revision of the requirements met by the USPHS/FDA regarding pasteurized Grade A milk; it was implemented in 1980 (U.S. Public Health Service/Food and Drug Administration, 1978).

Frozen desserts like ice creams, sherbets, ice milks, ices, and mixes from which frozen desserts are made should all conform to the sanitary standards set up by state and local regulations.

The dietitian or foodservice manager assuming duties in a new locality should consult with the local health authorities before setting up specifications. This is important, since some regulations differ from state to state, as well as from one locality to another.

Nondairy Products

In the FDA *Food Service Sanitation Manual* (1978a), it is stated that:

> Non-dairy creaming or whitening agents shall be provided in an individual service container, protected pour-type pitcher, or drawn from a refrigerated dispenser for such service.

> Non-dairy creaming, whitening, or whipping agents may be reconstituted on the premises only when they will be stored in sanitized, covered containers not exceeding 1 gallon in capacity and cooled to 45° F or below within four hours after preparation.

Meat, Poultry, and Products Made from Them

The perishability of mildly processed meat and poultry is of special interest here, since they are frequently mishandled regarding temperature control. These items, because they are not sterile, are vulnerable to warmth and should therefore be held under continuous refrigeration. While under refrigeration, chilled meats are vulnerable to spoilage by cold-tolerant bacteria. Raw meat may also be contaminated with pathogenic microorganisms, some of which are capable of multiplying under refrigeration, for example, *Yersinia enterocolitica*. In pasteurized meats the microbial balance is upset in that an assortment of heat-resistant forms may survive and grow when conditions allow this, while the forms that would normally multiply most vigorously and suppress pathogenic forms are absent.

The number of marketed items that fall into the category of mildly processed foods is on the increase. Included here are hams, other meats, and poultry. Because of the uncertainties in connection with the microbiological aspects of these and other items receiving light heat treatments, it is important that these items not be allowed to remain in the danger zone of bacterial multiplication except for brief periods. Carelessness in temperature control, anywhere and any time, may spell trouble.

Food items packaged under vacuum might require particular attention, since the anaerobic conditions would inhibit many spoilage bacteria, but not the anaerobics and the microaerophilics. However, this is a controversial issue and requires further study.

Specifications for shipment of frozen meats and poultry and products made from them should require that these items be kept at temperatures appropriate to maintain the quality of frozen foods.

It is evident, then, that the reliability of the vendor of highly perishable and potentially hazardous items is of utmost importance. This quality of reliability cannot be overestimated. Marginal dealers have been known to enhance their profits by selling items containing chemicals to retard food spoilage, which is an illegal practice. Institutions that are offered donated foods should refuse these donations on principle.

Eggs

"Only clean whole eggs, with shell intact and without cracks or checks, or pasteurized liquid, frozen, or dry eggs or pasteurized dry egg products shall be used, except that hard-boiled, peeled eggs, commercially prepared and packaged, may be used," according to the FDA *Food Service Sanitation Manual* (1978a).

Eggs cannot receive a grade when dirty, cracked, or broken. This is important, since eggs with dirty and broken shells cannot be trusted to be free from salmonellae. Eggs may be purchased by federal grades.

Eggs may also be graded according to the buyer's specifications under the supervision of federal graders, this being the acceptance-type inspection.

When writing specifications for eggs, the institutional buyer should be aware that egg quality deteriorates rapidly. Therefore, the maximum number of days allowed to lapse between grading and delivery should be specified; this period is usually restricted to a few days. Also, the temperature conditions under which the eggs are stored before delivery should be specified and should require that the eggs be held under refrigeration at all times. Ideally, the eggs should come from one and the same source known to produce eggs from a disease-free flock of hens under strictly sanitary conditions. Under conditions of competitive buying, contracting for eggs from one producer may be impractical. Processed eggs and egg products must be free from salmonellae.

Fish and Shellfish

Fish and shellfish are highly perishable and do not tolerate long holding. Quality standards developed for fish are administered by the National Marine Fisheries Service, U.S. Department of Commerce.

Most fresh fish is sold without labels, and, seemingly, some confusion exists about guidelines for writing specifications for fresh fish. A reliable local dealer should prove helpful; his or her advice might well be sought regarding the availability of the various fresh fish in season.

In writing specifications, the sanitary source and processing should be stressed as well as sanitary treatment in transit. This includes sanitary packaging and strict temperature control. Frozen fish must be kept solidly frozen at all times; wrappings and glazes should not indicate damage.

Shellfish, fresh or frozen, must come from unpolluted waters. The Food and Drug Administration is entrusted with the supervision of the shellfish industry, the catching, processing, and marketing. The requirements are stringent.

In the FDA *Food Service Sanitation Manual* (1978a) special recommendations are made regarding shellfish:

> Fresh and frozen shucked shellfish (oysters, clams, or mussels) shall be packed in nonreturnable packages identified with the name and address of the original shell stock processor, shucker-packer, or repacker, and the interstate certification number issued according to law. Shell stock and shucked shellfish shall be kept in the container in which they were received until they are used. Each container of unshucked shell stock (oyster, clams, or mussels) shall be identified by an attached tag that states the name and address of the original shell stock processor, the kind and quantity of shell stock, and an interstate certification number issued by the state or foreign shellfish control agency.

The certification by state shellfish agencies is made available through the Food and Drug Administration, which issues a periodic listing of certified shippers. The FDA honors only the certification of state shellfish agencies whose sanitary control measures are acceptable to them. This listing is an important and effective means of assuring the health authority that shellfish which originates outside its authority is wholesome.

As is true for other frozen items, frozen shellfish must be kept solidly frozen at all times.

Precooked Frozen Items

It is important to order from reliable vendors who handle items processed by reputable food processors. Since there have been almost no standards set up for these foods, buyers ordering items in very large quantities may wish to establish their own specifications, which may extend to formulation as well as to bacteriological quality. Strictest time–temperature control during transit is another important point to be stressed. Temperatures must be maintained at 0°F (-17.8°C) or lower to retain quality in a frozen product—in the processing plant, during transit, in warehouse storage, and on the premises of the foodservice establishment.

Foods Prepared Outside the Place of Service

When food prepared outside the hospital, school, or other place of service is purchased, it should be obtained from sources that comply with the regulations of the state, locality, or municipality. This is true whether the food is served in the conventional way or through vending machines. Such food should be wholesome and be processed, prepared, stored, and transported in a sanitary manner. This requirement includes that all good contact surfaces of containers should be protected from contamination and that strict time–temperature control be exercised during processing, preparation, and transport.

In vending, next to malfunctioning of the machines themselves, the most important hazard seems to be related to improper processing and mishandling of the items prior to introducing them into the machine.

PROTECTING FOODS IN STORAGE

Receiving and Checking

Promptly upon delivery, the purchased items should be checked and inspected to make certain that the products agree with specifications. Items that do not meet the requirements should be returned.

If cases or wrappings are damaged, or discolored, they should be opened and inspected. All deficiencies should be recorded.

Great speed is required in the inspection and subsequent storage of perishables requiring refrigeration, freezer storage, or hot holding. It is therefore essential to know the time when perishables are to be delivered and to be ready for them with adequate personnel and space. Speed protects the food received and reduces the length of time the refrigerator and freezer doors remain open. Food requiring hot holding must be checked and stored rapidly so that it does not cool.

As is true for other packaged goods, inspection for signs of physical damage is indicated. Signs of thawing should be looked for also. The experienced dietitian and food manager is familiar with these signs: coarse ice crystals, cavity ice, shrinkage, discoloration, leakage, and so forth.

Canned items are checked for abnormalities that might indicate that the product is not sterile or may not keep: broken seals, leaks, swells, rust, and so forth.

Storage

Storage serves to temporarily house the purchased food items. Storage facilities should provide quarters appropriate for the satisfactory preservation of food quality, including sanitary quality. For dry items such as staples and canned goods, "dry storage" is provided. For highly perishable items, refrigerator or freezer storage is necessary. Chilled storage is to be provided for dairy products, meat, poultry, eggs, fish, fruits, and vegetables; freezer storage for all frozen foods; and hot-holding equipment for hot food items.

The following recommendations are taken from the FDA *Food Service Sanitation Manual* (1978a):

> Food, whether raw or prepared, if removed from the container or package in which it was obtained, shall be stored in a clean covered container except during necessary periods of preparation or service. Container covers shall be impervious and nonabsorbent, except that linens or napkins may be used for lining or covering bread or roll containers. Solid cuts of meat shall be protected by being covered in storage, except that quarters or sides of meat may be hung uncovered on clean sanitized hooks if no food product is stored beneath the meat.
>
> Containers of food shall be stored a minimum of 6 inches above the floor in a manner that protects the food from splash and other contamination, and that permits easy cleaning of the storage area, except that:
>
> (1) Metal pressurized beverage containers, and cased food packaged in cans, glass or other waterproof containers need not be elevated when the food container is not exposed to floor moisture, and
>
> (2) Containers may be stored on dollies, racks or pallets, provided such equipment is easily movable.
>
> Food and containers of food shall not be stored under exposed or unprotected sewer lines or water lines, except for automatic fire protection sprinkler heads that may be required by law. The storage of food in toilet rooms or vestibules is prohibited.
>
> Food not subject to further washing or cooking before serving shall be stored in a way that protects it against cross-contamination from food requiring washing or cooking.
>
> Packaged food shall not be stored in contact with water or undrained ice. Wrapped sandwiches shall not be stored in direct contact with ice.
>
> Unless its identity is unmistakable, bulk food such as cooking oil, syrup, salt, sugar or flour not stored in the product container or package in which it was obtained, shall be stored in a container identifying the food by common name.

DRY STORAGE.   This type of storage serves for food items that do not require refrigeration but must be protected from freezing, excessive heat, dampness, rodents, and insects.

Dry storage rooms should be cool (50–70°F) (10–21.1°C), well ventilated, and dry; a relative humidity of 50–60% is satisfactory for many products kept in dry storage.

The construction should be such that cleaning is easy. The stored food should be protected against invasion of rodents, infestation with insects, and bacterial contamination. Therefore, the floors, walls, and windows should be rodent- and insect-proof. Places where pipes enter and leave the walls should be well sealed off.

Dry storage rooms are very frequently located in a basement and, therefore, are usually given the doubtful benefit of all sorts of pipes that run along the ceiling such as water, heating, and sewer pipes. Leakage from these pipes is a common source of trouble in basement storage rooms. Especially ominous is leakage from sewer pipes, which may have most serious consequences caused through contamination of foods with pathogenic bacteria and viruses present in sewage. Sewer pipes need frequent checking for leakage.

Hot water and steam pipes may create unfavorably high temperatures in the storeroom and should therefore be well insulated. The temperature can also be increased to an undesirable degree by sunlight entering through glass windows. Canned goods are not completely sterile and contain heat-loving, heat-resistant bacteria that survived the canning process; when temperatures rise to tropical heights, these survivors may begin to multiply, spoiling the contents of the cans.

Foods should never be placed directly on the floor; shelving should be provided. Both wood and metal shelves are used, each having its good and poor points. Wooden shelves may be cheaper but they absorb moisture and are difficult to sanitize, while noncorrosive metal shelves are easy to clean and vermin proof. Lightweight, sturdy, adjustable metal shelving is commercially available for storerooms and refrigerators. Just how far the lowest shelf should be placed above the floor is a matter of judgment. For easy cleaning, a minimum of 6–8 inches should be allowed in any case. For the storage of many types of foods, galvanized cans with lids provide excellent containers. For bags and case lots, slatted platforms raised at least 6 inches from the floor are often used.

The sanitary quality of the food stored should be constantly protected by providing excellent care of the storeroom. The physical structure, floors, walls, ceilings, and shelves, should be kept in excellent repair and immaculately clean. Frequent inspection for presence of rodents, insects, and leakage from pipes is mandatory.

Insects sometimes gain entrance with crates and boxes into otherwise well-maintained storerooms. To eradicate insects, a professional exterminator should be engaged. Professional services for the extermination of rodents are also recommended.

After every issue of food, spilled food items must be gathered up and eliminated, either by disposal in covered metal trash cans inside the storage area or by complete removal from the area.

The cleaning routine should be frequent. Highest sanitary standards for, and close supervision of, all activities in connection with storeroom use and care are absolutely essential to maintain the sanitary quality of the stored items.

Orderly procedures in the stocking and the withdrawal of foods are also necessary to assure that stocked items will be used within a reasonable period of time.

In many foodservice systems, prepared items are transported to the place of service as frozen, chilled, or hot foods.

FREEZER STORAGE.   To maintain the culinary quality of frozen foods, storage of 0°F (−17.8°C) or below is recommended, except for ice cream. At these temperatures, no bacterial hazards need be expected. Ice cream is usually stored at 6–10°F (−14.4 to −12.2°C), because it is more easily handled at these warmer temperatures and its culinary quality is enhanced.

Whenever possible, frozen foods should be stored in the original containers. If wrapping is done, moisture- and vapor-proof materials should be used.

Problems in connection with defrosting are discussed in Chapter 13.

CHILLED (REFRIGERATOR) STORAGE.   For the chilled storage of prepared foods, it is recommended in the FDA *Food Service Sanitation Manual* (1978a) that potentially hazardous food that is to be transported be prechilled and continuously held at a temperature of 45°F (7.2°C) or below. Safe chilling procedures of precooked foods are discussed in Chapters 11, 13, and 14.

In the FDA *Food Service Sanitation Manual* (1978a), the following statements concerning chilled storage are made:

> Enough conveniently located refrigeration facilities or effectively insulated facilities shall be provided to assure the maintenance of potentially hazardous food at required temperatures during storage. Each mechanically refrigerated facility storing potentially hazardous food shall be provided with a numerically scaled indicating thermometer, accurate to ±3° F [±1.67° C], located to measure the air temperature in the warmest part of the facility and located to be easily readable. Recording thermometers, accurate to ±3° F [±1.67° C], may be used in lieu of indicating thermometers.

The various items to be kept under refrigeration require somewhat different temperatures for storage. Dairy products and eggs are stored at 36–40°F (2.2–4.4°C); meat and poultry at 30–36°F (−1.1 to 2.2°C); fish is kept iced or at 30–32° F (−1.1 to 0°C); fruits and vegetables between 35 and 45°F (1.7 and 7.2°C).

The control of relative humidity is very desirable for cold storage of food items. A relative humidity of 75–85% is most frequently recommended for dairy products, meats, and poultry; for eggs, 80–85%; for fruits and vegetables, 85–95%.

Too high humidity causes sliminess in meats and poultry, the condition being due to excessive bacterial multiplication. The current trend is to include the feature of controlled humidity in refrigerators.

Temperature control is impossible without checking and rechecking the temperatures that actually prevail in a refrigerator. Too often a refrigerator is simply assumed to provide temperature conditions which, in reality, do not exist. The fact that a sign is affixed to the refrigerator door announcing a certain temperature does not necessarily mean that the refrigerator lives up to that expectation. Temperatures should be so adjusted that the warmest spot within the refrigerator is not higher than the maximum desirable for the particular food housed. Frequent regular checks are necessary, since the refrigerator temperature will fluctuate with such factors as size and temperature of the food loads placed in it and cooling capacity of the unit.

Dairy products and eggs absorb odors from other foods and should be stored separately. Milk and cream should be covered, butter and cheese kept wrapped, when stored. Eggs are stored with the pointed ends down and should not be disturbed more than is absolutely necessary. Crates should be stacked in a way to allow for circulation of air. Crates containing fruits and vegetables also should be stacked so as to allow for ventilation.

It goes without saying that, at best, cold storage will prolong but not improve the quality of perishable items. Even though properly refrigerated foods may remain bacteriologically safe for a remarkably long time, their culinary quality may not survive. Among the dairy products, fluid milk assumes off-flavors readily. Among the meats, lamb, pork, and poultry do not take kindly to prolonged storage, whereas aged beef may be held for 5–7 days, and fresh beef even longer.

Eggs, when stored at the proper temperature and relative humidity, will keep fresh remarkably long. At room temperatures, egg quality deteriorates quickly. It is, therefore, a deplorable procedure to hold eggs issued in the morning for a day's use in kitchens and bakeshops. Small refrigerator units should be installed in strategic areas of use, to receive and cold store the eggs.

Refrigerated fresh fish should be used within 24 hours if kept uniced. When held longer (3 days maximum), icing should be employed.

Since the keeping quality of fruits and vegetables is not as important from a public health point of view, it will not be discussed.

Metal shelves are recommended for refrigerators. Sanitary care of the refrigerated storage areas involves frequent inspections of the food supplies and removal of items suspected of quality deterioration; regular, if possible daily, cleaning of floors; regular, if possible weekly, cleaning of other surfaces such as walls and shelving. For cleaning shelves, which have direct contact with the food, hot water, soap, a brush, and "elbow grease" are recommended, followed by a thorough rinse with hot water containing baking soda.

HOT STORAGE. This topic is discussed in detail in Chapters 13 and 14. In principle, the FDA regulations as stated in the *Food Service Sanitation Manual* (1978a) require that:

> Enough conveniently located hot food storage facilities shall be provided to assure the maintenance of food at the required temperature during storage. Each hot food facility storing potentially hazardous food shall be provided with a numerically scaled indicating thermometer, accurate to $\pm 3°$ F [$\pm 1.67°$ C], located to measure the air temperature in the coolest part of the facility and located to be easily readable. Recording thermometers, accurate to $\pm 3°$ F [$\pm 1.67°$ C], may be used in lieu of indicating thermometers. Where it is impractical to install thermometers on equipment such as bainmaries, steam tables, steam kettles, heat lamps, cal-rod units, or insulated food transport carriers, a product thermometer must be available and used to check internal food temperature.

> The internal temperature of potentially hazardous foods requiring hot storage shall be 140° F [60° C] or above except during necessary periods of preparation. Potentially hazardous food to be transported shall be held at a temperature of 140° F [60° C] or above.

REFERENCES

Angelotti, R. (1975). "FDA regulations promote quality assurance." *Food Technol.,* 29(11):60–62.

Association of Food and Drug Officials and U.S. Department of Health and Human Services (1982). *Retail Food Store Sanitation Code.*

Clark, D. C. (1978). "The International Commission on Microbiological Specifications for Foods." *Food Technol.,* 32(1):51–54, 67.

Department of Defense; Office of Undersecretary of Defense for Research and Engineering (1978). *Defense Standardization and Specifications Program; Policies, Procedures and Instructions.* Manual DOD 4120. 3M. Naval Publ. and Forms Center, Philadelphia, PA.

Food and Drug Administration (1978a). *A Food Service Sanitation Manual. 1976.* U.S. Department of Health, Education and Welfare, Public Health Serv., DHEW Publ. No. (FDA) 78-2081. Washington, D.C.

Food and Drug Administration (1978b). *The Vending of Food and Beverages.* U.S. Department of Health, Education and Welfare, Public Health Serv., DHEW Publ. No. (FDA) 78-2091. Washington, D.C.

Food and Drug Administration (1982). *Compliance Policy Guides Manual.* No. PB-271176, Nat. Techn. Inform. Service, Springfield, VA.

Food and Drug Administration (1993). *Food Code 1993.* No. PB94-113941AS, Nat. Techn. Inform. Service, Springfield, VA.

Frooman, A. A. (1953). *Five Steps to Effective Institutional Buying.* Institutions Publications, Chicago, IL.

Labuza, T. P. (1983). "Regulation of mycotoxins in food." *J. Food Prot.,* 46:260–265.

Majorack, F. C. (1982). "FDA's industry quality assurance assistance program." *Food Technol.,* 36(6):87–88, 95.

Martin, R. E. and G. T. Pitts (1982). *Handbook of State and Federal Microbiological Standards and Guidelines.* National Fisheries Institute, Washington, D.C.

McLearn, D. C. and R. W. Miller (1985). "Airline food safety raises concerns." *FDA Consum.,* 19(1):4–9.

National Research Council (1985). *An Evaluation of the Role of Microbiological Criteria for Foods and Food Ingredients.* National Academy Press, Washington, D.C.

Olson, J. C., Jr. (1978). "Microbiological specifications for foods: International activities." *Food Technol.,* 32(1):55–57, 62.

Read, R. B. (1982). "Regulation enforcement as an aid to a safe, wholesome food supply." *Food Technol.,* 36(12):71–73.

Rowley, D. B., J. J. Previte, and H. P. Srinivasa (1978). "A radiometric method for rapid screening of cooked foods for microbial acceptability." *J. Food Sci.,* 43:1720–1722.

Sackett, I. D., Jr. (1982). "Quality inspection activities of the National Marine Fisheries Service." *Food Technol.,* 36(6):91–92.

Silliker, J. H. (1963). "Total counts as indexes of food quality." In *Microbiological Quality of Food.,* L. W. Slanetz, C. O. Chichester, A. R. Gaufin, and Z. J. Ordal, Eds., pp. 102–112. Academic Press, New York.

Slanetz, L. W., et al. (1963). "Microbiological quality of foods," Proceedings of a conference held at Franconia, NH, August 27–29, 1962. Academic Press, New York.

U.S. Public Health Service/Food and Drug Administration (USPHS/FDA) (1978). *Grade A. Pasteurized Milk Ordinance.* 1978 Recommendations, PHSI/FDA Publ. No. 229, U.S. Govt. Printing Office, Washington, D.C.

United States Public Law (1970). "Egg Products Inspection Act." U.S. Public Law 91-597, 91st Congress, H. R. 19888, Dec. 29, 1970.

Wehr, H. M. (1982). "Attitudes and policies of government agencies on microbial criteria for foods—An update." *Food Technol.,* 36(9):45–54, 92.

ADDITIONAL READINGS

Foster, E. M. "Interpretation of analytical results for bacterial standards enforcement." *Assoc. Food Drug Of. U.S. Q. Bull.,* 38:267–276. 1974.

Haveland, H. "Interstate travel sanitation." *FDA Pap.* 3(10):7–10. 1969.

International Commission of Microbiological Specifications for Foods. *Microorganisms in Foods.* Vol. 2, University of Toronto Press, Toronto. 1974.

Knight, J. B. and L. H. Kotchevar. *Quantity Food Production, Planning and Management.* CBI Publ. Co., Boston, MA. 1979.

Leininger, H. V., L. R. Shelton, and K. H. Lewis. "Microbiology of frozen cream-type pies, frozen cooked peeled shrimp and dry food-grade gelatin." *Food Technol.,* 25:224–226, 229. 1971.

Miskimin, D. K., K. A. Berkowitz, M. Solberg, W. E. Riha, Jr., W. C. Franke, R. L. Buchanan, and V. O'Leary. "Relationship between indicator organisms and specific pathogens in potentially hazardous foods." *J. Food Sci.,* 41:1001–1006. 1976.

Spears, M. C. and A. G. Vaden. *Foodservice Organizations.* John Wiley and Sons, New York. 1985.

WHO Expert Committee (with the participation of FAO). *Microbiological Aspects of Food Hygiene.* WHO, Geneva, Technical Report Series, No. 598. 1976.

CHAPTER 8

Contamination of Ingredients and Menu Items in the Foodservice Establishment

M icrobial contamination of menu items in a foodservice establishment may occur via human, animal, or environmental sources. Other sources include the food itself, contact surfaces, utensils, and equipment. To minimize contamination, some establishments are using outside sources of prepared foods for some or all menu items. A great many others are continuing to prepare food from scratch on site.

THE FOOD HANDLER

The food handler is an important source of contamination in a foodservice establishment. This fact bears repeating, even though the human reservoir of pathogens capable of causing foodborne illnesses was discussed in Chapter 5. Needless to say, the human reservoir is important whenever and wherever people handle food, be it in the processing plant, in shipment, in the kitchen, or in the dining room. It seems important to now take a closer look at the circumstances under which the transfer of microorganisms from people to ingredients and menu items may take place in the foodservice establishment, with regard to applying this information to effective control measures available to the foodservice manager, supervisor, and food handler.

Healthy humans are known to be a potential source of *Staphylococcus aureus,* both coagulase-negative and coagulase-positive, *Salmonella, Clostridium perfringens,* fecal streptococci (enterococci), and, less commonly, of

Campylobacter jejuni and *Yersinia enterocolitica.* The staphylococci are common inhabitants of the skin, nose, mouth, and throat, and may easily be transferred to food. This potential source is available throughout the working hours of the food handler. Every time his or her hands make contact with body parts harboring the staphylococci, they become contaminated, and subsequently contaminate food they touch. Direct transfer of these cocci from the respiratory tract to food is made when the food worker coughs and sneezes without covering his or her nose and mouth. If hands or a handkerchief are used to cover the cough, the hands become contaminated and unless they are immediately washed, they serve as a vehicle of transmission for many foods.

Hands with infected cuts or burns are a rich source of virulent staphylococci and so are infected sores on other body parts of a food handler, because he or she might scratch or otherwise touch them.

The intestinal organisms may get attached to the hands of a food handler who visits the toilet and does not thoroughly wash his or her hands before returning to work. Pathogens of intestinal origin that are capable of causing foodborne illnesses include the salmonellae, the fecal streptococci, *Clostridium perfringens,* enteropathogenic *Escherichia coli,* and shigellae. An outbreak of shigellosis involving 176 persons is illustrative of what dire consequences a food handler, sick with shigellosis *(S. boydii),* may have *(Morbidity and Mortality Weekly Report,* 1977). The food handler had become infected during a visit to Mexico. *Campylobacter jejuni* was isolated from the hands of an infected food handler who, while ill, prepared food for boys in a camp where an outbreak of foodborne illness occurred (Blaser et al., 1982). It is a well-known fact that viral pathogens, too, can be transmitted by way of hands soiled with human body wastes.

After washing, the worker may easily recontaminate his or her hands by touching soiled clothing, faucets, linen towels, doorknobs, and the like.

Respiratory as well as intestinal disorders are frequent causes of illness. Food handlers returning to work shortly after recovery from these disorders are likely to be especially rich reservoirs of the pathogens for a while.

The personal habits, also called "hand habits," of the food handler have a great deal to do with the chances of transfer of contaminants from person to food. These hand habits refer to involuntary movements of the hands, such as scratching the skin, rubbing the nose, smoothing or arranging the hair, touching the clothing, and the like.

Funk (1955) made a revealing study of certain habits of the foodservice employee that may lead to contamination of food. Habits believed to present sanitary hazards were under scrutiny. They were restroom procedures, including washing hands after visiting the toilet; washing hands before reporting to work and before returning to work after meals and coffee breaks; and washing hands after touching body parts. Also studied were certain working habits in the preparation of sandwiches and salads, in portioning desserts, in handling prepared foods, and in dishwashing. Observations were made in three units of a university food service and of a local luncheon counter. It was found that employees who executed a variety of duties had more undesirable habits than employees doing specific jobs. The employees of the lunch counter operation performed more undesirable acts than the employees of the college food service. On warm days, body parts were touched more frequently; in particular, the hair was brushed away from the face. Length of service of the employee was not a factor affecting the performance of undesirable habitual acts. Busy persons had less time for these undesirable habits. Hands were washed more frequently when hand-washing facilities were near the place of work.

A comparison of the bacterial flora on the hands of personnel engaged in nonfood and food industries was made by Seligman and Rosenbluth (1975). They found that coagulase-positive staphylococci changed from transient to resident status when food handlers were the contaminated persons. Staphylococci were more apt to demonstrate a transient status on persons occupied in nonfood industries. A correlation was noted between the flora of food handlers' hands and the foods that these contacted while working with them.

The opportunities for contamination of hands are endless and cannot possibly be enumerated. Examples are picking up a dangling shoe lace that needs to be tied, recovering a potholder from the floor, reaching into a drain that needs to be unplugged, and countless similar acts where contact is first made with unsanitary articles and surfaces and then with food. That foods themselves can be reservoirs of undesirable pathogens was discussed in previous chapters; handling of certain foods likely to bear pathogens may lead to serious contamination.

The bacterial flora of the hands of foodservice employees has been analyzed by Horwood and Minch (1951). Thirty-four food handlers were selected at random from 22 public eating places in Boston and Cambridge, Massachusetts. These establishments included cafeterias, lunchrooms, restaurants, and drugstores. No attempt was made to trace the origin of the bacteria. It is therefore likely that some bacteria were derived from the food that was handled. Extremely large numbers of bacteria were isolated. Among these, hemolytic staphylococci, streptococci, and *Escherichia coli* were types recovered frequently. The results of this study illustrated a dire need for education and supervision in matters of personal hygiene.

A food handler's habit of frequently touching her mouth while preparing cold sandwiches led to 105 cases of hepatitis A in a department store's basement restaurant. The sandwich-maker was the index person; the date of onset of her illness and the dates of food consumption and onset of illness of restaurant patrons were consistent with periods of infectivity and incubation for hepatitis (*Morbidity and Mortality Weekly Report,* 1974).

The smoking habit, from a sanitation point of view, may represent a potential danger because of possible transfer of saliva to the hands of the smoker. Also, when a cigarette is laid down on surfaces that are used in food preparation, the saliva will contaminate the surfaces with organisms originating in the human respiratory system.

The habit of tasting food from cooking utensils is an unsanitary one, because the taster will inoculate his mouth flora, which is apt to contain staphylococci, into food. This tasting habit is not only esthetically undesirable but potentially dangerous, especially when it concerns food that will not be heated or sufficiently reheated to destroy the organisms transferred. Kerr et al. (1993) and Snelling et al. (1991) examined the prevalence of *Listeria* on the hands of food workers and found that good hand-washing techniques, using soap and antibacterial agents, and using sufficient wash time as well as dry time with hot air was important in controlling the contamination. Coates et al. (1987) had shown similar results with *Campylobacter* and *Salmonella* bacteria.

RODENTS AND INSECTS

Rodents and insects are a menace to areas where food is stored and prepared. The danger of contamination with pathogens harbored by these animals was discussed in an earlier chapter.

Rodents and insect pests have been known to contaminate food in storage as well as in the preparation area. They have been found to contaminate menu items left in inappropriate places to cool, such as counters, equipment, utensils, and working surfaces—in brief, almost anything left unprotected. Opportunity for entrance and subsequent activities of these pests is afforded wherever and whenever access from the outside exists. The importance of excluding vermin from all areas where food is stored, prepared, and served cannot be overemphasized.

SOIL

Soil is carried into the food establishment on clothing, especially shoes. Soil may be blown in through doors and windows as dust. It may reach the kitchen by adhering to certain foods like celery, root vegetables, and potatoes. Depending on its source, soil may contain almost any microorganisms and parasites, including pathogens causing foodborne illnesses, especially spores, since these remain viable in soil for long periods of time. Reports of outbreaks involving food items, such as pudding, which were allowed to cool in dusty and drafty hallways, have indicated that soil is the source of the contaminants. Any food that drops to the floor may be considered contaminated by soil. Hands that pick up things from the floor become contaminated with soil.

McKillop (1959), who made a study of the bacterial contamination of food in a hospital over a period of 2½ years, found that cooked cold chicken was frequently contaminated with fairly large numbers of *Clostridium perfringens (welchii)* and gave as the probable source kitchen dust. Hobbs (1960) has stated that *Clostridium welchii (perfringens)* spores can be routinely cultured from kitchen floors.

WATER

The municipal water supply of our cities is, in general, excellent. However, the dangers involved in the use of water from unknown sources are great. Contaminated water will contaminate food either directly or by way of hands, equipment, utensils, and the like.

Here are some examples: contaminated tap water used in a public eating place in a small town was the cause of an outbreak of infectious hepatitis; through faulty plumbing, a connection had been established between the toilet and the drinking water (*Morbidity and Mortality Weekly Report,* 1970). Contaminated well water caused an outbreak of shigellosis in a camp; the water, which tasted bad, had not been chlorinated and the well was too shallow (*Morbidity and Mortality Weekly Report,* 1971).

If, in an emergency, water must be transported from an approved source to a foodservice establishment, it is important that contamination be avoided from unsanitary containers and through unsanitary methods of handling. The local health authority will give appropriate advice.

In some establishments, a supply of nonpotable water may be available by permission of the health authorities for special purposes such as fire protection and air conditioning. Such water is not intended as a food, and, if it is used in connection with food or drink, it may serve as a source of contamination.

AIR

Adequate ventilation is essential in a foodservice establishment, be it in the areas of food preparation, service, or storage. If adequately installed and well maintained, the ventilation system reduces condensation, which would otherwise be apt to promote microbial growth on walls and other surfaces. Contaminated water in the form of condensed droplets may fall into food and onto surfaces used in food preparation.

Ill-designed and ill-maintained ventilating systems, however, may cause a sanitary hazard in that they permit accumulation of condensates and grease, which may contaminate food and working surfaces. Faulty intake air ducts or ducts poorly maintained may admit contaminating materials such as dust, dirt, and insects.

Factors influencing airborne contamination of foods were discussed by Heldman (1974). He emphasizes the fact that air quality must be looked upon as including particle population, humidity, odor, microbial population, and temperature. Although the review concentrates on conditions prevailing in food-processing plants, application to food preparation and service establishments is appropriate. The sources of airborne microorganisms mentioned were the ventilation system; floor drains, when flooded; human subjects, the flora being closely related to the working environment of the subjects; particles lodged on exposed surfaces, which are swept into an air stream whenever one is created; and increased transport of airborne microbial particles by air turbulence at the opening between rooms.

SEWAGE

At first glance, it must seem shocking that sewage is even mentioned in connection with the area of food preparation, service, and storage. Unfortunately, sewage is known to have caused serious illness and gastroenteric foodborne outbreaks that originated in foodservice establishments. Plumbing, either improperly installed or ill-maintained, has given rise to a variety of troubles, such as cross-connections, back siphonage, overhead leakage, and drainage system stoppage. Due to faulty plumbing, sewage has contaminated water, food, equipment, and utensils. In basement storage areas, leaky overhead plumbing is a frequent source of trouble.

In areas where a nonwater-carried sewage system is used, improper disposal of sewage may cause havoc in many ways, but mainly by contaminating the water supply and by attracting flies, which in turn disseminate pathogens. Fortunately, nonwater-carried sewage systems are rarely used in connection with foodservice establishments, and if they are, they must have the approval of the health authorities.

FOOD SUPPLY

Cross-contamination may occur from raw to cooked foods in the storage area and kitchen. In the discussion of the various food groups, it was brought out that foods may carry microorganisms most unwelcome to the kitchen, be they part of the food's natural flora or a flora acquired during processing, transport, storage, or other handling.

Of special concern to the foodservice manager are the foods that are known to be potential bearers of microorganisms capable of causing foodborne illness. Even if these foods are basically clean, wholesome, from sources that are approved or considered satisfactory by the health authorities, and safe for human consumption, a potential danger still exists. Recognizing and accepting the fact that certain foods are potential sources of food-poisoning organisms is the first step in successfully dealing with the problem, since the contamination of cooked food with microorganisms from raw food has been the frequent cause of gastroenteric episodes.

Foods of Animal Origin

In the preceding chapters, the flora of the food supply has been discussed in detail, and the reader is referred back to them for information regarding the contaminants to be expected from specific food items.

Among the foods of animal origin, meats, poultry, and seafood stand out as important sources of contaminants capable of causing foodborne illnesses. These foods have been shown to be frequently contaminated with representatives of various strains of *Salmonella, Clostridium perfringens,* fecal streptococci, *Campylobacter jejuni, Yersinia enterocolitica,* and *Vibrio parahaemolyticus,* and to a lesser degree, *Staphylococcus aureus.* Naturally, all foods touched by human hands may at some time become contaminated with *S. aureus.*

COLD STORAGE.   Uncooked animal foods are usually stored in separate refrigerators. This is a good practice, since contaminants present on the meats are thus "kept to themselves."

When refrigerator space is limited and no provision exists for the separation of raw meats and cooked items, the chances for cross-contamination are greater. However, only the refrigerator that is poorly managed and ill-maintained will allow for such cross-contamination. The bacteria do not spread through the air to other substrates; rather, cross-contamination is usually performed by pieces of raw flesh foods and other food particles that happen to drop into unprotected, uncovered items. Undersides and rims of containers, soiled racks, and used covers transferred from one item to another may contain particles of food harboring bacteria that may serve as an inoculum in other food substrates.

FOOD PREPARATION AREA.   When raw meat, poultry, and seafood are handled, for example, in cutting, chopping, shaping, and portioning, the hands of the food handler, his or her clothing, the working surfaces, and equipment all may become contaminated with the bacterial flora of the meat. In cases of trichina-infested pork, the trichinae may be spread to cooked food items.

The literature abounds with examples of foodborne illnesses traced to the contamination of cutting boards with bacteria—salmonellae, in particular— and also with enterococci and *Clostridium perfringens.* Grinders, cutters, and similar equipment are frequently indicted, and so are wooden pushers for grinders. Kitchen practices that allow raw foods to come in contact with cooked food, either directly or by way of contaminated equipment, may lead to trouble. Cooked foods are sterile; when seeded with an inoculum of food-poisoning bacteria, the stage is set for this inoculum to find a medium particularly attractive because it is devoid of competitors. In the case of trichinae, no multiplication will occur; however, a wholesome cooked product can be rendered contaminated through simple contact with *Trichina*-infested surfaces and equipment.

In many large foodservice establishments, raw meats and poultry are handled in an area completely separate from the area where cooked foods are handled and the portioned meats are delivered to the kitchen ready to be cooked. The cutting, chopping, cubing, and slicing operations are carried out by employees who use implements solely reserved for this purpose. Meat-cutting areas that are air conditioned to low temperatures have the additional benefit of discouraging bacterial multiplication during the cutting operations. This is the ideal situation, but, unfortunately, it is not always possible, certainly not in small foodservice establishments. Therefore, it is very important for the operators, managers, and supervisors to fully understand and appreciate the potential dangers of cross-contamination from raw meats to cooked ingredients and menu items, and to pass the information on to their employees. They should either provide equipment and working surfaces that make possible complete separation of raw and cooked items or enforce rigorous rules regarding sanitation of contaminated surfaces and equipment.

If raw meats and poultry must be handled in the kitchen along with cooked foods, the most meticulous housekeeping practices should be followed: washing hands following contact with raw meats; using separate cutting blocks or boards; and thoroughly cleaning and sanitizing chopping blocks or boards, grinders, choppers, knives, and other implements immediately after use.

Cooked ingredients or menu items that have been contaminated and are not promptly reheated or cooled are a real health hazard.

Foods of Plant Origin

As was discussed earlier, plant foods, although washed before they are stored, are apt to be contaminated with some pathogens capable of causing food-borne illness.

COLD STORAGE. Uncooked plant materials such as fruits and vegetables should be stored in a separate refrigerator, if at all possible. If limited space prevents a complete separation, meticulous separation within the refrigerator is necessary so that cooked items will not be contaminated with the bacterial flora clinging to the plant material.

FOOD PREPARATION AREA.   Most foodservice establishments have a separate area for the cleaning of fruits and vegetables and for processes such as peeling and chopping. In establishments where such physical separation is not possible, meticulous housekeeping practices are indicated to avoid cross-contamination.

When raw vegetables are combined with an otherwise finished menu item that has received its terminal heat treatment, contaminants may be added along with the vegetables. Unless the contaminants are killed by reheating the item, they will remain viable and may even multiply, if the nature of substrate, temperature, and time permits this.

One example of a vegetable that is frequently added to a menu item "as the last thing" is parsley. Nuts are another ingredient frequently incorporated into finished menu items. Still other examples are celery and lettuce, ingredients frequently used in salads and sandwiches. Leaf lettuce and celery can be rich sources of soil-borne bacteria. Leaf lettuce has an open structure which provides excellent chances for contamination with soil. Multiplication of the contaminant would, of course, depend on the suitability of the substrate for bacterial activity and on prevailing temperatures. Actually, in this country, the dangers from contaminants of vegetable origin are less acute than those associated with foods of animal origin.

EQUIPMENT AND UTENSILS

Material, design, construction, and state of repair are all of sanitary importance in equipment, large and small. In large floor-mounted equipment, installation plays a role also, since liquids or solid particles may settle in spaces not easily accessible to cleaning.

Equipment and utensils made of materials difficult to clean, or so designed and constructed that thorough cleaning is inconvenient, are not apt to be cleaned regularly and thoroughly, and are therefore important sources of contamination in a foodservice establishment. But even equipment of sanitary construction and good cleanability may become a hazard if it is not maintained in a sanitary condition. Bacterial populations may build up to large numbers on first-rate equipment if this is not thoroughly and regularly cleaned. The ability of microorganisms to become more resistant to sanitizers and other antimicrobial agents once they become attached to the surface has been documented in aquatic environments and on glass, stainless steel, polypropylene, and rubber. The attached microorganisms are also known as biofilms and represent a potential problem when they involve pathogens;

the usual practice of disinfecting with sanitizers may not always be effective (Krysinski et al., 1992).

Cleanability of equipment generally depends, first, on the nature of the material used in construction and, second, on the general construction features and the ease with which the equipment is taken apart for cleaning purposes.

Examples of materials of poor wearability and sanitary quality are galvanized steel and iron, since the galvanized part wears off easily and soil gathers in its place. Wood, although light and popular as a chopping surface, does absorb and hold moisture, thus allowing penetration of bacteria; it is difficult to clean, especially when cracks are present, and it absorbs stains and odors. Wooden cutting surfaces and wooden pushers for grinders are still used a great deal in food preparation. The combination of wood and meat is very dangerous because meats and poultry are apt to be contaminated with microorganisms capable of causing foodborne illnesses, and the contaminants may easily be spread to the next item by way of wooden surfaces. They may also multiply on the board to enormous numbers, and there is danger that since the cells continue to multiply on the meat juices and food remnants, they would be especially efficient contaminants because their lag phase would be brief and they would continue without interruption as soon as they landed in the new substrate. Miller et al. (1994) compared wooden and plastic cutting boards for bacterial attachment and removal potential. Bacterial levels of *Listeria monocytogenes* and *Escherichia coli* were higher on wooden boards, regardless of contact time. Washing with any cleaner removed virtually all of the bacteria on both types, although results were less variable with plastic.

General construction is considered poor if it does not permit easy cleaning of the equipment and its immediate surrounding. Examples are large equipment poorly sealed to the floor; ill-fitting panels; poorly fitted steps and legs, drawers, and racks; fixed equipment too closely mounted to the wall; spouts that come out at an angle and do not empty effectively; ineffective draws; poorly fitted joints and seams; sharp corners and angles; screws, rivet heads, and other irregular protrusions that make direct contact with the food; food slicers, cutters, and grinders that are difficult to disassemble and reassemble; hollow handles on all kinds of utensils and equipment; ill-constructed rims of pots and pans; and seams that are rough or open and allow food particles to collect—in brief, all places where food particles may collect and where bacteria and vermin may feed.

The National Sanitation Foundation of Ann Arbor, Michigan, has been instrumental in stimulating interest in, and in giving directions regarding, the sanitary aspects of the design, construction, and installation of foodservice equipment. This organization is noncommercial and nonprofit. It conducts and sponsors research in order to form a basis for the establishment of minimum sanitation standards for equipment that are generally acceptable to health authorities.

Certain human traits make the sanitary maintenance of equipment more difficult. Many cooks tend to be jealous of their small equipment such as knives, whips, and other small pieces; they tend to keep them nearby, and, if possible, hidden when not in use. Thus, these implements may escape the regular washing and sanitizing treatments. Stauffer (1964) has rightly pointed out that many cooks become so attached to certain implements like knives that they will use them to the last, even when the handles are held together with string or tape and are no longer cleanable.

Another common and undesirable kitchen habit is to forget about the periodic cleaning of certain equipment that is used by a number of persons during a workday, such as can openers and cutting boards. Also, can openers, when provided in connection with vended food, represent a potential health hazard unless appropriate preventative provisions are made. More will be said about vending problems later.

Garbage disposers have been found to be potential sources of bacterial contaminants in the dishwashing area. Jopke et al. (1969) investigated this possibility and found that the disposers under study generated bacterial aerosols regardless of mechanical design. On the basis of studies in which the authors traced the path of a test organism, they warn that aerosols from disposers are a potential threat to clean dishes and utensils present in the area of the disposer. A box-type exhaust system properly installed was effective in trapping the contaminating aerosols.

Cleaning utensils such as wet mops can also be a source of contaminants. Westwood et al. (1971) found that mops stored wet supported bacterial growth to very high levels. By effective laundering and adequate drying procedures, decontamination of the mops could be achieved.

That common hand towels are a dangerously effective way of spreading microorganisms from person to person is a well-known fact, and their use fell into disgrace some time back. Dish towels are sanitary risks also because of the abuse they undergo, and they have no place in sanitary food-service.

FLOORS, WALLS, CEILINGS

Floors that are smooth and properly constructed are easily cleaned, whereas floors that are rough and absorbent are not. Especially in the food preparation area and in walk-in refrigerators where spilling may occur, an absorbent floor is a potential hiding and feeding place for bacteria which have gained entrance. It is not easy to keep clean, even if an effort is made toward that end. Floors originally smooth but in ill repair are a source of contamination for the same reason. Floors subjected to fluid wastes from cooking kettles and improperly drained may be a feeding ground for bacteria as well as insect pests.

Similarly, walls and ceilings that are rough or in a poor state of repair may harbor bacteria. *Staphylococcus aureus,* for example, may survive on such surfaces and contaminate food from these secondary sources. Floors, walls, and ceilings of poor basic construction are almost impossible to keep sanitary. However, even smooth structures are sources of undesirable contaminants unless they have regular and effective cleaning and repair.

Other places where contaminants may lodge are window sills, skylights, transoms, light fixtures, beams, rafters, joints, and the like. Kitchen and refrigerator shelves are of special importance as sources of contaminants of cooked foods. The significance of sanitary construction and effective maintenance is discussed further in Chapter 9.

Control measures include, first, an understanding of the dangers of the sources of bacterial contamination and the chances of multiplication, and an appreciation of the role of every employee in reducing the dangers of undesirable bacterial activity in the foodservice establishment; and second, meticulous housekeeping at every step of food preparation, service, and storage. If management fails to provide adequate sanitizing facilities for equipment used in food preparation, if no directions are given for sanitary maintenance, and supervision is lacking, the employees lose interest in maintaining high standards. Inadequate facilities and lack of interest on the part of any management induce dissatisfaction and fatigue in employees, and the foodservice employee is no exception in this respect.

REFERENCES

Blaser, M. J., P. Checko, C. Bopp, A. Bruce, and J. M. Hughes (1982). "*Campylobacter* enteritis associated with foodborne transmission." *Am. J. Epidemiol.,* 116:886–894.

Coates, D., D. Hutchison, and F. Bolton (1987). "Survival of thermophilic *Campylobacter* on fingertips and their elimination by washing and disinfection." *Epid. Infect.,* 99:265–274.

Funk, K. (1955). "A Study of Certain Habits of the Food Service Employee Which May Lead to Contamination." Master's thesis, University of Washington, Seattle, WA.

Heldman, R. D. (1974). "Factors influencing airborne contamination of foods." *J. Food Sci.,* 39:962–969.

Hobbs, B. C. (1960). "Staphylococcal and *Clostridium welchii* food poisoning." *Roy. Soc. Promotion Health J.,* 80:267–272.

Horwood, M. P. and V. A. Minch (1951). "The numbers and types of bacteria found on the hands of food handlers." *Food Res.,* 16:133–136.

Jopke, W. H., D. R. Hass, and A. C. Donovan (1969). "Food waste disposers and contamination." *Hosp. Prog.,* 50 (Oct.):47–50, 52.

Kerr, K., D. Birkenhead, K. Seale, J. Major, and P. Hawkey (1993). "Prevalence of *Listeria* spp. on the hands of food workers." *J. Food Prot.,* 56:525–527.

Krysinski, E., L. Brown, and T. Marchisello (1992). "Effect of cleaners and sanitizers on *Listeria monocytogenes* attached to product contact surfaces." *J. Food Prot.*, 55:246–251.

McKillop, E. J. (1959). "Bacterial contamination of hospital food with special reference to *Clostridium welchii* food poisoning." *J. Hyg.*, 57:31–46.

Miller, A., T. Brown, and J. Call (1994). "Comparison of wooden and plastic cutting boards for bacterial attachment and removal potential." Unpublished paper presented at the 1994 Annual Meeting of the Institute of Food Technologists, Atlanta, GA, June.

Morbidity and Mortality Weekly Report (1970). U.S. Department of Health, Education and Welfare, Public Health Serv., 19, July 25.

Morbidity and Mortality Weekly Report (1971). U.S. Department of Health, Education and Welfare, Public Health Serv., 20, October 23.

Morbidity and Mortality Weekly Report (1974). U.S. Department of Health, Education and Welfare, Public Health Serv., Cent. Dis. Control, 23, May 11.

Morbidity and Mortality Weekly Report (1977). U.S. Department of Health, Education and Welfare, Public Health Serv., Cent. Dis. Control, 26:107.

Seligman, R. and S. Rosenbluth (1975). "Comparison of bacterial flora on hands of personnel engaged in non-food and in food industries: A study of transient and resident bacteria." *J. Milk Food Technol.*, 38:673–677.

Snelling, A., K. Kerr, and J. Heritage (1991). "The survival of *Listeria monocytogenes* on fingertips and factors affecting elimination of the organism by handwashing and disinfection." *J. Food Prot.*, 54:343–348.

Stauffer, L. D. (1964). "Sanitation in hospital food service—from pots and pans to large appliances: Equipment and food safety." Part I. *Hospitals*, 38:80–87.

Westwood, J. C. N., M. A. Mitchell, and S. Legacé (1971). "Hospital sanitation: The massive bacterial contamination of the wet mop." *Appl. Microbiol.*, 21:693–697.

ADDITIONAL READINGS

Heldman, D. R. "Aerosol transport as influenced by a temperature gradient." *ASAE Trans.*, 11(5):613. 1968.

Heldman, D. R., C. W. Hall, and T. I. Hedrick. "The role of turbulence in bacterial aerosol transport." *Air Eng.*, 9(9):30. 1967.

Hobbs, B. C. *Food Poisoning and Food Hygiene,* 3rd ed. E. Arnold Publishers, London. 1974.

Kotschevar, L. H. and M. E. Terrell. *Foodservice Planning: Layout and Equipment,* 2nd ed. John Wiley and Sons, New York. 1977.

McDade, J. J., F. L. Sabel, R. L. Akers, and R. J. Walker. "Microbiological studies on the performance of a laminar airflow cabinet." *Appl. Microbiol.*, 16:1086–1092. 1968.

West, B. B., L. Wood, V. F. Harger, and G. S. Shugart. *Food Service in Institutions,* 5th ed. John Wiley and Sons, New York. 1977.

CHAPTER 9

Control: Preventing Contamination of Cooked Ingredients and Menu Items in the Areas of Preparation, Service, and Storage

C ontamination of menu items may occur after preparation during storage, display, service, or transport. This chapter is concerned with an examination of the protection of prepared food items after the preparation process has been completed and before the food has been consumed.

THE FOOD HANDLER

Attributes of a food handler that are important in connection with food sanitation are health, cleanliness, and willingness to learn. Good health reduces the chances for the food handler to be a dangerous reservoir of pathogens; cleanliness reduces the chances of spreading bacteria of which he or she may be a source; and willingness to learn about sanitation in the foodservice department and his or her role in it is a prerequisite for an effective sanitation program.

Health Control

A foodservice employee should not be on duty when he or she has an acute form of a communicable disease, or while he or she is a carrier. The acute form is likely to be noticed by the supervisor, whereas the carrier escapes notice; the person who is a carrier appears healthy.

Both ill people and carriers are menaces in the foodservice department in that they may transmit the disease to other employees and to customers through direct contact or through food that they have contaminated. Food may serve in the capacity of a mere vehicle of transmission (Chapter 3), in the same manner as doorknobs, money, and the like; or it may serve as a medium in which certain pathogens can multiply to enormous numbers, if conditions permit, causing outbreaks of food infections and food poisonings (Chapter 4). In the *Food Service Sanitation Manual* of the Food and Drug Administration (1978a) the following recommendation is made:

> No person, while infected with a disease in a communicable form that can be transmitted by foods, or who is a carrier of organisms that cause such a disease, or while afflicted with a boil, an infected wound, or an acute respiratory infection, shall work in a food service establishment in any capacity in which there is a likelihood of such person contaminating food or food-contact surfaces with pathogenic organisms or transmitting disease to other persons.

CONTINUOUS WATCHFULNESS. When a food handler is hired, he or she should come with a clean bill of health. This may or may not be supported by a statement from a physician. The medical checkup would show that the worker is not suffering from a communicable disease and is not a carrier at the time of the check. However, this clean bill of health would not prevent the worker from acquiring communicable diseases thereafter. Therefore, many foodservice operations try to get some protection by requiring periodic medical checkups of their food handlers. It seems desirable to require regular, frequent, fecal examinations of food handlers in geriatric institutions and hospitals, since salmonellosis is known to occur too frequently in such institutions. The very young, the old, and the enfeebled are seemingly more susceptible to salmonellosis than the public at large. The efficacy of periodic checkups cannot be a complete safeguard, however. This puts the burden of keeping track of their employees' health squarely on the shoulders of management.

There simply is no substitute for continuous watchfulness on the part of the supervisor for signs of illness in his or her employees, coupled with cooperativeness on the part of the employee.

It is the responsibility of the supervisor to see to it that employees are sent home when symptoms of illness are evident, to verify with the attending physician the nature of the illness, and to not allow the patient to return to work until the infectious stage has passed. In case of communicable diseases that may render a patient a carrier, this return may be delayed a long time.

It is the responsibility of the food handler to aid the supervisor in this endeavor. Some illnesses, such as intestinal illnesses, have symptoms not readily evident to other persons. Stauffer (1964), who called attention to the importance of health-conscious food handlers, stated that absenteeism is commendable whenever a foodservice employee has a condition as small as an inflamed hangnail. The reader is referred to this excellent series of five articles on sanitation in hospital foodservice.

Since the cooperation of the food handlers is so very essential, they must be or become health conscious. Interest can be stimulated by education, and so can the motivation to contribute to the sanitary condition of the establishment by not coming to work when afflicted with a contagious illness. As Stauffer (1964) rightly points out, in our present employment practices, continuous attendance is highly rewarded and absenteeism is frowned upon. There is also the employee's fear of losing pay because of days missed and of being removed from the job. The motivation to cooperate toward the goal of high sanitary standards is indeed handicapped by these fears and probably additional ones. The dietitian, food manager, or supervisor has the responsibility to instill in employees a health consciousness that will overcome such fears.

Cleanliness

Cleanliness and clean personal habits are extremely important in food handlers. They are not only desirable for esthetic reasons, but they are absolutely basic to sanitary food handling.

PERSONAL HABITS.   It has been said before, and must be reiterated here, that even the healthy person may carry microorganisms of public health significance on and in his or her body. These microbes, when allowed to contaminate food and multiply, may cause serious foodborne illnesses in persons who consume this food. These facts have been discussed in detail in Chapters 3 and 4.

Clean hair, skin, hands, nails, garments, and sanitary habits are essential to reducing contamination of food with the microbial flora for which the food handler is the primary source, as well as a "middleman," since his or her hands and garments may, of course, spread microbes from other sources also.

Sneezes and coughs may spread pathogens in two ways, directly through the air and indirectly through the hands. It is therefore mandatory that the mouth and nose be protected when coughing and sneezing to avoid the direct transmission of germ-laden droplets to food, food preparation surfaces, and equipment; it is also mandatory to subsequently wash hands thoroughly. Every use of the handkerchief should be followed by washing of hands, whether the handkerchief was previously used or not.

In the FDA *Food Service Sanitation Manual* (1978a) the recommendation is that:

Employees shall thoroughly wash their hands and the exposed portions of their arms with soap and warm water before starting work, during work as often as is necessary to keep them clean, and after smoking, eating, drinking, or using the toilet. Employees shall keep their fingernails clean and trimmed.

HAND WASHING.   Facilities for washing hands should be provided in dressing rooms, near the toilet room, and in the kitchen and the service area. A sink used in food preparation is not the place to wash hands. Many foodservice establishments lack a sufficient number of separate handwashing sinks in the kitchen, or lack them altogether in the food preparation area. Sanitation education cannot succeed if provisions are not made for practicing what is preached.

The importance of washing hands and cleaning nails cannot be overrated. Management has an obligation to provide handwashing facilities in strategic points, thus making it convenient for the food handler to do the frequent hand cleaning required in his job.

Hands should be washed before starting work, after the coffee break, after smoking, after visiting the toilet, and each time that hands have been soiled in work or by touching soiled surfaces. These include body parts such as hair, nose, mouth, and ears, and soiled clothing. As was discussed earlier, many persons perform certain involuntary movements with their hands, touching various body parts; these are the so-called hand habits and their control is difficult but essential.

Sinks for handwashing should be provided with warm water. If one faucet provides cold water and the other very hot, the cold will be preferable to most persons because of fear of getting scalded. Therefore, mixing valves providing warm water of 110–120°F (43–49°C) have been suggested by Stauffer (1964). This same author recommends the use of soaps designed for hand-washing in hospitals by physicians and nurses.

The FDA (1978a and 1993) recommends that a supply of hand-cleansing soap or detergent be available, that common towels be prohibited, and that a supply of sanitary towels or a hand-drying device be available. If disposable towels are used, waste receptacles should be placed nearby for convenient use. Miller et al. (1994) published an evaluation of the effectiveness of different hand soaps and sanitizers. The E2-rated hand soaps were significantly more effective in reducing bacterial numbers than others tested in the study.

USE OF TOBACCO.   The use of tobacco should be prohibited in the areas of food preparation and service, in storerooms, and in the area where dishes, pots, pans, and utensils are washed. Usually, certain areas are provided by management where the employees may smoke. However, the FDA recommendations (1978a and 1993) warn that a special area designated as a smoking room by employees should not be an area where use of tobacco might cause contamination of food, equipment, utensils, or other items needing protection. Employees should always thoroughly wash their hands after using tobacco.

CLOTHING.   Clothing must be clean, and if worn for more than one day, should be stored on the premises in clean lockers. Caps or nets should be used to prevent hair from contacting food surfaces and the food itself.

Management is responsible for an adequate, clean place in which the employee may change and store his or her clothing. In many institutions, uniforms are provided; in others, laundry service is available on the premises. It is, in general, undesirable to allow the worker to travel to the place of work in uniform, since the garments may become quite unsanitary en route.

Education in Principles of Personal Hygiene

Education in the principles of personal hygiene is basic to the success of a training program in food sanitation. Personal hygiene is what it says: personal. Interference with personal freedom is likely to arouse in almost everyone a feeling of resistance or even resentment, unless one understands and fully appreciates the reasons for the restrictions. Therefore, education in the principles of sanitation should precede or accompany actual training in "how-to-do-it" matters of personal hygiene.

A discussion of educational programs in food sanitation is presented in Chapter 15.

THE CUSTOMER

The customer may contaminate displayed food; therefore, displayed food must be protected from contact with him or her at all times. Wrapping food, when possible, will help. Where unwrapped food is displayed, however, devices must be used which are effective in guarding food from customers' hands, sneezes, or coughs and which are easily cleaned. Tongs, forks, spoons, or other devices suitable to allow the particular food to be picked up by the customer should be provided.

Protection from the hands and breath of the customer should be exercised whenever a food item is subjected to possible contact and ensuing contamination. Whenever customers have completely free access to food, as is true in a case of buffet-style service, food should be displayed in relatively small batches and replenished frequently.

Food that has been served once to a consumer, and has thus become a leftover item, shall not be served again, according to FDA recommendations (1978a and 1993), "except that packaged food, other than potentially hazardous food, that is still packaged and is still in sound condition, may be re-served."

ANIMALS

Pets

Pets, such as dogs and cats, may be rich sources of bacteria detrimental to public health, as discussed in Chapter 5.

The control of pathogens from pets is straightforward, in that pets absolutely must be kept out of all areas where food is stored, prepared, and served. These are the recommendations stated in the *Food Service Sanitation Manual* (FDA, 1978a):

> Live animals, including birds and turtles, shall be excluded from within the food service operational premises and from adjacent areas under the control of the permit holder. This exclusion does not apply to edible fish, crustacea, shellfish, or to fish in aquariums. Patrol dogs accompanying security or police officers, or guide dogs accompanying blind persons, shall be permitted in dining areas.

Persons who have handled pets should wash their hands and arms thoroughly before touching food. These precautions should also be observed when food is prepared in the home for community meal service.

Rodents and Insects

RODENTS.   The control of rats and mice is of great importance since rodents are hosts to many dangerous pathogens that they harbor in their intestinal tracts and carry on their feet and fur (Chapter 5). Among these pathogens are salmonellae, which are capable of causing outbreaks of foodborne infections in man.

In principle, rats and mice must be kept out of the foodservice department, including storage rooms, kitchen, bakeshop, pantry, dining room, and garbage-storage rooms. The all-out important control measure is to effectively protect all openings to the outside against the entrance of rodents. Conditions of the building that may permit entrance include windows near the ground; ventilation grills; holes in floors, walls, and ceilings, especially near pipe lines; and doors with a base not flush with the floor or threshold. The control measures consist of screening windows and ventilation grills, sealing openings with cement and/or metal plates or strips, and making doors flush with the floor threshold.

Further control measures require that harboring places where mice and rats might find temporary refuge should be eliminated. Such harboring places include unused crates, boxes, and rubbish piles. Good housekeeping practices should prevent these items from accumulating during the day, and inspection should be made each evening to assure that no such trash is being left around during the night.

Needless to say, food should never be left out during the night. Garbage should be protected from rodents at all times.

Eradication of rodents that have entered should be performed by an experienced professional exterminator. The local health authority should be consulted for advice.

Directions for the use of sanitation in the control of rodents have been given by Johnson (1960). Control methods against rodents are also discussed by Bjornson et al. (1968). Advice for rodent-proofing construction is made available through the Public Health Centers for Disease Control, Atlanta, Georgia.

INSECTS. Insects, especially flies and cockroaches, are pests most undesirable in any foodservice establishment. They must not be allowed in areas where food is stored, prepared, and served. Unfortunately, cockroaches sometimes enter hidden in crates and in other food containers and wrappings.

Basic to effective control of insect pests is an understanding of their life cycles and feeding habits. The reader is referred to Chapter 5 for information.

The control measures directed against insect pests should include, first, preventing these animals from entering the areas where food is stored, prepared, and served and where garbage is stored, and second, eradicating the specimens that have gained entrance to these areas.

Some insects can be kept out by screening windows, skylights, transoms, doors, vents, and other openings to the outside, provided the screening is sufficiently dense for the exclusion of the smaller specimens. Screened and other doors should be self-closing.

Cockroaches may enter also through cracks in walls and floors. Therefore, control measures must include the elimination of such entering places. Frequent harboring and feeding grounds for cockroaches are places where large equipment, such as a steam-jacketed kettle, is in poor contact with the floor or base. Food particles and moisture are apt to collect in cracks and crevices, providing food and drink, in addition to shelter, for the roaches. Through frequent inspection, such roach harbors must be located and appropriate action taken. These consist of sealing off cracks and crevices and eradicating the insect population. There is no doubt that constant vigilance in maintaining high standards of basic sanitation is an extremely important measure in the effective control of all vermin. Through effective basic sanitation, a buildup to large populations is prevented by depriving the insects of food, drink, and shelter, their three basic needs.

Whenever it is necessary to chemically eradicate insect pests present in a foodservice establishment, a professional exterminator should be retained. The suggestions of the local health authority will be helpful.

Besides flies and cockroaches, numerous other insects are apt to invade the foodservice department and cause a nuisance. Although these may not be as important as bearers of pathogenic bacteria as flies and cockroaches, they cannot be ruled out as disease carriers, and they can cause economic losses.

Moths, weevils, and beetles are insects often associated with dry foods such as flour, cereals, and dried fruit. They are typical pests of the "dry storage" area. Frequent inspection is necessary to prevent a buildup in population. Infestation can be recognized not only by the presence of the insects themselves but also by the fruits of their activities such as webbing, clumped-together food particles, holes in beans, holes in packaging, insect feces, and so forth.

Efforts should be made to (1) prevent infestation of the storage area by way of infested goods entering the area, although this is difficult when large shipments come in; (2) regularly and frequently inspect the storeroom; (3) avoid transfer of clean food to contaminated containers (in principle, food should be left in the original containers; if transfer is made, the previously infested container must be washed and sanitized); (4) avoid spills onto the floor, and immediately gather spilled food and place it in covered containers or completely remove it from the area; (5) regularly and frequently clean under bins, sacks, and other containers in which food materials are stored; and (6) if at all feasible, practice careful temperature control. Refrigerated storage provides excellent protection since none of the insect pests remain active at these low temperatures. In foodservice operations where refrigeration facilities are used for dry foods, items such as cereals, cocoa, chocolate, dried beans, powdered milk, dried fruit, nuts, and the like can be successfully stored for prolonged periods without risking losses caused by the activities of insects.

Control of insects in a foodservice establishment has been discussed by Johnson (1960), Scott and Littig (1962), and Scott (1963).

GENERAL ENVIRONMENTAL SANITATION IN THE CONTROL OF VERMIN.   Because of the great importance of environmental sanitation in the control of vermin, the following points need to be reemphasized:

1. Rats, mice, flies, and cockroaches, to mention the most important pests, are attracted to food and odors from food regardless of whether the food is fresh or whether it is beginning to decay, as may be the case when garbage is stored.

2. These vermin are also attracted to human feces and unsanitary toilets.
3. Basic sanitation serves rodent control as well as insect control:
   a. Incoming produce must be kept covered, preferably in a screened area. The area must be kept clean from spills and wastes.
   b. Empty containers, crates, boxes, and the like must be disposed of frequently and regularly, and never left accessible to vermin overnight.
   c. Garbage and rubbish must be stored in containers constructed of durable metal or other materials that do not absorb odors, do not corrode, and are easily cleaned. The containers should not leak. Garbage and rubbish cans should be covered with tight lids, unless they are stored in waste refrigerators or in vermin- and odor-proof rooms. Garbage should be removed frequently. Garbage containers should be cleaned thoroughly using special brushes and decontaminated using hot (180°F, 82°C) water or steam.
   d. Food waste grinders must be installed in accordance with the regulations of the state and local health authorities, be suitably constructed, and be operated properly to prevent insanitary conditions in the food preparation area.
   e. Toilet facilities must be kept immaculately clean and in excellent working order.
   f. The floors and equipment in the areas where food is stored, prepared, and served should be maintained in a state of excellent repair and cleanliness. Regular inspection and cleaning schedules and efficient methods of cleaning are basic sanitary measures that will deprive vermin of shelter, food, and drink.

SEWAGE, WATER, SOIL, AIR

Sanitary Sewage Disposal; Plumbing; Toilet Facilities

SEWAGE DISPOSAL.   Sewage is one of the most dangerous sources of human pathogens (Chapter 5) and should not make any contact whatsoever with food, drink, equipment, utensils, and any other surfaces that make contact with food. Therefore, sanitary sewage disposal is a prerequisite for good food sanitation. Sanitary sewage disposal should prevent the contamination of the ground and the water supply; it should also preclude access of rodents and flies to human feces. Proper sewage disposal is apt to be of special concern to those who operate temporary foodservice establishments. To prevent serious hazards from improper sewage disposal, the FDA, U.S. Public Health Service (1978a) recommends that:

> All sewage, including liquid waste, shall be disposed of by a public sewerage system or by a sewage disposal system constructed and operated according

to law. Nonwater-carried sewage disposal facilities are prohibited, except as permitted by sections 9-101 through 9-108 of this ordinance (pertaining to temporary food service establishments) or as permitted by the regulatory authority in remote areas or because of special situations.

PLUMBING.   Proper and sanitary plumbing is extremely important in food sanitation. If plumbing is not properly installed or maintained, serious trouble will ensue. Among these, flooding, back siphonage, stoppages, and cross-connections with the water system have frequently caused contamination in the food preparation and storage areas, with serious consequences. Leakage of sewer pipes is another common problem that must be kept under control. For the control of hazards from faulty plumbing, the FDA recommendations, as stated in the *Food Service Sanitation Manual* (1978a) are:

> Plumbing shall be sized, installed, and maintained according to law. There shall be no cross-connection between the potable water supply and any nonpotable or questionable water supply nor any source of pollution through which the potable water supply might become contaminated.

The FDA recommendations also state that the possibility of back flow be precluded and some specific directives are given. There are regulations for grease traps, which should be easy to clean; for garbage grinders, which should be installed and maintained according to law; for drains originating from equipment in which food, utensils, portable equipment, or other materials used in the preparation of food are placed, which should have no direct connection with the sewage system; and for connections from dishwashing machinery, which should be made according to law.

Drains should be prevented from causing back flow of sewage or flooding of floors. The latter trouble is a common one in some basements. Unfortunately, storage rooms are also frequently located in basements and may become subjected to flooding that contains raw sewage.

The recommendation for compliance with these regulations is that all plumbing should conform to applicable state and local plumbing laws, regulations, and ordinances.

The local health authority should be consulted regarding the appropriate solutions to problems arising in connection with the sanitary aspects of plumbing.

TOILET FACILITIES.   Toilets must be of sanitary design, maintained in good working order, used properly, and kept in clean condition. Unsanitary toilet facilities attract flies and other insects; they also are a hazard to clothing and hands of the food handler using the facility.

Procedures for cleaning are found in Longrée and Blaker (1982).

Management has a responsibility to see to it that toilets are adequate in number, construction, and maintenance. The following regulations are stated in the FDA (1978a) *Food Service Sanitation Manual:*

> Toilet facilities shall be installed according to law, shall be the number required by law, shall be conveniently located, and shall be accessible to employees at all times.
>
> Toilets and urinals shall be designed to be easily cleanable.
>
> Toilet rooms shall be completely enclosed and shall have tight-fitting, self-closing, solid doors, which shall be closed except during cleaning or maintenance, except as provided by law.
>
> Toilet fixtures shall be kept clean and in good repair. A supply of toilet tissue shall be provided at each toilet at all times. Easily cleanable receptacles shall be provided for waste materials. Toilet rooms used by women shall have at least one covered waste receptacle.

The recommendations also state that lavatories shall be at least the number required by law and shall be located in or immediately adjacent to toilet rooms or vestibules. Sinks used in the preparation of food or for washing equipment and utensils are not to be used for the purpose of washing hands soiled during a person's visit to the toilet.

Knee-operated faucets are more sanitary than hand-operated faucets. In principle foot-operated faucets should be sanitary also. However, cleaning of the area between the foot pedal and the floor is inconvenient and apt to be slighted.

WATER. The importance of potable water in a food facility has been discussed in Chapters 5 and 8. If contaminated water is used in a foodservice establishment, serious trouble will result.

In establishments where city water is used, the only control the food service manager needs to exert is to prevent the contamination of the potable water supply from faulty plumbing, as was discussed above. The recommendations in the *Food Service Sanitation Manual* (FDA, 1978a) are:

> Enough potable water for the needs of the food service establishment shall be provided from a source constructed and operated according to law.
>
> All potable water not provided directly by pipe to the food service establishment from the source shall be transported in a bulk water transport system and shall be delivered to a closed-water system. Both of these systems shall be constructed and operated according to law.
>
> Bottled and packaged potable water shall be obtained from a source that complies with all laws and shall be handled and stored in a way that protects it from contamination. Bottled and packaged potable water shall be dispensed from the original container.

> Water under pressure at the required temperatures shall be provided to all fixtures and equipment that use water.
>
> A nonpotable water system is permitted only for purposes such as air-conditioning and fire protection and only if the system is installed according to law and the nonpotable water does not contact, directly or indirectly, food, potable water, equipment that contacts food, or utensils. The piping of any nonpotable water system shall be durably identified so that it is readily distinguishable from piping that carries potable water.

The recommendations presented in the *Food Service Sanitation Manual* (FDA, 1978a and Food Code, 1993) are very specific regarding the plumbing of the potable water supply.

Soil, Air

Soil is carried into the foodservice establishment by way of doors, windows, airshafts, and ventilation systems, on employees' shoes and other clothing, and on certain foods and their wrappings (Chapters 5 and 8). Employees' street shoes can be eliminated as an important source of soil if they are exchanged for shoes worn only indoors. The control of soil in the kitchen is achieved by measures preventing its entry and by its prompt removal.

Root vegetables and other foods and wrappings that can be a source of soil should be kept out of the area where cooked food is prepared.

In general, the foodservice manager should analyze his or her establishment for actual or potential sources of soil and apply appropriate control measures. Daily cleaning of floors and frequent cleaning of walls, hoods, ceilings, and other dust-catching surfaces is a basic requirement for the control of soil. Foods that are allowed to be held in the kitchen before serving should be covered to protect them from dust. If the outdoor air is dusty, doors and windows may have to be shut and ventilation may have to be accomplished through intake systems equipped with filters. Filters, where used, must be readily removable for cleaning or replacement.

It is very important to maintain intake air ducts well, or they may admit contaminated particles and insects.

All ventilation systems must comply with applicable local or state laws pertaining to fire prevention. Also, ventilating systems should not constitute a nuisance to the neighborhood.

According to the recommendations of the FDA (1978a), "all rooms shall have sufficient ventilation to keep them free of excessive heat, steam, condensation, vapors, obnoxious odors, smoke and fumes"; they should be installed and operated according to law, and properly maintained.

Kitchens, storerooms, dining rooms, dishwashing rooms, storage rooms for garbage, locker rooms, dressing rooms, and toilets should all be well ventilated. Examples of ventilation systems are window exhaust fans, hood exhaust systems, unit blowers, and unit cooling systems.

Ventilation, although extremely necessary, may produce turbulence, which may be counteracting the positive benefits of ventilation. The benefits are reducing condensation; minimizing the soiling of ceilings, walls, and floors; reducing, or even regulating, high temperatures and humidities; and clearing the air of objectionable odors or toxic gases. On the other hand, if the renewal of air is accompanied by turbulence, some of the benefits are reduced. The intricacies of properly adjusting the ventilating system in kitchens with a view to minimizing possible dangers from a public health point of view were discussed by Pope (1976). A study of air-conditioning on microbial levels in hospital dishwashing facilities was reported by Jopke et al. (1972).

THE FOOD SUPPLY

Foods Serving as Potential Sources of Bacteria Capable of Causing Outbreaks of Foodborne Illnesses

Foods serving as important reservoirs of pathogens capable of causing foodborne illnesses were discussed in Chapter 6; the paths of contamination in the food preparation area were presented in Chapter 8; and purchasing procedures for the procurement of wholesome foods were outlined in Chapter 7.

In this chapter, the fact should be reemphasized that certain food items, even when produced and processed under high sanitary standards, must be treated as potential sources of pathogenic bacteria. Therefore, control measures directed at preventing these foods from contacting cooked and vulnerable food items are a must.

Meat, Poultry, Seafood

Among the foods of animal origin, three items stand out as carrying a microbial flora that may include bacteria capable of causing foodborne illnesses; these are meat, poultry, and shellfish that have not undergone processing during which pathogenic contaminants would have been destroyed. Pathogens frequently associated with these items are salmonellae, *Clostridium perfringens, Campylobacter jejuni, Vibrio parahaemolyticus, Yersinia enterocolitica,* fecal streptococci, and, to a lesser extent, strains of *Staphyloccocus aureus* and enteropathogenic *Escherichia coli.*

Canned products have all pathogenic contaminants removed. Products processed by mild heating are not sterile, however, and cannot be eliminated completely as a potential source of the above-named contaminants, however poor this source may be.

CONTROL IN STORAGE.   Meat, poultry, seafood, and the products made from them, except the canned (sterilized) products, should be kept in a separate refrigerator. If the raw items are stored along with cooked foods, there is danger of cross-contamination (see Chapter 8).

It is most important that cooked and partially cooked foods should always be stored in a refrigerator designated for the sole purpose of storing this kind of food. Even then, they must be protected from contamination from soil possibly adhering to containers and shelving. They should be covered, and containers should be stored off the floor, on dollies or racks.

Control in Food Preparation Area

PHYSICAL REMOVAL OF CONTAMINANTS.   Washing can be fairly effective in removing bacteria, provided that running water is used and the bacteria are flushed away. Not all foods can, or should, be washed. However, whenever washing is indicated to remove soil, many bacteria also will go down the drain. All raw fruits and vegetables must be washed before being cooked or served. Moldy foods should be discarded.

ELIMINATING CHANCES FOR CROSS-CONTAMINATION.   Separate surfaces should be used for the cutting, cubing, and portioning of raw meats and poultry, and for cooked food items. There is no easier way for cooked foods to become contaminated with such pathogens as *Salmonella* and *Clostridium perfringens* than by contact with contaminated work surfaces.

A report on an outbreak of salmonellosis originating in a drive-in restaurant (*Morbidity and Mortality Weekly Report,* 1973) is an example of the damage a cutting board used for multiple purposes can do. The board was used for absolutely everything, from cutting up chicken and catfish, to slicing cabbage, onions, and lettuce. An investigation revealed that salmonellae were not only isolated in massive numbers from the cutting board but also from knives, meat slicer, and sink; and from fresh chicken parts, catfish, and vegetables. The investigating authorities now found an explanation for the puzzling fact that many customers had fallen ill after eating cole slaw and onions: the vegetables had become contaminated while chopped on the work surface and were not subjected to subsequent heating, but eaten raw. This is just one example of the danger of cross-contamination from food containing a natural flora of pathogens to equipment and other foods; there are many others.

Other pieces of equipment, unfortunately often used for raw meat and poultry as well as for cooked items, are grinders, choppers, slicers, and the like. Separate equipment for raw and cooked items would be desirable, but at present is not commonly provided. Therefore, it is extremely important that they be cleaned and sanitized thoroughly between uses. Slicers are frequently not thoroughly cleaned because of the employees' fear of cutting themselves on the sharp blades. Jordan et al. (1973) discussed an outbreak of salmonellosis among restaurant patrons that was caused by the use of the meat slicer, which was not properly cleaned between uses because cleaning involved danger for employees' hands.

Because frequent cleaning is time consuming, some large institutions have a separate area where raw meats and poultry are handled and separate equipment is provided.

Eggs

Dirty cracked shell eggs and contaminated processed eggs and egg products could serve as a source of pathogens, especially of salmonellae. Control measures mentioned earlier are the purchase of clean, whole, uncracked, odorless shell eggs and the protection of processed egg products from recontamination.

Fish and Other Items

Fresh fish that needs cleaning and portioning is used in institutional food services in some parts of this country. If raw fish must be handled, it should be kept separate from cooked items; precautions used for raw meat and poultry apply to raw fish also.

All uncooked materials are unsterile and present a threat to cooked and sterile foods, especially the items that are good media for bacterial growth, namely, the "potentially hazardous" items.

THE FOOD WORKER'S HANDS

In handling foods that are potential sources of pathogens, the food handler's hands play a very important role. Hands and their significance in food sanitation have been discussed previously on several occasions; however, the importance of hands in connection with the transfer of pathogens from uncooked to cooked food items is so great that they must be mentioned again. Each time a worker has had contact with uncooked items, which must be suspected of carrying pathogens, he or she must wash his or her hands before handling cooked items. Unfortunately, the lack of a conveniently located sink is frequently the reason that this does not happen. If hand-washing facilities are distant, the worker will, instead of washing his or her hands, use an apron, a towel, dishcloth, or whatever is at hand. This kind of cleaning does not do the job. In fact, the cloth used may spread contaminants to the next person picking it up and using it.

In some foodservice establishments, it is customary to use food preparation sinks for hand washing. This is not a good idea, since the sink, as well as the food it is used for, becomes contaminated.

In principle, the use of hands in the preparation of potentially hazardous food is to be discouraged. The Food and Drug Administration (FDA, 1978a) recommends that "food shall be prepared with the least possible manual contact, with suitable utensils, and on surfaces that prior to use have been cleaned, rinsed and sanitized to prevent cross-contamination."

Management is responsible for making suitable utensils available to the employee for the task he or she is asked to perform, be it in the preparation or service of food.

SANITARY EQUIPMENT AND UTENSILS

Equipment and utensils have many chances of becoming contaminated. Knowing the source of contamination will aid in the understanding and the application of effective measures.

Equipment and utensils are known to have become contaminated with pathogens that come from the human reservoir, from rodents and insects, from sewage originating from faulty pipes and drains, from nonpotable water, from condensates created in connection with faulty ventilation, and from contaminated food.

The FDA *Food Service Sanitation Manual* (1978a) states:

> To avoid unnecessary manual contact with food, suitable dispensing utensils shall be used by employees or provided to consumers who serve themselves. Between uses during service, dispensing utensils shall be:
>
> (a) Stored in the food with the dispensing utensil handle extended out of the food; or
>
> (b) Stored clean and dry; or
>
> (c) Stored in running water; or
>
> (d) Stored either in a running water dipper well, or clean and dry in the case of dispensing utensils and malt collars used in preparing frozen desserts.

Furthermore,

> (a) Condiments, seasonings and dressings for self-service use shall be provided in individual packages, from dispensers, or from containers protected in accordance with section 2-508 of this ordinance.

(b) Condiments provided for table or counter service shall be individually portioned, except that catsup and other sauces may be served in the original container or pour-type dispenser. Sugar for consumer use shall be provided in individual packages or in pour-type dispensers.

Ice for consumers is to be dispensed only by employees with scooping devices or tongs, or through automatic self-service. And between uses, ice receptacles must be protected from contamination.

In 1976, according to the Centers for Disease Control (1977), out of a total of confirmed foodborne outbreaks of known etiology in which factors were reported, 17% were caused by unsanitary equipment.

Sanitary Design, Construction, Installation

The reasons equipment and utensils of poor design, construction, and installation may become important sources of contaminants were discussed in Chapter 8. It was shown that such equipment and utensils, poorly repaired and maintained, may harbor food residues which serve as media in which bacteria may multiply. It was also pointed out that food residues may attract vermin.

It has also been shown (Chapter 3) that equipment and utensils made with zinc, lead, and cadmium may lead to metal food poisoning if contact is allowed between the metal and acid foods or beverages. It is by recommendation of the FDA (1978a) that:

All equipment and utensils, including plasticware, shall be designed and fabricated for durability under conditions of normal use and shall be resistant to denting, buckling, pitting, chipping, and crazing.

(a) Food-contact surfaces shall be easily cleanable, smooth, and free of breaks, open seams, cracks, chips, pits, and similar imperfections, and free of difficult-to-clean internal corners and crevices. Cast iron may be used as a food-contact surface only if the surface is heated, such as in grills, griddle tops, and skillets. Threads shall be designed to facilitate cleaning: ordinary "V" type threads are prohibited in food-contact surfaces, except that in equipment such as ice makers or hot oil cooking equipment and hot oil filtering systems, such threads shall be minimized.

(b) Equipment containing bearings and gears requiring unsafe lubricants shall be designed and constructed so that the lubricant cannot leak, drip, or be forced into food or onto food-contact surfaces. Only safe lubricants shall be used on equipment designed to receive lubrication of bearings and gears on or within food-contact surfaces.

(c) Tubing conveying beverages or beverage ingredients to dispensing heads may be in contact with stored ice provided that such tubing is fabricated from safe materials, is grommeted at entry and exit points to preclude moisture (condensation) from entering the ice machine or the ice storage bin, and is kept clean. Drainage or drainage tubes from dispensing units shall not pass through the ice machine or the ice storage bin.

(d) Sinks and drain boards shall be self-draining.

Accessibility is also stressed, in that, unless they are designed for in-place cleaning, all food-contact surfaces must be accessible for cleaning and inspection by easy methods of disassembling, or by no disassembling at all. Specific recommendations for the designing of ventilation hoods and the installation of equipment away from unprotected sewer lines, open stairways, and other sources of contamination are also given.

All equipment should be so installed and maintained as to facilitate cleaning.

Single-service articles should be made of nontoxic materials.

Control measures pertaining to the design, construction, and materials have been greatly aided by some fundamental efforts in the development of standards. The Public Health Service cooperates with several agencies in developing these standards: the National Sanitation Foundation, the Baking Industry Sanitation Standards Committee, the Automatic Merchandizing Health Industry Council, and the Committee for 3-A Sanitation Standards for Dairy Equipment are examples. For foodservice equipment and utensils, the main points emphasized pertain to:

1. Durability and capability of withstanding scrubbing and the corrosive action of foods as well as of cleaning and sanitizing agents
2. Smoothness; good state of repair; cleanability of movable and in-place equipment
3. Nontoxicity of base materials and solders
4. Freedom from hard-to-clean corners and crevices
5. Accessibility for cleaning
6. Sanitary design of spouts, corners, seams, and lubricated bearings and gears

Of interest is the fact that in these recommendations the use of wooden cutting blocks and boards is not eliminated; this would probably be too unrealistic. However, it is recommended that cutting blocks and boards and bakers' tables be of hard maple or equivalent material that is nontoxic, smooth, and free of open places such as faulty seams, crevices, and cracks.

Actually, wood has been eliminated as a meat-contact surface in some institutions. Cutting boards of hard rubber, as well as metal pushers for grinders and choppers, have been substituted for the implements made of wood. Undoubtedly, wood is one of the most difficult materials to sanitize.

The FDA (1978a) recommendations specify that hard maple may be used for cutting blocks and boards, salad bowls, and bakers' tables. They also state that wood may also be used for such single-service articles as chopsticks, stirrers, and ice cream spoons, but that the use of wood as a food-contact surface under other circumstances should be prohibited. They also specify that

> safe plastic or safe rubber or safe rubber-like materials that are resistant under normal conditions of use to scratching, scoring, decomposition, crazing, chipping and distortion, that are of sufficient weight and thickness to permit cleaning and sanitizing by normal dishwashing methods, and which meet the general requirements of this ordinance are permitted for repeated use.

Control measures pertaining to installation of equipment on tables and counters include mounting which will facilitate cleaning of equipment itself as well as the surrounding area. Measures pertaining to floor-mounted equipment include sealing to the floor, or mounting on raised platforms of concrete, to control the seeping and settling of liquid and debris into inaccessible places; or elevating such equipment at least 6 inches from the floor. In any case, all mountings should be such that cleaning is easily achieved and no hidden places are left where food and moisture can collect.

Further specifications deal with aisle space and spaces between pieces of equipment; these should be large enough to allow the employees to move about freely without danger of contaminating food through contact with their body parts or clothing.

Attention is also called to a listing of National Sanitation Foundation Standards and Criteria (for sanitary equipment) presented under "Additional Readings" at the end of the chapter. The NSF has developed and implemented a method whereby uniform, nationally accepted standards are developed. These standards are based on a foundation of scientific facts and sound engineering, taking into account important aspects of public health. The standards and criteria are developed through cooperative efforts of groups of equipment manufacturers and appropriate NSF Joint and Advisory Committees. These Committees represent leading professional and official health, sanitation, and other related organizations; the Armed Forces and other user groups; and consultants.

The NSF authorizes the use of the NSF Seal of Approval for equipment that has been constructed in accordance with NSF criteria, tested in NSF laboratories, and approved.

Some other NSF Seal of Approval programs deal with tests and evaluation of plastics for containers for potable water and for various other purposes of interest from a sanitation point of view.

The buyer of institutional equipment and kitchenware should make use of the excellent services of the NSF and include NSF approval when setting up their specifications.

VENDING MACHINES.   Vending machines are moving into foodservice establishments in ever-increasing numbers. Therefore, the sanitary aspects of the design and construction of these machines need to be discussed. Many items dispensed from the machines are of a highly perishable nature.

Vending has introduced problems not normally encountered in conventional foodservice establishments. In the interest of uniformity, industry and health authorities (state and local) have requested the Public Health Service to develop an ordinance and code stating requirements for machine design and construction and for operation procedures. The ordinance and code have been adopted by numerous states and local jurisdictions.

Construction features of importance are these: The machine should be of sturdy construction and be so designed, fabricated, and finished as to facilitate its being kept clean externally and internally and to keep out rodents and insects. The interior should be so finished that all product contact surfaces are smooth, nontoxic, corrosion-resistant, relatively nonabsorbent, and able to withstand repeated cleaning and sanitizing treatments of accepted procedure. All food-contact surfaces should be protected against contamination. For compliance regulations, the reader is referred to the recommendations of the Food and Drug Administration (1978b and Food Code 1993).

Basic and special criteria for the evaluation of manually activated and/or coin-activated vending machines for food and/or beverages have been adopted by the Joint Committee on Food Equipment Standards in cooperation with representatives of industry, including users of such equipment; they were approved by the Council of Public Health Consultants, published in 1958 by the National Sanitation Foundation, and revised thereafter.

The local health authority should be consulted by foodservice operators who wish to install vending machines. Advice may be sought from the National Automatic Merchandising Association, Chicago, Illinois. This organization sponsors machine evaluation facilities at the Michigan State and Indiana University Schools of Public Health and maintains a listing of machines certified to meet code requirements. The first responsibility of the vending operator is to install only equipment that meets public health standards. Guidelines for institutions contracting with vending companies were published by Longrée (1969). For a discussion of other problems in connection with vending, see Chapter 13.

Cleaning of Equipment and Utensils

CLEANING AND SANITIZING.   The objective is to remove food particles and other soil, and to control bacteria. All equipment and utensils must be expected to contain food spoilage bacteria as well as pathogens. Proper cleaning removes soil. Sanitizing reduces the bacterial load to a safe level. Cleaning involves the liberal use of hot water, to which cleaning compounds are usually added to reduce friction. Proper water temperature and proper amounts of cleaning compounds must be used for an effectual job. The cleaning compound, or detergent, loosens the food remnants, but the use of brushes (mechanically or hand activated) is essential. Rinsing must follow, and it must be thorough, because the surfaces to be sanitized must be absolutely clean to achieve the bactericidal action desired.

The removal of food particles, fat, and other gross soil may leave equipment and utensils clean to the eye, but not bacteriologically safe. Therefore, a sanitizing process must follow the cleaning. Sanitizing involves "effective bactericidal treatment by a process that provides enough accumulative heat or concentration of chemicals for enough time to reduce the bacterial count, including pathogens, to a safe level on utensils and equipment" (FDA, 1978a and 1993).

Hot water is a common sanitizer, but chemicals have their place in certain situations, chlorine and iodine being the most commonly used sanitizing agents.

Both the "when" and the "how" of cleaning are essential. If the principles of sanitation are to be effectively applied, the time factor is of tremendous importance: not only is cleaning immediately after use more easily effected, but the time span, which might allow bacterial populations to increase greatly, is reduced. A grinder, for example, in which meat was ground, or a slicer, or a chopping board used for slicing and portioning of meat, if left unattended for more than the "danger time" may be teeming with bacteria and thus represent a dangerously rich source of contaminants in the food preparation area. The dangers of contamination of cooked, sterile food by soiled equipment, should be stressed. In gastroenteric episodes caused by *Salmonella* and *Clostridium perfringens,* contaminated equipment is frequently found to be an important link in the chain of events.

Therefore, cleaning must eliminate the contaminants. Effective cleaning involves the prompt removal of food particles after the close of the operation during which the equipment is used; or, if the equipment is used for extended periods, at predetermined intervals spaced to prevent microbial buildup. For example, if a piece of equipment is used all day, a cleaning schedule must insure well-spaced cleaning operations during the day. The higher the room or kitchen temperature, the shorter the intervals should be between cleanings. The cleaning schedule in such continuous operations should be acceptable to the health authority.

The general recommendations for cleaning stated in the FDA *Food Service Sanitation Manual* (1978a) are:

Tableware shall be washed, rinsed, and sanitized after each use.

To prevent cross-contamination, kitchenware and food-contact surfaces of equipment shall be washed, rinsed, and sanitized after each use and following any interruption of operations during which time contamination may have occurred.

Where equipment and utensils are used for the preparation of potentially hazardous foods on a continuous or production line basis, utensils and the food-contact surfaces of equipment shall be washed, rinsed, and sanitized at intervals throughout the day on a schedule based on food temperature, type of food, and amount of food particle accumulation.

The food-contact surfaces of grills, griddles, and similar cooking devices and the cavities and door seals of microwave ovens shall be cleaned at least once a day; except that this shall not apply to hot oil cooking equipment and hot oil filtering systems. The food-contact surfaces of all cooking equipment shall be kept free of encrusted grease deposits and other accumulated soil.

Non-food-contact surfaces of equipment shall be cleaned as often as is necessary to keep the equipment free of accumulation of dust, dirt, food particles, and other debris.

The requirements posed by local and state health authorities for cleaning, sanitizing, and storing equipment and utensils largely follow the recommendations of the FDA *Food Service Sanitation Manual* (1978a) and *Food Code 1993* (1993).

The foodservice manager has the responsibility of seeing to it that, in the establishment entrusted to him or her, sanitary rules are followed as required by law. This entails careful planning of every step, and relentless supervision. The foodservice manager is the person expected to be equipped with the knowledge to set up a workable sanitation program, to develop practical and effectual procedures for cleaning and sanitizing, to train the employees, to provide the necessary tools and compounds, and to follow through tirelessly. A checklist of all items should be developed and the method of cleaning meticulously worked out in writing, stating the time of cleaning, the "how" of cleaning, and the tools with which to do it. The directions must be very clear, very detailed.

Explicit directions for cleaning various pieces of equipment will be found in texts dealing with the applied aspects of foodservice sanitation (Longrée and Blaker, 1982; Kotschevar and Terrell, 1985; West et al., 1977).

1. Manual cleaning and sanitizing require:
   a. Prescraping and, usually, presoaking.
   b. Washing in the first compartment of a three-compartment sink, in hot detergent solution that is kept clean. The compartments should be large enough to accommodate the equipment to be washed.

   c. Rinsing in clean, hot water, using the second compartment.

   d. Sanitizing in the third compartment by one of the following methods (FDA, 1978a):

     (1) Immersion for at least $\frac{1}{2}$ minute in clean, hot water at a temperature of at least 170°F (76.7°C); or

     (2) Immersion for at least one (1) minute in a clean solution containing at least 50 parts per million of available chlorine as a hypochlorite and at a temperature of at least 75°F (23.9°C); or

     (3) Immersion for at least one (1) minute in a clean solution containing at least 12.5 parts per million of available iodine and having a pH not higher than 5.0 and at a temperature of at least 75°F (23.9°C); or

     (4) Immersion in a clean solution containing any other chemical sanitizing agent allowed.

For other allowable sanitizing agents consult the FDA *Food Service Sanitation Manual* (1978a), Appendix D, the FDA *Food Code 1993* (1993), or any text dealing with sanitary techniques. For large equipment, precleaning and sanitizing may require treatment with steam. Following the sanitizing process, equipment, utensils, and tablewear are air-dried, and then stored in a clean place protected from recontamination.

  2. Mechanical cleaning and sanitizing may be done by spray-type or immersing dishwashing machines, properly installed and maintained. The directions for pressure, water temperatures, type of chemicals, and amounts used for washing and sanitizing are very specific; it is beyond the scope of this book to reprint these. The reader is referred to the FDA manual (1978a) and the FDA *Food Code 1993* (1993); the earlier-mentioned texts dealing with cleaning and sanitizing; and to information provided by the National Sanitation Foundation (see also "Additional Readings"). Dishwashing machines must be kept immaculately cleaned and in good repair.

STORAGE OF CLEAN EQUIPMENT AND UTENSILS.   All cleaned implements must be kept clean and prevented from being recontaminated. By recommendation of the FDA *Food Service Sanitation Manual* (1978a), cleaned and sanitized utensils shall be stored as follows:

(a) Cleaned and sanitized utensils and equipment shall be stored at least 6 inches above the floor in a clean, dry location in a way that protects them from contamination by splash, dust, and other means. The food-contact surfaces of fixed equipment shall also be protected from contamination. Equipment and utensils shall not be placed under exposed sewer lines or water lines, except for automatic fire protection sprinkler heads that may be required by law.

(b) Utensils shall be air dried before being stored or shall be stored in a self-draining position.

(c) Glasses and cups shall be stored inverted. Other stored utensils shall be covered or inverted, wherever practical. Facilities for the storage of knives, forks, and spoons shall be designed and used to present the handle to the employee or consumer. Unless tableware is prewrapped, holders for knives, forks, and spoons at self-service locations shall protect these articles from contamination and present the handle of the utensil to the consumer.

The FDA (1978a) also recommends that

(a) Single-service articles shall be stored at least 6 inches above the floor in closed cartons or containers which protect them from contamination and shall not be placed under exposed sewer lines or water lines, except for automatic fire protection sprinkler heads that may be required by law.

(b) Single-service articles shall be handled and dispensed in a manner that prevents contamination of surfaces which may come in contact with food or with the mouth of the user.

(c) Single-service knives, forks and spoons packaged in bulk shall be inserted into holders or be wrapped by an employee who has washed his hands immediately prior to sorting or wrapping the utensils. Unless single-service knives, forks, and spoons are prewrapped or prepackaged, holders shall be provided to protect these items from contamination and present the handle of the utensil to the consumer.

Vending

Regular and efficient cleaning is essential to vending sanitation. Cleaning should pertain to the machines themselves as well as the surroundings.

GENERAL AREA.   The location of the machines is important since there should be no constant sources of dangerous contaminants such as overhead sewer pipes and excessive dust.

There should be a sufficient number of receptacles for trash, and these should be prevented from overflowing by regular servicing. If a sanitation room is provided by management where parts of the machine may be washed and sanitized, this room should be kept in an immaculate state of cleanliness.

VENDING OPERATIONS.   Almost all vending facilities are operated by vending specialists, or operators, who own and install the equipment, provide the food, and service the machines; the services include cleaning operations.

Supplemental Equipment and Utensils

Condiment dispensers sometimes create a sanitary nuisance because of spattering and use by many careless hands. Can openers not frequently cleaned may represent a real health hazard. All such equipment and utensils must be subjected to frequent and effective cleaning.

Recommendations are also made for the purchase, storage, and handling of single-service containers.

SANITARY PHYSICAL PLANT

Construction, Repair, and Cleaning

Proper construction, good repair, and appropriate cleaning of floors, walls, and ceilings are part and parcel of good plant sanitation (see Chapter 8).

In the *Food Service Sanitation Manual* (FDA, 1978a) the following statement is made:

> Floors and floor coverings of all food preparation, food storage, and utensil-washing areas, and the floors of all walk-in refrigerating units, dressing rooms, locker rooms, toilet rooms, and vestibules shall be constructed of smooth durable material such as sealed concrete, terrazzo, ceramic tile, durable grades of linoleum or plastic, or tight wood impregnated with plastic, and shall be maintained in good repair. Nothing in this section shall prohibit the use of antislip floor covering in areas where necessary for safety reasons.

> Carpeting, if used as a floor covering, shall be of closely woven construction, properly installed, easily cleanable, and maintained in good repair. Carpeting is prohibited in food preparation, equipment-washing and utensil-washing areas where it would be exposed to large amounts of grease and water, in food storage areas, and toilet room areas where urinals or toilet fixtures are located.

> The use of sawdust, wood shavings, peanut hulls, or similar material as a floor covering is prohibited.

> Properly installed, trapped floor drains shall be provided in floors that are water-flushed for cleaning or that receive discharges of water or other fluid waste from equipment, or in areas where pressure spray methods for cleaning equipment are used. Such floors shall be constructed only of sealed concrete, terrazzo, ceramic tile or similar materials, and shall be graded to drain.

It is furthermore stated that the juncture between walls and floors shall be sealed wherever concrete, terrazzo, ceramic tile, or such are used; and that in all other cases the juncture between walls and floors not present an open seam of more than $1/32$ inch. These recommendations have as their goal to facilitate easy cleaning. Another recommendation pertains to exposed utility service lines and pipes, which should be properly installed for easy cleaning; they should be prohibited in new facilities.

Recommendations for construction of walls and ceilings are also directed toward easy cleaning. Good maintenance and repair are emphasized. This includes, whenever possible, the elimination of exposed studs, joists, and rafters, especially in walk-in refrigerators, food preparation areas, utensil-washing and storing areas, and toilet rooms. For details, see texts dealing with the applied aspects of food sanitation given in the reference and additional reading sections.

Procedures for cleaning floors and walls were published by Longrée and Blaker (1982).

Refrigeration Equipment

The importance of sanitary care of refrigerators and freezers cannot be over-emphasized. Care should include these basic points: maintaining the mechanical parts in good working condition, preventing the accumulation of food items, and cleaning. Unfortunately, the care of refrigerator storage often leaves much to be desired. Refrigerators provide an environment that will support the growth of psychotrophs. Pritchard showed that *Yersinia* could grow in coolers and freezers (Pritchard et al., 1994).

Refrigeration units, whether they serve coolers or freezers, are complex and intricate mechanisms and require the know-how and skill of an expert for maintenance or repair of certain components. A schedule of systematic inspections by a specialist is recommended. The manufacturer or distributor should suggest the service agency to consult with regard to appropriate maintenance and repair. The manufacturer may also suggest points of refrigerator maintenance which can be scheduled by the regular staff employed by the foodservice establishment.

It is important to remember that the warm summer months place heaviest demands on refrigeration equipment; therefore, a thorough checkup before those months is desirable. Doors should be inspected for faulty gaskets, hinges, and latches. Drains must be kept clean at all times. Poor maintenance of drains causes foul odor, corrosion, and general unsanitary conditions, and may lead to the destruction of the insulating materials in the refrigerator. Regular, careful cleaning, followed by flushing with baking soda in warm water, is recommended.

Defrosting should precede cleaning of coolers and freezers unless these automatically defrost. Above-freezing temperature type refrigerators should be defrosted at least once weekly. Freezers need defrosting when the frost builds up to approximately ¼ inch. Heavy coats of ice on evaporators act as insulators and overwork the compressors.

Before cleaning refrigerating units, food items, as well as shelves, hooks, dollies, and other accessories, should be removed. Walls, floors, and accessories should be thoroughly washed. Baked-enamel or stainless-steel surfaces should be cleaned with a mild soap or detergent solution and then rinsed with clear water.

Coolers and freezers are not to be used as catch-alls. Coolers should be checked daily and freezers at regular frequent intervals to insure that food is being stored in appropriate containers or securely wrapped. Employees should be taught the proper procedure for storage.

Ventilation

Hoods should be regularly inspected for, and maintained in good working order and kept clean from, accumulations of dust and grease; regular cleaning schedules should be set up.

The *Food Service Sanitation Manual* (FDA, 1978a) states that ventilation systems shall be installed and operated according to law and, when vented to the outside, should not create an unlawful discharge. It also states that intake and exhaust air ducts need careful, regular maintenance.

Lighting

Ample, properly distributed light must be available for preparing and serving food in a sanitary way. Certainly, effective cleaning and hand-washing are not possible unless the employees see what they are doing. According to the manual of the FDA (1978a), compliance with the requirement of good lighting involves provision of at least 20 foot-candles of light on all working surfaces, less intense light being required for certain other strategic places where food is cooked, utensils washed, hands washed, and the like. The reader is referred to this important publication and the *Food Code 1993* for full details.

Garbage and Refuse

Improperly disposed garbage and refuse are not only a nuisance, they may represent an outright danger, because

1. They are ideal harboring places for rodents and insects.
2. They are a source of microbial contamination of food, food preparation surfaces, utensils, and equipment.
3. They make effective housekeeping impossible.

TABLE 9.1. *FDA Sanitary Inspection Form*

DEPARTMENT OF HEALTH, EDUCATION AND WELFARE
PUBLIC HEALTH SERVICE - FOOD AND DRUG ADMINISTRATION
FOOD SERVICE ESTABLISHMENT INSPECTION REPORT

Based on an inspection this day, the items circled below identify the violation in operations or Facilities which must be corrected by the next routine inspection or such shorter period of time as may be specified in writing by the regulatory authority. Failure to comply with any time limits for corrections specified in this notice may result in cessation of your Food Service operations.

OWNER NAME

ESTABLISHMENT NAME

ADDRESS

ZIP CODE

ESTABLISHMENT I.D.													CENSUS TRACT			SANIT CODE			DATE					INSPECT TIME (Min.)		
COUNTY		DISTRICT		TYPE		EST. NO.													YR		MO		DAY			
1	2	3	4	5	6	7	8	9	10	11	12	13	14	15	16	17	18	19	20	21	22	23	24	25	26	27	28

PURPOSE (29)
Regular 1
Complaint 3
Other 2
Investigation 5
Follow-up 4

ITEM	WT	COL
FOOD		
*01 SOURCE, SOUND CONDITION, NO SPOILAGE	5	30
02 ORIGINAL CONTAINER, PROPERLY LABELED	1	31
FOOD PROTECTION		
*03 POTENTIALLY HAZARDOUS FOOD MEETS TEMPERATURE REQUIREMENTS DURING STORAGE, PREPARATION, DISPLAY, SERVICE, TRANSPORTATION	5	32
*04 FACILITIES TO MAINTAIN PRODUCT TEMPERATURE	4	33
05 THERMOMETERS PROVIDED AND CONSPICUOUS	1	34
06 POTENTIALLY HAZARDOUS FOOD PROPERLY THAWED	2	35
*07 UNWRAPPED AND POTENTIALLY HAZARDOUS FOOD NOT RE-SERVED	4	36
08 FOOD PROTECTION DURING STORAGE, PREPARATION, DISPLAY, SERVICE, TRANSPORTATION	2	37
09 HANDLING OF FOOD (ICE) MINIMIZED	2	38
10 IN USE, FOOD (ICE) DISPENSING UTENSILS PROPERLY STORED	1	39

ITEM	WT	COL
18 PRE-FLUSHED, SCRAPED, SOAKED	1	47
19 WASH, RINSE WATER CLEAN PROPER TEMPERATURE	2	48
*20 SANITIZATION RINSE CLEAN, TEMPERATURE, CONCENTRATION, EXPOSURE TIME, EQUIPMENT, UTENSILS SANITIZED	4	49
21 WIPING CLOTHS CLEAN, STORED, RESTRICTED	1	50
22 FOOD CONTACT SURFACES OF EQUIPMENT AND UTENSILS CLEAN, FREE OF ABRASIVES, DETERGENTS	2	51
23 NON-FOOD CONTACT SURFACES OF EQUIPMENT AND UTENSILS CLEAN	1	52
24 STORAGE, HANDLING OF CLEAN EQUIPMENT/UTENSILS	1	53
25 SINGLE-SERVICE ARTICLES, STORAGE, DISPENSING, USED	1	54
26 NO RE-USE OF SINGLE SERVICE ARTICLES	2	55

ITEM	WT	COL
GARBAGE AND REFUSE DISPOSAL		
33 CONTAINERS OR RECEPTACLES, COVERED, ADEQUATE NUMBER, INSECT/RODENT PROOF, FREQUENCY, CLEAN	2	62
34 OUTSIDE STORAGE AREA ENCLOSURES PROPERLY CONSTRUCTED, CLEAN, CONTROLLED INCINERATION	1	63
INSECT, RODENT, ANIMAL CONTROL		
*35 PRESENCE OF INSECT/RODENTS - OUTER OPENINGS PROTECTED, NO BIRDS, TURTLES, OTHER ANIMALS	4	64
FLOORS, WALLS AND CEILINGS		
36 FLOORS, CONSTRUCTED, DRAINED, CLEAN, GOOD REPAIR, COVERING INSTALLATION, DUSTLESS CLEANING METHODS	1	65
37 WALLS, CEILING, ATTACHED EQUIPMENT CONSTRUCTED, GOOD REPAIR, CLEAN SURFACES, DUSTLESS CLEANING METHODS	1	66

WATER

No.	Item	Wt.	Box
*27	WATER SOURCE, SAFE, HOT AND COLD UNDER PRESSURE	5	56

SEWAGE

No.	Item	Wt.	Box
*28	SEWAGE AND WASTE WATER DISPOSAL	4	57

PLUMBING

No.	Item	Wt.	Box
29	INSTALLED, MAINTAINED	1	58
*30	CROSS-CONNECTION, BACK SIPHONAGE, BACKFLOW	5	59

TOILET AND HANDWASHING FACILITIES

No.	Item	Wt.	Box
*31	NUMBER, CONVENIENT, ACCESSIBLE, DESIGNED, INSTALLED	4	60
32	TOILET ROOMS ENCLOSED, SELF-CLOSING DOORS, FIXTURES, GOOD REPAIR, CLEAN, HAND CLEANSER, SANITARY TOWELS/TISSUE/HAND-DRYING DEVICES PROVIDED, PROPER WASTE RECEPTACLES	2	61

PERSONNEL

No.	Item	Wt.	Box
*11	PERSONNEL WITH INFECTIONS RESTRICTED	5	40
*12	HANDS WASHED AND CLEAN, GOOD HYGIENIC PRACTICES	5	41
13	CLEAN CLOTHES, HAIR RESTRAINTS	1	42

FOOD EQUIPMENT AND UTENSILS

No.	Item	Wt.	Box
14	FOOD (ICE) CONTACT SURFACES DESIGNED, CONSTRUCTED, MAINTAINED, INSTALLED, LOCATED	2	43
15	NON-FOOD CONTACT SURFACES, DESIGNED, CONSTRUCTED, MAINTAINED, INSTALLED, LOCATED	1	44
16	DISHWASHING FACILITIES DESIGNED, CONSTRUCTED, MAINTAINED, INSTALLED, LOCATED, OPERATED	2	45
17	ACCURATE THERMOMETERS, CHEMICAL TEST KITS PROVIDED, GAUGE COCK (¼ IPS VALVE)	1	46

LIGHTING

No.	Item	Wt.	Box
38	LIGHTING PROVIDED AS REQUIRED, FIXTURES SHIELDED	1	67

VENTILATION

No.	Item	Wt.	Box
39	ROOMS AND EQUIPMENT VENTED AS REQUIRED	1	68

DRESSING ROOMS

No.	Item	Wt.	Box
40	ROOMS CLEAN, LOCKERS PROVIDED, FACILITIES CLEAN, LOCATED, USED	1	69

OTHER OPERATIONS

No.	Item	Wt.	Box
*41	NECESSARY TOXIC ITEMS PROPERLY STORED, LABELED, USED	5	70
42	PREMISES MAINTAINED, FREE OF LITTER, UNNECESSARY ARTICLES, CLEANING MAINTENANCE EQUIPMENT PROPERLY STORED, AUTHORIZED PERSONNEL	1	71
43	COMPLETE SEPARATION FROM LIVING/SLEEPING QUARTERS, LAUNDRY	1	72
44	CLEAN SOILED LINEN PROPERLY STORED	1	73

RATING SCORE (100) (1 + Weight of Items Violated)

FOLLOW-UP   YES 1   NO 2   74

*CRITICAL ITEMS REQUIRING IMMEDIATE ACTION

RECEIVED BY (Name and Title)

INSPECTED BY (Name, Number and Title)

267

TABLE 9.1 (*continued*)

ITEM NO.	REMARKS	CORRECTED BY

Source: FDA, 1978a.

The responsibility of management is to provide durable, easily cleanable, insect- and rodent-proof containers. There are other very specific instructions listed in the *Food Service Sanitation Manual* (FDA, 1978a and 1993), and the reader is referred to these important publications.

Other Housekeeping Recommendations

These include general recommendations made by the FDA (1978a and 1993) for cleaning the physical facilities and the labeling, storing, and use of toxic materials, personal medications, and first aid supplies. Furthermore, recommendations are made for the care of the living areas, laundry facilities, linens, and clothes storage and storage of cleaning equipment.

Inspections

The reader of the *Food Service Sanitation Manual* (FDA, 1978a) will notice that the recommendations made therein are "keyed" for use in sanitary inspections. The form used for such inspections is reproduced in Table 9.1. It is recommended by the FDA that an inspection of a foodservice establishment be performed at least once every 6 months. Representatives of the regulatory authority, after proper identification, shall be permitted to enter any foodservice establishment at any reasonable time for the purpose of making inspections to determine compliance with this ordinance. The representatives shall be permitted to examine the records of the establishment to obtain information pertaining to food and supplies purchased, received, or used and to record the findings on the abovementioned form (Table 9.1) (FDA, 1978a). The rating score of the establishment is the total of the weighted point values for all violations subtracted from 100. Thus a perfect inspection score is 100.

The purpose of these inspections is, of course, to set in motion any corrections that may be necessary. A reasonable time would be allowed for this to occur, unless an imminent health hazard exists. In that case, the establishment must cease foodservice operation until the violations have been corrected. For the details of this point system, the reader is referred to the FDA *Food Service Sanitation Manual* (1978a). It is a useful tool for an establishment's self-inspection program.

REFERENCES

Bjornson, B. F., H. D. Pratt, and K. S. Littig (1968). "Control of Domestic Rats and Mice." U.S. Department of Health, Education and Welfare, Public Health Service. PHS Publication No. 563. Revised.

Centers for Disease Control (1977). U.S. Department of Health, Education and Welfare, Public Health Service. *Foodborne and Waterborne Disease Outbreaks,* Annual Summary, 1976.

Food and Drug Administration (1978a). *Food Service Sanitation Manual. 1976.* U.S. Department of Health, Education and Welfare, Public Health Serv. DHEW Publ. No. (FDA) 78–2081. Washington, D.C.

Food and Drug Administration (1978b). *The Vending of Food and Beverages.* U.S. Department of Health, Education and Welfare, Public Health Serv., Food and Drug Administration. DHEW Publ. No. (FDA) 78–2091. Washington, D.C.

Food and Drug Administration (1993). *Food Code 1993.* U.S. Department of Health and Human Services. PHS Pub. No. PB94-113941AS, Springfield, VA.

Johnson, W. (1960). *Sanitation in the Control of Insects and Rodents of Public Health Importance.* U.S. Department of Health, Education and Welfare, Communicable Disease Center. PHS Publ. No. 772. Training Guide: Insect Control Series Part 4.

Jopke, W. H., S. D. Sorenson, D. R. Hass, and A. C. Donovan (1972). "Airconditioning reduces microbiologic levels in hospital dishwashing facilities." *Hosp. Prog.,* 53(Aug.):22–24, 26, 28, 30.

Jordan, M. C., K. E. Powell, T. E. Corothers, and R. J. Murray (1973). "Salmonellosis among restaurant patrons: The incisive role of a meat slicer." *Am. J. Public Health,* 63:982–985.

Kotschevar, L. H. and M. E. Terrell (1985). *Food Service Planning: Layout and Equipment,* 3rd ed. John Wiley & Sons, New York.

Longrée, K. (1969). "Sanitation in food vending." *J. Am. Diet. Assoc.,* 54:215–220.

Longrée, K. and G. G. Blaker (1982). *Sanitary Techniques in Food Service,* 2nd ed. John Wiley & Sons, New York.

Miller, M., L. James-Davis, and L. Milanesi (1994). "A field study evaluating the effectiveness of different hand soaps and sanitizers." *Dairy, Food Environ. Sanit.* 14:155–160.

Morbidity and Mortality Weekly Report (1973). U.S. Department of Health, Education and Welfare, Public Health Serv., Cent. Dis. Control, 22, Jan. 27.

Morbidity and Mortality Weekly Report (1977). U.S. Department of Health, Education, and Welfare, Public Health Serv., Cent. Dis. Control, 26, Feb. 18.

Pope, H. H. (1976). "Food service ventilation." *Consultant,* 10(July):47.

Pritchard, T., C. Beliveau, K. Flanders, and C. Donnelly (1994). "Coolers and freezers as environmental niches of *Yersinia* contamination within the environment of dairy processing plants." Unpublished paper presented at the 1994 Annual Meeting of the Institute of Food Technologists, Atlanta, GA, June.

Scott, H. G. (1963). "Household and Store-Food Insects of Public Health Importance." U.S. Department of Health, Education and Welfare, Public Health Serv., Communicable Disease Center, Atlanta, GA. PHS Publ. No. 772. Training Guide: Insect Control Series Part 12.

Scott, H. G. and K. S. Littig (1962). "Flies of Public Health Importance and Their Control." U.S. Department of Health, Education and Welfare, Public Health Serv. PHS Publ. No. 772. Training Guide: Insect Control Series Part 4.

Stauffer, L. (1964). "Sanitation in hospital food service." *Hospitals,* 38:162–169, July 16; 80–87, Aug. 1; 84–88, Aug. 16; 116–121, Sept. 1; 88–97, Sept. 16.

West, B. B., L. Wood, V. F. Harger, and G. S. Shugart (1977). *Food Service in Institutions,* 5th ed. John Wiley & Sons, New York.

ADDITIONAL READINGS

Bell, I. "Rodent control is necessary for food protection." *J. Environ. Health,* 36:75–77. 1973.

Cichy, R. F. *Sanitation Management.* The Educat. Inst., Amer. Hotel Motel Assoc., East Lansing, MI. 1984.

DeWit, J. C., G. Broekhuizen, and E. H. Kampelmacher. "Cross contamination during the preparation of frozen chickens in the kitchen." *J. Hyg.,* 83:27–32. 1979.

Dunsmore, D. G., A. Twomey, W. G. Whittlestone, and H. W. Morgan. "Design and performance of systems for cleaning product-contact surfaces of food equipment: A review." *J. Food Prot.,* 44:220–240. 1981.

Heldman, D. R. "Factors influencing airborne contamination of foods. A review." *J. Food Sci.,* 39:962–969. 1974.

Jernigan, A. K. and L. N. Ross. *Food Service Equipment: Selection, Arrangement and Use.* The Iowa State University Press, Ames, IA. 1974.

Kotschevar, L. H. *Quantity Food Production, Planning and Management.* CBI Publication Co., Boston, MA. 1979.

Leggatt, A. G. "The effect upon bacterial surfaces of sanitizer residues on a soiled surface." *J. Milk Food Technol.,* 33:121–125. 1970.

Ley, S. J. *Foodservice Refrigeration.* CBI Publication Co., Boston, MA. 1980.

McKinley, T. W., W. C. Henning, and F. B. Hendrix. "The effectiveness of counterguards in preventing microbial contamination." *J. Environ. Health,* 31:232–235. 1968.

Minor, L. J. *Sanitation, Safety and Environmental Standards.* Avi Publishing Co., Westport, CT. 1983.

National Restaurant Association. *Sanitation Operations Manual.* Washington, D.C. 1984.

National Sanitation Foundation (testing laboratory). *Listing of Food Service Equipment.* NSF, Ann Arbor, MI. 1978.

National Sanitation Foundation (testing laboratory). *Listing of Plastic Materials, Pipe, Fittings, and Appurtenances for Potable Water and Waste Water.* NSF, Ann Arbor, MI. 1978.

National Sanitation Foundation (testing laboratory). *Listing of Special Categories of Equipment, Products and Services.* NSF, Ann Arbor, MI. 1978.
  No. 1   Soda Fountain and Luncheonette Equipment
  No. 2   Food Service Equipment
  No. 3   Commercial Spray Type Dishwashing Machines
  No. 4   Commercial Cooking and Hot Food Storage Equipment
  No. 5   Commercial Hot Water Generating Equipment
  No. 6   Dispensing Freezers
  No. 7   Food Service Refrigerators and Storage Freezers
  No. 8   Commercial Powered Food Preparation Equipment
  No. 12 Automatic Ice Making Equipment
  No. 18 Manual Food and Beverage Dispensing Equipment

No. 20 Commercial Bulk Milk Dispensing Equipment and Appurtenances

No. 25 Vending Machines for Food and Beverages

No. 26 Pot, Pan and Utensil Washers

No. 29 Detergent and Chemical Feeders for Commercial Spray Type Dishwashing Machines

No. 36 Dinnerware

No. 37 Air Curtains for Entranceways in Food Establishments

No. 51 Plastic Materials and Components Used in Food Equipment

C-2   Special Equipment and/or Devices

Wilkinson, Jule. *The Complete Book of Cooking Equipment,* 2nd ed. CBI Publishing Co., Boston, MA. 1981.

CHAPTER *10*

Multiplication and Survival of Bacterial Contaminants in Ingredients and Menu Items

PART I. EFFECT OF FOOD AS SUBSTRATE

The multiplication of microbial contamination is in part related to the composition of the food substrate. This chapter examines the effect of ingredients and menu items with respect to components, moisture, physical structure, and presence of inhibitors.

COMPOSITION

Food items can be grouped on the basis of their ability to support the multiplication of organisms that are dangerous from a public health point of view (see Chapter 7). Food items of vegetable origin support the growth of pathogens causing gastroenteric outbreaks less readily than do items of animal origin. The exceptions are vegetables of relatively high pH, such as peas and corn. The ability to multiply at low pH varies with the pathogen. Under anaerobic conditions, *Clostridium botulinum* grows well in a variety of vegetable media, including acid ones; the pH values of some common vegetables were given previously (Table 1.2).

Complete menu items vary much in composition and thus in ability to support bacterial multiplication. Items that contain a preponderance of ingredients of animal origin must be expected to be excellent media for the multiplication of pathogenic bacteria and to be potentially dangerous. The pH of some common menu items is discussed later.

273

Of increasing interest are the so-called "synthetic" foods—for example, cream fillings. It has been claimed by some manufacturers that pies made from these cannot support bacterial growth and that they can be marketed without refrigeration.

A synthetic cream filling contains, in general, these basic ingredients: starch, sugars, sodium chloride, artificial and natural flavoring, stabilizers, emulsifiers, preservatives, and other miscellaneous additives. Crisley et al. (1964) set out to check on the advisability of following the manufacturers' claims regarding safety. Using an enterotoxigenic strain of *Staphylococcus aureus,* they inoculated fillings and pies made from synthetic mixes. The results were enlightening. It was found that the fillings, in general, supported the inoculum of *S. aureus* poorly, unless a proteinaceous material was part of the powder. The natural contaminants of the powder showed abundant growth. However, since the powders, when made up with water, alone result in a product of poor culinary quality, they are usually improved by the baker through addition of some animal proteins such as milk and/or eggs. The authors found that synthetic fillings enriched this way supported growth of the staphylococci very well indeed.

Finally, these same workers studied the effect of the crust on staphylococcal growth. They found that profuse multiplication was achieved even when water alone was used in these fillings. Evidently, some nitrogenous material originating from the flour in the crust, probably wheat gluten, provided enough nourishment for the staphylococci. Since these small amounts were sufficient to support multiplication of *S. aureus,* the authors wondered whether in a meringued pie traces of egg white might not provide similar stimulation. More research is needed to clarify the safety of these so-called synthetic products.

McKinley and Clarke (1964) also tested the ability of an imitation cream filling to support growth of food-poisoning staphylococci, after two cases of food poisoning were attributed to doughnuts containing such filling, which were dispensed from an unrefrigerated vending machine. It was shown that the three cultures used for this test grew well on the imitation cream filling at 25 and 32°C (77 and 89.6°F). Therefore, it is advised that cooked synthetic fillings be kept refrigerated at all times.

Addition of permissible amounts of approved antimicrobial additives is made use of by some bakeries to prolong the shelf life of their products without the benefit of refrigeration.

MOISTURE

The moisture content of many potentially hazardous foods is sufficient for bacterial multiplication, except when these foods have been dehydrated. For example, contaminants of dried eggs or dried milk will not multiply. However, growth is resumed when the powders are reconstituted. Keeping dry foods dry is a very important sanitary measure.

Values for a_w of some common foods are: fruits and fruit juices, vegetables, eggs and meat, 0.97; cheese and bread, 0.96; dried fruit, 0.72–0.80; and crackers and cereal, 0.10 (Kaplov, 1970). Approximate water activity values below which growth of microorganisms usually does not occur are: many bacteria, 0.91; many yeasts, 0.88; many molds, 0.80; halophilic bacteria, 0.75; xerophilic fungi, 0.65; osmophilic yeasts (able to grow in high concentrations of solutes), 0.61 (Mossel and Ingram, 1955).

It has been pointed out by Adame et al. (1960) and McCroan et al. (1964) that lettuce added to dry sandwich fillings introduces moisture, which improves the conditions for bacteria to multiply. Lettuce, as commercially available, carries a heavy load of miscellaneous bacteria, many of them coliforms, including *Escherichia coli* (Silverman et al., 1975a, b; Maxcy, 1978). Contamination is especially heavy on the outer leaves.

PHYSICAL STRUCTURE

The effect of the physical structure of food must be considered. When food materials are cubed, chopped, minced, or ground, their surface area is much increased, and the contaminants are spread over these new surfaces. The spread of microorganisms is facilitated by the release of juices liberated by the processes of comminution, peeling, and skinning.

pH AND INHIBITORS

Soups

Research data pertaining to the response of *Staphylococcus aureus* to change in pH of certain menu items, including soups, were reported by Longrée et al. (1957). The investigation was initiated because information was needed as to the potential hazard of menu items likely to be served in camps, community meal service, social gatherings, and other types of foodservice in which cooling facilities are frequently inadequate, and where the persons entrusted with the handling of large batches of food are often unaware of bacteriological dangers. A potential source of trouble is the slow cooling and heating rates of large food batches which allow these foods to remain in the danger zone of bacterial multiplication for long periods of time.

The study was divided into two parts. In the first part, information was obtained on the effect on staphylococcal growth of adding various ingredients like meat, fish, and vegetables to liquid bases such as chicken broth, milk, and thin white sauce; the proportions of these ingredients were 3.3, 10, 16.6, 25, 33.3, and 50%. In the second part of the study, complete soups of

TABLE 10.1.   *Bacterial Growth and pH in Chicken Broth Mixtures as Affected by Kinds and Amounts of Added Ingredients*

Ingredient	pH of Ingredient	No Ingredient in Broth		16.6% Ingredient in Mixture		25.0% Ingredient in Mixture	
		pH	Log Final Count per mL	pH	Log Final Count per mL	pH	Log Final Count per mL
Carrot, fresh	5.6	7.2	7.6	5.3	5.1	5.2	4.4
Sweet green pepper, fresh	5.2	7.6	7.3	5.6	5.2	5.7	4.3
Okra, canned	4.1	7.0	7.2	4.9	4.5	4.8	3.1
Tomato, fresh	4.3	7.5	7.5	4.5	5.6	4.3	3.3
Veal, fresh	5.9	7.5	6.5	6.1	6.1	—	6.8
Green bean, frozen	5.8	7.0	8.0	5.4	7.2	5.2	7.7
Mushroom, canned	6.1	7.9	7.2	6.4	7.5	6.3	7.3
Pea, frozen	6.8	6.7	7.6	6.4	7.7	6.4	8.1

Source: Adapted from Longrée et al. (1957).

varying formulation were used as media for the staphylococci. All inoculated mixtures were incubated at 30°C (86°F). An inhibitory effect on bacterial growth was exerted by acid ingredients such as tomatoes, canned okra, and green peppers. In general, as the pH of the mixtures approached 4.5, bacterial counts became quite low. However, an inhibitory effect of carrots on bacterial growth of the staphylococci was also observed, and this effect could not be explained on the basis of low pH. Some of the data are given in Table 10.1.

In the second part of the study, complete soups of varying formulation were used as substrates for *Staphylococcus aureus*. Formulations were adjusted to include ingredients known to have an inhibitory effect (Table 10.2).

Entrees or Main Dishes

Most entrees are proteinaceous, and are therefore potentially hazardous menu items. Longrée (unpublished data) made a study of pH of some common entrees and inoculated them with *Staphylococcus aureus*. Menu items of relatively high pH, above 6, included beef stew, creamed dishes, scalloped eggs, meat loaves, meatballs, items made of fish and shellfish, meat and vegetable pies, fish and vegetable pies, chicken à la king, and turkey à la king. Bacterial growth was excellent in these items.

Low pH values (below 5) were found in mixtures such as chili con carne, creole spaghetti, and creole franks (the franks were cut into thin slices). Baked beans made with a high percentage of tomato juice and catsup were in the low pH class, and so were Spanish rice and vegetable chop suey. Bacterial growth was poor in these items.

In the intermediate pH range were items containing some small amounts of an acid ingredient, like tomato or mayonnaise. This group included items that are apt to vary a great deal in formulation; in some of them, the pH

TABLE 10.2. *Bacterial Growth and pH in Soups Prepared in Quantity*

	Proportion of Selected Ingredients (%)					
	Canned Tomato	Fresh Carrot	Fresh Green Pepper	Total	pH	Log Final Count per mL
Tomato bouillon	51.0	—	—	51.0	4.2	2.1
Consomme Madrilene	24.0	—	—	24.0	4.6	2.1
Creole	25.5	—	2.0	27.5	4.7	2.1
Mock turtle	18.6	4.7	—	23.3	4.8	3.2
Stockless vegetable	28.6	5.0	—	33.6	4.8	2.1
Dixie vegetable[a]	14.8	4.5	0.2	19.5	4.9	3.7
English beef broth	23.6	5.5	2.7	31.8	4.9	4.7
Minestrone	20.6	4.1	2.7	27.4	5.0	4.5
Spanish bean	24.5	—	—	24.5	5.0	4.2
Chicken gumbo	7.3	5.5	7.3	20.1	5.1	4.5
Cream of tomato	46.2	—	—	46.2	5.1	2.1
Cream of tomato and mushroom	47.3	—	—	47.3	5.1	2.1
Mulligatawny	—	—	—	0	5.5	4.3
	—	—	—	0	5.6	4.4
Split pea	18.6	10.0	—	28.6	5.6	5.1
Tomato–clam bisque	22.4	—	—	22.4	5.7	4.5
Cream of carrot	—	26.8	—	26.8	5.8	4.3

[a]Contained 0.7% peas.
Source: Adapted from Longrée et al. (1957).

increased with holding as the neutral and acid portions became more thoroughly mixed.

The pH of "made" dishes was greatly affected by the proportions of acid and nonacid ingredients. Items containing a high percentage of acid ingredients such as tomato sauce were of relatively low pH. It was found that the acid ingredients were effective in significantly lowering the pH of the entree only when the proportion of the acid ingredient was high and when the meat was in small pieces or finely divided. This allowed the acid to penetrate the meat thoroughly. On the other hand, entrees involving relatively large pieces of meat and small amounts of acid-containing sauce were of medium acidity. Besides, the pH had a tendency to change toward the neutral, as the juice from the meat oozed into the surrounding sauce.

It was not surprising, then, that a high proportion of the entrees allowed excellent growth of *Staphylococcus aureus*. Exceptions were chili con carne and "creole" dishes such as creole spaghetti, Spanish rice, and creole franks (meat was finely sliced), all of which contained a large proportion of tomato, no large pieces of meat, and were of a low pH (below 5). The formulas are available (Longrée et al., 1960). Only when the directions for the preparation of these menu items are carefully followed, especially regarding the proportion of acid and nonacid ingredients, will these formulas be an aid to the keeping quality and bacteriological safety of the items.

In conclusion, the author wishes to warn that all menu items made with a high proportion of proteinaceous ingredients are potentially hazardous, unless acid ingredients are incorporated in amounts sufficient to decrease the pH of the mixture to near 4.5. This is difficult to achieve and requires that a relatively large proportion of acid ingredients be used, and that the proteinaceous ingredients be finely divided to allow penetration of the acid into the meat.

Mayonnaise

Preliminary to a discussion of the effect of pH changes on bacterial multiplication in salads and sandwich fillings, a brief discussion on mayonnaise seems indicated. Mayonnaise is an important salad ingredient and is commonly used as a spread in sandwiches.

Mayonnaise has been defined by government identity standards as a semisolid emulsion of edible vegetable oil, egg yolk or whole egg, vinegar and/or lemon juice, with one or more of the following: salt, other seasoning used in preparation of the mayonnaise, and/or dextrose. It is required that the finished product contain not less than 50% edible oil.

Salad dressing looks similar to mayonnaise but may differ in oil content, which can be less than 50%. Rather than using egg alone to make the emulsions, water and fillers are also used.

Fabian and Wethington (1950) made bacterial and chemical analyses of mayonnaise, salad dressing, and related products. The samples were collected from all over the United States. It was found that in composition, mayonnaise varied least and French dressing most. The pH of the various samples are presented in Table 10.3.

Nunheimer and Fabian (1940) reported that, at a given pH, acetic acid was more inhibiting to food-poisoning organisms than other organic acids. According to Levine and Fellers (1940), the following concentrations of acetic acid were germicidal: a 3% solution for *Salmonella typhi,* a 4% solution for *Escherichia coli,* and a 9% solution for *Staphylococcus aureus.* These authors stated that acetic acid is more toxic to bacteria, at the same pH, than lactic acid or hydrochloric acid.

Mayonnaise is of special interest because salads made with mayonnaise have been indicted in food-poisoning episodes many times, and it has become simply customary to blame the mayonnaise. Wethington and Fabian (1950), who made a study of food-poisoning staphylococci and salmonellae in salad dressing and mayonnaise, found that the pathogens did not multiply in these media and finally died. In 1993, 40–50 people became ill with *E. coli* 0157:H7 after eating at restaurants of the same chain. The illnesses were linked to mayonnaise. Zhao and Doyle (1994) showed that the contamination of the mayonnaise was a result of abusive handling resulting in cross-contamination.

The salmonellae varied in their ability to withstand effects of low pH, *Salmonella typhimurium* and *S. schottmuelleri* being more resistant than *S. enteritidis, S. pullorum, S. parathyphi, S. cholerasuis,* and the staphylococci. The shortest survival time was 24 hours and the longest 144 hours. According to Lerche (1962), *S. typhimurium* and *S. thompson* were quite resistant to low

TABLE 10.3. *Acidity (pH Values) of Commercial Salad Dressings*

Product	Number of Samples	Range of pH Values
Mayonnaise	25	3.0–4.1
Salad dressing	40	3.0–3.9
French dressing	30	3.0–4.4
Tartar sauce	15	2.9–3.6

Source: Adapted from Fabian and Wethington (1950).

pH, while *S. senftenberg* was the least resistant among the strains tested. Another interesting observation was made by the same author: When mayonnaise was inoculated with *Salmonella* and the contaminated mayonnaise was then used for the preparation of meat salad, the meat became invaded by the contaminant. This implies that mayonnaise, although it will not support growth, could serve as a vehicle of contamination, provided the time elapsing between contamination of the mayonnaise and its use in food preparation is sufficiently short to allow for survival of the contaminants.

Smittle (1977), who presented a review of the microbiology of mayonnaise and salad dressing, concludes that the overall microbial content of mayonnaise and salad dressing is low, that lactobacilli, yeasts, and bacilli are the microorganisms most commonly encountered, and that mayonnaise and salad dressing commercially produced in the United States are inimical to bacteria, especially to food pathogens such as salmonellae and staphylococci. Numerous data obtained by other researchers attest to the fact that, owing to their low pH, mayonnaise and salad dressing are unfavorable media for growth and survival of most bacteria, especially pathogens.

Salads

Meat, egg, poultry, and potato salads have been indicted in many foodborne gastroenteric episodes. Although these menu items are acid, the degree of acidity will vary with formulation. Besides, the chances are excellent for the various ingredients to become contaminated with pathogens clinging to chopping boards, knives, choppers, and human hands.

In several studies, salads have been analyzed for total counts and specific pathogens. Lewis et al. (1953) called attention to the fact that a certain amount of contamination of poultry meat during deboning and cutting operations seems to be unavoidable. The extent of contamination varies considerably, as has been shown through microbial analyses of salads offered in retail markets. Total counts are sometimes as high as 1 billion bacteria per gram of protein salad. Staphylococci, including coagulase-positive strains, were said to be almost invariably present, at times in relatively high numbers, in protein salads analyzed by Shiffman and Kronick (1964), Rasmussen and Strong (1967), and Christiansen and King (1971). Although proteinaceous salads made with mayonnaise or other vinegar-containing dressings are on the acid side of the pH scale, the degree of product acidity will vary with formulation. Vegetable salads have lower counts than protein salads (Rasmussen and Strong, 1967). However, vegetable salads of high bacterial counts were reported by Silverman et al. (1975a, b).

A study of prepared salads, some of which were made with meat and others with vegetables, was made by Harris et al. (1975). The salads were procured from retail markets and microbiologically analyzed (1) when purchased; (2) after a holding period of three hours at 37°C (98.6°F); and (3) after a period of four days of chilled (9°C, 48°F) holding. They were tested for the presence of coliforms, *Clostridium perfringens,* and staphylococci. Total plate counts (TPC) were highest for meat salads, approximately 940,000 per gram, while vegetable salads had TPC counts near 100,000 per gram. The counts did not change much during the holding of the samples. Coliform counts were higher in meat salad and potato salad than in cole slaw; again, the counts did not change much during the holding of the samples. Only one sample, corned beef, contained *Clostridium perfringens. Staphylococcus aureus* was present in highest numbers in ham salad, and of 79 colonies analyzed, 31% were coagulase-positive.

Delicatessen salads were surveyed by Fowler and Clark (1975). Two studies were made. First, 12 different types of salads obtained from 11 convenience food manufacturers in eight geographic locations were sampled and the samples analyzed microbiologically. Two samples were taken, one on receipt, and again after 1–5 weeks of storage at 2°C (35.6°F). Total plate counts and the presence of coliforms, fecal coliforms, yeasts, molds, *Clostridium perfringens, Staphylococcus aureus,* and *Salmonella* were determined; pH values were measured also. The samples varied a great deal concerning their initial counts, but unfortunately, inspection reports of sanitary conditions in the plants were not available for the times at which the salads were prepared. Initial microbial counts remained rather stationary during storage. High plate counts were found in salads made with egg, shrimp, and macaroni. Microorganisms of public health significance were detected in a few samples when received, but their number decreased during chilled storage. The same authors followed up with a second survey in which 64 salads obtained from 13 manufacturers in 10 geographic locations were microbiologically analyzed. The purpose was to examine the data for compliance with Army and Air Force Exchange Service (AAFES) microbiological limits. These limits were: total plate count not exceeding 100,000 per gram, coliform counts of less than 10 per gram, and yeast and mold count of less than 20 per gram. Counts obtained from the commercially prepared samples exceeded AAFES limits in 56% of the samples. Violation in total plate counts, coliform counts, and yeast and mold limit, occurred in 16, 22, and 45% of the samples, respectively. Salmonellae, *C. perfringens* organisms, and staphylococci were isolated from several salads.

A survey of the bacteriological quality of seven types of delicatessen salads obtained from approximately 150 retail markets was made by Pace (1975). Chicken, egg, ham, macaroni, American potato, shrimp, and tuna salads were analyzed. A separate survey was made of a central production unit and the 18 retail establishments supplied by the unit. Results obtained from general retail outlets showed aerobic plate counts (APC values) to be less than 10,000 per gram in 26–85% of the samples. Thirty-six to 79% had coliform most probable number (MPN) levels of less than 100 per gram; and 83–100% of the samples contained less than 10 *Escherichia coli* per gram. Coagulase-positive *Staphylococcus aureus* was detected in some samples of each of the products. The APC values for the salads prepared in the central production unit were somewhat better, in that 71–96% had values less than 100,000 per gram, and their coliform MPN values were less than 100 per gram in 45–94% of the salads.

The shelf life of commercially prepared cole slaw was investigated by King et al. (1976), who found that initial total counts of cabbage were approximately 100,000 per gram. In cole slaw made from the cabbage using a dressing containing cultured sour cream, the original cabbage flora died off and was replaced by the flora of the sour cream. Cole slaw (pH of 4.2) stored at 14°C (57°F) deteriorated rapidly organoleptically and total counts increased. However, even when stored at a lower temperature, 7°C (44.6°F), organoleptic deterioration of the salad was just as rapid as that stored at the higher temperature. Physiological breakdown of the cabbage tissues seemed to be the determining factor in the spoilage of the slaw.

A microbiological profile of commercially prepared salads from nine different producers was established by Terry and Overcast (1976). Samples of chicken, ham, and potato salads, cole slaws, and pimiento cheese were collected. They were examined for aerobic plate count (APC), coliform count, psychrotrophic plate count (PPC), yeast, and mold count. Samples were taken within 48 hours of receipt and again after storage at 3–6°C (37–43°F), until 5 days after the expiration date given by the manufacturer for each salad. Samples without an expiration date were examined after chilled storage for 15 days. A number of bacterial genera were recovered, those found in largest numbers being *Bacillus, Lactobacillus, Leuconostoc,* and *Streptococcus.* Initial counts varied greatly, some having very high APC and PPC values, others had low counts. Upon receipt of the salads the pH values were as follows: chicken salad, 4.3–5.1; cole slaw, 3.9–4.8; ham salad, 4.2–5.0; potato salad, 4.1–5.1; pimiento cheese, 4.7–5.7; the values changed little during storage. The APC counts of chicken salad ranged from less than 100 per gram to more than 30 million per gram; cole slaw from 400 per gram to 700,000 per gram; potato salad from 300 per gram to 180,000 per gram; pimiento cheese from 3000 per gram to 8 million per gram. Coliform counts for all the salads ranged from less than 1 per gram to 7740 per gram. The authors concluded that the discrepancies in initial counts reflect the sanitary precautions, or the lack of them, taken during the production of the salads, and the microbial quality of the salad components.

Longrée et al. (1959a) made an investigation of potato and turkey salads. They studied the effect on pH and bacterial counts of varying formulation and of varying certain preparation procedures used for the salads. For the potato salads, the ingredients varied in amount of mayonnaise, pickle, and egg. For the turkey salads, the varied ingredients were mayonnaise, pickle, and celery. The highest amounts and lowest amounts of mayonnaise used were chosen on the basis of culinary acceptability of formulas. The variation in preparation procedures was that some inoculated samples were immediately marinated with part of the acid dressing, while others were held for several hours at room temperature following inoculation with the test organism, *Staphylococcus aureus.*

The results showed that in the high-mayonnaise salads the pH values and bacterial counts were lower than in the low-mayonnaise salads. The addition of a larger amount of pickle had a similar effect. On the other hand, the higher amounts of egg increased pH and bacterial counts. Marinating the ingredients with the acid dressing immediately after inoculation had a pronounced effect in that the final bacterial counts were relatively low. This treatment with acid was particularly effective in the salads made with a high amount of acid dressing. Some of these results are presented in Table 10.4.

Staphylococcal growth and enterotoxin production in chicken and chicken salad was investigated by McKinley et al. (1974). Three separate batches of chicken meat were inoculated with a known enterotoxin-producing strain (196 E) of the pathogen, at the rate of 1000, 10,000, and 100,000 cells per gram. Each batch contained saprophytic microorganisms at three levels: none, low number (3000 per gram), and high number (1,400,000 per gram). The batches were separated into several lots and incubated (temperature not stated) (1) directly; (2) mixed immediately into a salad, then incubated; (3) incubated for 6 hours, then mixed into a salad; or, (4) incubated for 18 hours, then mixed into a salad. Bacterial counts and determinations of enterotoxin were performed after 24 and 48 hours of incubation. The results showed that the quicker the chicken was mixed into salad after inoculation and the greater the competition from saprophytes, the less was the growth of *Staphylococcus* and the less were the chances for enterotoxin production. Doyle et al. (1982) later studied the inhibitory effect of mayonnaise on pathogens such as *Salmonella typhimurium* and *Staphylococcus aureus* in meat salads. The authors emphasize the fact that even a liberal use of mayonnaise is no alternative to refrigeration.

Sandwiches

Sandwiches are of interest because they are often made with mayonnaise and are frequently held at temperatures favorable for bacterial multiplication.

Commercially prepared sandwiches were surveyed for microbiological quality by Christiansen and King (1971). Among the 108 sandwiches analyzed, total counts varied greatly, not only with the type of sandwich, but also among

TABLE 10.4. *Bacterial Counts and pH Values of Potato Salads and Turkey Salads*[a]

	Not Marinated		Marinated	
	pH	Log Final Count per Gram	pH	Log Final Count per Gram
Potato				
High mayonnaise				
Plain	5.21	8.34	4.79	5.90
High egg	5.46	8.13	5.01	6.88
High pickle	4.60	5.28	4.60	3.51
Low mayonnaise				
Plain	5.51	9.10	5.15	8.29
High egg	5.91	8.85	5.41	8.59
High pickle	4.69	6.61	4.75	5.33
Turkey				
High mayonnaise				
Plain	5.70	8.30	5.52	8.01
High pickle	5.13	6.41	5.12	4.34
Low mayonnaise				
Plain	5.94	8.39	5.60	8.29
High pickle	5.65	8.61	5.79	7.16

[a] Inoculated potatoes or turkey were held at room temperature for 3 hours before remaining ingredients were added.
Source: Adapted from Longrée et al. (1959a).

samples of the same type. Most sandwiches sampled had been displayed at ambient temperature. The types of sandwiches analyzed were chicken salad, ham and chopped ham, ham salad, roast beef, egg salad, bologna, sliced turkey, cheeseburger, and smoked sausage. Median total counts were 100,000 per gram and 270,000 per gram. However, the range of total counts was very wide, from approximately 1000 per gram to several billion per gram; the highest count occurred in ham and chopped ham sandwiches. Approximately 60% of the samples contained coagulase-positive staphylococci.

Adame et al. (1960) undertook a bacteriological study of some selected commercially prepared, wrapped sandwiches. As the survey showed, sandwiches are frequently prepared 17–20 hours prior to sale and held during this period at ambient air temperatures, which for the Los Angeles area (the place of the survey) were given as 23–30°C (73–86°F). The sandwiches were prepared by hand. Analyses were made for total counts, coliforms, enterococci, spores, and staphylococci.

Among the salad-type or "wet" sandwiches, the egg sandwiches had higher counts than the tuna sandwiches. The pH of the egg sandwiches ranged from 4.90 to 6.20; the pH of the tuna sandwiches ranged from 4.60 to 5.35. The "dry" sandwiches were made of ham, cheese, salami, hot beef and cheese, and hot ham and cheese; the pH ranged from 5.40 to 6.30.

Staphylococcus counts were high, in general. No evidence of *Clostridium perfringens,* salmonellae, or shigellae were found. The authors were careful to point out that in spite of higher counts in the salad-type sandwiches, it should not be assumed that the "dry" type sandwiches were free from danger.

Several studies were made of bacterial multiplication in sandwich fillings of varying acidity.

Longrée et al. (1959b) changed the formulation of three basic fillings made with protein bases of ham, egg, or turkey. The fillings were varied to include different amounts of lemon juice as well as other ingredients, some of them acid, some spicy. Among the acid ingredients were pickle, cranberry, pineapple, raisin, and apricot; among the spicy were mustard, garlic (dry), onion (dry), and Worcestershire sauce. The test organism was *Staphylococcus aureus.* Culinary acceptability was determined. Highest pH values and highest bacterial counts were found in the egg-based fillings, and lowest pH and lowest bacterial counts in the turkey fillings. The addition of lemon juice, pickle, cranberry, and apricot reduced bacterial counts, but some of the acid additives were not acceptable organoleptically. Acceptable mixtures of low counts were egg filling with lemon juice and sweet relish pickle; ham with lemon juice and sweet relish pickle; ham with lemon juice and sweet pickle or raisin; and turkey with lemon juice and pickle, pineapple, and cranberry. Some of the data are presented in Table 10.5.

McCroan et al. (1964) called attention to the fact that although many sandwiches are bacteriologically abused by being transported in panel trucks and displayed for up to 96 hours on unrefrigerated shelves of filling stations, fruit stands, and the like, very few gastroenteric outbreaks caused by sandwiches have been discussed in the literature. However, these authors go on to say that if one chooses to review the food-poisoning history of sandwiches in general, the story is not as favorable: according to data gained by these authors from the *Morbidity and Mortality Weekly Report* of the Public Health Service, it is evident that between 1951 and 1963, sandwiches were incriminated in 133 foodborne outbreaks of gastroenteritis and that 5947 victims were involved.

These same authors made a study in Georgia, to measure the potential hazards of commercially prepared, wrapped sandwiches. They examined 820 fresh sandwiches from 15 different manufacturers for pH, average plate

TABLE 10.5.   *Bacterial Counts and pH Values of Protein-Base Sandwich Fillings*

| Type of Filling | Variable | No Lemon Juice in Filling | | Lemon Juice in Filling | |
		pH	Log Final Count per Gram	pH	Log Final Count per Gram
Egg base	Plain (control)	6.07	9.33	5.50	9.41
	Sweet relish pickle[a]	5.01	5.82	4.76	<4.50
Ham base	Plain (control)	5.90	9.06	5.85	8.43
	Sweet relish pickle[a]	5.13	<4.50	5.18	<3.50
	Raisins[a]	4.83	<4.50	4.70	<3.50
Turkey base	Plain (control)	6.00	8.97	5.65	7.41
	Cranberry[a]	5.36	4.66	5.12	5.20
	Dill pickle[a]	5.66	5.07	5.37	4.50
	Sweet relish pickle[a]	5.09	3.22	4.98	2.94
	Pineapple[a]	5.48	5.00	5.19	4.11

[a] 15.0% substitution.
Source: Adapted from Longrée et al. (1959b).

count, average coliform count, and coagulase-positive staphylococci, and again analyzed them after 48 hours of exposure to conditions of ambient temperatures routinely encountered. The average pH values of the blenderized sandwiches ranged as follows: chicken salad, 4.24–5.39; deviled egg, 4.83–6.18; spiced ham and cheese, 5.35–5.97; and ham and cheese, 5.51–6.21. The imitation chicken salad consisted of chopped pork, pork skins, pork stomachs, vinegar, and spices; pH values ranged from 5.02 to 5.11. It was found that coliform counts tended to decrease in salad-type sandwiches during holding and no salmonellae were isolated. Staphylococci were at times numerous, but few coagulase-positive types were detected, and no significant increase in these could be demonstrated upon holding.

In a laboratory study, a group of sandwiches, among them chicken salad, imitation chicken salad, spiced ham, and deviled egg, were inoculated with coagulase-positive staphylococci and held at room temperature for 48 hours. Multiplication did occur during this period in the chicken salad sandwiches, but none in the imitation chicken salad and deviled egg sandwiches. An impressive multiplication of these coagulase-positive staphylococci occurred in spiced ham and cheese sandwiches (Table 10.6). It is important to note that the pH values of these types were fairly high.

TABLE 10.6. *Average Findings for Commercially Prepared Wrapped Sandwiches Inoculated with Coagulase-Positive Staphylococci (Combined Results of 10 Sandwiches in Each Sample)*

Kind of Sandwich and Sample Number	Average Coagulase-Positive Staphylococci per Gram		Average pH	
	Fresh	48 Hours	Fresh	48 Hours
Spiced ham and cheese				
1	300,000[a]	6,200,000	5.78	5.74
2	170,000[a]	4,300,000	5.80	5.80
3	59,000[b]	62,000,000	6.78	6.12
4	53,000[b]	63,000,000	6.34	6.06

[a] Inoculum placed on the slice of spiced ham in contact with the bread and mayonnaise.
[b] Inoculum placed between the slice of spiced ham and the slice of cheese.
Source: Adapted from McCroan et al. (1964).

Of practical implication is the observation that the staphylococci grew far better when placed between the slices of ham and the slice of cheese, than when dropped onto the surface of a slice of ham, which, when the sandwich was completed, made contact with the mayonnaise and bread.

This information points again toward the inhibitory effect of mayonnaise and suggests that it may well be a good practice to spread perishable fillings on both sides with mayonnaise to discourage multiplication of food-poisoning bacteria.

In a later study (Swaminathan et al., 1981), an inhibitory effect of mayonnaise on *Salmonella typhimurium* inoculated into turkey sandwiches made with and without commercial mayonnaise was again demonstrated. However, mayonnaise did not prevent the pathogen from multiplying when the sandwiches were stored at 21 and 30°C (70 and 86°F) for as long as 8 hours.

Commercially prepared sandwiches purchased in retail markets were analyzed for coliforms by Hall et al. (1967). The sandwiches, which were prewrapped, came from various sources: coldboxes of chain stores, vending machines, and other miscellaneous places. Counts were fairly high, in general. In another study of sandwiches purchased in retail markets, Christiansen and King (1971) found that 60% of the items contained coagulase-positive staphylococci, and that in approximately 16% of the items the total counts were higher than a million cells per gram. Most sandwiches had not been under refrigeration at the time of purchase.

Poultry Stuffings

A special problem is posed by poultry stuffings, which have often been the critical foods in gastroenteric episodes. Many stuffings contain high-protein ingredients. In quantity foodservice it is considered good practice to bake the stuffing separately and to roast the turkey without stuffing. This is a sound rule, as will be discussed later, because heat penetration into the center of large stuffed turkeys is very slow. Within the long period of moderate temperatures prevailing in the stuffing during roasting, an opportunity for bacterial multiplication is afforded.

However, in view of the fact that to stuff poultry is unfortunately still a popular practice, Longrée et al. (1958) initiated an investigation to determine the effect on the growth of *Staphylococcus aureus* of varying certain ingredients in poultry stuffings. In three basic stuffings containing a bread base, onion, shortening, seasoning, and chicken broth, the bread base was varied to include white bread, bulgar wheat, and cornbread. The liquid was varied to change the pH of the mixture by using orange juice in place of part of the broth. In addition, substitution was made for part of the liquid and bread in the basic stuffing using apple, apricot, cranberry, celery, green pepper, parsley, ripe olives, walnut, raisins, egg, giblet, and oyster. The inoculated samples were incubated at 30°C (86°F) for 24 hours. The culinary quality of the mixtures was assessed before inoculation. A total of 117 different combinations of ingredients were tested. Some of the results are presented in Tables 10.7 and 10.8. In general, the bacterial counts were highest in the cornbread stuffing. Acid ingredients that were effective in keeping bacterial multiplication at a low level were apricot, cranberry, orange juice, and raisin. Very high bacterial counts were encountered in the mixtures containing egg, giblet, and oyster. Many mixtures of low pH and low counts were acceptable organoleptically.

Desserts

Of the varied items used as desserts, the cream-filled pastries, cream pies, and puddings fall under the category "potentially hazardous foods," because they consist in whole or in part of milk or milk products and eggs. These items are known to have caused gastroenteric outbreaks many times.

Plain unfilled cakes, unfilled pastry, and cookies will be omitted from the discussion because of their good record with respect to bacteriological safety. These items are heated to high terminal temperatures in baking.

Ryberg and Cathcart (1942) studied the response of bacterial pathogens to pure fruit fillings and custard fillings. The fruits and their juices used in fillings were lemon, pineapple, orange, strawberry, and apricot. Standard cus-

TABLE 10.7. *Bacterial Growth and pH of White Bread Stuffings*[a]

Stuffing	All Broth		Half Orange Juice and Half Broth	
	pH	Log Final Count per Gram	pH	Log Final Count per Gram
Basic[b] (controls)	5.26	7.41	4.54	4.16
Apricot[c]	4.50	3.00	4.40	3.00
	4.70	4.00	4.20	4.00
Cranberry[c]	4.62	3.92	4.10	3.64
	4.62	4.00	4.32	4.00
Egg[c]	5.30	7.61	4.68	3.88
	5.26	6.00	5.03	3.00
Giblet[c]	5.40	7.41	4.34	4.00
	5.48	6.00	4.56	3.00
Oyster[c]	5.10	7.44	4.52	3.96
	5.11	7.97	5.05	3.00
Raisin[c]	4.68	3.00	4.35	3.00
	4.49	4.00	4.69	3.00

[a]All stuffings were of acceptable palatability.
[b]Values are averages of all controls.
[c]At 5% substitution.
Source: Adapted from Longrée et al. (1958).

tards with varying amounts of added lemon juice and rind were also used in the experiments. Also investigated was the effect on bacterial growth of incorporating milk into the fruit fillings. The test organisms were *Staphylococcus aureus* and *Salmonella enteritidis.* The data showed that the growth of both organisms was decreased as the pH of the fillings were decreased from approximately 6.8 in the plain custard to approximately 3 in the lemon fillings. In the other fillings the pH values ranged like this: in apricot, 4.17–4.38; in strawberry, 4.02–4.15; in orange, 3.80–3.86; and in pineapple, 3.48–3.68. The inhibitory effect of the acid ingredients on the inoculum was greater for the salmonellae than for the staphylococci. Although the degree of inhibition paralleled, in general, a decrease in pH, there were some other effects at play. For example, when strawberry filling was prepared in such a way that its pH was similar to that of the pineapple filling, the strawberry had a greater inhibitory effect than the pineapple.

The addition of lemon juice and rind to a standard custard did not have a

TABLE 10.8.   *Bacterial Growth and pH of Cornbread Stuffings*[a]

Stuffing	All Broth		Half Orange Juice and Half Broth	
	pH	Log Final Count per Gram	pH	Log Final Count per Gram
Basic[b] (controls)	5.96	8.58	5.25	6.50
Apricot[c]	5.40	4.00	4.90	4.00
	5.20	4.00	4.40	4.00
Cranberry[c]	5.70	7.60	4.70	4.00
	5.20	7.89	5.00	4.00
Egg[c]	6.18	8.60	5.47	7.23
	6.30	7.96	5.40	7.31
Giblet[c]	6.00	8.78	5.40	6.84
	6.19	9.27	5.60	7.93
Oyster[c]	5.95	8.49	5.35	6.60
	5.90	7.84	5.26	3.94
Raisin[c]	5.47	5.00	4.93	4.00
	5.62	3.00	4.83	3.94

[a] All stuffings were of acceptable palatability.
[b] Values are averages of all controls.
[c] At 5% substitution.
Source: Adapted from Longrée et al. (1958).

marked retarding effect on the multiplication of *Staphylococcus aureus* until it was used in such high amounts that the acidified custard was no longer palatable, and even then the counts were not sufficiently decreased to make such an acidification of practical value. The addition of milk reduced the inhibitory action of the fruits on bacterial multiplication.

Cathcart and Merz (1942) studied the effect of chocolate and cocoa fillings on growth of *S. aureus*. Standard custards were prepared as control. The fillings were made with water, sugar, starch, butter, and chocolate or cocoa. Most formulas contained egg; some did not. The amounts and kinds of chocolate and cocoa were varied. The pH values were determined, and it was found that the amounts of the chocolate or cocoa had some effect on pH, the pH decreasing with increasing amounts of these ingredients. Their inhibitory action on bacterial multiplication was assumed by the authors as being due to a combination of decrease of the pH with some unidentified substance, or substances, in the nonfat part of the chocolate or cocoa. Omission of egg had a profound inhibitory effect on the growth of the inoculum.

Cathcart et al. (1947) investigated the growth of *S. aureus* in commercial dry-mix puddings, made with and without milk; prepared vanilla fillings; pie fillings made from pumpkin, squash, and sweet potato; fruit fillings; cheesecake mixes; and whipped-cream type mixes. Some of these items were modified by the addition of varying amounts of lactic acid, citric acid, and sodium propionate. The inoculated fillings and mixes were incubated for 24 hours at 37°C (98.6°F). The commercial dry-mix puddings, which included vanilla, chocolate, and butterscotch, when made with milk, supported the growth of the test organism very well. When water was substituted for milk, growth was poor but the products were unacceptable organoleptically. Good growth was found in the pie fillings made from pumpkin, squash, and sweet potatoes, the cheesecake fillings, and whipped-cream mixtures.

The fruit fillings made with peach contained sufficient acid to halt the multiplication of the test organism, and in those made with raspberry a substantial decrease of viable bacteria was noted. In another experiment, vanilla fillings and cheesecake fillings were altered in pH by use of various acids. In the vanilla fillings, the addition of citric acid in amounts sufficient to lower the pH to 3.43 and 3.65 successfully checked the proliferation of the staphylococci, but the products tasted sour and were therefore unacceptable. The filling supported growth well when no acid was added.

In the cheesecake fillings, a decrease of pH to below 5.12 was effective in gradually checking the multiplication of the test organism. It was observed that the use of lactic acid produced a filling of better flavor than the use of citric acid, and it effectively controlled the growth of the staphylococci at pH values between 4.42 and 4.87.

Castellani et al. (1955) reported that staphylococcal growth could be checked in unmeringued fruit cream fillings of pH 4 when incubated at 37°C (98.6°F) for 48 hours, but that in meringued pies prolific growth took place at the interface between the fillings and the meringue, and some bacterial penetration into the filling could be noted. At a pH of 3.5 and a temperature of 37°C (98.6°F), no staphylococcal multiplication was noted in the fillings, but extensive growth occurred at the meringue-filling interface. At a temperature of 30°C (86°F), no growth was observed at the interface of filling and meringue. With a filling at pH 3.8, a bactericidal effect was observed against *Salmonella meleagrides* and *Streptococcus faecalis* throughout the pie fillings.

The effect of baking time and temperature on heat penetration to the interface of filling and meringue, and temperatures attained at the interface, will be discussed in a later chapter.

ADJUSTMENT OF pH APPLICABLE TO QUANTITY FOODSERVICE

Among many other factors, the acidity (pH) of the food in which the contaminating bacteria find themselves controls the extent to which they multiply. This effect is discussed in Chapters 2 and 4. A pH of 4.5 is the approximate level below which little multiplication need be expected of bacteria which are capable of causing foodborne gastroenteric outbreaks.

A pH of 4.5 indicates a fairly acid condition. Many fruits, but only a few vegetables, have pH values as low as this (see Table 2.2). Fruits and vegetables, pickles, relishes, and vinegar can be combined with nonacid ingredients into mixtures that are of low pH and are poor supporters of bacterial growth.

Appropriate amounts of ingredients inhibitory to bacterial multiplication can be successfully incorporated in certain menu items if formulation is carefully worked out, provided attention is paid to the resulting pH as well as the culinary quality of the items.

Applicability to Community Mealservice

Formulation for high acidity (low pH) can have a purposeful and practical application in community mealservice. When facilities for meal preparation at the site of service are limited, and they frequently are, some menu items are usually prepared in the home. These home-prepared items are apt to be exposed to long holding periods. It is only logical that in planning community meals, menu items high in acid (of low pH) should be the ones prepared in the home, whereas the potentially dangerous ones, those of near neutral pH, should be prepared at the place of mealservice. In a Cornell Extension Bulletin by Longrée et al. (1960), information is presented along these lines and menu items are listed which are of low pH, if prepared with the formulas developed for this purpose.

Applicability to the Average Foodservice Operation

As a routine measure to control bacterial multiplication, adjustment of pH has several limitations under average conditions of foodservice. Although some acid menu items are well accepted by the public, most menu items cannot be readily acidified without becoming unpalatable. After all, menu items prepared for service to the public must appeal to the tastebuds of the average customer. Moreover, the number of ingredients sufficiently acid to effect a substantial change of pH is extremely limited; it would be very tiresome to see and taste, for example, tomato in almost everything.

It is difficult to measure acidity under conditions of actual food preparation. There is no gadget comparable to a thermometer which could be used by a cook to determine pH. And finally, even if determinations of pH were not required (measurements could be omitted if strictly standardized recipes were used), difficulties might arise in connection with general rules given to the employees for the sanitary handling of cooked foods, in that employees who have been educated to regard cooked foods as vulnerable, and who have been trained to act accordingly, would probably become confused by exceptions, and more harm than benefit would result.

Formulation with the intent to discourage bacterial growth is an excellent supporting measure in the control of bacterial multiplication, but is no substitute for vigilance in temperature control.

TIMING THE INCORPORATION OF ACID INGREDIENTS IN PREPARING SALADS

In the preparation of salads made with mayonnaise, such as potato, egg, turkey, seafood, or chicken salads, the time at which the acid ingredients are combined with the basic ingredients is of great importance. For information on the growth-inhibiting effect of mayonnaise and other acid dressings, the reader is referred to the earlier part of this chapter. In the past, mayonnaise has been unjustly blamed as the culprit in food-poisoning episodes. Mayonnaise, however, is a very acid ingredient and is inhibitory to bacterial multiplication if used at the right time and in sufficient amounts.

The acid should be put to work immediately after contamination is likely to have occurred. Opportunities for contamination are afforded through handling and through contact with soiled cutting boards, grinders, slicers, and the like. If the operations during which contamination is likely to occur are brief, the acid may well be added at the end. However, if these operations are drawn out over several hours, the acid should be added at regular intervals which should be sufficiently brief to prevent bacterial multiplication. The acid ingredient should be thoroughly distributed over the surfaces of the individual pieces. It is advised for potato, egg, seafood, meat, and poultry salads, to incorporate at least one-third of the acid dressing, possibly in the form of a simple vinegar and oil marinade, during or immediately following the cutting or slicing operations.

Acidification is to be looked on as an additional aid in discouraging bacterial multiplication, but it is not a substitute for other precautions: that hands and nails be thoroughly cleaned and food contact equipment sanitized, and that the period during which the food is held at warm temperatures be kept at a minimum. After the acid ingredient has been added, the food portions should be promptly cooled in shallow pans.

Salads made with meats, poultry, seafood, egg, and potato should be made using chilled ingredients.

CONTACT OF ACID INGREDIENTS WITH POTENTIALLY HAZARDOUS INGREDIENTS IN SANDWICHES

If acid ingredients, like mayonnaise, are to inhibit bacterial multiplication, they must be placed where they are needed, namely, on the food item likely to be contaminated and/or preferred as food by bacteria. For example, in the case of meat or egg sandwiches, the mayonnaise should make contact with the meat or egg, not necessarily with the lettuce, bread, or other less hazardous portions. In fact, spreading mayonnaise onto both sides of the meat, cheese, poultry, or egg is good procedure in making sandwiches. Pickle or acid ingredients would also restrain bacterial contaminants from multiplying. The sandwiches should be kept cold until served.

REFERENCES

Adame, J. L., F. J. Post, and A. H. Bliss (1960). "Preliminary report on a bacteriological study of selected commercially prepared, wrapped sandwiches." *J. Milk Food Technol.,* 23:363–366.

Castellani, A. G., R. Makowski, and W. B. Bradley (1955). "Inhibiting the growth of food poisoning bacteria in meringue-topped fruit cream pies." *Bact. Proc. Soc. Am. Bacteriol.,* 55:20.

Cathcart, W. H. and A. Merz (1942). "Staphylococci and *Salmonella* control in foods. III. Effect of chocolate and cocoa fillings on inhibiting growth of staphylococci." *Food Res.,* 7:96–103.

Cathcart, W. H., W. J. Godkin, and G. Barnett (1947). "Growth of *Staphylococcus aureus* in various pastry fillings." *Food Res.,* 12:142–150.

Christiansen, L. N. and N. S. King (1971). "The microbial content of some salads and sandwiches at retail outlets." *J. Milk Food Technol.,* 34:289–293.

Crisley, F. D., R. Angelotti, and M. J. Foter (1964). "Multiplication of *Staphylococcus aureus* in synthetic cream filling and pies." *U.S. Public Health Rep.,* 79:369–376.

Doyle, M. P., N. J. Bains, J. L. Schoeni, and E. M. Foster (1982). "Fate of *Salmonella typhimurium* and *Staphylococcus aureus* in meat salads prepared with mayonnaise." *J. Food Prot.,* 45:152–156.

Fabian, F. W. and M. C. Wethington (1950). "Bacterial and chemical analysis of mayonnaise, salad dressing and related products." *Food Res.,* 15:138–145.

Fowler, J. L. and W. S. Clark, Jr. (1975). "Microbiology of delicatessen salads." *J. Milk Food Technol.,* 38:126–149.

Harris, N. D., S. R. Martin, and L. Ellias (1975). "Bacteriological quality of selected delicatessen foods." *J. Milk Food Technol.,* 38:759–761.

Kaplov, M. (1970). "Commercial development of intermediate moisture foods." *Food Technol.,* 24:889–893.

King, A. D., Jr., H. D. Michener, H. G. Bayne, and K. L. Milhara (1976). "Microbial studies on shelf life of cabbage and cole slaw." *Appl. Environ. Microbiol.,* 31:404–407.

Lerche, M. (1962). "The viability of *Salmonella* bacteria in mayonnaise and meat salad." *Biolog. Abs.,* 37(5), No. 19212.

Levine, A. S. and C. R. Fellers (1940). "Action of acetic acid on food spoilage microorganisms." *J. Bacteriol.,* 39:499–515.

Lewis, M. N., H. H. Weiser, and A. R. Winter (1953). "Bacterial growth in chicken salad." *J. Am. Diet. Assoc.,* 29(11):1094–1099.

Longrée, K., R. F. Padgham, J. C. White, and B. Weismann (1957). "Effect of ingredients on bacterial growth in soups." *J. Milk Food Technol.,* 20:170–177.

Longrée, K., J. C. White, K. Cutlar, D. Hogue, and J. M. Hayter (1958). "Bacterial growth in poultry stuffings." *J. Am. Diet. Assoc.,* 34:50–57.

Longrée, K., J. C. White, K. Cutlar, and A. R. Willman (1959a). "Bacterial growth in potato and turkey salads: Effect of formula variation." *J. Am. Diet. Assoc.,* 35:38–44.

Longrée, K., J. C. White, and C. Lynch (1959b). "Bacterial growth in protein-base sandwich fillings." *J. Am. Diet. Assoc.,* 35:131–138.

Longrée, K., A. R. Willman, and M. Knickrehm (1960). *Soups and Main Dishes for Your Community Meals.* New York State College of Home Economics, Cornell University Miscellaneous Bulletin No. 35, Ithaca, NY.

Maxcy, R. B. (1978). "Lettuce salad as a carrier of microorganisms of public health significance." *J. Food Prot.,* 41:435–438.

McCroan, J. E., T. W. McKinley, A. Brim, and W. C. Henning (1964). "Staphylococci and salmonellae in commercial wrapped sandwiches." *U.S. Public Health Rep.,* 79:997–1004.

McKinley, T. W. and E. J. Clarke, Jr. (1964). "Imitation cream fillings as a vehicle of staphylococcal food poisoning." *J. Milk Food Technol.,* 27:302–304.

McKinley, T. W., W. C. Henning, and J. E. McCroan (1974). "Staphylococcal growth and enterotoxin production in chicken and chicken salad." *Assoc. Food Drug Of. Q. Bull.,* 38(1):56.

Mossel, D. A. A. and M. Ingram (1955). "The physiology of the microbial spoilage of foods." *J. Appl. Bacteriol.,* 18:232–238.

Nunheimer, T. D. and F. W. Fabian (1940). "Influence of organic acids, sugars and sodium chloride upon strains of food poisoning staphylococci." *Am. J. Public Health,* 30:1040–1049.

Pace, P. C. (1975). "Bacteriological quality of delicatessen foods: Are standards needed?" *J. Milk Food Technol.,* 38:347–353.

Rasmussen, C. A. and D. H. Strong (1967). "Bacteria in chilled delicatessen foods." *U.S. Public Health Rep.,* 82:353–359.

Ryberg, R. E. and W. H. Cathcart (1942). "Staphylococci and *Salmonella* control in foods. II. Effect on pure fruit fillings." *Food Res.,* 7:10–15.

Shiffman, M. A. and D. Kronick (1964). "Field studies on the microbiology of chilled foods: Chicken salad and tuna fish salad." *Assoc. Food Drug Of. U.S. Q. Bull.,* 28(3):144–149.

Silverman, G. J., E. M. Powers, and D. B. Rowley (1975a). *Microbiological Analysis of the Food Preparation and Dining Facilities at Fort Myer and Bolling Air Force Base.* Food Sciences Laboratory, Technical Report No. 75–53-FSL. U.S. Army, Natick Laboratories, Natick, MA.

Silverman, G. J., E. M. Powers, D. F. Carpenter, and D. B. Rowley (1975b). *Microbiological Evaluation of the Food Service System at Travis Air Force Base.* Food Sciences

Laboratory, Technical Report 75–110-FSL. U.S. Army, Natick Laboratories, Natick, MA.

Smittle, R. B. (1977). "Microbiology of mayonnaise and salad dressing: A review." *J. Food Prot.,* 40:415–422.

Swaminathan, B., J. M. Howe, and C. M. Essling (1981). "Mayonnaise, sandwiches and *Salmonella.*" *J. Food Prot.,* 44:115–117.

Terry, R. C. and W. W. Overcast (1976). "A microbiological profile of commercially prepared salads." *Food Sci.,* 41:211–214.

Wethington, M. C. and F. W. Fabian (1950). "Viability of food poisoning staphylococci and salmonellae in salad dressing and mayonnaise." *Food Res.,* 15:125–134.

Zhao, T. and M. Doyle (1994). "Fate of enterohemorrhagic *Escherichia coli* 0157:H7 in commercial mayonnaise." *J. Food Prot.,* 57:780–783.

ADDITIONAL READINGS

Kurtzman, C. P., R. Rogers, and C. W. Hesseltine. "Microbiological spoilage of mayonnaise and salad dressings." *Appl. Microbiol.,* 21:870–874. 1971.

Minor, T. E. and E. H. Marth. "Loss of viability by *Staphylococcus aureus* in acidified media. Inactivation by several acids, mixtures of acids, and salts of acids." *J. Milk Food Technol.,* 35:191–196. 1972.

Rappaport, H. and J. M. Goepfert. *Behavior of Salmonella and Staphylococcus aureus.* Annual Report—1975. Food Research Institute, Madison, WI. 1975.

Wright, C., S. D. Kominos, and R. B. Yee. "*Enterobacteriacae* and *Pseudomonas aeruginosa* recovered from vegetable salads." *Appl. Environ. Microbiol.,* 31:453–454. 1976.

CHAPTER 11

Multiplication and Survival of Bacterial Contaminants in Ingredients and Menu Items

PART II. TIME–TEMPERATURE RELATIONSHIPS

From a microbial perspective, it is convenient to group into zones the temperatures that foods see in the process of handling. These include (1) the freezing, defrosting and chilling zone—in this zone the temperatures should prevent multiplication of organisms causing foodborne intoxications and foodborne infections over an extended storage period; (2) the growth or hazardous temperature zone—in this zone the temperatures allow bacterial multiplication; (3) the hot-holding zone—in this zone the temperatures are aimed at preventing multiplication but usually do not kill the organisms; and (4) the cooking zone—in this zone the temperatures should be sufficiently high to destroy the bacterial cells within a brief span of time.

Research data presented in this chapter illustrate that, in reality, the hazardous temperature zone may extend into the refrigeration as well as the cooking zones, and that cooking temperatures used in routine preparation of menu items are not always sufficiently high or are not applied sufficiently long to kill pathogenic contaminants present in the food.

FREEZING ZONE

General Quality Aspects

Many ingredients and menu items can be frozen successfully. However, certain items deteriorate quickly; among these are hamburger, fatty kinds of fish, turkey, and pork.

Some prepared items do not lend themselves to freezing, since they suffer severely in quality.

Microbial Aspects

Some microorganisms may temporarily multiply in foods during the freezing process. Most foods are not solidly frozen at 32°F (0°C), and lower temperatures are required, the exact temperatures depending on the type of food. While food is not solidly frozen, the solutes are available for bacterial multiplication.

Elliott and Michener (1960) found 150 records of growth at subfreezing temperatures scattered over approximately 100 reports. Most of the records for vegetables are for temperatures above 20°F (−6.7°C) for bacteria, although molds may grow at lower temperatures. These authors state that microbial growth was reported to occur at temperatures as low as 10°F (−12.2°C), but that this is unusual. The psychrophilic bacteria may multiply at about 14°F (−10°C).

Bacteria of public health importance, such as *Staphylococcus aureus,* the salmonellae, and the fecal streptococci, are not known to multiply in solidly frozen foods. However, *Clostridium botulinum* type E and *Yersinia enterocolitica* are able to multiply below 40°F (4.4°C).

Survival and Death

Although there is a paucity of information regarding the mechanism determining death and survival of bacteria during the freezing process and freezer storage, it is known that during the freezing process the bacterial population may be expected to decline; further reduction takes place at freezer storage.

Elliott and Michener (1960, 1961) have reviewed important data available regarding the behavior of bacterial contaminants under conditions of freezing and freezer storage.

The killing effect of the freezing process varies with the type of microorganism, the rate of freezing, and other environmental conditions such as the substrate in which the organisms are frozen. Survival is apt to be higher in nonacid substrates; in menstrua containing protective substances such as meats, poultry, fish, and peas; and when freezing proceeds at a fast rate. Alternating freezing and thawing seems to have a detrimental effect on survival. In general, approximately 50% of the initial population dies off during the freezing process.

Unfortunately, conditions generally conducive to maintaining quality of frozen foods, such as fast freezing and storage at low nonfluctuating temperatures, are also conducive to the survival of contaminants. It is known that microbial contaminants have survived months of freezer storage.

It is difficult to generalize on the bacterial flora in precooked frozen foods when it reaches the consumer, because it is subjected to so many variables. Studies on the effect of frozen storage on fungi in foods made by Koburger (1981) have shown that the fungal population exhibited a sensitivity to freezing that was greater or less than that of the total aerobic flora, the outcome being dependent on the type of media used for analysis.

In conclusion, survival of part of the microbiological population, nonpathogenic as well as pathogenic, must be expected even after months of freezer storage. The survivors may resume growth following defrosting. However, appropriate freezing treatment kills some important meat parasites such as trichinae and tapeworms.

Precooked Frozen Foods

As the precooked frozen food industry expanded, specific microbiological problems emerged, including public health considerations. Precooked frozen items have, in general, an excellent record in regard to food-poisoning outbreaks. In spite of this record, potential danger exists from grossly mishandled products. Surveys have shown that some products that were obviously mishandled contained large numbers of bacteria, including forms of public health significance.

The cooking, blanching, and pasteurizing of the raw materials kills many microorganisms adhering to the food materials, but the chances for recontamination during subsequent handling cannot be ruled out. Many operations, such as deboning, sorting, and weighing, usually require the use of hands. Furthermore, during many operational steps the ingredients are at warm temperatures for some time.

The use of properly sanitized equipment, sanitary working habits of employees, proper heat treatment during processing, avoidance of recontamination after cooking, and avoidance of delays during the entire process, up to freezing, are important means to keep counts low and contaminants of public health significance out.

Numerous surveys of manufacturing processes employed in the production of frozen items such as meats, fish, shellfish, potato products, and cream-type pies have demonstrated this important relationship.

Pathogenic Bacteria

Pathogenic contaminants, and survivors, in frozen foods are known to include typhoid bacteria and other salmonellae, staphylococci, enterococci, and spore formers such as *Clostridium perfringens* and *botulinum*.

Proctor and Phillips (1948) showed that when *Staphylococcus aureus* and *Salmonella enteritidis* were added to cooked foods and these were frozen, the organisms survived for months (Fig. 11.1). Survival of *S. aureus* and enterococci in frozen chicken à la king was demonstrated by Buchbinder et al. (1949). In Figure 11.2 is shown a comparison of species of *Salmonella*. Survival varied with the species.

Research data involving frozen items inoculated with *Clostridium botulinum* (Saleh and Ordal, 1955) indicated that there was danger when the products were grossly mishandled, that is, when they were allowed to thaw and

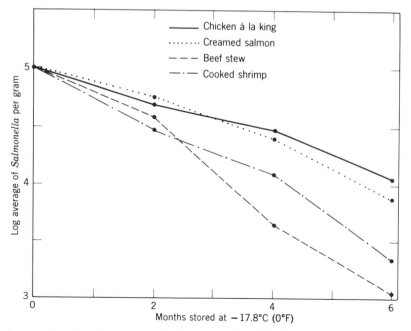

FIGURE 11.1.   Experimental inoculation studies. Survival of *Salmonella enteritidis* in foods stored at − 17.8°C (0°F), three samples per point. Adapted from Proctor and Phillips (1948).

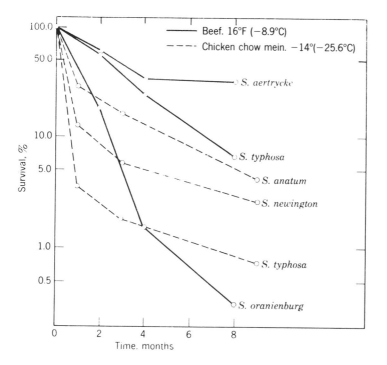

FIGURE 11.2.   Storage survival: comparison of species of *Salmonella*. Adapted from Elliot and Michener (1960).

stand at warm temperatures for hours or days. However, no toxin was found in the frozen items or in items defrosted and immediately refrigerated.

Woodburn and Strong (1960) studied survival of *Salmonella typhimurium, Staphylococcus aureus,* and *Streptococcus faecalis* in simplified food media and submitted these to freezer storage. The effect of freezer storage varied with the organism and temperature, survival being greater at −22°F (−30°C) than at 12°F (−11.1°C).

Georgala and Hurst (1963) reported that food-poisoning bacteria in frozen foods do not differ greatly from nonpathogens in their survival, that salmonellae are less resistant than are *S. aureus* or vegetative cells of *Clostridium,* and that bacterial spores and food-poisoning toxins are apparently unaffected. The protective effect of beef on the death of *S. aureus* is shown in Figure 11.3. Georgala and Hurst (1963) stated that food-poisoning bacteria die more rapidly when stored between 32 and 14°F (0 and −10°C) than at 1–4°F (−17.2 and −15.6°C).

Strong et al. (1963) examined 111 samples of commercially prepared frozen foods for *Clostridium perfringens*. The items included TV dinners, meat and poultry pies, and similar items; of these, three were positive for *C. per-*

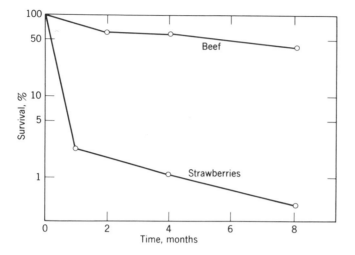

FIGURE 11.3.   Survival of *Staphylococcus aureus* at 0°F (− 17.8°C). Adapted from Elliot and Michener (1960).

fringens. In a laboratory experiment, Strong and Canada (1964) demonstrated the survival of this organism in frozen chicken gravy. The survival rate was high when the inoculum was mixed with sterilized soil before it was added to the gravy.

In summary, contaminants capable of causing foodborne illnesses have been demonstrated to survive for months in precooked freezer-stored items.

Studies on heat inactivation of *botulinum* toxin type A in some convenience foods after frozen storage have shown that the toxicity of that toxin remained the same throughout the frozen storage (Woodford et al., 1978).

Recognition of the inherent danger in the use of many types of precooked frozen foods has resulted in pressures for establishing standards for bacterial counts in these foods almost from the beginning. The pros and cons of setting up bacteriological standards for precooked frozen foods are still under scrutiny.

The microbiological criteria used, their merits, limitations, and attainability are discussed in Chapter 7.

The Food and Drug Administration is taking an active interest in the bacteriological quality of precooked frozen products, as indicated by their surveys and their close cooperation with industry. Industry is on the alert, and is working toward higher goals regarding the sanitary quality of these popular convenience foods.

Foter (1964) suggested the following guidelines to reduce contamination with microorganisms and their subsequent growth in foods during processing:

1. Use only raw materials that have been produced, stored, and transported with minimal contamination.
2. Keep human contacts with foods to a minimum through mechanization, and indoctrinate personnel with clean habits by provision of adequate hand-washing and sanitizing facilities and rigid supervision of all hand operations.
3. Provide food-processing equipment designed, constructed, installed, and maintained to facilitate cleaning. After cleaning, subject all food contact surfaces to germicidal treatment.
4. Maintain time–temperature conditions which will prevent the growth of any pathogenic or spoilage organisms that may gain accidental entry.

In foodservice management, the following principles are applicable:

1. Precooked frozen menu items should be purchased from reliable vendors, since even products processed under good conditions may lose their quality due to failure to observe proper temperature control during storage and transportation.
2. Upon arrival at the foodservice premises, frozen items should be immediately placed in appropriate cold storage (freezer) and held until needed. Holding time in freezer storage varies somewhat with the product, but is quite limited for precooked items.
3. At every step of preparation and service these items should be handled with the precautions due all potentially hazardous foods.

The hazard analysis critical control points (HACCP) concept has been used to establish models for the processing of frozen foods, including prepared items (Corlett, 1973, 1974). Critical control points included here were microbial data, time–temperature conditions, employee cleanliness, and general sanitation. The microbiological critical control points characterized by Peterson and Gunnerson (1974) were control and storage of the raw product, time–temperature conditions, microbiological population data during processing, employee cleanliness, sanitary equipment, and general sanitary maintenance of the facility itself.

The Food and Drug Administration (1976), using the approach of HACCP inspections, surveyed the frozen "heat and serve" type food industry. The evaluation was based on reports made after inspecting 100 frozen food establishments. The reports were divided into these categories: bakery products, agricultural products, nonmeat prepared dinners and/or dishes, seafood products, and cheese pizzas. On the basis of this evaluation, 78 critical control points were identified for the 100 processing establishments. The critical control points, presented in a very condensed form, are shown in Table 11.1.

Not all 78 critical control points were applicable to each individual processor. In the bakery processors group, 5% of the 59 critical control points appli-

TABLE 11.1.   *Critical Control Point Checklist for Frozen "Heat and Serve"*
Type Foods

Process	Number of Critical Control Points
Raw materials handling	
Agricultural, marine, meat, and processed or prefabricated materials	9
Water	3
Preparation of materials	11
Processing of materials and compounds	
Materials processing	9
Preparation of add-on components (i.e., sauces, gravy)	6
Addition of coating, batter, breading, and so on	6
Fabrication, processing, and handling of finished products	
Filling containers with components	6
Freezing process	6
Labeling, casing, and storage	7
Loading and transporting	4
Quality assurance during preparation, processing, and handling	
Finished products	6
In-line preparation, processing, handling	5
Total	78

Source: Food and Drug Administration, *Compliance Program Evaluation,* 1976.

cable were rated unsatisfactory in 50% or more of the firms rated for that point. In the seafood processors group, 16% of the 49 critical control points were rated unsatisfactory in 50% or more of the firms. In the agricultural product processors group, 36% of the 39 critical control points were rated unsatisfactory in 50% or more of the firms. In the group of nonmeat prepared dinners and/or dishes processors, 57% of the 44 critical control points were rated unsatisfactory in 50% or more of the firms. In the cheese pizza processors group, 39% of the 44 critical control points were rated unsatisfactory in 50% or more of the firms. It was concluded that the firms inspected in the group of processors of nonmeat prepared dinners and/or dishes had the highest number of unsatisfactorily controlled critical control points. An unsatisfactorily controlled critical control point indicates a potential cause for a hazardous product.

The report emphasizes the fact that the survey was a limited one in that it was restricted to products for which the only preparation prior to consumption is warming or heating, except for cream- and custard-filled pastries that require thawing. It also points out that although this sampling of firms may not be statistically representative of the frozen "heat and serve" industry, it can be viewed as a trend.

The application of the HACCP concept to the food service industry will be discussed in Chapter 14.

DEFROSTING ZONE

Foods not only freeze below 32°F (0°C) but also defrost below that temperature.

Bacterial growth is resumed when the food is thawed. If drip has formed during defrost or if condensed water has accumulated, the bacteria may spread on thawed items more readily than on their comparable unfrozen counterparts.

General Quality Aspects

Fanelli and Gunderson (1961), who made a study of defrost temperature of frozen fruit pies, frozen meat pies, and frozen soups, sum up their findings by saying that defrost of any degree adversely affects the quality of frozen foods; that the observed loss in quality which is due to various factors is even operative when the numbers of microorganisms are low; and that unless the products are held continuously in the frozen condition, chemical and physical changes take place that cannot be reversed and possibly are not halted when the products are refrozen.

The deterioration in quality of frozen foods at fluctuating temperatures below 32°F (0°C) may be due to the fact that these temperatures encompass the range of the actual defrost temperature of the product. Alternate partial thawing and refreezing may cause changes in cell tissue, enzyme systems, and microbial flora that result in loss of quality.

The effect of psychrophilic bacteria and their enzymes on the physical characteristics of the frozen product has been said to be a built-in indicator of defrost. Once the enzymes of psychrophilic bacteria are produced and liberated in the frozen product, lowering the temperature will not stop quality deterioration. In a very short time, enzymes of these bacteria can break down carbohydrates, protein, and fat with resultant protein digestion, fat rancidity, and acids from carbohydrate breakdown.

One of the problems with precooked frozen foods is the number of opportunities for defrost to occur, namely, during storage by the manufacturer, transportation and marketing, and on the consumers' premises. There is no way of estimating the amount of defrost that results from poor care. Studies conducted on temperatures of frozen food cabinets in retail markets show that the temperature of the cabinet does not necessarily reflect the temperature inside the carton of food.

Microbial Aspects

Defrost characteristics of frozen foods and interplay of bacterial populations have been discussed by Peterson et al. (1962). Temperatures between 0 and 31°F (-17.8 and -0.6°C) were observed. It was found that the changes in bacterial population varied greatly and were affected by these important factors: the length of time the product was held in the defrosted state, the refreezing procedure, the temperature attained by the defrosted product, and the kinds and numbers of bacteria initially present. Fourteen different products were studied, including dessert pies, meat pot pies, and soups. The items defrosted well below the freezing point of water, and defrost temperatures as low as 15.2°F (-9.3°C) were observed. In general, these products became organoleptically objectionable some time before they were bacteriologically unacceptable. The psychrophilic bacteria multiplied most actively and suppressed the staphylococci.

If defrosting is continued to the point that free water is available and if the temperatures are appropriate, multiplication of bacterial survivors is resumed. Which of the microorganisms present will multiply, and to what extent, depends on many factors such as types and number of microorganisms and their relationship with each other, the food substrate, ambient temperatures at which thawing takes place, and time.

Special danger exists in connection with food items that usually carry a flora of organisms capable of causing foodborne illnesses when these items require long thawing because of their bulk. Although it is fortunate that the lag period of bacteria surviving freezing and freezer storage is usually a long one (Hucker and David, 1957), it is also true that the opportunities are often present because of the long defrosting times that are required in the case of large-bulk food materials.

One example is frozen turkey. Turkeys are notorious carriers of salmonellae, and large turkeys thaw extremely slowly, the thawing time being influenced by the size of the turkey and by ambient temperatures. Defrosting in the refrigerator takes 3–4 times as long as defrosting at room temperature. Therefore, in spite of the dangers from salmonellae, turkey is frequently defrosted by "leaving it out." Moragne and Longrée (1961) found that when large turkeys were defrosted at kitchen temperatures, the skin of the birds remained over 40°F (4.4°C) for an average of 11 hours, and the leg meat for 7 hours. The body cavity was the last portion to defrost.

Bryan and McKinley (1974) studied time–temperature relationships of 20-pound, or heavier, turkeys that were thawed (1) in their original plastic wrappers at room temperature; (2) in double-layer Kraft® paper bags at room temperature; and (3) in a forced-air, reach-in refrigerator. Temperatures were measured in the thickest part of the breast and on the surface. Turkeys allowed to thaw at room temperature reached 32°F (0°C) internally in about 9 hours, and 50°F (10°C) in 18 hours. Surface temperatures were 62°F (17°C) at the end of holding. Turkeys thawed in double-layer Kraft paper bags at room temperature reached an internal temperature of 32°F (0°C) in about 16 hours, and after 22 hours (the end of holding) were still at 40°F (4.4°C). Their surface temperature was 55°F (13°C) at the end of holding. Turkeys allowed to thaw in a forced-air refrigerator of approximately 40°F (4.4°C) were still frozen (27°F, −3°C) after 40 hours. The authors concluded that for the turkeys thawed in the refrigerator and those thawed in paper bags at room temperature, no significant opportunities for multiplication of bacteria existed.

Precooked frozen foods are of interest in this connection. Hussemann (1951) studied the bacteriologic flora of some selected frozen precooked items as they reached the kitchen and followed the results during subsequent kitchen procedures. Total counts of bacteria were determined and analyses were made for *Staphylococcus aureus* as well as for bacteria of possible enteric origin, the coliforms. The menu items investigated were frozen chicken à la king, beef stew, and assorted creamed seafood items. Staphylococci appeared to be present in the majority of samples. Even in a refrigerator at 43°F (6.1°C), continued multiplication of bacterial cells was observed in the chicken à la king and in the beef stew during thawing.

Data on the growth of naturally occurring mixed populations in precooked frozen foods during defrost, with special emphasis on staphylococci in competition, were presented by Peterson et al. (1962). Commercially prepared frozen chicken pies were stored at defrost temperatures for varying periods and then tested organoleptically and analyzed bacteriologically. The results showed that at 41°F (5°C) the staphylococci failed to multiply, but the competitors multiplied to large numbers. At 68 and 99°F (20 and 37.2°C), the staphylococci did multiply, but they were outnumbered by numerous competitors.

In another experiment, higher defrost temperatures were used in order to give the staphylococci a better chance to multiply. The pies were defrosted for 24 minutes in a 425°F (218.5°C) oven. Under these conditions, the internal temperatures quickly went up to 86°F (30.3°C) and higher. The saprophytic bacteria developed to much higher numbers than the staphylococci. These results point to the fact that in a mixed population the staphylococci become suppressed, the repressive effect being definitely related to the proportion of staphylococci in the total population, to the total population level, and to the temperature of incubation.

While the presence of a mixed population seems at times to offer a certain degree of "protection" from staphylococcal growth, it should be remembered that the situation in freshly cooked, sterile foods may well be entirely different. When sterile foods are seeded with staphylococci, which may happen, for example, when a food handler's hands contaminate food items that have received a terminal heat treatment sufficient to eliminate other contaminants, the staphylococci reign alone; without competition, the staphylococcal population may build up to extremely high numbers.

The effect of thawing on growth of *Staphylococcus aureus* in 480 frozen convenience foods was investigated by Ostovar and Bremier (1975). Presence of *S. aureus* was observed in 18.3% of beef and poultry products; in 12.5% of seafood products, and in 8.3% of ready-to-eat frozen desserts. When samples of the various items were allowed to defrost at ambient temperature, the *Staphylococcus* populations were increased to numbers 100-fold of the initial numbers. Most of the isolates produced type A or B toxins.

Changes in microbial population during thawing of ground beef were studied by Beck and Milone (1972). The most rapid thawing was achieved by exposing the beef to forced air at room temperature, but this method was bacteriologically unsafe since *Clostridium perfringens* and *Salmonella typhimurium* multiplied rapidly once thawing was accomplished. Ground beef placed in stainless steel pans and allowed to thaw at room temperature thawed in 5–6 hours; and no multiplication of bacteria could be observed through even longer periods of holding (16 hours). The authors feel that, for birds of the size studied, if situations should arise when time for thawing in a refrigerator (18 hours) is not available and quick thawing must be achieved, this method is much safer than the one now frequently employed in foodservice, namely, thawing meat in its original container at room temperature. Also, the practice of using forced air at room temperature was discouraged by them. More research is needed in the area of thawing potentially hazardous items outside the refrigerator involving items of different type, and quantity thawed.

Recommendations for defrosting involve these simple principles: that vegetables not be defrosted before cooking, except corn on the cob; that fruit be defrosted in cold water or a refrigerator; that fruit juice concentrates not be defrosted before they are reconstituted; that poultry and large cuts of meat be defrosted in the refrigerator or, protected by a plastic covering, in cold water; that fish, shellfish, small parts of poultry, and small cuts of meat be thawed in the refrigerator or in cold water or that they be cooked from the frozen state unless breaded or covered with batter; that commercially precooked frozen items be handled in accordance with specific instructions given by the manufacturer.

Some warnings are in order. When the manufacturer states "cold" water, he refers most probably to water of temperatures below 70°F (21.1°C). However, water that flows out of a faucet labeled "cold" is not necessarily that cold. Even if it is, it must be kept flowing throughout the defrost operation to prevent a warmup. The reader is referred to the description of a food-associated outbreak of diarrhea and pharyngitis caused by a salad made from frozen shrimp thawed in "warm water" the night before the salad was prepared and served (*Morbidity and Mortality Weekly Report,* 1965b). Another warning concerns frozen meat pies. It should be made clear that for frozen meat pies the end point of heating is sometimes given by the manufacturer as "browning of the crust," and that this end point does not guarantee freedom from viable food-poisoning organisms. Ross and Thatcher (1958), who analyzed the bacterial flora of precooked frozen dinners and pies, point out that enterococci as well as staphylococci have been found to survive the heat treatment suggested by the manufacturer. It has been suggested that efforts be directed toward formulation of crusts that will brown slowly, because this would enable one to employ longer baking times. The problem of thermal destruction of pathogenic contaminants of menu items is further discussed in Chapter 13.

Handling precooked frozen foods produced under cook/freeze foodservice systems is discussed in Chapter 14.

CHILLED (REFRIGERATION) ZONE

Refrigeration is the process of removing heat, sensible and/or latent, from foods for the purpose of temporary preservation. As used in this presentation, the term "refrigeration" refers to chilling at above-freezing temperatures. And the term "refrigerator" refers to equipment that is used for the above-freezing storage of food items. The aim of refrigeration is to prevent microorganisms from multiplying and, in the case of fresh foods, to retard loss of quality due to other causes such as enzyme action. Since microorganisms differ widely in their temperature requirements for optimum, minimum, and maximum growth, the temperature at which food is stored greatly affects the kind of spoilage that will take place. Spoilage due to microbial activity may occur at any temperature between 23 and 158°F (-5 and 70°C), but the organisms of public health significance have narrower temperature ranges for growth. In quantity foodservice, temperatures ranging from 30 to -38°F (-1.1C to -3.3°C) are desirable for chilling. It is to be remembered that at 38°F (-1.1°C) *Clostridium botulinum* type E is able to grow, and so is *Yersinia enterocolitica* if sufficient time is allowed. At these temperatures the psychrophilic and psychrotrophic bacteria find conditions favorable for growth and strongly compete with pathogens. The factors affecting growth of psychrophilic microorganisms in foods have been reviewed by Elliot and Michener (1965).

Uncooked Foods

The purpose of chilling such items as fresh meats and poultry, fish, shellfish, dairy products, shell eggs, fruits, and vegetables is to retard their enzymatic activities and to prevent microorganisms from multiplying. This type of cold storage of fresh foods prolongs their shelf life considerably.

It is beyond the scope of this book to discuss the many aspects of chilled storage of fresh foods except those that are of significance from a public health point of view. It is for this reason that the discussion will be concentrated on some selected foods of animal origin.

MEATS AND POULTRY.   Chilling is a very important method of preserving meat and poultry and products made from them. The more promptly this chilling is applied in the packing and processing plants, and the more scrupulously it is maintained during transport to the consumer and on the consumer's premises, the less opportunity will be afforded for growth of mesophilic bacteria, among them the infectious and toxigenic types.

Storage temperatures for meats range from 30 to 36°F (-1.1 to 2.2°C). For beef the limit for cold storage may be a week or less, depending on the condition of the meat and the temperature and humidity of the storage. Shorter times are recommended for ground meat and organ meats—a maximum length of 2 days. Cured bacon and tenderized cured hams may be stored for 1–3 weeks, canned ham and dried beef up to 6 weeks. Storage time of cold cuts depends largely on moisture content, dry salami and the like being less resistant to spoilage than bologna-type products.

For mutton, lamb, and pork, maximum storage times are shorter than for beef. Veal and poultry should not be kept longer than 2 days. For quantity foodservice use, poultry is usually marketed in the frozen state. Preportioned meats are usually marketed in the frozen state also.

Carbon dioxide and ozone are sometimes used in addition to low temperature to discourage microbial activity during commercial storage of meats. Storage life in an atmosphere of CO_2 is prolonged with increasing concentration, but certain undesirable effects on the meat limit the amounts of gas that can be used. CO_2 hastens the loss of "bloom" or natural color through formation of metmyoglobin and methemoglobin. Recommendations for CO_2 concentration vary from 10 to 30% for meats and up to 100% for bacon. Ozone is used in a concentration of 2.5–3 parts per million.

Microorganisms that find the temperatures during cold storage to their liking are mostly the psychrophilic types such as *Pseudomonas, Achromobacter, Micrococcus, Streptococcus, Flavobacterium,* and *Proteus.* In meats stored at 40°F (4.4°C) or below, the microorganisms able to cause foodborne illnesses do not multiply; they may, however, resume growth when the temperature is raised above 40°F (4.4°C).

FISH AND SHELLFISH.   Fish and other seafoods are the flesh foods most susceptible to spoilage of many kinds, microbial, autolytic, oxidative, and others. Therefore, the requirements for chilling are that temperatures near 32°F (0°C) be promptly applied and strictly maintained and that cold storage be of short duration. Even chilled seafood has a short shelf life, as discussed in Chapter 6. Some unavoidable contamination is to be expected in seafood. Therefore, when outside temperatures are high and when distances of transport are great, freezing may be a bacteriologically safer method than chilling by ice or mechanical chilling.

DAIRY PRODUCTS AND SHELL EGGS.   Pasteurized milk and cream, cheese, butter, and shell eggs have excellent keeping quality under cold storage at approximately 40°F (4.4°C). Milk, cream, and cottage-type cheeses will keep for days; hard cheeses, butter, and shell eggs for weeks.

Cooked Foods: Growth of Pathogens

Cooked items such as partially prepared items, complete menu items prepared in advance, and leftovers deserve careful attention in connection with refrigeration. The principles of effective chilling are straightforward, yet are frequently slighted in practice. Too often cooked foods are simply placed in a refrigerator with the thought that now they are cold and safe, no consideration being given to the temperature conditions actually prevailing in the food. It is not surprising, then, that hazards have arisen in connection with chilled cooked food items under conditions of quantity foodservice.

Paramount to efficient cooling is the rapid transfer to the surrounding air of the heat contained in the food. This transfer should achieve a temperature drop in the center of the food mass to a bacteriologically safe level within as brief a span of time as possible. If cooling is slow and the foods remain in the "danger zone" for hours, bacteria multiply.

Heat transfer in food materials is affected by numerous factors, some of which are difficult to control. Among these are the nature of food, which determines its thermal conductivity, the area exposed to the coolant, and the temperature gradient between food and coolant. Cooling methods are discussed in Chapter 13.

As a first step to achieve efficient cooling applicable to conditions of quantity food preparation, these basic questions deserve attention: (1) What is a "bacteriologically safe" temperature level to which cooked food items should be cooled? (2) What are the cooling times of various foods when cooled by conventional methods under conditions of quantity foodservice, and how are these cooling times related to bacterial growth?

"Safe temperatures" are temperatures that are low enough to prevent multiplication of microorganisms capable of causing foodborne illnesses. Therefore, in a brief discussion, the minimum temperatures at which some common foodborne pathogens have been found to multiply in foods will be reviewed.

GROWTH OF STAPHYLOCOCCI.   To produce foodborne illness, staphylococci must have multiplied to large numbers and formed toxin in the food ingested. Early laboratory studies by Kelly and Dack (1936) have produced data which indicate that at temperatures as low as 46°F (7.8°C) toxigenic strains of *Staphylococcus aureus* multiplied, if slowly, in ham, tongue, and chicken sandwiches. Research results by Prescott and Geer (1936) have shown that refrigeration of foods at temperatures below 50°F (10°C) prevented the formation of *Staphylococcus* toxin for long periods of cold storage.

Angelotti et al. (1961) set up an experiment to study growth response of a mixture of two strains of *S. aureus* to temperatures between 40 and 50°F at 2° intervals (4.4 and 10°C at 1.1°), using three foods as media: custard, chicken à la king, and ham salad.

The incubation time was 5 days. In custard and chicken à la king, the staphylococci grew at 44°F (6.7°C) and above (Figs. 11.4 and 11.5). In ham salad, the increase in numbers was insignificant at a temperature range of 40–50° F (4.4–10° C).

GROWTH OF SALMONELLAE.   Angelotti et al. (1961) inoculated custard, chicken à la king, and ham salad with mixed cultures of *Salmonella enteritidis, manhattan,* and *senftenberg,* and subjected them to temperatures of 40–50°F at 2° intervals (4.4–10°C at 1.1°) for 5 days. In chicken à la king, multiplication occurred at 44°F (6.7°C) and above (Fig. 11.5). No multiplication was observed in the other two foods at the temperatures studied.

It is apparent from these results that storage of highly perishable foods at 50°F (10°C) does not preclude multiplication of these infectious organisms. Storage for prolonged periods may create hazardous conditions, especially if the foods are grossly contaminated at the start.

GROWTH OF FECAL STREPTOCOCCI.   Angelotti et al. (1963) explored the response of *Streptococcus faecalis* to temperatures between 40 and 50°F (4.4 and 10°C) using again the three menu items previously employed for their studies with staphylococci and salmonellae. This organism was able to multiply at a temperature as low as 42°F (5.6°C) when suspended in custard. In chicken à la king, the minimum temperature was 44°F (6.7°C) and in ham salad 50°F (10°C).

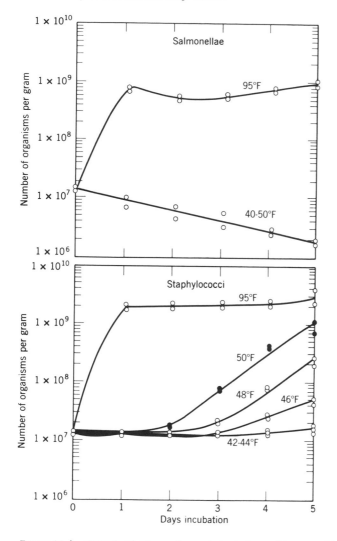

FIGURE 11.4. Growth of salmonellae and staphylococci in custard incubated at various temperatures. Adapted from Angelotti et al. (1961). *Note:* 42°F = 5.6°C; 44°F = 6.7°C; 46°F = 7.8°C; 48°F = 8.9°C; 50°F = 10.0°C; 95°F = 35.0°C.

OTHERS. It has been demonstrated (Schmidt et al., 1961) that *Clostridium botulinum* type E may grow and produce toxin at 38°F (3.3°C). At temperatures near 50°F (10°C), multiplication of types A and B is possible.

As reported for some strains of *C. perfringens* studied, practically no multiplication took place in the temperature range of 5–12°C (41–54°F) (Hall and

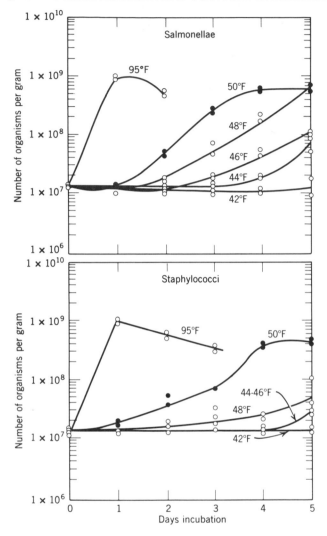

FIGURE 11.5.   Growth of salmonellae and staphylococci in chicken à la king incubated at various temperatures. Adapted from Angelotti et al. (1961). *Note:* 42°F = 5.6°C; 44°F = 6.7°C; 46°F = 7.8°C; 48°F = 8.9°C; 50°F = 10.0°C; 95°F = 35.0°C.

Angelotti, 1965). A summary of lowest temperatures reported for growth of some important pathogens is given in Table 11.2.

It is noteworthy that *Yersinia enterocolitica* is able to multiply at very low temperatures making it an important contaminant of milk, and that *Campylobacter jejuni,* although thermophilic in its requirements for growth, may survive for prolonged periods in refrigerated foods.

Cooked Foods: Cooling Times and Bacterial Growth

Research involving large pieces of meat and large batches of fluid foods has shown that cooling times are apt to be long and that bacterial populations may build up to large numbers during the cooling period, even under refrigeration.

Black and Lewis (1948) conducted a study observing the cooling rates and bacterial growth of hams, chickens, chicken broth, and custards cooled in several ways. These workers reported that, in general, cooling of the items was hastened and bacterial multiplication slowed by prompt chilling in a refrigerator. However, for the first 15–30 minutes, while the foods cooled from 180 to 150°F (82 to 65.6°C), the rate of heat loss was essentially the same in and out of the refrigerator. In general, the time in which foods remained in the temperature range 115–70°F (46.1–21.1°C) was lessened by moving the food to the cooler before its internal temperature reached 115°F (46.1°C).

Castellani et al. (1953) studied heat transfer in stuffed turkeys during heat-

TABLE 11.2. *Summary of Lowest Temperatures Reported for Growth and Toxin Production by Food-Poisoning Bacteria[a]*

	Lowest Reported Temperature			
	Growth		Toxin Production[b]	
	°C	°F	°C	°F
Staphylococcus aureus	4[c]–6.7	39[c]–44	4[c]–18	39[c]–64
Salmonella	6.7	44		
Fecal streptococci	5.6	42		
Clostridium botulinum				
Type A	10	50	10	50
Type B	10	50	10	50
Type E	3.3	38	3.3	38
Clostridium perfringens	12[d]–15	54[d]–59		
Bacillus cereus	10	50		
Vibrio parahaemolyticus	15	59		
Campylobacter jejuni	above 30	86		
Yersinia enterocolitica	0	32		

[a]These data have been compiled from different reports.
[b]Toxin production has not been reported in the absence of growth.
[c]Depending on substrate.
[d]Heavy inoculum.

ing and cooling. They found that when warm turkeys were chilled at 33°F (0.6°C), the drop in the internal temperature of the turkeys was slow. The authors emphasize the fact that for several hours the temperatures in these turkeys were capable of supporting bacterial growth and that these hours must be added to the number of hours during which temperatures will again be favorable for multiplication during roasting.

Chilling of cooked turkeys was studied by Bryan and McKinley (1974). Whole turkeys, turkey halves, and turkey rolls were used, various methods of cooling were employed, simulating methodology that is, and might be, practiced. These techniques include the following: A half-turkey was left in an unheated oven overnight; in that case, the surface and interior remained near the optimum growth temperature for pathogens for over 11 hours. Also, whole (20-pound) cooked turkeys were placed in refrigerators; in that case, the turkeys' internal temperatures remained for 10 hours within a temperature range conducive to the growth of pathogens. For another, a 4.6-pound cooked, half turkey roll was placed in a walk-in refrigerator; the meat remained within the growth range for *C. perfringens* for 6 hours, and within the growth range for staphylococci and salmonellae even longer. Methods for rapid chilling were devised: placing cut-up pieces of cooked turkey meat (8.5 pounds) in a pan placed on ice for an hour, followed by refrigeration; by this method, 8.5 pounds of meat cooled to temperatures that do not permit *C. perfringens* to grow in 3 hours and to 50°F (10°C) in 5 hours. Other methods achieving rapid cooling were: immersing meat (contained in a double plastic bag) in an ice bath, a half turkey roll chilled in ice cooled from 160 to 60°F (71 to 15.6°C) in 2½ hours, whereas the half roll placed in a refrigerator took 7 hours for the same drop in temperature. Turkey rolls are particularly hazardous items because of the handling they receive during deboning, and because contaminants that may stem from the turkey itself and also from the food handler and equipment may find their way into the internal portion of the roll.

Winter et al. (1954) inoculated different quantities of chicken salad with *Micrococcus pyogenes* var. *aureus (Staphylococcus aureus)*. The controls were left uninoculated but were not sterilized. The salads were held for various lengths of time alternately at room temperature and in a refrigerator. The time required for cooling was found to be related to batch size and container shape. A difference of several hours was noted between the cooling times of salad of large volume in a deep container as compared to the same volume when it was distributed into shallow pans. When the salads were kept below 50°F (10°C), little increase in bacterial growth was noted, even after 72 hours; at temperatures above 50°F (10°C), bacterial growth was rapid. Any change in environment resulted in a "lag" in increase or decrease of bacterial counts. This "lag," according to the authors, must be regarded as a potential danger when large quantities of warm food are refrigerated. It is interesting that in the controls, which were not inoculated, the bacterial counts were almost as high as in the inoculated samples.

Longrée and White (1955) determined cooling rates and bacterial growth in broth and white sauce prepared and chilled in large batches, from 110 to 115°F (43–46°C) to 55°F (12.8°C). Variables were type of container used for the storage of the food (tall, medium, and shallow); holding the food items at room temperature before refrigeration; batch size (2–8 gallons, 7.6–30.3 liters); and refrigerator temperatures (42 and 47°F, 5.6 and 8.3°C). The test organism was *Escherichia coli*. Extremely long cooling times were established for all batches. The longer the cooling times, the higher were the bacterial counts. Variables effecting the longer cooling times were: high viscosity of the food, large batch size, deep container, greater length of time that the food was held at room temperature preceding refrigeration, and higher refrigerator temperature. It was shown that even 2-gallon (7.6-liter) batches of broth that were refrigerated without previous holding at room temperature did not cool sufficiently fast to preclude some multiplication of the inoculum. But, in these cases, growth was slow and final counts, after 30 hours of refrigeration, were low.

The use of shallow containers was very effective in speeding heat transfer in 4-gallon (15.1-liter) batches of white sauce and in keeping bacterial counts low (Table 11.3).

The use of shallow containers is not practical for fluid foods, but it is applicable to solid and viscous semisolid items.

McDivitt and Hammer (1958) observed multiplication of a toxin-producing strain of *Micrococcus pyogenes* var. *aureus (Staphylococcus aureus)* related

TABLE 11.3. *Cooling Rates and Bacterial Counts of 4-Gallon[a] Batches of White Sauce Inoculated with* Escherichia coli *and Refrigerated at 47°F (8.3°C) in Containers of the Same Volume but of a Different Shape*

Shape of Container	Temperature Drop During Initial Cooling				Total Cooling Time to 60°F (15.6°C), hours	Count per Milliliter (Log Base of 10)
	5-hr period		10-hr period			
	°F	°C	°F	°C		
Shallow	36	20	50	27.8	10.5	2.5
Tall	14	7.8	31	17.3	20	3.2
Medium height	15	8.3	34	19	20	5.4

[a] 1 U.S. gallon = 3.785 liters.
Source: Adapted from Longrée and White (1955).

to the rate of heat loss in cornstarch pudding. The puddings were cooled in 9-quart*(100-portion) lots using stockpots of two sizes, and as 3-quart lots in shallow pans, at room temperature and in a 40°F (4.4°C) refrigerator. The results pointed toward a relationship between container size, area temperature, cooling rate, and bacterial development. Dividing the 100-portion lots into three parts and refrigerating them in shallow pans was the only method that did not allow extensive bacterial growth during cooling in the refrigerator.

Cooling and chilled holding of ground beef gravy were studied by Tuomi et al. (1974a) to determine time–temperature relationships during these procedures and their effect on bacterial counts. Sixty-six pounds of cooked gravy were allowed to cool in bulk to 158°F (70°C), then divided into 5.5-pound lots, using plastic bags, which were allowed to precool in chilled water for 1 hour. During this procedure the temperature of the gravy dropped to a mean temperature of 82°F (28°C). The bags were packed, six to each box, in cardboard cases and the cases moved to a 42°F (7.2°C) refrigerator for 16 hours of chilled storage. The gravy temperature dropped to 65°F (18.5°C) within 3 to 4 hours and had reached a temperature of 45.5°F (7.5°C) at the end of the 16-hour period of refrigeration. Bacteriological tests indicated that the number of viable cells was affected by the first 4–5 hours of cooling. During this period the gravy temperature was within the range of 122–65°F (50–18.5°C); the range of temperature for rapid multiplication included the 1-hour cooling in chilled water, which preceded refrigeration.

Another study of Tuomi et al. (1974b), again on ground beef gravy, involved the effect on *Clostridium perfringens* of chilling the gravy, packed in bags at an initial temperature of approximately 102°F (39°C) in a 42°F (5.6°C) refrigerator for 16 hours. The number of viable cells was influenced by the first 6 hours of cooling when the gravy was in the temperature range of 122–65°F (50–18.5°C), supporting multiplication of the *perfringens* organism as reported earlier (Hall and Angelotti, 1965). The final mean plate count which was 1.4×10^4 after inoculation, was 5.5×10^4 in one experiment, and 3.9×10^4 in another.

Cooling times were determined for a cooked ground beef product, both under actual food preparation conditions and in the laboratory, by Rollin and Matthews (1977). The data obtained under actual operating conditions are shown in Table 11.4. These data, as well as cooling times of a ground beef product when determined under laboratory conditions, showed that it was neither possible to chill cooked entrees to 45°F (7°C) within 4 hours when entrees were stored in walk-in refrigerators, nor to have them traverse the 120–60°F (49–16°C) temperature zone within 2 hours.

*1 quart = 0.946 liter.

TABLE 11.4. *Time–Temperature Relationships and Load in Refrigerator During Chilling of Nine Entrees under Actual Operating Conditions in a School Cook/Chill Foodservice System*

Entree	Temperature Range, °F (°C)	Cooling[a] Time, hours	Refrigerator Temperature, °F (°C)	Load, Number of Pans[b]
Turkey barbecue	93–45 (34–7)	7.0	39 ± 5 (4 ± 3)	72
Lasagna	90–46 (32–8)	7.0	39 ± 5 (4 ± 3)	72[c]
Macaroni and cheese	68–46 (20–8)	8.0	42 ± 8 (6 ± 4)	48
Chili II	94–45 (34–7)	8.0	44 ± 11 (7 ± 6)	96
Chili I	84–48 (29–9)	9.0	42 ± 6 (6 ± 3)	96
Barbecue ground beef	126–46 (52–8)	9.5	38 ± 6 (3 ± 3)	48
Hot beef sandwich	162–48 (72–9)	10.0	46 ± 13 (8 ± 7)	72
Spanish hamburger casserole	100–46 (38–8)	10.5	39 ± 8 (4 ± 4)	72
Beef stew	125–48 (52–9)	11.0	44 ± 11 (7 ± 6)	70

[a]Time required for the temperature at the geometric center of the entree to pass through the temperature range. Average of 10 pans of the entree.
[b]$10 \times 18 \times 3$-inch food mass in a $10 \times 18 \times 4\frac{1}{2}$-inch pan.
[c]72 ($23\frac{1}{4} \times 15\frac{1}{2} \times 2$ inch) pans.
Source: J. L. Rollin and M. E. Matthews, *J. Food Prot.* **40**(11): 782–784, 1977. Copyright © 1977, International Association of Milk, Food and Environmental Sanitarians, Inc. Reprinted by permission.

The problem of chilling food is discussed further in connection with cook/chill food systems in Chapter 14.

HAZARDOUS TEMPERATURE ZONE

This zone includes the temperature range within which more or less extensive bacterial growth must be expected.

Temperatures

In the older literature, the "danger zone" was, in general, spoken of as encompassing a narrower range than is now regarded as acceptable. The hazardous temperature zone covers the range of 45–140°F (7.2–60°C) (FDA, 1978). In establishing these terminal points, research findings on the multiplication of staphylococci, salmonellae, and fecal streptococci have been taken into account (Angelotti et al., 1961, 1963). The salmonellae and staphylococci were seen to tolerate lower maximal temperatures for multiplication (Fig. 11.6) than the fecal streptococci, which were shown to be capable of multiplying at relatively high temperatures, the extreme being 126°F (52.2°C).

The upper limit of the hazardous temperature zone, 140°F (60°C) gives a margin of safety. The lower one, 45°F (7.2°C), is only acceptable for brief holding. Staphylococci, salmonellae, fecal streptococci, and *Clostridium botulinum* type E and F have been demonstrated to grow, albeit slowly, at temperatures lower than 45°F (7.2°C). For prolonged chilled storage of hazardous foods, the hazardous temperature zone should be thought of as extending to temperatures below 38°F (3.3°C).

Holding Time

It is difficult, if not impossible, to state the exact number of hours for which a specific food item can be held safely within the zone of bacterial multiplication. A number of factors affect this time, such as the kind of organism, the physiological stage of the cells, the suitability of the food as substrate, and temperature. It is at present more or less agreed that the time for which a food may remain in the multiplication zone should not exceed 4 hours and that 2 hours would give a wider margin of safety at the period of very active multiplication.

Improper Holding

There is no doubt that these maximum holding times of 2–4 hours are frequently exceeded under practical conditions of quantity foodservice, as the reports and analyses of food-poisoning outbreaks have brought out. Only a few typical examples can be given:

1. Sliced, cooked meat contaminated by a food handler and held in the kitchen from noon to the night meal.
2. Ground meat patties shaped by hand, and held for "several hours" in the kitchen before cooking.
3. Ham, boned, sliced, and held at kitchen temperatures for "several hours" before serving.
4. Turkey, partially roasted, then held in the oven for "several hours," cooking being completed the next day.
5. Large stuffed turkeys; heat could not penetrate to the center of the stuffing during roasting.
6. Cream pies, brought to picnic grounds and subjected to warm temperatures for "long hours" before serving.

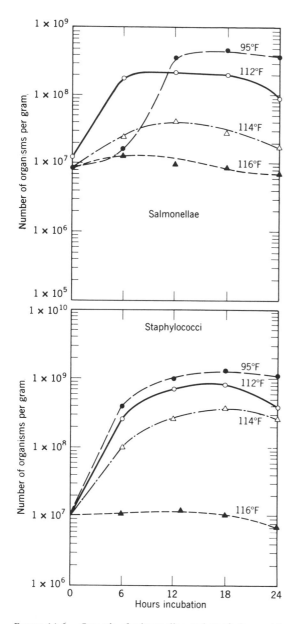

FIGURE 11.6. Growth of salmonellae and staphylococci in custard incubated at various temperatures. Adapted from Angelotti et al. (1961). *Note:* 95°F = 35.0°C; 112°F = 44.4°C; 114°F = 45.5°C; 116°F = 46.7°C.

7. Meat, chicken, and turkey salads made from leftovers that had not caused trouble when served for the first time, but had subsequently been held at kitchen temperatures for "prolonged periods of time."

8. Poultry salad made from meat removed from the bones and refrigerated in large batches overnight before the meat was used.

9. Poultry meat, removed from the bones and contaminated in the process, then held in a warm kitchen for "several hours;" then made into salads, casseroles, and creamed items.

10. Pudding, pie filling, and pastry filling held "several hours" in the bake shop for cooling.

11. Broth and gravy held overnight in the kitchen, or on the back of the stove.

12. Shrimp defrosted overnight in warm water, made into a salad the next morning, then held in a large "refrigerated" vat in which the salad was held until served (at noon); shrimp did not cool to below 65°F (18.3°C) except for the layer in immediate contact with the surface of the vat.

13. Baked potatoes, wrapped in foil, held at room temperatures for several days, then used in the preparation of nonheated menu items, such as salad.

In brief, bacterial populations may build up to tremendous numbers if contamination is heavy, if the food is an excellent substrate for growth, if the temperature conditions are conducive to bacterial growth, and if several hours are available for multiplication. When toxigenic strains are involved, toxins may be released during this active growth and accumulate in the food in quantities sufficient to cause food poisoning.

HOT-HOLDING ZONE

This zone encompasses temperatures which should prevent bacterial multiplication but would not necessarily kill the contaminants. The minimum temperature recommended by the U.S. Public Health Service (FDA, 1978) is 140°F (60°C) or above, "except that rare roast beef shall be held for service at a temperature of at least 130°F (54.5°C)." More will be said about rare roast beef later on when detailed recommendations for achieving a safe product are discussed.

Many prepared menu items are kept hot for prolonged periods before they are served. Hot-holding equipment is designed for keeping hot food hot, not for heating food. Therefore, menu items to be served hot should be at temperatures considerably higher than 140°F (60°C) when placed in the hot-holding equipment. That this is not always so was shown in a study by Blaker (1962), whose data are discussed in Chapter 13.

"Delayed service cookery" of meat has been recommended. The method involves long holding in hot-holding equipment. The microbiological aspects of delayed service cookery of loin cuts of beef were included in a study by Funk et al. (1966), whose other objectives were to compare heat penetration rates and culinary quality of roasts cooked by the delayed service method and the conventional dry-heat method. The delayed service method requires that the meat be first browned at high temperatures and then transferred to a temperature-controlled cabinet at 140°F (60°C) until needed. This method had been recommended for use when oven space was to be made available for other uses. Funk et al. (1966) roasted 10-kilogram (22-pound) loin cuts at 399°F (203.8°C) oven temperature when using the delayed roasting method, and at 300°F (148.9°C) when using the conventional method. All roasts were cooked to an internal temperature of 125.6°F (51.9°C). An average of 109 (90–120) minutes was required for delayed service roasts and 141 (120–160) minutes for the conventional roasts. The internal temperature of the roasts continued to rise after removal from the oven; a rise to 155°F (68.3°C) was noted in the delayed service roasts, and to 144°F (62.2°C) in the conventional roasts. In the delayed service roasts, which were placed in the hot-holding equipment upon completion of the roasting period, the internal temperature dropped to 133°F (56.1°C) within the 6-hour holding period; no further temperature variations were recorded for the remainder of an 18-hour holding period. Microbiological analyses were made of all roasts cooked by the delayed service method, and of two roasts injected in the center with 8 mL of a culture of 1×10^9 cells per milliliter of *Salmonella senftenberg,* then cooked by the delayed service method and held for 18 hours in the hot-holding equipment. In the noninjected roasts, counts of 0–183 cells per gram were obtained. In the *Salmonella*-injected roasts, no survivors were found under the conditions of this experiment.

COOKING ZONE

Temperatures

In this zone, no multiplication of bacteria should take place in any part of the food; in fact, vegetative bacterial cells are expected to be destroyed in the cooking process. The question remains whether in the cooking of lightly heated menu items heat-tolerant strains of pathogens are killed—especially when contamination is heavy or when the cells are shielded by the protective qualities which some food materials possess. To the food processor and the foodservice operator, death of a bacterium means that it has been rendered unable to reproduce.

Some of the factors that influence the heat resistance of cells are, besides the strain of organisms, the initial concentration of the cells—the higher the concentration, the higher the resistance to heat; the previous history and age of the contaminant—higher resistance being found in cells that grew in a medium to their liking and at maximum stationary growth; and whether the organism is present in the vegetative or spore stage—higher resistance to heat being offered by spores.

The presence of certain protective substances, such as proteins, fats, and a number of colloidal substances, diminishes the lethal effect of the heat treatment on bacterial contaminants.

Cooking temperatures range from very mild to intense. Some examples of menu items given light heat treatments on purpose are soft scrambled eggs where part of the egg usually remains under-coagulated, rare roast, meat patties, meat loaf, oyster stew, and hollandaise. A few examples of menu items that are sometimes undercooked through carelessness, lack of time, or lack of knowledge of heat penetration are warmed-over leftovers; fried patties and cakes, such as crab cakes; and meringued pies.

Heat used in quantity food preparation is essentially dry, moist, or a combination of both. Examples of dry heat are broiling, frying, baking, and roasting; of moist heat, steaming and boiling; of combination dry-moist, braising, and stewing. Actually, in all these forms of heating, the bacteria present in the food are subjected to moist heat some or all of the time, with the exception of the outside of items cooked by dry heat and items practically devoid of moisture.

Thermal Death of Bacteria in Foods

To cause thermal destruction of pathogens in food preparation, it is desirable to apply heat sufficient to kill the bacteria without interfering with the culinary and nutritive quality of the menu item, by either long or intense heat treatment. Fortunately, both temperature and time affect thermal death. Heating a food to a low temperature and holding it there for a long time may have the same lethal effect as heating it to a higher terminal temperature for a brief period. In determining thermal death times in the bacteriological laboratory, precautions can be taken and calculations can be made to eliminate errors produced by the fact that time will elapse before the coolest portion of the food has warmed up to the temperature whose effect is to be tested, and by the fact that some cells may die during the time necessary for heat to penetrate into the center of the food sample containing the bacteria. Very small food samples are exposed in tubes to a temperature-controlled bath, usually oil. The exposure time is corrected as follows: corrected exposure time = total time in bath − thermal lag time + lethality due to time of come-up and come-down.

When thermal death of bacteria is determined in a bulk of food, however, cognizance must be taken of the fact that the food warms up gradually and thermal death takes place gradually also, beginning at the instant when the minimum destructive temperature is reached and proceeding from then on. Since this time–temperature effect is an important factor that affects thermal death, it must be taken into consideration when evaluating thermal death data that have been collected under such conditions.

MENU ITEMS USUALLY HEATED TO 180°F (82.2°C) OR ABOVE. Heating foods to *boiling* suffices to kill the majority of vegetative cells of pathogens capable of causing gastroenteric illness, but does not necessarily kill bacterial spores. Heating foods to temperatures at or near boiling should eliminate *Staphylococcus aureus,* the salmonellae, the fecal streptococci, and the vegetative cells of the clostridia; also, spores of the non-heat-resistant strains of *C. perfringens.* The spores of *C. botulinum* types A and B are capable of enduring several hours of boiling; this fact has an important bearing on the methodology of heat-processing foods as to safety, safe holding conditions for vacuum-packed boiled potatoes (Sugiyama et al., 1981; Notermans et al., 1981), and safe holding of baked potatoes (Seals et al., 1981). The spores of type E are inactivated below boiling. The spores of *C. perfringens* vary in heat resistance with strain, some surviving high temperatures such as applied in boiling and roasting. A certain degree of heating may actually activate the spores to germinate.

Many menu items reach temperatures near 212°F (100°C) before the stage of doneness is reached, even though the method of their preparation and cooking equipment used may vary.

Breads, cakes, cookies, and similar *baked* items have been shown to reach temperatures near 212°F (100°C) or higher (Lowe, 1955). Knight and Coppock (1957) studied the influence of the baking process on the destruction of heat-resistant salmonellae in certain baked products containing egg albumin, and found that an inoculum of 10^9 cells per gram of mixings was destroyed with a wide margin of safety in all baked products including angel food cupcakes and layer cakes.

Hussemann and Tanner (1947) reported that staphylococci in sponge cake batter were killed when a temperature of 75.2°C (167°F) was reached; this temperature is well below the usual terminal temperature attained in this type of cake.

Breads, cakes, and cookies may be regarded as bacteriologically safe at the end of the baking period. However, after cream fillings or toppings are added, the picture changes completely. Cream fillings and toppings of bakery products are excellent media for bacterial growth and have been indicted many times as the cause of gastroenteric episodes. Sometimes bakers rebake cream-filled products to destroy contaminants possibly added with the filling.

Soups, broths, and *gravies* are usually *boiled* and the destruction of the vegetative cells of pathogens should be assured by this heat treatment. Spores of *Clostridium perfringens* are not necessarily killed. Items made from meat, or containing meat, have repeatedly been shown to contain spores of this pathogen, which may have been survivors; some strains of this organism are extremely heat resistant.

Recontamination of cooked items may, of course, also occur in consequence of handling, or of adding contaminated ingredients. For example, gravies have become recontaminated with salmonellae introduced with chopped giblets that had picked up the pathogens when in contact with contaminated chopping boards, and when the gravy was not reheated after the addition of the giblets. The records of gastroenteric outbreaks attest to the fact that an opportunity for extensive multiplication of the contaminants was afforded by holding contaminated gravies at lukewarm temperatures. A hazard analysis of roast beef jus made by Bryan and McKinley (1980) points toward the danger of lukewarm holding and stresses the importance of rapid cooling of jus and gravy and of reheating to boiling of items exposed unduly to hazardous, lukewarm temperatures at which bacteria are able to multiply.

The survival of spores of *Clostridium perfringens* on chicken parts subjected to *water cooking* was demonstrated by Craven et al. (1975); vegetative cells were eliminated by cooking chicken thighs and breasts at 82°C (180°F) for 2 minutes and at 93°C (199°F) for 15 minutes. Heat-sensitive spores were reduced to low levels after 43 minutes at 82°C (180°F). But spores of heat-resistant strains were not reduced when the meat was water cooked at 82°C (180°F) for 50 minutes, nor completely destroyed after 45 minutes at 93°C (199°F). This information is important in connection with holding such items for later reheating and service. The ubiquitous presence of *Clostridium perfringens* and the failure of heat-resistant spores to become completely eliminated by boiling, freezing, and subsequent heating must be recognized and dealt with, whatever foodservice system is used.

From *roasts* and *broiled meats,* surface contaminants in the vegetative stage of growth should be eliminated in the process of broiling, frying, and roasting. Spores of *C. perfringens* may resist death by roasting (*Morbidity and Mortality Weekly Report,* 1965a).

Among the menu items that are usually *broiled* is bacon. Thatcher et al. (1962) studied the effect of broiling on bacterial and toxin destruction in bacon grilled at 401°F (204.6°C) for 6 and 12 minutes. The authors report 190°F (87.8°C) as the approximate terminal temperature that was reached in the bacon. However, it is not clear from the description whether this was the temperature reached by the bacon at the crisp or at the flaccid stage, or whether it represents an average of both. Staphylococci were destroyed at each treatment. After the lighter heat treatment, the somewhat flaccid stage, small amounts of toxin were found; no toxins were detected after the longer cooking period. Grilled bacon has an excellent record in connection with foodborne gastroenteric outbreaks.

Among the bulkier meats, poultry is usually heated to internal temperatures above 180°F (82.2°C), because most persons like poultry well done. The terminal temperature varies somewhat with the site at which the temperature is taken; it lies within the range of 185–195°F (85–90.6°C).

Hussemann and Wallace (1951) cooked parts of chickens that were known to have viable cells of *Salmonella typhimurium* in their bloodstream, collected heat penetration data, and analyzed the cooked meats for survivors (Table 11.5). A very great reduction in inoculum was achieved by *broiling* to terminal internal temperatures of 93–96°C (199–205°F); and by *roasting* to internal temperatures above 80°C (176°F) in the breast and leg, and to 100°C (212°F) in the shallow parts of the carcass. An exceptional situation might arise when exceedingly high numbers of contaminants are involved.

The effect of *deep fat frying* on internal temperatures reached in chicken parts (leg, breasts, wings) coated with batter was investigated by Mabee and Mountney (1970). The parts were fried for 11 minutes in 400°F (209°C) oil; some were fried at atmospheric pressure, some under 15-pound (1.05 kg/cm^2) pressure. The initial temperature of the parts was made a variable also; some of the parts were fried in the frozen state (19°F, −7.2°C); some when chilled (53°F, 11.7°C); and some when lukewarm (77°F, 25°C). In one trial, survival of *Salmonella senftenberg* 775W inoculated into the parts was determined. It was found that higher internal temperatures were reached in parts fried under 15-pound pressure than in those fried at atmospheric pressure; they ranged from 212 to 255°F (100–124°C), as compared to 178–216°F

TABLE 11.5. *Number of Viable Salmonella in Chicken Tissue Before and After Broiling*

Tissue	Before Broiling		After Broiling		
	Salmonella per gram	Number of Samples	*Salmonella* per gram	Number of Samples	Percent Reduction
Breast	3.75×10^9	13	9.05×10^7	10	97.59
	$(1.0 \times 10^8 - 2.9 \times 10^{10})$		$(0 - 1.37 \times 10^9)$		
Leg	2.7×10^9	12	3.8×10^7	8	98.59
	$(1.0 \times 10^8 - 2.0 \times 10^{10})$		$(0 - 1.8 \times 10^8)$		
Tail region	3.15×10^9	11	5.6×10^6	10	99.82
	$(1.0 \times 10^8 - 2.48 \times 10^{10})$		$(0 - 4.21 \times 10^8)$		
Liver	1.1×10^9	15	1.24×10^8	13	88.73
	$(9.0 \times 10^7 - 6.23 \times 10^9)$		$(0 - 5.26 \times 10^8)$		

Samples plated on SS agar after 24 hours at 37 C° in tetrathionate broth.
Source: Adapted from Hussemann and Wallace (1951).

(81.1–102.2°C). Under all conditions, the temperatures reached were sufficiently high to kill heat-resistant salmonellae.

Craven et al. (1975) submitted precooked chicken parts containing surviving spores of a heat-resistant strain of *Clostridium perfringens* first to freezing, then to reheating to 192°C (378°F) for 30 minutes, and then to flash frying at 192°C (378°F) for 30, 45, or 60 seconds. Ninety percent of the spores that had survived the freezing process were eliminated by this heating.

The present trend is to heat *pork roasts* to end points below 180°F (82.2°C). In the past, the recommendation was to heat pork to an internal temperature of 180–185°F (82.2–85°C). Working with loin roasts, Carlin et al. (1965) found that roasts heated to 170°F (76.7°C) were juicier than those heated to 185°F (85°C) and cooking losses were lower. At the 170°F (76.7°C) end point, *Trichinella spiralis* is no longer viable.

Stews allowed to simmer or boil should become devoid of living vegetative bacterial cells. As was stated for gravy, heat-resistant spores of *Clostridium perfringens* may survive the heat treatment given these menu items.

In *meat pies,* the temperatures attained have been found to vary greatly. Kereluk and Gunderson (1961) studied thermal death of bacteria during baking of chicken pies inoculated with *Staphylococcus aureus, Streptococcus faecalis, Escherichia coli,* and *Bacillus subtilis.* The pies, which reached 214°F (101.1°C) were practically sterile; there was a maximum of 0.1% survival of nonspore-forming bacteria, *S. faecalis* surviving in the greatest numbers. The spore-forming *B. subtilis* showed a 0.35% survival. The baking time needed to reach this internal temperature was 40 minutes at 425°F (218.5°C) oven temperature.

Omelets are cooked on top of the stove. Gibbons and Moore (1944) prepared omelets from reconstituted dried eggs containing salmonellae and cooked these items for 4–5 minutes to a terminal temperature of 94–98°C (201–208°F); they found no survivors.

Souffles are cooked in the oven. Time–temperature relationship data of souffles were collected by Longrée et al. (1962a), who used formulas and procedures applicable to quantity food preparation. Variables were batch size and use of water bath in baking. The authors found that the average temperature at doneness was 195.5°F (91.4°C) and that the cooking times were long.

Hard-cooked eggs were studied by Licciardello et al. (1965). The authors determined the destruction of salmonellae in eggs of various sizes. Four serotypes of *Salmonella* were employed: *S. senftenberg* 775W, which is extremely heat resistant, *S. derby, S. newport,* and *S. typhimurium.* Thermal resistance was determined on these organisms suspended in egg yolk, using miniature thermal death time tubes. Also, the rates of heat penetration during cooking into shell eggs were determined when two methods of cooking shell eggs were used. By integrating the thermal resistance and heat penetration data, the authors calculated the theoretical cooking times that would be required to destroy the salmonellae. By comparing these data with cooking times recommended for eggs in cookery under household and institutional conditions, the authors found that the cooking times recommended exceed the calculated times that are necessary to destroy salmonellae. On the basis of these data, therefore, hard-cooked eggs may be regarded as being safe from salmonellae. However, this does not preclude that hard-cooked eggs cannot be recontaminated by pathogen-carrying chilling water used to cool hot eggs after cooking. A food-poisoning outbreak following an Easter egg hunt attests to this fact (Merrill et al., 1984). It has also been demonstrated experimentally by Harbrecht and Bergdoll (1980) and Merrill et al. (1984) that *Staphylococcus* cells are able to enter the shells of cooked eggs since these are no longer protected by their natural resistance to bacterial penetration (see Chapter 6).

For *cooked salad dressing,* Kintner and Mangel (1953) found that cooking dried egg in the dressing to a temperature of 183–186°F (84.9–85.6°C) rendered the product free from staphylococci and salmonellae.

Desserts other than cakes and cookies, which were discussed earlier, are a very diversified group. Many desserts are made with egg and do not tolerate intense or prolonged heat treatment without undesirable changes in culinary quality. It is not surprising, then, that much research in connection with thermal death has been devoted to desserts such as custards, pie fillings, puddings, and pastry fillings.

Bakery custards were studied by Cathcart et al. (1942). The mixtures were inoculated with salmonellae and *Staphylococcus aureus.* The inoculum was killed when the custard mixture was brought to a boil after adding the egg–starch mixture to the liquid base. However, custards and puddings made by accepted methods are not boiled; the heating is usually terminated as soon as the mixture has "sufficiently thickened" (see Chapter 13).

Kintner and Mangel (1953) investigated the survival of staphylococci and salmonellae in puddings and custards prepared with experimentally inoculated dried egg. Killing was achieved between 91 and 93°C (195.8 and 199°F), but not at the minimum temperatures required for the egg to coagulate.

Time–temperature relationships in oven-baked custards made with whole egg solids and prepared in quantity were studied by Longrée et al. (1961). Two variables, among others, were oven temperature and depth to which the pan was filled. The data showed that heating times were long and temperatures at doneness near 190°F (88°C). Although no bacteriological analyses were made, the time–temperature relationship indicated that all the custards received heat treatments that should suffice to kill salmonellae, if present.

MENU ITEMS USUALLY HEATED TO TEMPERATURES BELOW 180°F (82.2°C). Among the *broiled and fried meats,* the steaks, chops, cutlets, and other small cuts are likely to be contaminated on the surface. However, they are exposed to very high temperatures when broiled, pan broiled, and fried. Therefore, this treatment should eliminate vegetative cells clinging to the outside, even in cuts cooked to the rare stage.

However, in ground, chopped, or otherwise comminuted meats such as hamburger, ham patties, fish cakes, and the like, surface heating does not necessarily eliminate contaminants, which are apt to include pathogens of human source because of the handling these items have received.

Moragne et al. (1962) reported that oven-cooked patties made from fresh, raw beef, heated to an internal temperature as low as 145°F (62.8°C) were judged "acceptable" in doneness; yet these items would probably not have been rendered bacteriologically safe by the heat treatment they received. The authors point out that doneness in this case was not a criterion for bacteriological safety.

It has been shown that soy protein added to beef increased the heat resistance of salmonellae present in the mixture; this increase could be related to an increase in pH (Craven and Blankenship, 1983).

Campylobacter jejuni, inoculated into meatballs, which were subsequently oven-cooked to an internal temperature of 70°C (158°F), was inactivated 10 minutes after this temperature was attained (Stern and Kotula, 1982).

Bernarde (1957) studied penetration of heat into commercially prepared precooked frozen crab cakes of initial internal temperature of 19 to 23°F (−5 to −7°C) and found that, when the directions given on the wrapper were followed in heating these cakes, very low terminal temperatures were achieved and that the heat treatment left much to be desired from a public health point of view.

Menu items made from cooked ingredients and reheated in deep fat are also apt to be lightly heated. This was proven for croquettes, for example. Deskins and Hussemann (1954) prepared ham croquettes from uncooked cured ham and heated them for 2 minutes in deep fat at 376°F (191.1°C) to a deep golden brown color. It was found that the internal temperature in the finished product varied from 133 to 145°F (56.1–62.8°C), and that although browning reduced the bacterial counts, the products contained survivors. The number of survivors depended on the bacterial load present previous to browning.

Beef and lamb roasts may be cooked to varying internal temperatures, 130–140°F (54.4–60°C) for rare, 160°F (71.1°C) for medium, and 170°F (76.7°C) for well done. In unboned roasts, danger from staphylococci and salmonellae is remote, the outside being exposed to high heat, the inside being practically sterile. However, the possibility exists that spores of heat-resistant *Clostridium perfringens* will survive the roasting process.

Sylvester and Green (1961) studied the effect of different types of cooking on artificially contaminated meat roasts. The organisms used were *C. welchii (perfringens), Salmonella typhimurium,* and *Staphylococcus.* The roasts reached an internal temperature of 150°F (65.6°C); salmonellae and staphylococci were killed, but *C. welchii (perfringens)* survived. From the data it is not clear whether or not the roasts remained at the terminal temperature of 150°F (65.6°C) for a prolonged period of time.

Funk et al. (1966) studied the fate of *Salmonella senftenberg* injected into loin cuts of 10-kg cuts of beef roasted at 399°F (203.8°C) to an internal temperature of 125.6°F (51.8°C) and then held for 18 hours in heat-holding equipment at 140°F (60°C). The maximum internal temperature reached in the center of the roasts during their history of roasting plus hot holding was 152.6°F (66.9°C), recorded 1 hour after placing the roasts in the 140°F (60°C) "warmer." The lowest temperature attained in the roast during the 18-hour hold in the "warmer" was 132.8°F (56°C). There were no survivors under the conditions of this experiment.

Heat resistance of *C. jejuni* in beef roast was studied by Christopher et al. (1982), who inoculated a heavy cell load into roasts at depths of 3.2 and 2.5 cm (1.18 and 0.98 in.). When baked at 177°C (350°F) oven temperature to 50°C (122°F) and 55°C (131°F), no survivors were recovered when the final internal temperature of the roasts was 57°C (134.6°F); but at a final internal temperature of 53°C (127.4°F), survivors were found. It would be interesting to test for survivors in rolled roasts in which contamination could occur at the center, and at much greater depths than those used in the above study.

The thermal sensitivity of *C. jejuni* in autoclaved ground chicken breast meat was determined by Blankenship and Craven (1982), who concluded that, under the conditions of this experiment, poultry meat heated to, and held at, 60°C (140°F) for 10 minutes would be freed from these contaminants.

Roast beef is often a deboned, rolled piece of beef. Common contaminants of beef are *Salmonella* and *Clostridium perfringens*. Rare roast beef is a favorite entree in restaurants, and commercially processed roasts are sold to delicatessen and fast-food establishments for sandwiches and cold platters. Roast beef has had a worrisome history in recent years in that it has been one of the most frequently reported items indicated in foodborne outbreaks in the United States (Bryan, 1975; Cohen and Blake, 1977). From 1976 through 1978, commercially processed roast beef caused a number of food-poisoning incidents traced to salmonellae (*Morbidity and Mortality Weekly Report*, 1976, 1977, 1978, 1981).

For boned rolled roasts, chances for inside contamination from hands, knives, and cutting surfaces that had prior contact with the outside of raw meat are afforded; common pathogens introduced with raw meat are salmonellae, *Clostridium perfringens*, and *Campylobacter jejuni*.

In the commercial preparation of roast beef from frozen chunks, the chunks are frequently thawed in water during defrosting, then heated while hanging on stainless steel racks in the oven. It is possible that the salmonellae penetrate through cracks and crevices into the interior of the meat during these procedures. Low roasting temperatures used to avoid shrinkage may contribute toward the survival of the pathogens. Another way for contaminants to enter the internal parts of a roast is the rolling up of the edges of a slab of beef, thus incorporating outside contaminants into the inside of the roast. Following these food-poisoning incidences and as an emergency measure, the USDA immediately issued regulations requiring processors of roast beef to cook roasts to an internal temperature of 145°F (63°C) (*Federal Register,* 1977). This made the processors very unhappy, because they no longer could fill the customers' demand for rare beef; at an endpoint of 145°F (63°C) the color of the beef was no longer as desirably red. As a result of this unpopular situation, several roast beef producers decided to collaborate with independent laboratories in developing roasting procedures whereby time and temperature were adjusted in such a way that salmonellae were eliminated and yet a rare appearance of the meat was attained. After thorough scrutiny of the suggested procedures, the USDA then rescinded its previous ruling and allowed 15 alternative time and temperature formulas for the production of beef (*Federal Register,* 1978). Thermal destruction of bacteria is a function of both time and temperature: at higher temperatures bacterial death occurs within a short time, whereas at lower temperatures longer heating is required. On the other hand, the change in the color of beef muscle, myoglobin, from red to gray is affected by a different time–temperature relationship. For example, a temperature of 145°F (63°C) causes a rapid change in color of the myoglobin, while a temperature of 135°F (57°C) for a prolonged period produces little change in meat color. Therefore, it is possible to destroy salmonellae by exposing roasts to low heat for extended time periods without causing the meat to turn gray. Moisture is also important in the death of salmonellae; they are more resistant to heat in a dry environment. This fact had to be considered in setting up regulations. Another safety factor requiring consideration of proposing long, slow cooking of beef roasts was the potential danger from growth of *Clostridium perfringens.* This possibility was carefully considered by Angelotti, Administrator of Food Safety and Quality Service (*Federal Register,* 1978). The situation was considered safe, provided that the roasting process is very carefully monitored. The directions are presented in Chapter 13.

Veal is usually cooked to the well-done stage and can be expected to be bacteriologically safe.

Ham and other cured pork pose a problem because of the handling they undergo with certain methods of processing. Micrococci have been frequently associated with the interior of hams that are cured by pumping brine into them. Deskins and Hussemann (1954) found center slices of hams more contaminated than end slices. These few examples point toward the hazard from internal contamination of cured pork. McDivitt and Hussemann (1957) made a study of micrococci in hams and reported that micrococci predominated in uncooked rolled hams. Cooking boned hams at oven temperature of 300°F (149°C) to a temperature of 77°C (170.6°F) was not sufficient to eliminate micrococci, according to these authors. Ham seems to exhibit a particularly protective action, making the micrococci quite resistant to the effect of heat.

Fresh pork may contain live *Trichinella spiralis* unless the meat is heated to at least 137°F (58.6°C). At that end point, the meat looks pink.

According to an FDA 1976 recommendation in the *Food Service Sanitation Manual* (1978), pork should be heated to an end point of at least 150°F (66°C). If every particle of pork and food mixtures containing pork is heated to that end point, *Trichinella spiralis* should no longer be viable. The current trend is to use an end point of 170°F (76.7°C), according to Carlin et al. (1965), Bowers and Goertz (1966), and Holmes et al. (1966).

Stuffed roasted turkey has been a frequent cause of food-poisoning outbreaks in the past. Some of the reasons are presence of salmonellae in the cavity of the carcass serving as a source of contaminants of the stuffing; contamination of the stuffing during its preparation; slow rate of heat loss from the interior of the stuffed turkey being refrigerated prior to cooking; slow rate of heat penetration into the interior of the stuffed turkey; mishandling and poor temperature control of leftover meat and stuffing. In quantity food preparation turkeys are roasted unstuffed, the stuffing being baked separately. However, since stuffed turkeys might still be prepared by and for groups of people such as at family gatherings, community meals, and church suppers, turkeys continue to be stuffed, and food-poisoning outbreaks caused by them continue to be reported.

Stuffing baked separately in shallow pans is quickly penetrated by heat, is portioned easily, and cools fast as a leftover. To prepare turkey unstuffed is thus a highly commendable practice.

Meat, turkey, and fish loaves and similar items are of particular interest because proteinaceous ingredients when comminuted are known to often harbor bacteria in high numbers. Contaminants may also be contributed by the binding ingredients like flour and breadcrumbs.

Deskins and Hussemann (1954) investigated the effect of cooking on thermal death of *Staphylococcus aureus* in ground ham mixtures. Ham loaves were baked in a 350°F (176.7°C) oven to an internal temperature of 80°C (176°F). The finished product was not sterile, but counts were low.

Beloian and Schlosser (1963) studied the heat penetration into salmon loaf inoculated with a heat-resistant strain of *Salmonella senftenberg*. Under the conditions of the experiment, lethality was achieved at a terminal temperature of 160°F (71.1°C).

Longrée et al. (1963) studied the time–temperature relationships of beef, turkey, and salmon loaves under conditions of quantity food preparation. Variables included oven temperature, use of a water bath, depth of the mixture in the pan, and terminal temperature to which the loaves were baked.

Beef loaves and salmon loaves baked to a low terminal temperature of 155°F (68.3°C) were acceptable in culinary quality. It is therefore questionable whether such loaves would receive heat treatments sufficient to eliminate even vegetative cells of possible pathogens. Higher terminal temperatures were required to render the turkey loaves acceptable to the judges. These results point out the fact that "doneness" on a culinary basis is not necessarily a satisfactory end point from a bacteriological point of view.

Whether *meat pies, poultry pies,* and *casseroles* made with proteinaceous solid ingredients reach internal temperatures sufficient to kill pathogenic contaminants depends on many factors. The nature of the food is one. In general, heat transfer is slow into mixtures consisting of proteinaceous solids held together by starchy sauces. The depth of the material in the pan is another factor, and so are initial temperatures of the materials to be heated. Two other important factors are oven temperature and time of heating.

Individual meat pies were inoculated with salmonellae by Miller and Ramsden (1955) and baked at various oven temperatures. In 4-ounce (113.4-gram) pies, when heating was rapid and oven temperatures above 400°F (204.4°C), the crust was browned before the interior of the pies got sufficiently hot to kill the inoculum; the interior temperature of the fillings reached only 47.2°C (117°F). At oven temperatures near 320°F (160°C), applied for one hour, kill was effected and an internal temperature of 86.6°C (188°F) was reached; however, the pie crust was not acceptable because of sogginess. Application of an intermediate oven temperature of 380°F (193.3°C) also achieved kill and resulted in an acceptable crust. The internal temperature reached under these conditions was not stated by the authors.

Wiedeman et al. (1957) baked three chicken casseroles inoculated with one strain each of *Micrococcus pyogenes* var. *aureus, Streptococcus faecalis,* and *Salmonella typhimurium,* at 350°F (176.7°C) for 40 minutes. The terminal internal temperature of the casseroles at the end of baking was 135°F (57.2°C) and the temperature rose after removal from the oven to 145°F (62.8°C). Although the numbers of vegetative cells were reduced considerably during cooking, the mixtures were not sterile. The streptococci were most resistant to the heat treatment, the salmonellae least.

Thermal destruction of *Staphylococcus aureus, Streptococcus faecalis, Escherichia coli,* and *Bacillus subtilis* in baking artificially contaminated chicken pies was studied by Kereluk and Gunderson (1961). Only one species of bacteria was inoculated into each pie. The contaminated pies were frozen, then baked in a 425°F (218.3°C) oven for 20, 30, or 40 minutes. The pies baked for 20 minutes to an internal temperature of 124°F (51.1°C) had a "just thawed" appearance; in these pies the nonspore formers exhibited survival rates of 14–100%, and the spore formers a survival rate of 150% or higher, indicating possible multiplication. In the pies baked for 30 minutes to 170°F (76.7°C), survival ranged from 0 to 3.6%, *S. faecalis* surviving in the greatest numbers. In the pies baked for 40 minutes to 214°F (101.1°C), survival of nonspore formers was negligible, the highest percentage (0.1%) being found for *S. faecalis;* of the spore former *B. subtilis,* 0.35% survived. The data pertaining to *S. faecalis* indicate that the heat treatment applied to a terminal temperature of 170°F (76.7°C) was just about as effectual as the heat treatment applied to a terminal temperature of 214°F (101.1°C).

Hussemann (1951) studied the effect of heating on the bacteriologic flora of chicken à la king, beef stew, and creamed seafood. These foods were heated from refrigerator temperatures to 85°C (185°F) in a double boiler, not in an oven. The heat treatment reduced the number of bacterial cells, including micrococci, but did not eradicate any type completely from a food in which it had been shown to be present originally.

In oven heating, "bubbling at the top" is not a sure sign that the pie or casserole has reached the boiling point in the center. In fact, items that are "run under the broiler" have been shown to be cool in the center when tested with a thermometer. Longer heating times at a moderate oven temperature would therefore be more effective in achieving heat penetration into the center without burning the top. The use of a thermometer is encouraged, especially for deep pies and casseroles. The terminal temperature should be at least 165°F (73.9°C).

Shellfish is usually lightly heated, if heated at all; some being acceptable in the uncooked state. To be safe, shellfish must be harvested from approved sources. The hazard of consuming lightly heated, contaminated shellfish has been demonstrated many times. A recent example is the case of virus-contaminated steamed clams: an outbreak of hepatitis was traced to clams that had been heated to the stage when the shells just opened (*Morbidity and Mortality Weekly Report,* 1972). Clams steamed to that stage have not reached an internal temperature sufficiently high to inactivate hepatitis virus (Koff and Sears, 1967); important bacterial pathogens may survive such light heating also.

Creamed menu items have been indicted many times as the offending food in gastroenteric outbreaks. Creamed meat, poultry, fish, shellfish, and eggs are potentially dangerous for several reasons: their proteinaceous nature and near neutral pH; the handling which the solid ingredients usually receive before they are incorporated into the sauce; and, last but not least, the temperatures prevailing in the combined mixture.

The temperature of the base, a "cream" or white sauce, will vary with the method of preparation and batch size. Longrée (1953) found that when scalded milk of 188–194°F (86.7–90°C) was used in the preparation of the sauces, the temperatures of the finished products ranged from 166 to 180°F (74.4–82.2°C); such a product would be practically sterile. However, when the solid ingredients are combined with the sauce, the temperature of the resulting mixture will decrease, the extent of the decrease depending on the temperature of the solid ingredients. If the temperature does not fall below 140°F (60°C), no multiplication of pathogenic contaminants needs to be expected. However, danger arises when the temperature falls below 140°F (60°C) and lingers within the temperature zone favorable to multiplication.

To achieve thermal death of contaminants, reheating the combined mixture to appropriate temperatures is required. Knowledge and skill are necessary to do this without interfering with some culinary quality characteristics of the items heated. To aid heat transfer, a certain degree of agitation is required, and this may break up solid ingredients. Also, curdling upon harsh heat treatment may be a problem in creamed menu items.

Studies on *soft-cooked shell eggs* were made by Rettger et al. (1916), who inoculated eggs with *Salmonella pullorum,* then boiled the eggs for periods up to 4 minutes. Viable salmonellae were recovered from some of the eggs that received the maximum heat treatment. Survival of salmonellae in 25% of eggs inoculated with *S. pullorum* was also reported by Stafseth et al. (1952).

Although only clean sound shelled eggs are to be used in quantity foodservice (FDA, 1978) and although eggs to be frozen or dehydrated must be pasteurized first to eliminate salmonellae, the fate of occasional *Salmonella* contaminants in cooked items made with eggs is of interest; recontamination of a sterilized product is known to have occasionally occurred.

Information on the bacteriological safety in scrambled eggs made with whole egg solids is limited. Gibbons and Moore (1944) inoculated whole egg solids with *S. bareilly, S. oranienburg,* and *S. typhimurium.* The eggs were reconstituted and used in preparing "scrambles" cooked on top of the stove. The batch containing the first contaminant was cooked to a maximum temperature of 68°C (154°F). Batches containing the other two contaminants were cooked to a maximum temperature of 82°C (180°F). No salmonellae organisms could be detected in the products after cooking. Scrambled eggs cooked to an internal temperature of 180°F (82°C) are of dry consistency (Longrée et al., 1962b).

Solowey and Calesnick (1948) inoculated reconstituted egg with *S. oranienburg, S. pullorum,* and a heat-resistant strain of *S. senftenberg.* Some of the inoculated batches were immediately scrambled, and some were held at room temperature and at refrigerator temperature before cooking. All "scrambles" were cooked to a moderately soft stage. Salmonellae were recovered from the "scrambles" at all ranges of the time–temperature interval. These results prove that when scrambled eggs are cooked to a soft, underdone stage, survival of salmonellae must be expected. It was found by Baker et al. (1983) that scrambling for 1 minute at 74°C (165.2°F) and 2 minutes at 78°C (172.4°F) were required for the complete destruction of *Salmonella typhimurium* and *Staphylococcus aureus,* respectively.

Fried and poached eggs are among the items often cooked to a soft, underdone stage. Survival of *Salmonella pullorum* in fried and poached eggs was studied by Stafseth et al. (1952). Survival was favored by brief heating. The data showed that survival must be expected under heat treatments usually applied in frying and poaching eggs. Heat penetration data were not collected. Survival of *Salmonella typhimurium* and *Staphylococcus aureus* in eggs cooked by frying, poaching, and boiling was studied by Baker et al. (1983). They found that except for poaching, commonly recommended procedures were not adequate for killing these contaminants. For fried eggs, complete kill depended on the method of cooking—4 minutes at 70°C (158°F) for covered eggs, and 3 minutes on each side at 64°C (147.2°F) for turned-over eggs. In sunnyside eggs cooked for 7.5 minutes at 64°C (146.2°F), both test organisms were not destroyed.

Hollandaise receives an exceedingly light heat treatment. In fact, bacteria are likely to multiply in the sauce while it is held warm. Many food-poisoning outbreaks have been traced to this highly perishable item. To safeguard against excessive bacterial multiplication, hollandaise should not be held longer than 3 hours and desirably for briefer periods than that. If the holding time has reached the maximum limit of a 3-hour hold, the batch must be discarded. To guard against a bacteriological risk and financial loss, hollandaise sauce ought to be made in batches small enough to ensure use within an hour.

Stirred (soft) custards receive light heat treatments in their preparation. Such custards have been indicted many times as the food item in food-poisoning outbreaks, the causative organism being frequently *Salmonella* contributed by the eggs.

To determine the effect of certain quantity preparation procedures on the extent of heating which soft custards receive, Miller et al. (1961) undertook two studies. In the first study, a bain-marie water bath was used as the source of heat. Variables were batch size of custard, amount of egg in the formula, initial temperature of the milk before the egg was added, method of combining the ingredients, and interval of agitation. In general, the factor that was effective in producing temperatures just above 170°F (76.7°C) within the custards was a short interval between agitations. In the second study, a steam-jacketed kettle was used as the source of heat and steam pressure was made a variable also. Higher terminal temperatures, near 180°F (82°C), were reached with this source of heat; at high steam pressures the custards curdled, however. Longer heating times were achieved when the egg was added along with the thickening agent (two-step method) instead of waiting until the starch had thickened (three-step method); the latter method is, at present, the conventional one.

Puddings were studied by Kintner and Mangel (1953), who prepared puddings with reconstituted dried eggs that had been inoculated with *Salmonella typhimurium, S. enteritidis, S. pullorum,* and *S. anatum,* and with a toxigenic strain of *Staphylococcus aureus.* The authors found that cooking stirred custards made with egg containing salmonellae and staphylococci to 196–199°F (91.1–92.8°C) sterilized the product. The total cooking time was 3–6 minutes. These terminal temperatures seem unusually high and perhaps not entirely applicable to quantity food preparation.

Cream fillings were studied by Hussemann and Tanner (1947). The authors used the thermal death tube method to determine the thermal death times for *S. aureus* in cream filling and found that the organism was killed by 8 minutes (lag time of 142 seconds) exposure at 149°F (65°C), less than 4 minutes (lag time of 148 seconds) exposure at 167°F (75°C), and by less than 3 minutes (lag time of 151 seconds) exposure at 185°F (85°C). Cream filling prepared by the accepted technique was found to be a sterile product, and it appeared that during its preparation the milk, flour, and sugar were maintained at above 149°F (65°C) for much longer than 8 minutes, found in thermal death tube experiments to be necessary to kill the staphylococci; after the egg was added to the hot mixture the temperature remained above 167°F (75°C) for a sufficient length of time to render the product free of staphylococci; at no time did the mixture boil.

Meringued pies in quantity food preparation are usually made using frozen egg whites in the meringues. In the past, frozen egg whites have been shown to be contaminated with salmonellae and to have caused foodborne infections when used in meringues that were not sufficiently heated to destroy the contaminants. The terminal temperatures attained in meringued pies and survival of *Streptococcus faecalis* and *Escherichia coli* have been studied by Mallman et al. (1963). These authors varied the conditions of preparation as follows: the meringues were placed on cold, 39°F (3.9°C), and hot, 158°F, (70°C), or warm, 122°F (50°C), fillings; the pies were baked at 3 oven temperatures, 325, 350, and 400°F (162.7, 176.7, and 204.4°C); and baked for varying lengths of time, 8–24 minutes. The temperatures of filling and interface of the cold-filled pies remained considerably lower than the temperatures of their hot-filled counterparts. Meringues placed on cold fillings contained viable contaminants after baking under any conditions of the experiment. The safeness and servability of meringues cooked on hot and warm fillings were similar. Meringues baked at 400°F (204.4°C) were either unsafe or they were unservable because they were dark, tough, and shrunken.

When the meringues were placed on hot fillings and the pies baked at 350 or 325°F (176.7 or 162.7°C) for 16–20 minutes, or at 325°F (162.7°C) for 24 minutes, the internal temperatures reached were sufficiently high to destroy the inoculum; these meringues were all palatable. Felt et al. (1956) also found that higher interface temperatures were reached when meringues were placed on hot, 158°F (70°C), rather than cold, 50°F (10°C), fillings. The interface temperature tended to be higher when the pies were baked for a longer period at the low, 325°F (162.7°C), temperature than when baked for a shorter period at the medium, 375°F (190.6°C), and high, 425°F (218.3°C), oven temperatures.

Leftover items may have a varied history. It is sound thinking to assume that leftovers are apt to become contaminated with human pathogens because of the handling they receive. Additional danger, that of multiplication, may arise during long holding periods. Precautions must therefore be taken to prevent additional multiplication of contaminants during rewarming before service.

Reheating practices vary, and so do the thoroughness of the heating process and the temperatures attained. Blaker (1962) studied the temperatures of foods held in hot-holding equipment and determined the temperatures of the items before they were placed in the equipment. She made the interesting observation that the temperatures of menu items prepared from precooked and cooled ingredients reheated just prior to serving time ranged from 82 to 140°F (27.8 to 60°C); these temperatures fall within the danger zone of bacterial multiplication.

The same author also observed that the end points of cooking for items reheated in the oven was frequently determined by the cook on the basis of the degree of brownness, not internal temperature attained, and that brownness was a poor criterion of internal temperature, especially if the items were at refrigerator temperature when placed in the oven. The author warned that such items when placed in hot-holding equipment might well become subjected to prolonged exposure at unsafe temperatures during the production period. The reader should again be reminded that the time periods for which food is held within the danger zone are cumulative regardless of whether the food was held in the oven (at supposedly hot, and safe, temperatures) or in the refrigerator (at supposedly cold, and safe, temperatures).

Leftovers are discussed further in Chapter 13.

A study of bacterial growth at foodservice operating temperatures was made by Rivituso and Snyder (1981). They concluded that, because of the diversity of foods prepared and methods of preparation employed, complex time–temperature relationships are possible. Therefore, a great number of study data need to be compiled and analyzed as a meaningful basis for effective microbiological control, the goal being effective HACCP programs (see Chapters 7 and 14) and quality-assured recipe procedures.

Time–temperature relationships under conditions of microwave heating are presented in Chapter 12.

REFERENCES

Angelotti, R., M. J. Foter, and K. H. Lewis (1961). "Time-temperature effects on salmonellae and staphylococci in foods. I. Behavior in refrigerated foods. II. Behavior at warm holding temperatures." *Am. J. Public Health,* 51:76–83, 83–88.

Angelotti, R., K. H. Lewis, and M. J. Foter (1963). "Time-temperature effects on fecal streptococci in foods. II. Behavior in refrigerated foods and at warm holding temperatures." *J. Milk Food Technol.,* 26:296–301.

Baker, R. C., S. Hogarty, W. Poon, and D. V. Vadehra (1983). "Survival of *Salmonella typhimurium* and *Staphylococcus aureus* in eggs cooked by different methods." *Poultry Sci.,* 62:211–1216.

Beck, W. J. and N. A. Milone (1972). "Changes in microbial population during thawing of ground beef." *J. Environ. Health,* 35:39–42.

Beloian, A. and G. C. Schlosser (1963). "Adequacy of cooking procedures for the destruction of salmonellae." *Am. J. Public Health, Nations Health,* 53:782–791.

Bernarde, M. A. (1957). "Heat penetration into precooked frozen crab cakes." *J. Milk Food Technol.,* 20:307–311.

Black, L. C. and M. N. Lewis (1948). "Effect on bacterial growth by various methods of cooling cooked foods." *J. Am. Diet. Assoc.,* 24:399–404.

Blaker, G. (1962). "Holding Hot Foods Before They Come to the Steam Table." Unpublished paper presented at the 90th Annual Meeting of the American Public Health Association, Miami Beach, FL, Oct.

Blankenship, L. C. and S. E. Craven (1982). "*Campylobacter jejuni* survival in chicken meat as a function of temperature." *Appl. Envir. Microbiol.,* 44:88–92.

Bowers, J. R. and G. E. Goertz (1966). "Effect of internal temperature on eating quality of pork chops. I. Skillet and oven-braising." *J. Am. Diet. Assoc.,* 48:116–120.

Bryan, F. L. (1975). "Status of foodborne disease in the United States." *J. Environ. Health,* 38:74–83.

Bryan, F. L. and T. W. McKinley (1974). "Prevention of foodborne illness by time–temperature control of thawing, cooking, chilling, and reheating turkeys in school lunch kitchens." *J. Milk Food Technol.,* 37:420–429.

Bryan, F. L. and T. W. McKinley (1980). "Hazard analysis and control of roast beef jus preparation in foodservice establishments." *J. Food Prot.,* 43:512–513; 519.

Buchbinder, L., V. Loughlin, M. Walter, and G. Dangler (1949). "A survey of frozen precooked foods with special reference to chicken à la king." *J. Milk Food Technol.,* 12:209–213.

Canale-Perola, E. and Z. J. Ordal (1957). "A survey of the bacteriological quality of frozen poultry pies." *Food Technol.,* 11:578–582.

Carlin, A. F., D. M. Bloemer, and D. K. Hotchkiss (1965). "Relation of oven temperature and final internal temperature to quality of pork loin roasts." *J. Home Econom.,* 57:442–446.

Castellani, A. G., R. R. Clarke, M. I. Gibson, and D. F. Meisner (1953). "Roasting time and temperature required to kill food poisoning microorganisms introduced experimentally into stuffing in turkeys." *Food Res.,* 18:131–138.

Cathcart, W. H., A. Merz, and R. E. Ryberg (1942). "*Staphylococcus* and *Salmonella* control in foods. IV. Effect of cooking bakery custards." *Food Res.,* 7:100–103.

Chen, T. C., J. T. Culotta, and W. S. Wang (1973). "Effects of water and microwave energy precooking on microbiological quality of chicken parts." *J. Food Sci.,* 38:155–157.

Christopher, F. M., G. C. Smith, and C. Vanderzant (1982). "Effect of temperature and pH on the survival of *Campylobacter fetus.*" *J. Food Prot.,* 45:253–259.

Cohen, M. L. and P. A. Blake (1977). "Trends in foodborne salmonellosis outbreaks 1963–1975." *J. Food Prot.,* 40:798–800.

Corlett, D. A., Jr. (1973). "Freeze processing: Prepared foods, sea food, onion and potato products." Presented at the HACCP Inspector Training Course, Food and Drug Administration, Aug. and Sept., Chicago, IL.

Corlett, D. A., Jr. (1974). "Frozen food processing technology." Presented at the HACCP Inspector Training Course, Food and Drug Administration, Sept. and Oct., Denver, CO.

Craven, S. E. and L. C. Blankenship (1983). "Increased heat resistance of salmonellae in beef with added soy proteins." *J. Food Prot.,* 46:380–384.

Craven, S. E., H. S. Lillard, and A. J. Mercuri (1975). "Survival of *Clostridium perfringens* during preparation of precooked chicken parts." *J. Milk Food Technol.,* 38:505–508.

Crespo, L. and H. W. Ockerman (1977). "Thermal destruction of microorganisms in meat by microwave and conventional cooking." *J. Milk Food Technol.,* 40:442–444.

Crespo, F. L., H. W. Ockerman, and K. M. Irvin (1977). "Effect of conventional and microwave heating on *Pseudomonas putrefaciens, Streptococcus faecalis,* and *Lactobacillus plantarum* in meat tissue." *J. Milk Food Technol.,* 40:588–591.

Culkin, K. A. and D. Y. C. Fung (1975). "Destruction of *Escherichia coli* and *Salmonella typhimurium* in microwave cooked soups." *J. Milk Food Technol.,* 38:8–15.

Deskins, B. B., and D. L. Hussemann (1954). "Effect of cooking on bacterial count of ground ham mixtures." *J. Am. Diet. Assoc.,* 30:1245–1249.

Elliott, R. P. and H. D. Michener (1960). *Review of the Microbiology of Frozen Foods.* Conference on Frozen Food Quality, U.S. Department of Agriculture, Albany, CA, pp. 40–61.

Elliott, R. P. and H. D. Michener (1961). "The microbiology of frozen foods, I, II, and III." *Frosted Food Field,* 32(5):26–27, 49; 33(1):16; 33(2):38–40, 53.

Elliott, R. P. and H. D. Michener (1965). "Factors Affecting the Growth of Psychrophilic Microorganisms in Foods. A Review." USDA Agricultural Research Service Technical Bulletin No. 1320.

Fanelli, M. J. and M. F. Gunderson (1961). "Defrost of prepared frozen foods. I. Defrost temperatures of frozen fruit pies, frozen meat pies and frozen soups." *Food Technol.,* 15:419–422.

Federal Register (1977). 42:44217, Sept. 2.

Federal Register (1978). 43:30793, July 18.

Felt, S. A., K. Longrée, and A. M. Briant (1956). "Instability of meringued pies." *J. Am. Diet. Assoc.,* 32:710–715.

Food and Drug Administration (1976). *Compliance Program Evaluation. FY 74. Hazard Analysis and Critical Control Point (HACCP) Inspections, Frozen "Heat and Serve Type Foods"* (7320.7). Food and Drug Administration, Washington, D.C.

Food and Drug Administration (1978). *Food Service Sanitation Manual.* U.S. Department of Health, Education and Welfare, Public Health Serv. DHEW Publ. No. (FDA) 78–2081. Washington, D.C.

Foter, M. J. (1964). "Bacteriology of frozen foods during processing." *J. Environ. Health,* 25 (Jan.–Feb.):273–280.

Funk, K., P. J. Aldrich, and T. F. Irmiter (1966). "Delayed service cookery of loin cuts of beef." *J. Am. Diet. Assoc.,* 48:210–215.

Gibbons, N. E. and R. L. Moore (1944). "Dried whole egg powder. III. The effect of drying, storage and cookery on the *Salmonella* content." *Can. J. Res.,* 22F:58–62.

Georgala, D. L. and A. Hurst (1963). "The survival of food poisoning bacteria in frozen foods." *J. Appl. Bacteriol.,* 26:346–358.

Goresline, H. E. (1962). "Historical development of the modern frozen food industry." In Proceedings, *Low Temperature Microbiology Symposium,* 1961. Campbell Soup Company, Camden, NJ, pp. 5–25.

Hall H. and R. Angelotti (1965). "*Clostridium perfringens* in meat and meat products." *Appl. Microbiol.,* 13:352–357.

Harbrecht, D. F. and M. S. Bergdoll (1980). "Staphylococcal enterotoxin B. production in hard-boiled eggs." *J. Food Sci.,* 45:307–309.

Holmes, Z. A., J. R. Bowers, and G. E. Goertz (1966). "Effect of internal temperature on eating quality of pork chops. II. Broiling." *J. Am. Diet. Assoc.,* 48:121–123.

Hucker, G. J. and E. R. David (1957). "The effect of alternate freezing and thawing on the total flora of frozen chicken pies." *Food Tech.,* 11(7):354–356.

Hussemann, D. L. (1951). "Effect of cooking on the bacteriologic flora of selected frozen precooked foods." *J. Am. Diet. Assoc.,* 27:855–858.

Hussemann, D. L. and F. W. Tanner (1947). "Relation of certain cooking procedures to *Staphylococcus* food poisoning." *Am. J. Public Health,* 37:1407–1414.

Hussemann, D. L. and M. A. Wallace (1951). "Studies on the possibility of the transmission of *Salmonella* by cooked fowl." *Food Res.,* 16:89–96.

Kelly, F. G. and G. M. Dack (1936). "Experimental *Staphylococcus* food poisoning. A study of the growth of a food poisoning *Staphylococcus* and the production of an enterotoxic substance in bread and meat." *Am. J. Public Health,* 26:1077–1082.

Kereluk, K. and M. F. Gunderson (1961). "Survival of bacteria in artificially contaminated frozen meat pies after baking." *Appl. Microbiol.,* 9:6–10.

Kintner, T. C. and M. Mangel (1953). "Survival of staphylococci and salmonellae in puddings and custards prepared with experimentally inoculated dried eggs." *Food Res.,* 18:492–496.

Knight, R. A. and J. B. M. Coppock (1957). "The influence of the baking process on the destruction of salmonellae in certain baked products containing egg albumen." *Roy. Soc. Prom. Health J.,* 77:528–532.

Koburger, J. A. (1981). "Effect of frozen storage on fungi in foods." *J. Food Prot.,* 44:300–301.

Koff, R. S. and H. S. Sears (1967). "Internal temperature of steamed clams." *N. Engl. J. Med.,* 276:737–739.

Licciardello, J. L., J. T. R. Nickerson, and S. A. Goldblith (1965). "Destruction of salmonellae in hard-boiled eggs." *Am. J. Public Health,* 55:1622–1628.

Longrée, K. (1953). "Viscosity of white sauces prepared in quantity." *J. Am. Diet. Assoc.,* 29:997–1003.

Longrée, K. and J. C. White (1955). "Cooling rates and bacterial growth in food prepared and stored in quantity." *J. Am. Diet. Assoc.,* 31:124–132.

Longrée, K., M. Jooste, and J. C. White (1961). "Time-temperature relationships in custards prepared in quantity with whole egg solids. III. Baked in large batches." *J. Am. Diet. Assoc.,* 38:147–151.

Longrée, K., J. C. White, and B. Y. Sison (1962a). "Time–temperature relationships of souffles: baked foamy omelets made with whole egg solids." *J. Am. Diet. Assoc.,* 41:107–110.

Longrée, K., J. C. White, B. Y. Sison, and K. Cutlar (1962b). "Scrambled eggs made with whole egg solids: Time-temperature relationships." *J. Am. Diet. Assoc.,* 41:213–216.

Longrée, K., L. Moragne, B. A. Bell, and J. C. White (1963). "Time-temperature studies of baked loaves; meat, fish, poultry." *J. Am. Diet. Assoc.,* 42:500–504.

Lowe, B. (1955). *Experimental Cookery, From the Chemical and Physical Standpoint,* 4th ed. John Wiley & Sons, New York.

Mabee, M. S. and G. J. Mountney (1970). "Time–temperature patterns during deep fat frying of chicken parts and their relation to the survival of *Salmonella.*" *Food Technol.,* 24:808–811.

Mallman, W. I., P. J. Aldrich, D. M. Downs, and G. Houghtby (1963). "Safeness and servability of meringued pie." *J. Am. Diet. Assoc.,* 43:43–47.

Martin, S. (1968). "The rise of prepared and precooked frozen foods." In *The Freezing Preservation of Foods,* D. K. Tressler, W. B. vanArsdel, and M. C. Copley, Eds. 4th ed. Avi Publishing Co., Westport, CT.

McDivitt, M. E. and M. L. Hammer (1958). "Cooling rate and bacterial growth in corn-starch pudding." *J. Am. Diet. Assoc.,* 34:1190–1194.

McDivitt, M. E. and D. L. Hussemann (1957). "Growth of micrococci in cooked ham." *J. Am. Diet. Assoc.,* 33:238–242.

Merrill, G. A., S. B. Werner, R. G. Bryant, D. Fredson, and K. Kelly (1984). "Staphylococcal food poisoning associated with an Easter egg hunt." *J. Am. Med. Assoc.,* 252(Aug. 24):1019–1022.

Miller, A. A. and F. Ramsden (1955). "Contamination of meat pies by *Salmonella* in relation to baking and handling procedures." *J. Appl. Bacteriol.,* 18:565–580.

Miller, C., K. Longrée, and J. C. White (1961). "Time-temperature relationships of custards made with whole egg solids. I. In the Bain Marie. II. In the steam jacketed kettle." *J. Am. Diet. Assoc.,* 38:43–48; 49–53.

Moragne, L. and K. Longrée (1961). "Defrosting times of frozen turkeys." *Hosp. Mgt.,* 92(1):64–67.

Moragne, L., K. Longrée, N. L. Fuller, and J. C. White (1962). "Time-temperature relationships of beef patties made with whole egg solids." *J. Milk Food Technol.,* 25:274–276.

Morbidity and Mortality Weekly Report (1965a). U.S. Department of Health, Education and Welfare, Public Health Serv., 14, June 26.

Morbidity and Mortality Weekly Report (1965b). U.S. Department of Health, Education and Welfare, Public Health Serv., 14, Oct. 16.

Morbidity and Mortality Weekly Report (1972). U.S. Department of Health, Education and Welfare, Public Health Serv., 21, Jan. 15.

Morbidity and Mortality Weekly Report (1976). U.S. Department of Health, Education and Welfare, Public Health Serv., Cent. Dis. Control, 25, Feb. 7; Oct. 29.

Morbidity and Mortality Weekly Report (1977). U.S. Department of Health, Education and Welfare, Public Health Serv., Cent. Dis. Control, 26, Aug. 26.

Morbidity and Mortality Weekly Report (1978). U.S. Department of Health, Education and Welfare, Public Health Serv., Cent. Dis. Control, 27, Aug. 25.

Morbidity and Mortality Weekly Report (1981). U.S. Department of Health, Education and Welfare, Public Health Serv., Cent. Dis. Control, 30:391–392.

Notermans, S., J. Dufrenne, and M. J. H. Keijbets (1981). "Vacuum-packed cooked potatoes toxin production by *Clostridium botulinum* and shelflife." *J. Food Prot.*, 44:572–575.

Ostovar, K. and M. J. Bremier (1975). "Effect of thawing on growth of *Staphylococcus aureus* in frozen convenience items." *J. Milk Food Technol.*, 38:337–339.

Patterson, J. T. and P. A. Gibbs (1973). "Observation on the microbiology of cooked chicken carcasses." *J. Appl. Bacteriol.*, 36:689–697.

Peterson, A., J. J. Black, and M. F. Gunderson (1962). "Staphylococci in competition. I. Growth of naturally occurring mixed populations in precooked frozen foods during defrost." *Appl. Microbiol.*, 10:16–22.

Peterson, A. C. and R. E. Gunnerson (1974). "Microbiological critical control points in frozen foods." *Food Technol.*, 28(9):37–44.

Prescott, S. C. and L. P. Geer (1936). "Observations on food poisoning organisms under refrigeration conditions." *Refrig. Eng.*, 32:211–212; 282–283.

Proctor, B. E. and A. W. Phillips (1948). "Frozen precooked foods." *Am. J. Public Health*, 38:44–49.

Rettger, L. F., T. G. Hull, and S. W. Sturges (1916). "Feeding experiments with *Bacterium pullorum*. The toxicity of infected eggs." *J. Exper. Med.*, 23:475–489.

Rivituso, C. P. and O. P. Snyder (1981). "Bacterial growth at foodservice operating temperatures." *J. Food Prot.*, 44:770–775.

Rogers, R. E. and M. F. Gunderson (1958). "Roasting of frozen stuffed turkeys. I. Survival of *Salmonella pullorum* in inoculated stuffing. II. Survival of *Micrococcus pyogenes* var. *aureus* in inoculated stuffing." *Food Research*, 23:87–95; 96–102.

Rollin, J. L. and M. E. Matthews (1977). "Cook/Chill foodservice systems: Temperature histories of a cooked ground beef product during the chilling process." *J. Food Prot.*, 40:782–784.

Ross, A. D. and F. S. Thatcher (1958). "Bacteriological content of marketed precooked frozen foods in relation to public health." *Food Tech.*, 12(7):369–371.

Saleh, M. A. and Z. J. Ordal (1955). "Studies on growth and toxin production of *Clostridium botulinum* in a precooked frozen food. I. Some factors affecting growth and toxin production." *Food Res.*, 20:332–339.

Schmidt, C. F., R. V. Lechowich, and J. F. Folinazzo (1961). "Growth and toxin production of type E *Clostridium botulinum* below 40°F." *J. Food Sci.*, 26:626–630.

Seals, J. E., J. D. Snyder, T. A. Edell, C. L. Hatheway, C. J. Johnson, R. C. Swanson, and J. M. Hughes (1981). "Restaurant associated Type A botulism: Transmission by potato salad." *Am. J. Epidemiology*, 113:436–444.

Solowey, M. and E. J. Calesnick (1948). "Survival of *Salmonella* in reconstituted egg powder subjected to holding and scrambling." *Food Res.*, 13:216–226.

Stafseth, H. J., M. M. Cooper, and A. M. Wallbank (1952). "Survival of *Salmonella pullorum* on the skin of human beings and in eggs during storage and various methods of cooking." *J. Milk Food Technol.*, 15:70–73.

Stern, N. and A. Kotula (1982). "Survival of *Campylobacter jejuni* inoculated into ground beef." *Appl. and Envir. Microbiol.*, 44:1150–1153.

Stoychew, M. G., G. Djejewa, and R. I. Ilieva (1971). "Influence on some pasteurization temperatures on the dynamic evolution and breathing activities of *Streptococcus faecalis.*" *Proceedings of the 17th Meeting of European Meat Research Workers,* Bristol, England.

Strong, D. H. and J. C. Canada (1964). "Survival of *Clostridium perfringens* in frozen chicken gravy." *J. Food Sci.,* 29:479–482.

Sugiyama, H., M. Woodburn, K. H. Yang, and C. Movroydis (1981). "Production of botulinum toxin in inoculate pack studies of foil-wrapped baked potatoes." *J. Food Prot.,* 44:896–898.

Sylvester, P. K. and J. Green (1961). "The effect of different types of cooking on artificially infected meat." *Med. J. Australia,* 2(19):765.

Thatcher, F. S., J. Robinson, and I. Erdman (1962). "The 'vacuum pack' method of packaging foods in relation to the formation of the botulinum and staphylococcal toxins." *J. Appl. Bacteriol.,* 25:120–124.

Tressler, D. K., W. B. van Arsdel, and M. J. Copley, Eds. (1968). *The Freezing Preservation of Foods.* 4th ed. Avi Publishing Co., Westport, CT.

Tuomi, S., M. E. Matthews, and E. H. Marth (1974a). "Temperature and microbial flora of refrigerated ground beef gravy subjected to holding and heating as might occur in a school foodservice operation." *J. Milk Food Technol.,* 37:457–462.

Tuomi, S., M. E. Matthews, and E. H. Marth (1974b). "Behavior of *Clostridium perfringens* in precooked chilled ground beef gravy during cooling, holding, and reheating." *J. Milk Food Technol.,* 37:494–498.

Wiedeman, K., M. A. Watson, J. Neill, and W. G. Walter (1957). "Effect of holding time on bacteria in chicken casserole." *J. Am. Diet. Assoc.,* 33:37–41.

Winter, A. R., H. H. Weiser, and M. Lewis (1954). "The control of bacteria in chicken salad." *Appl. Microbiol.,* 1:278–281.

Woodburn, M., M. Bennion, and G. E. Vail (1962). "Destruction of salmonellae and staphylococci in precooked poultry products by heat treatment before freezing." *Food Technol.,* 16:98–100.

Woodburn, M. J. and D. H. Strong (1960). "Survival of *Salmonella typhimurium, Staphylococcus aureus* and *Streptococcus faecalis* in simplified food substrates." *J. Appl. Microbiol.,* 8:109–113.

Woodford, A. L., E. J. Schantz, and M. J. Woodburn (1978). "Heat inactivation of botulinum toxin Type A in some convenience foods after frozen storage." *J. Food Sci.,* 43:620–624.

ADDITIONAL READINGS

Baer, E. F., A. P. Duran, H. A. Leininger, R. B. Read, Jr., A. H. Schwab, and A. Swartzentruber. "Microbiological quality of frozen breaded fish and shellfish products." *Appl. Environ. Microbiol.,* 31:337–341. 1976.

Beuchat, L. R. "*Escherichia coli* on pecans. Survival under various storage conditions and disinfection with propylene oxide." *J. Food Sci.,* 38:1063–1066. 1973.

Blankenship, L. C., C. E. Davis, and G. J. Magner. "Cooking methods for eliminating of *Salmonella typhimurium*-experimental surface contaminant from rare dryroasted beef roasts." *J. Food Sci.,* 45:270–273. 1980.

Bradshaw, J. G., D. W. Francis, and R. M. Twedt. "Survival of *Vibrio parahaemolyticus* in cooked seafood at refrigeration temperatures." *Appl. Microbiol.,* 27:657–661. 1974.

Bryan, F. L. "*Clostridium perfringens* in relation to meat products." *Proc. 25th Ann. Reciprocal Meat Conf., Am. Meat Sci. Assoc., Ames, Iowa,* 25:323–341. (Published by the National Livestock and Meat Board, Chicago, IL. 1972).

Bryan, F. L., C. A. Bartleson, and N. Christopherson. "Hazard analysis, in reference to *Bacillus cereus,* of boiled and fried rice in Cantonese-style restaurants." *J. Food Prot.,* 44:500–512. 1981.

Bryan, F. L. and E. G. Kilpatrick. "*Clostridium perfringens* related to roast beef cooking, storage, and contamination in a fast food service restaurant." *Am. J. Public Health,* 61:1869–1885. 1971.

Craven, S. E. and A. J. Mercuri. "Total aerobic and coliform counts in chicken-soy patties during refrigerated storage." *J. Food Prot.,* 40(2):112–115. 1972.

Dahl, C. A. and M. E. Matthews. "Forced-air convection ovens: Temperature range in oven and in beef loaf during heating." *School Food Serv. Res. Rev.,* 3(1):11–15. 1979.

Dawson, E. "Heat penetration, quality and yield of turkeys roasted to an internal temperature of 195°F." *J. Home Econom.,* 57:188–191. March, 1965.

Decareau, R. V. "Foodservice equipment: Technological trends." *J. Food Prot.,* 41:459–463. 1978.

Heidelbauer, R. J. and P. R. Middaugh. "Inhibition of staphylococcal enterotoxin production in convenience foods." *J. Food Sci.,* 38:885–888. 1973.

Hobbs, B. C. "Microbiological hazards of international trade." In *Microbiology in Agriculture, Fisheries and Food,* F. A. Skinner and J. G. Carr, Eds. Academic Press, London, New York, San Francisco. 1976.

Hussemann, D. L. and F. W. Tanner. "Relation of certain cooking procedures to *Staphylococcus* food poisoning." *Am. J. Public Health,* 37:1407–1414. 1947.

Jul, M. *The Quality of Frozen Foods.* Academic Press, Orlando. 1984.

Kennedy, J. E., Jr., J. L. Oblinger, and R. L. White. "Fate of *Salmonella infantis, Staphylococcus aureus,* and *Hafnia alvi* in vacuum packaged beef plate pieces during refrigerator storage." *J. Food Sci.,* 45:1273–1277; 1300. 1980.

Ley, S. J. *Foodservice Refrigeration.* CBI Publ. Co., Boston. 1980.

Livingston, G. E. and C. M. Chang. "Second-generation reconstitution systems." *Cornell Hotel Rest. Adm. Q.,* 13(1):57–64. 1972.

Longrée, K. and G. G. Blaker. *Techniques in Sanitary Food Service.* John Wiley & Sons, New York. 1971.

Mercuri, A. J., G. J. Banwart, J. A. Kinner, and A. R. Sessums. "Bacteriological examination of commercial precooked Eastern type turkey rolls." *Appl. Microbiol.,* 19:768–771. 1970.

Minor, T. E. and E. H. Marth. "*Staphylococcus aureus* and staphylococcal food intoxication. A review. IV. Staphylococci in meat, bakery products and other foods." *J. Milk Food Technol.,* 35:228–241. 1972.

Morbidity and Mortality Weekly Report. U.S. Dept. of Health and Human Services, Public Health Serv., "Nutritional outbreak of yersiniosis." Centers for Disease Control, 31:505–506. 1982.

Naik, H. S. and C. L. Duncan. "Thermal inactivation of *Clostridium perfringens* enterotoxin." *J. Food Prot.,* 41:100–103. 1978.

Peterson, A. C., J. J. Black, and M. F. Gunderson. "Staphylococci in competition. I. Growth of naturally occurring mixed populations in precooked frozen foods during defrost." *Appl. Microbiol.,* 10:16–22. 1962.

Peterson, A. C. and M. F. Gunderson. "Microbiological control points in frozen foods." *Food Technol.,* 28(Sept.):37–44. 1974.

Peterson, A. C. and M. F. Gunderson. "Role of psychrophilic bacteria in frozen food spoilage." *Food Technol.,* 14:413–417. 1960.

Reichert, C. A. and D. Y. C. Fung. "Thermal inactivation and subsequent reactivation of staphylococcal enterotoxin B in selected liquid foods." *J. Milk Food Technol.,* 39:516–520. 1976.

Rowley, D. B. "Microbiological aspects of certain military feeding systems." *J. Milk Food Technol.,* 39:280–284. 1976.

Schwab, A. H., B. A. Wentz, J. A. Jagow, A. Swartzentruber, A. P. Duran, J. A. Lanier, R. J. Barnard, and R. B. Read, Jr. "Microbiological quality of cream-type pies during processing." *J. Food Prot.,* 48:70–75. 1985.

Seligman, R. and H. Frank-Blum. "Microbiological quality of barbecued chickens from commercial rotisseries." *J. Milk Food Technol.,* 37:473–477. 1974.

Smith, L. D. S. "Factors affecting the growth of *Clostridium perfringens.*" In *SOS/70 Proc. 3rd Int. Congr. Food Sci. Technol., Inst. Food Technol.,* Chicago, IL. 1971.

Solomon, H. M., R. K. Lynt, T. Lilly, Jr., and D. A. Kautter. "Effect of low temperatures on growth of *Clostridium botulinum* spores in meat of the blue crab." *J. Food Prot.,* 40:5–7. 1977.

Sundberg, A. B. and A. F. Carlin. "Relation to final internal temperature to *Clostridium perfringens* destruction in beef loaves cooked in a crockery pot or conventional oven." *J. Food Sci.,* 43:285–288. 1978.

Surkiewicz, B. F., M. E. Harris, and R. W. Johnston. "Bacteriological survey of frozen meat and gravy produced at establishments under federal inspection." *Appl. Microbiol.,* 26:574–576. 1973.

Sylvester, P. K. and J. Green. "The effect of different types of cooking on artificially infected meat." *Med. J. Australia,* 2(19):765. 1961.

Thomas, C., J. C. White, and K. Longrée. "Thermal resistance of salmonellae and staphylococci in foods." *J. Appl. Microbiol.,* 14:815–820. 1966.

Todd, E. and H. Pivnick. "Public health problems associated with barbecued food." *J. Milk Food Technol.,* 36:1–19. 1972.

Trachulchang, S. P. and A. A. Kraft. "Survival of *Clostridium perfringens* in refrigerated and frozen meat and poultry items." *J. Food Sci.,* 42:518–521. 1977.

Troller, J. A. *Sanitation in Food Processing.* Procter and Gamble Co., Cincinnati, OH. 1981.

vanArsdel, W. B., M. J. Copley, and R. L. Olson, Eds. *Quality and Stability in Frozen Foods: Time-Temperature Tolerance and Its Significance.* Wiley-Interscience, New York. 1969.

Woodburn, M. and C. H. Kim. "Survival of *Clostridium perfringens* during baking and holding of turkey stuffings." *Appl. Microbiol.,* 14:914–920. 1966.

Woodburn, M. and A. E. Ellington. "Choice of cooking temperature for stuffed turkeys. Part II. Microbiological safety of stuffing." *J. Home Econom.,* 59:186–190. 1967.

Zottola, E. A. and F. F. Busta. "Microbiological quality of further-processed turkey products." *J. Food Sci.,* 36:1001–1004. 1971.

CHAPTER *12*

Microwave Heating

T he use of microwave heating for foodservice applications has been considered since the 1940s, when microwave appliances became available
for the first time. Decareau (1992) states that there is growing interest in this
form of heating in the 1990s.

BASIC PROPERTIES OF MICROWAVES

The behavior of radio frequency waves and their ability to produce heat was
recognized in the late nineteenth century. However, the application of this
knowledge to food preparation was not attempted until the 1940s and 1950s.

Among the earliest users of microwave ovens were a few restaurants in the
late 1940s, which installed them for use in heating foods. The first significant
use of microwave ovens began in the late 1960s, when vending foodservice
facilities began to install them. By 1977, Decareau (1977) reported that the
penetration of microwave ovens in foodservice installations was 22%.

Microwave heating, or electronic heating, as it was called in the 1940s, is
also dielectric heating. Two frequencies have been allocated by the Federal
Communications Commission (FCC) in the United States for this application,
915 and 2450 MHz. The 915-MHz frequency, however, is rarely used today.

In microwave heating, foods are placed in an electromagnetic field when
they are placed in the oven and the oven is turned on. Heat is generated by
the molecular friction produced primarily in free water molecules in the

food. Except for salts, other molecules in foods are relatively unaffected dielectrically; they are heated primarily by conduction from the water molecules. The friction provided thus results in heat energy that cooks or heats the food. The term used to describe the degree to which a food will absorb dielectric energy is "loss factor" or sometimes "lossiness."

THAWING OF FOODS

In frozen foods, a large part of the water in the food has been changed to ice. While water readily absorbs microwaves, ice does not. Some of the water in frozen foods does not freeze; this may be due to the salt content. This unfrozen water absorbs microwaves readily in thawing. As a consequence, use of microwaves to thaw and cook food may result in "runaway heating," a situation in which the unfrozen water containing salts is boiling while, next to it, areas of solid frozen ice exist.

To prevent this, use of a defrost program is recommended; this feature exposes the food load to microwave energy for a short time, then turns microwaves off for a slightly longer time, allowing the heat to be conducted to the ice. This cycle is repeated until thawing is completed, and it does not usually produce runaway heating.

HEATING PATTERNS

Microwave heating is faster than conventional heating. Time is the most widely used method to control the cooking process. Power level can also be manipulated to control cooking time. The cooking time is determined by the food's composition, size and shape, initial temperature, and final temperature when cooked. Temperature probes can be inserted into foods, and cooking can be programmed to stop when the desired final temperature is reached.

Large food loads usually require more cooking time than small loads. However, the relationship depends also on the shape and size of each load. Doubling the load size usually requires less than twice as much time to heat to the same temperature. The optimum shape for food for microwave cooking is round and shallow (Cook, 1972). This allows for large surface area exposure.

The material used for cookware in microwave heating must be chosen with consideration of its behavior when exposed to a microwave field. Materials may absorb or reflect microwaves or may be transparent. Those that absorb microwaves compete with the food for microwave energy; those that reflect will shield the food from microwave absorption. The ideal cookware is transparent to microwaves. Materials that have a high degree of transparent properties include paper, heat-resistant glass, ceramics, and plastics.

The container or cookware material may affect time, as well as uniformity, of heating. Materials that have high transmission properties shorten the cooking time; those that are more absorptive will lengthen the cook time. This is particularly true when foods are being heated to serving temperature in the microwave oven, as is the case in much foodservice microwave use. Cookware materials with high transmission properties will result in more uniform temperature distribution in the cooked or heated foods.

An example of cookware material designed to be used for microwave heating and thermalizing food is a composite based on a polymer, pulp, and cellulose mixture, which has excellent performance characteristics and yields more uniform heating patterns than those observed when other materials such as paper, plastics, or ceramics are used. For more information about composite cookware, contact the Society of the Plastics Industry, Inc. (1025 Connecticut Avenue, NW, Suite 409, Washington, DC 20036).

Frequently, when poor heating patterns are observed in foods at the end of the heat cycle, the oven may be blamed for the problem when it is the cookware. Some early models of microwave ovens suffered from design problems that resulted in nonuniform heating (often called "hot spots"). Many new microwave oven models that have come onto the market in the 1980s have been redesigned, with the result that hot spots have been eliminated in the majority of ovens available today. Uneven heating patterns may, however, be encountered when the container material chosen has poor transmission properties.

The use of a cover on foods during microwave cooking aids in a uniform heat distribution pattern (Armbruster and Haefele, 1975). Sawyer et al. (1984) examined the internal temperature and survival of bacteria on meats with and without a polyvinylidene chloride wrap during microwave cooking and found that the wrap improved the counts of *Staphylococcus aureus* and *Salmonella senftenberg* on meats.

Microwave heating of food does not usually produce browning comparable to that observed with conventional cooking. Nutritionally, this is not a negative. The loss in nutrition due to browning is well known. The introduction of browning mixes, browning devices, and browning dishes and susceptors made it possible to achieve browning in microwave cooking.

EFFECT ON MICROBIAL LIFE

The question of whether microwaves are lethal to microbial life because of a specific effect of microwave energy per se on the microorganisms has been asked a number of times; the heart of the question is whether microwave radiation is similar to ionizing radiation and as such is possibly lethal.

It is difficult to apply microwave energy to microorganisms without heating, inasmuch as microorganisms are systems made up of a large amount of water. Wang and Goldblith (1967) placed *E. coli* organisms into a flask at

−18°C (0°F) and then exposed the flasks to microwave energy for one minute without raising the temperature above 30°C (86°F), and found that the *E. coli* were not killed. When a similar flask at room temperature was exposed to microwave energy for the same time, the temperature was raised to 93°C (199°F) and the bacteria were destroyed. These data indicated that the sterilizing effect of microwaves was due solely to the heat generated by the microwaves. Mudgett (1985) stated that microbial lethality in microwave processing was subject to the same time–temperature relationship as in conventional heating.

Dessel et al. (1960) made a quantitative comparison of electronic and conventional cooking in the destruction of several bacterial species artificially inoculated into foods. Baked custards were inoculated with *Serratia marcescens, Staphylococcus aureus,* and *Bacillus cereus;* scrambled eggs with *S. aureus* and *B. cereus;* and ground beef patties with *Salmonella typhi.* An electronic range and two conventional ovens—electric and gas—were used. The results showed that cooking in the electronic range was at least as effective in destroying vegetative cells as conventional cooking and that spores were not eliminated with either method.

MICROWAVE APPLICATIONS IN FOODSERVICE

Use of microwave ovens in foodservice systems is an attractive concept. Oaks (1981) stated that microwave ovens were used 80% of the time for heating in foodservice systems.

Snyder and Matthews (1986) reviewed 12 major studies of microbial quality of foodservice microwave oven usage. Included were (1) studies of microwave use in actual foodservice facilities, (2) microwave studies in foodservice laboratories, (3) time and temperature surveys of menu items produced under actual operating conditions in hospital foodservice, and (4) postprocessing temperature rise in microwave reheating of food. The studies reviewed showed that temperatures below 165°F (74°C) were observed in microwave-reheated food, but that the "microbiological quality of microwaved menu items was good, even though temperatures reported were not always in compliance with federal guidelines for reheating cooked foods."

Decareau (1992) and Heddleson and Doores (1994) reviewed research examining microwave destruction of pathogens in foods in foodservice applications. The research studies cover more than 40 years and include a wide range of pathogens, foods, and microwave systems. The reviews indicate that concern for microbial safety in microwave-heated foods may be justified. Many of the cases examined could be revisited using the emerging technology in concert with the state of the art microwave units that are on the market today. With that approach, the results could be more acceptable. Decareau concludes his review with the following guidelines for cook/chill and cook/freeze microwave foodservice systems:

1. Begin with high quality foodstuffs.
2. Use prescribed sanitation practice during preparation.
3. Cook to 73.8°C (165°F) or higher.
4. Chill rapidly to 7.2°C (45°F) or less in four hours or less.
5. Package and store at 4.4°C (40°F) or lower, or freeze and store at −17.7 to −23.3°C (0 to −10°F).
6. Plate foods, cover with a plastic film or plastic banquet cover, hold at 7.2°C (45°F) or lower and microwave heat to 73.8°C (165°F) before serving.

COOKING OF PORK

The USDA recommendation for cooking pork states that a temperature of 170°F (76.7°C) must be reached in all parts of the product in order to devitalize any possible contamination by *Trichinella spiralis.*

Zimmerman (1983) conducted a study of microwave cooking methods using *Trichinella spiralis*-infected pork. Four different brands of microwave oven were included. The output wattages of the ovens ranged from 625 to 700 watts. Roasts were covered during cooking and all roasts were allowed to stand for 20 minutes after cooking with an aluminum foil tent covering the meat.

The study showed that *T. spiralis* in pork could be consistently devitalized in microwave ovens. Based on the study, recommendations for devitalizing *T. spiralis* in microwave cooking were as follows:

1. Use 50% or less power.
2. Use roasts weighting 2 kg or less.
3. Boneless loin and bone-in-center loin are preferred cuts.
4. Allow roasts to stand covered with foil, or use the temperature-hold feature available on some ovens, with temperature probe inserted, and set for 170°F (76.7°C) for 10 minutes or more.
5. Measure the temperature of the roast at several locations—if any temperature is below 170°F (76.7°C), recook until all temperature readings are at least 170°F.
6. Make visual observations of cut-up product; if any pink or red meat is evident, cook longer.

FDA *FOOD CODE 1993* RECOMMENDATIONS

In 1993, the FDA *Food Code* recommended the following procedure for microwave cooking:

Raw animal foods cooked in the microwave shall be:

A. Rotated or stirred throughout or midway during cooking to compensate for uneven distribution of heat
B. Covered to retain surface moisture
C. Heated an additional 14°C (25°F) above the temperature

63°C (145°F) For shell eggs that are broken or fish and meat
68°C (155°F) For pork, game, comminuted fish and meats and other methods used for eggs
74°C (165°F) For field dressed wild game, poultry, stuffed fish, stuffed meat, stuffed pasta, stuffed poultry, or stuffing containing fish, meat, or poultry

D. Allowed to stand covered for 2 minutes after cooking to obtain temperature equilibrium.

REFERENCES

Armbruster, G. and C. Haefele (1975). "Quality of foods after cooking in 915 MHz and 2,450 MHz microwave appliances using plastic film covers." *J. Food Sci.,* 40:721–723.

Cook, R. (1972). "Plastic containers for microwave and conventional oven use." In *Proceedings, Consumer Microwave Oven Systems Conference,* G. Armbruster and M. Purchase, Eds. Association of Home Appliance Manufacturers, Chicago, IL.

Decareau, R. V. (1977). "Microwave ovens big in commercial food service." *Microwave Energy Appl. Newsl.,* 10(4):2.

Decareau, R. (1992). *Microwave Foods: New product development.* Food and Nutrition Press, Inc. Trumbull, CT.

Dessel, M. M., E. M. Bowersox, and W. S. Teter (1960). "Bacteria in electronically cooked foods." *J. Am. Diet. Assoc.,* 37:230–233.

Heddleson, R. and S. Doores (1994). "Factors affecting microwave heating of foods and microwave induced destruction of foodborne pathogens—A review." *J. Food Prot.,* 57:1023–1037.

Mudgett, R. E. (1985). "Modeling microwave heating characteristics." In *Microwaves in the Food Processing Industry,* R. V. Decareau, Ed. Academic Press, New York.

Oaks, D. W. (1981). "Institutional ovens: Industry predicts nine percent growth for foodservice oven sales." *Microwave World,* 2(6):8–9.

Sawyer, C. A., S. D. Biglari, and S. S. Thompson (1984). "Internal end temperature and survival of bacteria on meats with and without a polyvinylidene chloride wrap during microwave cooking." *J. Food Sci.,* 49:972–974.

Snyder, P. O. and M. E. Matthews (1986). "Microwave reheating of menu items in foodservices." *Microwave World,* 7(1):5–8.

Wang, D. I. C. and S. A. Goldblith (1967). "Effects of microwaves on *E. coli* and *B. subtilis.*" *Appl. Microbiol.,* 15:1371–1375.

Zimmerman, J. (1983). "An approach to safe microwave cooking of pork roasts containing *Trichinella spiralis.*" *J. Food Sci.,* 48:1775–1777.

ADDITIONAL READINGS

Copson, D. A. *Microwave Heating.* Avi Publishing Co., Westport, CT. 1962.
Decareau, R. V. *Microwaves in the Food Processing Industry.* Academic Press, New York. 1985.
VanZante, H. J. *The Microwave Oven.* Houghton Mifflin Co., Boston. 1973.

CHAPTER 13

Time–Temperature Control: Preventing Multiplication and Achieving Death of Contaminants in Ingredients and Menu Items

The foodservice manager is aware that microbial multiplication can occur during preparation, storage, transport, and service of menu items due to favorable temperatures. The control measures discussed in this chapter are designed to retard or eliminate growth by controlling the potential contaminants and the environmental temperature.

FROZEN FOODS

In frozen foods, no multiplication of bacteria should be possible. Frozen foods must be freezer stored at 0°F (-17.8°C). At temperatures between 32 and 19°F (0 and -17.2°C) certain food-spoilage bacteria, the psychrophilic or cold-loving ones, may multiply. Although these are not pathogenic, they mar or ruin the quality of the frozen product. Bacteria capable of causing food-borne illnesses are able to survive freezing and freezer storage and may resume growth when the food thaws.

Purchased Items

In general, the frozen food industry endeavors to produce products of high sanitary quality, and is successful. In this effort it is effectively supported by the Food and Drug Administration and state and local health agencies. The

FDA, through its District Office and resident inspection posts, inspects freezing plants. Also, it samples processed products and analyzes them for their microbiological quality. These inspections, carried out throughout the nation, provide excellent protection to those foodservice establishments that purchase frozen products shipped across state lines.

RECOMMENDATIONS.   Order frozen food from a reliable vendor who handles items processed by reputable processors. Beware of "bargains" from unknown sources.

Purchase only the amount of the food item that can be used in the immediate future. The quantity ordered depends on such factors as inventory on hand, present needs, amount of freezer space available, and frequency of delivery. In general, rapid turnover is preferable over long holding, less than 1 month being a desirable holding time with 3 months being the maximum acceptable time. After this length of time, the quality of the food may deteriorate; the degree of deterioration will vary with the nature of the food frozen.

Specify transit conditions; frozen foods should be held at 0°F (-17.8°C) or lower during the entire period.

When receiving frozen foods, have the necessary freezer space ready; check for signs of mishandling. If there is suspicion of defrost, the delivery should be refused. Do not allow frozen food to remain on loading docks; store promptly at 0°F (-17.8°C) or below.

Prepared Items Frozen on the Premises

In the United States, as well as in some European countries, the trend is toward the freezing of kitchen-prepared or commissary-prepared menu items in preference over preparing food for one day's use. Some foodservice operations prepare part or even all of their freezable menu items well in advance, package and freeze them, and reheat them as needed. Some of the advantages voiced by the proponents of the freeze-it-yourself method are: better utilization of labor and equipment, better culinary-quality control, better microbiological control, wider menu choice, use of unskilled labor in final reheating, and lower operating cost in general.

This type of food-freezing system is very common in commercial foodservice and is finding use in institutional foodservice also. In commercial foodservice, some chain-type establishments are active in this type of operation, employing factory equipment and processing methods in central kitchens or commissaries. The individual foodservice establishment within the chain receives the frozen items prepared and ready to be reheated (see Chapter 14).

Besides professionally operated and streamlined freezing operations, much freezing of leftovers and food items prepared in advance goes on in conventional foodservice establishments. Unfortunately, the quality of the freezing operations often leaves much to be desired.

A foodservice establishment considering the wisdom and feasibility of freezing prepared foods must consider this venture from many angles. One important consideration is that of sanitation. One risk is that, in a foodservice operation where the processing of frozen food is practiced concurrently with the production of food for immediate consumption, the freezing operations are apt to be slighted in favor of food preparation for the day; the latter obviously takes precedent, while the former "can wait." This may lead to holding food at hazardous temperatures for prolonged periods of time, presenting an opportunity for contaminants to multiply and to form toxins.

Long holding also affords an opportunity for additional, undesirable contamination; where people work and move the presence of staphylococci must be anticipated. *Clostridium perfringens* and *Campylobacter jejuni* are ubiquitous microorganisms, likely to be around also. These organisms are capable of causing foodborne illness. Food should not be exposed to such contaminants any longer than is absolutely necessary.

For the sake of keeping potentially hazardous contaminants under reasonable control, preliminary preparation, such as cutting and trimming of raw ingredients, should be performed in a separate room, removed from the area where the food is cooked and packed for freezing. Hazardous bacteria such as salmonellae are likely to be contaminants of raw meats, and a variety of soilborne organisms adhere to raw vegetables. If the raw ingredients are handled indiscriminately along with cooked foods, there is danger from these contaminants also.

The foodservice establishment where prepared food is frozen as a sideline may not have ready access to a reputable bacteriological laboratory, which is equipped to analyze the prepared food and provide reliable information on its bacteriological quality.

In conclusion, this warning is reiterated: the production of precooked frozen food must not ever be handled in a haphazard fashion. Unless the freezing operation can be a continuous, streamlined, bacteriologically controlled, short-time process, the bacteriological hazards could be formidable.

Unless a foodservice operator is willing and able to process frozen foods as a separate physical unit of operation using separate and adequate equipment, specially trained personnel, and microbiological control, he or she should refrain from planning further and give up the idea of going into the frozen prepared food business.

Once this basic issue has been decided in the positive, the foodservice operator has to plan in detail. To make these detailed plans for establishing a frozen food operation, he or she needs to appreciate the fact that the freezing of precooked food needs very special know-how. If he or she does not have it, it must be acquired. The problems are chemical, physical, and microbiological in nature, and they need to be fully understood and taken into consideration if the venture is to be a successful one. Many precooked foods are greatly changed by freezing, freezer storage, or reheating, or combinations of these. Some items freeze well but deteriorate in storage. Others do not even freeze successfully. Still others—which do not freeze well when formulated in the conventional way—can be adapted to freezing when reformulated. For example, items containing gelatinized (cooked) starch need to be reformulated by substituting special, freezable starches for the regular (corn, wheat) starches, which do not tolerate freezing well.

Equipment to be used in the preparation and further processing of frozen food must conform to high standards of cleanability and sanitary installation. It must be suitable to batch cooking. Cooling equipment must be available to effect a rapid drop of temperature in the cooked products. Efficient cooling is extremely important from a sanitation point of view. The many facets of packaging must also be understood.

Freezers must be available which are capable of freezing the food in a very short time, preferably within ½ hour. Many institutional freezers would not be capable of performing that efficiently, although they might be very adequate for the storage of food already frozen.

Reheating equipment must be considered also. Reheating can be done by various methods and a method most suitable to the nature of the food, the quantity packaged, the method of packaging, and other considerations peculiar to a specific foodservice must be chosen. Reheating equipment includes ovens—conventional, convection, and electronic; hot water baths for boil-in-bag packages; steamers; and other special devices.

Fortunately, management can get professional help in the selection and installation of appropriate pieces of equipment by contracting reputable firms that manufacture rapid-chill, rapid-freeze, and rapid-thaw equipment exclusively designed for multipurpose foodservice operations. The food is chilled, frozen, or thawed in cabinet units. The emphasis is on rapidity of processing in order to inhibit microbial multiplication, and on flexibility, which allows the cabinets to be used for processing as well as storage. This equipment is useful for use in conventional foodservice as well as in commissary foodservice systems.

Personnel to be entrusted with the freezing operation should be selected with care. Reliability, neatness, and interest in this type of work would be important assets. The personnel should be carefully instructed, so that they understand the reasons for every step of the processing procedure and the necessity for strict adherence to the sanitary measures prescribed. They must develop the skills under constant, careful supervision before going into production by themselves, and continued checking is advisable after the formal training period is over. Potential sources of undesirable contamination are, among others: ingredients; soiled or malfunctioning equipment; ill or carrier food handlers; careless fabricating methods such as insufficient heating, slow cooling, and faulty packaging; and unduly slow freezing rates. Cook/freeze systems as applied to institutional foodservice are discussed further in Chapter 14.

RECOMMENDATIONS. Start by providing available, appropriate equipment that ensures that the food can be chilled, frozen, and thawed rapidly. Process food material of excellent quality only.

Prepare raw ingredients such as meats and fresh vegetables in a separate room away from the cooking, cooling, and packaging areas.

Keep working surfaces, food-contact equipment, and utensils in sanitary condition by cleaning and sanitizing these at 2-hour intervals, or more often if indicated.

Have employees exercise strict personal hygiene, including periodic hand-washing (a minimum of 2-hour intervals is suggested), and meticulous hand-washing after visiting the toilet, touching anything soiled, and handling raw ingredients (especially meat).

Exercise scrupulous kitchen sanitation. Use a germicidal agent in wall cleaning solutions and in water for mopping the kitchen floor. Use freshly laundered floor mops.

Maintain strict time–temperature control throughout processing to ensure that the ingredients and/or menu items will not remain in the hazardous temperature zone of bacterial growth (45–140°F; 7.2–60°C) more than 2 hours.

Remember that the period of 2 hours for which food may "safely" remain at hazardous temperatures is a composite of every minute of warm holding, not necessarily one continuous 2-hour span of time, and that hazardous temperatures may prevail during handling as well as cooling.

Be cognizant of the fact that many frozen foods that need to be cooked again before being served receive minimum heat treatment before they are frozen, and that bacterial survivors may remain.

Prevent recontamination of the food during cooling and packaging.

Use appropriate durable, sanitary containers or wrappings, which are moisture-vapor resistant and do not impair the quality of the food being frozen. Packagings should be adapted to the nature of the food, the intended use of the food, and the method of reheating.

Freeze food in small (shallow) batches for fast heat transfer. The food should be solidly frozen with ½ hour of exposure to freezing temperatures.

Defrosting Foods

In the *Food Service Sanitation Manual* (FDA, 1978a), it is stated that frozen foods must be stored at such temperatures as to remain frozen, except when being thawed for preparation or use. Furthermore, it is required that potentially hazardous foods be thawed at refrigerator temperatures of 45°F (7.2°C);

> or, under potable running water of a temperature of 70° F (21 C°) or below, with sufficient water velocity to agitate and float off loss food particles into the overflow; or in a microwave oven only when the food will be immediately transferred to conventional cooking facilities as a part of a continuous cooking process or when the entire, uninterrupted cooking process takes place in the microwave oven; or, as part of the conventional cooking process.

The main principles underlying these recommendations are that unless defrosting is absolutely necessary, it should be omitted, and that the utmost precautions should be taken to assure that potentially hazardous foods do not unduly warm up during the defrosting process.

It should always be remembered that, if defrosting is continued to the point that the ice crystals have been converted to free water and if temperatures are above 45°F (7.2°C), bacterial multiplication is possible. It should be reiterated that, for the purpose of rapid and safe thawing, specially designed rapid-thaw cabinets, in which the air is circulated at high velocity and in which the fans stop automatically upon completion of the thaw cycle, are available. Make sure that the unit purchased has the approval of the National Sanitation Foundation, Ann Arbor, Michigan.

It is important to use all defrosted items promptly. Holding defrosted items under refrigeration more than a day may lead to a buildup of cold-loving bacteria. Even pathogenic contaminants, if present in large numbers, may multiply to dangerously high populations.

Refreezing of defrosted items is not recommended in principle. The frozen food industry has wisely protected the quality of its products by discouraging this practice since the culinary as well as the microbiological quality usually suffers in defrosting.

GUIDELINES.   It is the responsibility of the foodservice manager or dietitian to set up detailed guidelines concerning defrosting procedures, which should include these major points:

1. Type of food; whether it should be defrosted or not
2. Place
3. Equipment

4. Details of defrosting procedures
   a. Length of time (approximate)
   b. Protection against contamination during period of defrost
   c. Protection against chances of warmup beyond the point where bacterial multiplication can be resumed (above 45°F; 7.2°C)

If thawing turkeys in bags at room temperature should be necessary, Bryan and McKinley (1974) advise that not more than 1 hour per pound be allowed if one double-layer bag is used; or 1¼ hour per pound, if two double-layer bags are used. Close monitoring is advised.

RECOMMENDATIONS

Fresh Frozen Foods Served Unheated. *Fruit juice concentrates:* Reconstitute from frozen state and chill at once. *Fresh fruit:* Defrost in original container in the refrigerator, or in a tightly sealed moisture-proof container in cold running water.

Fresh Frozen Foods to Be Heated. *Fruits:* Defrost just enough for convenience in handling; defrost in a refrigerator or in a tightly sealed moisture-proof container in cold running water. If the fruit must be thawed at room temperature, it should be kept in the original closed container. Prolonged warming will cause mushiness of the fruit and may allow microbial multiplication in mildly acid fruits.

Vegetables: Do not defrost before cooking, except corn on the cob.

Fish, shellfish, meats (small cuts), and poultry (small cuts): Do not defrost unless breaded or covered with batter. If defrosting is necessary, place item in refrigerator or, enclosed in tightly sealed moisture-proof bag, in cold running water.

Whole turkeys, large roasts, frozen egg: Defrost in a refrigerator or, provided that the item is protected by a tightly sealed moisture-proof container, in cold running water.

Precooked Frozen Foods. The nature of the item will determine whether it needs defrosting.

CHILLING COOKED FOODS

Efficient chilling of cooked food is one of the most important tools in keeping microbial growth—and toxin formation—at bay. It has been estimated that 60% of all outbreaks of foodborne illness is caused by insufficient chilling. The chilling of uncooked foods may extend to other purposes also. For items prepared in the foodservice establishment, chilling is used to protect items prepared in advance to be used later as ingredients, complete menu items, and leftovers.

Chilling does not necessarily ensure complete microbiological safety, however, even at low refrigerator temperatures. For example, *Yersinia enterocolitica* may multiply at very low temperatures, and so may *Clostridium botulinum* type E. Also, *Campylobacter jejuni* survives better in foods at refrigerator temperature than at room temperature, although the pathogen needs higher temperatures for growth.

Items prepared outside the foodservice establishment that need chilling may include canned goods that have been opened, and otherwise packaged perishables; frozen foods destined to defrost; and items received in a partially prepared or fully prepared state, awaiting further preparation and/or service, including leftover baked potatoes wrapped in foil and vacuum-packed boiled potatoes. The latter two items are potentially hazardous since they might be contaminated with *Clostridium botulinum.*

For items sold through vending machines, refrigeration must be applied to readily perishable items that are to be served cold.

Refrigeration Needs

The refrigeration needs of a foodservice operation depend on many managerial factors (West et al., 1977; Kotschevar and Terrell, 1977). Certainly no perishable foods classified as potentially hazardous should be stored at room temperature because of lack of refrigeration, although this is all too frequently done. When setting up refrigeration requirements, space must be allowed for defrosting of frozen items.

In order to be used effectively, refrigerators should be placed near the appropriate preparation centers. At present, salad centers usually have refrigeration units nearby. For green, gelatin, and many other types of salad the benefit of refrigeration is obvious, since visible deterioration is prevented. Not obvious to the eye is the need for refrigeration in connection with ingredients and menu items that are vulnerable to warmth because of their capacity to serve as media for multiplication of bacterial pathogens.

Refrigerators should be available near working areas where hazardous items are handled ahead of time of final preparation—for example, where poultry, meat, and seafood are boned, cut, sliced, or cubed—and where these items (combined with other ingredients) are shaped into croquettes, patties, cakes, loaves, and the like. Food handlers who are expected to keep potentially hazardous foods out of the danger zone of bacterial multiplication should be provided with adequate refrigeration nearby, readily accessible to them.

Temperature Required for Chilling Cooked Food

Multiplication of the majority of important foodborne pathogens is very slow at temperatures at and below 45°F (7.2°C), although growth of common foodborne pathogens is possible below 45°F (7.2°C), as was shown in Table 11.2. The food should be cooled rapidly to 40–45°F (4.4–7.2°C). The warmest part of the food mass should reach 45°F (7.2°C) within a time span of 4 hours, preferably less, and the food should not linger in the temperature range of 120–60°F (48.9–15.6°C) for more than 2 hours, preferably less. Fast cooling cannot be achieved unless the temperature of the refrigerator is considerably lower than 45°F (7.2°C). However, the air temperature should not go so low as to cause the food to freeze.

Length of Storage

In general, the maximum length of refrigerator storage is influenced by the ability of the various contaminating pathogens to multiply at low temperatures. Some of the more common food pathogens are cold-loving—for example, *Yersinia enterocolitica. Staphylococcus aureus,* and the salmonellae, too, are able to multiply under refrigeration, as well as *Clostridium botulinum* type E (see Table 11.2). Therefore, if the period of refrigerator storage is kept brief, the danger from microbial growth is lessened.

In summary, cooked foods should be chilled rapidly to at least 45°F (7.2°C), preferably to 40°F (4.4°C); stored at 38°F (3.3°C); and used as soon as possible. Storage for one day is ideal. Unless highly efficient cooking procedures are used, prolonging storage time will increase microbial hazards. However, in some highly streamlined, rigidly controlled cook/chill foodservice systems, where chilling is achieved in less than 1 hour to temperatures lower than 40°F (4.4°C), markedly long periods of safe cold storage can be achieved. Refrigerator temperatures, just above those at which the food would freeze, are provided in these highly controlled systems.

Cold Foods Prepared Outside the Place of Service

As the number of foodservices, including health care and school foodservices, which contract for food from outside, grows, the sanitary hazards connected with lack of time–temperature control gain in importance. The dangers lie in the fact that foods which should be kept under constant refrigeration are apt to be subjected for prolonged periods to temperatures at which bacterial growth may take place. Although specifications made by the food contracting establishment may state strict time–temperature control during preparation and transit, this control is up to the vendor in the end. The reliability of the vendor cannot, therefore, be overestimated.

Another trend is for schools, hospitals, and other institutions to prepare the food they serve in centralized kitchens or commissaries, and to have it transported to the participating satellite establishment for service. Frequently the food is transported while chilled. Items to be served hot are reheated at the place of service.

In addition to the hazards innate in chilling and storing large quantities of food, other hazards to be considered and eliminated are increase of food temperature in transit, and long periods of storage. All items should be kept chilled prior to transit, in transit, and at the place of arrival—regardless of whether they are served cold or are reheated before service.

Cooked food to be sent to satellite establishments is frequently prepared one or two days prior to service. Foods served Mondays, however, may well have to be prepared on Fridays. Cook/chill systems are discussed in Chapter 14.

Refrigerators for Chilling Cooked Food

SANITARY FEATURES.   The cleanability of materials used for walls, ceilings, floors, and shelves and construction features should be considered. Floor drains are a sanitary hazard. It is beyond the scope of this book to discuss the component parts and principles of refrigeration.

Certain principles pertaining to refrigerators and their use apply to all types of walk-in and reach-in refrigerators; the *temperature* through appropriate refrigeration units is reduced to a predetermined level, the *air flow* is usually controlled, and the *moisture content* of the air (relative humidity) is sometimes controlled. Actually, these three factors are interdependent.

TEMPERATURES.   The colder the refrigerator air, the faster the food will cool. The temperature of a refrigerator used for the cooling and storage of cooked foods should be kept as low as is feasible without causing the food to freeze; the maximum temperature should not exceed 40°F (4.4°C). The thermometer should be numerically scaled, accurate to ±3°F (1.7°C).

Before adjusting the temperature of a refrigerator, experimentation is necessary to determine its temperature conditions over a number of days, including those of peak production and those of no production. These points should be kept in mind:

1. Ascertain the warmest area, or areas, and the coldest area, or areas, where food is stored; check the temperature there; never place the thermometer on a wall.

2. Record temperatures frequently throughout the testing days, and possibly nights; this way one should find the lowest as well as the highest temperatures that are likely to occur; it is important to include periods when the refrigerator carries a typical "full load" and a small load.

The results may look like these:

1. The warmest and coldest areas are similar; this indicates good ventilation throughout the refrigerator. Controls should be tentatively set to allow for a maximum of 40°F (4.4°C) and a minimum of 32°F (0°C) or above, and checks made to find out whether these temperatures are maintained at times of a capacity warm load. If at capacity load the refrigerator temperatures do not rise, all is well.
2. The warmest and coldest areas are quite dissimilar even when the load is light and cold; adjustment will be difficult, because poor circulation is probably the cause of this discrepancy. Refrigerators with poor circulation respond poorly to a large load, especially when the load is warm. When using such a refrigerator, it is essential that the load be precooled before it is introduced. If possible, a refrigeration system with adequate circulation should be provided.
3. The warmest and coldest areas are similar when the food load is light and cold, and the circulation seems adequate; after food is introduced there are peaks of unduly high temperature rises in the warmest as well as the coolest areas. The controls should be set as low as possible without risking the danger of freezing the food. If the temperature at peak load rises above 40°F (4.4°C) and lingers there for hours, the capacity of the refrigerator obviously does not meet the requirements of the load. In this case, precooling the warm food outside the refrigerator may solve the problem. Precooling methods are discussed below.

Longrée and White (1955) continuously recorded for six working days the temperature fluctuations in six locations within a walk-in refrigerator equipped with a forced-air unit. The cooler was used for the storage of cooked foods. The lowest temperature recorded during this period was 39°F (3.9°C), and the highest was 55°F (12.8°C). Two distinct temperature peaks were observed: one following the close of the noon meal, the other following the night meal. At night, the employees rushed, and much of the food placed in the cooler came from the steam table and other hot-holding equipment. At noon, some effort was made to precool some items. This may explain the somewhat lower peak temperatures following the lunch hour. The data showed clearly that (1) the load of warm food had a tremendous effect on the temperatures prevailing in the refrigerator; (2) the refrigerator temperatures decreased very slowly; in fact, temperatures continued to drop until high noon of the following day; and (3) opening and closing of the refrigerator door during the busy morning hours had little if any effect on the temperatures.

AIR FLOW.   Refrigeration works by the removal of heat. Circulation plays a very important role in removing the blanket of warm air and in supplying cold air to the food to be cooled. The effect of forced air was demonstrated by Moragne et al. (1959a) for a 55-cubic-foot (1.55-cubic-meter) reach-in refrigerator, in which loads of 8, 16, and 32 gallons (30.3, 60.5, and 121 liters) of white sauce were cooled from 140 to 80°F (60 to 26.7°C). See Tables 13.1 and 13.2.

More efficient circulation of air is provided when the air intake is near the ceiling and the exit is near the floor, below the bottom shelf.

HUMIDITY.   The relative humidity of the refrigerator has an effect on moisture changes in the food stored. If the relative humidity of the air is lower than that of the stored items, moisture will be drawn from them and the food surfaces may take on a dry appearance. If the relative humidity of the air is higher than that of the food, the food will pick up moisture, and sliming and bacterial deterioration will result.

Since cooked items stored in a refrigerator range in relative humidity from high to low, it follows that losses or gains in moisture must be prevented by covering each item.

Heat Transfer Problems in Foods

In principle, refrigeration should remove the heat from foods at a rate that effects cooling to safe temperatures within a span of time sufficiently brief to

TABLE 13.1.   *Effect of Total Load and the Effect of Forced Air on the Temperature Range of the Refrigerator Air*[a]

| Total Load (gallons)[b] | Number of Stock Pots | Size of Batch (gallons)[b] | Air Temperature | | | |
| | | | Fan On | | Fan Off | |
			°F	°C	°F	°C
8	8	1	32–42	0–5.6	63–65	16.7–18.3
16	8	2	32–41	0–5.0	64–75	17.8–23.9
32	8	4	30–52	−1–11	68–85	20.0–29.4

[a] Sauce was cooled from 140 to 80°F (60–26.7°C).
[b] U.S. gallon = 3.785 liters.
Source: Adapted from Moragne et al. (1959a).

TABLE 13.2. *Effect of Forced Air on the Total Cooling Time of White Sauce*[a]

Total Load (gallons)[b]	Number of Stock Pots	Size of Batch (gallons)[b]	Total Cooling Time			
			Fan On		Fan Off	
			Hours	Minutes	Hours	Minutes
8	8	1	2	26	3	55
16	8	2	4	43	9	21
32	8	4	7	45	16	46

[a] Sauce was cooled from 140 to 80°F (60 to 26.7°C).
[b] U.S. gallon = 3.785 liters.
Source: Adapted from Moragne et al. (1959a).

prevent bacterial multiplication in the foods cooled. The methodology applied will vary with the nature of the food cooled, the quantity of the food cooled, and the cooling facilities.

SOLID FOODS.   Solid foods are, in general, more difficult to cool than fluid foods. Research data on heat transfer in solid foods are scant. Therefore, cooling times are largely anticipated on the basis of experience rather than scientific knowledge. Heat transfer is affected by the thermal properties of a food, the geometry of a food, and the thermal processing conditions. An important contribution is the work by Dickerson and Read (1968) dealing with calculation and measurement of heat transfer in various foods and also the data on meat by Hill et al. (1967) and by Qashou et al. (1970).

FLUID FOODS.   The viscosity of fluid food plays an important role in heat transfer. In low-viscosity items, convection currents help to continually mix the fluid as long as a temperature difference exists within a batch. In high-viscosity items, cooling takes place largely by conduction, a relatively slow process of heat transfer. As a food becomes more viscous while cooling, as many foods do, the convection currents are increasingly suppressed and conduction cooling takes over gradually.

Fatty and starchy foods are slow to cool. As the temperatures decrease, a dense film forms at the wall of the container surrounded by the coolant, be this air or water; this film constitutes a barrier to heat transfer.

Cooling Procedures Pertaining to the Quantity of Food Cooled

The quantity of warm food to be cooled may prolong cooling times in several ways: (1) the total warm load may be too large for the particular refrigerator to handle; (2) the individual batch may be too large, even if the refrigerator maintains the desired low temperature; or (3) a combination of these conditions may exist.

CONTROL OF TOTAL LOAD.   The size of the total load of warm food that may be placed in a refrigerator without raising the temperature of the refrigerator air to an extent that makes rapid cooling of the food to 45°F (7.2°C) impossible must be established by the food manager. Frequent checks of the refrigerator temperature in a manner described previously in this chapter are necessary to do this.

Overloading can be remedied by using another refrigerator to accommodate the excess load or decreasing the temperature of the food before the load is introduced into the refrigerator.

Data showing the effects of total load and of initial temperature on the temperature range prevailing in a refrigerator and the cooling time of the food were reported by Moragne et al. (1959a). These data are presented in Tables 13.3 and 13.4. Methods of precooling foods outside the refrigerator are discussed later.

CONTROL OF DEPTH OR SIZE OF BATCH.   Even if the total load is sufficiently small, sufficiently cool, or both, and thus will not cause a rise in the temperature of the refrigerator air above the desirable low level, batch depth or size must be controlled whenever warm food is introduced into a refrigerator (as discussed in Chapter 11) to assure that the food will cool from 140 to 45°F (60 to 7.2°C) within 2–4 hours.

Solid foods lend themselves well to being cooled in shallow layers. A few

TABLE 13.3.   *Effect of Placing White Sauce in the Refrigerator at Two Initial Temperatures on the Temperature Range of the Refrigerator Air*[a]

Total Load (gallons)[b]	Number of Stock Pots	Size of Batch (gallons)[b]	Air Temperature			
			Sauce at 140°F (60°C)		Sauce at 80°F (26.7°C)	
			°F	°C	°F	°C
8	8	1	32–41	0–5.0	33–44	0.5–6.7
16	8	2	32–39	0–4.0	33–41	0.5–5.0
32	8	4	31–51	−1–10.5	31–41	−1–5.0

[a] Sauces were cooled to 60°F (15.6°C).
[b] U.S. gallon = 3.785 liters.
Source: Adapted from Moragne et al. (1959a).

TABLE 13.4. *Effect of Total Load and Effect of Placing the Sauce in the Refrigerator at Two Initial Temperatures on the Total Cooling Time of White Sauce*

Total Load (gallons)[a]	Number of Stock Pots	Size of Batch (gallons)[a]	Total Cooling Time			
			140–60°F (60–26.7°C)		80–60°F (26.7–15.6°C)	
			Hours	Minutes	Hours	Minutes
8	8	1	3	57	2	33
16	8	2	7	11	2	51
32	8	4	11	20	5	7

[a]U.S. gallon = 3.785 liters.
Source: Adapted from Moragne et al. (1959a).

examples should suffice: meats can be sliced, poultry sliced or divided into smaller pieces, fish placed in shallow layers, and so forth; salads, such as potato and poultry, placed in shallow pans and refrigerated, cool faster than when cooled in deep containers. They can be refrigerated either without precooling or following precooling on ice.

Cooling cooked items, such as turkeys, by immersing them in water may cause serious recontamination, as was shown by Kelsay (1970).

Semisolid foods must be handled according to the judgment of the food manager; some semisolid items would be treated like solid foods, others like fluid ones.

Fluid foods are difficult and impractical to handle in shallow containers. Regular stock pots are more suitable and less liable to spill the food. Since the cooling surface cannot be increased vertically, it must be extended horizontally; this means that a large batch must be broken up into several small ones of 2 gallons or even less. The smaller the batches are, the faster cooling will proceed.

For food that has been effectively precooled to a low temperature, separation into small batches may be eliminated. Precooling to 60°F (15.6°C) or lower is desirable; the process should not take longer than 1 hour.

Precooling Methods

Precooling methods should be efficient. If the methods are slow, more harm than benefit may result. Ideally, the combined cooling from 140 to 45°F (60 to 7.2°C) outside and inside the refrigerator should be achieved in a maximum of 4 hours, preferably within 2 hours.

USING ROOM TEMPERATURE.   Precooling in the kitchen, at room temperature, is a deplorable, yet all too popular, practice. This method is unacceptable from a sanitation point of view, because the process is slow and temperature conditions favorable to bacterial multiplication are likely to be created. Furthermore, recontamination may occur easily when food is left for hours in a place as busy as a kitchen.

At best, temporary holding at room temperature may be applied to hot foods (above 140°F; 60°C) provided the batches are small and the holding times are brief, and provided the food is protected from contamination. These conditions usually cannot be fulfilled and dangerous conditions are created whenever potentially hazardous foods are allowed to precool on kitchen floors or other warm and unsuitable places. Research data are available to prove the microbial dangers of this practice (Black and Lewis, 1948; Lewis et al., 1953; Longrée and White, 1955; McDivitt and Hammer, 1958; Miller and Smull, 1955).

USING LOW-TEMPERATURE COOLANTS.   Low-temperature coolants that can be applied are ice, cold water, and cold air.

It is the responsibility of the foodservice manager or dietitian to set up the appropriate procedures and to see to it that they are carried out. It will take some experimentation on the part of the person in charge of food preparation to work out procedures to fit the refrigeration situation of his foodservice operation. If the refrigeration space available for the storage of cooked foods is such that refrigerators are easily overloaded and unduly warmed up when average or large loads are introduced, precooling must be carried to lower temperatures than would be necessary if refrigeration space were adequate.

Experimentation would also be necessary to determine the approximate cooling times for specific quantities of specific foods cooling in specific containers, because all these factors affect cooling times. Experimentation should be accurate and results reproducible. A reliable thermometer should be used and measurements made in the warmest part of the food mass. The combined cooling times outside the refrigerator and inside should be shorter than 4 hours. Factors affecting cooling are:

1. Type of food
2. Type of container
3. Amount placed in each container
4. Type of covering used
5. Length of time for which the food should be precooled, terminal temperature to be achieved in the warmest part of the food mass, and approximate location of the warmest part
6. Treatment following precooling

For solid foods, ice is a very practical coolant. The foods to be cooled should be placed in shallow layers in shallow pans or trays and covered as protection against contamination.

Some semisolid foods may lend themselves to precooling like a solid food item; others would have to be treated like fluid foods. The foodservice manager will need to make that decision.

For fluid foods, cold running water can be used successfully in precooling even when batch size is large. A prerequisite to successful cooling is that the water actually be cold, at least 70°F (21.1°C) or lower. In some areas or seasons, cold water is not as cold as is necessary for an effective cooling job. The importance of water temperature in precooling has been demonstrated by Moragne et al. (1959a), who found that the cooling times of the foods were prolonged one and a half times when the water temperature was increased from 35 to 42°F (1.7–5.6°C) and that, at a summer water temperature of 70°F (21.1°C), the food rarely cooled to below 75°F (23.9°C) and cooling proceeded at an extremely slow pace.

Steam-jacketed kettles can be constructed to be used as cooling kettles. Some manufacturers of steam-jacketed kettles make such equipment available. Cooling kettles should be designed and constructed in such a way that the coolant circulates all around the kettle. Special baffles installed between kettle and jacket are effective in directing the flow of the coolant. Finally, provision should be made for slowly agitating the food during cooling. Agitation is discussed in detail below.

Stockpots containing food to be precooled can be placed in sinks, in converted bains-marie, or in other water baths supplied with cold running water. Under practical conditions of foodservice, sinks are usually used for various other purposes in food preparation; therefore, the danger exists that sooner or later the stock pot containing the food will end on the kitchen floor and cooling will become an illusion. Also, the food would now become subjected to increased chances for contamination.

In contrast to a much used kitchen sink, a bain-marie converted to a water bath and supplied with cold water at a fast rate of flow is a very desirable piece of equipment (Moragne et al., 1959b). Preferably, all cooling equipment should be installed in a separate cooling room maintained at a low temperature. Food precooled should be agitated, at least at certain intervals, say every 15–20 minutes.

USING AGITATION.   Agitation is known to be a powerful tool in hastening heat transfer in fluid materials, including foods. Agitation is used extensively in heating of foods. Unfortunately, the foodservice industry has not made much use of agitation in cooling, probably because of force of habit to "simply refrigerate" or because of lack of suitable equipment to do the job.

To show the application of agitation in the precooling of fluid foods, some research data is now presented.

Manual Agitation. The beneficial effect of manual agitation on cooling times of white sauce was studied by Moragne et al. (1959b). White sauces were cooled in stock pots immersed in cold running water in a bain-marie water bath. Of the implements compared for effectiveness, a wire whip proved most efficient; however, this whip was not employed for whipping, but rather to remove the cooled portion of food away from the container wall, using a complete circle agitation technique. Intervals of agitation were 15 and 30 minutes. The two intervals achieved similar reductions in cooling time, approximating one-half the time required by the batches cooled without the use of agitation.

However, helpful as manual agitation may be, it cannot be expected to be very effective when applied to a large food mass.

Manual agitation with kitchen utensils such as whips, spoons, spatulas, and similar implements is not very effective in removing the layers of cold food which tend to build up on the inside wall of the vessel containing the food, and which interfere with the transfer of heat into the surrounding coolant. Agitation by hand increases labor cost. Also, agitation may be forgotten because of more pressing demands on employees. After all, an employee who fails to apply agitation in certain heating processes sees and smells the consequences of his negligence, whereas nothing so startling will happen when he or she omits agitation during cooling, for no one sees or smells the activity of food-poisoning bacteria.

Methods of rapidly cooling turkey stock were evaluated by Bryan and McKinley (1974). They cooled broth from an initial temperature of 160°F (71°C), in 2.4-gallon (8-liter) lots contained in 5-gallon (18.92-liter) stock pots by chilling them in the following ways: (1) placing the stock pot into a pan of ice; (2) placing the stock pot into a sink filled with running water; (3) placing the stock pot in a walk-in refrigerator (50°F, 10°C); (4) at room temperature; and (5) under continuous agitation. Batches undergoing treatments 1, 2, and 4 were stirred by hand every 5 minutes. Here are the results: In the icebath, the temperature dropped from 160 to 60°F in 42 minutes; cooling times of the batch cooled in running water were slightly longer. Mixing stock at low speed was of some aid in reducing cooling time. Storage in a refrigerator (no stirring, no mixing) was very slow, and so was, of course, cooling at room temperature.

Mechanical Agitation. Mechanical agitation has the advantage over manual agitation of being more efficient and more predictable.

The effect of mechanical agitation on cooling of puddings was studied by

McDivitt and Hammer (1958), who used an electric mixer at slow speed. The coolant in this case was therefore air of room temperature. The cooling times of the agitated batches were reduced as compared with those of unagitated ones. The 9-quart (8.5-liter) batches of pudding cooled from 142 to 77°F (61.1–25°C) in a 1¾-hour period of stirring.

Cooling effects of an agitator consisting of a cold tube which contained refrigerated water was studied by Longrée et al. (1960) and Moragne et al. (1961), using white sauce and pudding as foods. Cooling times were reduced to one-half or one-third of the time required by nonagitated batches.

The efficacy of the agitator was further improved by applying a scraper–lifter attachment as described by Moragne et al. (1963). The foods cooled were custards and puddings. Using this gadget, the cooling times of the foods were approximately one-sixth of the time needed to cool comparable batches in the conventional manner, namely, under refrigeration.

A difficulty encountered with fatty foods in tube cooling was solidification of the fat on the surface of the tube. An entirely different approach was tried; agitation was applied to foods while they were cooling in a refrigerator (Longrée et al., 1963). The refrigerator air served as the coolant, and the agitator used was a scraper-type gadget.

When 4-gallon (15.2-liter) batches of custard and pudding were scraper-agitated in a refrigerator of 37°F (2.8°C) air temperature, the times required for the foods to cool from 140 to 50°F (60–15.6°C) were reduced considerably. While nonagitated batches of custard cooled in 10.7 hours, equivalent batches, when agitated at 16 or 38 rpm, cooled in 3.8 and 3.5 hours, respectively. For puddings, the cooling times were 11 hours when not agitated; when agitated at 16 or 38 rpm, cooling times were 4 and 3.8 hours, respectively. The cooling times of 2-gallon (7.6-liter) batches of soups such as chowders, cream soups, navy bean soup, and vegetable soup, and of entrees such as chop suey and meat and vegetable stew, were upon agitation (at 38 rpm) reduced to one-third and one-fourth of the cooling times required by comparable unagitated batches. Use was made of the fact that properly designed scrapers are highly efficient in removing films from cooling surfaces and markedly improve the rates of heat transfer of viscous materials (Ackley, 1960).

There is a danger when using agitation of creating undesirable changes in the consistency of the foods; such changes may pertain to viscosity, to breaking up of solid ingredients, and the like. Therefore, it is essential that the rate of agitation be kept as low as is absolutely essential to achieve the desired degree of cooling. Nowrey et al. (unpublished) studied heat transfer in large agitated batches and found that rates of agitation below 10 rpm were sufficiently rapid. When purchasing a cooling kettle equipped with an agitator, it is essential to specify that the agitator be capable of being operated at very slow speeds and be of the scraper type. The importance of appropriate construction features which allow the cooling water to completely circulate around the food has been pointed out earlier.

It is the responsibility of foodservice management to make its needs known to the manufacturers of equipment. If there is sufficient demand, the manufacturing industry will endeavor to fill these needs. The initiative, however, must come from the foodservice industry.

For food that is to be refrigerated in single-service units, as is done when a cook/chill food system is used, rapid-chill cabinets in which high air velocity is used are available. As was suggested for rapid-freeze cabinets, the use of units that have the approval of the National Sanitation Foundation, Ann Arbor, Michigan, is recommended.

RECOMMENDATIONS. Provide appropriate and sufficient facilities for chilling.

Provide the facilities in locations where potentially hazardous food items are handled during preparation and service. Use these facilities. Do not hold food at kitchen temperature other than during actual manipulation.

Be sure that the air temperature of the refrigerator is below 40°F (4.4°C), but not cold enough for the food to freeze. Check temperature frequently, especially at times of peak load and low load; make adjustment if indicated.

Make provisions that ensure that cooked items do not remain in the hazardous temperature range of 45–140°F (7.2–60°C) for more than 2 hours, an absolute maximum being 4 hours. Remember that the safe temperature span is a composite of all the minutes for which the cooked food was exposed to bacteriologically hazardous temperatures.

To aid rapid cooling, do not introduce large food batches into the refrigerator, and keep batch size small.

Solid foods like whole cooked (steamed, simmered) turkeys may be cut into halves lengthwise and placed in single layers on trays to cool. When cut into smaller pieces, the poultry will cool faster yet. Leftover roasts and hams also will cool faster when not refrigerated whole, but when first cut into smaller portions and refrigerated in shallow layers on trays. Bones interfere with cooling. Unless meats and poultry have been deboned prior to cooking, the cooked items should, if possible, be deboned as an aid to fast transfer of heat. Deboning should be performed as soon as the cooked items have cooled sufficiently to be handled.

Precool foods to avoid overloading the refrigerator with warm food and to speed cooling. Solid foods are precooled on trays or shallow pans set on ice, fluid foods in stock pots immersed in very cold running water. Fluid food should be agitated at frequent and regular intervals. For large quantities, jacketed cooling kettles equipped with slow-speed scraper agitators and an efficient cooling system are appropriate.

Do not allow food to precool to room temperatures in the kitchen because cooling is very slow at the temperatures prevailing in the food preparation area. At 140°F (60°C) the hazardous temperature zone is entered, and food must be cooled down rapidly to at least 45°F (7.2°C), using efficient procedures.

Use cooked food held in cold storage as soon as possible. It is a desirable practice to limit holding time to 24 hours.

Food should be protected from recontamination at all times.

Cold Foods Dispensed from Vending Machines

Cold foods, such as milk, ice cream, pastries, pies, salads, sandwiches, meat items, combination platters, puddings, custards, cream-filled cakes, and many other potentially hazardous items sold through vending machines may be purchased from local sources or prepared in special commissaries.

According to the FDA recommendations for the vending of food and beverages (1978b),

> while being prepared, stored, loaded, displayed, or transported, food intended for sale through vending machines shall be protected from contamination by all agents, including dust, insects, rodents, unclean equipment and utensils, unnecessary handling, coughs, sneezes, flooding, draining, and overhead leakage or condensation.
>
> The temperature of potentially hazardous foods shall be 45°F (7.2°C) or below.
>
> Milk and fluid milk products offered for sale through vending machines shall be pasteurized, shall meet the Grade A quality standards as established by law, and shall be dispensed only in individual original containers.
>
> Milk and fluid milk products and fluid non-dairy products (creaming agents) shall not be dispensed in vending machines as additional ingredients in hot liquid beverages or other foods.

Further recommendations deal with packaging potentially hazardous items and proper temperature control.

> Potentially hazardous food offered for sale through vending machines shall be dispensed to the consumer in the individual, original container or package into which it was placed at the commissary or at the manufacturer's or processor's plant. Potentially hazardous food shall not be dispensed from bulk food machines.
>
> Potentially hazardous food shall be maintained at safe temperatures except as follows:
>
> (1) During necessary periods of preparation and packaging; and
>
> (2) During the actual time required to load or otherwise service the machine and for a maximum machine ambient temperature recovery period of 30 minutes following completion of loading or servicing operation.

Vending machines dispensing potentially hazardous food shall be provided with adequate refrigerating (or heating) units and thermostatic controls which insure the maintenance of safe temperatures at all times. Such vending machines shall also have automatic controls which prevent the machine from vending potentially hazardous food until serviced by the operator in the event of power failure, mechanical failure, or other condition which results in noncompliance with temperature requirements in the food storage compartment.

Potentially hazardous food that has failed to conform to the time–temperature requirements of this ordinance shall be removed from the vending machine, and be denatured or otherwise rendered unusable for human consumption.

Vending machines dispensing potentially hazardous food shall be provided with one of more thermometers which, to an accuracy of ±3° F (1.7° C) indicate the air temperature of the warmest part of the refrigerated food storage compartment, (or the coldest part of the heated food storage compartment, whichever is applicable).

In this writer's opinion, a temperature-recording device would be even more effective, since it would accurately determine the time–temperature conditions prevailing in the machine every minute of the day, every day of the week, and the record would be there for everyone to inspect.

According to Hartley (1975), recent improvements have been made in automatic cut-off controls, which inactivate vendors of perishable items when safe temperatures are not maintained for some reason.

Items to be consumed hot are reheated by the customers in special heating devices provided by the vendor. Although the vending company is responsible for the sanitation of the product and the machine, it is in the interest of the foodservice establishment where the machines are set up that the items dispensed be prepared under sanitary conditions and that strict time–temperature control be maintained throughout their preparation, transport, and holding in the machine. As has been pointed out by Tiedeman (1958), placing stacks of sandwiches prepared at room temperature in a cold compartment in the expectation that they will be cooled in a short time is no more than wishful thinking.

HANDLING AND HOLDING FOODS AT HAZARDOUS TEMPERATURES

During precooking operations, potentially hazardous foods are frequently held at kitchen temperatures for several hours. This is serious, since the temperature range of 70–100°F (21.1–37.8°C) is particularly favorable to bacterial multiplication of the pathogens capable of causing foodborne illnesses, except that the optimum temperature range for growth of *Clostridium perfringens* lies higher, 112–116°F (44.4–46.7°C).

The practice of holding foil-wrapped baked potatoes and vacuum-packed boiled potatoes at room temperature is a dangerous one; outgrowth of *Clos-*

tridium botulinum spores followed by the multiplication of new, toxin-producing vegetative cells is possible under such anaerobic, warm conditions if sufficient time is allowed (see Chapter 4).

Another menu item likely to be held at room temperature for long hours in order to preserve its texture is boiled rice. Hazard analyses in reference to *Bacillus cereus* in cooked rice have shown (Bryan et al., 1981) that whenever cooked rice was held at room temperature for a few hours, the temperatures were such that considerable growth of this microorganism could have occurred. Staggered preparation of small batches is advised.

Exact timing of the holding of perishable food items may seem to be a difficult task. Actually it is not, provided thoughtful and purposeful management is put to work and careful monitoring exercised.

Control measures, although varying in the details of execution, do not vary in principles. Therefore, food managers have to use their resourcefulness in putting this all-important principle to work in a manner suitable to the specific setup of the foodservice operations to which they lend their services. The principles underlying the control measures pertain to food prepared on the premises as well as to food prepared outside the foodservice establishment and transported to the place of service.

Recommendations (General)

Reduce to a minimum the time during which the potentially hazardous foods such as milk (fresh and reconstituted from powder), poultry, meat, eggs (fresh and reconstituted from powder), seafood, and all items made with milk, poultry, meat, eggs, and seafood are held at kitchen temperatures.

Move those operations that can be performed in an area other than the kitchen, to cool surroundings.

Stagger preparation procedures as much as is feasible. Keep potentially hazardous food cold (45°F; 7.2°C or lower); or hot (140°F; 60°C), except for required manipulations. Items which have been ground, sliced, shaped, mixed, or otherwise handled, are especially apt to be contaminated and should not be held at kitchen temperatures except for a brief period of time.

Food items transported from central kitchens and commissaries to places of service must be handled in a manner that assures that hot items remain hot, and cold foods cold.

In community foodservice, too, all highly perishable menu items that must be transported over long distances, or are for other reasons subjected to prolonged holding, need to be protected. If no provisions can be made to safeguard vulnerable food by effective temperature control, menu items should be chosen that are not likely to support bacterial growth well because of their low pH (Longrée et al., 1960).

Prepared Menu Items in Transit

Prepared menu items that are transported from central kitchens or commissaries to satellite establishments, contracting foodservices, or vending machines must be maintained at safe hot or cold temperatures. Insulated containers are used to control temperatures of food in transit. Their efficacy of performance should not be blindly trusted; rather, it should be ascertained under a variety of conditions. Temperature of the food at arrival is subjected to variables such as type of food, batch size, insulating capacity of the container, and ambient temperature. Measurements should be repeatedly made on food temperatures at the time of departure and arrival. Such checks are to be made at different seasons. Warm and hot weather is apt to endanger the chilled items; winter weather, the hot items. Air-conditioned trucks, because of their expense, are not used as widely as is desirable. Attention must also be given to the fact that closeness of hot and chilled food in transit may cause undesirable transfer of heat from hot to chilled items and vice versa.

Recommendations (Specific Hazardous Items)

Sandwiches made with potentially hazardous ingredients (e.g., meat, poultry, egg, fish):

1. Use ingredients of excellent sanitary quality.
2. Prepare sandwiches from cold ingredients, except butter, which should be soft for spreading.
3. Maintain hands, working surfaces, equipment, and utensils in sanitary condition.
4. Work rapidly to minimize time during which ingredients and sandwiches remain at hazardous temperatures.
5. Stagger production: place finished sandwiches on shallow trays no more than approximately 3 or 4 inches high; refrigerate. Start a new batch.

Salads made with potentially hazardous ingredients:

1. Use ingredients of excellent sanitary quality. A minimum of handling is essential to keep them sanitary. For example, deboning poultry before cooking reduces the chances for contaminating the meat after it has been cooked.
2. Have ingredients chilled.
3. Maintain hands, working surfaces, equipment, and utensils in sanitary condition.

4. Incorporate part of the acid dressing into potentially hazardous ingredients immediately after these have been handled and, probably, contaminated (see Chapter 10).
5. Work rapidly and stagger production, thereby minimizing the time for which ingredients remain at hazardous temperatures.
6. Chill promptly in shallow pans.

Nourishments made with uncooked eggs: nourishments involving uncooked eggs, such as eggnog, are usually prepared for the sick, convalescent, or otherwise invalid. Special precautions in preparation and service of nourishments are in order because these persons are particularly sensitive to salmonellae. The pathogens may cling to the outside of shell eggs, and are occasionally present in the inside of shell eggs also. Even tiny pieces of shell falling into the broken-out egg may contaminate the nourishment with salmonellae. Processed eggs made from properly pasteurized eggs should be free from salmonellae unless the products are recontaminated after pasteurization, which, unfortunately, has occasionally happened. If nourishments involving egg are prescribed at all, these precautions are recommended:

1. Commercial eggnog mixes manufactured for hospital use should be employed when preparing nourishment—not shell eggs, frozen eggs, and powdered eggs intended for general kitchen use.
2. The dry eggnog mix should be kept in a closed container, protected from contamination.
3. Advance preparation of the liquid nourishment should be kept to a minimum period of time. The shorter the time between reconstitution of the dry mix and consumption of the product, the fewer are the chances for bacterial contamination and growth. Egg mixtures are excellent media for bacterial multiplication.
4. Nourishments should not be allowed to remain on patients' bedstands beyond the time when they have warmed up. Once warm, such aids to health may become the opposite of what they are intended to be—they may become a menace.

A bacteriological study of liquid nourishments in hospitals was made by Sperber et al. (1969).

Leftovers:

1. Plan to have no or little food left over. Leftovers can be wasteful and are a bacteriological hazard; they are handled often and are thus subjected to many chances for contamination. Moreover, leftovers are usually subjected to various cycles of holding, cooling, and warming and are often held for many hours at temperatures at which bacteria may multiply.

2. Stagger menu item production of combination items involving protein-aceous ingredients such as poultry, meat, egg, fish, and seafood with cream sauces, gravies, and the like. Keep the hazardous ingredients refrigerated and add to hot sauces as needed.
3. Before storage reheat lukewarm leftovers to boiling, if possible, or to at least 165°F (74°C) to destroy contaminants; precool and refrigerate. This rule applies in particular to items which come back from counters and the like.
4. Precool and refrigerate leftover items following the methods stated above under Recommendations (General).
5. Use leftovers within a day.

FOODS HELD IN HOT-HOLDING EQUIPMENT

The recommendations of the FDA (1978a) are as follows:

> Enough conveniently located hot food storage facilities shall be provided to assure the maintenance of food at the required temperature during storage. Each hot food facility storing potentially hazardous food shall be provided with a numerically scaled indicating thermometer, accurate to ±3° F[±1.67° C], located to measure the air temperature in the coolest part of the facility and located to be easily readable. Recording thermometers, accurate to ±3° F [±1.67° C], may be used in lieu of indicating thermometers. Where it is impractical to install thermometers on equipment such as bainmaries, steam tables, steam kettles, heat lamps, cal-rod units, or insulated food transport carriers, a product thermometer must be available and used to check internal food temperature.

> The internal temperature of potentially hazardous foods requiring hot storage shall be 140° F [60° C] or above except during necessary periods of preparation. Potentially hazardous food to be transported shall be held at a temperature of 140° F [60° C] or above.

Menu items that cannot tolerate holding at this temperature without serious damage to their culinary quality—for example, hollandaise—should be made in small quantities to ensure that they are consumed within a 2-hour period. If they are not used, they must be discarded.

When placed in hot-holding equipment, items should be at temperatures considerably above 140°F (60°C). Hot-holding equipment is principally designed to keep food hot rather than to heat it. Test food temperatures, using a thermometer. Careful monitoring is important.

Steam Tables

Blaker (1961) observed the temperatures at which hot foods were being held in four types of foodservice establishments, including a college pay cafeteria, a commercial cafeteria, an industrial cafeteria, and a table-service dining room. She surveyed the kind of hot-holding equipment being used and recorded visible quality changes in the foods held, changes in color and consistency, surface drying, scum formation, and the like. The types of steam tables used included the "wet" as well as the electric "dry" kind. She found that the temperatures of foods brought to the steam table at 160°F (71.1°C) or above remained well above 140°F (60°C) for an extended holding period, 45 minutes or longer.

In separate laboratory studies, longer holding periods were applied to determine the effectiveness of the steam tables in maintaining temperatures. The menu items studied included cream soups, meats, potatoes, and "made" entrees and/or baked vegetables. It was found that if the foods were placed on the steam table at 170°F (76.7°C) or above, their temperatures gradually declined, but seldom did they drop below 140°F (60°C) within a 2-hour holding period, provided the steam was not turned off during holding.

It was found that the wet steam table was efficient in maintaining temperatures with minimum damage to the quality of the menu items studied. However, wet steam tables are often not operated at temperatures necessary to maintain safe temperatures in the foods, sometimes because of a tendency of the steam to escape around the inserts. Blaker calls attention to the situation and recommends that methods should be investigated for sealing sectored surfaces. It seems that the buyers and users of such equipment should make their dissatisfaction known to the manufacturing industry, and insist on equipment that can be operated at the capacity necessary to produce safe temperatures without creating a nuisance to employees and guests.

Other Hot-Holding Equipment

Blaker (1962) determined the temperatures of food items held warm in hot-holding equipment other than steam tables. The equipment included these types: electric holding cabinet, bain-marie, steam-jacketed kettle, top of range (solid grill top; open burner), and steamer. When such primary equipment was converted to keep food hot prior to being served, the following conditions were fulfilled: ovens and steam-jacketed kettles were turned off, solid-grill-top range units were turned low, and open-burner range units were turned low or were turned off.

These important observations were made on the temperatures of items subjected to holding: Items that had been prepared in one continuous cooking operation were at high temperatures, 170°F (76.7°C) or above. However, those prepared from ingredients that had been precooked, then cooled, and finally reheated prior to being served were at low temperatures, 140°F (60°C) or even lower.

In food prepared in one continuous operation and at an approximate temperature of 170°F (76.7°C) or above, and held in electric holding cabinets set at 175°F (79.4°C), the temperature rarely fell below 140°F (60°C) during prolonged (1½ hours) holding. However, in cabinets set at 150°F (65.6°C), the food temperatures often decreased to temperatures as low as 130°F (54.4°C).

In primary cooking equipment used as "makeshift" hot-holding equipment, food temperatures were observed to be fairly adequately maintained. The open-burner range was the least satisfactory primary equipment used for hot-holding because of severe changes in quality, whereas the solid grill top did a more satisfactory job in maintaining adequate temperatures without such severe quality changes.

In summary, the studies showed that both conventional hot-holding equipment and primary cooking equipment used for hot holding were capable of keeping cooked food items at temperatures of 140°F (60°C) and higher for a prolonged period of time, 1½ hours at least, provided the initial temperature of the food was at least 170°F (76.7°C). Therefore, a special effort must be made to reheat all precooked and cooled foods to 170°F (76.7°C) before they are allowed to go into hot-holding equipment.

Recommendations

Plan menu item production to keep hot-holding time at a minimum, insure bacteriological quality, and retain nutritive value as well as other culinary quality characteristics such as color, texture, and flavor.

Be sure the food is hot, preferably near 170°F (76.7°C), before it goes into the hot-holding equipment. Do not use hot-holding equipment for heating lukewarm foods.

Maintain hot-holding equipment in good working condition. Check its heat-holding capacity periodically using a thermometer placed in the coolest portion of the batch at the beginning and close of hot holding; perform this test on various types of foods prepared by different heating procedures. Repeat the tests in order to obtain typical, average temperature values. Food temperature should be maintained at 140°F (60°C) during holding.

Special equipment for maintaining proper temperature of large roasts of beef, which also prevents surface dehydration, was designed by Berry and Dickerson (1975). A stainless deep-well serving pan was installed in the wet-well opening of the serving table. The pan could be raised as the roast was sliced away. Thermal protection is afforded by the pan for the sides of the roast and an infrared lamp or lamps keep the surface of the meat protected. The temperature(s) of the wet well and the number and distance(s) of the lamp(s) are specified for accurate performance.

Hot Foods Dispensed from Vending Machines

The recommendations of the Food and Drug Administration (1978b) are, in general, similar for cold and hot foods. Units should be in good operating order, ensuring maintenance of the required temperatures at all times; for hot food this temperature is 140°F (60°C). Vending machines should have automatic controls to prevent the machine from vending potentially hazardous foods in the event of power failure.

Concerning the vending of hot foods, the trend is toward dispensing most items to be consumed hot (except some canned items, such as soups) in the chilled state and to have patrons reheat their selections in microwave ovens. The cavities and door edges of microwave ovens must be cleaned at least once a day with nonabrasive cleaners.

COOKING FOODS

Many menu items, but not all, are heated sufficiently to render them free from pathogens if these should be present.

End Point of Heating Adequate to Destroy Pathogens

At this time, it is almost universally accepted that for all practical purposes, internal temperatures of 165–170°F (73.9–76.7°C) in food will be sufficient for the effective reduction in number, or even elimination, of nonspore-forming pathogens such as the salmonellae and staphylococci. The spores of *Clostridium perfringens* are most probably not eliminated by such heat treatments; nonheat-resistant spores of this organism have been demonstrated to survive, at least in part, an exposure to 176°F (80°C) for 10 minutes. The spores of heat-resistant strains of this organism may endure prolonged boiling for as much as several hours. Fecal streptococci in food heated to terminal temperatures of 165–170°F (73.9–76.7°C) also may survive, in part.

The degree of heating applied in many routinely used cooking methods eliminates pathogenic contaminants and parasites such as trichinae from menu items, as shown in Chapter 11. In thoroughly heated menu items, the pathogens might be killed, but bacterial toxins preformed in the food are not necessarily eliminated by this heating. Heating spores of *C. perfringens* up to 176°F (80°C) may simply heat-shock them, thus stimulating them to subsequent germination (Hall and Angelotti, 1965). Moreover, food sterilized by heating and subjected to recontamination would be an excellent medium for pathogens that are sensitive to microbial competitors, such as *Staphylococcus aureus*.

It is therefore evident that even thorough heating is not a cure-all, rather a supportive sanitary measure.

Microbial death under conditions of microwave heating was discussed in Chapter 12.

Recommendations

Items that do not suffer a decrease in culinary quality upon heating to high temperatures should be heated to 165–170°F (73.9–76.7°C). Metal stem-type numerically scaled indicating thermometers, accurate to ±2°F (±1.1°C) are recommended by the FDA (1978a), to check the temperature reached.

In cases in which heating to safe temperatures is not applicable, the control measures directed at preventing bacterial contamination and bacterial multiplication can and must be used effectively.

Items Given Mild Heat Treatments, Routinely or Arbitrarily

It was shown in Chapter 11 that certain menu items are routinely or occasionally heated to temperature end points that would not ensure the elimination of pathogens. Among these are bulky items such as hams and stuffed turkeys.

Under discussion are those items that are apt to be contaminated with pathogens, and items that are potentially hazardous because of their composition and previous history, or items that are hazardous for a combination of these reasons.

For the sake of discussing appropriate control measures, the food likely to receive mild heating to unsafe terminal temperatures is categorized as follows:

1. The item becomes less desirable or attractive or is completely ruined when heated to high temperatures; mild heating is applied by the cook on purpose.
2. The item is bulky and penetration of heat to the center is slow; unless an effort is made to ascertain the internal temperatures reached and a thermometer is used, the cook does not know how hot the center has become; heating is haphazard.
3. The item is cold when heating is started and the heat source is intense (broiler, very hot oven); the cook uses as the end point of heating the appearance of the outside; the center may become hot or just lukewarm; heating is haphazard.
4. Cold ingredients are incorporated into a warm base resulting in a lukewarm mixture; the combined mixture, unless purposely reheated to a definite safe end point, may never get hot; heating is haphazard.

MEATS COOKED TO THE RARE STAGE.   Meats, especially beef, are frequently cooked to the rare stage, a terminal temperature of 130–140°F (54.4–60°C) or even lower. The inside of roasts that have not been deboned or otherwise handled should not pose a sanitary problem. Rolled roasts, however, may be contaminated on the inside because of the handling they have received. This is true for the meat and the meat juice.

Contaminants may resume multiplication as soon as the meat has sufficiently cooled to make this possible and will continue this activity until the temperature has dropped to below 45°F (7.2°C). Rare, deboned, and rolled roasts may contain spores of *Clostridium perfringens;* they may also be contaminated with salmonellae, *Campylobacter jejuni,* and *Clostridium perfringens,* which may survive this heat treatment (see Chapter 4). According to Blankenship (1978), a heavy inoculum of *Salmonella typhimurium* was not always eliminated by cooking the roasts to 137–147.5°F (58.3–64.1°C).

Recommendations.   A hazard analysis of roast beef preparation in foodservice establishments was made by Bryan and McKinley (1979), and control measures for the production of roasts were suggested. Since raw beef must be expected to be contaminated with foodborne pathogens, no matter where the contamination has occurred, any mishandling and neglect of strict time–temperature control may lead to an outbreak of foodborne illness. The above authors assessed opportunities for survival of foodborne pathogens during cooking and reheating, postcooking contamination, and bacterial multiplication during the holding of cooked meat at room temperature, hot-holding, refrigerator storage, and reheating, as practiced in several different types of foodservice operations. It was found that besides raw beef, dry beef-jus mix and workers' hands contributed pathogens. Surface bacteria in the vegetative stage were killed during cooking, with one exception. Geometric centers of roasts, other than those barbecued, seldom reached time–temperature values lethal to vegetative food-borne pathogens, but postoven rise in temperature was an aid in reducing survivors.

Hot storage tends to decrease the number of vegetative survivors, but may lead to germination of spores. The authors suggest that sterilized thermometers should be used to make sure that the geometric center of hot-stored roasts does not drop below 130°F (54°C). Temperatures favorable for bacterial activity also prevailed when roasts were held at room temperature or refrigerated in large bulk. The authors feel that rapid cooling is one of the most critical control procedures for roast beef operations. One procedure suggested is to wrap roasts and store them singly away from other warm roasts, or cut them to reduce their bulk.

For reheating roasts, the authors suggest:

1. For rolled roasts and roasts that have been fabricated of chunk and ground meat, cut roast into portions, wrap these in foil, and reheat the portions to at least 71.1°C (160°F). The use of this type of leftover roast in stews and similar dishes is also recommended; for these, a final temperature of at least 73.9°C (165°F) is indicated.
2. For leftover whole cuts of beef that are not subjected to internal contamination, pasteurization of the roasts' surface is suggested. Several surface-penetrating procedures were found effective:
   a. Immersing whole roasts in boiling stock, or reheating roasts in stock, up to the boiling point.
   b. Heating foil-wrapped whole roasts or slices of roasted meat in an oven of at least 325°F (162.7°C).
   c. Heating whole roasts or sliced, individual portions, in boiling-water-heated steam tables for at least 1 hour.
   d. Immersing slices of roast in hot (92.8–100°C; 199–212°F) jus.
   e. Heating slices of beef in enclosed steam-injected steamers.

With these methods, the authors state that heat will not penetrate deeply and the interior of the roast can be kept medium rare. These recommendations, which were made by Bryan and McKinley (1979) following the hazard analysis of roast beef preparation in several foodservice establishments, deserve attention.

The same authors (1980) also analyzed the microbiological hazards connected with the handling of roast beef jus. The analysis pointed to holding at warm temperatures as a dangerous practice. Control measures suggested are rapid cooling, as well as reheating, of jus and gravy.

It was pointed out in Chapter 11 that heating meat to 140°F (60°C) does not allow meat to have the rare appearance so cherished by persons who wish to see a bright red color in rare beef. As was stated, time–temperature relationships affecting death of bacteria, and time–temperature relationships determining changes in the color of beef muscle (myoglobin) from red to gray, are different. Therefore, by carefully adjusting heating times and temperature, it was possible to work out roasting times for roasts of specific weight which result in a safe product of "rare" appearance. The cooking requirements, as presented in the *Federal Register* (1978) by the Food Safety and Quality Service of the USDA, are given below:

Cooking Requirements for Cooked Beef and Roast Beef

(a) Cooked beef and roast beef shall be prepared by a cooking procedure that produces a minimum temperature of 145°F (63°C) in all parts of each roast or prepared as provided in paragraphs (b) and (c) of this section.

(b) Cooked beef may also be prepared by any one of the cooking procedures described in the following table and in paragraphs (c)(1) and (d), and roast beef may also be prepared by any one of the cooking procedures described in the following tables and in paragraph (c)(2) and (d) provided that the procedure produces and maintains the minimum temperature required, in all parts of each roast, for at least the stated period:

(c)(1) Bag cook: each roast to be moist cooked shall be placed in a moisture impermeable film, either vacuum packaged or excess air removed, and the bag sealed prior to immersion cooking in a water bath or cooking in an oven.

(2)(i) Unbagged cook (netted or racked roasts): Roasts processed entirely by dry heat must weigh 10 pounds or more before processing and must be dry cooked in an oven maintained at 250°F (121°C) or higher throughout the process; or

(ii) An oven temperature less than 250°F (121°C) may be used for dry cooking of roasts of any size provided that the relative humidity, as measured in either the chamber or exit vent of the oven in which they are prepared, is greater than 90 percent for at least 25 percent of the total cooking time for the process, but in no case for a lesser period than 1 hour. This relative humidity may be achieved by use of steam injection or by sealed ovens capable of producing and maintaining the required 90 percent relative humidity.

(d) A processor who selects any of the alternative procedures specified in paragraphs (b) and (c) of this section must have equipment designed to insure that beef roasts do not contact each other during processing and shall have sufficient monitoring equipment to assure that the time (within 1 minute), temperature

Alternative Processing Procedures for Cooked Beef and Roast Beef

Minimum Internal Temperature		Minimum Processing Time in Minutes
°F	°C	
130	54.4	121
131	55.0	97
132	55.6	77
133	56.1	62
134	56.7	47
135	57.2	37
136	57.8	32
137	58.4	24
138	58.9	19
139	59.5	15
140	60.0	12
141	60.6	10
142	61.1	8
143	61.7	6
144	62.2	5

(within 1°F), and relative humidity (within 5 percent) limits required by this process are being met. The processor shall provide proper recording devices, and make the data from these available to the Food Safety and Quality Service inspection officials upon request, as provided in Part 320 of the regulations in this subchapter. Continuous recording devices with the prescribed accuracies will be acceptable for all products prepared under paragraphs (a) and (b).

MEAT LOAF, POT ROAST, GRAVY, JUS.   Treat the products made from ground meat like rolled roasts since they must be expected to be contaminated all the way through. Meat loaf and meat patties have been shown to be acceptable when heated to a medium rare stage and they are frequently served that way.

For beef pot roast production it is recommended that large roasts be exposed to hazardous temperatures for the briefest time only. Also, cooling should be speeded by quartering the roasts and quick-chilling them promptly (Powers and Munsey, 1980).

To cool gravy and jus, separate them from meat, reheat to boiling, then cool rapidly to safe temperatures. Before reusing, reheat to boiling.

SHELLFISH.   Oysters, clams, and mussels are usually lightly heated to preserve their culinary quality, and much seafood is eaten raw. Therefore, one must not rely on heating as an effective measure in the control of pathogenic contaminants.

Recommendations.   Procure shellfish from sources approved by the State Shellfish Authority; if the source is outside the state, the source must be certified by the state of origin. Keep shellfish cold, near 32°F (0°C) as long as feasible. Stagger production for lightly heated menu items and reduce hot-holding to a minimum. Avoid having leftovers.

EGGS AND PRODUCTS MADE WITH EGG.   Shell eggs, unless dirty and/or cracked, should be free from salmonellae and therefore may be given mild heat treatment in preparing boiled, poached, fried, and scrambled eggs and sauces.

In the food preparation area, contamination of products with salmonellae from the shells of eggs is a possibility that should not be overlooked.

All processed eggs must be pasteurized to remove salmonellae. However, recontamination is a possibility.

Hard-cooked eggs should be cooled in freshly drawn, uncontaminated water, since penetration of contaminants into the shell is possible.

Scrambled eggs can be heated up to 180°F (82.2°C), or a dry stage, then remoistened through incorporation of a medium white sauce; for 50 servings of egg use 1 quart (0.946 liter) of sauce. Also, baked scrambled eggs can be moistened by serving them with a creole sauce.

Hollandaise is now fortunately excluded from the menu list of most institutions. It is a very hazardous item, consisting largely of egg and butter, slightly acidified with lemon juice. It is an excellent medium for bacterial growth, and does not tolerate high heat. Therefore, heating as a control measure is not applicable to this potentially dangerous sauce. As a control measure its holding time must be kept very brief, 2 hours at the most, and when the specified time has gone by, the unused portion must be discarded.

For *custards, cream fillings, and puddings,* the procedures directed toward rendering these vulnerable items safe from pathogens that might be present involve heating to high terminal temperatures and/or prolonged heating. Not all procedures routinely used ensure that the egg is thoroughly cooked. In these potentially unsafe procedures, the egg is added at the end of the cooking period, after the other ingredients have been cooked to doneness. This conventional and much used procedure for making custards, fillings, and puddings is the "three-step method." The milk is heated (no definite terminal temperature is usually given); the starch and suger are added and the mixture cooked until it has thickened; finally the egg is incorporated, the end point of cooking being usually brief and uncertain. In the two-step method, developed by Billings et al. (1952), the egg is added early and higher temperatures as well as longer cooking times are assured. In this method, three-fourths of the milk, all the sugar, and the salt are heated to 190–200°F (87.8–93.5°C) and a suspension prepared from one-fourth of the milk, all the starch, and the egg are added to the hot milk. This method is applicable to custards, fillings, and puddings. The studies on custards made by Miller et al. (1961) showed that in a steam-jacketed kettle higher terminal temperatures were achieved than in a bain-marie, the terminal temperatures being 180 and 170°F (82.2 and 76.7°C), respectively. In the steam-jacketed kettle, the steam pressure had to be kept low to prevent scorching. Fillings cooked in a steam-jacketed kettle had terminal temperatures of 172–182°F (77.8–83.3°C) (Billings et al., 1952).

Meringued pies are items which are often lightly heated in the interior portion because the cooks are interested in producing a pretty meringue. Brief heating at high oven temperature could be hazardous, because this procedure results in undercooking of the lower portion of the meringue. An attractive and safe meringue may be produced by using a procedure worked out by Mallman and co-workers (1963); the meringue should be placed on a hot (approximately 158°F, 70°C) filling, and the pie baked at 325°F (162.7°C) for 24 minutes or at 350°F (176.7°C) for 16 minutes.

Custard-filled puffs and eclairs can be rendered safe by pasteurization, *Staphylococcus aureus* being known to be a potential, hazardous contaminant of such items. It is recommended procedure that the filled pastries be rebaked at an oven temperature of at least 425°F (218.3°C) for at least 20 minutes, followed by prompt cooling to 45°F (7.2°C).

Recommendations. Use high-quality, clean, sound-shelled eggs. Prevent contamination of eggs broken out of the shell, and of eggs reconstituted from powder, and do not allow them to remain at lukewarm temperatures for any length of time, because of danger from bacterial multiplication; use promptly, or keep refrigerated until used. The heating recommendations presented below will be an aid to achieving either high terminal temperatures or long heating times at moderate temperatures. The methods are effective in reducing or eliminating bacteria in the cooking process. Menu items in which egg is used as a binder should be baked in shallow layers to insure complete heat penetration.

Hollandaise: Stagger production. Discard portion not used within 2 hours.

Custards, cream fillings: Use the two-step method of preparation as described in the text, which involves incorporating the egg early in the cooking process so that it receives a thorough heat treatment.

Meringued pies: Place filling in shells while filling is hot (at least 158°F; 70°C); use the hot-process method for preparing meringue, which involves incorporating the sugar as a hot syrup; bake the pies at a moderate temperature, 325 or 350°F (162.7 or 176.7°C) for 24 or 16 minutes, respectively.

TURKEY.   The dangers of the practice of stuffing and roasting large turkeys are discussed in Chapter 11.

The only control measure recommended is that large turkeys should not be stuffed for several reasons. (1) Bacteriological safety. The cavity of the turkey is apt to be contaminated with salmonellae; if the bird is roasted without stuffing, the heat penetrates easily into the cavity and kills the contaminants, whereas the temperatures prevailing in the stuffing during roasting may even allow bacterial multiplication. (2) Labor is saved. (3) The finished product looks neat and is easy to portion and serve. (4) Cooking time is short. (5) The cavity of the bird cannot possibly accommodate all the stuffing needed for the number of servings which the turkey itself provides; therefore, additional dressing must be baked outside the turkey. (6) Heat penetration is fast in stuffing baked in pans. Even potentially hazardous stuffings, such as those made with giblets, oysters, and so on, can be heat treated efficiently when baked in separate pans.

Recommendations.   Do not stuff turkey. Bake dressing in separate, shallow pans to an internal temperature of at least 165–170°F (73.9–76.7°C). Cook turkeys to an internal temperature of at least 165°F (74°C). Higher temperatures are recommended for breast meat (170–180°F; 77–82°C), and for thighs 180–185°F (82–85°C). Detailed recommendations for time–temperature control of thawing, cooking, chilling, and reheating turkeys in school lunch kitchens were made by Bryan and McKinley (1974); see Chapter 14.

Hams. Hams are available untenderized or tenderized, and may be labeled partially cooked, fully cooked, or ready to eat (see Chapter 6). The minimum heat treatment for the cooked hams required by USDA regulations is 150°F (65.6°C), which is adequate to destroy trichinae, but not necessarily all bacterial pathogens.

Recommendations. Heat all hams to an internal temperature of 165–170°F (73.9–76.7°C).

Cold Precooked Items Requiring Terminal Heating. In this group are included the "made" dishes, meat, poultry and fish pies, casseroles, croquettes, meat cakes, fish cakes, and the like. Leftovers served hot, and combination items made with leftovers and served hot, belong here. The group includes precooked frozen foods such as meat pies and chicken pies.

The ingredients used in the preparation of these items are usually handled considerably in the course of their preparation, and adequate time–temperature control is often wanting. Use of leftovers may pose a special problem because of their history, which may include long exposures to lukewarm temperatures during their previous preparation, holding, cooling, and subsequent rewarming. It is sound thinking to assume that all these items have been contaminated, probably with pathogens, before they are served. The extent to which heating should be carried varies somewhat with the ingredients. Certainly, all menu items should attain internal temperatures of at least 165°F (73.9°C), and items made with meat should be brought to boiling, if feasible.

In light of research data on *Clostridium perfringens* (Hall and Angelotti, 1965), it is necessary to require that all meats, especially beef, and menu items made with beef should be reheated to boiling if at all feasible. This precaution, however, is not effective toward heat-resistant strains. As has been reported earlier, a high percentage of meats must be expected to be contaminated with *C. perfringens*. Cooked meats and gravy may prove contaminated because of survival of heat-resistant spores or because of recontamination after cooking with the spores and vegetative cells of this organism.

To achieve the desired internal temperatures in the food without ruining the outside portion, it is often necessary to apply moderate temperatures and longer heating times. The internal temperatures should be checked in the coldest portion of the food with an accurate thermometer.

"Running under the broiler" is the worst way to reheat food, and "bubbling at the top" and "browning" are the most unreliable criteria for determining the end point of heating required to kill pathogenic contaminants.

In a well-managed foodservice establishment where standardized quantities, procedures, equipment, and temperatures are used, it should not prove difficult to work out specific directions for the reheating of cold precooked menu items and frozen precooked items. Some experimentation on the part of the manager or dietitian will have to precede the setting up of appropriate workable directions that should result in a safe and otherwise acceptable product. (See also Chapter 14.)

It may not prove feasible to achieve terminal temperatures of 165°F (73.9°C) or above in items fried in deep fat (see Chapter 11), such as croquettes and crab cakes. Control measures applicable to all foods, but of specific aid here, are: Provide and use only ingredients of the highest sanitary quality. Keep them cold until ready for heating. Prepare mixtures, cool if required, shape, bread, heat, and serve with a time span sufficiently brief to prevent bacterial multiplication. Apply time–temperature control measures using your knowledge of bacterial growth and good judgment.

Recommendations. Items made with beef should be heated to boiling, if at all feasible. All other items should be heated to at least 165–170°F (73.9–76.7°C) internal temperature.

Items that are heated in deep fat may not reach internal temperatures sufficiently high to kill contaminants. Use every precaution to prevent contamination, and exercise strict time–temperature control. Use high-quality ingredients, *do not use leftovers,* minimize contamination from hands during shaping, keep shaped items cold until ready to heat, and heat in small quantities for immediate service.

CREAMED ITEMS. When preparing cream soups and creamed entrees, danger exists that the cold solid ingredients, when incorporated into the cream base, may create temperature conditions in the combined mixture that are conducive to bacterial multiplication. The problem is greater in connection with entrees than soups, heat transfer being rather easily achieved in soups. It is essential that the combined mixture be reheated at once. In cases where reheating to 165–170°F (73.9–76.7°C) proves difficult because of poor heat transfer, the procedure of mixing the cream base and solid ingredients has to be staggered. It is absolutely essential that the temperature of food before it goes to the hot-holding equipment be well above 140°F (60°C), preferably 160°F (71.1°C) or higher, in order to have it remain at the required temperature of 140°F (60°C) during the holding period. It must be remembered that the solid ingredients incorporated into the cream base have frequently undergone considerable handling, deboning, cutting, and cubing. Therefore, if it was not reheated to at least 165°F (73.9°C) and bacterial kill was not achieved, the mixture will harbor these contaminants. Holding at 140°F (60°C) will prevent their multiplication, true, but the potential danger remains.

Leftover creamed items must be reheated to at least 165°F (73.9°C) and then cooled rapidly to a safe temperature, 45°F (7.2°C) or below. Store below

40°F (4.4°C) and use within a day. In many foodservice operations, it is required that creamed leftovers be discarded.

Recommendations. Have cream sauce as hot as possible. Use only ingredients of excellent sanitary quality. *Do not use leftovers.* Reheat the mixture to 165–170°F (73.9–76.7°C); in the coolest part of the batch the temperature should never be below 140°F (60°C). Stagger production unless you are sure you will serve the entire batch. Creamed items are particularly poor risks as leftovers. Creamed leftovers, if any, should be discarded.

RICE. Rice is frequently contaminated with spores of *Bacillus cereus* which survive the cooking procedures applied to rice. Since cooked rice kernels have a tendency to stick together when chill-stored, cooked leftover rice is often held over at room temperature. This provides favorable conditions for outgrowth of surviving spores and the production of a population of vegetative cells which may multiply to large numbers, accompanied by the formation of heat-stable toxins.

Recommendations. Prepare rice in small quantities as needed. Keep cooked rice hot (140°F; 60°C) until it is served. Manage production to avoid having rice left over. Chill leftover rice quickly, refrigerate, and reheat thoroughly before using it.

REFERENCES

Ackley, E. J. (1960). "Film coefficients of heat transfer for agitated process vessels." *Chem. Eng.,* 67:133.

Berry, M. R., Jr. and R. W. Dickerson, Jr. (1975). "Apparatus for maintaining holding temperature while serving cafeteria rounds of beef." *J. Food Sci.,* 40:1095–1096.

Billings, M. N., A. M. Briant, K. Longrée, and K. W. Harris (1952). "Cream pie fillings prepared in multiples of an eight-pie batch." *J. Am. Diet. Assoc.,* 28:228–229.

Black, L. C. and M. N. Lewis (1948). "Effect on bacterial growth of various methods of cooling cooked foods." *J. Am. Diet. Assoc.,* 24:399–404.

Blaker, G. (1961). "Holding temperatures and food quality." *J. Am. Diet. Assoc.,* 38:450–454.

Blaker, G. (1962). "Holding hot foods before they come to the steam table." Unpublished paper presented at the 90th Annual Meeting of the American Public Health Association, Miami Beach, FL. Oct.

Blankenship, L. C. (1978). "Survival of a *Salmonella typhimurium* experimental contaminant during cooking of beef roasts." *Appl. Environ. Microbiol.,* 35:1160–1165.

Bryan, F. L. and T. W. McKinley (1974). "Prevention of foodborne illness by time–temperature control of thawing, cooking, chilling, and reheating turkeys in school lunch kitchens." *J. Milk Food Technol.,* 37:420–429.

Bryan, F. L. and T. W. McKinley (1979). "Hazard analysis and control of roast beef preparation in foodservice establishments." *J. Food Prot.,* 42:4–18.

Bryan, F. L. and T. W. McKinley (1980). "Hazard analysis and control of roast beef jus preparation in foodservice establishments." *J. Food Prot.*, 43:512–513; 519.

Bryan, F. L., C. A. Bartleson, and N. Christopherson (1981a). "Hazard analysis in reference to *Bacillus cereus*, of boiled and fried rice in Cantonese-style restaurants." *J. Food Prot.*, 44:500–512.

Bryan, F. L., M. Harvey, and M. Misup (1981b). "Hazard analysis of party-pack foods prepared at a catering establishment." *J. Food Prot.*, 44:118–123.

Dickerson, R. W., Jr. and R. B. Reed (1968). "Calculation and measurement of heat transfer in foods." *Food Technol.*, 22:1533–1535; 1545–1548.

Federal Register (1978). 43:30793, July 18.

Food and Drug Administration (1978a). *Food Service Sanitation Manual.* U.S. Department of Health, Education and Welfare, Public Health Serv. DHEW Publ. No. (FDA) 78–2081. Washington, D.C.

Food and Drug Administration. (1978b). *The Vending of Food and Beverages.* U.S. Department of Health, Education and Welfare, Public Health Serv. DHEW Publ. No. (FDA) 78–2091. Washington, D.C.

Hall, H. E. and R. Angelotti (1965). "*Clostridium perfringens* in meat and meat products." *Appl. Microbiol.*, 13:352–357.

Hartley, D. E. (1975). "Recent trends in vending." *J. Milk Food Technol.*, 39:59–62.

Hill, J. E., J. D. Leitman, and J. E. Sunderland (1967). "Thermal conductivity of various meats." *Food Technol.*, 21:1143–1148.

Kelsay, R. C. (1970). "Food poisoning outbreak in Kentucky traced to creamed turkeys." *U.S. Public Health Rep.*, 85:1103–1108.

Kotschevar, L. H. and M. E. Terrell (1977). *Foodservice Planning: Layout and Equipment,* 2nd ed. John Wiley & Sons, New York.

Lewis, M. N., H. H. Weiser, and A. R. Winter (1953). "Bacterial growth in chicken salad." *J. Am. Diet. Assoc.*, 29(11):1094–1099.

Longrée, K. and J. C. White (1955). "Cooling rates and bacterial growth in food prepared and stored in quantity. I. Broth and white sauce." *J. Am. Diet. Assoc.*, 31:124–132.

Longrée, K., L. Moragne, and J. C. White (1960). "Cooling starch-thickened food items with cold tube agitation." *J. Milk Food Technol.*, 23:330.

Longrée, K., L. Moragne, and J. C. White (1963). "Cooling menu items by agitation under refrigeration." *J. Milk Food Technol.*, 26:317–322.

Mallman, W. L., P. J. Aldrich, D. M. Downs, and G. Houghtby (1963). "Safeness and servability of meringued pie." *J. Am. Diet. Assoc.*, 43(1):43–47.

McDivitt, M. E. and M. L. Hammer (1958). "Cooling rates and bacterial growth in cornstarch pudding." *J. Am. Diet. Assoc.*, 34:1190–1194.

Miller, C., K. Longrée, and J. C. White (1961). "Time–temperature relationships of custards made with whole egg solids. I. In the Bain-Marie. II. In the steam-jacketed kettle." *J. Am. Diet. Assoc.*, 38(1):43–48; 49–53.

Miller, W. A. and M. L. Smull (1955). "Efficiency of cooling practices in preventing growth of micrococci." *J. Am. Diet. Assoc.*, 31:469–473.

Moragne, L., K. Longrée, and J. C. White (1959a). "Heat transfer in refrigerated foods." 33rd Annual Report, New York State Association of Milk Sanitarians. 5 pp. Dec.

Moragne, L., K. Longrée, and J. C. White (1959b). "Heat transfer in white sauce cooled in flowing water." *J. Am. Diet. Assoc.*, 35:1275–1285.

Moragne, L., K. Longrée, and J. C. White (1961). "Cooling custards and puddings with cold-tube agitation." *J. Milk Food Technol.*, 24:207–210.

Moragne, L., K. Longrée, and J. C. White (1963). "Effect of a scraper–lifter agitator on cooling time of food." *J. Milk Food Technol.*, 26:182–184.

Nowrey, J. E., K. Longrée, E. J. Race, and S. A. Wald (unpublished). "Batch cooling with slow-speed scraper agitator."

Powers, E. M. and D. T. Munsey (1980). "Bacteriological and temperature survey of ginger beef pot roast production at a central food preparation facility." *J. Food Prot.*, 43:292–294.

Qashou, M., G. H. Nix, R. D. Vachou, and G. W. Lowry (1970). "Thermal conductivity values of ground beef and chuck." *Food Technol.*, 24:493–496.

Sperber, S. S., S. Dudowitz, and A. Mazel (1969). "A bacteriological study of liquid nourishment in hospitals." *Hospital Mgt.*, 108(Oct.):29–33; 77.

Tiedeman, W. D. (1958). "Implications of new developments in food and milk processing-packaging, storing and vending." *Am. J. Public Health*, 48(7):854–860.

West, B. B., L. Wood, V. F. Harger, and G. S. Shugart (1977). *Food Service in Institutions*, 5th ed. John Wiley & Sons, New York.

ADDITIONAL READINGS

Beyer, C. E. "Hospital converts to Ready Foods." *Cornell Hotel Restaurant Adm. Q.*, 12:39–46. 1971.

Bradshaw, J. G., J. T. Peeler, and R. M. Twedt. "Thermal inactivation of ideal loop-reactive *Clostridium perfringens* type A strain in phosphate buffer and beef gravy." *Appl. Environ. Microbiol.*, 34:280–284.

Brown, D. F. and R. M. Twedt. "Assessment of the sanitary effectiveness of holding temperatures on beef cooked at low temperatures." *Appl. Microbiol.*, 24:599–603. 1972.

Bryan, F. L. "Microbiological food hazards today—based on epidemiological information." *Food Technol.*, 28(9):52–54; 58–60; 62–64; 84. 1974.

Bryan, F. L. "Prevention of foodborne diseases in foodservice establishments." *J. Environ. Health*, 41:198–206. 1979.

Craven, S. E., H. S. Lillard, and A. J. Mercuri. "Survival of *Clostridium perfringens* during preparation of precooked chicken parts." *J. Milk Food Technol.*, 38:505–508. 1975.

Desrosier, N. W., Editor-in-chief, and D. K. Tressler, Pres. *Fundamentals of Food Freezing*. Avi Publishing Co., Westport, CT. 1977.

Johnson, K. M. "*Bacillus cereus* foodborne illness—An update." *J. Food Prot.*, 47:145–153. 1984.

Litman, C. D. "Refrigeration for convenience foods." *Cornell Hotel Restaurant Adm. Q.*, 12(1):64–68. 1971.

Mallman, W. L. "Insulated server packs for transporting food from commissary to the table." *J. Milk Food Technol.*, 33:105–108. 1970.

Newcomer, J. L., E. W. Ramsey, and H. D. Eaton. "Effect of air flow in a refrigerator on cooling rate." *J. Am. Diet. Assoc.*, 40:39–40. 1962.

Plotkin, S. "Keep your roast beef bacteria safe with time-temperature control." *J. Environ. Health*, 38:230–234. 1976.

Sullivan, R., R. M. Marnell, E. P. Larkin, and R. B. Read, Jr. "Inactivation of polio virus 1 and coxsackie virus B-2 in broiled hamburgers." *J. Milk Food Technol.,* 38:473–474. 1975.

Vanderzant, C. and R. Nickelson. "Survival of *Vibrio parahaemolyticus* in shrimp tissue under various environmental conditions." *Appl. Microbiol.,* 23:34–37. 1972.

Willardsen, R. R., F. F. Busta, C. E. Allen, and L. B. Smith. "Growth and survival of *Clostridium perfringens* during constantly rising temperatures." *J. Food Sci.,* 43:470–475. 1978.

CHAPTER *14*

Microbiological Considerations in Connection with Some Specific Categories of Foodservice Systems

T his chapter considers special situations related to the foodservice system. New developments in the way in which food is delivered under these conditions are also addressed.

DESCRIPTION OF FOUR MAJOR TYPES OF FOODSERVICE SYSTEMS

Along with constant developments in the technology of commercial food processing, changes continue to take place in the foodservice industry—primarily because of the increasing use of foods that are prepared outside the place of service, some partially and fully, and because of the availability of innovative and sophisticated equipment. Foodservice establishments where all or most of the menu items are prepared "from scratch" are well on their way to becoming a rarity.

Microbiological problems will vary with the type of service system used, and analyses of the potential danger points deserve the attention of the foodservice manager. No matter which direction developments in the foodservice industry take, the sanitary aspects of feeding the public need to be understood and sanitary control needs to be relentlessly applied. This is a "must" wherever food is served, be it a commercial establishment; a hospital, nursing home, or other health care facility; a school, college, or university; an industrial dining facility or a mess hall for the Armed Forces; or foodservice on ships, airplanes, and trains. Regardless of whether the service is rendered on a permanent or temporary basis, for example, foodservice in summer camps, or whether food is dispensed from vending machines, or consumed in space flight, all food must be safe from a public health point of view.

The foodservice industry has some sanitary problems in common with the food-processing industry. However, the former is still so much less streamlined in operation, so much more complex and diversified, that the analysis of microbiological hazards and the pinpointing and monitoring of critical control points is far more difficult to perform than in the food-processing industry. Yet, a beginning has been made through the use of the HACCP approach in the foodservice industry.

In 1977, Unklesbay et al. published the results of a study that was concerned with the identification of food product flow through various forms of foodservice systems and with the identification of critical areas for effective managerial control, or monitoring of time–temperature relationships, for microbial quality and safety. As an important prerequisite to the study, the authors reviewed and classified the various foodservice systems. Food product flow is a specific path "within a foodservice operation which food components and menu items may follow, beginning with receipt of food items and ending with service of food to the client" (Unklesbay et al., 1977). The authors emphasize the impact of the food-processing industry on foodservice systems. The food-processing/foodservice relationship, or interface, as characterized by Dwyer et al. (1977) and Unklesbay et al. (1977), is illustrated in diagrammatic form in Figure 14.1. The "food processing continuum" represents the amount of processing applied to the items, from no processing (far left) to completely processed (far right). In this particular case, the foodservice used items that had received no or little processing. Other illustrations will follow, which characterize four categories of foodservice systems delineated by the authors. These are conventional, commissary, ready-prepared, and assembly-serve.

Conventional Foodservice Systems

These conventional systems have been used for many years. They are labor intensive. Conventional systems have developed from traditional systems with their own kitchen, bake shop, butcher shop, vegetable preparation area, and so forth; foods were purchased raw. As more processed foods were made available, procured, and used, such as precut meats, dessert mixes, frozen, dehydrated, or prepeeled potatoes, frozen vegetables, and prepared fresh salads, the traditional system gave way to a conventional-type foodservice that is still characterized by the fact that preparation was completed in a kitchen located on the premises (Rappole, 1973), but where preparation "from scratch" was no longer true for all items. For conventional systems, the flow

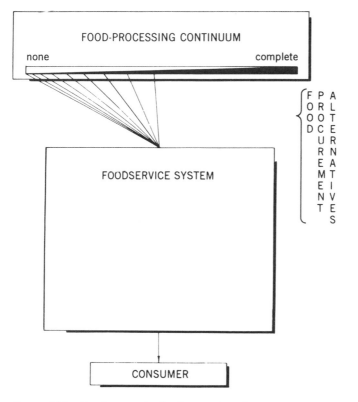

FIGURE 14.1. Food-processing/foodservice interface. From Dwyer et al. (1977), reprinted with permission.

of food products as characterized by Dwyer et al. (1977) and Unklesbay et al. (1977) is illustrated in Figure 14.2. Food is procured over the entire food-processing continuum, from unprocessed to fully processed. The authors point to hot-holding (hold-heated) as a critical control point, since prolonged hot-holding may have adverse effects on the culinary quality of a product. They also mention that the items prepared in advance and chilled (hold-chilled) may have an adverse effect on sensory as well as microbial quality. More will be said about microbiological aspects later on.

Commissary Foodservice Systems

Unklesbay et al. (1977) characterize these systems as having "centralized food procurement and production functions with distribution of prepared menu items to several remote areas for final preparation and service." The commis-

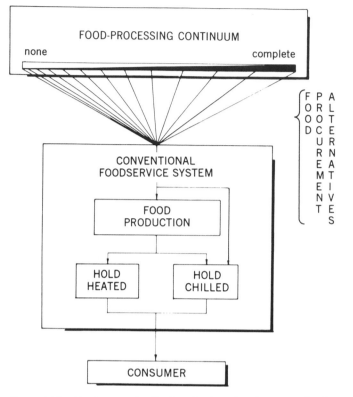

FIGURE 14.2.   Food-processing/foodservice interface for conventional systems. From Dwyer et al. (1977), reprinted with permission.

sary systems, according to the authors' definition, include operations called satellite, central commissary, commissariat, and food factory. Commissary kitchens are usually equipped with technologically advanced equipment for production and holding. As to product flow, Unklesbay et al. (1977) state:

> ... actual product flow may vary with different commissary adaptations; however, the distinct feature of all commissaries is that the food production center and service areas are located in separate facilities. Therefore, the function of food distribution must receive considerable emphasis for the effective operation of these food service systems.

The food product flow as illustrated by Dwyer et al. (1977) and Unklesbay et al. (1977) is illustrated in Figure 14.3. It shows that there is a trend for procuring foods that are unprocessed or processed to a limited extent. These are then completely processed in the central kitchen. Following preparation, the items may be stored in several ways, frozen, chilled, or hot-held. The distance between kitchen and place of service may be as great as 100 miles (Balsley,

1973). Some of the new equipment used in connection with the production and service of food was described by Schukraft (1972), Sell (1973), Hartman (1975), Kotschevar and Terrell (1977), West et al. (1977), and Seligsohn (1978), to name only a few references on the subject. Equipment and methodology employed in the system is a vast subject in itself which goes beyond the scope of this book. The microbiological aspects are discussed in another section.

Ready-Prepared Foodservice Systems

These are systems in which food production takes place largely on the premises and foods are stored ready for final assembly, either with or without heating (Unklesbay et al., 1977). The systems were developed because of high labor cost and lack of skilled labor required to meet the pressure of meal

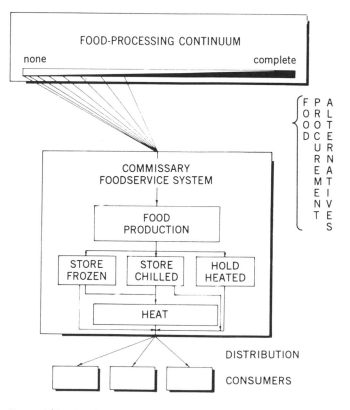

FIGURE 14.3.   Food-processing/foodservice interface for commissary systems. From Dwyer et al. (1977), reprinted with permission.

preparation deadlines. They provide the variety of foods desired and reflect the individuality of a food-production operation, in that the items used are not dependent on completely prepared food offered on the market. Ready-prepared menu items are stored, either chilled or frozen, for final use, either with or without previous heating, depending on the nature of the item. The product flow characterizing these systems is presented in Figure 14.4, which shows that food items may be procured from all along the food-processing continuum, from unprocessed to completely processed.

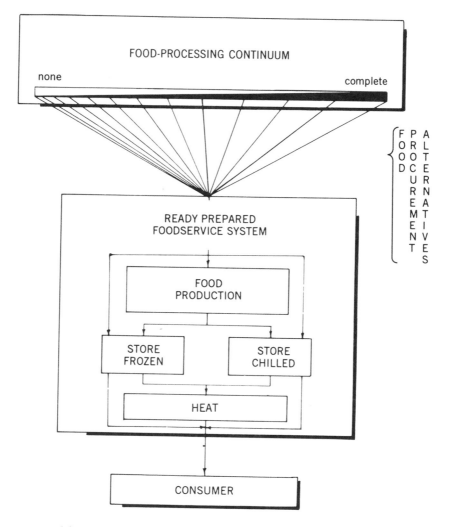

FIGURE 14.4.   Food-processing/foodservice interface for ready-prepared systems. From Dwyer et al. (1977), reprinted with permission.

The ready-prepared food systems are of two main types: the *cook/freeze system* and the *cook/chill system.*

In the cook/freeze system, batches of food are usually prepared on a convenient schedule established by the foodservice manager, preplated, frozen, and freezer-stored. One of these systems was described as "ready foods" by Rappole (1973). A blast freezer is used for freezing, and sufficient low-temperature storage is required. For single-portion packs, conventional freezers were found to be adequate. Reheating of frozen items can be performed by boiling in the bag or in the microwave oven.

Another cook/freeze system, developed by the United Leeds Hospitals in Leeds, England, is similar to the ready-foods system. Foods are slightly undercooked to avoid overcooking during reheating prior to service. Reheating is performed in forced-air convection ovens (Millross et al., 1974; Hill and Glew, 1974). The latter authors emphasize the need for special recipe formulation of certain menu items to offset possible damage to their flavor and texture.

The cook/chill system is similar to the cook/freeze system in general methodology, except that the cooked food is chilled, then refrigerator stored, usually in bulk. The duration of storage varies from one to several days.

Following storage, the product is individually portioned, chilled again, and finally reheated before service. It is important that food to be chilled should be somewhat undercooked to avoid overcooking in reheating. Reheating may be done by microwave energy, convection heat, or integral heat.

Microbiological control is very essential in the use of the cook/chill system. An early example of this system is the Nacka System developed in Sweden and practiced at the Nacka Hospital, Stockholm (Bjorkman and Delphin, 1966). Another older system, the A.G.S. System, which was fashioned after the Nacka System, was developed by the McGuckian (1969) for use in hospitals in Anderson, Greenville, and Spartansburg, South Carolina.

Heating prior to service is an important step since its methodology affects culinary quality, nutrient content, and microbiological safety. Armstrong et al. (1974) discussed factors entering decision making in the selection of heating equipment appropriate for ready-prepared foodservice. Microwave ovens, convection ovens, and immersion procedures are commonly used (Bobeng and David, 1975; Bernsten and David, 1975; Ringle and David, 1975). Integral heat systems can also be used. These were described by Schukraft (1972) and by Fries and Graham (1972).

Rinke (1976) reviewed and evaluated the conventional, the cook/freeze, and the cook/chill systems, and concluded that a combination of on-premise-produced chilled and frozen subsystems, supported by automated high-volume production assembly, transportation, and distribution subsystems, is probably the foodservice system of the future.

Some fast-food companies and food production equipment companies have developed, and endeavor to consistently refine, their own cook/chill systems, in which all steps—from planning and designing a central food production facility to steps in processing and delivery of the final product—are carefully thought out and executed. Microbiological control plays an important part in the development of a system and in its application to the needs of an individual foodservice establishment.

Assembly-Serve Foodservice Systems

The food-processing/foodservice relationship for assembly-serve foodservice systems is illustrated in Figure 14.5. It demonstrates that, in this system, processed foods are used exclusively. According to Unklesbay et al. (1977), three market forms of frozen entrees are commonly employed in these systems—bulk, preportioned, and preplated. A very small labor force is required, since the preprocessed items merely require storage, assembly, heating, and ser-

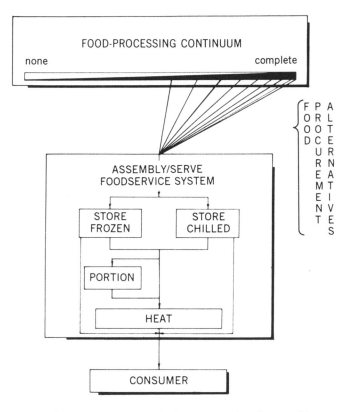

FIGURE 14.5.   Food-processing/foodservice interface for assembly-serve systems. From Dwyer et al. (1977), reprinted with permission.

vice. Thawing or tempering, when needed for some items, is to be done under strictly controlled temperature conditions, which are aimed at holding temperatures at the surface of the product at 4°C (40°F).

New-Generation Refrigerated Foods

Included among the new-generation refrigerated foods is a processed product called "Sous Vide," meaning under vacuum. This product is processed by a new technology that offers a high-quality product with fresh eating and tasting parameters. For foodservice applications, this product offers high quality without the need for large kitchen staff and expensive equipment. It is predicted that this will make kitchenless foodservice facilities possible.

The process starts with high-quality raw food ingredients packaged under vacuum in impermeable pouches. Sealed pouches are cooked slowly in hot water at low temperatures for up to 4 hours using strict controls. The cooked product is held at refrigerator or freezer temperatures until it is used. No preservatives are used. Strict control of time and temperatures throughout the processing, storage, and end use are considered critical. No problems of foodborne illnesses associated with this product have been observed.

The concept was developed and is being used in Europe, but it has been slow to move into the North American market. Concerns about the product center around the fact that the product is not commercially sterile or shelf stable. Spores of *Clostridium botulinum* would not be destroyed by the process used. Also of concern is the question of whether refrigeration can guarantee microbial safety; *Listeria monocytogenes, Yersinia enterocolitica,* and *Escherichia coli* can grow at refrigerator temperatures, and *Campylobacter jejuni* can survive for long times at refrigerator temperatures. It is well known that a common problem associated with the distribution of foods is temperature abuse. It is clear that, if this product is to succeed, a HACCP approach has to be incorporated into the processing, marketing, and distribution of the product (Baird, 1990 and Rhodehamel, 1992).

Livingston (1990) recommended that refrigerator temperatures used in the Sous Vide system are only as dependable as the individual who is monitoring the system. He was acknowledging that refrigeration services may fail and that the manager in charge must prepare for it by controlling other variables, such as pH, water activity, and other factors that inhibit the growth of anaerobes.

MICROBIOLOGICAL CONSIDERATIONS AND CONTROL POINTS

Outbreaks of foodborne illnesses associated with quality food preparation and service are discussed at length in Chapter 4 and will not be repeated

here. However, it is emphasized that a breakdown of food-poisoning incidences on the basis of the four categories of foodservice systems established
by Unklesbay (1977) is not available. In each of the categories, the potential
for the presence of microorganisms of public health significance undoubtedly exists, although differences can be expected because of the peculiarity
of each system, and, before all, because of differences in the degree of monitoring applied at critical control points. As was shown in earlier chapters of
this book, sources of pathogens may be raw food, food items that are insufficiently heated (undercooked), and foods that were sufficiently heated but
contaminated after cooking by food handlers, equipment, and other sources.
The overwhelming effects of time and temperature on microbial multiplication and their control was discussed in preceding chapters. Since in currently
evolving food systems the time between incipient handling and final service
to the customer is increased, it is important to be aware of the identity of
the critical control points before these can be appropriately and effectively
monitored. Nine areas requiring monitoring within foodservice operations
were presented by Unklesbay et al. (1977); they are food procurement, food
storage, food packaging, preprocessing, heat processing, food storage following heat processing, heat processing of precooked menu items, food distribution, and foodservice.

Food Procurement

Food procurement and its microbiological aspects have been discussed in
earlier chapters of this book. The principles of purchasing a safe food supply
are applicable to all four systems discussed above—conventional, commissary, ready-prepared, and assembly-serve. Microbiological criteria were also
discussed previously (Chapter 8).

Food Storage

Food storage needs monitoring in each of the four categories of foodservice.
In the case of conventional and assembly-serve systems, the items are stored
immediately upon delivery. Storage of various food items has been discussed
in earlier chapters. Storage before, as well as after, the production of various
food items is required under the commissary and ready-prepared systems.
Detailed instructions are necessary concerning temperature conditions and
length of storage. The reader is referred to Chapters 8, 11, and 13. Much
more research is needed in this critical area.

Food Packaging

Packaging plays an important role in two foodservice systems, the commissary and the ready-prepared. Proper packaging facilitates handling and protects the food from contamination and unwanted changes in texture. Inadequate packaging gives false security and may alter the quality of the product and render it unsafe.

Preprocessing

Excepting the assembly-serve systems, preprocessing activities take place in every one of the foodservice systems. Cross-contamination from raw to processed items is a danger that must be eliminated by all controlled methods available. These involve, before all, strict separation of raw food and processed food in storage as well as in food preparation areas (Chapters 8 and 9).

Heat Processing

This is a production activity applicable to the conventional, commissary, and ready-prepared systems. From a public health point of view, most contaminants, before all, the pathogenic ones, should be destroyed in the process. Potentially hazardous items require special attention. In the *Food Service Sanitation Manual* of the FDA (1978) it is stated that:

> Potentially hazardous foods requiring cooking shall be cooked to heat all parts of the food to a temperature of at least 140°F [60° C], except that:
>
> (a) Poultry, poultry stuffings, stuffed meats and stuffings containing meat shall be cooked to heat all parts of the food to at least 165°F [74° C] with no interruption of the cooking process.
>
> (b) Pork and any food containing pork shall be cooked to heat all parts of the food to at least 150°F [66° C].

In ready-prepared systems, a period of storage at low temperatures follows initial heating to 140°F (60°C) before the items are again heated before service, the second time to at least 165°F (73°C).

Heating to 140°F (60°C) is a relatively mild treatment and food heated in this manner cannot be considered sterile. If consumed soon after preparation, as is commonly done in a conventional foodservice, and held hot in the meantime, the food should be safe. However, when the ready-prepared system is used, and the heated items are cold-stored (chilled or frozen) until reheated, the cooling and storing procedure must be closely monitored so as to preclude bacterial proliferation and, possibly, formation of toxins of survivors. Second heating, which precedes service, should raise the food temperature to at least 165°F (74°C). Unless heat-stable toxins are present, this heating should reduce bacterial numbers to low levels.

Survival of contaminants following heating to 60°C (140°F) was shown in a study by Bunch et al. (1976) on acceptability and microbiological characteristics of 5.2-kilogram beef-soy loaves when processed according to a hospital chill foodservice system. A convection oven operating at 121 ± 8°C (250°F) was employed. Viable bacteria remained in the center of the loaves, but the counts were low (Table 14.1). The data presented in the table are discussed further under "chilled storage."

In a subsequent investigation, Bunch et al. (1977) followed the fate of *Staphylococcus aureus* inoculated into uncooked beef-soy loaves that were then subjected to procedures typical of a hospital chill foodservice system, as

TABLE 14.1.   *Numbers of Aerobic Bacteria in Beef-Soy Loaves During Three Sampling Stages in a Chill Foodservice Simulation*

Sampling Stage and Location	Aerobic Bacteria (number per gram)		
	Length of Chilled Storage		
	24 Hours[a]	48 Hours[b]	72 Hours[c]
Trial One			
After cooking, corner of loaf 1[d]	2,700	2,700	2,100
After cooking, center of loaf 3[e]	59,000	57,000	50,000
After chilled storage, center of loaf 3	110,000	110,000	150,000
After microwave reheating, center of loaf 3	5,100	5,100	8,100
Trial Two			
After cooking, corner of loaf 1	4,400	3,600	3,500
After cooking, center of loaf 3	70,000	65,000	59,000
After chilled storage, center of loaf 3	100,000	120,000	130,000
After microwave reheating, center of loaf 3	4,000	4,500	6,700
Trial Three			
After cooking, corner of loaf 1	4,200	3,900	2,900
After cooking, center of loaf 3	65,000	68,000	55,000
After chilled storage, center of loaf 3	110,000	120,000	140,000
After microwave reheating, center of loaf 3	4,900	5,200	6,900

[a]Raw ground beef was held at 5 ± 3°C for 48 hours.
[b]Raw ground beef was held at 5 ± 3°C for 24 hours.
[c]Raw ground beef was used day purchased.
[d]Loaf 1 (side of pan).
[e]Loaf 3 (center of pan).
Source: Bunch et al. *J. Food Sci.* **41**:1273–76, 1976. Copyright © 1976, Inst. Food Technologists. Reprinted by permission.

described in their earlier publication (Bunch et al., 1976). They found that the number of staphylococci of an inoculation of 5.0×10^3 cells per gram was considerably reduced after the loaves were cooked to an end point of 60°C (140°F), using a convection oven at 121 ± 8°C (250°F).

A study of microbiological quality of beef loaf prepared under the cook/chill system was made by Dahl et al. (1978). Microbiological quality was evaluated at five stages—preparing ingredients, mixing ingredients, initial heat processing, chilled storage, and terminal processing. The variable in the study was the end point of initial heating, no heating, and heating in a convection oven at 121°C (250°F) to 45, 60, 75, and 90°C (113, 140, 167, and 194°F). The lack of heating, as well as the end point of heating, had a distinct effect on the microbial load in terms of aerobic plate counts, greatest reduction being achieved by heating to higher end points, although no statistically significant differences were noted after microwave heating to 74°C (165.2°F).

Food Storage Following Heat Processing

In commissary and ready-prepared systems, and also to some extent in conventional systems, food storage follows heat processing. The storage may be hot-holding, chilled storage, or freezer storage.

HOT FOOD STORAGE.   The safe temperature for this type of storage has been recommended (FDA, 1978) and accepted to be at least 140°F (60°C). Culinary quality is apt to deteriorate with prolonged holding at this temperature, however.

CHILLED FOOD STORAGE.   This type of storage is used in those commissary and ready-prepared foodservice systems in which items are cooled down following the first heating and held in the chilled condition until reheated for service. It is used to a limited extent in conventional systems also. Quick chilling to safe temperatures is essential. In the FDA (1978) *Food Service Sanitation Manual* the recommendation is made that

> Enough conveniently located refrigeration facilities or effectively insulated facilities shall be provided to assure the maintenance of potentially hazardous food at required temperatures during storage. Each mechanically refrigerated facility storing potentially hazardous food shall be provided with a numerically scaled indicating thermometer, accurate to ± 3°F [± 1.7° C], located to measure the air temperature in the warmest part of the facility and located to be easily readable. Recording thermometers, accurate to ± 3°F [± 1.7° C], may be used in lieu of indicating thermometers. Potentially hazardous food requiring refrigeration after preparation shall be rapidly cooled to an internal temperature of 45°F [7.2° C] or below. Potentially hazardous foods of large volume or prepared in large

quantities shall be rapidly cooled, utilizing such methods as shallow pans, agitation, quick chilling or water circulation external to the food container so that the cooling period shall not exceed 4 hours. Potentially hazardous food to be transported shall be prechilled and held at a temperature of 45°F [7.2° C] or below.

The necessity for rapid cooling preceding chilled storage is well documented (see Chapters 11 and 13), but more research data are needed on which to base practical recommendations for systems using the cook/chill system.

Microbiological characteristics of beef-soy loaves prepared in a hospital using a cook/chill foodservice system were determined by Bunch et al. (1976). The loaves were baked to 60°C (140°F) using a convection oven, then chill-stored at 5 ± 3°C (41°F) for 24, 48, and 72 hours; then portioned and chill-stored again at 5 ± 1°C (41°F) for 2 hours; thereafter, they were heated for 55 seconds in a microwave oven to an internal temperature of 80°C (176°F). Bacterial numbers increased most during the cooling period and viable bacteria were recovered from the center of the loaves. The greatest number of bacteria was recovered after the 72-hour storage period (Table 14.1). A small number of bacteria survived the final heating; spores would survive this heat treatment. Bacterial loads were low, in general. The authors concluded that by the procedure described loaves of excellent microbiological quality could be served.

Bunch et al. (1977) inoculated uncooked beef-soy loaves with *Staphylococcus aureus,* subjected them to an initial heat treatment by cooking them to an internal temperature of 60°C (140°F) at an oven temperature of 121°C (250°F) which reduced the number of staphylococci considerably. The loaves were then held at 41°F (5°C) for 24, 48, and 72 hours. Further reduction of *Staphylococcus* cells took place during chilled holding.

Cremer and Chipley (1977a) assessed two foods produced in a commissary cook/chill system, spaghetti and chili. The items were chilled after they were cooked and transported, in the chilled condition and in chilled trucks, from the commissary to various schools for reheating and service. Microbiological and culinary quality were determined in order to identify critical control points in processing. The authors reported that critical phases were indicated in wide—at times unacceptably wide—ranges in time and temperature for about half the phase of product flow. Microbial quality was considered to be good in general, average total plate counts at time of service being 1500 or less per gram, but numerous genera of pathogens were identified, albeit small in number. Clostridia were the most numerous contaminants.

The effects on bacterial counts of chilling 5.5-pound lots of ground beef gravy, in plastic bags, for an initial period of 1 hour in chilled water, thereafter in lots of 6 bags to a carton in a refrigerator (42°F, 5.6°C), were investigated by Tuomi et al. (1974a). The gravy temperature reached 65°F (18.5°C) within 3–4 hours, and had fallen to 45.5°F (7.5°C) at the end of the 16 hours of refrigeration. Samples of gravy for bacteriological analyses, taken at six stages, were analyzed for total aerobic counts, coagulase-positive staphylococci, and *Clostridium perfringens*. None of the samples yielded the latter organism. Coagulase-positive staphylococci were found in some samples, the numbers being very low. Total aerobic counts increased mostly during the first 4–5 hours of cooling, which included the first hour in chilled water. All counts were low.

The same investigators (Tuomi et al., 1974b) studied the effect on *Clostridium perfringens* of cooling ground beef gravy in lots of 5.5 pounds, from 102°F (39°C) to 65°F (18.5°C), in a refrigerator (42°F, 5.6°C). Precooling in chilled water was omitted this time. The cartons, each containing six lots, were refrigerated. The number of viable cells after 16 hours of refrigeration was influenced by the first 6 hours of chilling, during which the gravy was within a temperature range permitting growth of *C. perfringens* (65–122°F; 18.5–50°C). The time–temperature relationships in this experiment were more favorable for growth of *C. perfringens* than in the previous one (Tuomi et al., 1974a), when precooling in chilled water preceded refrigeration. It must be remembered that, in the first experiment (Tuomi et al., 1974a), the gravy was precooled as 5.5-pound lots, which allowed for fast initial cooling, thereafter packed in lots of 6 bags into cartons and refrigerated in bulk. This first method of cooling was evidently a more effectual method to shorten the danger zone for growth of *C. perfringens* than the second one.

Time–temperature control of chilling turkeys in school lunch kitchens was investigated by Bryan and McKinley (1974). Twenty-pound carcasses were thawed by various methods and then baked, either whole or as half-turkeys, the latter being the faster and more practical method. The birds were allowed to precool at room temperature for an average of 1–3 hours prior to being refrigerated; some turkeys, while warm, were deboned, cut into bite-size pieces, and placed in swallow pans. Refrigerated whole turkeys cooled slowly. Immersing double-plastic bagged turkey meat and halved turkey rolls in an ice bag and slicing turkey meat onto ice-cooled pans speeded cooling. The authors isolated *Clostridium perfringens* from both cooked turkey meat and stock. Its origin was doubtful; either survival or postcooking contamination could explain its presence. Whatever the mode of contamination, the presence of the pathogen on the cooked meat demonstrates the importance of efficient chilling and chilled storage. Staphylococci and salmonellae were not found in samples of cooked turkey. Unfortunately, cutting up whole turkey for the purpose of faster cooling, involves handling and contamination of the cooked meat from handlers and equipment. Thus strict enforcement of sanitary handling methods is necessary. Prompt refrigeration in shallow pans is advised. As the authors so aptly summarize: "Rapid cooling of cooked products is the most important step in preventing outbreaks of foodborne illness from turkeys." They further advise that following chilled storage, stock should be boiled and turkey meat reheated to at least 165°F (74°C) to nullify inadequacy in cooling practices.

A study of cooling of the surfaces and internal portions of beef roasts while refrigerated was included in a hazard analysis of roast beef preparation in foodservice establishments, made by Bryan and McKinley (1979). During cooling the geometric centers of 83% of the roasts, and the surfaces of 79%, were exposed to incubation temperatures long enough to have permitted growth of mesophilic bacteria, including *Clostridium perfringens*, if they had been present. The period during which temperatures were within 7.2–60°C (45–140°F) frequently exceeded 4 hours; in fact, it usually was 8 hours or more. Little difference was noted in roasts that were wrapped in foil or plastic film. Very slow cooling was observed when several roasts were stored in plastic pans covered with lids in walk-in refrigerators, and data are presented that show that internal portions of roasts were frequently at temperatures at which foodborne disease bacteria can multiply.

Cooked food items prepared using the Nacka System and the A.G.S. System (see Chapter 13) are chill-stored for extended periods, but monitoring of the bacteriological quality is systematic and, according to Bjorkman and Delphin (1966), it is satisfactory. The A.G.S. System is fashioned after the Nacka System (see page 403). Rowley et al. (1972), comparing cook/chill and cook/freeze methods (commissary system) of preparing and using food, concluded that chilled items were superior to frozen items in terms of both microbiological and culinary quality.

More recent studies were made by Cremer et al. (1985) on a widely used type of foodservice system in which the finished menu items are packaged, hot from the kettle, in plastic bags, sealed, and chill-stored for as long as 1 month. Chicken and noodles was the menu item analyzed for time–temperature data and for microbial and sensory quality. Mesophilic, psychrotropic, coliform, and staphylococcal counts, as well as anaerobic spore counts, were made. Samples were taken of the food at the end of cooking, after its transfer to plastic bags, during cooling prior to chill-storage, at the end of various storage periods, at the end of reheating, during hot-holding (in pans, in convection oven), and at the time of portioning. Although with up to four weeks of chill-storage, microbial and sensory quality were judged as being satisfactory, the temperatures after heating and cooling were not always at acceptable levels. Mean total plate counts increased with length of storage time. The authors warned that temperatures at initial cooking, cooling, and heating for service should be rigidly monitored.

FROZEN FOOD STORAGE.   Commissary as well as ready-prepared food systems utilize the cook/freeze concept. Prerequisites for properly freezing precooked menu items are a sound background in the mechanics of freezing and use of adequate equipment. The period for which food is held in the danger zone of bacterial growth (40–140°F) (4.4–60°C) must be reduced to a minimum. If food to be frozen must be stored for a while in the chilled condition, that period, too, should be short; Rowley et al. (1972) considered 24 hours to be the maximum. Handling operations require streamlining to keep the period of rapid bacterial proliferation, which ranges from 68 to 122°F (20–50°C), very brief (Millross et al., 1974). Microbiological monitoring is considered desirable when setting up freezing and freezer-storage operations, and strict adherence to microbiologically acceptable methodology is a must (see also Chapter 13).

Heat Processing of Precooked Menu Items

Whether the precooked menu items are reheated from the chilled, frozen, tempered, or thawed stage, the process should be fast and an internal food temperature of 165°F (74°C) should be reached. Tempering differs from thawing in that the final temperature desired is 28–30°F (−2.2 to −1.1°C) or slightly below (Decareau, 1978). This is the recommendation stated in the Food and Drug Administration *Food Service Sanitation Manual* (1978):

> Potentially hazardous foods that have been cooked and then refrigerated, shall be reheated rapidly to 165°F [74° C] or higher throughout before being served or before being placed in a hot food storage facility. Steam tables, bainmaries, warmers, and similar hot food holding facilities are prohibited for the rapid reheating of potentially hazardous foods.

The implications are that, with inefficient heating equipment, the products may remain in the danger zone for bacterial growth unduly long and spores must be expected to survive the heating. Frozen foods are frequently thawed and then reheated in microwave ovens. In the FDA *Food Service Sanitation Manual* (1978) the recommendations are that:

> Potentially hazardous foods shall be thawed:
>
> (a) In refrigerated units at a temperature not to exceed 45°F [7.2° C]; or
>
> (b) Under potable running water of a temperature of 70°F [21.1° C] or below, with sufficient water velocity to agitate and float off loose food particles into the overflow; or
>
> (c) In a microwave oven only when the food will be immediately transferred to conventional cooking facilities as part of a continuous cooking process or when the entire, uninterrupted cooking process takes place in the microwave oven; or
>
> (d) As part of the conventional cooking process.

Time, temperature, and quality of hamburger patties purchased as a frozen item, stored, and assembled in a commissary establishment, and reheated at the place of service (schools) were investigated by Cremer and Chipley (1977b). Samples for microbiological analysis were taken from patties when received, after assembly, after storage, and after heating for service. Internal temperatures of the heated patties ranged from 152°F (67°C) to 192°F (89°C). When received from the supplier, the patties showed contamination with clostridia and staphylococci. These, as well as the total bacterial population were reduced but not eliminated by the heating process in a forced convection oven (Table 14.2). A potential for public health hazard exists, if pre-cooked food is mishandled by insufficient time–temperature control before reheating and if reheating temperatures are inadequate.

The effect on bacterial counts of heating preportioned slices of beef-soy loaves, which were processed according to a hospital cook/chill foodservice procedure, was investigated by Bunch et al. (1976). The results, presented in Table 14.1, showed that aerobic counts, which had increased during chilled storage, were considerably reduced after 55 seconds of heating in a microwave oven to an approximate temperature of 80°C (176°F).

Bunch et al. (1977) also studied the survival of *Staphylococcus aureus* in beef-soy loaves that were subjected to an initial heating to an internal temper-

TABLE 14.2. *Microbiological Evaluation of Frozen Hamburger Patties Reheated in a Forced Convection Oven*

Phase of Process	Total Plate Count	Coliform	Clostridial	Staphylococcal
As received	5330[a]	223[b]	2650[a]	290[b]
First assembly	4850	190	2140	210
Middle assembly	5200	195	2300	265
Last assembly	5450	225	2460	300
Before reheating	5100	205	2380	220
After reheating[c]	1540	33	480	75
After reheating[d]	1270	20	300	40
After reheating[e]	1340	28	375	60

[a] Expressed as microbial counts per gram of product. Averages of three experiments.
[b] Expressed as microbial counts per 10 gram of product. Averages of three experiments.
[c] Top back of reheating oven at an internal product temperature of 159°F (70.5°C).
[d] Top front of reheating oven at an internal product temperature of 179°F (82°C).
[e] Bottom front of reheating oven at an internal product temperature of 164°F (73.5°C).
Source: M. L. Cremer and J. R. Chipley, *J. Food Prot.,* **40**(9):603–607, 1977. Copyright © 1977, International Association of Milk, Food and Environmental Sanitarians, Inc. Reprinted by permission.

ature of 60°C (140°F) and thereafter to 1–3 days of chilled storage at 5°C (41°F). They found that the number of staphylococci, already considerably reduced by heating and chilled storage, amounted to less than 3 per gram after portioning and heating in a microwave oven to 80°C (176°F). Preformed toxins would not be destroyed by this terminal treatment.

HEATING EQUIPMENT.   Initial and final heating are being performed in conventional (deck) ovens, convection ovens, and microwave ovens. The latter are largely used for the reheating of preportioned items in ready-prepared and assembly-serve systems. The performance of heating equipment has an important bearing on the microbiological quality of the final product when served.

Convection Ovens.   Convection ovens have been recommended over deck ovens because of their versatility and because they occupy relatively less floor space than deck ovens. Yet, a distinct disadvantage of forced-air ovens has been claimed to be variation in temperature in the oven cavity (Decareau, 1978; Livingston and Chang, 1972; Bryan et al., 1978).

Temperatures of spaghetti after heating in convection ovens in a commissary foodservice system were studied by Cremer (1978). The effects of equipment model and the position of the food were investigated to determine temperature variability in the food. Significant differences were found when spaghetti was heated in four oven models and when 12 food positions were compared. Differences in temperature were affected by oven thermostat setting, oven power rating, and heating element location; also by the number of meals heated, the presence of an oven floor, and number of fans. Overall, temperature variability was found be related to model of oven and position of food in the oven. The author concluded that forced-air convection ovens can be effectively used in commissary food systems, but emphasized the opinion that ovens of this type need careful engineering, need to be selected with caution, and must be properly operated.

Performance of convection ovens was also studied by Dahl and Matthews (1979) who used beef loaf as the food being heated. Temperature patterns of the oven air and of the beef loaves were determined and water evaporation tests were performed. Considerable variation in temperatures was detected. The water evaporation test was useful in detecting "hot spots." The authors felt that the tests were easy to perform and an aid in determining oven positions that should be avoided in a practical food production situation. A description of the test in the author's own words follows:

> A practical method to determine temperature patterns in forced-air convection ovens, which could be used in kitchens supplying meals to schools, was developed. One hundred milliliters of distilled water at 65–75° F (18–24° C) were placed in each of 27 prenumbered aluminum containers (Ekco, Wheeling;

16.5 × 12.5 × 3.5 cm). Containers were placed in the oven (in a certain pattern). The oven was not preheated. Its setting was 325° F (162.8° C); load, 6; damper, open. Temperature at the center of the oven was monitored with a potentiometer. Containers of water were heated for 30 minutes and then the doors were opened. Containers of water were permitted to cool for 30 minutes in the oven. One container was selected randomly and the remaining water was poured into a 1000 ml glass pyrex beaker. Water was transferred into a 100 ml graduated cylinder for measurement. This procedure was repeated for each container. Milliliters of water which remained after heating were subtracted from 100. The number obtained was considered to be the percent of relative evaporation of water which had occurred at each of 27 locations in the oven.

With this method, "hot spots" could be avoided, because their use might cause overcooking, whereas the "cold spots" would serve as areas where the temperatures of food during cooking would be monitored, insuring a safe product.

Food Product Distribution

Foods prepared in central kitchens must be transported to the places of service, which may be quite distant. The products may be transported as chilled or hot foods. Chilled food should be maintained at 45°F (7.2°C) or below, hot food at 140°F (60°C) or above, and frozen food at 0°F (−17.8°C) or below, as recommended by the Food and Drug Administration (1978). Adequate equipment must be available and careful managerial control exercised. Contamination of items must be prevented by keeping food protected.

In school foodservice, on-site food preparation and service is still the most common system used. However, new systems of preparation and distribution are used to an increasing extent, for various reasons. Central kitchens and commissary-type food preparation and distribution are taking the place of the conventional foodservice system, and the problems inherent in the satellite foodservice system must be dealt with (VanEgmond-Pannel, 1985).

Foodservice

During service, foods must be monitored in regard to contamination and temperature control. Hot food must be kept at or above 140°F (60°C) and cold food at or below 45°F (7.2°C). Covering food aids in protecting it against contamination and surface evaporation. As stated by Unklesbay et al. (1977), "if monitoring is not effective at the point of service, the effectiveness of all previous managerial controls throughout the flow of food products from procurement to consumption may be nullified."

A case in point are the findings of a study made by Ridley and Matthews (1982) on temperature histories of menu items during meal assembly, distribution, and service in a hospital foodservice in which the cook/chill/reheat/ serve system was used. The findings showed a need for stricter observation of time–temperature control; most chilled items had not been reheated to 170.6°F (77°C), the temperature recommended by Bobeng and David (1978a, b) for a hospital situation; they had not even attained the somewhat lower final temperature, 165°F (74°C) recommended by the FDA (1978). Another example is a study by Sawyer et al. (1983) of the microbiological quality and end-point temperature of chilled beef loaf, peas, and potatoes reheated by conduction, convection, and microwave radiation. The authors found that, although the reheated products were similar microbiologically, their internal temperatures frequently failed to meet the standards set by the FDA for reheated products. Human error and mechanical problems were thought to partially explain this poor performance. The microwave subsystem was the most successfully controlled one (see also Chapter 12).

HACCP MODELS

The HACCP concept refers to a system for quality control largely used in the food-processing industry (see Chapter 7), with special emphasis on microbial control. As defined by Bauman (1974), hazard analysis is concerned with identifying microbiologically sensitive ingredients, critical control points during processing, and human factors that may affect the microbiological safety of a product. Critical control points are characterized "as those processor determiners whose loss of control would result in an unacceptable safety risk."

Bryan (1981) has defined hazard analysis in foodservice establishments as the investigation directed at disclosing the potentially hazardous nature of a food; the presence, at any stage of handling, storage, or processing, of pathogenic foodborne organisms; employee practices that could result in transfer of pathogens to food; time–temperature conditions that might allow survival or multiplication of pathogens in or on the food, or would be inadequate to destroy a sufficient proportion of pathogens during reheating; procedures that might contaminate potentially hazardous foods after heat processing; environmental conditions that would allow maintenance and transfer of pathogenic foodborne microorganisms on food contact surfaces; and finally, environmental conditions that would allow for contamination of food with toxic substances and pathogens by water, air, or vectors (e.g., rodents or insects). The reader will profit from studying this publication in detail, since procedures for hazard analyses are outlined and well illustrated. The FDA *Food Code 1993* provides a section titled "HACCP Guidelines" and is intended for those who are using a HACCP system or for those who will implement this form of monitoring and control. Bryan (1994) reviewed the present status and future of HACCP systems.

Examples of hazard analyses made on different menu items and under different conditions of foodservice operations are presented under Additional Readings at the end of this chapter. These hazard analyses of food production under conditions of various foodservice systems have shown clearly that insufficient cooling of potentially hazardous cooked food is one of the most important causes of creating conditions which may lead to outbreaks of foodborne illnesses. Another common flaw is failure to sufficiently reheat cooked, chilled food, namely, to the recommended (FDA, 1978) temperature of 165°F (74°C).

To assure high microbiological and sensory quality of food served in space, NASA has successfully developed and used a HACCP system. Eighteen critical control points were identified and are monitored in the procurement, processing, and delivery of each component of the food system (Heidelbaugh et al., 1973a). Microbiological testing of Skylab foods was described in another publication (Heidelbaugh et al., 1973b). A hazard analysis of *Clostridium perfringens* in the Skylab food system was presented by Bourland et al. (1974). The foods were manufactured using critical control point techniques of quality control combined with appropriate hazard analysis. After a hazard analysis, which included many factors affecting the possibilities for growth of the pathogen under the conditions of Skylab feeding, the specification limit of not more than 100 cells of *C. perfringens* per gram was established, and proved to be adequate to protect the astronauts. This limit was based on a sampling plan and enumeration of the organisms by a previously tested procedure (Heidelbaugh et al., 1973a).

The military services in the United States have sponsored and are carrying on an important research program designed to constantly improve military food and the foodservice systems under which the food is prepared and served to the military personnel. Microbiological studies and development of equipment are an important basis for the sanitary procedures used in their foodservice systems. There are various types of feeding systems within the military services, ranging from field feeding systems to highly structured, highly automated foodservice employing highly sophisticated equipment. But whatever the system used, whatever the facilities are, great efforts are made to turn out appetizing meals prepared, stored, transported, and served under sanitary conditions. The basic principles and standards for foodservice sanitation are essentially the same as those stated in the recommendations of the Food and Drug Administration *Food Service Sanitation Manual* (1978). Specific guidelines are available, however, for each military service in the various manuals and regulations, such as Army Regulation 40–5 (Anonymous, 1974). Inspection is an important part of the sanitary control system. Inspections, as described by Silverman et al. (1975a, b), involved visual appraisal of sanitary conditions, microbiological analyses by RODAC (replicable organism detection and counting) plates, monitoring of temperatures during storing, preparation, transporting, and serving of food, and an assessment of the microbial quality of the prepared items on the serving line. It also involved the microbial aspects of dish and ware washing. In the two studies just mentioned, the hazard analyses were basic to important improvements in sanitary practices in the establishments inspected.

Rowley (1976), in his article on the microbiological aspects of certain military feeding systems, mentions that the Army has under consideration a centralized food preparation facility, which would be capable of supporting the serving of 25,000 meals per day, in satellite dining halls. The design is described by Tuomy and Byrne (1974). Precooked chilled and precooked frozen entrees would be reconstituted in the dining halls. The distinct advantage of this system is that the microbiological quality of the foods can be closely monitored by trained personnel at predetermined control points, which have already been established (Rowley et al., 1972). The fact that major emphasis is placed on critical control points, such as raw materials, time–temperature control, and general sanitation, renders microbiological analysis of the finished product to a control point of minor importance.

If critical control points are not carefully established and then scrupulously monitored, microbiological guidelines alone, be they ever so stringent, do not necessarily guarantee a safe as well as palatable product. This was shown in a report released by the Natick Research and Development Command (Anonymous, 1976) on a microbiological evaluation of production procedures for frozen foil pack meals at the central preparation facility of the Francis E. Warren Air Force Base. The microbial constraints imposed by the Strategic Air Command were total aerobic count, less than or equal to 100,000 per gram; coliforms, less than or equal to 100 per gram; *Escherichia coli,* zero per gram. The study brought out these facts: that the final products met the microbiological restraints at the cost of organoleptic quality, which was reduced because of excessive heating. The authors felt that a hazard analysis which would be of aid in production guidance was not really possible because of a lack of predictability of production procedures. There were some evidences of lack of sanitation as food was prepared, although sanitation was satisfactory, in general. Recommendations were made for improving current production procedures and for a new program of consistent routines and time–temperature monitoring. These changes would form a basis for a realistic HACCP analysis to be made in the future.

HACCP models for quality control of entrée production in hospital food systems were developed by Bobeng and David (1978a) and, thereafter, the quality of beef loaves was assessed utilizing these models (Bobeng and David,

1978b). To establish the models, hot entrée production was critically observed in three on-premise hospital foodservice systems: conventional, cook/chill, and cook/freeze.

In the *conventional system* studied, entrées were stored in bulk during hot-holding, then portioned; assembled in a centralized location, then distributed to patient units. In the *cook/chill system,* entrees were chilled in bulk immediately following production and chill-stored overnight. On the day of service, they were portioned, assembled, and chilled again until reheated prior to service, using microwave ovens. In the *cook/freeze system,* hot entrees were produced on premises in advance of service, packaged in bulk, frozen, and freezer stored. Following storage, they were thawed, then treated as described for the cook/chill system.

HACCP models were developed for the three systems described above in three steps: identification of control points, using flow diagrams; identification of critical control points; and establishment of monitors for control. Twelve control points were established and four critical control points identified: ingredient control and storage, equipment sanitation, personnel sanitation, and time–temperature relationships (Table 14.3). Each of these points is critical in that they affect the microbiological hazard of an item by reducing or eliminating it. The authors point out that control must be exercised at these critical control points by applying specific standards to be determined by each hospital.

According to Silverman (1982), the difficulty in using HACCP models in relatively small foodservice operations can be explained by the fact that—in contrast to the production of large batches—a variety of food items is prepared in a variety of forms and in small batches. The author has devised a modified Quality Assurance Program adapted to hospital operations of the military; by this system products are classified into categories according to processing, for example, freezers, ovens, kettles, and so forth. Within these categories, temperature constraint can be monitored with ease for each product prepared. The author has found this method a successful one in that excessive counts of microbial contaminants could be reduced to low levels.

Microbiological analysis as a tool of monitoring the quality of ingredients and products at critical control points might be desirable if it were possible to use it in foodservice. It has its limitations, however, even in the food-processing industry, where microbiological testing is an important tool. Results cannot be obtained and used immediately.

Regarding equipment and personnel sanitation, Bobeng and David (1978a) could not establish universal critical control point parameters, because each foodservice is different from another in types, sizes, and models of equipment, and has varying kinds and numbers of positions for personnel. The authors suggest that each foodservice operation needs to establish its own standards suitable to its situation and must then use them to monitor sanita-

TABLE 14.3. *Critical Control Points During Entree Production in Conventional, Cook/Chill, and Cook/Freeze Hospital Foodservice Systems*

| Control Points | System | Critical Control Point | | | |
		Ingredient Control and Storage	Equipment Sanitation	Personnel Sanitation	Time–Temperature Relationship
Procurement	1,2,3[a]	x			
Preparation	1,2,3		x	x	x
Heating	1,2,3				x
Hot holding	1				x
Chilling and chilled storage	2		x		x
Freezing and frozen storage	3				x
Thawing	3		x		x
Portioning and assembly	2,3		x	x	x
Portioning, assembly, and distribution	1		x	x	x
Cold holding and distribution	2,3		x		x
Heating	2,3				x
Serving	1,2,3		x	x	x

[a] 1 = conventional; 2 = cook/chill; 3 = cook/freeze.
Source: Bobeng and David, 1978a. Copyright © The American Dietetic Association. Reprinted by permission from *Journal of the American Dietetic Association,* **73**:524–529, 1978.

tion of equipment and personnel. In the models developed, of the four critical control points, time–temperature control is common to 11 of the 12 control points established, procurement being the one exception. Time–temperature critical control points during entrée production in the three systems studied are presented in Table 14.4. The authors suggest that establishing time–temperature standards is a practical method for monitoring entrée production in hospital foodservice. Time–temperature control had also been suggested by Peterson and Gunnerson (1974) as an effective tool in the microbiological control applied at critical control points during processing of frozen foods.

Having developed HACCP models for quality control of entrée production in three hospital systems, Bobeng and David (1978b) tested them in the production of beef loaves, made of beef, eggs, milk, and bread crumbs and

TABLE 14.4. *Time–Temperature Critical Control Points During Entree Production in Conventional, Cook/Chill, and Cook/Freeze Hospital Foodservice Systems*

Control Points	Conventional		Cook/Chill		Cook/Freeze	
	Time	Temperature[g]	Time	Temperature[g]	Time	Temperature[g]
Preparation	Minimal	45–140°F[a]	Minimal	45–140°F[a]	Minimal	45–140°F[a]
Heating	—[b]	≥140°F[i,b]	—[b]	≥140°F[i,b]	—[b]	≥140°F[i,b]
Hot holding	—[b]	≥140°F[b]	N.A.[j]	N.A.	N.A.	N.A.
Chilling	N.A.	N.A.	≤4 hours[k]	≤45°F[c]	N.A.	N.A.
Chilled storage	N.A.	N.A.	≤20 hours[k]	≤45°F[c]	N.A.	N.A.
Freezing	N.A.	N.A.	N.A.	N.A.	≤1.5 hours	≤ −4°F[e]
Frozen storage	N.A.	N.A.	N.A.	N.A.	≤8 weeks	≤0°F[f]
Thawing	N.A.	N.A.	N.A.	N.A.	Minimal	≤45°F[c]
Portioning, assembly, and distribution	Minimal	≥140°F[b]	N.A.	N.A.	N.A.	N.A.
Portioning and assembly	N.A.	N.A.	Minimal	≤45°F[c]	Minimal	≤45°F[c]
Cold, holding and distribution	N.A.	N.A.	—[b]	≤45°F[c]	—[b]	≤45°F[c]
Microwave heating	N.A.	N.A.	—[b]	165–170°F[d]	—[b]	165°–170°F[d]
Service	Minimal	≥140°F[b]	Minimal	≥140°F[b]	Minimal	≥140°F[b]

[a] 7.2–60°C.
[b] 60°C.
[c] 7.2°C.
[d] 74–77°C.
[e] −20°C.
[f] −17.8°C.

[g] Internal temperature at completion of control point activity.
[b] Time will vary with entree, equipment, and/or system.
[i] Minimum temperature; will vary with entree.
[j] Control point not applicable for system.
[k] Combined time of chilling and chilled storage should be ≤24 hours.

weighing 900 grams, in the three systems simulated in a laboratory. The purposes were to evaluate the effectiveness of the models and to assess the quality of the entrée produced.

Cooking

The loaves were baked at 315°F (157°C) to end points representative of the three systems used: to 165–170°F (74–77°C) for the conventional system and to 140–145°F (60–63°C) for the cook/chill and cook/freeze systems.

Holding

For hot-holding, to simulate holding in the conventional system, a chamber maintained at 181°F (82°C) and 50% relative humidity was used, and the internal temperature of the loaves was maintained at 160°F (71°C) during a 1-hour hold. The temperature dropped to not lower than 140°F (60°C) during portioning, assembly, and service.

Simulating holding in the cook/chill system, the loaves were covered with tagboard lids, sealed, chill-stored for 24 hours, portioned, placed on styrofoam plates, and covered with plastic, disposable covers. The portions were stored in a reach-in refrigerator for 2 hours at 39°F (3.9°C).

Simulating holding in the cook/freeze system, the loaves, covered with tagboard lids and sealed, were placed in a still-air freezer at −24°F (−31°C), freezer stored for 28 days; thawed for 24 hours at 40°F (4.4°C), portioned, and the portions treated like those of the cook/chill system.

Heating

For the portions produced under the cook/chill and cook/freeze systems, heating prior to service was performed in a microwave oven. The electric field distribution had been studied prior to the study. Heating times to achieve internal temperatures of 165–170°F (74–77°C) were determined. After heating the portions, they were allowed to set for 60 seconds before final temperatures were recorded.

Quality measurements included determination of weight loss, nutritional quality, sensory quality, and microbiological quality. The results of the latter are presented in Table 14.5. They indicate that aerobic plate counts went down to very low levels after the first cooking and kept low thereafter, regardless of the food system used.

Continuous surveillance of time–temperature as a monitor during produc-

TABLE 14.5. *Aerobic Plate Counts of Beef Loaves Produced in Three Simulated Hospital Foodservice Systems*

Control Point	Aerobic Bacteria per Gram[a]		
	Conventional	Cook/Chill	Cook/Freeze
Preparation	3.5×10^6	3.1×10^6	3.1×10^6
Baking	290	270	340
Storage	370	320	340
Thawing	—	—	340
Microwave heating	—	230	260

[a] Mean of three replications.
Source: Bobeng and David, 1978b. Copyright © The American Dietetic Association. Reprinted by permission from *Journal of the American Dietetic Association,* **73:**530–535, 1978.

tion of an entree had been analyzed in an earlier study by Bobeng and David (1978a). The time–temperature data at control points determined during production of the beef loaves are given in Table 14.6. With the exception of the time needed to chill the loaves in the cook/chill system, time–temperature standards were maintained at the control points developed for the HACCP model. For the cook/chill system, a chilling time to 45°F (7.2°C) in 4 hours had been established, but actual chilling time of the loaves was 5 hours. However, the loaves remained in the danger zone of 120–60°F (49–15.6°C) for 2 hours or less, an acceptable length of time. The authors emphasize the importance of time–temperature critical control points for monitoring control points in the three systems studied. Certainly, the study shows that if time–temperature controls were meticulously applied, a product of acceptable microbiological quality could be produced. The authors recommend the implementation of the HACCP system for hospital foodservices.

From the body of data presented in this chapter, it is evident that more research is needed in certain areas of quality food production. Some of the problems that have come to light in connection with researching critical control points of the various foodservice systems have to do with microbiological implications related to inefficiency of chilling equipment, microwave ovens, and air-forced convection ovens, and a lack of standardization of equipment and utensils in general. Foodservice designers and equipment managers can be of help if they know what foodservice managers need and want.

The reader is again referred to the examples of hazard analyses, conducted for various foodservice systems, that are listed at the end of this chapter under Additional Readings.

A review of publications dealing with the microbiological quality of menu items produced and stored by cook/chill, cook/freeze, cook/hot-hold, and

TABLE 14.6. *Actual Time–Temperature at Control Points for Beef Loaves Produced in Three Simulated Hospital Foodservice Systems*

Control Point	Conventional		Cook/Chill		Cook/Freeze	
	Time	Temperature[a]	Time	Temperature[a]	Time	Temperature[a]
Preparation	30 minutes	50–52°F	30 minutes	50–52°F	30 minutes	50–52°F
Heating	44.2 minutes[b]	165–170°F	34.9 minutes[b]	140–145°F	37.6 minutes[b]	140–145°F
Hot holding	60–90 minutes	160±3°F	N.A.[c]	N.A.	N.A.	N.A.
Chilling	N.A.	N.A.	5 hours[b]	45°F[b]	N.A.	N.A.
Chilled storage	N.A.	N.A.	19 hours[b]	41°F[b]	N.A.	N.A.
Freezing	N.A.	N.A.	N.A.	N.A.	—[d]	—[d]
Frozen storage	N.A.	N.A.	N.A.	N.A.	28 days	—[d]
Thawing	N.A.	N.A.	N.A.	N.A.	24 hours	39–43°F
Portioning, assembly, and distribution	10 minutes	≥140°F	N.A.	N.A.	N.A.	N.A.
Portioning and assembly	N.A.	N.A.	15 minutes	≤45°F	15 minutes	≤45°F
Cold holding and distribution	N.A.	N.A.	2 hours	38–42°F	2 hours	38–42°F
Microwave heating	N.A.	N.A.	90 seconds	165–170°F	90 seconds	165–170°F
Service	3 minutes	140–145°F	8 minutes	140–145°F	8 minutes	140–145°F

[a]Internal temperature of beef loaves at completion of control point activity. For conversion to C see Appendix B.
[b]Mean of three replications.
[c]Control point not applicable for system.
[d]Device for recording temperature at <0°F was not available.

Source: Bobeng and David, 1978b. Copyright © The American Dietetic Association. Reprinted by permission from *Journal of the American Dietetic Association,* **73:**530–535, 1978.

heat/serve methods has been published by Snyder and Matthews (1984).

Special attention to strict monitoring of time–temperature conditions during processing is advised when prolonged chill-storage in commonly used systems up to one month is used (Cremer et al., 1985).

But there are many more areas in need of information. Unklesbay et al. (1977), in their summary and suggestions for future research, state that there is a need for:

1. Investigating the effects of alternate methods of food procurement, storage, preparation, and service upon the microbial, nutritional, and sensory qualities of selected menu items in foodservice operations
2. Determining the effects of innovative materials handling techniques and/or foodservice equipment in each type of foodservice system upon the growth and survival of pathogenic microorganisms of public health significance
3. Formulating procedures to be used as managerial tools for decision making about preparing and serving quality menu items within each of the foodservice systems
4. Identifying factors within the physical environment of the foodservice system that directly affect food quality and safety, and correlating the effect of the interrelationships among these influential factors with food quality
5. Determining methods through which the systematic control of food quality and safety can be achieved by automated and computerized methods

REFERENCES

Anonymous (1974). *U.S. Army Regulation No. 40–5, Chapter 6, Food Service*. Medical Services, Health and Environmental Headquarters, Department of Army, Washington, D.C.

Anonymous (1976). *Microbiological Evaluation of Production Procedures for Frozen Foil Pack Meals at the Central Preparation Facility of the Francis E. Warren Air Force Base*. U.S. Army Natick Research and Development Command, Natick, MA. Technical Report 76-37-FSL.

Armstrong, J. F., D. C. Dorney, and G. Glew (1974). "Reheating and service." *Hospitals,* 48(Aug. 1):94–97.

Baird, B. (1990). "Sous Vide: What's all the excitement about." *J. Food Tech.,* 44:92–98.

Balsley, M. B. (1973). "Central commissaries: three examples of an evolving food service concept." *J. Am. Diet. Assoc.,* 63:422–426.

Bauman, H. E. (1974). "The HACCP concept and microbiological hazard categories." *Food Technol.,* 28:30; 32; 34; 74.

Bernsten, W. T. and B. D. David (1975). "Determining the electric field distribution in a 1250 watt microwave oven and its effect on portioned food during heating." *Microwave Energy Appl. Newsl.,* 8(July/Aug.):3.

Bjorkman, A. and K. A. Delphin (1966). "Sweden's Nacka Hospital Food System centralizes preparation and distribution." *Cornell Hotel Restaurant Adm. Q.,* 7(3): 84–87.

Bobeng, B. J. and B. D. David (1975). "Identifying the electric field distribution in a microwave oven: A practical method for food service operators." *Microwave Energy Appl. Newsl.,* 8(Nov.–Dec.):3–6.

Bobeng, B. J. and B. D. David (1978a). "HACCP models for quality control of entrée production in hospital food service systems. I. Development of hazard analysis critical control point models." *J. Am. Diet. Assoc.,* 73:524–529.

Bobeng, B. J. and B. D. David (1978b). "HACCP models for quality control of entrée production in hospital food service systems. II. Quality assessment of beef loaves utilizing HACCP models." *J. Am. Diet. Assoc.,* 73:530–535.

Bourland, C. T., N. D. Heidelbaugh, C. S. Huber, P. R. Kiser, and D. B. Rowley (1974). "Hazard analysis of *Clostridium perfringens* in the Skylab food system." *J. Milk Food Technol.,* 37:624–628.

Bryan, F. L. (1981). "Hazard analysis of food service operations." *Food Technol.,* 35 (Feb.):78–80; 82–87.

Bryan, F. L. and T. W. McKinley (1974). "Prevention of foodborne illness by time–temperature control of thawing, cooking, chilling, and reheating turkeys in school lunch kitchens." *J. Milk Food Technol.,* 37:420–429.

Bryan, F. L. and T. W. McKinley (1979). "Hazard analysis and control of roast beef preparation in food service establishments." *J. Food Prot.,* 42:4–18.

Bryan, F. L., K. A. Seabolt, R. W. Peterson, and L. M. Roberts (1978). "Time–temperature observations of food and equipment in airline catering operations." *J. Food Prot.,* 41:80–92.

Bryan, F. (1994). "HACCP: Present status and future in contribution to food safety." *Dairy, Food Environ. Safety,* 14:650–655.

Bunch, W. L., M. E. Matthews, and H. H. Marth (1976). "Hospital chill food service systems: Acceptability and microbiological characteristics of beef-soy loaves when processed according to system procedures." *J. Food Sci.,* 41:1273–1276.

Bunch, W. L., M. E. Matthews, and E. H. Marth (1977). "Fate of *Staphylococcus aureus* in beef-soy loaves subjected to procedures used in hospital chill food service systems." *J. Food Sci.,* 42:565–566.

Cremer, M. (1978). "Temperatures of spaghetti after heating in convection ovens at service locations in a commissary food service system." *J. Food Sci.,* 43:1062–1065; 1070.

Cremer, M. L. and J. R. Chipley (1977a). "Satellite food service system assessment in terms of time and temperature conditions and microbiological and sensory quality of spaghetti and chili." *J. Food Sci.,* 42:225–229.

Cremer, M. L. and J. R. Chipley (1977b). "Satellite food service system: Time and temperature and microbiological and sensory quality of precooked frozen hamburger patties." *J. Food Prot.,* 40:603–607.

Cremer, M. L., T-K. K. Yum, and G. J. Banwart (1985). "Time, temperature and sensory quality assessment of chicken and noodles in a hospital foodservice system." *J. Food Sci.,* 50:891–896.

Dahl, C. A., M. E. Matthews, and E. H. Marth (1978). "Cook/chill foodservice systems: Microbiological quality of beef loaf at five process stages." *J. Food Prot.,* 41:788–793.

428		MICROBIOLOGICAL CONSIDERATIONS

Dahl, C. A. and M. E. Matthews (1979). "Forced-air convection ovens: Temperature range in oven and in beef loaf during heating." *School Food Serv., Res. Rev.,* 3(1):11–15.

Decareau, R. V. (1978). "Foodservice equipment: Technological trends." *J. Food Prot.,* 41:459–463.

Dwyer, S. J., K. Unklesbay, N. Unklesbay, and C. Dunlap (1977). "Identification of major areas of energy utilization within the food processing/foodservice industry." Research Report to the National Science Foundation, NSFSIA 75-16222. Washington, D.C.

Food and Drug Administration (1978). *Food Service Sanitation Manual.* U.S. Department of Health, Education and Welfare, Public Health Serv. DHEW Publ. No. (FDA) 78–2081.

Food and Drug Administration (1993). *Food Code 1993.* U.S. Department of Health and Human Services, Public Health Serv. Publ. No. PB94–113941AS, Springfield, VA.

Fries, J. A. and D. M. Graham (1972). "Reconstituting preplated frozen meals with integral heat." *Food Technol.,* 26(11):76–77; 80; 82.

Hartman, J. (1975). "Innovations in food service equipment." *Hospitals,* 49(March 16):126–128.

Heidelbaugh, N. D., M. C. Smith, Jr., and P. C. Rambout (1973a). "Food safety in NASA nutrition programs." *Am. Vet. Med. Assoc. J.,* 163:1065–1070.

Heidelbaugh, N. D., D. B. Rowley, E. M. Powers, C. T. Bourland, and J. L. McQueen (1973b). "Microbiological testing of Skylab foods." *Appl. Microbiol.,* 25:55–61.

Hill, M. A. and G. Glew (1974). "Recipe development." *Hospitals,* 48(June 16):124–125.

Kotschevar, L. H. and M. E. Terrell (1977). *Food Service Planning: Layout and Equipment,* 2nd ed. John Wiley & Sons, New York.

Livingston, G. E. and C. M. Chang (1972). "Second generation reconstitution systems." *Cornell Hotel Restaurant Adm. Q.,* 13(1):57–64.

Livingston, G. (1990). "Foodservice: Older Than Methuselah." *Food Tech.,* 44:54, 56, 58–59.

McGuckian, A. T. (1969). "The A.G.S. Food System—Chilled pasteurized food." *Cornell Hotel Restaurant Adm. Q.,* 10(1):87–92; 99.

Millross, J., M. A. Hill, and G. Glew (1974). "Consequences of a switch to cook-freeze." *Hospitals,* 48(Aug. 16):118; 124–126.

Peterson, A. C. and R. E. Gunnerson (1974). "Microbiological critical control points in frozen foods." *Food Technol.,* 28(9):37–44.

Rappole, C. L. (1973). "Institutional use of frozen entrees." *Cornell Hotel Restaurant Adm. Q.,* 14(1):72–87.

Rhodehamel, E. (1992). "FDA's concerns with Sous Vide processing." *J. Food Tech.,* 46:73–76.

Ridley, S. J. and M. E. Matthews (1982). "Temperature histories of menu items during meal assembly, distribution and service." *J. Food Prot.,* 46:100–104.

Ringle, E. C. and B. D. David (1975). "Measuring electric field distribution in a microwave oven." *Food Technol.,* 29(12):46; 48; 50; 52–54.

Rinke, W. J. (1976). "Three major systems reviewed and evaluated." *Hospitals,* 50(Feb. 16):73–78.

Rowley, D. B. (1976). "Microbiological aspects of certain military feeding systems." *J. Milk Food Technol.,* 39:280–284.

Rowley, D. B., J. M. Tuomy, and D. E. Westcott (1972). *Fort Lewis Experiment, Application of Food Technology and Engineering to Central Preparation.* Food Laboratory, United States Army, Natick Laboratories, Natick, MA. Technical Report 72–46–FL.

Sawyer, C. A., Y. M. Naidu, and S. Thompson (1983). "Cook/chill foodservice systems: Microbiological quality and end-point temperature of beef loaf, peas, and potatoes after reheating by conduction, convection, and microwave radiation." *J. Food Prot.,* 46:1036–1043.

Schukraft, B. (1972). "Integral heat system for volume food preparation." *Food Technol.,* 26(Sept.):27–28.

Seligsohn, M. (1978). "Walter Reed's mighty little food factory." *Food Eng.,* 50(April):80–81.

Sell, W. (1973). "New equipment and systems in mass feeding." *J. Am. Diet. Assoc.,* 63:413–416.

Silverman, G. (1982). "Assuring the microbial quality of hospital patient feeding systems." In *Hospital Feeding Systems.* National Academy Press, Washington, D.C.

Silverman, G. J., E. M. Powers, D. F. Carpenter, and D. B. Rowley (1975a). *Microbiological Evaluation of the Foodservice System at Travis Air Force Base.* U.S. Army Natick Research and Development Command, Natick, MA. Technical Report 75-110-FSL.

Silverman, G. J., E. M. Powers, and D. B. Rowley (1975b). *Microbiological Analysis of the Food Preparation and Dining Facilities at Fort Myer and Bolling Air Force Base.* U.S. Army Natick Research and Development Command, Natick, MA. Technical Report 75–53–FSL.

Snyder, O. P. and M. E. Matthews (1984). "Microbiological quality of foodservice menu items produced and stored by cook/chill, cook/freeze, cook/hot-hold and heat/serve methods." *J. Food Prot.,* 47:876–885.

Tuomi, S., M. E. Matthews, and E. H. Marth (1974a). "Temperature and microbial flora of refrigerated ground beef gravy subjected to holding and reheating as might occur in a school foodservice operation." *J. Milk Food Technol.,* 37:457–462.

Tuomi, S., M. E. Matthews, and E. H. Marth (1974b). "Behavior of *Clostridium perfringens* in precooked chilled ground beef gravy during cooling, holding, and reheating." *J. Milk Food Technol.,* 37:494–498.

Tuomy, J. M. and R. J. Byrne (1974). *Design of a Central Food Preparation Facility for the Army.* U.S. Army Natick Research and Development Command, Natick, MA. Technical Report 74–25–OS/SA.

Unklesbay, N. (1977). "Monitoring for quality control in alternate foodservice systems." *J. Am. Diet. Assoc.,* 71:423–428.

Unklesbay, N. F., R. B. Maxcy, M. E. Knickrehm, K. E. Stevenson, M. L. Cremer, and M. E. Matthews (1977). *Foodservice Systems: Product Flow and Microbial Quality and Safety of Foods.* University of Missouri-Columbia, College of Agriculture, Agriculture Experiment Station, Columbia, MO. North Central Regional Research Publication No. 245.

VanEgmond-Pannel, D. (1985). *School Foodservice,* 3rd ed. Avi Publishing Co., Westport, CT.

West, B. B., L. Wood, V. F. Harger, and G. S. Shugart (1977). *Food Service in Institutions,* 5th ed. John Wiley & Sons, New York.

ADDITIONAL READINGS

Anonymous. *Quality Control Inspection Manual.* U.S. Army Troop Support Agency, Fort Lee, VA. 1975.

Bryan, F. L. "Hazard analysis of food service operations." *Food Technol.,* 35(Feb.):78–80; 82–87. 1981.

Bryan, F. L. "Foodborne disease risk assessment of foodservice establishments in a community." *J. Food Prot.,* 45:3–100. 1982.

Bryan, F. L., C. A. Bartleson, M. Sugi, L. Miyashiro, and S. Tsutsumi. "Hazard analyses of fried, boiled and steamed Cantonese-style foods." *J. Food Prot.,* 45:410–421. 1982.

Bryan, F. L. and C. A. Bartleson. "Mexican-style foodservice operations: Hazard analyses, critical control points, and monitoring." *J. Food Prot.,* 48:509–524. 1985.

Bryan, F. L. and J. B. Lyon. "Critical control points of hospital foodservice operations." *J. Food Prot.,* 47:950–963. 1984.

Bryan, F. L., M. Harvey, and M. C. Misup. "Hazard analysis of party-pack foods prepared at a catering establishment." *J. Food Prot.,* 44:118–123. 1981.

Bryan, F. L. and T. W. McKinley. "Hazard analysis and control of roast beef jus preparation in food service establishments." *J. Food Prot.,* 43:512–513; 519. 1980.

Bryan, F. L., K. A. Seabolt, R. W. Peterson, and L. M. Roberts. "Time–temperature observations of food and equipment in airline catering observations." *J. Food Prot.,* 41(2):80–92. 1978.

Davies, H. "The need for training to fill a technological gap in the catering industry." In *Catering Equipment and Systems Designs,* G. Glew, Ed. International Ideas Publ., Philadelphia. 1977.

Donaldson, B. "Food service." *Hospitals,* 45(April 1):81–86. 1971.

Dorney, D. C. and G. Glew. "The selection of forced convection ovens for reheating precooked frozen food." *HCIMA Rev.,* 1:39. 1974.

Dorney, D. C. and G. Glew. "Rapid thawing of precooked frozen food in catering." *J. Food Technol.,* 12:523–534. 1977.

Livingston, G. E. and C. M. Chang, Eds. *Food Service Systems, Analysis, Design and Implementation.* Academic Press, New York. 1979.

Matthews, M. E. "Quality of food in cook/chill foodservice systems: A review." *School Foodserv. Res. Rev.,* 1(1):15–19. 1977.

Nicholanco, S. and M. E. Matthews. "Quality of beef stew in a hospital chill system." *J. Am. Diet. Assoc.,* 72:31–37. 1978.

The Pillsbury Company. "Food Safety Through the Hazard Analysis and Critical Control Point System." The Pillsbury Co., Minneapolis, MN. 1973.

Ridley, S. J. and M. E. Matthews. "Temperature histories of menu items during meal assembly, distribution and service." *J. Food Prot.,* 46:100–104. 1982.

Shea, L. A. "Heat retaining capabilities of selected delivery systems." *J. Am. Diet. Assoc.,* 65:430–436. 1974.

Snyder, P. O. "A model food service quality assurance system." *J. Food Technol.,* 35(2):70–76. 1981.

Spears, M. C. and A. G. Vaden. *Foodservice Organizations—A Managerial and Systems Approach.* John Wiley & Sons, New York. 1985.

Unklesbay, N. "Hospital foodservice, 1978 and beyond." *J. Food Prot.,* 41:471–475. 1978.

White, J. C. "The national conference on food protection in foodservice." *Cornell Hotel Restaurant Adm. Q.,* 18(3):77–78. 1977.

CHAPTER *15*

Educating Foodservice Personnel
in Food Sanitation

OPPORTUNITY FOR EDUCATION

Opportunity for education in matters of foodservice sanitation is offered on several levels, from the four-year colleges and two-year junior and community colleges to vocational schools, and through courses given under the sponsorship of professional organizations, and federal, state, and local agencies concerned with matters of health. However, there is a lack of uniformity regarding breadth and depth. Even at the highest level, the four-year colleges, discrepancies regarding education in matters of food sanitation exist. Woodburn (1978) made a survey of 20 professional foodservice programs and found to her surprise that only one-third of the schools surveyed required a course in microbiology, and that only three schools appeared to have specific sanitation courses that would have direct application to foodservice. The same author discusses the role of junior colleges in the education of students desiring an A.A. degree in foodservice, with a view to qualifying for positions as dietetic technicians or for supervisory jobs regarded as "middle management." The author lists three objectives that should be followed in the education of these students: (1) the arousal of an awareness of the importance of foodborne hazards and acceptance of the fact that these can be controlled; (2) the building of a scientific basis for sanitary control; and (3) the identification of control procedures, with a possible emphasis on the HACCP concept.

In connection with the education of middle management personnel, the role of the Hospital, Institution and Educational Food Service Society deserves to be—at least briefly—discussed. This society, also referred to as HIEFSS, is a national organization, founded by the American Dietetic Association (ADA) approximately 20 years ago. It is now an independent society with a strong liaison with ADA. Its aim is to provide an opportunity for affiliation on the technical level of persons of similar education background in dietetics. Among its objectives are the promotion of education in foodservice and nutrition practices, and the development of continuing education opportunities for its members. Eligible for membership are people who meet the standards of HIEFSS concerning both education and experience, and who are recognized as being members of the supportive personnel in dietetics, that is, dietetic technicians and dietetic assistants.

The job responsibilities of a dietetic technician are in two main areas, foodservice management and nutritional care. In foodservice management, a dietetic technician works under the supervision of an administrative dietitian or an administrator and consultant dietitian. His or her education includes the successful completion of an Associate Degree program meeting the standards established by ADA.

The job responsibilities of a dietetic assistant are to provide supervision in foodservice and nutritional care services under the supervision of a dietitian, a dietetic technician, or an administrator and consulting dietitian. His or her education includes the successful completion of a Dietetic Assistant program, of approximately 1-year duration, which meets the standards established by the ADA.

A national certification and recertification program has been developed by HIEFSS to attest to the qualifications of dietetic technicians and assistants. Recertification depends on the completion of certain requirements in continuing education.

Members of HIEFSS are individuals who frequently have the responsibility for training food handlers. Therefore, their own knowledge of, and proficiency in, sanitary practices in foodservice is of great importance. Knowledge in matters of sanitary foodhandling requires regular updating in order to be in step with new developments in the rapidly changing field of foodservice.

Basic to any training of nonprofessional food handlers are an appreciation by top and middle management of the importance of sanitary quality control in foodservice and the knowledge of how to achieve it in the establishment they serve.

KEEPING UP ON DEVELOPMENTS IN THE PROFESSION

It is a human trait to support causes in which one believes and to slight those that seem unimportant. Fortunately, matters on which one keeps well informed tend to gain in importance; this applies to the field of food sanitation. It is therefore desirable that management keep well informed on the various aspects of sanitation: developments in food processing, food microbiology, foodservice equipment, detergents and sanitizers, and the like. For instance, specific microbiological hazards are arising in connection with new food-processing methods as well as with new methods of merchandising prepared menu items. And, of course, a new era in food production, now well established, is characterized by the increasing use of production systems such as cook/freeze, cook/chill, and assembly-serve. These new systems have new microbiological hazards connected with them. Management also needs to keep informed on current problems in epidemiology, and on local, state, and federal legislation as they relate to preparing and serving food to the public. In the equipment field, developments regarding improved heating, cooling, and hot-holding equipment should not only be watched but should be stimulated by requesting them. Well-informed management has the responsibility of making known their need for equipment appropriate for dependable heating of food, for fast cooling, for efficient cold storage, and for efficient hot holding. Management is also responsible for procuring this equipment and for training employees in using it.

To keep abreast of current developments in the food field, including sanitary aspects, is no easy task even for those who have the benefits of professional associations, professional journals, and attendance at professional meetings. Fortunately, the health authorities, from the federal level to the local, are eager to be of constructive assistance to the foodservice industry.

Continuing education in matters of sanitation is the concern of everyone engaged in the preparation and service of food to the public, from top management down the line: supervisors (middle management), food handlers, foodservice personnel, and warewashers.

TRAINING OF NONPROFESSIONAL PERSONNEL

In the more distant past, few foodservice establishments seemed to have the benefit of a well-structured training program in sanitation for employees. In many localities the health authority does not have sufficient staff time to conduct classes in sanitation. In the foodservice establishment itself, qualified teachers are frequently not available, or if they are available, these persons are usually so busy with other responsibilities that this "one more thing" cannot be shouldered.

This is an unfortunate situation, since training employees in sanitation is absolutely essential to the success of a sanitation program. New employees should become convinced of the importance of sanitation, a subject probably initially foreign to them. To accomplish this, new employees must learn about the fundamentals: bacterial growth, foodborne illness, personal hygiene, temperature control, and so forth. Food handlers have to become imbued with the fact that they play an important role in sanitation and need to understand and become trained in sanitary techniques in handling food. It is essential that they be informed on matters of sanitation at the very start of working in an establishment.

To develop a successful training program for employees, these points should be considered by management:

1. Knowing the fundamentals of sanitary practices acceptable to the health authority.
2. Supplying the new employee with background information which will enable him or her to understand the concept of sanitation. This information should be supplied as part of his or her orientation.
3. Teaching the employee the techniques of sanitary food handling; this instruction should start the day the employee begins work.
4. Supplying proper and adequate equipment, tools, and supplies.
5. Supplying supervision on the job.
6. Supplying refresher sessions in sanitation.
7. Giving recognition to the employee for information well learned and techniques well performed.

The number of new foodservice employees who have to be trained is staggering because of a high turnover rate. Foodservice employees often come from lower socioeconomic levels and have not received formal training for the trade. Many of them are not easy to teach, have language difficulties, or read poorly. Consequently, they advance slowly, earn poorly, feel insecure and dissatisfied, and leave their jobs frequently to seek employment elsewhere.

Teaching sanitation to unskilled employees of a poor socioeconomic background is a hard task, and the concepts "cleanliness" and "sanitation" may prove difficult to convey. Yet the advantages of training unskilled foodservice employees are obvious. For management they are: chance of foodborne illness is reduced; labor turnover is reduced; supervision of employees is reduced; the working standards are improved; production is increased; and a larger supply of skilled employees is created for the particular foodservice as well as the foodservice industry as a whole.

It has been rightly stated by Gravani (1982, 1983) that "training programs do not need to be boring," and that when certain basic principles are followed, they can be made interesting, informative, and effectual. Since learning is affected by a multiplicity of factors, only a few important ones are mentioned: the capability, attitude, and educational background of the audience; and the importance of presenting complex material simply and straightforwardly, especially when the audience has a poor educational background and lacks previous training and experience.

There are also distinctive advantages for the employee: job satisfaction, the chance for advancement, and the greater sense of security that comes with recognition, advancement, and job satisfaction.

The Instructor

A successful instructor knows his or her subject matter; is alerted to current changes in the food field relevant to sanitary aspects; has time and is willing to plan and prepare lessons, including visual aids, in detail; is able to hold the attention of a trainee or group of trainees; is apt to be tired after a full day's work; is tactful yet frank in handling subjects touching on such intimate matters as personal hygiene; and always seeks ways of improving his or her teaching.

In institutions that employ professionally trained managers who are qualified to be instructors, these persons are frequently overburdened with other duties. It seems that it is responsibility of top management to relieve these persons of those duties that could be taken over by others and to free them for the important task of instructing employees in food sanitation. But it also seems that professionally trained managers might well take the initiative and make it known to top management that they wish to conduct a well-structured training program in sanitation, and for what reasons. They should be prepared to suggest which duties could be taken on by someone else to free them for the teaching responsibility. Nothing succeeds like conviction, initiative, and perseverance. The need for delegating duties and responsibilities in dietary departments to nonprofessional personnel has been emphasized by the American Dietetic Association for years.

Training Methods

The methods used include on-the-job training, conferences, lectures, discussions, and the use of visual aids such as posters, slides, films, videotapes, and demonstrations. Videotape training is a relatively new method that can be effective if properly designed and effectively used. Gravani (1984) notes that video has several advantages in that it displays actual scenes, has a strong emotional and personal appeal, repeats information for reinforcement, and generates interest and excitement. The author stresses the fact that there is a need for developing appropriate, high-quality video programs for nonprofessionals in food protection, and for professionals as well.

Programmed instruction in sanitary food handling using teaching machines was discussed by Carter (1963).

All teaching methods require that follow-up instruction take place and that supervision on the job be employed, to reemphasize what was learned.

ON-THE-JOB TRAINING. On-the-job training is probably the most frequently used method today in foodservice establishments. Its success depends on how carefully the program is planned and executed.

The most knowledgeable teachers are just good enough for this important job. Unfortunately, the on-the-job trainee is all too frequently simply assigned to another employee who shows him "how to do it." Faulty and bacteriologically unacceptable methods are perpetuated in this manner.

Lukowski and Eshbach (1963) have pointed out that there are four major steps based on the principles of habit formation, which include motivation, demonstration, and practice, and that these steps are preparation, presentation, application, and follow-up.

In the first step, preparation, trainees should be motivated to learn. They should become convinced that their person is an important link in the chain of events and that they may play a dual role—providing contaminants and controlling contaminants—and that successful cooperation in the program will affect their job performance record and chances of advancement.

The second step, presentation, includes the "whys" and "hows." A clear understanding of the reasons underlying sanitary handling techniques is fundamental to their application.

The third step, application, gives trainees a chance to prove to the instructor that they have understood the lesson and are using the appropriate techniques on the job.

The fourth step, follow-up, involves checks on the part of the instructor. Naturally, frequent and thorough checks would be more effective than infrequent and superficial ones.

It should be remembered that recognition of a job well done is essential to keeping employees' performance at a high level.

CONFERENCES, LECTURES, DEMONSTRATIONS, AND VISUAL AIDS. An early conference on sanitation with the new employee is extremely important and should be scheduled as part of orientation. Naturally, instruction given on the first day cannot possibly convey to the employee all the basic information he or she needs about bacteria, their reservoirs, activities, and so forth, except, possibly, when programmed instruction is applied (see below). Additional conferences, lectures, demonstrations, and visual or audiovisual aids should accompany the employee's on-the-job training as soon as possible. In these sessions, "old" employees might be included. Regular refresher sessions in sanitation are needed by all foodservice workers.

PROGRAMMED INSTRUCTION.   Programmed instruction by machines is a relatively new teaching method. The subject matter is prepared by a specialist in a well-organized, simple, effective manner. The learner teaches himself or herself using the material and an appropriate machine.

Teaching machines and programs have, according to Carter (1963), this in common: that continuous active response is required by the learner; that provision is made for informing the student immediately whether each response made is correct, making it possible for him or her to immediately correct mistakes; and finally, that the rate at which the learner proceeds is determined by his or her own capabilities.

Objectives and Course Content

The major objectives of a sanitation training course for a nonprofessional foodservice employee are to create an awareness of the public health aspects of the job and to create a feeling for the importance of his or her role within the total sanitation program and an eagerness to do his or her part.

The subject matter would include, in concise form, the following:

1. Elements of microbiology, with emphasis on microorganisms that are important from a public health point of view: size, shape, spores, reproduction; time–temperature relationships of growth and death; and importance of food as a medium for bacteria. Principles of food preservation.
2. Parasites in foods.
3. Transmission of pathogens.
4. Foodborne illnesses: causative organisms, circumstances associated with outbreaks, symptoms, reporting, and the role of the health authority.
5. Reservoirs of microorganisms: humans (the food handler, the customer), animals (livestock, pets, rodents, insects), environment (sewage, soil, air, water), and food supply.
6. Contamination of food in the foodservice area from the above reservoirs and from secondary sources, such as soiled hands, soiled equipment, utensils, and an ill-maintained physical plant. Control measures: personal hygiene; rodent and insect control; efficient plumbing; potable water; removal of soil; avoidance of cross-contamination from raw to cooked food; equipment and utensil sanitation; housekeeping in the areas of storage, food preparation, and service.
7. Multiplication of bacteria in foods and factors affecting multiplication. The meaning of "potentially hazardous foods." Time–temperature relationships; the meaning of "danger zone." Control measures; time–tem-

perature control for all potentially hazardous foods at all stages of storage, preparation, and service.
8. Agencies concerned with food protection. Cooperation with the local health authority.

According to Snyder (1978),* employees who handle food, serve food, and clean working surfaces and equipment should—when properly trained in sanitation—have the information and skills listed below.

Food-Handling Personnel

1. Can specify how to produce food and keep hands sanitarily safe
2. Can describe how to look for rodents and insects and what action to take
3. Can specify safe food preparation processes
4. Can specify how to inspect incoming food products for wholesomeness
5. Can describe how to measure process temperatures and prescribe safe time–temperature procedures
6. Can conduct a Hazard Analysis Critical Control Point analysis of food handling and kitchen cleaning
7. Can describe safe storage methods for raw and cooked foods and foodservice materials
8. Know how to set up a Quality Control (QC) system in their own work centers
9. Know how to conduct a QC check of his/her own procedures and measure QC indicators
10. Know what to do in an emergency when a utility has failed
11. Can specify how to keep food hot or cold for service
12. Can prescribe how to handle leftovers from kitchen operations
13. Understand advantages to investigating sources when ordering for quality and safety
14. Can specify how to operate a temporary foodservice

Foodservice Personnel

1. Know how to conduct a hazard analysis and inspect critical control points in holding and serving food
2. Can describe personal health symptoms that are cause to stay out of the food, food utensil, and food storage area
3. Understand and can apply the regulations regarding use of food served to customers
4. Know how to measure food temperatures
5. Can describe safe storage methods for foods in the service area
6. Know the importance of proper operation of foodservice equipment and can describe proper operation of the equipment for which they are responsible

7. Understand the requirements for microbial growth and the relation of time and temperature for major illness microorganisms
8. Can differentiate the hazard risk of different foods

Cleaning Personnel

1. Know how to clean themselves preparatory to work and follow proper personal hygiene work habits
2. Can describe how to wash, sanitize, and dry a work surface or piece of equipment with cleaner and sanitizer
3. Know how to perform hot water cleaning, sanitization, and drying
4. Know how to work out concentrations of cleaners and sanitizers and test for concentration levels
5. Know how to judge if a utensil or piece of equipment is sanitary and safe to use
6. Know how to clean facilities and know what is adequately clean
7. Know how to keep serving utensils and areas clean and sanitized
8. Can describe ways to prevent cross contamination in the service, ware and pot washing, and garbage areas
9. Understand how food can become contaminated with hazardous chemicals and know how to deal with pesticides and chemicals
10. Know how to dispose of rubbish and garbage properly
11. Know the major causes of foodborne illness and can relate this to their own operation
12. Understand how chemical poisoning can occur and how it can be prevented
13. Know and understand the role of the sanitarian

Self-Inspection

Self-inspection is a valuable tool for assuring that efforts toward creating and maintaining high sanitation standards in a foodservice operation have been attained and are being maintained. These self-inspections need to be performed regularly and systematically, and should be carried out by trained and reliable persons such as foodservice operators or managers or, in the case of a large foodservice operation, supervisors of the various departments. All areas and activities of the operation—from receiving, storing, preparing, holding, transporting, serving, and caring for leftovers, to maintenance of equipment used in preparation, holding, and serving menu items, to personal hygiene of food handlers and the handling practice of these, to the sanitary aspects of the physical plant, to dishwashing and garbage disposal—must be included in the scrutiny, with critical control points given more frequent checking. A useful sample checklist for sanitation self-inspection was developed by the National Restaurant Association (1983). Training aids are discussed at the end of this chapter.

A listing of training and certification programs in food protection is kept up to date by the Food and Drug Administration. This registry contains listings of government organizations (local, state, and federal), industry organizations, and academic institutions. Sponsors are listed by FDA region, and addresses of contact persons are given for each region (see Appendix A).

FOOD PROTECTION AND CERTIFICATION PROGRAM
FOR FOODSERVICE MANAGERS AND OPERATORS

History

A growing awareness of the need for higher standards of sanitation in food-service establishments—partly stimulated by a disturbing number of food-borne outbreaks in public eating places—has resulted in an increase in formal training programs. Historically, New York City has been a municipality that has shown an active interest in upgrading the sanitary standards in its many foodservice establishments. Its history of trying to succeed in this effort has had its ups and downs—successful at times, then again fraught with disappointments and setbacks caused by lack of interest and cooperation on the part of the operators and managers of the foodservice establishments concerned. Courses offered by the Health Department on a voluntary basis were popular at first, but as the years went by, were attended by increasingly fewer participants, while food-poisoning outbreaks were on the increase. Finally, beginning in 1973, the Health Department of New York City required that managers, or operators, of foodservice establishments being cited for serious violations of the Health Code take a course in food protection set up by the city's Department of Health (Hinkley, 1974).

In the meantime, in 1971, a conference was conducted by the U.S. Food and Drug Administration, the Public Health Association, and representatives of the foodservice industry. The purpose of this conference was to scrutinize existing food protection programs. The consensus was that foodservice management personnel should become more knowledgeable in sanitation and sanitary food-handling practices.

In 1973, the Ohio Department of Health developed the first statewide foodservice manager training and certification program in the United States. The FDA showed an interest in Ohio's activities of training and certification, and since then, the concept of foodservice manager training and certification has spread rapidly. The foodservice industry became increasingly motivated to improve foodservice sanitation through manager training and certification (Palmer et al., 1975; Bower and Davis, 1976; White, 1977; Davis, 1977; Sandler, 1978). It was felt that an industry as large as the foodservice industry—it ranks fourth in sales behind grocery stores, the automobile industry, and general merchandising (Hall, 1977)—has an obligation to raise its sanitary standards and to uphold them. To uphold high sanitary standards is no easy task, because the foodservice industry employs approximately 4 million persons and has an extremely high turnover of employees, possibly one of the highest in any major industry in the United States.

The National Institute for the Foodservice Industry (NIFI) has now become the Educational Foundation of the National Restaurant Association. In close cooperation with the Food and Drug Administration, it has been instrumental in working toward the goal of educating and training foodservice personnel. NIFI was successful in bringing together the foodservice industry, regulatory agencies, and educational institutions. As stated by Hall (1977), NIFI's goals were the professionalization of the foodservice industry through education and the development of management certification that is based on both education and experience. To achieve this, NIFI developed a plan geared to satisfy the need for competent managers. The plan included the development of training courses, creation of scholarships, and establishment of teacher training grants. It also included distribution of informative material, and research. These activities, greatly expanded, are still carried out by the Educational Foundation.

Two other interstate organizations also offer programs leading to certification. They are the Educational Institute of the American Hotel and Motel Association (AHMA), and the Foodservice Certification Society. Manager training and certification can be either mandatory or voluntary. On the local level, the state may leave the decision to the local authorities.

In the mid-1970s, a need for a *uniform* plan for sanitation training and certification for managers and operators of foodservice establishments was felt, and the National Institute for the Foodservice Industry set out to create such a plan.

Uniform National Plan for Sanitation Training and Certification of Foodservice Managers and Operators

In 1976, the National Institute for the Foodservice Industry was awarded a contract by the Food and Drug Administration to develop a plan for the implementation of a uniform national program of sanitation training and certification of owners, operators, and managers of foodservice establishments. As a first step, a nationwide investigation was made of existing foodservice manager certification programs. The survey revealed that at least 27 major programs could be identified. Besides the programs that were offered on a statewide basis, a number of similar programs were found to exist on a local level. In some instances, educational institutions were involved in that they sponsored, planned, and conducted the programs. Junior colleges and community colleges that were training students majoring in foodservice to be managers gave these students a foundation in foodservice sanitation that led to certification.

The survey also showed that a number of food chains and companies sponsored and conducted training courses and sought certification in foodservice sanitation for their own employees engaged in foodservice managerial activities. The U.S. Armed Services have their own training program.

The texts used in the various training courses are not uniform. It seems that some states, colleges, and food companies use their own teaching materials. Also used are teaching aids published by the FDA and by the Educational Foundation, and a text by Longrée and Blaker (1982), to name a few (see Appendix A for details; see also Teaching Aids).

To assist with the development of a uniform national training plan, a Project Coordinating Committee was chosen, which consisted of representatives of the foodservice industry and government, many with affiliations with educational institutions. In 1977, NIFI submitted the "Final Report" (National Institute for the Foodservice Industry, 1977) to the Food and Drug Administration.

The "Final Report" was divided into two parts. Part I consists of a plan to implement uniform national sanitation training and certification of foodservice managers. Part II deals with recommendations for the establishment of minimum standards of course content and program administration for foodservice manager sanitation training and certification.

The major elements were:

1. Acceptance and promulgation of a minimum standard of training content, as described in the *Report,* along with flexibility in training design.
2. Use of a meaningful examination process.
3. Joint sponsorship of training and certification by the foodservice industry and regulatory agencies.
4. Recognition of training leading to certification, provided certain minimum standards are met.
5. Establishment of reciprocal recognition of training and certification among mandatory and voluntary programs, provided certain minimum standards are met.
6. Establishment of the National Council for Accreditation of Foodservice Managers.
7. Encouragement, promotion, coordination and support of the uniform sanitation training and certification plan by the U.S. Food and Drug Administration.

The steps in certification were:

1. Training the manager, operator, or owner in operating a safe foodservice establishment.
2. Requiring completion of an examination which tests the trainee's knowledge of the course content.

   3. A test of the trainee's performance in an actual day-to-day working situation into which he or she is placed. This is a concluding requirement.

Educational tools are provided to the trainee during the course that should enable him or her to conduct self-inspection and to also be a valuable aid in training nonprofessional foodservice workers.

According to Snyder (1978),* the outcomes for management of an educational program covering the prevention of foodborne illness should be:

Management

1. Can prepare a sanitation creed or policy for the organization.
2. Understands that some levels of food contamination are unavoidable and can prescribe acceptable limits posing no real risk to the public.
3. Knows what is needed for sanitary design of a food facility and is able to specify design policy.
4. Is able to specify policy on purchasing of supplies.
5. Can specify and establish a self-inspection system/quality control system with adequate record keeping and action feedback for operating components not within control limits.
6. Can prescribe an accept–reject policy for marginal food products.
7. Can perform an accurate hazard analysis and critical control point inspection of the establishment.
8. Can specify a training program policy in sanitation and qualifications for certification.
9. Can prescribe a personal hygiene policy.
10. Is able to specify a cleaning and sanitizing policy.
11. Knows the cost-benefits of sanitation.
12. Can prescribe a policy of reward and punishment for good–bad employee performance.
13. Can prescribe an emergency operations policy in case of utility failure.
14. Can prescribe an organizational policy to be followed when notified that the organization is suspected of being a source of foodborne illness.

UNIFORM FOOD PROTECTION CERTIFICATION PROGRAM OF 1985

While the still young programs for manager and operator training and certification progressed, there emerged a new idea, namely, that of making testing for certification uniform. The possibility of developing a national Food Protection Certification Program requiring a nationally standardized test was discussed as to its pros and cons by persons in industry and regulatory agencies. A test was envisioned that would reliably assess the knowledge and skills of

---

*Copyright © 1978 by the International Association of Milk, Food and Environmental Sanitarians, Inc. Reprinted by permission.

candidates seeking certification, and no formal training prerequisites would be required, although there was considerable disagreement voiced in regard to that part of the testing program-to-be.

In 1982, the FDA contacted the Center for Occupational and Professional Assessment (COPA), a division of the Educational Testing Service (ETS), to determine whether it would be feasible to develop the envisioned national testing program. By 1984, the FDA concluded that, on the basis of a report submitted by the ETS, such a program was indeed feasible, and it was developed thereafter.*

An Advisory Board, made up of a cross-section of experts, provides policy guidance and reviews and approves all test materials. The board consists of a consumer representative as well as federal, academic, industry, local, and state representatives.

When this uniform certification program was established, one of the objectives was the creation of an examination by which all candidates were tested on their concepts about sanitary food management. It should be a program that would be acceptable to state and local regulatory agencies throughout the country. It should be easy to understand. It should be available to a variety of foodservice personnel, from persons with a degree from a 4-year college to those whose entire training might have been on the job. Candidates failing the test should have an opportunity to better their knowledge and be tested again.

The Test

The test consists of 60 multiple-choice questions that cover the important aspects of food protection such as *food:* procurement, receiving, storing (dry storage and refrigeration), processing, including preparation, holding, displaying, and handling of leftovers, serving or dispensing; *employees:* personal hygiene and health; and *facilities, equipment,* and *maintenance* of these.

Test Development

A team of experts, which was assembled by COPA, helped define content specifications, and aided in the formation of the test questions. This team included experts from the FDA, state and local public health officials, educators, trainees, and representatives of the foodservice industry.

---

*Center for Occupational and Professional Assessment, Educational Testing Service, Princeton, NJ. 08541.

Test Administration

The Certification Test is administered by trained ETS personnel at designated test sites. The scores are reported to the candidates and those who pass will receive a certificate. Candidates who fail the test receive, in addition to their score report, a critique that outlines topics for further study.

National Registry of Certified Persons

This registry is of value not only to the candidates themselves, but also to personnel managers, administrators, and participating jurisdictions on a national basis.

Persons interested in becoming more informed about the Food Protection Certification Program may write to COPA/ETS, CN 6515, Princeton, NJ 08541-6515. For candidates interested in taking the test, a Candidate Bulletin of Information is available; it provides an overview of the program, a test content outline, sample questions, and a test registration form.

The decision as to whether the above-described testing and certification program is mandatory or voluntary rests with state and local regulatory agencies. One of the outstanding benefits that the National Food Protection Certification Program provides is that successful candidates will be in the possession of a certificate that has recognition beyond the limits of their institution, company, or jurisdiction.

The many-faceted subject of education and training was an important part of the Second National Conference for Food Protection. Papers presented and committee recommendations were published in the *Proceedings* (1984) of the Conference. Subjects presented were educating the consumer in food protection; can video be used as an effective training tool in food protection?; training and use of professional and nonprofessional person power—the intervening years; certification programs: their effectiveness and future; and education and training committee recommendations.

TEACHING AIDS

Films, slides, posters, and manuals are available through federal and state health agencies as well as through commercial channels. Some materials are free; others, like films and slides, may have a rental charge attached; still others need to be purchased.

Before showing visual aids to a class, the instructor will profit by previewing them critically. Even the best material becomes outdated as research continues to produce new pertinent data. The instructor would do well to correct outdated information and be prepared for questions from the audience.

Information on sources of audiovisual aids is available through the Retail Food Protection Branch of the FDA. The agency has compiled a *Program Information Manual* (PIM), which offers its references of information concerning food safety and sanitation in the foodservice, food vending, and retail food store industries. The PIM contains:

1. Organizational charts, directories, lists and bibliographies
2. The three model codes (cross-referenced to subsequent interpretations)
3. All current code interpretations (bulk food, sulfites, dishwasher conversion, etc.)
4. Manager training and certification information
5. A guide to the FDA's automated data processing system—SPIF
6. Agency procedures for conducting investigations and evaluating food chains
7. A complete course on facility planning and plan review

Some Selected Teaching Materials and Sources

1. The *Program Information Manual* (PIM) published by the FDA is available only on microfiche from:

   National Technical Information Service (NTIS)
   5285 Port Royal Road
   Springfield, VA 22161
   (703) 487-4650

2. FDA's *Food Code 1993,* Publication No. PB94-113941AS from:

   U.S. Department of Commerce
   Technology Administration
   National Technical Information Service
   Springfield, VA 22161
   (703) 487-4650

The FDA also maintains training aids (e.g., 16-mm films, filmstrips, and slides) and provides training courses on food sanitation topics in support of federal, state, and local regulatory personnel. Inquiries should be directed to:

FDA State Training Branch, HFC-153
Room 1536
5600 Fishers Lane
Rockville, MD 20857-1706

In addition, the FDA has available a wide variety of brochures, pamphlets, and other materials on food. Information about what is available can be obtained from:

Consumer Inquiries, HFE-88
FDA Office of Consumer Affairs
5600 Fishers Lane
Rockville, MD 20857-1706

The Centers for Disease Control have available, on loan, two training kits. CDC Training Kit LL-059 (1980) consists of a narration guide titled "Control of Foodborne Diseases in the Foodservice Industry" and a set of slides dealing with the recognition and solution of foodborne disease problems.

Another kit, CDC Training Kit LL-219 (1983) consists of two manuals and a set of slides, "Prevention of Foodborne Diseases—Procedures for Foodservice Workers." One manual serves as a teacher's guide, the other as a narration guide.

The slides and guides may be borrowed for a period not to exceed 6 weeks. Since these materials are in the public domain, they may be copied. They are available through:

The Centers for Disease Control
Center for Professional Development and Training
Division of Continuing Education and Training
Non-resident Instruction Branch
Still Picture Archives/Training Resources
Bldg. 2, Room B 46
Atlanta, GA 30333

Other teaching aids have been developed by various agencies. The sponsors or distributors of educational materials include, among others, the American Dietetic Association; the American Hospital Association; the American Public Health Association; the International Association of Milk, Food and Environmental Health; the National Institute for the Foodservice Industry; the National Sanitation Foundation; the National Restaurant Association; and the health departments of the various states, municipalities, regions, and counties. A listing of some selected sources of teaching aids follows:

Home Study Program
Cornell University
247 Warren Hall
Ithaca, NY 14853-0399

The Educational Institute of the
American Hotel and Motel Association
1407 South Harrison Road
East Lansing, MI 48823

Food Marketing Institute
1750 K Street, NW
Washington, DC 20006

Food Protection Certification
  Program
Center for Occupational and Profes-
  sional Assessment
Educational Testing Service, CN
  6515
Princeton, NJ 08541-6515

National Sanitation Foundation
P.O. Box 1468
Ann Arbor, MI 48106

Independent Study by Correspon-
  dence
The Pennsylvania State University
3 Shields Building
University Park, PA 16802

Department of Food Science
Att: Cooperative Extension
Cornell University
Stocking Hall
Ithaca, NY 14853-0399

National Automatic Merchandising
  Association
20 North Wacker Drive, Room 3500
Chicago, IL 60606

National Educational Media, Inc.
15760 Ventura Boulevard
Encino, CA 91436

Educational Foundation of the National Restaurant Association
250 South Wacker Drive, Suite 1400
Chicago, IL 60606

National Restaurant Association
311 First Street, NW
Washington, DC 20001

REFERENCES

Bower, W. F. and A. S. Davis (1976). "The federal food service program." *J. Milk Food Technol.,* 39:128–131.

Carter, E. J. (1963). "A preliminary investigation of the effectiveness of programmed instruction in teaching sanitation to non-professional food service employees." M.S. thesis, University of Missouri, Columbia, MO.

Davis, A. S. (1977). "A new era in food service sanitation." *Food Technol.,* 31(8):69.

Gravani, R. B. (1982). "Training programs: They need not be boring." *Dairy and Food Sanit.,* 2:96–99.

Gravani, R. B. (1984). "Video tape training—The future is now." *Dairy and Food Sanit.,* 4:216–220.

Hall, C. G. (1977). "National program for food service sanitation." *Food Technol.,* 31 (Aug.):72.

Hinkley, W. J. (1974). "Restaurant sanitation: A new approach." *J. Environ. Health,* 36:449–466.

Longrée, K. and G. G. Blaker (1982). *Sanitary Techniques in Food Service,* 2nd ed. John Wiley & Sons, New York.

Lukowski, R. F. and C. E. Eshbach (1963). *Employee Training in Food Service Establishments.* Food Management Program Leaflet 7, GPC 3/63 AMA, Coop. Ext. Service, College of Agriculture, University of Massachusetts.

National Institute for the Foodservice Industry (NIFI) (1977). *Development of a National Plan for Sanitation Training of Foodservice Managers.* Final Report, FDA

Contract 223-76-2072. NIFI, Chicago, IL; or Food and Drug Administration, Division of Retail Food Protection, Washington, D.C.

National Institute for the Foodservice Industry (NIFI) (1985). *Applied Food Service Sanitation,* 3rd ed. Wm. C. Brown Publishers, Dubuque, IA.

National Restaurant Association (1983). *Sanitation Self-Inspection Program for Food Service Operators.* Washington, D.C.

Palmer, B. J., J. B. Hatlen, and B. B. Jackson (1975). "The implementation and evaluation of management training in a fast food restaurant chain." *J. Environ. Health,* 37:364–368.

Proceedings of the Second National Conference for Food Protection (1984). U.S. Department of Health and Human Services, Food and Drug Administration, supported by FDA Contract No. 223-84-2087. pp. 273–324.

Sandler, C. H. (1978). "Sanitation training and certification: A national trend." *Cornell Hotel Restaurant Adm. Q.,* 19(1):23–27.

Snyder, O. P. (1978). "The need for standards in foodservice sanitation education." *J. Food Prot.,* 41:295–301.

White, J. C. (1977). "The national conference on food protection in foodservice." *Cornell Hotel Restaurant Adm. Q.,* 18(3):77–78.

Woodburn, M. J. (1978). "Educating to prevent foodborne illness." *Food Technol.,* 32(2):56–58; 70.

*Manager, Training and Certification Programs in Food Protection, Regions**

*Compiled by U.S. Department of Health and Human Services, Public Health Service, Food and Drug Administration, Retail Food Protection Branch, 1983.

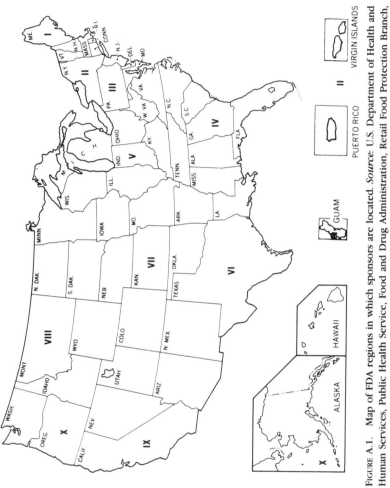

FIGURE A.1.   Map of FDA regions in which sponsors are located. *Source:* U.S. Department of Health and Human Services, Public Health Service, Food and Drug Administration, Retail Food Protection Branch, 1983.

Contact Offices for Regions

Region I

Senior Food Specialist
Food and Drug Administration
585 Commercial Street
Boston, MA 02109

Region II

Senior Food Specialist
Food and Drug Administration
830 Third Avenue
New York, NY 11232

Region III

Program Coordinator
Food and Drug Administration
Baltimore, MD 21201

Region IV

Program Director
Food and Drug Administration
1182 West Peachtree, N.W.
Atlanta, GA 30309

Region V

Senior Food Specialist
Food and Drug Administration
West Jackson Boulevard,
   Room A-1945
Chicago, IL 60604

Region VI

Senior Food Specialist
Food and Drug Administration
1200 Main Tower Building,
   Room 1545
Dallas, TX 75202

Region VII

Senior Food Specialist
Food and Drug Administration
1009 Cherry Street
Kansas City, MO 64104

Region VIII

Senior Food Specialist
Food and Drug Administration
U.S. Customhouse, 19th Street
Denver, CO 80202

Region IX

Senior Food Specialist
Food and Drug Administration
50 United Nations Plaza
San Francisco, CA 94102

Region X

Senior Food Specialist
Food and Drug Administration
909 1st Avenue Room 5003
Seattle, WA 98174

APPENDIX *B*

Temperature Conversion Table

T he numbers in the body of the table give in degrees Fahrenheit the temperature indicated in degrees Celsius at the top and side.

To convert 178°C to Fahrenheit scale, find 17 in the column headed degrees C. Proceed in a horizontal line to the column headed 8, which shows 352°F as corresponding to 178°C.

Range: $-29°C(-20°F)$ to $309°C(588°F)$

To convert 352°F to Celsius (Centigrade) scale, find 352 in the Fahrenheit readings, then in the column headed degrees C, find the number which is on the same horizontal line (i.e., 17). Next, fill in the last number from the heading of the column in which 352 was found (i.e., 8), resulting in 178°C, which is equivalent to 352°F.

Conversion formulas: $T°C = 5/9 \ (T°F - 32)$; $T°F = 9/5T°C + 32$

Degrees C	0	1	2	3	4	5	6	7	8	9
−2	−4°F	−6°F	−8°F	−9°F	−11°F	−13°F	−15°F	−17°F	−18°F	−20°F
−1	14°F	12°F	10°F	9°F	7°F	5°F	3°F	1°F	0°F	−2°F
−0	32°F	30°F	28°F	27°F	25°F	23°F	21°F	19°F	18°F	16°F
0	32°F	34°F	36°F	37°F	39°F	41°F	43°F	45°F	46°F	48°F
1	50°F	52°F	54°F	55°F	57°F	59°F	61°F	63°F	64°F	66°F
2	68°F	70°F	72°F	73°F	75°F	77°F	79°F	81°F	82°F	84°F
3	86°F	88°F	90°F	91°F	93°F	95°F	97°F	99°F	100°F	102°F
4	104°F	106°F	108°F	109°F	111°F	113°F	115°F	117°F	118°F	120°F
5	122°F	124°F	126°F	127°F	129°F	131°F	133°F	135°F	136°F	138°F
6	140°F	142°F	144°F	145°F	147°F	149°F	151°F	153°F	154°F	156°F
7	158°F	160°F	162°F	163°F	165°F	167°F	169°F	171°F	172°F	174°F
8	176°F	178°F	180°F	181°F	183°F	185°F	187°F	189°F	190°F	192°F
9	194°F	196°F	198°F	199°F	201°F	203°F	205°F	207°F	208°F	210°F
10	212°F	214°F	216°F	217°F	219°F	221°F	223°F	225°F	226°F	228°F
11	230°F	232°F	234°F	235°F	237°F	239°F	241°F	243°F	244°F	246°F
12	248°F	250°F	252°F	253°F	255°F	257°F	259°F	261°F	262°F	264°F
13	266°F	268°F	270°F	271°F	273°F	275°F	277°F	279°F	280°F	282°F
14	284°F	286°F	288°F	289°F	291°F	293°F	295°F	297°F	298°F	300°F
15	302°F	304°F	306°F	307°F	309°F	311°F	313°F	315°F	316°F	318°F
16	320°F	322°F	324°F	325°F	327°F	329°F	331°F	333°F	334°F	336°F
17	338°F	340°F	342°F	343°F	345°F	347°F	349°F	351°F	352°F	354°F
18	356°F	358°F	360°F	361°F	363°F	365°F	367°F	369°F	370°F	372°F
19	374°F	376°F	378°F	379°F	381°F	383°F	385°F	387°F	388°F	390°F
20	392°F	394°F	396°F	397°F	399°F	401°F	403°F	405°F	406°F	408°F
21	410°F	412°F	414°F	415°F	417°F	419°F	421°F	423°F	424°F	426°F
22	428°F	430°F	432°F	433°F	435°F	437°F	439°F	441°F	442°F	444°F
23	446°F	448°F	450°F	451°F	453°F	455°F	457°F	459°F	460°F	462°F
24	464°F	466°F	468°F	469°F	471°F	473°F	475°F	477°F	478°F	480°F
25	482°F	484°F	486°F	487°F	489°F	491°F	493°F	495°F	496°F	498°F
26	500°F	502°F	504°F	505°F	507°F	509°F	511°F	513°F	514°F	516°F
27	518°F	520°F	522°F	523°F	525°F	527°F	529°F	531°F	532°F	534°F
28	536°F	538°F	540°F	541°F	543°F	545°F	547°F	549°F	550°F	552°F
29	554°F	556°F	558°F	559°F	561°F	563°F	565°F	567°F	568°F	570°F
30	572°F	574°F	576°F	577°F	579°F	581°F	583°F	585°F	586°F	588°F

Source: *Handbook of Food Preparation*, 9th ed., p. 41. Copyright © 1993, American Home Economics Association, Alexandria, VA.

Index

457